BANK

G CCC BOM (LONDON , ALDWYCH)   334914

DAMAGE IN SOUTHERN ENGLAND. BY ENEMY ACTION.

37440. A WRECKED CAR IN THE DAMAGE.
S & G.

MINISTRY

12 JUL 1944

19
NOT
TO BE PUBLISHED
INITLD.........................
GENERAL   PRESS AND
SECTION   CENSORSHIP BUREAU

3 JUL 1944

& GENERAL
PRESS AGENCY, LIMITED,
LONDON.

THE V-WEAPONS
THEN AND NOW

The long-range bombardment of England will begin in the middle of June.

FÜHRER ORDER, MAY 16, 1944

After months of waiting, the hour has come for us to open fire. Führer and Fatherland look to us; they expect our crusade to be an overwhelming success.

OBERST MAX WACHTEL, JUNE 12, 1944

THE V-WEAPONS
THEN AND NOW

Edited by Winston Ramsey

Credits

ISBN: 9 781870 067 997
© *After the Battle* 2020

PUBLISHERS
Battle of Britain International Ltd
The Mews, Hobbs Cross House,
Hobbs Cross, Old Harlow,
Essex CM17 0NN
Telephone: 01279 41 8833.
Fax: 01279 41 9386
E-mail: hq@afterthebattle.com
Website: *www.afterthebattle.com*

PRINTERS
Printed by Ozgraf S. A., Olsztyn, Poland.

FRONT COVER
In 1944, the August 15 edition of *Der Adler* featured this photo on the cover by Kriegsberichter Vieth with this caption: 'For many weeks, with only short interruptions, day after day and night after night, Greater London and the southern part of England lie under the heavy revenge fire of the V1. Again, one of the remote-controlled rocket bombs is rolled out of secure cover to the launching site in order to begin its calamitous flight from there to the ordered target area.' (see also pages 148-150).

REAR COVER
On Friday, November 10, a rocket hit Middlesex Street — better known as Petticoat Lane. It landed on Brunswick Buildings just as the Prime Minister was giving a somewhat belated announcement stating that V2s had been falling on Britain since September (see page 222).

FRONTISPIECE
The un-named photographer from *The Star* was up early on Sunday, June 25, as a flying bomb struck the junction of Blackfriars Bridge Road and The Cut, in Southwark at 4.12 a.m. (see page 83). The tall structure behind Waterloo Bridge is the Shot Tower which was demolished following the Festival of Britain in 1951.

FRONT ENDPAPER
On June 30, the flying bomb that exploded in the roadway at the Aldwych caused the third largest death toll. The official record states that 48 persons were killed and 150 seriously injured (see pages 87-91).

REAR ENDPAPER
The censored caption reads: 'Children look at the wrecked flats in southern England after a flying bomb had dropped on August 22, 1944'.

ACKNOWLEDGEMENTS
The author is indebted to the following for their invaluable help: Denis Bateman. Nick Catford. Ron Gamage. Chris Goss. Adam Grounds, Chiswick & Feltham Libraries. Andrew Hyde. Kevin Lamberth. Norman Longmate. Jean Paul Pallud. Terry Parsons. Andy Saunders. Colonel Roy Stanley.

PHOTOGRAPHS
Nick Catford, 179 both. Ted Carter, 223. Bob Collis, 198 bottom. Dienst Stadsontwikkeling en Volkshuisvesting Den Haag, 253 top left. Downsview Monumental Company, 113 bottom. Haags Historisch Museum, 230 top left, bottom left. H.G.L. Schimmelpenningh-collectie Haags Gemeentearchief, 224 top. Muriel Maddox, 160 bottom. Karel Margry, 230 top right, bottom right, 253 top right. Andy Saunders, 101 all, 123 bottom, 141 top right. Peter Schenk, 50 bottom right, 51 top. Colonel Roy Stanley, 56, 57 bottom, 58 centre. Chris Thomas 47 top, 48 both. Alan Tomkins, 135 bottom. Simon Yiend, 107 bottom right.

EDITORIAL NOTE

At the end of the war, the Air Historical Branch of the Air Ministry set out to produce RAF Narratives on specific aspects concerning the air defence of Great Britain. The reports were for internal use only and classified as 'Secret'. Volume 6, covering the flying bomb and rocket campaigns of 1944-45, was completed in August 1948 but it was to be another 30 years before it was declassified.

Never published before, it is reproduced here under the Open Government Licence v3.0 (www.nationalarchives.gov.uk). Minor editorial changes in style or for clearer understanding have been incorporated yet the integrity of the report as a unique historical document has not been compromised.

As far as the illustrations are concerned, the late Roger Bell had spent many years building up a huge collection of photographs that had been issued by now-defunct Press agencies. In many cases they bear the wartime red obliterations made by the censor before they could be published but none gave the location other than the general term 'southern England'. This is where Chris Ransted gave invaluable help in tracking down evidence in wartime incident reports from official files. Andy Saunders came to the rescue with a large collection of maps, over-printed with the military grid in use during the war, which enabled us to confirm precise map references to incidents. Peter Gunn, our indexer, waded through hundreds, if not thousands of names, listing every V1 and V2 landing in Britain. An additional valuable source was the website: *https://www.v2rocket.com* and the researchers are to be congratulated in compiling a comprehensive listing detailing every V2 fired from launch sites on the Continent. Another important website was *https://www.wrsonline.co.uk.*

Rob Green, my typesetter and IT expert, has suffered my demands for over 30 years, and his patience and cheerful attitude to solving our many problems makes it a real pleasure to work together. Marty Black also generously gave of his time, and not forgetting the invaluable expertise of our Editor, Karel Margry.

Finally, I extend my grateful appreciation to my wife Gail Ramsey for spending many hours trawling through the internet for relevant material. She was also successful in solving many queries, in particular the iconic photo on our frontispiece for which we required detailed captioning as to which particular incident was depicted.

WINSTON RAMSEY, 2020

A US Signal Corps photo taken on June 19 of 'Robot Bomb' damage in Mortimer and Goodge Streets, London. This picture was not released until September 5, 1944 (see also pages 74-75).

Contents

7 INTRODUCTION

8 RAF Narrative: The Flying Bomb and Rocket Campaign
9 Early Intelligence. 10 The Sandys Investigation. 11 Estimations of the Size and Effect of the Weapon. 13 Criticisms by Lord Cherwell. 14 The Beginning of Counter-Measures, Selection of Targets for Attack. 16 Attacks on Suspected Production Centres: Watten and Peenemünde.

18 September to December 1943
19 Early Intelligence on the Flying Bombs. 20 Confusion between the Rocket and the Flying Bomb. 21 Transfer of Full Responsibility to the Air Ministry. 22 The Emergence of the Flying Bomb and the Identification of Launching Sites. 28 The Organisation of Counter-Measures. 29 Attack of Large Sites, Attack of Production Centres. 32 Attack of the Ski Sites. 33 Conclusion.

34 January to June 12, 1944
34 First Plans for Defence against 'Crossbow'. 35 Radar, Sound-Ranging and other Prospective Counter-Measures. 38 The Place of Air Defence of Great Britain (ADGB). 39 Estimates of the Direct Effect of Flying Bomb Attack. 40 Effect on 'Overlord' of Defence against 'Crossbow'. 41 The Concurrent 'Overlord' and 'Diver' Plan of Air Defence. 42 Bombing Counter-Measures. 44 Intelligence on the German Site Programme. 46 The Problems of Attacking Sites. 47 Progress of the Attacks, January — March 1944. 50 Progress of the Attacks, April — June 1944. 52 The Situation prior to the Commencement of Flying Bomb Attacks, Estimates of the Scale and Time of Flying Bomb Attack. 54 Appearance of the Modified Sites. 56 Final Reports on the Prospects of Flying Bomb Attack.

60 The First Attacks: June 13 to July 15, 1944
60 Action taken in the United Kingdom. 63 The Attack of June 15/16. 65 Counter-Measures of June 16 by the War Cabinet and the Chiefs of Staff. 66 By the Operational Commands. 67 Expansion of the 'Diver' defences. 68 Formulation of a Bombing Policy; First Effects of Bombardment. 72 Intelligence on the Flying Bomb Organisation. 76 First Attempts at Solution. 77 Improvements in Equipment and Tactics. 78 *Guns*. 79 *Balloons*. 80 *Radar*. 83 Progress of Counter-Measures, June 17 — July 15. 92 The Bombing of Sites in northern France. 93 *Organisation*. 94 *Operations*. 96 The Attack on London; Work of the Defences. 98 *Fighters*. 102 *Guns*. 104 *Balloons*. 105 Difficulties of Co-ordinated Defence. 110 The Redeployment of the Guns. 114 Reactions at the Air Ministry.

116 The Attack on London: July 16 to September 5
117 The Offensive against 'Crossbow' Targets, July 16 — August 15. 122 Scale of the German Attack, July 15 — August 15. 123 The Development of the Coastal Gun Belt. 126 Defence against Attack from the East. 130 The Protection of London. 155 Scale of German Attack, August 16 — September 5. 161 The Defence of London, August 16 — September 5. 167 The Contribution of Ground Forces.

171 Rocket and Flying Bombs attacks: September 5 to November 25
172 Intelligence on the Rocket, January — July 1944. 173 The Polish Trials, Evidence from Prisoners of War and the Swedish Rocket. 175 Renewed Interest of the War Cabinet. 176 The Final Reconstruction of the Rocket, Report by A.D.I. (Science) on August 27, Counter-Measures, June — August. 179 Radar and Radio. 182 Public Warning System, Offensive Action and Plans. 183 Events Immediately prior to the First Rocket Attack. 186 Reactions to the First Rockets. 188 First Couner-Measures. 190 Counter-Measures prior to Arnhem. 194 Effect of the Attack on Arnhem. 198 Switch to the Attack on Norwich; Rocket Attacks on the Continent. 200 Renewed Attacks on London. 204 Further Attacks by Flying Bombs. 205 Flying Bombs, September 15 — October 14. 206 Counter-Measures, September 15 — October 14. 209 Rocket and Flying Bomb Attacks, October 15 — November 25, Relative Effort against England and the Continent. 211 Counter-Measures against Flying Bombs. 215 Counter-Measures to Rockets.

224 November 25, 1944 to March 29, 1945
224 Fighter-Bomber Attacks against The Hague, November 25 — December 16. 226 Rocket Attacks, November 25 — December 16. 228 Continued Offensive against The Hague; Request by Home Secretary for Stronger Counter-Measures. 229 Consideration of Stronger Counter-Measures. 232 Fighter-Bomber Attacks against The Hague, December 17 — February 1. 236 Rocket Attacks, December 17 — February 1. 241 Defensive Reactions. 244 The Last Air-Launched Flying Bomb Attacks, November 25 — January 14. 246 The Attack on Manchester, Defensive Reactions. 250 Heavier Attacks against The Hague, February 17 — March 16. 256 Scale of Rocket Attacks, February 17 — March 16. 260 March 3-29: The Last Flying Bomb Attacks from Sites in German-occupied Territory. 261 Defensive Preparations. 262 The Attacks; Success of the Defences. 264 The Last Rocket Attacks on London, March 17-27. 269 Enemy Activity; Reactions of the Defences. 272 Withdrawal of the German Batteries; Cessation of Counter-Measures.

274 INDEX

This striking picture was taken by Westminster photographers Hobbs Offen & Co Ltd and released for publication by the Press and Censorship Bureau on November 1, 1944, some four months after attacks by V1 flying bombs began. No other caption information was provided but the quality leads one to suppose that the camera had been set up to picture the Clarket tractor when the alert sounded. Or was it fiddled in the dark-room by superimposing the diving doodlebug? We discovered the print in 1975 but with no clues as to where it had been taken, it took a strenuous effort to track down the location.

INTRODUCTION

It turned out to have been taken in the yard of the A.C.E. Machinery Company on Westmoor Street, Charlton, the two fitters being Ken 'Curly' Whittaker on the ladder and Arthur Brown with his hand on the klaxon.

The Germans began launching V1 flying bombs from France on June 13, 1944 with a salvo of four 'doodlebugs', as they were called, the only one to reach London exploding at Bethnal Green at 4.25 a.m. Ten days later, as a young child, I had personal experience of these weapons. I was at my Auntie Doris's house in St Alban's Crescent, South Woodford, with my Grandmother when we heard a throbbing noise overhead. We rushed out into the garden to see a small plane put-putting across the sky towards the west. Suddenly the engine cut out and it dived out of our view. A huge explosion followed.

My Gran quickly got her hat and coat and we rushed up to the High Road where a column of smoke showed where it had landed. The V1 had come down on the corner of Empress Avenue (see page 83) but it was only 40-odd years later, while researching our *Blitz* volumes, that I discovered that five people had been killed: three-year-old Hannah Coronell at No. 3; Dorothea Foot, 31, of the National Fire Service and Violet Foot, 72, both at No. 7; Mary Ridgewell, 68, at No. 9 and Harry Burgrove, 70, at No. 11.

Another incident that we visited a day or so after it had happened was the V1 that landed on the corner of Eagle Lane and Woodford Road at Snaresbrook on July 19. Two people were killed: Commander Leslie Griffiths and his wife Mabel.

Less than a week later I was playing in the back room of our house in Onslow Gardens, South Woodford, when the blast from another explosion blew the glass from the French doors in on me. This was the flying bomb that crashed on the Fir Trees pub on Hermon Hill, Wanstead, on July 26 killing Albert Hopkins.

The next incident I remember Mum taking me to was at Cowslip Road on August 1. The school had been badly damaged but as it was the holidays, only one person was killed. We stood behind the usual striped knife-rest barrier at the end of the road looking down to where the ruins were still smoking. (The same road received a V2 rocket on January 20, 1945, killing 18 persons and injuring nearly 100.)

Those days are now from another century, and experienced by a generation getting smaller every year, but before the memory fades I thought we should produce this lasting record of V1s and V2s crashing in Britain. There were over 9,000 of the former, most flying bombs ending their journey by their own accord, although guns, fighters and the balloon barrage managed to account for over 4,000 before they reached the capital.

The V2 campaign, also targeted at London, opened on September 8 with two rockets being launched from The Hague in the Netherlands. This time there was no defence as the missile reached a speed of over 3,000 mph and arrived at more than the speed of sound. Thus one only heard it coming after it had landed. Just over 1,000 were fired at Britain, the last one killing Ivy Millichamp at Orpington, Kent, on March 27, 1945.

Hitler's 'revenge' weapons had resulted in the deaths of 8,938 persons and the injuring of a further 58,000, nine-tenths of these casualties being caused in the London Civil Defence Region.

WINSTON RAMSEY, 2020

By 1942, Britain was building up a four-engine bomber force to be able to bring the war to Germany. On February 23, Sir Arthur Harris *(left)* was appointed AOC-in-C of Bomber Command and the following month the RAF attacked Lübeck in force. The operation on the night of March 28/29 was the Command's first major success against a German target. Hitler, on the other hand, was incensed and on April 14 ordered that 'retaliatory terror attacks' were to be carried out against civilian life in Britain. The Lübeck raid re-awakened his interest in the possibility of long-range bombardment of London and his Minister of Munitions, Albert Speer *(right)*, filled him in on the progress to develop a rocket with a one-ton warhead currently underway at Peenemünde in northern Germany.

RAF Narrative: The Flying Bomb and Rocket Campaign

The decline in the fortunes of Germany which set in during the last months of 1942 was nowhere more clearly displayed than in the air. In the three years prior to the war the German Air Force had been perhaps the most important single military factor in Europe. Instructed and uninstructed alike were impressed by its potential striking power which to no small extent explained the success of German policy. Nor did war deflate its reputation. The first two years demonstrated that the force was well trained and well equipped. It was certainly checked in the August and September of 1940 but during the following winter and spring the night attack of Britain continued. In the Mediterranean the same efficiency as had marked the earlier campaigns in Poland, Scandinavia and Western Europe was displayed in the Balkans and Crete. However, this turn on the part of Germany first to the south-east and then to Russia eased the pressure of the air offensive against the United Kingdom. Thereafter the Luftwaffe was at worst a nuisance, and chiefly a mere threat. Moreover, from the end of 1942 the offensive strength of the force declined — or was so much needed for other tasks — that a repetition of attacks on the scale of 1940-41 became practically impossible.

Thus, throughout the period preceding the Allied invasion of France, it was unlikely that the economy of this country and the forces assembling here would be subjected to a scale of attack so heavy that it might jeopardise the plans that had been laid.

However, by using flying bombs and rockets, the bombardment of London was made possible at a time when more-orthodox methods were almost out of the question. This does not mean that the Germans had this object clearly in mind throughout the phase in which the weapons were developed. It is certainly untrue for the A4 rocket for experiments directly linked with this weapon were taking place in Germany before war broke out. The intensive development of both weapons dates from the middle of 1942 when the Germans may well have realised that they were committed to the Russian campaign for much longer than they had visualised and that, in consequence, heavy bomber attacks on the United Kingdom, in reply to those which were beginning to be made on Germany, were problematical.

Then, on May 18, Sir Arthur approached Sir Charles Portal, the Chief of the Air Staff, with the idea of mounting an operation using a thousand bombers to attack just one German city. This was something that the Luftwaffe had never achieved and to which the Prime Minister Winston Churchill had given his enthusiastic approval. Although Harris's front-line strength was in the order of 400 aircraft, in the end he managed to assemble 1,043 bombers: 598 Wellingtons, 131 Halifaxes, 88 Stirlings, 79 Hampdens, 73 Lancasters, 46 Manchesters and 28 Whitleys. To reach the total it meant that over 350 of the bombers were manned by instructors and crews under training. Operation 'Millennium' took place on the night of May 30/31; it was the first large massed attack, and it was bound to lead to retaliation, especially as the RAF had now upped the ante by using 4,000lb blast bombs (cookies in RAF parlance but dubbed 'blockbusters' by the Press) with the promise of an 8,000-pounder to come.

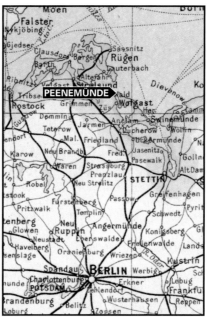

Oberst Walter Dornberger *(left)*, a First World War artillery officer, had been in charge of the rocket project since the 1930s although there was yet to be a successful test of what was officially termed the A4. Nevertheless, Hitler now demanded that the rocket offensive must begin with the launch of 5,000 missiles. Apart from the difficulty of manufacturing that number of rockets, Dornberger explained that the production of the fuel required — 2,700 tons of hydrogen peroxide and 75,000 tons of liquid oxygen — was beyond the country's capability. The location for the testing ground at Peenemünde on the Baltic coast had been selected by Dr Wernher von Braun *(right)* who had been recruited by Dornberger in 1932 to develop the engine for the rocket.

Early Intelligence

The first serious evidence to fall into British hands that the Germans were developing rockets for military purposes came as early as November 1939 in the form of information which became known in this country as the 'Oslo Report'. Later events proved this to be an especially reliable document on prospective German weapons some of which were in the very early stages of development. For example, the Henschel Hs 293 glider bomb, which the report mentioned, did not come into use until the summer of 1943.

It was not until the end of 1942 that fresh information was received. Then, on December 18, 1942, a hitherto untested source of intelligence sent in the first of three reports that together indicated that at the end of November 1942, trials of a long-range rocket had been carried out near Swinemünde on the Baltic coast. At least four more reports were received in the first quarter of 1943 linking similar trials more precisely with Peenemünde. This place was known to be important as a research centre and three photographic reconnaissance sorties had been flown over it between May 1942 and March 1943. The whole story was given added credibility through the unwitting indiscretions of two high-ranking German prisoners.

The firing of the first A4 prototype in 1942 was set for March 18 but it exploded prematurely during a test of the combustion chamber. After undergoing alterations to hopefully rectify the problem, a second launch was carried out on June 13. This time, although the rocket lifted off safely, it began to rotate and came down in the sea a mile from the launch stand. The third test took place on August 16 but at a height of 35,000 feet and at twice the speed of sound, the rocket suddenly exploded. It was not until October 3 that the first successful launch of an A4 took place. Following a perfect lift-off and a flight of 118 miles along the Baltic coast, it came down less that 4,000 yards from its intended target. Here, Dornberger and von Braun read a telegram of congratulations.

In Britain, General Sir Hastings Ismay, Churchill's Chief of Staff and chief military adviser, minuted the Prime Minister on April 15, 1943: 'The Chiefs of Staff feel that you should be made aware of reports of German experiments with long-range rockets. They are of the opinion that no time should be lost in establishing the facts and, if the evidence proves reliable, in devising counter-measures. They feel this is a case where investigation directed by one man who could call on such scientific and intelligence advisers, as might be appropriate, would give the best and quickest results. They suggest for your consideration the name of Mr Duncan Sandys, who they think, would be very suitable if he could be made available.' Sandys was 35 years old and had served in an anti-aircraft unit in Norway in the early days of the war and had been closely involved with the creation of British 'Z' Batteries using 3-inch projectile rockets as an anti-aircraft weapon. Following a serious road accident that left him disabled, he was first appointed Financial Secretary to the War Office and was now the Joint Parliamentary Secretary at the Ministry of Supply responsible for all weapons research. Churchill wrote that 'in both these offices he had had considerable responsibility for the general direction of weapon development, and had consequently been brought into close contact with the Chiefs of Staffs Committee. As he was my son-in-law I was naturally glad that the Chiefs of Staff should wish to give him this important work though I had in no way suggested it.'

However the government already had a Scientific Officer and a full-time member of the Air Ministry staff accredited to the Royal Aircraft Establishment at Farnborough. Dr Reginald Jones, a 32-year-old physicist, was the Assistant Director of Intelligence (Science) and also MI6's principal scientific adviser who had analysed the so-called 'Oslo Report'. This had been written by German mathematician and physicist Hans Ferdinand Mayer during a business trip to Oslo and had been secretly delivered to the British Embassy in November 1939. It described several German weapons, some in service and others being developed, so was passed on to MI6 in London for further analysis. Although at the time Jones had no idea who had compiled it, unlike some of the intelligence fraternity who thought it might be a plant, he believed in its authenticity. Having lived with the study of German secret weapons for several years, Jones was therefore somewhat peeved when he heard belatedly of Sandys' appointment. He said that 'it did not seem to occur to the Chiefs of Staff that they already had a Scientific Intelligence component inside their organisation. How had the Chiefs of Staff overlooked us? We decided to stay in the background and see that Sandys got all the information; but, just in case he or his organisation were not up to it, we would continue to keep an eye on everything so to be able to step in if there were signs of a breakdown.' It appears that Sandys was unaware of the resentment caused by this appointment.

The size and performance of the rocket that was being tested was doubtful. Most reports indicated that it had a range of some 130 kilometres and a warhead containing five tons of explosive had also been mentioned although the latter was thought at first to be an exaggeration. According to Dr Alwyn Crow, Director of Projectile Development at the Ministry of Supply, the weight of the warhead was more likely to be about one ton.

By April 1943, there appeared to Military Intelligence at the War Office to be sufficient evidence to justify informing the Vice-Chief of the Imperial General Staff, Lieutenant-General Sir Archibald Nye, who after consultation with Professor Charles Ellis, the Scientific Adviser to the Army Council, and Dr Crow, brought the matter before the other Vice-Chiefs of Staff on April 12,

1943. This would have been a serious step to take on any matter where only preliminary and imprecise intelligence was available. It was especially grave when the threat that was apprehended had such extensive implications both for the defence of the country and for the security of the projected invasion.

The Sandys Investigation

It is not surprising, therefore, that the main result of the meeting of the Vice-Chiefs was that a special investigation was set in train. Its direction, however, was put in the hands, not of a serving officer, but of a member of the government: Duncan Sandys, the Joint Parliamentary Secretary to the Ministry of Supply. His appointment dated from April 19, 1943.

At the outset, he was required to answer a number of specific questions:

whether a rocket of the dimensions and performance indicated was technically possible; what stage of development the Germans had reached, and what counter-measures were possible. He was instructed to report back to the Chiefs of Staff and it was with their authority that he could call upon scientists in other departments besides his own for advice and help. It soon became clear, however, that the process of obtaining conclusive answers to the various questions was likely to take a long time. Consequently, the various individuals and branches of departments on which Sandys relied upon for assistance were embraced during May and June 1943 in an extraordinary organisation which overrode the usual divisions of responsibility, the whole being under his direction.

Estimations of the Size and Effect of the Weapon

As was to be expected, the most difficult problem facing the investigators was to discover exactly what sort of weapon the Germans were developing. Their approach took a dual form: first, to collect, collate and analyse all the relevant intelligence that was obtained from our sources in Germany and elsewhere, and from photographic reconnaissance; secondly, to reconstruct the sort of weapon which the Germans might well have developed bearing in mind the existing state of scientific knowledge and technical skill.

The first of these tasks was principally in the sphere of existing agencies of intelligence. Mr Duncan Sandys requested photographic reconnaissance and the special interrogation of prisoners of war, and he also arranged that all intelligence information should be passed to him and to the scientists and technicians whom he consulted. The collection of intelligence was entirely the work of those sources and contacts that supplied us with information from Europe, and the role of photographic reconnaissance was chiefly to follow up lines of investigation which came first from agents on the ground.

For four months, from April to July 1943, nothing came from these sources to make it possible to establish beyond doubt what size of weapon the Germans were developing. A general picture emerged, however, the main features of

To gather intelligence about the goings-on at Peenemünde, one avenue was to glean information from Axis prisoners of war. With the war in North Africa now in its final stage, Britain had captured a large number of high-ranking German and Italian officers. They were shipped to the UK and held at the Combined Services Interrogation Centre based around two country estates in Buckinghamshire. Unfortunately, the wartime buildings in both Wilton Park and Latimer House no longer survive, the cell-block *(above)* at the latter being demolished in the late 1980s.

which were that a rocket was certainly being developed and that Peenemünde was undoubtedly the main experimental station and possibly also a centre of production. A photographic reconnaissance on April 22, 1943 gave the information necessary for a comprehensive report tracing the structural developments that had taken place at Peenemünde during the previous year. It told us nothing about long-range weapons, but at least it showed that a great deal of heavy construction had already taken place and that more was in progress.

Jones makes no bones of the fact that he was put out by the introduction of a rank outsider into what he felt was his own particular sphere of influence. He had already been keeping a close eye on all the evidence seeping through from agents, photo-reconnaissance and prisoner-of-war interrogations, and he wrote that the one thing that marked the turning point in his investigations occurred on March 27, 1943. At the time, two German generals, Wilhelm von Thoma *(left)* and Ludwig Crüwell *(right)*, both former commanders of the Afrikakorps, who had been captured in North Africa, were being held in the secure interrogation centre. While no overt attempt was made to grill high-ranking prisoners, 30 of the cells were specially bugged with microphones in the hope of picking up titbits of information, sometimes induced by employing stool-pigeons. In the case of high rankers, it was customary that these officers arranged amongst themselves that each newcomer should deliver a lecture to his fellow officers on his experiences, which was another very useful opportunity of gleaning information. All these conversations were recorded by the staff and transcribed. The deliberations between von Thoma and Crüwell when translated ran as follows: '. . . but no progress whatsoever can have been made in this rocket business. I saw it once with Feldmarschall Brauchitsch, there is a special ground near Kunersdorf (?) . . . They've got these huge things which they've brought up here . . . They've always said they would go 15kms into the stratosphere and then . . . You only aim at an area . . . If one was to . . . every few days . . . frightful . . . The major there was full of hope — he said "Wait until next year and the fun will start!". There's no limit (to the range).'

We were to discover during the next few weeks that large numbers of foreign workers were employed there, most of whom had been recruited in Belgium and Luxembourg.

Two more reconnaissance sorties on June 12 and 23 supplied photographs showing two large objects which appeared to be rockets, some 40 feet long and seven feet wide. One of them surprisingly called attention to itself by its light colour; but both were sufficiently unobtrusive as only to be recognised on photographs of excellent quality.

Photographic reconnaissance also confirmed reports of heavy constructions taking place in northern France. As early as July 1943, suspicious and large excavations were detected at Watten, near Calais, at Wizernes and at Bruneval, although there was nothing to connect them for certain with what was taking place at Peenemünde. Certainly there was nothing definite about the size and performance of the weapon.

During the same four months, the approach of Mr Sandys' scientific advisers also yielded no results. Early in the investigation it was calculated that the very approximate characteristics of the rocket might include a length of 20 feet, a diameter of ten feet, and a total weight of 70 tons with a warhead of up to ten tons. This implied a much more destructive projectile than that postulated in the initial report by the Vice-Chiefs. Quite apart from the scientific factors involved, the estimate was in fact more in line with such vague information as had been obtained up to that time from agents. Nor was it much amended when the rockets photographed at Peenemünde were examined for these were reckoned to be nearly 40 feet long, seven feet wide, 60 to 100 tons in weight, and containing two to eight tons of explosive.

Although Sandys vetoed any Photographic Reconnaissance Unit (PRU) material on Peenemünde being seen by anyone but his own investigators, Jones' good relations with both pilots and staff at the Central Interpretation Unit at Medmenham built up during the early years of the war, resulted in Peter Stewart, chief of the Assistant Directorate of Intelligence (Photos), continuing to send him the results of photographic sorties. The first pictures taken on April 22 showed 'a large establishment with an enormous cloud of steam'; as Jones later commented with hindsight: 'probably the condensed exhaust from the test of a rocket jet'. The next sortie — N/853 — was mounted on June 12, with an interpretation report being issued by Medmenham two days later but without the mention of anything significant. Jones received his prints *(above)* on the 18th and he soon spotted something that looked suspiciously like a rocket (annotated to the left of building). Highly critical of the omission by the principal interpreter assigned to Peenemünde, Jones sent a diplomatic note to Sandys 'to draw your attention to the fact — should you not already have noticed it — that a rocket seems to be visible on Sortie N/853 of Peenemünde; it is about 35 feet long'.

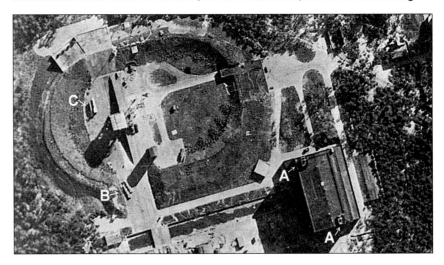

Dr Jones writes that he did not receive a reply but that the photo-interpreter concerned issued an addendum, two or three days later, to his previous report. 'This experience', wrote Jones in 1978, 'certainly confirmed my impression that my help was being avoided, and that Sandys wished to have others think that his arrangements were working well.' The next reconnaissance photos from Sortie N/860, flown by Flight Sergeant Ernest Peek in a Mosquito of No. 540 Squadron, were taken on June 23 *(above)* — pictures which clearly showed rockets and a pair of low loaders 'B' and 'C'. These were introduced as evidence at a special meeting of the War Cabinet Defence Committee convened on June 29 with Churchill in the chair. The end result of the conference was that Peenemünde was seen as a threat which should be bombed at the earliest opportunity.

Now the decision had been made that a major attack had to be carried out against Peenemünde, annotated target maps were prepared indicating the primary buildings to be bombed. The attack was planned in the greatest secrecy over several weeks.

The main difficulty in estimating the weight of the warhead and the performance of the weapon was that almost nothing was known of the propellant that the Germans had developed. It was suspected that they had evolved an entirely new fuel, and the calculations mentioned above were based on the assumption of a propellant with twice the calorific content of cordite. Yet it was known that no variant of cordite could possibly have been produced to give such results. The probability was, therefore, that some form of liquid fuel had been developed and one of Mr Sandys' committees sat under Sir Frank Smith to investigate the possibilities.

If the Germans had indeed succeeded in producing a rocket of these dimensions the implications were truly terrible. Early in June the Ministry of Home Security estimated that a rocket containing ten tons of explosive might cause complete or partial demolition over an area of radius of 850 feet and might kill 600 people. Two months later the Home Secretary Herbert Morrison informed the Prime Minister that if one such rocket fell in the London area every hour for a month, the cumulative casualties might be 108,000 killed and as many seriously injured. The figures made no allowance for overlap of craters nor for the large-scale evacuation, official and unofficial, that would take place. But even if the estimates were discounted by as much as a half or even three-quarters, the results might well be such that it would be impossible to maintain London as a centre of government and an area of production.

Criticisms by Lord Cherwell

As the implications were so grave, yet nothing positive was known about the weapon which might bring about this disastrous situation, it is not surprising that a determined effort was made between June and September 1943, chiefly by Lord Cherwell, the government's scientific adviser, to shake the foundations of the rumours regarding the rocket. His arguments were partly scientific. He focussed on what was a weak point in the case as presented up to that date, namely that the Peenemünde rockets were clearly single stage, which meant, according to the best informed opinion in this country, that its maximum range would only be 40 miles. He also pointed out that most of the agents' reports mentioned that the rockets would be steered by radio. This seemed to him practically impossible as the projectile would be rotating so rapidly. There was also the point that the only conceivable fuel for such a large body was one that was unknown to scientists in this country.

His arguments were partly based on the grounds of common sense. He could not believe that the Germans would develop a weapon of 60 tons or more that would require huge launching instal-

A. EXPERIMENTAL STATION.
    1. Elliptical Earthwork.
    2-6. Experimental Sites.
B. ELECTROLYTIC HYDROGEN PEROXIDE PLANT.
    1. Production.
    2. Concentration.
    3. Loading Point.
C. POWER PLANT AREA.
    1. Steam and Power Plant.
    2. Electrolytic Hydrogen Plant.
D. ELECTROSTATIC HYDROGEN PEROXIDE PLANT.
E. EXPERIMENTAL ESTABLISHMENTS.
F. SLEEPING AND LIVING QUARTERS.
G. AIRFIELD.
    1. Experimental Site.
    2. Airfield Buildings.
    3. Test Houses.
    4. Launching Track.

When Churchill became Prime Minister Professor Frederick Lindemann (later Lord Cherwell) was appointed his scientific adviser. His belief that Peenemünde was a hoax led to a protracted dispute with Sandys because he refused to accept the notion that the building of a long-range rocket was possible.

lations which would be impossible to conceal and would therefore be heavily attacked. Also the firing trials of such a missile would surely be accompanied by terrific flashes of light, yet there had been no such reports from the Baltic area. Finally, his suspicions that the whole story was a hoax were heightened by what appeared to be remarkable negligence on the Germans' part that they had failed to camouflage the rocket-like objects that had been photographed at Peenemunde, If the Germans were attempting a hoax, he thought it probable that they hoped thereby to conceal some other project, possibly, he suggested, the development of pilotless aircraft.

Events were to show, of course, that there was no hoax. The rocket was certainly being developed, and those who believed this were not convinced by Lord Cherwell's arguments. In fairness to him, however, it should not be forgotten that some of his objections were quite valid; not for the rocket that the Germans actually developed and used, but for the hypothetical rocket of far greater dimensions with which Sandys and his advisers were, so to speak, threatening the country at this time.

Although there were nine launch pads at Peenemünde ranged behind the eastern beach, it was Prüfstand VII at the northern end from where the first successful test had been carried out. P-7 was surrounded by a high sloping earth bank to protect it from wind-blown sand, and a wide concrete trench, which could be drenched with water, served as a flame pit for the rocket exhaust. The last launch from here took place in February 1945.

itself, next to nothing was known in the spring and summer of 1943 about any other experimental stations, centres of production, or launching sites. The Ministry of Economic Warfare thought that certain extensions to the I.G. Farben factories at Leuna, Ludwigshafen, and Oppau might be connected with the fuel of the rocket. Friedrichshafen was also suspected of being a centre for the manufacture of electrical components. These factories were already listed for attack as part of the main bomber offensive against German industry (Operation 'Pointblank'). Watten and the other new constructions in northern France were also thought to be possible targets.

The question of an attack on Peenemünde was first seriously considered towards the end of June, when it was decided to despatch a strong Bomber Command force as soon as there were sufficient hours of darkness which would not be until early August. A directive to this effect, in which the Leuna and Ludwigshafen factories were also specified for attack, was issued to Bomber Command early in July. General Ira C. Eaker, who was commanding the US Eighth Air Force at this time, was also consulted and he agreed to follow up with attacks on these targets in daylight as soon as possible after the RAF attack.

Also early in July the preparation of the special charts required for the 'Oboe' technique of radio-aided bombing was put in hand against the possibility that attacks would be called for against launching sites in northern France. This was entirely a preliminary measure. So little was known of the purpose of the suspicious works in that region, or of the details of their construction, that no decision to attack them was made until early August. In any case, it seemed likely that the best method of

The Beginning of Counter-Measures

It was in this atmosphere of belief in the rocket as a threat, yet without any certain knowledge of the nature of the rocket, or the organisation of supply and production that must undoubtedly have been behind it, that the first counter-measures were planned and carried out. As far as civil defence and radar were concerned, the work of planning and establishing what would be required went on chiefly through two committees, one presided over by Sir Findlater Stewart of the Home Defence Committee and the other, the Inter-Departmental Radio Committee, by Sir Robert Watson-Watt. Photo-reconnaissance was also a vital part of counter-measures, and a beginning was also made in formulating a policy of counter-bombing.

Selection of Targets for Attack

It had been obvious from the moment that the investigation began that the only means readily at hand by which the German preparations might be interfered with was the bombing of all relevant targets. So much was clear but, with the exception of Peenemünde

In May 1945, Peenemünde was overrun by the 2nd Belorussian Front and Soviet infantry under Major Anatole Vavilov found the test site in ruins. He had orders to completely destroy the facility which thereafter remained hidden away behind the Iron Curtain. Two years after the fall of the German Democratic Republic in 1989, surviving employees from the rocket programme were allowed to enter the former sealed area for the first time since the end of the war. Today this marker has been erected to mark the spot from where the first V2 was launched in Test Stand VII.

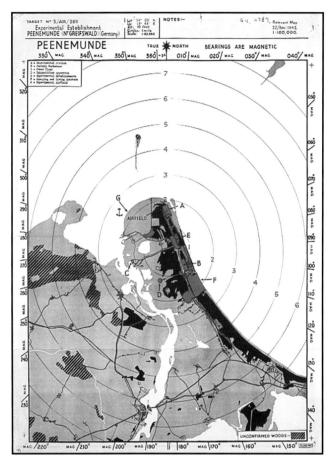

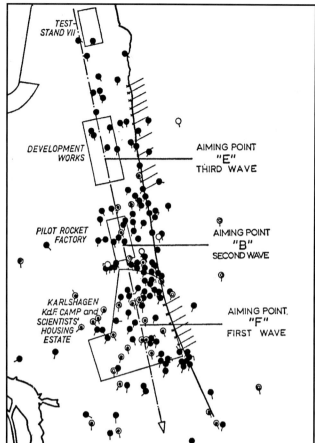

The special Peenemünde attack, Operation 'Hydra', was one of the rare occasions when the whole weight of Bomber Command was brought to bear at night against a pin-point target. A new innovation was the designation of one man to act as 'Master Bomber' to control the raid from his flying command post right over the target, and Group Captain John Searby of No. 83 Squadron carried out the task on the night of August 17/18. It was a moonlit night over northern Germany and the three aiming points — the living quarters (F), rocket factory (B) and experimental station (E) — were identified. However, the initial target markers fell 1½ miles to the south on a labour camp, killing some 500 foreign workers, before the Master Bomber could get the bombing redirected on the main targets. Another 180 people were killed in the plant area. Estimates vary, but it is believed the raid set back the development of the V2 by about two months.

attack would be to employ Lancasters using 'Oboe' dropping 12,000lb or 20,000lb earth displacement bombs, neither of which was expected to be available before September at the earliest. Meanwhile, Flying Fortresses of the Eighth Air Force, attacking in daylight and dropping 2,000lb demo-lition bombs, would be the most suit-able aircraft, and it was this type that was actually used for the first attacks against Watten.

Meanwhile a new construction site hidden in a forest between Calais and St Omer had been spotted on photographs taken over the Pas-de-Calais on May 16. Its purpose was unknown but as any suspicious object was now under the spotlight, it was decided to play safe and bomb it. The task was given to the Eighth Air Force and their daylight attack went in on August 27, just at the time when the workings had reached a critical phase before the concrete had set. This German model shows the intention: a bomb-proof launch pad for the V2, scheduled to enter service in December.

The chief engineer in charge of the construction programme in France was Werner Flos and we had the opportunity to visit the remains of the bunker in the Forêt d'Éperlecques at Watten with him in June 1987. He explained that the attack came when only the lower level had been built and that 'Kraftwerk Nordwest' was so badly smashed up that the idea of complet-ing the launch bunker (on the left) had to be abandoned. Instead it was decided to press ahead with a bomb-proof factory alongside (right) to manufacture the liquid oxygen needed to fuel the rockets.

Attacks on Suspected Production Centres: Watten and Peenemünde

Friedrichshafen, Ludwigshafen and Oppau were all attacked during this period. Little damage was thought to have been caused to the suspicious extensions at the I.G. Farben factories, but reports filtered through in August that the attack on Friedrichshafen, which had been carried out by 60 Lancasters on the night of June 20/21 had affected the production of radio and electrical components for the rocket. The Askania electrical plant in Berlin, which may have been engaged on the same sort of work, was also heavily damaged in an attack on the city in July.

Watten was not attacked until August 27 when 185 Fortresses dropped 326 tons of bombs. Nineteen direct hits were observed. A further attack was made by 58 Fortresses on September 7 but the weather was poor and only five direct hits were obtained. Nevertheless, work on the site was practically suspended for over two months, and not until December did the Germans once more make big efforts to complete it. In the interval Watten was not further attacked.

The heaviest blow at the German preparations was rightly reserved for Peenemünde. The night of August 17/18 was the first one that was suitable and 597 aircraft were despatched by Bomber Command with 1,937 tons of bombs being dropped for the loss of 40 aircraft. Photographic reconnaissance after the attack and such information as came out of Germany showed that very heavy damage was caused, especially in one of

Mass production of V2s was just about to begin at Peenemünde when Operation 'Hydra' took place. Having inspected the extent of the damage, ten days later Speer called a meeting to propose the immediate evacuation of the site. Now that it was obvious that the Allies were aware of the purpose of the installation, he considered it far too vulnerable to further attacks. (In fact the Eighth Air Force carried out raids in July and August 1944 as it was thought it was then being used for the production of the rocket fuel, hydrogen peroxide.) Early in September, machinery and personnel were transferred to an underground factory being excavated in the Harz mountains in central Germany. At the same time a back-up test range was set up at Blizna in south-west Poland.

the two works areas, in the camps for workers and technicians and to the railway system. Numerous technical and administrative officers were also believed to have been killed. Two large production sheds and a number of suspected firing points were undamaged, but, as the other damage was so heavy, and as the sheds presented a difficult target, it was decided not to repeat the attack until more was known of what the Germans would continue to do there. While the place remained in use, it is unlikely that it functioned with the same efficiency, and there is good reason to believe that the considerable dispersal of research and development which subsequently occurred was at least partly due to the bombing. In any case the attack was well conceived if only from the psychological point of view in that it represented the first direct attack on the enemy's preparations after four months of indecisive analysis and conjecture.

In May 1990, the Peenemünde Historical Museum was opened in the control room of the former power station which had been spared destruction by the bombing and had been preserved by the Soviets.

When the Royal Air Force was created in 1918, the newly-formed Air Ministry established itself in this building at the southern end of Kingsway in central London and, with deference to the RAF motto, they named it Adastral House. From October 1940 the Chief of the Air Staff was Marshal of the Royal Air Force Sir Charles Portal *(below)* and it was during his tenure that the Germans came just yards from achieving a direct hit on his headquarters as we shall see later on pages 88-92.

When, in 1954, the Independent Television Authority awarded contracts for the new ITV commercial broadcasts, the building was purchased from the government for a studio complex for Associated-Rediffusion and renamed Television House. In the 1970s, it returned to the government for use as the General Register Office in what became St Catherine's House. Further change came in the 1990s when it became the HQ of ExxonMobil and, more latterly, an office block simply called 61 Aldwych.

September to December 1943

To begin with, it was the long-range rocket which almost entirely exercised all those connected with Mr Sandys' investigation. Originally their attention had been directed specifically to the rocket and, as there was indeed evidence of its development, it had remained in their minds the prime threat to the country.

However, during the summer of 1943 reports were received which indicated another type of weapon. Its precise form was not known. As early as June there was a report of an 'air mine with wings, long distance steering and a rocket drive' which would be launched against London by catapult. Other reports received during July and early August also suggested the use of pilotless aircraft; while one of late July stated that there were two long-range weapons under development, a rocket and something akin to the Queen Bee (the radio-controlled light aircraft that had been developed by the Royal Air Force). It was not until the end of August that reports were received of such authority to make it fairly clear that some form of pilotless aircraft was just as real and immediate a threat as the rocket.

Up to that time, the study of this sort of weapon, and even of glider bombs and jet-propelled aircraft, although clearly within the sphere of the Air Ministry and the Ministry of Aircraft Production, had also come into Mr Sandys' orbit, but on September 6 he pointed out to the Chief of the Air Staff, Sir Charles Portal, that his responsibilities were becoming so wide that some rationalisation was necessary. At his request, the Air Ministry formally took over responsibility for investigating German jet propulsion, in which pilotless aircraft were included.

Thus, within a short time of our first knowledge of the new weapon, the Air Ministry were responsible for obtaining further information about it and devising counter-measures against it, though all the intelligence data on flying bombs continued to be examined by Mr Sandys and his staff, as well as by the Intelligence staffs at the Air Ministry and War Office, for some months to come. Any differentiation on the basis of the two sorts of weapon would in fact have been impossible, so confused and confusing were the reports.

The problem in Britain that summer was to try to discover a coherent theme running through all the various bits of information coming in from a variety of sources, some of it conflicting and contradictory with well-meaning agents mixing up the rocket with the pilotless aircraft. From the end of July, reports to the Secret Intelligence Service began to refer more frequently and more distinctly to pilotless aircraft, and right up until the end of August the information being collected had done more to confuse the attempt to establish the characteristics of the long-range rocket than to realise that the Germans were developing two separate weapons for the bombardment of England. On August 22, a test launch of a scale model of the Flak-Zielgerät, or FZG 76 (as the V1 was called), went awry and it crashed on the Danish island of Bornholm in the Baltic.

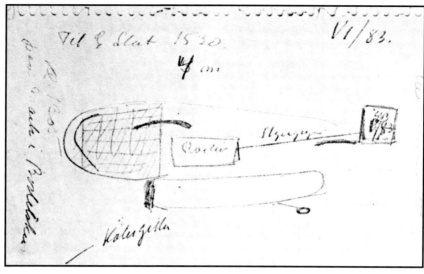

Early Intelligence on the Flying Bombs

A report dated August 12, 1943 from a particularly reliable source and one unusually well placed to learn of new weapons developed by the German Army reinforced all that had been suspected of the rocket and at the same time corroborated the reports that had been received of pilotless aircraft. The source mentioned two weapons: a rocket officially called 'A4', and a pilotless aircraft, 'PH17'. He claimed to know very little about the latter as it was not being developed by the Army, and the designation he gave it turned out later to be false. Moreover, he misled us by attributing to the rocket the launching procedure of the flying bomb. Even so, coming from him the report was of great value, the more so as it reached London shortly before another report which embodied a hurried sketch made of a pilotless aircraft which had landed on the Danish island of Bornholm in the Baltic. From this it appeared that the aircraft contained an explosive charge, probably of the order of 1,000 lbs, and that it had some form of rocket propulsion. Much about the weapon remained conjectural, notably the form of propulsion and the method of steering, but by the end of September 1943 it was fairly certain that a flying bomb was being developed and had reached an advanced stage. There were strong indications that the German Air Force were responsible for it, probably in rivalry with the German Army and the A4 rocket.

It was a small pilotless aircraft and the wreckage was promptly photographed by Lieutenant Commander Hasager Christiansen, the Danish officer in charge on the island. He also made a sketch *(top)*, noting that the warhead was a dummy filled with concrete. He sent copies of his photographs to the Chief of the Danish Naval Intelligence Service who, in turn, forwarded them to Britain. As Christiansen had had to get the film processed at a local shop, it is believed that extra prints were run off by the owner which then fell into German hands. The policeman standing beside the wreckage was recognised leading to Christiansen being identified as the photographer. He was arrested on September 5 and horribly tortured but held out and was transferred to hospital on October 8 from where he was rescued and taken to neutral Sweden. In London the photo and the accompanying sketch indicated a length of only four metres, further confusing the issue. An Enigma message decoded on September 7 revealed that Luftflotte 3 had requested the immediate bringing up of anti-aircraft forces to protect the ground organisation of Flak-Zielgerät 76. The C-in-C West reported that an enemy agent had been captured who had the task of establishing the position of the new rocket weapon. The report also stated that 'the English have information that the weapon is to be employed in the near future and they intend to attack the positions before this occurs'.

Hitler had already visited Peenemünde and inspected both weapons, and he told his military leaders that by the end of 1943 London would be levelled to the ground and Britain forced to capitulate. After the devastating RAF raid on Hamburg that had taken place in the last week of July and resulted in the deaths of tens of thousands of its inhabitants, Hitler was anxious to retaliate and according to an intelligence report of August 12, he had ordered the production of 30,000 rockets and had set October 30 as the day to begin the attacks on England. At the same time, he instructed Generalfeldmarschall Erhard Milch, in charge of production for the Luftwaffe, to prepare 2,000 aircraft for a gas attack on England. Milch was already decrying the lack of a four-engined bomber and had to reply that aviation reserves were already exhausted. Hitler then ordered experiments to be made for the A4 rocket to be filled with poison gas. Meanwhile, it was planned to build 1,500 V1s a month by November.

Confusion between the Rocket and the Flying Bomb

However, there was still some confusion between the two weapons. Within a few weeks more certain information had been obtained about the flying bomb than of the rocket over a much longer period and there was still a tendency to disbelieve the latter. The position was not made any clearer by a detailed report received in late September of information obtained in July and August. It purported to refer exclusively to the long-range rocket; mentioned Peenemünde and the neighbouring village at Zempin where an experimental unit, led by an Oberst Wachtel, was carrying out firing trials. It was said that this unit would form the basis of a unit known as 'Flak-Regiment (Anti-Aircraft) 155 (W)' which was expected to move to northern France in late October or early November. Regimental headquarters would be at Amiens and it would operate 108 'catapults' sited in a belt Amiens—Abbeville—Dunkirk. The report thus forecast with considerable accuracy the organisation that was eventually to launch flying bombs, but the connection that was erroneously traced between Oberst Wachtel and the rocket was not finally cleared up until the end of November.

In the meantime, a determined effort was made through an examination of such concrete evidence as there was, related to the scientific and technical problems involved, to establish the nature of the rocket. During the late summer of 1943, a British fuel expert, Isaac Lubbock of the Asiatic Petroleum Company, had visited the United States and examined a liquid fuel which was being produced there and which was suitable for rocket propulsion. The main constituents were aniline and nitric acid. Using a fuel of this sort it was possible to build a single-stage rocket, such as those that had been photographed at Peenemünde, with sufficient range to attack the United Kingdom from north-west Europe.

The dimensions of such a weapon that were advanced as a possibility by a committee of eminent British scientists included a warhead of five to 15 tons if the maximum range was 130 miles, and of one to five tons if it was 200 miles. If extra thrust was given to the fuel (and a 15 per cent increase was possible judging from laboratory tests in the United States), a warhead of ten to 20 tons at the shorter range and of five to 12 tons at the longer range might be achieved. The overall weight of the projectile would be over 50 tons.

As to its accuracy, the scientists reported that half the rounds fired might fall within a circle of about five miles radius round the mean point of impact at a range of 150 miles. The estimates, it should be noted, were the work of 11 men whose claim to eminence in this particular field of science was uncontested in this country. There was just one dissenter — Dr Alwyn Crow of the Ministry of Supply.

Unfortunately, there was little reliable evidence from the usual intelligence sources with which the hypothetical estimate could be compared. One detailed report had arrived late in August from the source that had first brought the terms 'A4' and 'PH17' to our notice. According to him, the Peenemünde rocket was 16 metres long and 4.5 wide (this was obviously an error). He did not know its weight but the explosive charge was equivalent in effect to a British four-ton bomb. Its range was about 200 kilometres and it reached an altitude of some 35,000 metres. This indicated a less-destructive weapon than that had been visualised by the scientists, but in the circumstances confirmatory reports were needed.

The contradiction between the two sorts of estimate had not been resolved when, towards the end of October, Mr Sandys reported the possibility of an

After the pulse-jet engine had been started, the flying bomb was then propelled by a steam-driven piston along an inclined ramp, 150 feet long. These stills are taken from a German training film showing the complete launch procedure being carried out at the Luftwaffe test centre at Karlshagen.

Having gained a speed of 105 metres a second, the piston dropped away to be re-used if undamaged, the plane continuing to its target at a speed of 640 kph (400 mph).

Transfer of Full Responsibility to the Air Ministry

Already in October the Chiefs of Staff had instructed their Joint Intelligence Sub-Committee to examine all relevant intelligence; which made a second authority — that of Mr Sandys — examining the same body of evidence and reporting to the Chiefs of Staff unsatisfactory. On this account Sandys himself suggested to the Chiefs of Staff that the machinery of investigation should be rationalised, either by the Joint Intelligence Sub-Committee being placed under him for this particular question or by himself dropping out of the investigation altogether. As the Chiefs of Staff were by this time anxious to pursue intensive operational counter-measures, they preferred the second course, and on November 11 they recommended to the Prime Minister that all Sandys' responsibilities should be transferred to the Air Ministry in the person of the Deputy Chief of Air Staff.

Nominally, the Air Ministry had been responsible for the study of flying bombs since early September but, as the two types of weapon were part of the same intelligence problem, Sandys had continued to play an important part in respect of each. Moreover, by the middle of November, although the rocket was still unsubstantial enough for its very existence to be doubted by some exceptionally experienced and capable officers, the flying bomb and the organisation behind it was being identified rapidly and a programme of counter-measures against it was taking shape. It was, therefore, proper that a service department should be responsible for counter-measures and for further investigation. And as there was a close connection between the two sorts of weapon, especially in intelligence work, so it was best to make the same authority responsible for both. The transfer of responsibilities from Sandys to the Deputy Chief of Air Staff, Air Marshal Norman Bottomley, was effected by November 18.

attack at an earlier date than had been estimated previously. During September and October evidence of production had been accumulating and there was some reason to believe that up to 500 rockets had been manufactured. In consequence, Mr Sandys advised the Chiefs of Staff on October 24 that there was a possibility of an attack on London with the equivalent of some 2,500 to 10,000 tons of bombs during any single week in November or December, while by the early months of 1944, by which time the rocket might be in full production, heavier and sustained attacks might be possible.

On the evidence that was available at the time this was undoubtedly the worst case from the British point of view, and not surprisingly it caused no little concern. A special meeting of the Defence Committee was held on the following day: the Prime Minister presided and Field-Marshal Jan Smuts, the South African statesman, who had been invited to join the Cabinet, was present.

In many respects the meeting traversed the same ground as the last conference on rockets held by the Prime Minister in June. There were still three sorts of opinion. There were those who disbelieved in the rocket, or at any rate in a rocket of the specifications suggested by the scientific committees, and those who said that intelligence pointed unmistakably to a rocket but that its nature was not yet clear. Field-Marshal Smuts, bringing a fresh mind to the subject, thought that something was certainly being developed; while the Prime Minister himself was so far convinced that he decided to make a statement in a secret session of the House of Commons. It was also decided that some of the scientists previously consulted should examine with Lord Cherwell the scientific factors involved. On the operational side, attacks were to be made on the suspicious constructions in northern France and on factories believed to be involved in rocket production. Photographic reconnaissance of northern France was to be given priority.

The results of a series of meetings of scientists held during the last week in October were summarised in a report compiled by Sir Stafford Cripps, the Minister of Aircraft Production. As far as the hypothetical rocket of some 60 tons was concerned, the conclusion was that it was theoretically possible and capable of construction. As for the objects photographed at Peenemünde, there were certain objections to accepting them as rockets. For one thing they were fitted with fins which would add greatly to the difficulty of firing them if, as had been assumed so far, some form of mortar was necessary. Furthermore, the objects had hemispherical heads that would seriously reduce their range, although they might be simply practice warheads. On the other hand, the Germans appeared to be making some kind of preparations for attack from northern France so therefore they had confidence either in a weapon already developed or in their ability to overcome any practical difficulties that might arise. Consequently, the rocket could not be discounted.

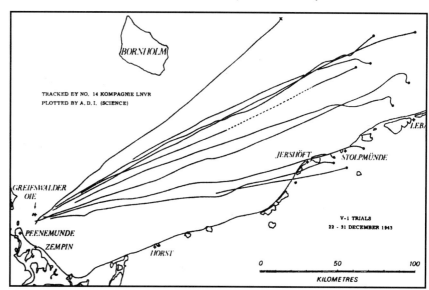

By intercepting plots from the German radar stations situated along the Baltic coast, British intelligence was able to continuously assess the threat of the V1. This is the plot for December 1943. This enabled Dr Jones to report that the accuracy and reliability of the weapon was still poor and, if launched from the French coast, it was estimated that only one in six flying bombs would have reached London.

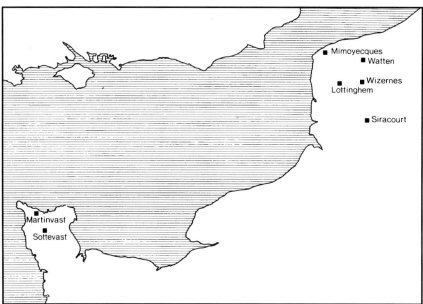

On August 30, intelligence received information from a French officer stating that a special Anti-Aircraft Regiment 155 (W), under an Oberst Max Wachtel *(left)*, was being posted to France in October or November to operate the launch catapults that had been prepared. At the same time, an intercepted signal from the commanding officer at Peenemünde-West (the Luftwaffe airfield) reported that an FZG 76 had been successfully released from a Heinkel He 111. This seemed to indicate that the Germans were developing a fall-back plan in the event that the surface sites were destroyed. *Right:* Apart from the complex at Watten which had already been bombed by the Americans, photo-reconnaissance was now identifying other suspicious construction sites in northern France.

The Emergence of the Flying Bomb and the Identification of Launching Sites

To understand how it was that the flying bomb, having started later than the rocket, had now overhauled and passed it, it is necessary to take up the intelligence story in early October of 1943. At that date Oberst Wachtel's projected organisation in northern France had not been connected with flying bombs, but reports were coming in of numerous unexplained emplacements in the Pas-de-Calais and Cherbourg areas. Some of these referred to what became known eventually as 'large sites', of which Watten and Wizernes had been the first to come under suspicion, and also large sites at Siracourt and Marquise-Mimoyecques in the Pas-de-Calais, and at Martinvast in the Cherbourg peninsula. In addition to Watten and Wizernes, all were under observation by the end of October 1943.

Ingenieur Flos, the Chief Engineer of Organisation Todt, explained that because it was impossible to build anything on the large scale required without air superiority, he conceived a radical new method of construction called 'Erdschalung'. First a massive slab of reinforced concrete would be cast flat on the ground giving very little for the enemy to destroy. Once this had been increased to the required thickness to make it bomb-proof, workmen could then burrow underneath and excavate underground chambers while protected at all times from air attack. As these large sites for the storage, assembly and launch of the FZG 76 had to be served by rail, any new railway lines were looked at as suspicious by the RAF photo interpreters. Construction at a site near St Pol was first reported in September and it was photographed on October 3.

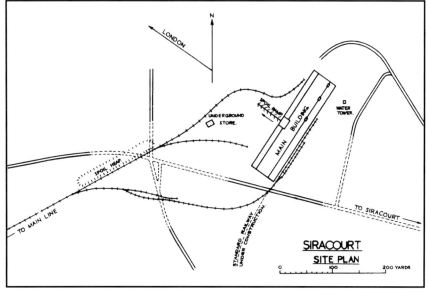

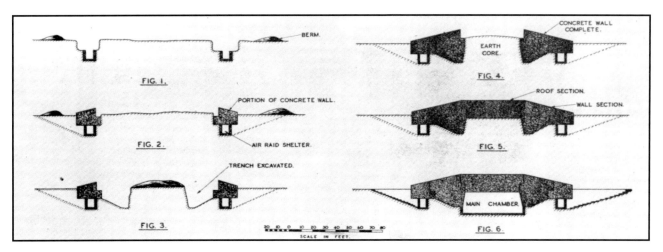

The various phases of Flos' plan for the construction of what was deceivingly called 'Wasserwerk St Pol'.

Siracourt was believed to be part of the V-weapon programme as the orientation of the building appeared to be angled towards London. Although the site was bombed long before it had been completed, in November 1944 Colonel Terence Sanders, a civil engineer at the Ministry of Supply, led a team to survey various bunker sites that had been captured, and his report included these sketches *(opposite and right)* of how it would have looked in operation. *Below left:* Between January and May 1944, the installation had been well and truly bombed by B-24s of the Eighth Air Force which attacked the target on 13 separate occasions, this picture being taken by the RAF's No. 540 Squadron on April 22. Then on June 25 it was subjected to 'Tallboy' earthquake bombs from Lancasters of No. 617 Squadron. They claimed three direct hits although Sanders found no evidence to substantiate this. Further attacks were mounted on July 6 and August 4.

An amazing transformation of the moon-like landscape. The uncompleted concrete slab still remains to be seen in one of the pastures.

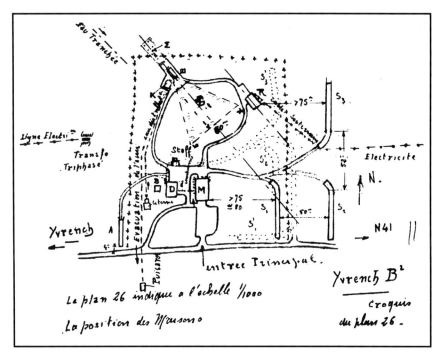

Back in December 1942, when the first of the FZG 76 pilotless aircraft had been successfully test flown, the method of launch was still being debated. Generalfeldmarschall Erhard Milch, the Inspector General of the Luftwaffe, favoured the massive bomb-proof bunkers from which an unremitting fire could be kept up against London. However, Generalleutnant Walter von Axthelm (Chief of Flak) felt the bunkers were so vulnerable that they would be bombed before they were completed. Instead he proposed a hundred small dispersed sites. No firm decision was reached so both options were proceeded with as well as plans being laid for air launches from Heinkel He 111s. Oberst Max Wachtel's misleadingly-titled organisation 'Flak-Regiment 155 (W)' was formed in August and, by September, 58 of the first 64 dispersed sites were nearing completion. Such intensive construction work could hardly be hidden from spying eyes, although intelligence on the dispersed sites was initially lost amongst the huge defensive works then underway in northern France along the Atlantic Wall. Not until October 28 did a positive report reach London — this time from the Resistance network controlled by Michel Hollard in Picardy. There he had identified six places where unusual buildings, all to the same pattern, with one aligned on London, were being erected and he managed to infiltrate one of his contacts, André Comps, a qualified engineer, as a draughtsman at a site near Yvrench. Comps succeeded in not only preparing this sketch (above) of the layout, but in copying the plans of every building. Unaware of the real importance of the tremendous coup he had achieved, Hollard personally took the drawings to Switzerland, from where they were sent on to London.

Agents were being briefed as thoroughly as available information would permit but their task was complicated by the enormous amount of defence construction being carried out in northern France. Not until October 28 was a really useful report obtained. It referred to work going on at Bois Carré, ten miles north-east of Abbeville, and described a rough plan made by a workman showing 'a concrete platform with a centre axis pointing directly to London'. Photographs were obtained from a reconnaissance flown on November 3 showed a concrete platform some 30 feet long and 12 feet wide with its axis aligned on London, two rectangular buildings and one square one, and three buildings shaped like skis. It was from this last characteristic that the term 'ski site' arose. There were no defences at Bois Carré and nothing to connect the site either with rockets or flying bombs. Nevertheless, previous photographs were scrutinised and further reconnaissance flown; and in less than a fortnight 29 ski sites had been identified, while agents' reports gave the approximate location of 70 to 80 more. The great

majority were disposed in a band between Dieppe and Calais. They bore no discernible relation to the coastline or to any orthodox scheme of defence but they were all between 130 and 143 miles from London. There was also a group of a maximum of ten sites within ten miles of the north coast of the Cherbourg peninsula.

What was obviously required at this juncture was to establish a firm link between this large programme of constructions in France and what was happening at Peenemünde, This link came after many months of careful work in Germany.

Early in 1943 it had been appreciated that if the Germans were developing long-range projectiles they would want to track them in flight beyond visual range, for which radar would be necessary. For the skill and experience required they would almost certainly call upon the 14. Kompanie of the Luft-Nachrichten-Versuchs-Regiment, which specialised in radar. The regiment was well known to Air Intelligence for the part it had played in developing and operating radio beams during the night attacks on this country, so a watch had been maintained on its later activities. Until October, however, all that could be discovered was that the company was deployed round the shores of the Baltic on the islands of Rügen and Bornholm and as far east as Stolpmünde. Then one of our sources succeeded in transmitting a detailed report from which it was clear that the company was plotting flying bombs launched from Peenemünde and also from Zempin, a few miles along the coast from Peenemünde.

During October a small aircraft with a wing-span of about 20 feet had been photographed at Peenemünde. Previous cover was re-examined and a similar aircraft was identified on photographs taken on July 22 and September 30.

When the RAF photographed the site in the square wood called Bois Carré on November 3, the accuracy of Comps' sketch was seen to be remarkably accurate.

It was due to André Comps' bravery in taking a job at the site that he was able to obtain copies of the contractor's plans. This one headed 'Maison R', shows the square building, built parallel to the launch ramp. It had no iron in its construction and the seven-metre-wide entrance allowed the assembled FZG 76 to be taken inside where an arc inscribed on the floor enabled the compass to be 'swung'. Once aligned on London, the autopilot, controlled by gyroscopes, then maintained the course to within one degree and also kept the altitude between 300 and 2500 metres. A small propeller on the nose rotated a preset number of turns before forcing the elevators to depress. It was this sudden application of G force that then caused the engine to cut out at the start of the dive.

In view of the other reports that were being received, it was fairly certain that this was a flying bomb, although this was not finally confirmed — nor was a connection established with the ski sites in northern France — until the activities of the radar company had been followed up by photographic reconnaissance. Unfortunately, the weather during most of November was unsuitable and it was not until the 28th that photographs could be obtained but they were worth waiting for. The sortie was so timed as to stand a good chance of catching an aircraft on a launching ramp and one was in fact identified in this position at Peenemünde. At Zempin there were buildings closely resembling the characteristic structures associated with the ski sites, and there were also ramps elevated at about 10 degrees and pointing in the direction along which the German trials were known to have been carried out.

After these photographs had been interpreted, there was no longer much doubt that the ski sites in northern France were intended for the launching of flying bombs. On December 4 photographic reconnaissance of the whole of northern France within 143 miles of London and Portsmouth was ordered.

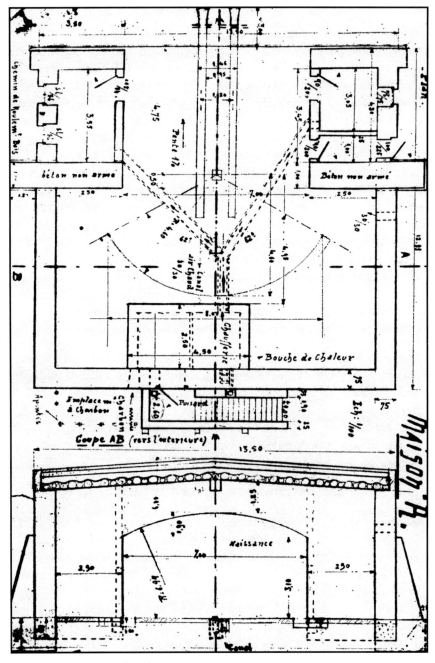

We visited Bois Carré — the first of the 'ski' sites to be identified using André Comps' plan — in 1974 when it was possible to picture the buildings but now the wood has taken over preventing clear views. We checked the angle of the ramp at 315 degrees — directly towards London where the aiming point was Tower Bridge. The buildings, constructed out of crude concrete blocks, clearly showed evidence of the bombing that soon followed.

By November, the Central Interpretation Unit (CIU) at Medmenham was working hard to identify the launch sites, No. 541 Squadron bringing back the first photograph of Bois Carré.

Below left: **A week later this low-level oblique captured the ski-shaped storage building that gave these sites their nickname.** *Below:* **It was soon singled out for attack.**

The range of this reconnaissance was later extended to 150 miles. By the end of 1943 this enormous task was three-quarters finished; 80 ski sites had been identified and at least 50 more were suspected.

By the same date other details of the general picture had been filled in.

Chiefly on the basis of the trials plotted by the 14. Kompanie and of photographs, an estimate of the performance and dimensions of the flying bomb was prepared which, in most part, proved accurate. The only point on which there was some doubt was the size of the warhead. This was due to lack of evidence concerning the engine.

As for production, a number of factories connected with rockets and flying bombs had been correctly identified but on the whole very little was known. This is not surprising. In the first place,

The 'square wood', a mile or so east of Yvrench, has a unique place in history yet Bois Carré is now overgrown and forgotten.

Then on November 28 Squadron Leader John Merifield *(left)* of No. 540 Squadron was tasked with a photo-reconnaissance mission to Berlin but found the city covered in cloud so he turned instead to the secondary locations along the Baltic coast. He ended the flight at the island of Usedom with the airfield at Peenemünde-West. When the print from the last exposure on the reel was examined at Medmenham, the interpreter spotted a tiny, cruciform aircraft at the bottom of a ramp facing the sea.

output may well have been kept low throughout 1943 in case technical modifications were required. Secondly, the Germans went to extreme lengths to disperse the manufacture of components through the engineering and electrical industries. Lastly, it is now known that final assembly was not carried out by industrial concerns but by a number of German Air Force munitions depots.

One feature, however, was fairly clear and that was the unit that would be responsible for the actual launchings. This was quite definitely Flak-Regiment 155 (W) under the command of Oberst Max Wachtel. It was known that besides a headquarters at Zempin there were four Abteilungen either at full strength or in cadre form. It was also known that Colonel Wachtel had arrived in France with elements of the unit about the middle of November 1943. On the other hand, Air Intelligence had been led to believe that the regiment would operate 108 'catapults', which seemed too many even for a regiment containing four Abteilungen (three was more usual), and the discrepancy led to a mistaken search for a larger organisation than in fact existed.

As the Germans actually built approximately that number of ski sites, the explanation may be that a number of reserve sites were constructed as an insurance against bombing, though there is also the possibility, for which evidence only became available late in 1944, that a further firing regiment was planned.

To sum up, by the end of 1943 real progress had been made by Air Intelligence in identifying the nature of the weapon and the organisation that would operate it. Enough was now known for a big programme of counter-measures to be embarked upon. Moreover, the last three months of the year had seen the flying bomb replace the rocket as the more immediate menace. Not until the summer of 1944 was there to be quite the same concern about the rocket as had been shown between April and November 1943.

Dr Jones, who claimed to have initiated this particular sortie, was ill in bed at the time but had the prints brought out to him at home. In his account published in 1978, Jones writes that 'all credit to a photographic interpreter who, not knowing the story leading up to the sortie, then found the V1 and thought the discovery was accidental; but in reality it was no accident. We had caught a flying bomb in position, just as I had hoped when I specified the optimum time of day for the sortie to be flown.' The photo-interpreter, not named by Jones, was Flight Officer Constance Babington-Smith and in her book published in 1958 she gives a lengthy explanation of the events of December 1 at the Central Interpretation Unit and how her discovery of the bomb was confirmed by her chief, Wing Commander Douglas Kendall. It was the missing link with the ramps in the ski sites in France, confirming that these were for launching pilotless aircraft.

Thirty kilometres due south of Calais lay the second of the massive bunker sites being constructed by the 'Erdschalung' method. Like Siracourt it was also disguised under the innocent-sounding title of 'Wasserwerk [Waterworks] Desvres' after the town six kilometres to the west. Work began in August 1943 but this was soon spotted by Medmenham and considered as suspicious. *Left:* The site was earmarked for attacking and this is how it appeared in April 1944 after further work had been abandoned. *Right:* The same area today, the bunker having been totally swallowed up by the forest.

The Organisation of Counter-Measures

From the middle of November 1943, the Air Ministry was responsible for the study of long-range weapons, the planning of counter-measures and, through the Deputy Chief of Air Staff, for the co-ordination of the work that was going on in civil as well as service departments. Until the end of the year this responsibility was expressed in a somewhat unorthodox form. A new directorate, the Directorate of Operations (Special Operations), was set up in the Air Ministry to co-ordinate all intelligence work on 'Crossbow' (the code-name now in use to describe all German long-range weapons) and to plan operations. The Director was responsible to the Deputy Chief of Air Staff but he was also responsible to a body outside the Air Ministry: the Joint Intelligence Sub-Committee of the Chiefs of Staff, in his capacity as chairman of a specially created offshoot of the Chiefs of Staff: the 'Crossbow' Sub-Committee. This was an inter-departmental intelligence committee that analysed all relevant intelligence data. Certain practical difficulties arose in the daily working of this committee so it was abolished early in January 1944. Its functions were then transferred to the Director of Operations who remained responsible both for co-ordinating intelligence and formulating counter-measures. Thus, except for the closing months of 1943, it was this Directorate

that was responsible, through the Deputy Chief of Air Staff to the Chiefs of Staff and the Defence Committee, for most of the detailed planning and intelligence of 'Crossbow'.

On the civil side, the Deputy Chief of Air Staff exercised his general responsibility through an inter-departmental co-ordinating committee. This tended to be a body that simply reviewed progress; the details of civil defence, evacuation and security schemes being in the hands of the Ministry of Home Security and the Home Defence Executive.

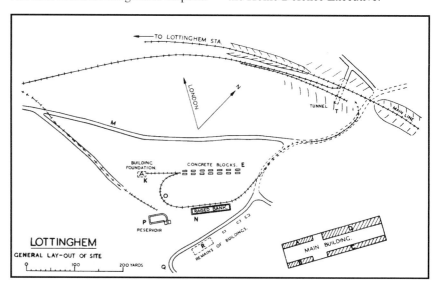

Colonel Sanders' team visited the site in December 1944 — this is the sketch plan included in his report. The main bunker was being built in sections marked A, B, C and D with air raid shelters beneath each. A spur was built from the Boulogne—St Omer railway line, ready to deliver the pilotless aircraft direct to the site, but Ingenieur Flos said that he realised that however bomb-proof the bunker was, the weakest link was the rail line which was always going to be vulnerable to being destroyed.

Attack of Large Sites

In addition to the large sites at Watten, Wizernes, Marquise-Mimoyecques and Martinvast, which had been located before the end of August, three more suspicious constructions were discovered in the next two months and were put in the same category. They were at Sottevast in the Cherbourg peninsula and Siracourt and Lottinghem in the Pas-de-Calais. Watten had been badly damaged by the Eighth Air Force in August and early September. As there was so great a demand for Fortress attacks against Germany, and since the most economical attacks against this sort of target would only be possible when the 12,000lb bomb became available, it was decided that an attempt should be made to interfere with the work at the sites by fighter-bombers of Fighter Command and Marauders of the Ninth Air Force. Their attention was confined to Mimoyecques and Martinvast and, when intense activity recommenced there in December, to Watten. Construction at the other sites was not sufficiently advanced to warrant attack.

In addition, the village of Audinghem, which had been taken over by the Todt organisation, was heavily attacked. By the middle of December, 2,060 tons of bombs had been dropped on these four targets, and the damage at each was so great that attacks were temporarily suspended. A close watch was maintained on all sites, however, for although their purpose was not yet known they could not be connected with orthodox means or requirements of warfare.

After Watten was bombed, the replacement site chosen for a launch bunker was ten miles to the south in a quarry at Wizernes where work on a rocket storage facility had been under way since April. This was now expanded as a combined storage/launch complex called 'Schotterwerk Nordwest'. Werner Flos constructed a massive concrete cupola, five metres thick, on the hillside beneath which rockets could be prepared before being rolled out to the floor of the quarry for firing.

Attack of Production Centres

The attack on the production centres of long-range weapons was largely a matter of reliable and precise intelligence. Throughout the last months of 1943, agents were reporting many firms that were manufacturing rocket components. This could have meant that production was planned on a large scale; that it was widely dispersed, or that false information was being put out in Germany. In September the Ministry of Economic Warfare compiled a list of seven firms that might be building rocket casings and four that might be making electrical and other components. Seven of those were damaged, four of them severely, in Bomber Command attacks

Left: Flos revisited the Wizernes site in 1987 where he was able to greet his adversary in the V-weapon campaign, Dr, now Professor, Reginald Jones (see After the Battle No. 57). Daylight raids on Wizernes were begun by the Eighth Air Force in March 1944, over 1,000 tons of bombs being dropped over the following three months. Although only one bomb hit the dome itself, disruption of the surrounding area made communications all but impossible. Flos had also not bargained for the genius of the inventor of the special bomb which had knocked down the Ruhr dams.

Barnes Wallis's next toy was the 'Tallboy' — a streamlined 12,000lb bomb with offset fins to spin it like a rifle bullet to penetrate the ground before erupting like an earthquake beneath its target. After No. 617 Squadron had dropped 32 Tallboys on Wizernes in June and July, completely dislodging the dome, any further development was impossible and Hitler instructed that the site was to be abandoned. Right: Then in 1986, the Nord-Pas-de-Calais region of France decided to restore the workings as a Second World War Museum which was opened in 1997.

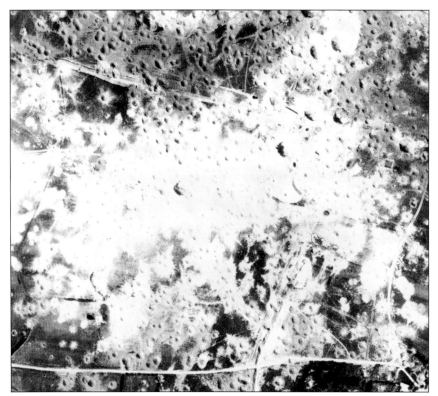

Closer to the coast, and midway between Calais and Boulogne, another construction had been identified as a possible launch site near the village of Mimoyecques so it was bombed by the US Ninth Air Force on November 5 with two follow-up raids during the next five days. However, over the next three months, the Germans managed to complete the protective concrete slab so a further ten raids were carried out by the Eighth Air Force between March 19 and June 22, 1944. RAF Bomber Command stepped in with four attacks and No. 617 Squadron dropped 16 Tallboys on it on July 6. The site appeared to be totally obliterated, the concrete slab obscured midst the mass of craters, although all the Tallboys had missed the target save one that just clipped it. No. 541 Squadron took the reconnaissance photo on August 4, the same day that the Eighth Air Force sent an 'Aphrodite' (a radio-controlled B-17 packed with explosives) against the Mimoyecques installation, but it was not until the site was captured the following month that its true purpose was revealed.

would affect rocket production. Secondly, the navigational equipment of Bomber Command, while it was accurate enough to put a force over an urban area, would not permit the bombing of specific factories. As for the American heavy bombers, their primary task was to destroy the industry behind the German fighter force, and unless there was definite knowledge of some particular focus of rocket production which if damaged would severely limit output, he considered it unjustifiable to divert the American effort. He suggested that the Ministry of Economic Warfare and the Joint Intelligence Sub-Committee should re-examine the question of rocket production and produce a short list of relevant factories. These would be allotted the same degree of importance as targets in the German aircraft industry and would be attacked as conditions allowed. The Chief of the Air Staff pointed out, however, that Bomber Command would probably be able to attack only those factories located within an industrial area.

The suggested inquiry was put in hand and was completed by the middle of November. By that time the flying bomb had assumed far greater importance than before, and the search for factories connected with 'Crossbow' was, therefore, not confined to those thought to be providing just rocket components. Five factories were advanced as profitable targets, though simply on the grounds that they were the most frequently referred to of the many factories that had been mentioned in intelligence reports. Each was thought to be making either A4 rockets or flying bombs.

They were the Maybach works and the Zeppelin works at Friedrichshafen; Julius Pintsch at Fürstenwalde near

in September and early October. Three factories in Schweinfurt, which were also thought to be involved in rocket production, were heavily damaged by the Eighth Air Force on October 15, but in each case the damage was a subsidiary effect of attacks that were primarily designed to injure German industry in general and the aircraft industry in particular. As late as the end of October, neither Bomber Command nor the Eighth Air Force had clear instructions on the place which attacks on rocket production should occupy in their respective offensives.

At the meeting of the Defence Committee on October 25 on the subject of rockets, Sir Charles Portal, the Chief of the Air Staff (CAS), agreed to arrange for all suspected factories to be included 'on a high priority' in the targets to be attacked by the British and American heavy bombers. Yet when he had examined the matter further, the CAS felt bound to conclude that it was practically impossible at this stage to brief the bombers to attack specific factories and he informed the Prime Minister to this effect on November 4.

There were a number of reasons. In the first place, there was not enough evidence to show that the destruction of any one of the factories so far named

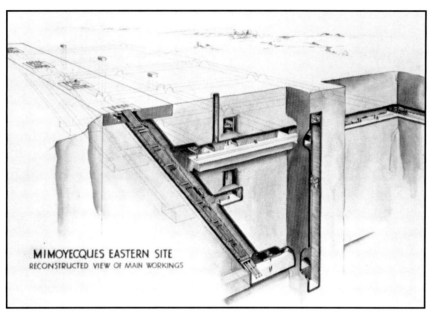

MIMOYECQUES EASTERN SITE
RECONSTRUCTED VIEW OF MAIN WORKINGS

Dr Jones: 'Under the name of "Hoch-Druck-Pumpe" (High Pressure Pump), it was to contain 50 smooth-bore barrels approximately six inches in diameter and 416 feet long, firing finned projectiles, each weighing about 300 lbs, at a combined rate of up to ten per minute at London. A final muzzle velocity of about 5,000 feet per second was to be achieved by igniting further propellant charges in side ports up the main barrel, as the projectile passed them on the way out.'

Berlin; Klein Schanzlin Becker at Frankenthal near Mannheim, and the Henschel works at Wiener Neustadt. Work was also thought to be going on at the Opel works at Rüsselsheim and the Volkswagen works at Fallersleben, both in the Mainz area, and at the Hanomag works in Hannover. Eleven other factories were added to this list as secondary targets.

The first four of the primary targets were passed to Bomber Command with instructions that they were to be attacked in the course of their current operations against German industry. The new significance of the fifth factory at Wiener Neustadt was brought to the notice of the Mediterranean Air Command. No attacks were carried out, however, during the rest of 1943. Sufficient damage had already been caused at Friedrichshafen and Wiener Neustadt to justify delay but the factories at Fürstenwalde and Frankenthal were unsuitable targets for Bomber Command. Both were in isolated positions and to attack them was only practicable when special navigational equipment (3cm H2S) was available. Even then a large force would be necessary and, as the rate of fitment of the new equipment was expected to be only three a week, the prospects of heavy attack were not favourable.

This unsatisfactory situation caused little concern, which would be remarkable except that the 'Crossbow' situation had changed so much since October with the positive identification of the flying bomb and the extensive programme of ski sites. From November 1943, attention was concentrated far more on northern France, where there appeared to be targets of undeniable validity, than on the production centres in Germany, on which information was fragmentary and imprecise.

As the third of Hitler's 'revenge' weapons, it was inevitably dubbed the 'V3'. (There was even a V4 consisting of a four-stage rocket but this never progressed beyond the experimental stage — see *After the Battle* No. 114.) Colonel Sanders spent four months examining the workings of what was a unique weapon, and in his report dated February 21, 1945 he concluded that the installation could still be repaired and pose a threat to London. Duncan Sandys showed the report to Churchill and urged Mimoyecques's immediate destruction 'to ensure that it is demolished whilst our forces are still in France'. However, the Foreign Office asked for a delay as there were soundings about a possible Anglo-French 'treaty of friendship' and they considered that demolition could alienate French feelings. On April 25 Churchill was warned that 'it is very unlikely that the French will ever agree to the destruction of these installations and unilateral action becomes more difficult with every day that passes'. The advice was that it would be better for Britain to act first and to discuss its action with General de Gaulle afterwards. Yet the prevarications continued right until the end of the war. Finally, Royal Engineers were ordered in and on May 9, 1945 they began the destruction using 35 tons of explosives to seal the entrances and demolish the firing slots *(above)*.

Attack of the Ski Sites

The identification of the ski sites and their connection with flying bombs marked the biggest advance in our knowledge of German preparations since the threat had first been realised. Before any bombers were diverted to attack them, a survey of the construction of the sites and the degree of completion in each case was carried out in order to determine what was the most economical weight of attack and in what order the sites were best attacked.

A report was rendered to the Chiefs of Staff on December 2. All available information indicated that the degree of reinforcement of the various ski site buildings was very light and, judging by the accuracy achieved in attacks on large sites, it was estimated that the following scales of effort would be necessary before a site was so badly damaged that it required almost complete reconstruction. Fortresses would require 25 sorties to drop 90 tons, and Lancasters, bombing by night using 'Oboe', would

need to carry out 28 sorties and drop 129 tons. Marauders would need to drop 170 tons (95 sorties) and Mitchells 390 tons (215 sorties) to destroy one site.

At this time some 30 of the 60 sites so far identified were estimated to be half complete for civil engineering but no military engineering appeared to have been started at any of them. Initial attacks were to be carried out by the Second Tactical Air Force and the American IX Bomber Command against sites

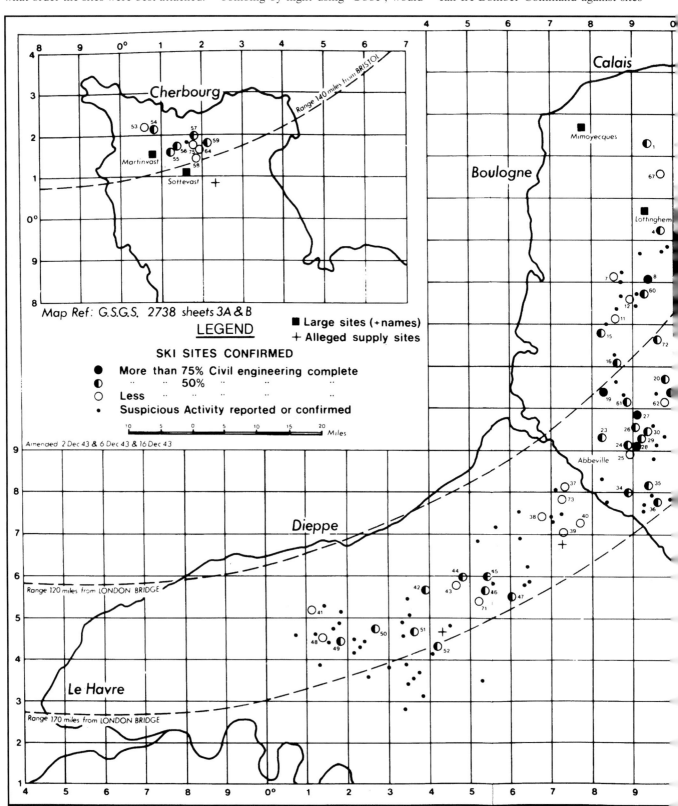

Map Ref: G.S.G.S. 2738 sheets 3A & B

LEGEND

■ Large sites (+names)
+ Alleged supply sites

SKI SITES CONFIRMED

● More than 75% Civil engineering complete
◐ " " 50% " " " "
○ Less " " " " "
• Suspicious Activity reported or confirmed

Amended 2 Dec 43 & 6 Dec 43 & 16 Dec 43

at least half completed in order to discover what were the best methods of attack. Thereafter all sites were to be bombed as they reached this stage of completion. A few attacks of an experimental kind were also to be carried out by heavy bombers but, unless the medium and fighter-bomber attacks proved insufficient, it was not intended to divert heavy bombers to this type of target. The training of the two forces would be interfered with by this programme but was expected to be offset by the increase in battle experience. Moreover, it was hoped that the attacks would provoke the German fighters in northern France to battle and thus give escorting British and American fighters the opportunity of destroying the defensive power of the German Air Force in the west.

When Second Tactical Air Force and IX Bomber Command began their attacks on December 5, the expectation was that 25 ski sites would have been neutralised by the end of 1943 but this expectation was soon belied. The very

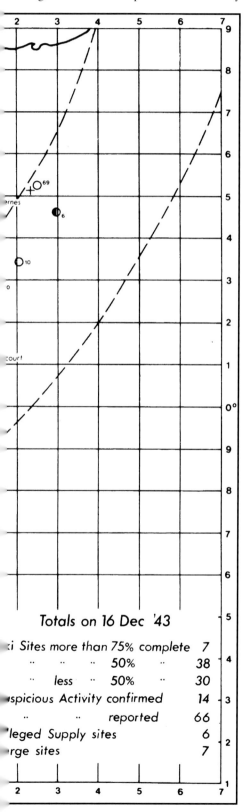

The plan (see identification lists, pages 57-59) was produced on November 29, 1943 to indicate the order of priority of the ski sites to be bombed. This is Croisette, No. 22 just south of Siracourt, following massive attacks to wipe out the site.

first operation in which 198 Marauders were despatched against three sites, demonstrated how difficult it would be for medium bombers to find and attack their targets in winter weather and with the bomb-sights available at this time, for only 52 Marauders dropped their bombs and these were without success. Heavy ground haze persisted during the next seven days and at least seven operations had to he cancelled or were aborted. Three sites which had been allotted to Bomber Command for attack by night were also left alone because of the weather. In view of the delay, General Ira Eaker, the Eighth Air Force Commander, was asked to consent to a heavy attack on as many sites as possible using his heavy bombers. For the moment, however, all that was contemplated was an isolated operation as there was no question of interfering with the attack of the German aircraft industry.

The weather improved a little during the third week in December and more attacks were made by medium and fighter-bombers with one by Bomber Command. On December 20 and 21, a total of about 200 German fighters came up to meet our attacks and 12 were believed to have been destroyed. Thereafter there was rarely any attempt on the part of the enemy fighter force to oppose attacks on ski sites. Not until December 24 was the weather suitable for the Eighth Air Force. On that day 672 Fortresses attacked 24 sites,

dropping nearly 1,400 tons of bombs, and serious damage was believed to have been caused at 13 sites.

No more attacks were carried out by the Eighth Air Force during the last week of the year yet the Second Tactical Air Force and IX Bomber Command were active. Twenty-five sites were attacked with over 500 tons and, in addition, Bomber Command attacked four sites at night. Altogether, between December 9, when the attacks began, and the end of the year 52 ski sites had been attacked with 3,200 tons of bombs. Twelve sites were thought to have been neutralised in these attacks and nine more seriously damaged. Fifteen others had been affected, six were untouched, and ten had not been photographed.

Conclusion

These then were the beginnings of a bombing campaign that was eventually to bring about the abandonment of the ski sites, although the policy governing the bombing of ski sites had not been properly defined by the end of 1943. There was still doubt concerning the role of the heavy bombers, both American and British, and it was still not clear what proportion of bombing effort was to be allocated between 'Crossbow' and German industry. Nor was it clear how the forthcoming Operation 'Overlord' might be affected. It was in fact to be an influence on bombing policy, and even more on air defence, for the areas from which the invasion of France was to be launched were not those which were principally threatened by 'Crossbow', and the question of allocating the resources of air defence was thereby complicated.

This lack of clarity about operational plans at the end of 1943 was only to be expected. Up to that date 'Crossbow' had been primarily an intelligence problem and it was only in the last few weeks of the year that the problem had been solved so that it could be passed on to the operational staffs.

Totals on 16 Dec '43

ki Sites more than 75% complete 7
"   "   " 50%   " 38
"   less " 50%   " 30
spicious Activity confirmed 14
"   " reported 66
leged Supply sites 6
rge sites 7

Meanwhile, the public were completely unaware of what was going on behind the scenes in an attempt to counter the impending threat of the new weaponry. Hitler gave a clue that something was in the wind in his address to the Old Guard on the evening of November 8, 1943. This get-together always used to be held in Munich in the Burgerbräukeller on Rosenheimerstrasse, from where the 'putsch' was mounted in 1923, but after its meeting hall was seriously damaged in 1939 by the explosion of Georg Elser's bomb in his attempt to kill Hitler, the venue had been changed to the Löwenbräu beer cellar on Stiglmaierplatz. In view of the devastating air raids now being inflicted on Germany, Propaganda Minister Dr Joseph Goebbels was especially pleased that Hitler was going to give a morale-boosting speech so he arranged to have it recorded for broadcasting later that evening. In closing his address, Hitler gave this portent of things to come: 'Believe it or not but the hour of revenge will come! For thank God, even if we cannot reach America for the time being, another State lies well within our reach and this one we will deal with.'

January to June 12, 1944

First Plans for Defence against 'Crossbow'

One result of the first vague rumours of long-range rockets had been the formation of a special committee of the Home Defence Executive under Sir Findlater Stewart to consider various questions of civil defence: e.g., a system of public warning, the deception and confusion of the enemy, control of the Press, evacuation from London, transfer of Government departments, provision of additional shelters and the reinforcement of existing casualty and rescue services.

Numerous plans were made and embodied in a report that was approved by the Defence Committee on June 30, 1943. A warning system had been devised which was to be ready by October 15; a plan had been prepared to confuse the enemy by the extensive use of smoke and flash simulators although as it entailed a good deal of labour and material, it remained a paper scheme.

Plans were also ready for the evacuation of 100,000 of London's priority classes and 20,000 were also to be evacuated from Portsmouth and Southampton. Accommodation in the London area had been earmarked for half a million homeless people, and reserves of Morrison shelters were being concentrated near London and in the Solent area.

This sort of problem, however, could only be tackled satisfactorily if there was fairly definite information, first about the likely scale of attack and second, the date at which it could be expected to begin although nothing certain was known on either of these points during 1943. As the year went by, the civil departments became less disposed to commit themselves to big preparations for meeting a threat which might not materialise, and which, if it did, might not be so terrible as had at first been thought. By November 1943 the original

The Löwenbräukeller was bombed in 1944; became a food warehouse which was looted in 1945, and was gutted by fire in 1986. It has since risen from the ashes although the architecture of the meeting hall where Hitler spoke is now totally different.

Up to the date of this meeting the main danger appeared to be the rocket that, with its short time of flight and invulnerability to the usual means of air defence, created a special and difficult problem. It is significant that with the lessening apprehension of rocket attack, and of the increasing concern with flying bombs, that between November 1943 and June 1944 little was added to the policy laid down by the Defence Committee at the earlier date. Only when flying bomb attacks began did questions of civil security become once more a major concern of government.

Radar, Sound-Ranging and other Prospective Counter-Measures

A number of counter-measures other than bombing and orthodox air defence were also considered. In the months when the only threat appeared to be rockets, it was appreciated that the only way in which it might be possible to diminish the enemy's rate of fire would be to bomb the centres of production, the lines of communication between Germany and the areas from which the projectiles were being launched, and the firing points or launching sites themselves. Very little was known about the first of these three types of target nor had the firing points themselves been identified. Something could be done, however, for it seemed practically certain that the attack would come from northern France, and counter-measures would be greatly simplified if equipment was prepared that would locate firing points within that area.

The obvious means that lay at hand was radar. Consequently, one of Duncan Sandys' earliest measures was to set up a committee under Sir Robert Watson-Watt to see whether existing radar equipment could track rockets and plot the

One can read Hitler's threat in two different ways: either he was intimating the introduction of his secret 'Vengeance' weapons, then under trial, or he could have been referring to the Lufwaffe's long-awaited response against Britain. Ten days after Hitler's veiled warning, the RAF began an all-out operation against Berlin, and over the next four months the German capital was to receive 16 major raids in Bomber Command's attempt to bring about a decisive victory from bombing alone. Retaliation could no longer wait for the new V-weapons to be ready so Reichsmarschall Hermann Göring, the head of the Luftwaffe, convened a meeting on November 28 with General-major Dietrich Peltz (seen here on the right), recently appointed Angriffsführer England.

estimates of casualties had been scaled down to between ten and 20 killed by each rocket that fell in London, and there was general agreement that the very earliest date at which attack might begin was January 1944. Consequently, at a meeting of the Defence Committee on November 18, it was decided that all plans covering the security of the population in general and the government in particular should be completed on paper but should remain at that stage. The decision was the more willingly made in view of the Chief of Air Staff's advice that if heavy attacks began, the whole weight of the British and American bomber forces would be diverted to the bombing of the firing points.

Operation 'Steinbock' — known to the British as the 'Little' or 'Baby' Blitz — began on the night of January 21/22, 1944. Göring wanted to open the assault with a force of 300 aircraft and every available bomber in the West was pressed into service, including around 30 of the new four-engined bombers, the He 177, which could each carry a pair of SC 2500 bombs. The raid was mounted in two phases, yet of the 500 tons of bombs carried, only half that total came down on the British mainland and less than ten per cent on London. Twenty-one aircraft failed to return.

Britain already had a very efficient early warning network of radar stations for identifying aircraft approaching the coast in its Chain Home system, and this was considered quite adequate for tracking pilotless aircraft. This is RAF Poling, 2½ miles east of Arundel in Sussex, circa 1942. The three large transmitter (TX) towers were not aerials in themselves but had the aerial array strung between them, whereas the four receiver (RX) towers on the right had aerials mounted directly on the latticework.

positions from which they had been fired. It appeared that the requirements of long-range and a wide field of view were best met by the existing Chain Home stations round the south and south-east coasts. However, except in rare cases and with highly-skilled operators, they could not be expected to identify rocket tracks unless special apparatus was installed. Fortunately, such was due to come into service in the summer of 1943 in the form of Cathode Ray Direction Finding (CRDF) equipment. This had been developed to improve the location of aircraft and displayed instantaneously, and in a form suitable for automatic photography, the range and bearing of all targets within a field of view of 120 degrees in front of the Chain Home station.

Early in July 1943, the first of these sets was installed at Rye, and by August five Chain Home stations between Ventnor and Dover had been fitted. From July onwards operators were trained to identify the characteristic trace that was to be expected from a rocket. A continuous watch was also maintained at these stations which, with three more to the west of the Isle of Wight, were the basis of the public warning system that had been devised. In December, however, the watch was abandoned subject to reinstitution at eight hours notice.

Flying bombs were not thought to demand special radar measures to the same extent as rockets. If they flew at 3,000-4,000 feet, as the majority were expected to do, and on a straight and steady course, the radar equipment in service on the south and south-east coasts for normal aircraft tracking was expected to suffice. A procedure for identifying flying bombs and transmitting data was laid down early in 1944 and operators were trained in it.

Preliminary measures were taken in the summer of 1943 to locate rocket firing points by means of flash spotting and sound-ranging. Coastal artillery units between Folkestone and Dover were responsible for the first. For sound-ranging, four troops of the 11th Royal Artillery Survey Regiment were allotted two deployment areas in Kent from which they could cover the area Calais—Boulogne and, less efficiently, Abbeville—Fécamp. Like most early measures against rockets there was a period between the end of 1943 and the summer of 1944 in which little was done in this field.

Two other sorts of proposed counter-measures are also worth noting even though little came of them. The background to their consideration was the lack of intelligence about what the Germans were preparing in northern France. It was therefore suggested as early as July 1943 that a Commando raid might be launched against the suspected firing points in the Pas-de-Calais. The operation would have been extremely hazardous and there was a likelihood that information obtained would be delayed in reaching England.

The Reporting Room was installed in a Nissen hut, 60 feet by 16 feet, and located around 200 feet from the aerial array. It contained display apparatus, three plotting tables, three vertical display boards, a dead reckoning board and recording map. Its role was to give accurate tracks of formations within range of the station and displaying the height on a cathode ray screen.

Left: **Back in October 1940, Herbert Morrison (seen here with Mrs Churchill) became the Home Secretary and Minister of Home Security, and on February 11, 1941 he announced to Parliament the introduction of a new type of indoor shelter. The 'Morrison', as it became known, doubled as a table and a place of refuge, and it meant that two adults and a child could sleep in their own homes with a considerable degree of** safety. **Erected on the lowest floor, it gave protection against the collapse of the house and additional supplies were now being manufactured in anticipation of the bombardment to come.** *Right:* **This picture was taken in All Soul's Avenue, Willesden, although the censor deleted the location, only permitting 'an air raid shelter, practically undamaged, seen amid the debris of houses wrecked in last night's raid'.**

So little was known about the sites or likely launching technique that it would have been difficult to give our men the precise briefing that is a necessary preliminary to this sort of venture. Consequently, nothing was arranged.

However, when the ski sites had been identified and connected with flying bombs, the Air Ministry again suggested that a Commando raid might bring back some valuable information. On this occasion Major-General Robert Laycock, the Chief of Combined Operations, reported that simultaneous raids by parties of four or five men on eight to 12 sites might have some chance of success, but he considered such an oper-

ation justified only if intelligence could be obtained in no other way. There the proposal was dropped. It came up again towards the end of June 1944 but it was still considered impracticable. In any case the Commandos were fully committed at that time.

The second type of operation that was proposed was not dissimilar. It was to obtain information from a captured German technician about the purpose of the large sites in northern France. This was a task that came within the sphere of the Special Operations Executive (SOE). It involved even more than the usual difficulties. Not only had an SOE agent to be dropped in one of the most heavily

guarded areas of occupied Europe and picked up again, he had to capture a suitable technician and bring him back to this country for interrogation. An agent suitable for the job of kidnapping would not be the man to ask the right technical questions and ensure that the answers he received were reliable and accurate. SOE reported unfavourably on the project but such importance was attached to it that a suitable individual was selected for capture. It turned out, however, that he and others like him were so closely guarded that the enterprise would have been too hazardous even for the determined and resourceful men upon whom SOE could call.

'Last night' was March 3/4, 1943, and the location was Nos. 22 and 24 — here six people lost their lives.

Following the creation of the RAF's Second Tactical Air Force in 1943 specifically to support the 'Overlord' operation, the rump of Fighter Command was renamed Air Defence of Great Britain (ADGB). This designation was not new as it had been in use since 1925 and was only abolished in 1936 when Fighter Command came into being. Chief of the Air Staff was Sir Charles Portal (see page 18), his deputy being Air Marshal Sir Norman Bottomley *(left)*. The former head of Fighter Command, Air Chief Marshal Sir Trafford Leigh-Mallory *(centre)*, was now the Allied Air Commander-in-Chief for the invasion, and Air Marshal Roderic Hill *(right)* the commander of ADGB. (Air Defence Great Britain reverted to its previous name in 1944.)

The Place of Air Defence of Great Britain (ADGB)

All these plans and proposals for defence, both on the civil and military side, were necessary but it was on the air defences already in being that the security of the country chiefly depended. This was not actually the case to begin with. Fighters (at any rate in a defensive role), guns and balloons were helpless against rockets, and only the radar stations appeared to have any value and that was entirely passive.

The position was altered, however, when the threat took the form of a pilotless aircraft. Against this sort of attack the existing defences could expect some success. The indications were that the new weapon would not be directed by radio so jamming by radio counter-measures was out of the question. The possibility of diverting the missiles by setting up a powerful magnetic field near London was also considered, but the amount of copper and electric power that would have been required was so great that the scheme was pronounced quite impracticable.

Thus, within a fortnight of the purpose of the ski sites becoming known, the Deputy Chief of Air Staff, Air Marshal Sir Norman Bottomley, reported to the Chiefs of Staff that 'an appreciation of the threat from pilotless aircraft has been forwarded to Air Chief Marshal Sir Trafford Leigh-Mallory, the Air Commander-in-Chief, Allied Expeditionary Air Force, with instructions to consider, in consultation with the C-in-C of Anti-Aircraft Command, the counter-measures possible with the resources at his disposal and to prepare plans accordingly'.

By the end of December 1943 Air Marshal Roderic Hill commanding ADGB, had prepared an outline plan which was approved by Leigh-Mallory and submitted to the Chiefs of Staff. Fighters, guns and balloons were to be deployed in three separate areas on the approaches to London and deployments were also proposed to cover Bristol and Southampton. No important changes in the disposition of searchlights, which already covered London and the other threatened areas, were visualised.

Frederick Pile had been commissioned into the Royal Artillery in 1904 serving in a variety of roles until appointed General Officer Commanding Anti-Aircraft Command in 1939, a position he held throughout the war. On him would rest a hugely important responsibility for the country's defence against the flying bomb.

In the London defence scheme, the fighter area was nearest to the South Coast. By day, standing patrols were to be maintained over the coast and inland. By night, similar patrols would be organised and intruder aircraft would be employed to intercept the flying bombs near the point of launching. On the North Downs all available anti-aircraft weapons — some 500 heavy guns and 700 light — would be deployed. Immediately behind the guns would be a balloon belt where as many balloons as possible would be kept permanently at a suitable operational height.

The scheme at once raised the problem of providing the necessary guns and balloons without seriously weakening defences already in being or budgeted for the future. In the case of balloons, the Chiefs of Staff were at the time considering the reduction of the balloon defences in the United Kingdom, so if the saving proposed was devoted to defence against flying bombs the problem could be solved.

The question of guns was more difficult. The most convenient sources of supply was 21st Army Group and the anti-aircraft training and firing camps, but the army group was part of the forces required for the invasion of France and most of its guns would only be available until D-Day at the latest. Consequently, the plan for defence against flying bombs had to be so arranged that as few guns as possible were taken from this source, which made it necessary to find the majority from formations of Anti-Aircraft Command in remote areas not threatened by flying bombs. In all, 264 heavy guns were to be provided in this way but to this the Chiefs of Staff objected and in February the plan was abandoned.

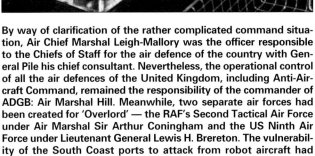

By way of clarification of the rather complicated command situation, Air Chief Marshal Leigh-Mallory was the officer responsible to the Chiefs of Staff for the air defence of the country with General Pile his chief consultant. Nevertheless, the operational control of all the air defences of the United Kingdom, including Anti-Aircraft Command, remained the responsibility of the commander of ADGB: Air Marshal Hill. Meanwhile, two separate air forces had been created for 'Overlord' — the RAF's Second Tactical Air Force under Air Marshal Sir Arthur Coningham and the US Ninth Air Force under Lieutenant General Lewis H. Brereton. The vulnerability of the South Coast ports to attack from robot aircraft had already been considered by the 'Overlord' Chief of Staff, Lieutenant-General Frederick Morgan *(left)*, but Eisenhower *(right)* as Supreme Commander, stated in March that he had no thought of re-locating the troops away from the danger area. The plan for the bombing of suspected V-weapon sites was prepared by Hill, before being approved by Leigh-Mallory, then Eisenhower, followed by the British Chiefs of Staff and lastly by the Prime Minister. Code-names were also used for various aspects of the campaign: 'Crossbow' covered German long-range attacks in general; 'Diver' for assault by flying bombs, 'Big Ben' for attack by rockets, and 'Noball' for Allied operations againsts V-weapon sites.

Estimates of the Direct Effect of Flying Bomb Attack

To understand why this was done it must be appreciated to what extent the requirements of the invasion of France were dictating military plans during the closing months of 1943 and early 1944. The invasion was a project long and carefully prepared. The Atlantic powers were committed to it for, despite the hazards, it offered the one means of early victory. And not only were they committed to the project in general, they were committed by the end of 1943 to a particular plan which was inflexible in most of its essential parts if the invasion was to take place at the appointed date.

For most of 1943 the obstacles to its success were appreciated and had been discounted as much as possible. As far as the preparatory period and the actual seaborne expedition were concerned, the most obvious threat was air attack but the position in the air was such that it could be faced with confidence. Although an attack as heavy and sustained as the Luftwaffe in the West could launch might well cause serious damage at the invasion ports and the shipping concentrated there, the new German weapons created an unforeseen — and largely unforeseeable — problem. Not much could be done about it until more was known of the likely form

and direction of attack, but as soon as the ski sites had been identified, and it was known that the immediate threat was attack by flying bombs, the possible effect on 'Overlord' was examined.

A first report was produced by Lieutenant-General Frederick Morgan, Chief of Staff to the Supreme Commander, on December 20, 1943. It was based on a number of assumptions, two of which reflected the inadequate intelligence of the scale and direction of the German attack. These were first, that 100 launching sites would be used against the 'Overlord' ports and assembly areas, and second, that the maximum German effort would be equivalent to 2,000 tons of bombs each 24 hours. This was quite the worst case from the defenders' point of view as at the time only ten per cent of the identified ski sites were aligned on Bristol. One third of the remainder were in range of Southampton and the rest at London — not so much as an 'Overlord' port but as a centre of population and government.

However, the conclusions were that the present invasion plan was impossible unless it was carried out from the South Coast; that movement of the assault force westwards from Southampton, where it would be in less danger of attack, would require transport and supply re-arrangements that could

hardly be completed if the expedition was to be launched punctually; that the existing plan should stand and the risk of casualties be accepted; but that if it was decided to amend it the decision must be taken immediately to allow as much time as possible for new arrangements to be made.

No major changes were in fact made, and with the mounting success of the operations against the ski sites during the first three months of 1944, the danger of attack appeared to recede. The final verdict came at the end of March from General Dwight D. Eisenhower, the Supreme Allied Commander, who stated that 'a "Crossbow" attack will not preclude the launching of the assault from the south coast ports and the probable incidence of casualties does not make it necessary to attempt to move assault forces west of Southampton. Though some interference with the loading of shipping, and aircraft in the Thames and Southampton areas must be expected, it is not sufficient to justify plans for displacement of shipping and craft from these areas.'

This remained the authoritative statement of the effect to be expected from flying bombs. In the event, no attempt was made to attack the invasion fleet by these means, and altogether the direct effect of 'Crossbow' on the expedition was negligible.

Increasingly throughout these pages we shall see the importance of the service chiefs in the decision-making process so here they are with the Prime Minister, the photo being taken in the garden of No. 10 Downing Street in May 1945. L-R: Sir Charles Portal, Chief of the Air Staff, and General Sir Alan Brooke, the Chief of the Imperial General Staff, promoted to Field-Marshal in January 1944. On Churchill's left sits Admiral of the Fleet and First Sea Lord Sir Andrew Cunningham who took over from Sir Dudley Pound who resigned through ill health on September 20, 1943. Pound died a month later.

Effect on 'Overlord' of Defence against 'Crossbow'

However, there were a number of less direct ways in which the two projects were related for, although invasion might not itself be seriously threatened, it made such demands upon the forces, both American and British, in the United Kingdom, that both defensive and offensive counter-measures against 'Crossbow' were inevitably affected.

It was on this account that the original defensive plan against flying bombs was modified. This as it stood could only have been carried out at the expense of the defences of numerous towns in south and south-west England and of the training of anti-aircraft units of 21st Army Group. Moreover, when the question of special defences against flying bombs was being considered early in 1944, the disposition of the air defences of the 'Overlord' ports had already been agreed upon, leaving what was regarded as the minimum number of fighters and ancillary defences for the rest of the United Kingdom. Consequently, if flying bomb attacks began when the 'Overlord' defences were required as might well happen, either these would have to be reduced — which was hardly to be accepted when so much depended on the expedition — or the defences of the rest of the country, already reduced, would have to be reduced still further.

It was in an attempt to overcome this difficulty that, on the instructions of the Chiefs of Staff, a revised plan was prepared during February 1944 to take the place of the original one for defence against flying bombs prepared two months earlier. It was designed to make the most of the available air defences in a situation where defences were required at the same time both for the invasion expedition and against flying bombs, with the former receiving prior attention. In other words, it met a situation where flying bomb attacks coincided with the final preparations for invasion or with invasion itself.

In the early 1970s, when the Irish Republican Army began a campaign of bombing in Britain, security in Whitehall was stepped up including the building of a police guard post and the erection of gates to seal the entrance to Downing Street in 1988. Regardless of these measures, in February 1991 the Provisional IRA carried out a daring mortar bomb attack in an attempt to kill Prime Minister John Major and his Cabinet. Three bombs were fired from a van parked 250 yards away, one exploding in the back garden of Number 10 where the wartime chiefs had sat for their photograph. It was an operation that was described by one anti-terrorist officer as 'quite brilliant'.

The Concurrent 'Overlord' and 'Diver' Plan of Air Defence

The plan, which was prepared at Headquarters, ADGB, adhered to the same disposition of the various components of air defence as the original discarded plan. That is to say that fighters were to be the first line of defence against flying bombs and would man patrol lines by day and night over the coast and inland as far as the gun belt. This, for the defence of London, would be on the North Downs, and, for the defence of Bristol, in the Yeovil—Shaftesbury area. London was also to be protected by a belt of balloons on the high ground between Caterham in the west and Cobham in the east. Additional searchlights were to be placed forward of the gun belt south of London to assist the gunners at night. In the Solent area the defences allotted for the protection of the invasion expeditions were, with the addition of two searchlights batteries (48 lights), reckoned sufficient to deal with flying bombs as well as conventional aircraft.

The plan involved allotting eight day fighter squadrons specially to flying bomb patrols. Six would be drawn from No. 11 Group and would man the patrol lines forward of the gun belt on the North Downs. Two others from No. 10 Group would defend the Bristol area, using normal methods of interception, i.e. standing patrols would not be flown. As for fighter patrols at night, it was hoped that five squadrons would be available in the south-east and three further west.

Similarly, the balloons and searchlights that the plan earmarked for 'Diver' involved little or no reduction in the defences of 'Overlord'. The London balloon belt was to contain 480 balloons, most of which were available by the end of March 1944 as a result of reductions in the static balloon barrages of the United Kingdom. The only balloons still in operation that would be required were those in the barrages at Swansea, Cardiff and Newport. Those were to be withdrawn for the belt only when flying bomb attacks began. The 11 batteries of searchlights, additional to those already deployed in the south, that the plan entailed could be found without much difficulty from existing defences in South Wales and north-east England.

Altogether, as far as it allotted fighters, balloons and searchlights to flying bomb defence, the Concurrent Plan was little more than a re-statement of the original plan and involved no special problems. The disposition of the gun defences, however, was another matter. Three situations had to be considered. The first — Case A — was that which would apply prior to April 1, 1944, the date at which the defences of the 'Overlord' bases were to be at full strength. The guns that it was planned to allot to flying bomb defence under Case A included 128 American heavy guns; and Case B covered the situation that would arise if for some reason these guns were not available. Case C concerned the situation which might apply after April 1 when there was some likelihood that more American guns could be utilised.

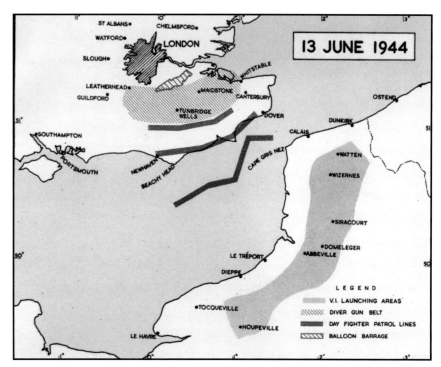

The anti-'Diver' measures envisaged by Air Marshal Hill and General Pile saw fighters being the first line of defence, backed up by a concentrated belt of guns in front of a greatly thickened balloon barrage.

In each of these three situations there were three main requirements for anti-aircraft guns in the United Kingdom. First and foremost, the defence of the 'Overlord' bases; second, defence against flying bombs, and in particular the defence of London; third, the defence of the rest of the country, including London, against attacks by piloted aircraft. That the latter was necessary was a sufficient reminder of the night attacks of January to March 1944.

Under Case A, i.e. before April 1, the complete anti-aircraft defences of the 'Overlord' bases were not required, for not until that date would the last and most important stages of assembly be reached. When they were, some 600 heavy anti-aircraft guns and 800 light guns were to reinforce the defences already in position giving a total of no less than 1,442 heavy and 1,122 light guns. Thus, between the date by which the Concurrent Plan had been prepared (March 4), and the beginning of April, a large number of guns were available to be called upon if flying bomb attacks began. Nevertheless, the allotment of guns for the latter purpose under Case A was numerically the same as in Case B, partly because the time in which Case A would apply was so short, partly because the Chiefs of Staff were determined to let nothing interfere with what they regarded as an adequate defence for the invasion expedition. If a large number of guns went into action against flying bombs before the 'Overlord' preparations reached their peak, it might have been difficult to redeploy any of them for the defence of the 'Overlord' bases.

With insignificant exceptions, the total gun resources before and after April 1 but prior to D-Day were the same. They amounted to 2,735 heavy

guns and 1,870 light guns. The 21st Army Group and 1st US Army Group accounted for 432 heavy and 670 light guns. The rest were in Anti-Aircraft Command and Home Forces.

Under Case B, which was the worst possibility in that it envisaged separate deployments, both for 'Overlord' and 'Diver', and also the absence of 128 American guns, the 'Overlord' defences and the guns in anti-aircraft regiments detailed to move on or shortly after D-Day, embraced 1,258 heavy and 950 light guns, leaving some 1,400 heavy guns and 900 light weapons for defence against flying bombs and the rest of the country.

The needs of the latter dictated the scale of the former. Thirty-two gun-defended areas in Anti-Aircraft Command at which 910 heavy guns were deployed, were selected as suitable areas from which withdrawals could be made for the needs of invasion as well as 'Diver'. Not all these guns could be withdrawn while the threat of normal air attack remained, and the minimum security was estimated to be some 546 guns.

A more drastic reduction was planned in the defences of vital points protected by light guns. Forty-two were to be stripped of all protection, thus making available some 200 guns. Out of these resources of Anti-Aircraft Command, 192 heavy and 138 light guns were held in readiness to man the 'Diver' gun belt defending London. If American heavy guns could be called upon (and by April 15 it appeared that 96 might be available), they would replace a similar number of Anti-Aircraft Command guns, not be additional to them. All told, the gun belt was planned to contain these 192 heavy guns and 246 light guns, 108 of the latter being provided by 21st Army Group.

The original anti-aircraft plan envisaged the deployment of 600 heavy and 800 light guns but as the policy of the Chiefs of Staff was to ensure the fullest possible protection for the invasion forces for 'Overlord', numbers were reduced to 192 heavy and 246 light guns. General Pile was hoping that American anti-aircraft weapons could be provided to bolster the numbers. Here a British officer instructs an American crew on the 40mm Bofors.

Bombing Counter-Measures

At the end of 1943 no comprehensive policy had been formulated for counter-bombing, the Allied effort being applied almost entirely against the ski sites in northern France. The large sites were also receiving some attention, although their purpose was not yet known, and certain suspected centres of rocket and flying bomb production had been attacked, but only insofar as they were centres of piloted aircraft production. Little was known of this aspect of German preparations.

What forces ought to be employed against 'Crossbow'; what sort of attacks should be carried out; what size of effort would be required, were not easy questions to answer at the beginning of 1944. It had first been thought that the best instruments would be the American Ninth Air Force and the British Second Tactical Air Force, (including No. 2 Group of Bomber Command), which were the offensive components of the Allied Expeditionary Air Forces (AEAF). If these formations had been capable of neutralising the sites in northern France, the main obstacle to the efficient distribution of the Allied bomber resources in the United Kingdom would have been overcome. Not that this would have been easy for the two forces had an essential part to play in the bombing preparatory to invasion, and even more in the invasion itself and the subsequent battles. Moreover, their tactical role demanded a high and peculiar standard of training to fit them for the task of co-operating with ground forces, and their own commanders were loath to allow their training schedules to be interfered with. Against this, however, could be set the experience that would be gained, and was gained, in actual operations.

At first the attacks by the medium bombers and fighter-bombers were disappointing. Their performance could be expected to improve with practice, especially that of the Ninth Air Force which was a new and inexperienced formation. Nevertheless, it was calculated early in January 1944 that AEAF squadrons were not likely to destroy more than 14 ski sites a month and, as the existence of 96 sites had already been confirmed, this meant that AEAF would be forced to maintain a heavy scale of attack well into the summer which would seriously affect its role in invasion. Consequently, it was impossible to escape the conclusion that regular attacks would have to be carried out by heavy bombers if the German preparations were to be restrained. The main body of the heavy bomber forces of Bomber Command was hardly a suitable instrument for the attack of pinpoint targets, though good results could be expected from some of the specially trained squadrons of the Command. On the other hand, the B-17s and B-25s of the Eighth Air Force were admirably suited to the task and it was estimated that six sites could be expected to be destroyed in any one major attack by this force.

However, Lieutenant General James Doolittle (who succeeded General Ira Eaker in January 1944) and Air Chief Marshal Harris were committed to the attack of German industry, which they considered vital to the success of the invasion of France and the defeat of Germany, and both men were loath to

The Americans introduced the 90mm M1 as it had longer range, greater muzzle velocity, and a larger effective shell-burst area. Photo taken in April 1944 deployed near the English coast.

Another bone of contention lay in the priorities of the British and American bomber forces. Air Chief Marshal Harris of RAF Bomber Command and Lieutenant General James Doolittle *(left)*, the legendary leader of the morale-boosting attack on Tokyo in April 1942 and since January 1944 chief of the Eighth Air Force, were both committed to pursuing the goal of destroying German industry (Operation 'Pointblank'). Now their forces were also wanted for bombing 'Overlord' targets as well as being asked to help destroy V-weapon sites. *Right:* Harris received a visit from King George VI and Queen Elizabeth on February 7 but it was not until April 14 — less than two months before D-Day — that the Combined Chiefs of Staff directed that 'Overlord' should now take priority.

direct their forces to any other task. Nor was Portal, the Chief of Air Staff who exercised a responsibility for the strategic air offensive to the Combined Chiefs of Staff, convinced that 'Crossbow' was such a threat that it warranted any major change in bombing policy. Yet the fact remained that the American heavy bombers would have to be employed if the Germans were not to have a good proportion of sites ready for use by the time that the invasion of France would be launched, if not earlier. The principle was therefore agreed upon between the British Chiefs of Staff, and Lieutenant General Carl Spaatz, Commanding General of the US Strategic Air Forces, that the sites in northern France should only be attacked by the Eighth Air Force 'whenever weather conditions over Germany do not allow of major attacks

there but permit precision bombing over northern France'. In addition, Air Chief Marshal Harris was instructed to regard the destruction of eight selected ski sites as the primary task of his Stirling squadrons whenever these were not operating against targets in Germany. The principle, as we shall see, was only departed from in exceptional circumstances, and only a little more than one tenth of the effort of the Eighth Air Force was devoted to 'Crossbow' targets between December 1943 and June 1944. Nevertheless, it is abundantly clear that both Doolittle and Harris were antagonistic to what they regarded as a commitment of far less importance than either the offensive against Germany or against the enemy forces in the West.

However, there was at least one type of target that they were allowed to

ignore: namely, suspected centres of flying bomb and rocket production. Allied intelligence on this subject remained weak throughout the period under review — January to June 1944. Consequently, the Chiefs of Staff agreed on February 1 that production centres should not be attacked until more definite evidence was available. Where a suspected factory was also a part of the German aircraft industry, attacks were made on it in virtue of its latter function. For example, on April 24 the Dornier assembly works at Löwental in Friedrichshafen was attacked by 98 B-17s, and 291 Lancasters bombed Friedrichshafen on the night of April 27. Similarly, hydrogen peroxide plants were attacked more by virtue of their importance to the German production of jet-propelled piloted aircraft than to that of flying bombs and rockets.

The last line of defence was to be the balloon barrage. The officer in charge of Balloon Command was Air Marshal Sir Leslie Gossage, seen here in April 1943 on an inspection tour with Mrs Margaret Sloan Colt of the American Red Cross.

The parade was held in the dry moat of the Tower of London, the venue for a stunning display of ceramic poppies in August 2014 to mark the 100th anniversary of the outbreak of the First World War.

Intelligence on the German Site Programme

By the beginning of January 1944, 96 ski sites had been identified in northern France. There was some evidence from ground sources that the Germans would build as many as 150 but this number was never constructed. By the same date, seven large sites had been found at Watten, Wizernes, Mimoyecques, Siracourt, Lottinghem, Sottevast and Martinvast, of which the last two were on the Cherbourg peninsula. All were within 150 miles of London on which all seemed to be oriented (with the exception of Martinvast which was aligned on Bristol), and none of them could be connected with any ordinary military or industrial purpose. As agents' reports almost invariably connected them with rockets, it was assumed that they were intended to play some important part in the German attack as at every site much labour and material was being expended. An eighth site at Hidrequent, near Calais, had also come under suspicion but even less could be deduced from the construction there than at the other large sites.

There was also a third category of site. The fact that none of the ski sites were served by railways of normal gauge had early suggested that the Germans probably intended to deliver supplies to them by road from supply depots which would be linked with railway communications with Germany. Ground sources offered no relevant information but towards the end of 1943 evidence of what came to be

Other suspicious sites in France were kept under surveillance. Eight miles south of Cherbourg this construction at Sottevast raised concerns even though its purpose was unknown.

called 'supply sites' began to accumulate from successive photographic reconnaissance. It was not until February 1944, however, that the evidence was sufficiently conclusive for a report on the subject to be passed to the Chiefs of Staff. This specified seven places where supply sites appeared to be under construction. One of them was on the Cherbourg peninsula. The others extended in

an arc just inland from the belt covered by the ski sites, and with one exception were evenly spaced at intervals of 20 miles. All were served by rail and had good road communications. Work on them had started about the same time as on the ski sites and certain standardised buildings were common to them. All were heavily defended by anti-aircraft guns.

It was a proposed storage and launch site similar to those in the Pas-de-Calais area, built by the same Verbunkerung method to create a bomb-proof complex underneath a massive concrete slab. Beginning in February 1944, Sottevast was bombed several times to halt the construction work and before

it could be completed, it was captured by US forces within 20 days of landing in Normandy. *Left:* No. 541 Squadron brought this photo back on May 7. *Right:* Little remains to identify the same area today although the concrete slab still remains to be seen in a pasture.

The limestone quarries at Hidrequent in the Pas-de-Calais region, which stretched for some two miles on either side of the Calais—Boulogne railway line, also came under suspicion. Air reconnaissance had first drawn attention to the quarries in April 1943 where the presence of two railway turntables [1] indicated possible use as firing platforms for railway guns.

A great deal of activity was also reported in this area during the summer and it was also significant that the site was well protected by flak posts. However, its secrets only came to light after it was captured when it was discovered that the tunnel entrances [2], were sealed by heavy steel doors cut into the deep vertical face,

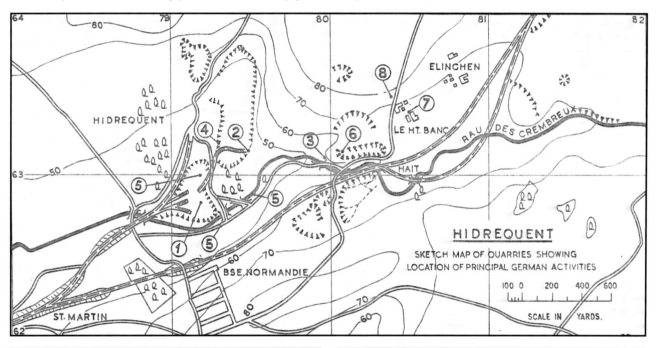

HIDREQUENT
SKETCH MAP OF QUARRIES SHOWING
LOCATION OF PRINCIPAL GERMAN ACTIVITIES

100 0   200   400   600

SCALE IN YARDS.

For a time, the location was believed to be connected with activities concerning V-weapon operations, yet it appeared after inspection in November 1944 that the quarries had only been used as a dump for 'Crossbow' stores *(left)* and a pile of

massive steel cover plates *(right)* were found at [4] which had been delivered for the Mimoyecques project. Other locations were a transformer building [3]; various huts and shelters [5]; tunnels [6]; a disused mine [7], and a gas filter station [8].

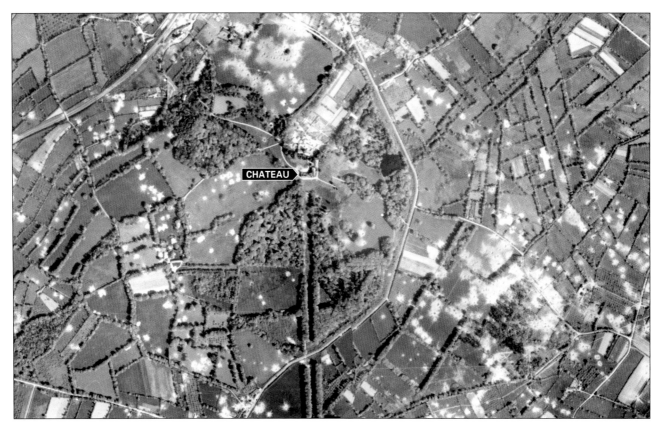

The difficulty of identifying targets is perfectly illustrated by these photos taken by No. 541 Squadron on May 11, 1944.

Sticks of bomb craters cover the landscape but what is the actual target?

The Problems of Attacking Sites

Thus the first half of 1944 saw attacks confined to ski sites and large sites. Neither presented easy targets. Each type was contained within a square of 300 to 400 yards and only a small proportion of this area was occupied by essential constructions. Accurate visual attack therefore depended to a great extent on good visibility. For example, the bomb-aimer in the Marauder, which was the most up-to-date of the medium bombers, had to identify his target at a range of at least six miles if he was to bomb accurately. Blind bombing with the aid of radio navigational devices had to be no less accurate and only 'Oboe' of the various aids in service at the time was sufficiently precise for the task.

Low-level and dive-bombing had their advocates and both methods were comparatively successful, especially the former, but the success was at the cost of higher casualties than those suffered by the medium and heavy bombers. Although it was only on rare occasions that the German fighter reaction to our attacks was at all spirited, anti-aircraft defences were increased to the point at which the Pas-de-Calais and the Cherbourg peninsula were amongst the most heavily defended areas in Europe. In the ski site belt between Dieppe and St Omer, there were only some 60 heavy and 60 light anti-aircraft guns in December 1943, but by the end of the following May there were about 520 and 730 respectively. The sites in the Cherbourg peninsula were already covered by strong anti-aircraft defences and these were further increased until there were at least 200 guns in the area.

Moreover, in the case of the large sites, the problem of how to attack successfully and economically was made especially difficult by the strength of the main constructions. Few attacks with 12,000lb bombs were carried out before June 6; until then 2,000lb bombs were normally used, more to smash rail and road communications at the sites and to interfere with work than to destroy the massive concrete buildings. The ski sites were not so robustly constructed so 500lb — and even 250lb — bombs were sufficient to cause serious damage.

One can hazard a guess that the bombers were trying to hit the ski installation in the grounds of the château at Martinvast in the Cherbourg peninsula.

In January 1944, pilots of No. 245 Squadron return to their base at Westhampnett after having attacked 'Noball' sites in northern France.

Progress of the Attacks, January — March 1944

During the first half of January, 79 ski sites, but no large sites, were attacked (some more than once), the bulk of the effort being made by the squadrons of AEAF. RAF Bomber Command carried out eight attacks but the Eighth Air Force only attacked a site on January 14. Results were not very good. Only eight sites were classified with Category A destruction, four by the Eighth in their single operation and four by AEAF squadrons, so the rate of neutralisation would have to be increased, otherwise the Germans would have as many as 60 sites ready by the end of February. This was even more certain in view of evidence that the repair of damaged sites had begun. Moreover, there were good reasons for using some of the heavy bomber resources against the large sites, four of which — Siracourt, Watten, Sottevast and Lottinghem — had reached, or would reach within a month, a state of development where they could well be attacked again.

All this meant that an increased scale of effort, or alternatively a more accurate one, was required. For a whole week, however, further operations were held up by bad weather and it was not until January 21 that attacks recommenced, both by the Eighth during the day and Bomber Command by night. Forty-five sites were attacked but first reconnaissance showed that only four had been made Category A, all as the result of attacks by the American force. Six Fortresses, two Mosquitos and two fighters had been lost, but there was some compensation as out of approximately 60 German fighters that came up to meet our aircraft, 18 were claimed as destroyed.

Yet despite the fact that B-17s had so far been the most successful aircraft employed, Portal was still loath to divert heavy bombers from their other tasks. Indeed, the Stirling squadrons of Bomber Command, which had met with little success in their night attacks, were diverted from sites at the end of January in order to drop arms to French resistance groups in Haute-Savoie. It was held that while the attack on sites had not come up to expectations, nearly one-third had been neutralised since December 5 and another third damaged less severely. More-accurate bombing by AEAF could be expected as experience accumulated and the weather improved.

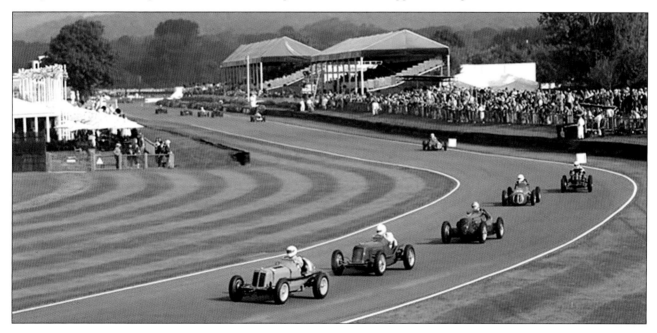

In September 1948, the first motor race was held on the aerodrome's perimeter track. Now this is the Goodwood racetrack and it is the only classic circuit in the world to remain in its original form. It also hosts the annual Goodwood Revival Meeting.

Armourers fit 500lb bombs to one of the squadron's Typhoons in readiness for another attack on the ski sites.

The performance of the AEAF squadrons did in fact improve during the last week in January even though the weather over northern France was still poor. At least six sites were made Category A in attacks on which only 900 tons of bombs were dropped. Four aircraft were lost. Unfortunately, during the week from January 30 to February 5, the weather was bad and only a very small effort (248 tons, dropped entirely by AEAF squadrons) was possible and no sites were vitally damaged.

By this time, a good deal of data had been accumulated on the damage that had been caused to sites and on the rate of repair of damaged sites which allowed a prediction of the progress that could be expected under varying conditions. On the assumption that the Germans were working to a programme of 120 sites, the Operational Research Centre at the Air Ministry calculated that if attacks were carried out by AEAF on all suitable days, and if the Germans maintained the existing rate of repair, no less than 89 sites would probably be complete at the end of March. If double sorties were carried out, as would be possible with the longer days, the number completed would be about 72. If the Eighth Air Force participated on all days that were suitable for visual bombing over northern France but not over Germany, 62 sites would be ready. If they participated on all suitable days, irrespective of the conditions over Germany, the figure would fall still further to 28. In the two latter cases, if AEAF made double sorties between February 15 and the end of March, the number of sites that would be completed would be 46 and 12 respectively.

The implications of this prediction were obvious enough: that AEAF must continue, and if possible increase, their effort and that the Eighth Air Force must operate more frequently than hitherto. However, no new instructions were issued to either force that would have ensured a heavier scale of attack.

In February the total weight of bombs dropped on the sites was 5,527 tons, which was less by 1,200 tons than that dropped in January. In the same month, 67 per cent of AEAF bomber sorties were against sites compared to nearly 94 per cent in the previous month. The Eighth's effort fell by comparatively little in terms of sorties and bombs but it was only 13 per cent of its total effort as compared with 23 per cent in January. In March the effort of the two forces against sites fell still more. The Eighth's heavy bombers made a total of 11,000 sorties of which only 970 were against V-weapon sites. The comparable figures during the same month for the bombers of AEAF were 6,100 and 2,300.

The weather during those two months was often a hindrance to operations over northern France but there were other factors that contributed to the fall in the scale of attack. The Eighth Air Force had first claim on the fighters of the Ninth Air Force whenever targets in Germany were to be attacked, which meant that on those days there were fewer fighters left for covering operations by the Ninth bombers. For example, operations against Berlin in early March employed practically all the Ninth Air Force's fighters, and there was a period during the same month when a complete group of medium bombers (54 aircraft) was only allowed a fighter escort of one squadron. Secondly, with the increase in the anti-aircraft defences of the ski site area, and in particular round Abbeville and St Pol, medium-altitude and low-level attacks became increasingly hazardous, which led to representations by Air Chief Marshal Leigh-Mallory that certain heavily defended sites, including most of the large sites, should be attacked only by heavy bombers. But it was not until the middle of March that the Eighth Air Force took over this responsibility; in the meantime, the scale of effort by AEAF against such sites was low.

Finally, as the time for invading France drew nearer, more of the Marauders of the Ninth Air Force were required for preliminary bombardment, especially of railways. While from the beginning of March a minimum of 70 Marauders was allotted to the attack of sites, inevitably the AEAF effort decreased.

However, an improvement in bombing accuracy during February and March compensated for the somewhat lower effort compared to that of the preceding two months. 'Oboe'-equipped Mosquitos were used to lead formations of medium bombers, and good results continued to be obtained by B-17s and Mosquitos and

On February 15, No. 19 Squadron undertook their first operational sortie over the Continent in their new Mustang IIIs. Although it turned out to be an uneventful flight, all the pilots liked the ability of the new machine to cruise at 250 knots at 25,000 feet.

Bostons of No. 2 Group in low-level attacks. Mitchells also began to improve. Altogether, by the end of March, 65 sites were deemed Category A and another 20 Category B. A number of sites had been repaired but there was good reason to believe that although our scale of attack had not been as heavy as it might have been, it was still heavier than the Germans had budgeted for. Labour appeared to have been seriously disorganised to the point at which repair work was chiefly carried out by pioneer companies of the German Army and only at about a half of the original 96 sites.

At a Chiefs of Staff meeting on April 4, Portal said that providing the number of completed sites could be kept down

Although the flying bomb ski sites had borne the brunt of the attacks, the progress of the large bunker constructions was worrying. At Wizernes, work was obviously proceeding out of view of aerial reconnaissance beneath Ingenieur Flos's massive bomb-proof dome.

to less than 20, a concentrated bombing attack should see the whole of the ski site programme neutralised.

The situation in respect of large sites was not considered to be as satisfactory. Attacks on these had been carried out since the end of January, chiefly by the Eighth and Ninth Air Forces. Thirty-nine attacks were made and nearly 4,000 tons had been dropped. At Martinvast, the damage was such that the site could be ignored for three months, even if vigorous repairs were undertaken. Lottinghem and Wizernes had also been seriously

damaged and were reckoned to be out of action for at least six weeks. At the four others, however, only slight damage appeared to have been inflicted. It was true, of course, that as far as was known, these sites were connected with rockets, not flying bombs, and that the former was not believed to be as immediate a threat as the latter. As construction went ahead at the large sites, the massive main buildings became progressively less vulnerable to attack. Consequently, from the end of March a heavier weight of attack was brought to bear upon them.

Now this is the location of the La Coupole Museum opened in 1997 (see page 29).

Progress of the Attacks, April — June 1944

How quickly the rate of neutralisation could be altered became evident during the second week in April. The reduced effort of March had been more successful proportionately in neutralising sites than any previous month, but it seemed to give the Germans an opportunity to improve the rate of repair. Also, where in the middle of March it had been estimated that there would only be the equivalent of ten sites ready for action by April 15, by that date it seemed that as many as 25 might be completed. The Chiefs of Staff felt compelled to take action and in late March and April they addressed a number of communications to the air force commanders which were designed to bring down a bigger weight of attack on the flying bomb sites.

After their meeting on March 21, both Air Chief Marshal Leigh-Mallory and Lieutenant General Spaatz were requested to intensify the attacks of their forces to which they responded that bad weather continued to hinder operations. After their meeting a fortnight later, Bottomley again wrote to Leigh-Mallory and emphasised the importance of maintaining attack on the sites but the latter pointed out on April 11 that on nearly half the days in the previous month operations had been impossible owing to the weather. In addition, targets other than ski sites had been given priority of attack. Also most of the ski sites still intact were in heavily defended areas where tactical bombers were liable to heavy losses. Leigh-Mallory asked, therefore, that the Eighth Air Force should make at least one full-scale effort each week against ski sites in order to ensure that the menace was kept under control.

A week later the Chiefs of Staff pursued the matter further in a letter addressed still higher up in the chain of command: to General Eisenhower. The Supreme Allied Commander had by this time taken over the direction of the operations of the strategical and tactical air forces in the United Kingdom but responsibility to the War Cabinet for

action effecting the security of the United Kingdom still remained with the British Chiefs of Staff. Accordingly, on April 18, a letter was sent to him in which the Chiefs of Staff expressed the War Cabinet's concern at the deterioration of the ski site position. The Supreme Commander was told that unless action was taken immediately to bring to bear a heavy scale of attack, the enemy might be able to recover from previous bomb-

ing and build up a threat which would divert strong Allied air forces, perhaps at a time when the invasion of France called for our greatest effort in the air. Eisenhower was also made aware of the dissatisfaction of the Chiefs of Staff at the failure to seriously damage the majority of the large sites. However, the Chiefs fought shy of demanding a reduction of the effort against German industry which was the biggest obstacle to

While counter-measures were being taken against the threat in north-western France, we must not forget that the Germans were taking equal measures of their own to redress the position in eastern Europe. After the devastating raid on Peenemünde in August 1943, another test site was urgently required. Within ten days a new firing range — albeit overland — was chosen in Poland. Heidelager (Heath Camp) was an exercise area, roughly midway between Krakow and Lublin, in the middle of extensive woodland at Blizna that had originally been a Polish ordnance depot. It was inspected by Reichsführer-SS Heinrich Himmler on September 28 and, taken over by the SS, facilities for test-firing A4 rockets were quickly built, with a railway spur leading directly into the site.

At the end of October an experimental rocket unit, Lehr- und Versuchs-Batterie 444 under Major Wolfgang Weber, was set up to train soldiers to fire the weapons.

Today the concrete access road is the most obvious relic at Heidelager together with a small section of narrow-gauge railway crossing it.

However, the first test on November 5 was a failure as the launch pad was only resting on sand. After ignition the blast from the exhaust blew away the sand from one of the supporting legs causing the rocket to take off at an inclined angle, crashing two miles away. As a result, concrete launch pads had to be built; Peter Schenk photographed this one in 1994.

During May and early June attacks on ski sites continued to be as successful as those on large sites were not. The number of ski sites reckoned Category A was now 86, eight were Category B and only two were undamaged. Considering that the relative effort of the Eighth Air Force was only a little more than five per cent and that of the AEAF 25 per cent for the first half of the month and only ten per cent during the second half, this was very satisfactory. The fall in the second half of the month itself reflected the success of previous attacks and was the response of AEAF to a request from the Chiefs of Staff that more effort should be put into preparations for 'Overlord' There were, however, still four large sites which were reckoned virtually undamaged, but after May 30 no further attacks were made upon them until after flying bomb attacks had begun.

increasing the weight of attack on 'Crossbow'. Their requirement was phrased thus: '[The Chiefs of Staff] request that you give attacks on "Crossbow" objectives priority over all other operations except "Pointblank" [attacks to destroy German fighter aircraft and its industry] until such time as the threat is overcome and that both the Eighth Air Force and the Tactical Air Forces be instructed to take the fullest advantage of any opportunities to attack both large sites and ski sites from now onwards.'

The close relationship between the two operations was certainly appreciated by the Supreme Commander and his deputy. On April 19, Air Chief Marshal Sir Arthur Tedder wrote to Leigh-Mallory, with reference to the Chiefs of Staffs request to General Eisenhower. He agreed that both the ski sites and large sites could not be allowed to develop at their present rate but he did not indicate any interference with the heavy bomber offensive. Tedder simply laid down that 'attacks on "Crossbow" objectives by the Tactical Air Forces should be given priority over all other air operations'.

The tonnage notably increased from the middle of April. Over 4,000 tons of bombs were dropped on ski sites during the second half of the month compared with the whole of March. Sixteen hundred tons of bombs were also dropped on large sites during the same period. Results were good in the case of the ski site attacks and 75 were now claimed as Category A and 17 Category B by the end of the month. At the large sites, however, no fresh major damage could be discerned. Accordingly, on May 2 the Chiefs of Staff agreed that attacks on large sites should be carried out in preference to those on ski sites. It is not untypical that far from this resulting in a larger effort, only 1,100 tons were dropped on large sites during the first half of May which was only two-thirds the tonnage dropped during the second half of April. A similar weight of bombs was dropped in the second half of May.

The museum now established at Blizna has had to make do with a full-size replica of a V2 rocket.

The testing ground was soon located by the Polish resistance movement, and members attempted to recover pieces of crashed rockets before the Germans arrived as most were blowing up on re-entry. The Poles also even had a plan to try to capture a complete unexploded V2 rocket. Although it is jumping ahead in our story, in May 1944 a rocket came to earth on the bank of the Bug river near the village of Sarnaki (see map opposite), and the resistance managed to retrieve much of it including the very heavy combustion chamber.

The Germans initially called the V1 the Fi 103, the main contractor being Fieseler, but it also had a cover name 'Flakzielgerät 76' (Anti-Aircraft Aiming Device 76) abbreviated to FZG 76. The Ministry of Home Security first referred to the weapon as a Pilotless Aircraft, shortened to P.A.C., but after a meeting on June 19 the official name became 'flying bomb' although popularly known to Britons as the Doodlebug or Buzz-Bomb.

The Situation prior to the Commencement of Flying Bomb Attacks

Of the two types of 'Crossbow' target that were attacked in 1944 prior to D-Day, the ski sites were known to be for the launching of flying bombs while the large sites were only thought to be connected with rockets. Definite information of the first, compared to the lack of certainty concerning the second, only reflected the state of intelligence on all aspects of the two weapons.

Investigation into rockets had gone on during the winter of 1943 and in the following spring new and important information had been coming in. Fresh evidence of development had been found and new channels of intelligence had been opened but the main problems had yet to be solved: i.e. the weight of the rocket and in particular that of the warhead; the propellant fuel or fuels, and the method of launching. Consequently, the few rocket targets that were known or suspected remained an objective subsidiary to the flying bomb sites. Large sites, as we have seen, were attacked, although rather as an insurance against a possible failure on the part of intelligence, and in order to delay the time when successful attack upon them would be exceptionally difficult rather than because rockets were deemed as immediate a menace as flying bombs.

Estimates of the Scale and Time of Flying Bomb Attack

It is significant that in all the estimates made during the first months of 1944 of the possible scale of attack against the United Kingdom, rockets were not taken into account. The calculations were worked out in terms of flying bombs only with some allowance being made for attacks by piloted aircraft. The possibility of dependable assessments was largely determined by what was known of the characteristics of flying bombs, what stage their development had reached, how many had been produced, and what was the rate of fire at the launching sites.

Thanks to the information that had been coming through since the autumn of 1943 on the trials that the Germans were conducting on the Baltic coast, most of the details of the performance of the weapon had been established and, as it turned out, with fair accuracy. The height of 3,000 feet, at which the majority of the flying bombs that were launched against London flew, was lower than had been anticipated, but otherwise there were no serious discrepancies between estimated and actual performance.

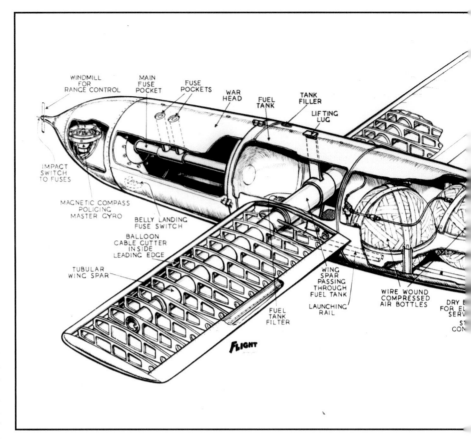

The V1 had a wing span of 17 feet 6 inches and an overall length of 25 feet 4½ inches, constructed largely of thin sheet steel and plywood. Armed with an explosive nose, the missile was propelled by a pulse-jet engine using 150 gallons of petrol for fuel and compressed air as the oxidizer. The direction, altitude and range of flight were governed automatically by a gyroscopic unit that initiated signals to the air-operated rudder and elevator which stabilised the bomb in all three attitudes, directional information being obtained from a pre-set compass. An air-log driven by a small nose airscrew measured the pre-set distance after which the elevators were depressed and the missile dived into its target. Before launching, the missile was taken to a non-magnetic building, where it was aligned and the desired bearing for the flight was set. For the launch (see pages 20-21), the V1 and cradle were placed on an inclined ramp, 150 feet long, beneath which was a slotted tube containing a piston in a combustion chamber. A fin projected through the slot in the firing tube and was fixed to the underside of the fuselage. Hydrogen peroxide and calcium permanganate were injected by compressed air into the firing-tube combustion chamber. When the chemical reaction had supplied enough gas pressure behind the piston, a quarter-inch retaining bolt gave way, and the piston travelled up the firing tube with increasing acceleration, carrying with it the missile. At the same time, as the fuel was injected into the combustion chamber, a current was supplied to the spark plug on the missile's propulsion unit, which proceeded to run at full power for about seven seconds. At the end of the ramp, the piston and cradle fell to the ground and were used again.

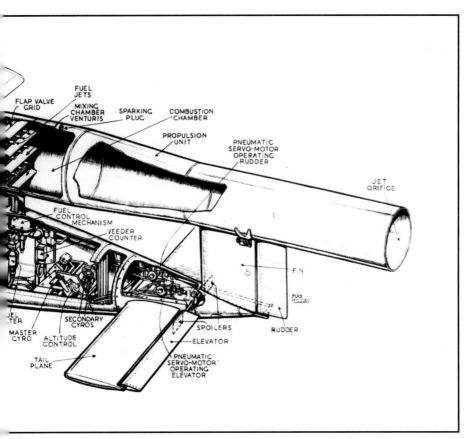

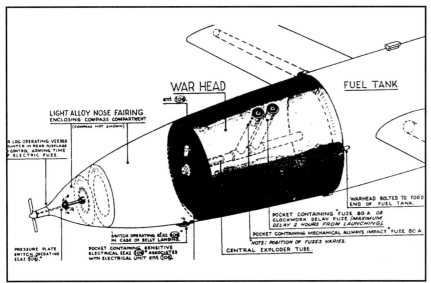

The warhead contained 850kg of high explosive and was bolted to the forward end of the fuel tank. A steel exploder tube ran longitudinally through the centre of the warhead; this tube had a fuze pocket in the forward end and two fuze pockets at right angles to the exploder tube. The fuzing system consisted of one electrical impact fuze El.A.Z 106*, one mechanical all-ways impact fuze 80 A, and a mechanical clockwork delay fuze of the 17 B type. The El.A.Z 106* was a new design of a sensitive electrical impact fuze, primarily designed to detonate on impact with the minimum penetration and the maximum blast effect. This was charged from a 30-volt dry battery and was armed by means of the air-log veeder counter switch approximately 40 miles after take-off. It was placed in the forward end of the exploder tube, and could operate by a sensitive pressure-plate nose switch operated by an extension to the propeller shaft of the air-log which functioned upon nose impact — the switch making an electrical connection to the fuze. The time-delay fuze 17 B had a clockwork movement but it was armed mechanically, not electrically as in the case of the bomb fuze. The fuze was armed immediately on take-off by the withdrawal of a pin by remote control, causing the clockwork delay mechanism to start working. The maximum delay of this fuze was two hours. In the event of a belly landing, another electrical switch was positioned on the underside of the fuselage in front of the warhead. There was also an inertia bolt within the fuze which operated on nose impact if for any reason the fuze did not function by either of the other two methods.

The method of propulsion remained uncertain until late in May 1944 when officers of Air Intelligence were able to examine a flying bomb that came down in Sweden and for this reason it was not possible to be precise about the size of the warhead until a short time before the attacks begun. However, a warhead weighing approximately one ton was usually assumed which was not far removed from its actual size.

Intelligence sources on the Baltic coast continued to transmit details of successive trials, from which it followed that development work was still taking place, and from which Dr Jones and his staff were able to work out the factor of accuracy for the weapon. Stated in terms of bombs launched that would reach the London area, this changed from 30 per cent in January to nearly 60 per cent in April, reflecting improved performance in the German trials.

The fact that trials were still going on during the early part of 1944, presumably in order to improve the accuracy of the weapon and perfect the technique of launching, did not mean — nor was it taken to mean — that flying bombs were not already being produced. How many had been produced and what was the rate of production was simply not known; and, in the absence of this information, estimates of the likely scale of attack were little more than guesses. However, some sort of estimate was called for and one was proffered by the Joint Intelligence Committee through the Chiefs of Staff on February 2, 1944. Mid-March was the date by which the flying bomb might become operative, an initial attack of 400 tons of bombs spread over a period of 10 hours was thought possible. Thereafter 600 tons a month could be expected of which at 400 tons at most could arrive in ten hours.

With the advance in the knowledge of the extent of the ski site programme, and as the bombing of sites achieved notable results, a further estimate was advanced in the middle of March, even though there was no evidence of the scale of German production. However, assuming that 2,000 flying bombs had been produced, and that monthly production was in the region of 1,000, it was calculated that the Germans would have so few completed ski sites (probably about ten) by the middle of April that they would be capable of mounting only a very reduced scale of attack.

The Air Staff, for it was they who were responsible for the estimate, pointed out that on the night of February 18/19, German bombers had dropped 135 tons of bombs on London, the implication presumably being that prospective attacks by flying bombs would be no worse than the raids that London had been suffering.

And indeed as April and May went by, and the number of ski sites capable of firing remained at less than ten, there is no reason to doubt that the scale of attack from this sort of site would have been negligible. This is, of course, an index of the success that had attended the Allied bombing as it had neutralised almost completely the machinery of ski sites from which the Germans had originally planned to launch their attack.

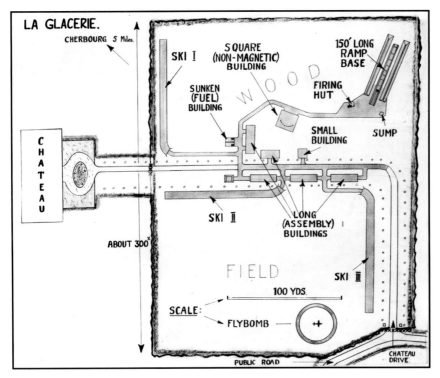

LA GLACERIE.

CHERBOURG 5 Miles.

SKI I

SQUARE (NON-MAGNETIC) BUILDING

150' LONG RAMP BASE

SUNKEN (FUEL) BUILDING

WOOD

FIRING HUT

CHATEAU

SMALL BUILDING

SUMP

SKI II

LONG (ASSEMBLY) BUILDINGS

ABOUT 300'

FIELD

SKI III

100 YDS.

SCALE:

FLYBOMB

PUBLIC ROAD

CHATEAU DRIVE.

The attacks on the ski sites had demonstrated to the Germans just how vulnerable they were so it was decided that the 96 launch sites already built would be abandoned, although efforts would still be made to repair them to divert attention from their replacements. Consequently, Allied air operations continued against the ski sites for over three months with 23,000 tons of bombs dropped on useless targets. (This is 'ski site' No. 57 — see list on page 58.)

Appearance of the Modified Sites

Nevertheless, it equally became clear that long before the Allied attacks had begun to show such dividends, the Germans had decided on an amended policy of site construction but Air Intelligence knew nothing of this until the end of April 1944. It was on April 27 that scrutiny of the results of a photographic reconnaissance of the Cherbourg peninsula revealed what was suspected to be a new type of site near the village of Belhamelin.

During the next fortnight the examination of previous photographs and fresh reconnaissance showed that an extensive programme of new sites was indeed being carried out. On May 13, it was reported that 20 of the new sites had already been identified: nine in the Pas-de-Calais and 11 in the Cherbourg peninsular. They were termed 'modified sites' by Air Intelligence for a good reason, that while they included certain essential features of the ski sites, they had none of the ski-shaped buildings that had been such a distinguishing feature of the latter. Apart from the launching ramp and the square non-magnetic building, in which the gyro compass of the flying bomb was adjusted, the other buildings of the modified site were not standardised as they were at ski sites, Furthermore, to confuse reconnaissance and hinder identification, many of the sites embodied innocuous farm buildings.

During the next three weeks intense photographic reconnaissance revealed many more sites. By June 12, the day before the first flying bombs were launched against London, 66 modified sites had been identified. Forty-two were in the area Somme—Pas-de-Calais, all aligned on London, and 24 in the Cherbourg peninsula and the Calvados department, all aligned on South Coast ports and Bristol.

This implied a far swifter rate of construction than at the ski sites and the explanation was, so Air Intelligence reported on June 9, that prefabricated units were used for the square building and the foundations of the launching ramp, the two essential components of the site. Once these structures had been placed in position, the whole site could be completed within a fortnight.

The threat was obvious enough but the modified sites were an even more difficult target than ski sites. An experimental attack was carried out by Typhoons of the Second Tactical Air Force on a site in the Cherbourg peninsula on May 27, but met with little success, the pilots reporting that it had been extremely difficult to locate. However, there was some doubt whether the new launching system was best attacked at the sites themselves. The size and construction of a typical modified site included no facilities, so far as could be seen, for storing and assembling flying bombs. Therefore, the rate of fire might be most affected if the sources from which missiles and fuel were transported to the sites were identified and attacked. Hence the eight so-called supply sites came into the picture once more.

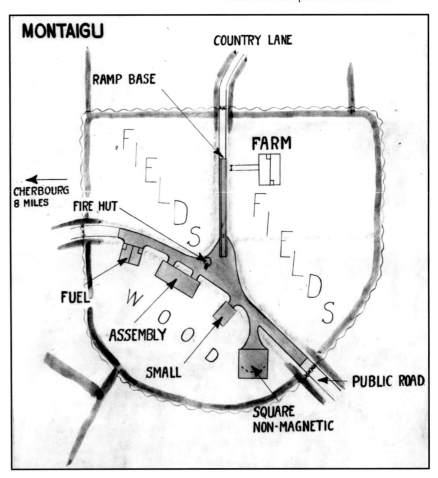

MONTAIGU

COUNTRY LANE

RAMP BASE

FIELDS

FARM

CHERBOURG 8 MILES

FIRE HUT

FUEL

WOOD

ASSEMBLY

SMALL

FIELDS

PUBLIC ROAD

SQUARE NON-MAGNETIC

The new launch sites were of a much simpler design without the tell-tale ski building. Partly prefabricated and well dispersed and camouflaged, it was intended that the 'modified sites' would not be easy for the Allies to find and destroy.

The two launch sites illustrated opposite were both located near Cherbourg, but as the city was in American hands by the end of June, V1 sites in the peninsula saw little action.

This ski site at Château du Pannelier (La Sorellerie II), No. 58 on the list on page 59, was pictured on June 20, the day it was captured.

Up to the middle of May, these had remained inactive; nor was there any correlation between their location and that of the modified sites. Some were as close as three miles but others were as far away as 25 miles. Presumably the large sites had been erected for a purpose, which seemed to be that of supply, and presumably the Germans intended to use them for all were well defended. Thus, on May 16, the Chiefs of Staff invited the Air Ministry to examine and report on the desirability of attacking supply sites rather than the new type pilotless aircraft sites. Ten days elapsed before a report was rendered. In it, it

was admitted that no relationship between the two types of site could be established, but as photographic reconnaissance alone could not settle what was the purpose of the supply sites, it was recommended that an attack by heavy day bombers be made against a selected site. This would at least display the enemy's reaction and, if it was followed closely by photographic reconnaissance, might indicate the contents of the various buildings. To this the Chiefs of Staff agreed.

The first attack was made against the site at Beauvoir on May 29 by 64 Marauders of the Eighth Air Force, a

second attack by their Liberators taking place a few days later. In all, 293 tons of bombs were dropped. Results were not considered satisfactory but there was one thing that was thought to be significant: that up to June 10 the Germans had made no attempt to repair a number of breaches that had been made in the railway line that led to the site. Nor had there been any indications at other supply sites that the Germans were moving in supplies. Therefore, the supply sites were still an unknown quantity with no connection established between them and the modified sites.

This modified site constructed on a farm near the hamlet of La Sorellerie, five miles to the south-east of Cherbourg.

The iron rails have been camouflaged with hay against aerial observation.

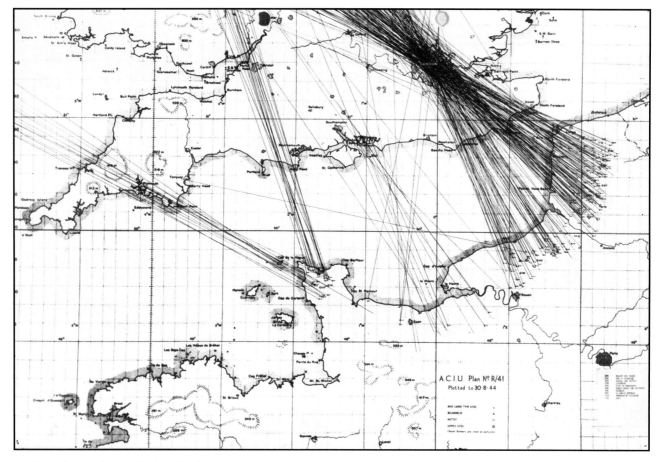

By the end of April, the Chiefs of Staff believed that practically all the launch sites (ski-type) had been neutralised, but in fact by then the Germans claimed to have built 95 of the new modified sites. The first one was identified at Belhamelin, near Cherbourg, and by June 9 over 47 of the modified sites had been logged by the Allied Central Interpretation Unit at Medmenham where they were plotted with their firing lines to London, Plymouth and Bristol.

Final Reports on the Prospects of Flying Bomb Attack

It had always been appreciated that an indication that attack was imminent would be obtained partly from the state of preparedness at the launching sites, and more particularly from reports of the movement of supplies towards the sites. Up to and including June 11 there was no evidence that supplies were on their way so the Deputy Chief of Air Staff Sir Norman Bottomley reported that the general position was as follows:

'It is estimated that the fire-power which might be developed from those ski sites aligned on London is equivalent to that of approximately eight completed sites. This is on the assumption that all the necessary technical equipment and weapons are available at sites; there is as yet no confirmation of this. On this basis it is estimated that the scale of attack on Greater London by pilotless aircraft does not amount to more than the equivalent of 90 tons of bombs in a period of ten hours. The number of times it will be possible for the enemy to repeat such a scale of attack will depend upon the reserve of weapons he is able to accumulate in firing areas. It is likely that the damage caused to his communications, and the fact that other transport commitments have over-riding priority, will so affect the delivery of pilotless aircraft from Germany that, for the time being, he will not be able to sustain more than minor harassing attacks.

'The above estimate of the scale of attack does not take into account the modified sites. From an examination of the evidence received to date, it does not appear probable that these sites will be completed and capable of operating pilotless aircraft on any appreciable scale within the next three or four weeks.'

Fortunately for the credit of Air Intelligence this was not the last forecast before the attack opened. On the same day as the report was submitted, photographic reconnaissance were flown over a number of modified sites in the Pas-de-Calais. They were the first since June 4, the weather having been bad during the intervening week. Photographs of nine sites were immediately examined by the Central Interpretation Unit and the results were embodied in a report that was made to the Chiefs of Staff on the morning of June 12.

It appeared that there was much activity at six out of the nine sites; rails had been laid on the launching ramps at four sites and at six sites the square non-magnetic building had been completed. A report had also been received on the 11th from a usually reliable source that on the 9th/10th, a train of 33 wagons, each nearly 60 feet long, and each loaded with three 'rockets' had passed through Ghent for Tourcoing. According to our agent, further trains were expected.

In the view of Air Intelligence, the objects were more likely to be the fuselages of flying bombs rather than A4 rockets. 'Without further evidence no definite conclusion can be arrived at in regard to the intended scale and timing of an attack on this country, but the indications are that the Germans are making energetic preparations to bring the pilotless aircraft sites into operation at an early date'.

The next question was what scale of attack would the modified sites be capable of? In a brief that was prepared on June 12 for the use of the Deputy Chief of Air Staff at a meeting of the Chiefs of Staff to be held on the following day, this was assessed at much the same figure as had been arrived at early in February, i.e. an initial heavy attack equivalent to 400 tons of bombs in ten hours, two repeat attacks of the some scale at intervals of 48 hours, and thereafter 600 tons a month. This was expected to be the maximum weight of attack but it was not anticipated that the Germans would be able to achieve it because of the unreliable communications between northern France and Germany.

Nevertheless, the signs that attack was imminent were not to be ignored, and the Deputy Chief of Air Staff intended to ask the Chiefs of Staff on the 13th to agree to attacks on the four supply sites in the area Somme—Pas-de-Calais but by that time the first flying bombs had been launched against the United Kingdom. The threat so long apprehended had at last materialised.

15.12.43

APPENDIX A

J.I.C. NO.	NAME	MAP REF. OF SQUARE BUILDING	JULY 27-AUGUST % DATE	SEPTEMBER % DATE	OCTOBER % DATE	NOVEMBER % DATE	DECEMBER % DATE	ESTIMATED STATE OF COMPLETION 11.12.43
28	YVRENCH/BOIS CARRE	926914	2 16.8.43	No cover	No cover	65 3.11.43 / 90 26.11.43		99
19	LIGESCOURT/BOIS DE ST.SAULVE	816042	2? 16.8.43	No cover	No cover	58 3.11.43 / 80 26.11.43		94
8	BELLEVUE	946305	0 30.7.43	15 24.9.43	No cover	63 19.11.43	78 2.12.43	90
22	CROISETTE	111095	No cover	No cover	5 3.10.43	73 26.11.43		89
27	GUESCHART	915978	0 16.8.43	4 16.9.43	No cover	55 3.11.43 / 74 30.11.43		86
30	MAISON PONTHIEU I	935936	0 16.8.43	No cover	No cover	49 3.11.43 / 69 24.11.43		86
	FORET D'HESDIN	947162	0 16.8.43	2? 16.9.43	No cover	48? 3.11.43		86 ?
31	LE MEILLARD	0.9908	No cover	2 16.9.43	No cover	72 28.11.43		84
52	LE PETIT BOIS LOBERT	443430	No cover	5 23.9.43	No cover	No cover		84 ?
61	LABROYE	898039	No cover	4 16.9.43	No cover	44 3.11.43		82
15	BRUNEHAUTPRE FME	810181	0 30.7.43	0 6.9.43	No cover	36 3.11.43 / 64 26.11.43		79

On December 15, the Central Interpretation Unit at Medmenham produced these listings of known V1 launch sites, although unfortunately they are not of the best quality. Nineteen of them, in the early stages of construction, had been identified by November 7 although at that stage they were still considered as being connected to the rocket or storage sites. The tally had risen to 26 by November 10 but there was still a failure to connect these sites with pilotless aircraft. By November 24 the number of sites that had been identified was 38, the final total being 96. (See also plan on pages 32-33.)

Broadly speaking, however, from November 1943 to June 1944 the rocket was, as it were, in eclipse. The main concern was the flying bomb and the sites from which it was expected that attack would be launched. The offensive against the latter began on December 5 and lasted until the end of May. The progress that was made in destroying sites was never constant, varying principally according to the weight of attack that was brought to bear. Nor were the arrangements that were made between each of the attacking forces, AEAF and the Eighth Air Force, satisfactory.

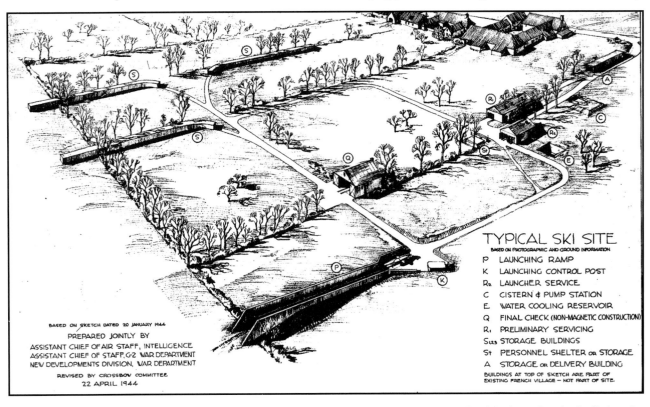

BASED ON SKETCH DATED 20 JANUARY 1944

PREPARED JOINTLY BY
ASSISTANT CHIEF OF AIR STAFF, INTELLIGENCE
ASSISTANT CHIEF OF STAFF, G-2 WAR DEPARTMENT
NEW DEVELOPMENTS DIVISION, WAR DEPARTMENT

REVISED BY CROSSBOW COMMITTEE
22 APRIL 1944

TYPICAL SKI SITE
BASED ON PHOTOGRAPHIC AND GROUND INFORMATION

P   LAUNCHING RAMP
K   LAUNCHING CONTROL POST
R₂ LAUNCHER SERVICE
C   CISTERN & PUMP STATION
E   WATER COOLING RESERVOIR
Q   FINAL CHECK (NON-MAGNETIC CONSTRUCTION)
R₁ PRELIMINARY SERVICING
S₁₂₃ STORAGE BUILDINGS
S₁ PERSONNEL SHELTER or STORAGE
A   STORAGE or DELIVERY BUILDING

BUILDINGS AT TOP OF SKETCH ARE PART OF EXISTING FRENCH VILLAGE - NOT PART OF SITE

Maisoncelle (Site No. 14) was chosen by the Crossbow Committee as a good example to show photo-interpreters — and aircrews — a typical ski site, and this schematic drawing was produced as an aid to identification in April 1944. However, after the intensive bombing campaign to neutralise the sites, it came as a huge shock to learn late in April that the Germans had abandoned the idea of using the ski sites (except perhaps for two of them) in favour of a much simpler 'modified' type of launch site, much harder to identify and knock out.

J.I.C. NO.	NAME	MAP REF. OF SQUARE BUILDING	JULY 27-AUGUST (DATE)	SEPTEMBER (DATE)	OCTOBER (DATE)	NOVEMBER (DATE)	DECEMBER (DATE)	ESTIMATED STATE OF COMPLETION 11.12.43
49	BONIFTOT	183440	No cover	No cover	No cover	40 3.11.43		78%
23	AGENVILLERS	845924	0 16.8.43	10 16.9.43	No cover	65 29.11.43		77%
34	AILLY-LE-HAUT-CLOCHER	890809	0 16.8.43	4 16.9.43	No cover	45 3.11.43 / 65 30.11.43		76%
16	ST. JOSSE-AU-BOIS	853107	0 16.8.43	8 16.9.43	No cover	53 17.11.43 / 60 26.11.43		75%
46	FUCHERVIN	531576	0 28.7.43	No cover	No cover	55 23.11.43 / 60 26.11.43		75%
14	MAISONCELLE	032204	0 30.7.43	No cover	½ 20.10.43	5 3.11.43 / 50? 19.11.43	65? 2.12.43	74%?
17	COLMEUX	055149	0 30.7.43	0 4.9.43	No cover	58 26.11.43		73%
36	DOMART-EN-PONTHIEU	966775	0 26.7.43	No cover	No cover	37 3.11.43 / 57? 26.11.43		72%?
47	LE MESNIL-ALLARD	592559	No cover	No cover	No cover	50? 19.11.43		72%?
24	YVRENCHEUX/BOIS DE MARIPEL	892920 / 834923	0 16.8.43	10 16.9.43	No cover	37 3.11.43 / 54 29.11.43		72%
29	MAISON PONTHIEU III	929927	0 16.8.43	No cover	No cover	34 3.11.43		72%
1	LOSTEBARNE/ARDRES	941642	0 15.8.43	0 22.9.43	No cover	20? 5.11.43 / 55? 25.11.43		71%?

Nevertheless, by the end of April the ski sites were so badly damaged that their potential rate of fire was no serious menace; and this was the position when the invasion of France began. What was

After the first of the new sites was discovered at Belhamelin, photo interpreter Wing Commander Douglas Kendall issued a memo on June 6 for an urgent investigation into what he then called 'Belhamelin' sites (rather than the term 'modified' adopted later). He wanted to know if the firing ramps were the same length as the one at Bois Carré. He also warned that a number of the latter sites were being sufficiently repaired and could be used as Belhamelins, and that if an attack should develop, it could come from well over 100 sites.

J.I.C. NO.	NAME	MAP REF. OF SQUARE BUILDING	JULY 27-AUGUST (DATE)	SEPTEMBER (DATE)	OCTOBER (DATE)	NOVEMBER (DATE)	DECEMBER (DATE)	ESTIMATED STATE OF COMPLETION 11.12.43
33	BEAUVOIR	117963	0 16.8.43	10 16.9.43	No cover	54? 25.11.43	60? 1.12.43	70%?
45	PRESUSVILLE	592559	0 28.7.43	2 4.9.43	No cover	45 3.11.43 / 55 26.11.43		70%
50	FREVAL	271473	No cover	No cover	No cover	30 3.11.43		68%
35	GORENFLOS	935810	0 16.8.43	4 16.9.43	No cover	30? 3.11.43		68%?
20	VACQUERIETTE	975076	0 16.8.43	4 16.9.43	No cover	No cover	57 1.12.43	67%
3	CORMETTE	074548	0 15.8.43	No cover	5 3.10.43	30? 19.11.43 / 55 29.11.43		67%
2	COCOVE	005635	No cover	1 23.9.43	No cover	No cover	60? 5.12.43	66%?
57	LA GLACERIE	184179	No cover	0 13.9.43	2 3.10.43 / 25 28.10.43	No cover	58 2.12.43	66%
65	AUDINGHEN	049369	No cover	No cover	No cover	No cover	55 1.12.43	65%
4	DRIONVILLE	982429	No cover	No cover	No cover	45 19.11.43	55 1.12.43	65%
21	VACQUERIE-LE-BOUCQ	059002	0 16.8.43	5 16.9.43	No cover	50 26.11.43		65%
41	HERBOUVILLE	113516	No cover	No cover	10 30.10.43	25 3.11.43		63%
26	NOYELLE-EN-CHAUSSEE	904954	0 16.8.43	1 16.9.43	No cover	27? 3.11.43 / 50? 29.11.43		62%?

J.I.C. NO.	NAME	MAP REF. OF SQUARE BUILDING	JULY 27-AUGUST DATE	SEPTEMBER DATE	OCTOBER DATE	NOVEMBER DATE	DECEMBER DATE	ESTIMATED STATE OF COMPLETION 11.12.43
32	BONIERES	102974	0 16. 8.43	4. 16. 9.43	No cover	50? 29.11.43		62 ?
63	QUOEUX	993043	0 16. 8.43	5 16. 9.43	No cover	50 29.11.43		62
6	BOIS DES HUIT RUES	301476	No cover	No cover	0 22.10.43	45? 25.11.43		61 ?
5	HEURINGHEM	162482	0 15. 8.43	0 16. 9.43	No cover	25? 5.11.43		61 ?
42	ST. AGATHE D'ALIERMONT	323569	No cover	No cover	6 3.10.43	45 26.11.43		60
51	POMMERVAL	395462	No cover	15 23. 9.43	No cover	45 26.11.43		60
55	LA BRISTELLERIE	117168	No cover	0 3. 9.43	20 27.10.43	46 25.11.43		60
59	MESNIL-AU-VAL/LA BORDONNERIE	214175	No cover	No cover	2 3.10.43	44 10.11.43	50 2.12.43	59
44	ST. PIERRE-DES-JONQUERES	492587	0 28. 7.43	No cover	No cover	39 3.11.43 / 48 30.11.43		55
54	FLOTTEMANVILLE-HAGUE II	088215	No cover	2 3. 9.43	6 2.10.43 / 12 20.10.43	42 25.11.43		58
60	BOIS DE CREUX	939278	0 30. 7.43	2 24. 9.43	No cover	No cover	45? 2.12.43	54 ?
64	LA SORELLERIE III	195164	½ 15. 8.43	No cover	2 3.10.43	No cover	45? 2.12.43	53 ?
38	LONGUEMONT	681749	0 13. 7.43	No cover	6 20.10.43	30? 19.11.43		52 ?
53	FLOTTEMANVILLE-HAGUE I	068222	No cover	2 15. 9.43	20 20.10.43	35 25.11.43		51

not least notable about this victory was that it had been achieved without interfering to any notable extent with bombardment preliminary to invasion.

This attack on ski sites was indeed an Allied victory in that it forced the Germans first to amend and finally to abandon their original system of sites, none of which, or possibly only one, was actually used. It appears that the Germans appreciated the vulnerability of the ski sites almost as soon as attacks upon them had started — one would have thought they might have appreci-

ated this even earlier — but it was not until the end of March 1944 that they began the construction of the modified type of site which they had designed in the meantime. While this was evidence of the success of Allied bombing it was also proof of the German determination to bring their novel weapon into action; and it was in fact from the modified sites that the main attack upon London was launched. Thus it cannot be claimed that the victory of the Allied bombers was absolute. On account of the bombing the Germans were forced

to alter their plans; but their plans were sufficiently flexible for an alternative system of sites to be constructed and brought into operation. On the whole, however, there was much to be thankful for on June 12, 1944. For the invasion of France had been successfully launched and Allied troops were established there; whereas when the threat from the new German weapons had first appeared there seemed to be the possibility that it would force at least the amendment of the invasion plans if not their abandonment.

J.I.C. NO.	NAME	MAP REF. OF SQUARE BUILDING	JULY 27-AUGUST DATE	SEPTEMBER DATE	OCTOBER DATE	NOVEMBER DATE	DECEMBER DATE	ESTIMATED STATE OF COMPLETION 11.12.43
39	MARQUENNEVILLE / Le Plouy Ferme	733717	0 15. 7.43	No cover	4 20.10.43	36 26.11.43		51
11	LE PLOUY	869231	0 16. 8.43	1 6. 9.43	No cover	34 25.11.43		50
18	BOIS DE LA JUSTICE	139187	No cover	No cover	No cover	35? 26.11.43		50 ?
56	HARDINVAST-LA-MOTTERIE	129173	No cover	0 3. 9.43 / 2 13. 9.43	No cover	35 25.11.43		49
58	LA SORELLERIE II	181154	No cover	No cover	2 9.10.43	No cover	40? 2.12.43	48 ?
62	MONTORGUEIL	978032	No cover	6 16. 9.43	No cover	35 29.11.43		47
	BEHEN	722794	0 26. 7.43	No cover	20 20.10.43	21? 3.11.43 / 30? 25.11.43		46 ?
9	FRUGES/BOIS DE COUPELLE	028305	0 30. 7.43	No cover	No cover	30? 25.11.43		46 ?
48	BELLEVILLE-EN-CAUX	143451	0 28. 7.43	No cover	No cover	30? 25.11.43		46 ?
13	RUISSEAUVILLE	018244	0 28. 7.43	2 24. 9.43	No cover	25 25.11.43		41
43	BAILLY-LA-CAMPAGNE	475594	0 28. 7.43	No cover	10 30.10.43	15 3.11.43 / 25 26.11.43		40
12	BOIS DE POTHIER	896266	0 30. 7.43	No cover	No cover	2 3.11.43 / 10? 19.11.43		38?
40	BOIS COQUEREL	777736	0 26. 7.43	No cover	10? 20.10.43	20 26.11.43		35 ?
66	ZUDAUSQUES	No square building	0 15. 8.43	0 16. 9.43	No cover	No cover	15? 5.12.43	20 ?

MOST SECRET

R.A.F. STATION, MEDMENHAM

+ NOTE: Where assessments have been affected by poor quality photographs, trees, shadows, etc. a ? has been added.

The first flying bomb to fall in the United Kingdom came down at 04.13 hours on June 13 at Swanscombe, four and a half miles west of Gravesend. Six minutes later a second fell at Cuckfield in Sussex, followed by one at Bethnal Green, where the LNER bridge over Grove Road was hit. A fourth bomb fell at 05.06 hours at Platt, near Sevenoaks. The only casualties were at Bethnal Green where six people were killed and nine seriously injured.

These were the only flying bombs to fall on British territory until the night of June 15/16. First reports from the radar stations and the Royal Observer Corps indicated that as many as 27 were launched, including four from the Cherbourg peninsula towards Lyme Bay but, after analysis, this figure was reduced to 11. A well-informed prisoner who was captured in April 1945 said that only four or five were despatched; while according to the war diary of Flak-Regiment 155 (W), seven were launched, four of them unsuccessfully.

What is beyond doubt, however, is that the attack was not a mere trial. It was intended to be the beginning of a full-scale offensive, with piloted bombers of the Luftwaffe participating in at least the initial attack. One Me 410 was certainly over the London area on the morning of the 13th, and was shot down by anti-aircraft fire near Barking at 03.05 hours, but the enemy found it impossible either to carry out the joint operation or to bring more than one or two sites into action.

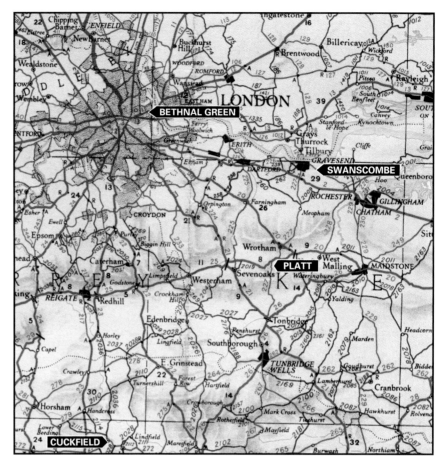

The locations of the first four V1s to come down in Britain on June 13, 1944.

The First Attacks: June 13 to July 15, 1944

Action taken in the United Kingdom

At the meeting of the Chiefs of Staff Committee on the morning of the 13th, the Chief of the Air Staff reported that it was not certain whether the attack had come from such ski sites as were complete or from modified sites. As the evidence pointed to the latter, the question was whether the modified sites should be attacked. Forty-two of these had been identified in the area Somme—Pas-de-Calais, and it was estimated that some 3,000 Fortress sorties or 5,000 by Marauders would be required to neutralise them. This meant a large diversion from the needs of the battle in Normandy.

On the other hand, the four supply sites in the same area — Domléger, Beauvoir, Sautrecourt and Renescure — might be neutralised in 900 to 1,000 Fortress sorties. Consequently, although there was still no established connection between this type of site and either the ski or modified sites, the Chief of the Air Staff recommended that the four sites in question should be heavily attacked immediately, and that all launching sites should also be attacked whenever effort could be spared, but he made it quite clear that the needs of the Battle of France should not be prejudiced.

The new series of attacks against supply sites was initiated by the Eighth Air Force when aircraft bombed Beauvoir

After months of waiting, the hour has come for us to open fire! Today your wait and your work will have their reward. The order to open fire has been issued. Now that our enemy is trying to secure at all costs his foothold on the Continent, we approach our task supremely confident in our weapons; as we launch them, today and in the future, let us always bear in mind the destruction and the suffering wrought by the enemy's terror bombing.

Soldiers! Führer and Fatherland look to us, they expect our crusade to be an overwhelming success. As our attack begins, our thoughts linger fondly and faithfully upon our native German soil. Long live our Germany! Long live our Fatherland! Long live our Führer!

OBERST MAX WACHTEL, Flak-Regiment 155 (W), June 12, 1944

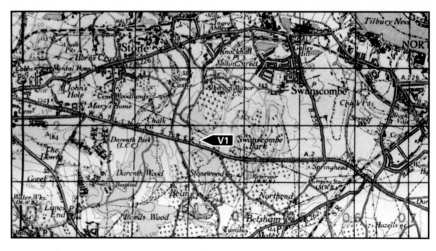

The very first V1 crashed here, close to Watling Street at Swanscombe, in Kent at 04.13.

We were the permanent fire-picket at Woolwich's Royal Military Repository. On June 13, the air raid sirens sounded just before the first light of dawn flecked the eastern horizon. It was the first time the sirens had sounded since D-Day, a week before.

The early morning was warm and we simply donned battledress trousers, shirts, socks and gym shoes to be at our places as quickly as possible. Hitherto, a lapse of a least ten minutes, often more, came between the first intermittent warning wail and the sounds of approaching enemy planes, with the sound of distant anti-aircraft fire preceding even that sound but Tuesday's dawn on the 13th of June 1944 was to be the exception to break precedent in all future air raid alarms — pilotless warfare had arrived!

The fire-picket hut stood a little apart from the rest of the workshop and administration buildings, with a tarred parade ground and roadway between the hut and the main buildings, where stood the simple brick, concrete roofed 'air raid shelter' fire station, so typical in WW2 Britain. In less than a minute we of the duty fire crew tumbled out of the hut and headed to the fire station, quickly, but not unduly hurried.

Then we all stood looking south-eastwards towards the slopes of the high ground of Shooters Hill towards Bexley, about a mile or so away, which lay obscured to our view behind the main office building.

Although still not loud, the sound of the ack-ack guns was unusual, the clatter of Bofors light anti-aircraft guns rather than the heavier boom of the usual 3.7-inch guns that usually tackled high-flying bombers. Looking towards the rapidly closing sound of the Bofors and their exploding shells, we saw searchlight beams crossing under the low cloudy sky — crossing purposefully, rather than sweeping the sky to spot the enemy. It was such an unusual sight and we stopped in our tracks and stared at the strange transition of events, so different to the usual events of an air raid on London.

Each twinned searchlight pair crossed on their obvious target from south-eastwards to north-eastwards as the rapidly approaching enemy aircraft closed in on us at incredible speed, so much faster than our Spitfires or the Luftwaffe Messerschmitts that we were suddenly aware that something extraordinary was happening.

In less than a minute the searchlights within London's south-east suburbs had opened up and our 'local' searchlight had illuminated and immediately found the fast-approaching aircraft, and we glimpsed the enemy plane briefly before it disappeared behind the low workshop building. In that split-second we could see flames from the aircraft's tail. We all ran to get a better view of what we thought was a fast German fighter-bomber making a sneak attack on Central London.

In the time it took us to run the 100 or so yards from our billet hut to the vantage point overlooking the artificial lakes on the Charlton side of the Repository grounds, the strange sounding plane was over Blackheath Park and less than two miles away from us, flying low at a height of about 1,000 feet with its tail ablaze and leaving a short trail of brilliant flame. 'They've hit the bastard,' cried someone. A great cheer went up at the thought that the anti-aircraft batteries had hit the fast-flying 'Jerry' but it continued on its direct unswerving track and was hurtling towards the dome of St Paul's Cathedral that already stood out clearly in early dawn light.

The reverberating throb of the plane's engine sounded much like a plumber's blowlamp that instinctively one thought of some odd sort of rocket engine. That sound was to haunt us for rest of our lives, those who suffered the trauma of hearing the approaching sound, hearing it close overhead, then the abrupt cease of the deafening pulsation, followed by those dreadful seconds of silence until the ear-shattering explosion came.

Somewhere over Rotherhithe the flame went out, just as all the crowded shipping in the Pool of London opened fire. We were sure that the aircraft was doomed and stood waiting for the flash of its ground impact and explosion, somewhere in Central London but none came.

It took many seconds after the exhaust flame disappeared before we heard the sudden end to the engine and the sound of the gun-fire from the ships and shore batteries by the Pool of London. We all stood in puzzled silence, watching in fascination to see what part of the City or Westminster would suffer the blast of the downed enemy plane. Our vigilant watch was rudely ended when shrapnel from the anti-aircraft guns started to pepper the area; luckily a corrugated iron-roofed lean-to shed was close by and we took refuge under its open-ended awning still with a view over towards Central London. Silently the six or so of us watched and waited for the flash of the explosion.

A minute, maybe more elapsed, but no sign of any explosion came and we all fell to wondering about the strange sights and sounds we had witnessed. Then, it came . . . the boom of a relatively distant explosion. Then silence, until several minutes later the air raid sirens sounded the 'All Clear.'

ALEC SAVIDGE, SEPTEMBER 24, 2003

The first casualties were Dora Cohen, aged 55; Connie Day, 32; Willie Rogers, 50; Lennie Sherman, 12; Mrs Ellen Woodcraft, 19, and her eight-month old baby, Tom. All were killed here in Grove Road, Bethnal Green, where the third V1 fell.

It is believed that there was an earlier salvo of nine V1s that were fired just after 11 p.m. on June 12 although none reached England. On the following night, Oberst Wachtel launched ten bombs (although the number varies in the records), four of which crashed soon after take-off, two came down in the Channel and four reached Britain. A spotter plane — a Messerschmitt 410 — sent to observe, was shot down over East London by anti-aircraft fire. It crashed at 4 a.m., near Choats Manor Way, the two crewmen being killed.

That morning, Dr Jones said, 'I went to the Cabinet office to see Lindemann [Churchill's scientific adviser] who was tending to chuckle at the insignificance of the German effort and who said: "The mountain hath groaned and given forth a mouse". I told him that last night's effort had in my opinion been an organisational hiccup and that within a few days we should see a major effort. I asked him to persuade Churchill to warn the country.' Jones had never been to the railway bridge at Bethnal Green so in June 1987 we took him there.

and Domléger on the 14th. Results were poor, however, in each case. Another attack on Beauvoir on the 15th by Fortresses was unsuccessful, but on the 16th good concentrations of bombs were reported after attacks by RAF Bomber Command on each of the four sites. However, as no modified sites were attacked between the 13th and 16th, the Germans were able to complete their preparations for the start of heavy attacks without interference from bombing.

On the defensive side, equally little was done. The defences allotted to the invasion ports and bases were in position and nothing was done to weaken them in order to protect London. Air Marshal Hill did not press for it as it would have been surprising if so light an attack had been made the occasion for the large and complicated deployment which was entailed in the existing plan of defence against flying bombs. From the 13th, however, intruder aircraft of

ADGB were sent out to patrol the area of the launching sites. For the same reason — that the attack was so light — the War Cabinet at their evening meeting on the 13th decided to wait for a heavier attack before any announcement of the arrival of the new weapon was made to the general public. It was agreed that the term 'Southern England' should henceforth be used in reporting any incidents that occurred south of a line from the Bristol Channel to the Wash.

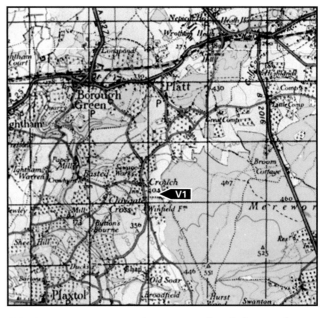

These are the precise locations where the other two flying bombs fell on the 13th. *Left:* The Cuckfield V1 landed at 04.19 two miles to the north-west on Sparks Farm (now Mizbrooks Farm) at grid reference 733 457 as recorded using the Modified British System then in use during the war.

This does not equate to the present day Ordnance Survey map reference which is TQ 294 268. *Right:* The V1 described as coming down at Platt actually fell at 05.06 two miles to the south of the village on Winfield Farm at grid reference 061 741 (OS map reference TQ 623 555).

Early on it was agreed that 'Southern England' would be the only reference given in Press reports but even then this photo was stopped from publication. Terms like 'P-Plane' and 'Henschel' were used although the latter were not the manufacturers. *Bottom:* The Air Ministry collated reports giving the locations and time of V1s reaching Britain which were listed for the period 21.00 hours up to 20.59 hours the following day. Hence this is the list for June 15/16.

The Attack of June 15/16

On the night of June 15/16, a heavy and sustained attack began. Between 22.30 hours and 22.39 hours on the following night, 151 flying bombs were reported by the defences, 144 crossing the coast and 73 reaching the London area. Of those that fell outside London, 14 were shot down by anti-aircraft guns, seven by fighters and one was destroyed by combined gun and fighter action. Anti-aircraft guns of the Inter Artillery Zone were in action and brought down 11 flying bombs inside the built-up area. There were a number of gross errors in accuracy as one flying bomb fell near Chichester and another as far north as Framlingham in Suffolk. Inside London, 70 per cent of the bombs fell south of the river.

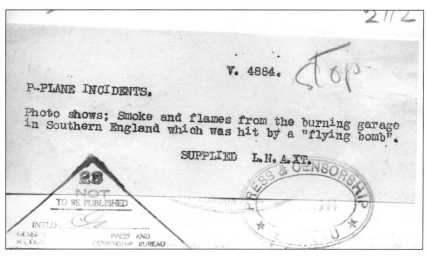

IN LONDON BETWEEN 21.00 ON THURSDAY, JUNE 15, TO 20.59 ON FRIDAY, JUNE 16							
23.43	Epsom	03.10	Bexley	05.30	Woolwich	07.35	Coulsdon & Purley
23.46	Camberwell	03.10	Lewisham	05.45	Beckenham	07.36	East Ham
00.05	Bermondsey	03.30	Lewisham	05.45	Yiewsley	07.45	Deptford
00.15	Finchley	03.45	Beckenham	05.46	Croydon	08.09	Dagenham
00.20	Poplar	03.50	Dagenham	05.50	Woolwich	08.20	Beckenham
00.40	Hornsey	04.00	Bromley	06.00	Woolwich	08.47	East Ham
00.45	Orpington	04.15	Dagenham	06.04	Croydon	09.12	Southwark
01.00	St Pancras	04.15	Woolwich	06.10	Woolwich	09.15	Bexley
01.25	Greenwich	04.15	Enfield	06.15	West Ham	09.35	Epsom
01.30	Bromley	04.30	Orpington	06.30	Croydon	09.45	Croydon
01.40	Wandsworth	04.30	Chislehurst	06.40	Poplar	10.00	Acton
01.40	Lewisham	04.30	Beddington & Wallington	06.40	Beckenham	10.29	Chislehurst
02.20	Chislehurst	04.35	Bexley	06.55	Chislehurst	11.10	Coulsdon & Purley
02.22	Ilford	04.38	Croydon	07.00	Croydon	11,15	Coulsdon & Purley
02.29	Chislehurst	04.50	Walthamstow	07.20	Woolwich	13.12	Lewisham
02.30	Lewisham	04.55	Barking	07.20	Tottenham	14.00	Staines
03.00	Chislehurst	05.20	Bromley	07.26	Woolwich		
03.08	Crayford	05.25	Bermondsey	07.30	St Pancras		

FRIDAY, JUNE 16, 1944

Evening Standard

37,366 BLACK-OUT: 11.4 pm to 4.57 am MOON: Sets 5.17 p.m.; Rises 4.6 a.m. ONE PENNY

FINAL NIGHT EXTRA

Morrison Announces New German "Air Weapon"

PILOTLESS PLANES NOW RAID BRITAIN

WATCH THE LIGHT IN THE TAIL

The Ministry of Home Security offers the following advice to the public:

When the engine of the pilotless aircraft stops, and the lights at the end of the machine are seen to go out, it may mean that the explosion may soon follow, perhaps in five to 15 seconds.

So take refuge from blast; even those indoors should keep out of the way of blast, and use the most solid protection immediately available.

THIS IS HOW THE ROBOT WORKS

From HARRY ASHBROOK, who saw the opening of the pilotless airplane attack from the coast.

Already the picture of the German pilotless airplane can be seen in general outline.

Here are some of the answers to the questions you have been asking:

Q. *How fast does the airplane fly?*

A. Probably between 220 and 250 miles an hour.

Q. *What is its size?*

A. It is smaller than a fighter. It has a wing-span of about 20 feet and is about 25 feet long.

Scenic Railway

Q. *How does the airplane take off?*

A. It is believed to be attached to a railed runway, not unlike a fair ground scenic railway. Reports say that the airplane is hooked on a single up-grade rail and hauled up a few hundred feet by a cable or winch machine.

At the top on the up-grade rail the airplane is switched to a down-run rail and released.

Reports say that the second rail is like a switchback.

The airplane rushes down at a great speed and becomes airborne as the rail bends upwards at the end of the run.

Good Night Target

Q. *Is the airplane vulnerable?*

A. Extremely so. It flies on a fixed, straight course and cannot take evasive action when attacked by fighters or A.-A. guns.

It probably flies low to avoid radio-location listening posts.

Because of this it ought to be possible to bring it down even by machine-gun fire.

It is a good night target. Observers have noted that the airplane carries a clear white light on its tail.

Q. *What effect is caused when the airplane explodes? Is it more serious than a large-size block-buster?*

A. Reports on damage caused by pilot-less airplanes are not yet complete.

Q. *Is the pilotless airplane a new invention?*

A. No. It is a development of the radio-controlled Queen Bee airplane used in this country before the war.

Q. *What do they sound like?*

A. They have a distinctive [illegible] note, giving the effect of a pulsating low throb.

They appear to be painted a dark brown or black; the smoke issues from them in small thick puffs.

Q. *How is the attack being met?*

A. The recent heavy raids on the Pas de Calais area probably gave the clue to the way we are tackling this new form of air warfare.

The scenic rail runways are being

(Continued on Back Page, Col. Two)

'Counter-measures Are Vigorous'

The Germans have begun sending pilotless airplanes over this country. This was announced by Mr. Morrison, Home Secretary, in the House of Commons to-day.

THESE PILOTLESS AIRPLANES WERE USED IN THE RAIDS HERE LAST NIGHT AND TO-DAY. MR. MORRISON SAID:

It has been known for some time that the enemy was making preparations for the use of pilotless aircraft against this country.

He has now started to use this much-vaunted new weapon.

A small number of these missiles were used in the raids on Tuesday morning and their fall was scattered over a wide area.

A larger number was used last night and this morning.

OUR REPLY

The enemy's preparations have not, of course, passed unnoticed, and counter-measures have already been and will continue to be applied with full vigour.

It is, however, probable that the attacks will continue.

Subject to experience the usual siren warning will be given for such attacks.

On the first occasion they caused a few casualties.

But the attack was light, and the damage on the whole was inconsiderable.

Last night's attack was more serious and I have not as yet full particulars of the casualties and damage, nor the number of pilotless aircraft destroyed before they could explode.

Meanwhile, it is important not to give the enemy any information which would help him in directing his shooting by telling him where his missiles have landed.

It may be difficult to distinguish these attacks from ordinary air raids, and therefore it has been decided that for the present information published about air raids in Southern England, that is to say south of a line from The Wash to the Bristol Channel, will not give any indication where the air raid has taken place beyond saying it has occurred in Southern England.

While I thought it right to give the House, at the earliest opportunity, information about the use of this new weapon by the enemy, available information does not suggest that exaggerated importance need be attached to the development.

All possible steps are, of course, being taken to frustrate the enemy's attempts to supplement his nuisance raids by means which do not imperil the lives of his pilots.

Meanwhile the nation should carry on with its normal business. (Cheers.)

Further, as the raids by pilotless aircraft may occur during daylight when the streets are full of people and A.-A. guns will be used to shoot down the machines, I must impress on the public the importance of not exposing themselves unnecessarily to danger by remaining in the streets out of curiosity instead of taking the nearest cover whilst the guns are firing.

For the time being, at any rate, the guns will shoot, but that is liable to review as we go along in the light of experience and what is expedient.

Members will notice the arrangement we have made with the Press

(Continued on Back Page, Col. One)

R.A.F. Heavies Strike Again At E-Boats

Another deadly blow was struck last night against the E-boat menace to our convoys across the Channel.

At 10.30 p.m., precisely 24 hours after the first of two great blows struck against the E-boats at Le Havre, about 300 R.A.F. heavies hit at E-boats in Boulogne harbour.

E-boat pens, R-boats and mine-sweepers were also attacked. The attack was at least as heavy as the worst of the two against Le Havre—probably between 1500 and 2000 tons—and is believed to have been as effective.

Twelve thousand pound bombs were dropped and the Germans to-day admitted heavy damage to the port.

Photographic reconnaissance shows that the attack on Le Havre was tremendously effective. Previous to it ten E-boats and some other craft were seen afloat. Afterwards only two E-boats were visible. Both were aground.

Le Havre Shelled

It is almost certain that the rest in the harbour were destroyed. Three torpedo-boats also disappeared.

It is now known that while the R.A.F. attacked Le Havre it was shelled heavily by the Royal Navy.

Despite rain and limited visibility over many parts of France yesterday, the Allied air forces flew 3000 sorties, many of them by aircraft based in France, attacking targets indicated by Advanced Air Force and Army Headquarters.

Among the targets were troops and tanks sheltering in woods and orchards east of Caen.

W. GERMANY BOMBED

R.A.F. bombers last night attacked objectives in Western Germany, and mines were laid.

One aircraft is missing.

The Germans reported that bombs were dropped on several points of the Rhineland and Westphalia.

To-day the German Achtung service reported "enemy battle formations over the Lower Danube," and single airplanes over Franconia.

Intruders were also reported over North-West Germany.

Weather Improves

The weather in the Straits of Dover early to-day was dull, with a low ceiling of cloud and mist, but it improved a little towards noon. It was still overcast but visibility was better. The thermometer at 8 a.m. registered 60 degrees. A light southerly wind, which veered to the west at mid-day, was not strong enough to ruffle the sea.

'ALL ENEMY ATTEMPTS TO TAKE INITIATIVE FRUSTRATED'

ADVANCE OF 1½ MILES ACROSS PENINSULA

THE ALLIED THREAT TO CUT THE CHERBOURG PENINSULA IS INCREASING. OUR TROOPS ARE NOW ONLY THREE MILES EAST OF ST. SAUVEUR AND SIX MILES FROM CUTTING THE ROAD AT LA HAYE.

To-day's Allied communiqué reports "no major change in any sector" but mentions the advance in the Peninsula by saying that Allied troops have made further progress west of Pont l'Abbé.

"All attempts by the enemy to gain the initiative have been frustrated, and counter-attacks have been successfully repelled, says the communiqué.

"Our striking power grows steadily."

The Allied advance westward amounts to about one and a half miles. Probably the most westerly point of our advance is in the area of the little village of Reigneville, near St. Sauveur, writest a reporter at Supreme Headquarters.

NAZI QUANDARY

But the peninsula will not be cut until we have taken La Haye, or the high ground to the north of it, because there is an alternative route branching out from La Haye and going up the west coast.

The enemy must be in a quandary what to do about the Cherbourg Peninsula. The more reinforcements they push up the more will be cut off if and when we sever the communications.

In the Quineville area, it seems that our troops are over or are approaching the line of the Sinope River, which reaches the sea just north of Quineville.

The Allies are now well to the north-east of Montebourg, although the situation in the town itself is still obscure, and it is by no means certain who holds it at the moment.

BURNED OUT

But William Stringer, Reuter's correspondent with the American forces, reported in a message despatched last night, that U.S. patrols had entered Montebourg—now a mere burned-out shell of a town—and captured townships on the outskirts.

He also reported patrols less than 4000 yards from the River Douve, which runs through St. Sauveur.

"The Germans in this sector and along the western bulge of the peninsula bridgehead continued to stiffen their resistance and hurl in an increasing number of tanks, principally Mark IIIs," said Stringer.

"The Germans are believed to

(Continued on Back Page, Col. Four)

Channel Isles Very Strong

There is no evidence that the Germans are evacuating the Channel Islands, which are probably among the most heavily fortified places in the world, it was stated at Supreme Headquarters to-day.

LAVAL TAKES UP RESIDENCE

From D. A. ROBERTSON
Evening Standard Correspondent

MADRID, Friday.

Laval has taken up permanent residence in Paris at Chateaudun, where he is bringing Vichy leaders and collaborationists into daily consultations.

Meetings of council ministers are also a regular feature at his home.

Chateaudun has been frequently bombed by Allied aircraft, particularly in recent days.

New Vice-Admiral

The Admiralty announce that Rear-Admiral Frederick Hew George Dalrymple-Hamilton, C.B., is promoted to Vice-admiral in His Majesty's Fleet, to date June 15, 1944.

Vice-admiral Dalrymple Hamilton was Captain of the Rodney when she helped to sink the Bismarck, for which he got the C.B.

Counter-Attack

Last night, and in daylight to-day, the Allied air forces counter-attacked secret military installations in Northern France.

Monty Gets His Hammer Ready

From LESLIE RANDALL
Evening Standard War Reporter with the 21st Army Group,
Friday.

While the battle ranges over the eighty miles front from Montebourg to beyond Caen, we are piling up our strength for a smashing blow.

Behind the British lines thousands of sappers and pioneers are toiling. They are clearing up our beaches, building airfields and improving communications.

They are paving the way for the next big step in the liberation of Europe.

We are now in Phase Two of the invasion plan. Phase One was the landing, the storming of the West Wall and the occupation of a long strip of the coast line. This has been accomplished.

GIVING NO REST

Phase two, it was always known, would have to be a period of hard fighting to consolidate our gains. We are pressing forward, giving the enemy no rest. And all the time we are building up powerful striking forces.

Phase three, if all goes well, will be a blow that will send the enemy reeling.

But do not expect our big offensive to be launched in a hurry. That is not Montgomery's way of fighting battles. He believes in intensive preparation. Nothing will persuade him to start an attack until he is ready.

But when he does strike, he strikes with everything he has got. The battle order is: "Hit the enemy for six." That is what he is now preparing to do.

BUILDING UP

While the enemy are pinned down and compelled to throw in their reserves as soon as they reach the battlefield, Montgomery is building up for his hammer blow.

Men and equipment are leaving our invasion ports in a steady flow. Those of us who have been able to drive about the coastal invasion belt have been staggered by what we have seen.

A great part of England is to-day crammed with tanks, trucks, ammunition and warlike stores of every description. Much has already gone over to the other side, but there is very, very much more to follow.

Soon after the assault troops had landed, bulldozers, cranes and excavators were brought ashore. I saw scores and scores of them in the great convoys rolling towards the ports.

With them went Army, Navy and Air Force technicians. These men and machines are now doing a great job of work which is an essential prelude to the big offensive.

The term 'Southern England' was meant to prevent the Germans finding out the accuracy of the flying bomb. After the big attack rumours abounded so it was pointless to sustain the news black-out. Therefore, on June 16 Herbert Morrison, the Minister of Home Security, announced details of the new weapon in Parliament.

In 1940, the War Cabinet had been provided with bomb-proof accommodation in the basement of the New Public Offices in Whitehall, the windows facing St James's Park being sealed and shuttered.

Counter-Measures of June 16 by the War Cabinet and the Chiefs of Staff

Clearly the country was faced with a very different situation to that of June 13. The Germans had obviously got sufficient sites in action to subject London to a serious scale of attack, though how long this could be sustained was, of course, not known. The Home Secretary made a statement in the House of Commons on the morning of the 16th, which had the merit of correcting the more extravagant speculations of Londoners. The Chiefs of Staff agreed on the morning of the same day that the 'Diver' deployment of guns and balloons should be put into effect. The searchlights demanded by the plan were already deployed as part of the ordinary defences of the south-east. The full deployment of balloons was expected to take about a fortnight to complete, but some of the guns which it had been intended to use were still in their 'Overlord' positions and the Deputy Chief of the Air Staff, as the officer responsible in general for 'Crossbow', did not give a date by which the gun deployment would be completed.

On the evening of the same day a Staff Conference was called by the Prime Minister and the following decisions were made:

'1. To request the Supreme Commander, Allied Expeditionary Force, to take all possible measures to neutralise the supply and launching sites, subject to no interference with the essential requirements of the battle in France.

'2. That the air raid warning should not be sounded on the approach of a single pilotless aircraft. At night, the sounding of the siren should be reduced to the minimum and the warning should be only sounded on the approach of the first "covey".

'3. That for the time being, pending further experience, the anti-aircraft guns, both inside and outside the London area, should continue to engage pilotless aircraft.

'4. That the Air Marshal Commanding, Air Defence Great Britain (ADGB) in consultation with the GOC-in-C, Anti-Aircraft Command, should re-distribute the gun, searchlight and balloon defences, as necessary, to counter the attacks.

'5. That the Air Marshal Commanding, ADGB, should consider the use of armed cables on those balloons deployed against piloted aircraft.'

In short, these decisions meant that counter-measures were to be applied immediately; the defensive deployment was to go ahead as planned; counter-bombing was to be begun on as large a scale as possible so long as the battle in Normandy did not suffer; and the general public were to be encouraged to carry on as normally as possible.

Now preserved by the Imperial War Museum, Churchill's seat in the Cabinet War Rooms is the one in front of the wall map.

Hitler had wanted the launch of his 'vengeance' campaign to coincide with the anticipated invasion of France but missed the date by just a week. Nevertheless, Oberst Wachtel had virtually opened up a second front at a time when the Allies needed to concentrate on securing a foothold in Normandy. Air operations over the battlefield were being carried out by the two air forces specially created for 'Overlord': the RAF's Second Tactical Air Force under Air Marshal Sir Arthur Coningham *(left)* and the US Ninth Air Force commanded by Lieutenant General Lewis H. Brereton. Now they were to be pressured into attacking 'Noball' targets as well. *Right:* This Spitfire of No. 132 Squadron is being bombed-up with two 250lbs and one 500lb at the newly-constructed airstrip B11 at Longues in Normandy (see *Invasion Airfields Then and Now*).

By the Operational Commands

Fighters of ADGB and guns of Anti-Aircraft Command were both in action on the night of the 15th/16th and the following day. Eleven fighter squadrons, including two of Mosquitos that operated at night, carried out 80 patrols. The London guns and those deployed between London and the coast were frequently in action and claimed 27 flying bombs destroyed. Thirteen of these came down inside the London area.

On the same day, the first moves were made to put the planned deployment into effect. The project entailed moving 192 heavy and 192 light guns and 480 balloons. Not much could be done until the evening of the 16th owing to the needs of invasion traffic. On the following day, however, Anti-Aircraft Command reported that one regiment had taken up its new positions in the early hours of the 17th and that three regiments of each type of gun would be deployed by that night. It was expected that the full deployment would be completed within three or four days. For the time being, all guns were drawn from Anti-Aircraft Command.

Balloon Command also reported on the same day that their deployment was going ahead and would be finished in about a week. (It was, in fact, completed on June 21 whereas under the Concurrent Plan a full fortnight had been allowed.)

Energetic offensive action was also called for by the opening of the attacks, all the more so as the deployment of the defences would take some time. By the 16th Air Chief Marshal Leigh-Mallory had been informed by the Air Ministry that the four supply sites in the Pas-de-Calais were regarded as priority targets, followed by 11 of the original ski sites

and 12 modified sites which were believed to be in operation. In response, he arranged with Air Chief Marshal Harris that the four supply sites should be attacked that same night, but beyond a warning to Air Marshal Sir Arthur Coningham that the fighter-bombers of his Second Tactical Air Force might have to be diverted to the attack of modified sites, he gave no further instructions.

This was not surprising as the same bad weather that was hindering the invasion made it impossible to launch effective attacks against targets in the Pas-de-Calais, and it was still not clear what were the best sites to attack. The target list issued by the Air Ministry (see pages 57-59) specifying of ski sites is proof enough that it was not yet aware that only modified sites were in action. It was not until the following day that Leigh-Mallory was informed of the true state of things. Meanwhile on the night of the 16th/17th, and again on the following night, Bomber Command attacked the four supply sites.

There was a decline in the scale of flying bomb attacks in the 24 hours following dusk on the 16th. Only 83 crossed the coast of which 48 came down in London, but the following 24 hours saw as heavy an attack as that of the 15th/16th.

The Formation of the War Cabinet 'Crossbow' Sub-Committee

On the evening of the 18th the Prime Minister held another Staff Conference to review what had already been done and what was planned. Again it was emphasised that the supply and launching sites (including the large sites) should be hit as hard as the battle in Normandy would allow. Also every

effort should be made to improve the efficiency of the various arms of defence, and the public should be encouraged to carry on as usual with the proviso that they should sleep in as safe a place as they could find. The Prime Minister also decided that he would hold a daily meeting at which the departments and operational commands most concerned in countering the attack would be represented.

It was the Prime Minister's initial intention to preside over this body personally, giving it that same powerful authority as earlier special committees that he had established to consider vital operations like the Night Air Defence Committee and the Battle of the Atlantic Committee. On June 19 such a meeting was held and among those present were Field-Marshal Smuts, the Home Secretary, the Secretary of State for Air, the three Chiefs of Staff and the Deputy Supreme Commander, Air Chief Marshal Sir Arthur Tedder. However on the 20th, after consulting with the Chiefs of Staff, the Prime Minister came to the conclusion that the day-to-day consideration of plans and policy would be better carried out by a smaller body.

The connection with himself as Minister of Defence was retained by instructing the new body to report to him as well as to the Home Secretary and the Chiefs of Staff. Its chairman was Duncan Sandys, and ADGB, Anti-Aircraft Command, the Air Staff, the Supreme Allied Commander, and the Ministry of Home Security were represented on it. It was not an executive body but, as it reviewed the progress of every sort of counter-measure, its deliberations form one of the most important records of the campaign.

IN LONDON BETWEEN 21.00 ON FRIDAY, JUNE 16, TO 20.59 ON SATURDAY, JUNE 17

21.35 Sutton & Cheam	01.28 Lewisham	03.55 Croydon	08.40 Epsom
00.55 Orpington	01.50 Lewisham	04.15 Kensington	14.15 Surbiton
01.00 Beckenham	02.32 Croydon	04.15 Epsom & Ewell	16.04 Battersea
01.00 Lewisham	02.36 Banstead	04.30 Sutton &. Cheam	16.09 Woolwich
01.00 Wood Green	02.50 Coulsdon & Purley	05.00 Sutton & Cheam	16.15 Malden
01.02 Orpington	02.57 Banstead	05.15 Wallington & Beddington	16.46 Lewisham
01.03 Ruislip & Northwood	03.15 Sutton & Cheam	05.39 Croydon	17.05 Uxbridge
01.05 Croydon	03.20 Wimbledon	05.40 Banstead	18.12 Lewisham
01.09 Croydon	03.20 Camberwell	05.55 Surbiton	18.34 Wandsworth
01.10 Orpington	03.25 Croydon	06.00 Coulsdon & Purley	20.08 Barking
01.20 Croydon	03.29 Croydon	06.00 Banstead	20.15 Hackney
01.25 Beckenham	03.40 Sutton & Cheam	06.08 Wallington & Beddington	

Expansion of the 'Diver' defences

During this first week of the attack, the deployment of guns and balloons and the allocation of fighter squadrons to flying bomb patrols was rapidly carried out. As we have seen, the planned balloon deployment had been completed by June 21. The deployment of guns was also virtually complete by the same date. Eight single-seater fighter squadrons of No. 11 Group, ADGB, and four Mosquito squadrons were being employed on flying bomb patrols but already Air Marshal Hill, General Frederick Pile and Air Vice-Marshal William Gell of Balloon Command, had appreciated that more weapons were required than the Concurrent Plan had envisaged. By the 21st, Anti-Aircraft Command were examining a plan to increase the number of guns in the gun belt to 376 heavy, almost double the planned deployment, and nearly treble for the number of light guns at 540.

Balloon Command were organising an increase of their deployed strength from 480 to 1,000.

No increase in the number of fighters was contemplated. The problem here was not one of numbers but of increasing the efficiency and effectiveness of the equipment already in use, and not only in fighters but throughout the whole system: radar stations, Royal Observer Corps and operations rooms by which fighter operations were controlled.

Because 'Southern England' encompassed the whole area south of a line from the Bristol Channel to the Wash, many original British-captioned pictures of the period are difficult to identify. However, the US Signal Corps were not so constrained, describing this picture as St John's Hill, Battersea on June 17. From Air Ministry records we can pinpoint the time of the incident as 16.04 on Saturday. Twelve people were initially reported as being trapped but the eventual death toll reached 24.

On June 13 the Chief Intelligence Officer at AEAF headquarters informed Leigh-Mallory that the Home Secretary was going to make a fuss at the War Cabinet meeting that evening but that the Chiefs of Staff were not unduly worried about 'Crossbow' and that they did not wish air support to be diverted to it from 'Overlord'. Five days later, when the effects of the massed attack on London was inescapable, Eisenhower minuted Tedder: 'In order that my desires, expressed verbally at the meeting this morning, may be perfectly clear and of record, with respect of 'Crossbow' targets, they are to take first priority over everything except the urgent requirements of the battle.'

SECRET   M. of H.S., R... E. Dept.   BOMB   FORM   Serial No...............

and AIR MINISTRY   CENSUS   B.C.4.   Sheet No....1.............

Region	5. County: Group 4 London	Total Casualties:			Date: 17/18 6/44
Adminis-trative Area	Greenwich	Killed M S/I M L/I M	F F F	C C C	Warnings P. home and R 23.22 Times W 06.31

A	B	C	D	E	F
Bomb No & time of fall	Size & type of bomb & X or UX	Judged by F. C or D	Crater size and type of soil	Location and damage notes ——— (Grid reference if no plot is made)	Additional notes by R. & E. Dept. Technical Officers
1 04.17	P.A.C. X	F Casing Tubes Y Part Engine	Water-logged appr: 10' X 1'6"	Border, edge of roadway, R.A.F. property (No1 Balloon Centre) Kidbrooke 550' North of SR elec railway & 700' West of Kidbrooke Pk Rd. Blast damage up to 500'	85 19 49
2 01.15	P.A.C. X	F wing	D.H.	D.H. top of gas-holder. Gas Efficiency works Norman Rd East side 45' & 184' South of junc Thornham St. Damage:– Top of gas-holder fractured, 2 holders caught fire, appr 131,000 cubic ft of gas destroyed. Odessa Wharf (opposite side of road) 5 storey building 18" brick (flour store) partly demolished by bomb, now burned out by fire which broke out some 4 hrs after detonation (fire still burning (19th pm) P.T.O.	82 19 65

Formulation of a Bombing Policy; First Effects of Bombardment

An examination of what form the future counter-offensive should take was being made during the same period by the Allied Expeditionary Air Force (AEAF), RAF Bomber Command, and the US Eighth Air Force under the surveillance of Tedder, the Deputy Supreme Commander. The necessary intelligence came to the operational commands through the Directorate of Operations (Special Operations) at the Air Ministry. On June 18, Tedder, with the full approval of the Supreme Commander, directed that a big effort should be made against 'Crossbow' targets in the near future while the battle on land was still going well. The latter was still to have first claim upon the Allied bomber resources, but once its needs had been provided for, 'Crossbow' had priority over all other tasks.

Apart from the general listing of flying bomb incidents reproduced on these pages, detailed reports were produced by the Air Ministry covering each one — quite a massive task bearing in mind the number of V1s involved. This one describes the two at Greenwich on the morning of June 18.

IN LONDON BETWEEN 21.00 ON SATURDAY, JUNE 17, TO 20.59 ON SUNDAY, JUNE 18

21.35	Wimbledon	01.00	Wandsworth	04.20	Walthamstow	08.15	Wandsworth
21.35	Lewisham	01.10	St Pancras	04.24	Chiswick	08.15	Camberwell
23.20	Lewisham	01.15	Greenwich	04.30	Sutton	08.44	Battersea
23.34	East Ham	01.17	Mitcham	04.35	Lambeth	08.50	Westminster
23.40	West Ham	01.30	Esher	04.35	Mitcham	09.11	Orpington
23.45	New Malden	01.40	Wandsworth	04.40	Bexley	09.20	Islington
23.45	Banstead	01.43	Bermondsey	04.50	Beddington	10.20	Wandsworth
23.47	Coulsden & Purley	01.55	Stepney	05.00	Wandsworth	11.20	Westminster
00.15	Ealing	02.00	Sutton	05.01	Fulham	12.12	Hackney
00.22	Southwark	02.07	Greenwich	05.03	Kensington	12.40	Lambeth
00.22	Merton & Malden	02.30	Croydon	05.03	Bermondsey	12.48	Battersea
00.27	Banstead	02.50	Ilford	05.30	City of London	13.40	Woolwich
00.35	New Malden	03.15	Merton & Malden	05.40	Battersea	14.17	East Ham
00.45	Wandsworth	03.30	Chislehurst & Sidcup	05.40	Paddington	15.12	Penge
00.45	Merton & Malden	03.36	City of London	05.52	Finsbury	15.20	Epsom
00.45	Wandsworth	03.45	Penge	06.00	Beddington & Wallington	16.20	Malden & Coombe
00.50	Croydon	03.45	Bermondsey	06.58	Stoke Newington	16.36	Woolwich
00.50	Croydon	03.50	Beddington & Wallington	07.30	Twickenham	17.50	Wandsworth
00.55	Bromley	04.10	Lambeth	07.55	Hackney	20.35	Bromley
01.00	Esher	04.17	Greenwich	08.09	Bromley	20.40	Dagenham

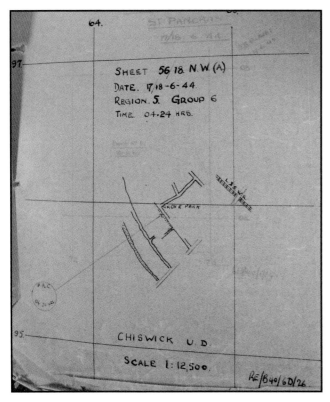

A sketch plan was produced for each incident, indicating the exact impact point and streets affected. This one at Grove Park, Chiswick, at 04.24 hours on the morning of the 18th is at map reference 645 959.

Of the various types of 'Crossbow' targets, large sites were considered the most important. Then came the supply sites followed by the 47 modified sites that had by now been identified in the area Somme—Pas-de-Calais. To these was added on June 21 a suspected railhead for flying bomb supply at Nucourt, 15 miles north-west of Paris, and also the electricity system in the Pas-de-Calais which was thought to be important to the functioning of large sites and supply sites.

During this first week of heavy flying bomb attack, the counter-offensive was not satisfactory as the weather severely curtailed flying. It was also the case that neither Air Chief Marshal Harris nor Lieutenant General Doolittle were convinced that their forces could as yet play a useful part in countering the enemy's attack as both of them were not satisfied about the selection of targets. After Bomber Command aircraft had attacked supply sites on successive nights (June 16/17 and 17/18), Harris intimated that he was unwilling to attack this type of target again until photographic reconnaissance had established the need. Nor were he and Doolittle happy about the attack on the modified sites.

Meanwhile a much more attractive operation was projected: a massive attack on Berlin by 1,200 aircraft of the Eighth Air Force and 800 from Bomber Command. Tedder was in favour of it, pointing out that one of its advantages would be to damp the spirits of the German people which had been temporarily raised by the exaggerated accounts of flying bomb damage in London. In this sense, so it was argued, such an attack would play its part in the flying bomb campaign although Tedder did not regard it as a substitute for the attack of the flying bomb organisation proper, and on June 23 he instructed the Allied

air commanders that they must seize even a fleeting opportunity for the attack of sites. He suggested that the American force be permanently standing by for 'Crossbow' work for which Doolittle agreed to set aside 200 aircraft.

Up to June 23 the counter-offensive, for one reason and another, had not settled down although it had hot been devoid of results. On the 23rd, three supply sites — Domléger, Sautrecourt and St Martin-l'Hortier — were suspended from further attack and Watten, Wizernes, Siracourt and Mimoyecques had been badly damaged. One attack on Watten by No. 617 Squadron had been particularly successful with an attack at dusk on June 19. Fifteen 12,000lb

bombs were dropped, 12 falling within 100 yards of the aiming point.

The first attack on the believed supply depot at Nucourt was also successful when 250 tons were dropped by Fortresses on June 22. Buildings and railway facilities were damaged and the ground subsided in three places indicating that the roofs of underground store chambers had collapsed.

In addition, at least six and possibly nine ski and modified sites had been damaged to Category A standard during the week, much of this being the work of Second Tactical Air Force, but Air Marshal Coningham was already seeking permission to be allowed to concentrate on the support of the battle on land.

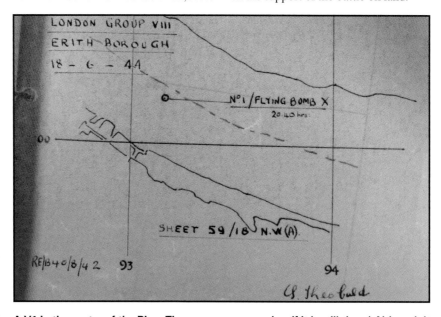

A V1 in the centre of the River Thames . . . one wonders if it is still there! Although it is marked as landing at 20.40 hours just over the boundary between Erith in Kent and Dagenham in Essex, it appears that it was logged under the latter district.

Central London suffered grievously on that first weekend. At 04.10 on Sunday, June 18, Wachtel first scored a direct hit on Hungerford Bridge *(above)*; then at 08.50 another V1 struck Rutherford Street *(below)*, both incidents being photographed by US Signal Corps cameramen. The fire was not brought under control until later in the afternoon when Home Security was advised there were four killed, four persons missing, and 20 injured. However, the final death toll was ten, with over 50 seriously injured.

Flak-Regiment 155 (W) was getting into its stride, and by that Sunday morning had achieved its 500th launch against London. It could well have been the actual 500th that caused the worst incident of the whole nine-month-long flying bomb campaign. In view of the hit or miss nature of the weapon, a direct hit on a military target was almost more than could be hoped for, but Oberst Wachtel's men scored a bull's-eye at 11.20 a.m. with a bomb on the chapel at Wellington Barracks, the home of the Brigade of Guards in Birdcage Walk. This picture was taken by the late David Gurney just seconds after the bomb had exploded and shows musicians still on the parade ground having just returned with the King's Guard from Buckingham Palace just across the road.

We sat near the back of the chapel and watched the people come in. I remember some of the people I saw, in particular a young Canadian lieutenant who eagerly surveyed his surroundings as if to memorise the details that he might write them down in his next letter home. In the gallery, a band of Guardsmen began to play. Instead of an organ, we sang the opening hymn. My mind must have wandered during the reading of the first lesson, I dare say I was thinking about my forthcoming leave. 'Here endeth the first lesson', the Guards' colonel who had been reading it must have said. The congregation rose to its feet. In the distance hummed faintly the engine of a flying bomb. 'We praise thee, O God: we acknowledge Thee to be the Lord', we, the congregation, sang. The dull buzz became a roar, through which our voices could now only faintly be heard. 'All earth doth worship Thee: the Father everlasting.' The roar stopped abruptly as the engine cut out. The Te Deum soared again into the silence. 'To Thee all Angels cry aloud, the Heavens, and all the Powers therein.' Then there was a noise so loud it was as if all the waters and the winds in the world had come together in mighty conflict and the Guards' Chapel collapsed upon us in a bellow of bricks and mortar. One moment I was singing the Te Deum and the next I lay in dust and blackness, aware of one thing only — that I had to go on breathing.

I felt no pain, I was scarcely aware of the chunks of massed grey concrete that had piled on top of me, nor did I realise that this was why breathing was so difficult. My whole being was concentrated in the one tremendous effort of taking in long struggling breaths and then letting them struggle out again. It may have been an hour later, perhaps two or three or more, that I was suddenly aware that somewhere far above me, above the black emptiness, there were people, living, helpful people whose voices reached me, dim and disembodied as in a dream. 'Please, please, I'm here', I said and I went on saying it until my voice was hoarse and my throat ached with the dust that poured down it. Somewhere not far away from me someone was screaming, screaming, screaming, like an animal caught in a trap. My eyes rested with horror on a blood-stained body that, had my hands been free, I could have reached out and touched the body of a young soldier whose eyes stared unseeingly at the sky. I tried to convince myself that this was truly a nightmare, one from which I was bound soon to wake up. I think I must have been given a morphia injection for I still felt no pain, but I did begin to have an inkling that I was badly injured. I turned my freed head towards a Guardsman who was helping with the rescue work, and hysterically I cried out: 'How do I look? Tell me how I look!' 'Madam', he said, 'you look wonderful to me!'

ELIZABETH SHEPPARD-JONES, 1981

When the final death toll was compiled, 58 civilians and 63 Service personnel had lost their lives, with 68 more being seriously injured, like ex-ATS Subaltern Elizabeth Sheppard-Jones, her spine fractured and paralysed from the waist down. Among those killed was the Commanding Officer of the Scots Guards, Lieutenant-Colonel John Cobbold, and Lieutenant-Colonel The Lord Edward Hay of the Grenadier Guards, and the Director of Music, Major James Causley-Windram. Almost immediately

plans were made for worship to continue. A Romney hut was erected on the floor of the chapel and the first service was held on Christmas Day 1945. In 1962 rebuilding began to the design of architect Bruce George after Harry Goodhart-Rendel died in 1959 before completing his plans. The most significant proposal was to enclose the portico of the undamaged east end within the shell of the new, the whole concept forging a link with that which was, with that which is, to that which shall be.

Evidence was in fact accumulating during this third week in June that pointed to the direct delivery of bombs and equipment from storage depots at railheads direct to the modified sites thus avoiding the use of supply sites. Two such depots, the one at Nucourt and another at St Leu-d'Esserent, had been identified by June 24 and others were suspected. Supplies were delivered by rail to these depots, which included much underground storage capacity, and from there by road to the modified sites, usually, and probably entirely, at night.

Summing up the position, the Assistant Chief of Air Staff reported on June 26 that 'it must be expected that the enemy's scale of attack will be maintained at its present level and might even increase. Against this, however, must be set the damage being done to the supply sites, depots and other elements of the enemy's rear organisation. On balance it seems unlikely that the scale of attack will increase greatly before it declines.'

The scale of attack was one thing but the effect of the attack was another element, and it was the aim of the defenders to reduce the latter even if the former remained the same. Height and speed, the two features that most affected the defending guns and fighters, varied appreciably. Bombs were observed at heights of between 1,000 and 4,000 feet, flying at speeds which appeared to vary between 250 and 400 mph. Their accuracy was such that if not intercepted approximately 65 per cent of the bombs launched reached the London area. This meant that the majority of the bombs, after crossing the coast between Beachy Head and the South Foreland, converged upon the line Dorking to Gravesend and thence into the London area.

After the initial fears of the massive destructive power of Hitler's secret weapon, it was some relief to find that in reality it was less severe than had been anticipated. Analysis of the blast damage at Bethnal Green led Morrison to advise the Cabinet that the effect was no greater than that of a parachute mine. The caption to this picture, not released until May 1945, explains that it shows three V1 incidents in Lewisham. Top right 14 houses and many others damaged on Lewisham Hill where 12 people were killed, 17 seriously injured and 22 slightly on June 17. In the centre, another flying bomb on Granville Park damaged over 200 houses and commercial property including a cinema although the casualties were just one person taken to hospital. In the foreground, one person was killed in another incident on Cressingham Road in July.

Intelligence on the Flying Bomb Organisation

Available intelligence, while it was by no means complete, pointed unmistakably to a well-prepared organisation on behalf of the Germans. Up to June 24, 50 modified sites had been discovered in the Pas-de-Calais; 34 were complete and 21 had been identified as having been in operation. Only two modified sites had been spotted between the Seine and the Somme but it was evident from radar plots that there were other sites in that area that were in use.

What was the next link in the chain of the German organisation was not quite clear. Logically it could well have been the supply sites but even after two such locations at Valognes and Bricquebec in the Cherbourg peninsula had been captured and inspected, it was still not possible to confirm this. It seemed probable that special fuels were stored at supply sites and also that spare parts and equipment were kept there. Air Intelligence however, could not and would not say that the destruction of this type of site would seriously affect the scale of attack; nor did they say that it would not.

After the war local councils took the opportunity to redevelop bomb-sites with new estates and high-rise blocks of flats.

21.00	Lambeth	00.20	Esher	04.00	East Barnet	10.07	Wandsworth
21.05	Harrow	00.33	Feltham	05.00	Twickenham	12.42	Kensington
21.45	Fulham	00.35	Southall	06.00	Wandsworth	12.50	St Pancras
21.50	Croydon	00.55	Finchley	06.35	Wimbledon	17.10	Stepney
22.02	Staines	01.12	Staines	06.40	Banstead	18.37	Merton & Malden
22.12	Southall	02.20	Southall	07.20	Twickenham	18.37	Twickenham
22.20	Carshalton	02.20	Twickenham	07.31	Westminster	19.15	Twickenham
22.35	Enfield	02.32	Kensington	07.35	Mitcham	19.50	Erith
23,07	Staines	02.35	New Malden	07.50	Heston and Isleworth	20.35	Willesden
00,20	Staines	02.40	Hayes & Harlington	07.55	Twickenham		
00.20	Richmond	03.53	Wimbledon	08.38	Wimbledon		

Norman Longmate, the foremost historian of the Home Front, spent five years collecting material for his book *The Doodlebugs*. Compiling his many eyewitness recollections, one contributor wrote that 'the noise is what everyone remembers best: the distant hum, growing to a raucous and deafening rattle, which either diminished as the aircraft disappeared into the distance, or jerked abruptly to a stop, to be followed by an explosion. It was this interval which was the hardest to bear. It seemed interminable but from the numerous recordings made at the time — one unsung hero of the summer spent his time on the roof of Broadcasting House holding a microphone towards any approaching flying bomb — it is clear that it was actually about 12 seconds. When the engine stopped it seemed that everything stopped. "It was", thought one 12-year-old girl in East Ham, "as if the world stood still and held its breath." Many attempts have been made to find the right adjective for those vital, and sometimes fatal, few moments.

An "ominous silence", felt one woman, who first heard it while taking her bull terrier for a walk on Chipperfield Common in Hertfordshire. A "dread silence" suggests her husband whom it had caused to order "the examinees to fall flat on their faces in the aisles between the desks" during a school certificate examination at Kilburn Grammar School. A "terrifying silence" considers one from Sidcup. But probably the best choice of all was that of a schoolgirl from Lake in the Isle of Wight, conscious of "a deafening silence when the engine cut out".' The US Signal Corps caption claims this as the first photo of Hitler's 'secret' weapon. It was taken by photographer Neuman on June 22 with the caption adding that it was 'over the Piccadilly section of London'. The dome in the foreground is that of the Central Hall, Westminster. Note Nelson's Column in Trafalgar Square on the left. The flying bomb crashed on Shelton Street in the borough of Holborn at 6.50 p.m. killing Sylvia Lyons and her son Paul.

When the capital began to suffer air raids in 1940, the architect's department of the London County Council prepared overlays on the Ordnance Survey sheets of 1914-16 showing the varying degrees of destruction, represented in five different colours ranging from yellow for slight damage to purple denoting totally destroyed. Buildings slightly damaged were assigned to the Special Repair Service (SRS) of the Ministry of Health, but in February 1941 the responsibility for requesting assistance from the SRS shifted to the newly-formed Directorate of Emergency Services. A surveyor would assess the damage and provide an approximate cost for the repairs. A depot would then be established in the vicinity of the work. When the flying bombs began to take their toll, each V1 and V2 impact site was illustrated with different size circles. This section of Map Sheet 61 shows the flying bomb that struck Whitfield Street, midway between Goodge Street and Windmill Street in the borough of St Pancras, at approximately 12.50 on June 19.

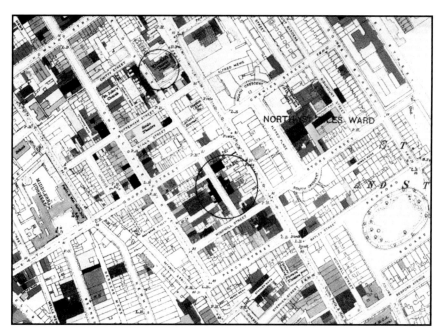

The official report on the incident states that the V1 'fell on old brick and timber properties at rear of Tottenham Court Road Police Station. Damage extensive and severe but impossible to assess at time of investigation. Street filled with debris and rescue work in progress. Casualties feared heavy — many trapped.'

The Air Raid Precautions controller reported that heavy and light rescue parties were on the scene within minutes and that the heavy equipment such as cranes and skips was available shortly after. A cameraman from Pathe News was quickly on the scene as the emergency services carried out rescue work.

The Situation Report at 18.00 the following day stated that 21 had been killed, 79 seriously injured, 146 slightly injured, with about eight people still missing. An updated report on June 21 stated: 'Four further bodies recovered, three missing. Rescue work still proceeding.'

The minutes of the St Pancras Borough Council ARP Committee of July 4 reveal that casualties from the attack had risen to 35 dead, 76 seriously injured and 163 slightly injured. The attack had caused 200 people to become homeless, many being accommodated in the council's rest centre.

Apart from personnel from the emergency services, there was even a contingent of US Military Police lending a hand.

The Ministry of Works Flying Squad were on site the day after the V1 exploded. The next step was to make a detailed inspection and prepare a schedule of repairs and approximate cost for each house. In preparing the schedule, the Assistant Surveyor paid careful attention to the criteria established by the Ministry of Health for what were called 'First Aid Repairs'. This approach for slightly damaged houses had been set out by the Minister of Health, Malcolm MacDonald, in October 1940. Explaining the powers of local authorities to make houses fit for housing purposes, he stated that 'first-aid repairs will be carried out as speedily as possible, the question whether it is necessary or wise to proceed with more-permanent repairs depends on a number of considerations, particularly the possibility of further damage in the immediate future, and the availability of labour and materials'. Sites were then cleared, many areas in central London becoming one of the ubiquitous bomb-site car parks which graced the capital in post-war years.

The Greater London Council replaced the car park at Colville Place with public gardens in 1985.

First Attempts at Solution

The speed of the bombs, combined with their low altitude, made the work of guns and fighters, separately and in co-operation, more difficult than in the case of attacks by piloted aircraft. At a height of 3,000 feet, the bomb presented a target almost equally awkward for both heavy and light anti-aircraft gunners, being on the low side for the one and too high for the other. The heavy anti-aircraft regiments were trained and equipped principally to deal with attacks by piloted bombers at high altitudes. The flying bomb, however, crossed the field of vision far more rapidly than any bomber flying at normal operational height. Predictor operators had therefore to work much more quickly than usual to obtain the necessary fire data for the guns, which in turn had to be traversed and elevated at a speed that proved to be too much for manual laying. The light guns suffered from some of the same disadvantages, with the additional one that this type of anti-aircraft weapon is best used for the close defence of specific and small objectives, whereas in these novel circumstances they had to be widely deployed well away from the target area of London.

Up to June 18, both the heavy and light guns that were sited for the close defence of London were allowed to engage flying bombs. Thereafter this was prohibited. For one thing, their patent lack of success was not calculated to improve the morale of Londoners; for another, even when successful, the bombs they hit usually came down and exploded in the built-up area.

As for the fighters, their small margin of speed over the flying bombs, coupled with the short time in which interception had to be made, demanded that they should be quickly and accurately directed on to the course of the bomb. Otherwise, the pursuing fighter reached the gun and balloon belts — and London itself — before the bomb could be attacked. There was thus a problem of warning and control to be solved of the same sort, though different in degree, as that which the co-ordinated working of radar stations, the Royal Observer Corps and the system of telecommunications and operations rooms had been solving with fair success for the interception of piloted aircraft since the outbreak of war.

The RAF's No. 11 Group was responsible for south-east England but as its Operations Room at Uxbridge was fully committed to the battle over France, instead all the 'Diver' defences were controlled by the ops room at Biggin Hill. Following the intensive attacks on the airfield in August 1940, operations had been temporarily moved to an empty shop in the village, but later a country house *(left)* was requisitioned at Keston Mark, two miles from the airfield. *Right:* Today, Towerfields has been subdivided into flats, the tower being demolished in the late 1970s.

The same was true of the defence system as a whole. It was not just a matter of improving the efficiency of the guns, searchlights, balloons and fighters as separate weapons but of co-ordinating their activities so as to obtain the optimum effect. This was especially so in respect of guns and fighters.

All the 'Diver' defences were controlled from the operations room of the Biggin Hill sector as the operations room at No. 11 Group Headquarters was fully occupied in controlling operations over France. To it was passed all information from the radar stations and the Royal Observer Corps, and to it were linked the operations rooms of the guns in the 'Diver' area, but the control that was exercised from Biggin Hill was general and not specific. Thus, radar stations and the Royal Observer Corps centres at Horsham and Maidstone were used as fighter direction stations. The reason for such decentralisation was that the time available for interception was shorter than in the case of attack by piloted aircraft.

Similarly, Anti-Aircraft Command found that to control the firing of individual batteries from gun operations rooms was impracticable. Instead batteries were allowed to fire independently except where the operations rooms ordered fire to cease, for example to safeguard friendly aircraft. In both the Biggin Hill operations room and, through the transmission of information, in the gun operations rooms a complete picture of the state of the battle was progressively recorded, but neither was used for the minute control of fighters and guns.

This system needed supplementing by a number of standing orders designed to avoid mutual interference between the guns, fighters and balloons, and the weather was an important factor to be considered when framing them.

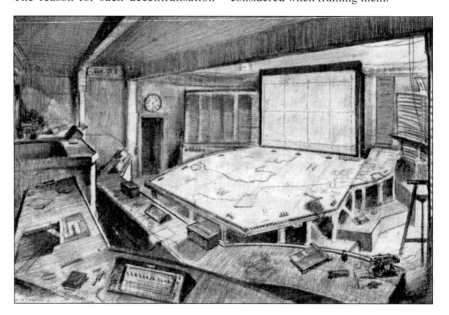

The Operations Room was located in the ground-floor lounge with the Met office on the first floor. In a broadcast from Towerfields on September 15, 1945, Richard Dimbleby told listeners that 'it is one room in which you could say: "This is where they won the war".'

As early as June 16, Air Marshal Hill decided that fighters would patrol over the Channel and the land between the coast and the southern limit of the gun belt. They could pass over the gun belt only when in pursuit of a flying bomb, in which case the guns were not to open fire. On June 19 it was decided that on days of very good visibility only fighters would operate; on bad days only the guns, while on moderate days both guns and fighters would operate, each in their own areas. These principles were expanded on the 26th under the code-names, 'Flabby', 'Spouse' and 'Fickle'.

FLABBY: Condition: Weather suitable for fighters. Effect: Total prohibition of gun-fire.

SPOUSE: Condition: Weather unsuitable for fighters. Effect: Complete freedom to guns.

FICKLE: Average weather conditions. Effect: In the 'Diver' belt, guns allowed to fire up to 8,000 feet. Fighters prohibited entry except when making a visual interception. Outside the 'Diver' belt, fighters given freedom of action. Light anti-aircraft guns allowed to fire by day against visual targets if no fighters present.

It cannot be claimed, however, that these rules solved the problem. Fighter pilots were frequently reporting that they had been engaged by the guns and the gunners no less frequently reported that fighters had hindered their shooting. As will be seen, it was not until the whole scheme of defence was radically altered in the middle of July that these difficulties were overcome.

Improvements in Equipment and Tactics

The first weeks of the attack were the more difficult for the defenders because the equipment that was available proved unsatisfactory in many respects and was subjected to numerous experiments and changes. Moreover, the novel form of attack demanded novel tactics to counter-act it.

Fighters. Tempest Vs, Spitfire XIVs, XIIs and IXs, Typhoons and, at night, Mosquitos were the first type of fighter aircraft to be used. Of the day fighters, the first two were the fastest and, for this reason, the most suitable. The Mustang III was also satisfactory and from July 3 onwards this aircraft began to play an important part. Mosquitos were used at night with good results to the end of the campaign but they were not as fast as the job demanded and, almost from the beginning of the attack, day fighters were also employed at night. They proved unsatisfactory at first, partly because pilots were also required to fly by day, partly because they were not well trained in night flying, and it was not until volunteers from Mosquito squadrons had been given short conversion courses on Tempests that the faster day fighter achieved good results at night.

As for the actual interception of flying bombs, this was largely a matter of obtaining accurate information on the course of the missile and transmitting it rapidly from the sources on the ground through the fighter controller to the patrolling pilot. Having been told where to look for his target, the pilot then had to find it. By day, this was not easy even in good weather for the flying bomb was small and it travelled fast. Experience quickly showed that it could most easily be identified, in twilight and 'Flabby', i.e. complete freedom of action for the fighters, was frequently instituted at dawn and dusk for this reason. At night, the task of spotting the bomb was relatively easy, thanks to the glare from the propulsion unit, though this also made it difficult to bring accurate fire to bear.

By the end of June, the methods for controlling fighters were of two main sorts, one being used solely for controlling fighters over the Channel, the other chiefly for fighters patrolling overland. The first of these — the 'Close Control' method — entailed the direction of individual fighters by controllers located at radar stations on the coast. Approaching flying bombs were plotted in the control room and the controller, who was in R/T communication with the patrolling fighter, would then issue detailed instructions on course so as to bring the pilot into a position to intercept. The factor limiting the extent to which the method could be used was the number of control points available. Four radar stations — Fairlight (MEW — Microwave Early Warning), Fairlight

Unfortunately, the American caption to this remarkable photograph does not specify a date, only saying that 'a Spitfire [in actual fact it is a Hawker Tempest!] chases robot (V1) over the quiet countryside of England. Only fast low-level ships, such as the P-51, P-47 and Spitfire XIV are good for this work, as robots have been clocked as high as 440 miles per hour and average well over 300.'

(CHL — Chain Home Low), Swingate (CHL), and Beachy Head (CHL) — were being used for this work by the middle of July. The principal practical difficulty was that existing types of radar station could not, for technical reasons, provide sufficiently early warning of an approaching bomb. The best of the stations rarely detected the bombs at ranges of more than 50 miles which meant that the fighter had only six minutes to intercept before a bomb reached the coast but in practice it had less. First, because there was a time lag between the initial detection of a bomb and the transmission of interception data from the fighter controller to the pilot, and secondly because patrols could not be carried out at the limit of radar detection because of the danger of being surprised by enemy fighters. This was especially the case in the Straits of Dover, where fighters had at most three minutes in which to intercept a bomb before the Kent coast was reached.

However, 'Close Control' was persevered with as it usually resulted in bombs falling harmlessly into the sea, but it was no use overland where there were no low-looking radar facilities. Here the 'Running Commentary' method was used. The controllers using this technique were located at three radar stations (Beachy Head, Hythe and Sandwich) and at two Royal Observer Corps Centres (Horsham and Maidstone). In the 'Running Commentary' method, the position and course of flying bombs was passed by the controller to all patrolling fighters working on the same frequency, who then worked out their own course to their target. The method was also used for seaward patrolling fighters but it was at its best overland where landmarks, shell-bursts, rockets from observer posts, and searchlight beams all helped the pilots to make speedy interceptions. The chief fault that arose was that more than one fighter frequently went after the same flying bomb.

Engaging and destroying the bomb had also its problems. Chasing a flying bomb from astern meant a long and probably fruitless pursuit unless the fighter pilot had an advantage in height at the moment of sighting. The best method of closing to attack was, therefore, to fly on the same, or nearly the same course, as an approaching flying bomb so that it came to the fighter, rather than the fighter to the bomb. Usually it was possible to employ only brief deflection shots as the speeds at which combat took place were so high, so the vast majority of destructions were the result of fire from astern. In this position the effect of the slipstream of the flying bomb made it difficult to hold a steady aim, and short bursts of fire and frequent aiming corrections were necessary. For the same reason, the shorter the range the more effective the fire, with the proviso that the fighter did not approach closer than 200 yards otherwise the blast from an exploded bomb might be fatal.

As far as the guns were concerned, the new measures gave the gunners a far better sight of their targets and, more important, authorisation to use shells fitted with the new VT proximity fuze which, as the name implied, was designed to 'detect' the presence of its target before exploding. The conception, development and mass production in America of this fuze is a whole story in itself; suffice it to say that, together with the gun-laying radar and searchlight radar, it improved the kill rate against the flying bomb from 33 per cent in the first week of operations to a staggering 80 per cent by September.

Guns. The problems that Anti-Aircraft Command faced were no less difficult than those of the fighters. During the first fortnight of the attack they were partly matters of organisation arising out of certain modifications in the Concurrent Plan that were found to be necessary. Under this plan the sites that had been selected for the heavy guns were located in hollows and folds in the ground so that gun-laying radar might be as free as possible from enemy jamming. Counter-measures to jamming, which had been taken prior to the invasion of France, had reduced this possibility, and sites on higher ground could thus be utilised. This meant relaying the extensive network of telecommunications that had been established under the earlier plan. Signals detachments from Anti-Aircraft Command and engineers of the GPO telephone network had completed the task by June 28.

Light guns had also to be re-sited. Originally, the intention was to deploy these at searchlight sites over the whole of the 'Diver' Defence Area so that they could make use of the radar equipment of the searchlights for the engaging of unseen targets. However, after the attack had started, Anti-Aircraft Command changed their requirement and the light guns were then concentrated in a belt forward of the heavy guns in order to make the best use of their fire-power. This redeployment was still taking place on June 26.

The deficiencies of equipment that rapidly became apparent were mainly the result of the high speed of the flying bomb and its ability to operate at all times and in all weathers. The first deployment

Left and below: **This was claimed to be the first flying bomb brought down by a balloon at Tatsfield in Surrey, right in the centre of the balloon belt, that covered what became popularly** known as 'Doodlebug Alley'. *Right:* **We are reliably informed that it came down on Clarks Lane Farm, although a new residential development makes for a poor comparison.**

during June 15-21 had been made entirely by mobile units that were fully equipped with transport. Unfortunately, the 3.7-inch mobile guns with which these regiments were equipped were manually controlled when firing and proved in practice to be too slow to obtain good results. Hence it became essential to reinforce them by the static 3.7-inch guns which could be automatically loaded and remotely controlled, i.e. the gun was traversed and elevated electrically as data was fed into it from the predictor. They were also fitted with the No. 11 Mechanical Fuze Setter that allowed a higher rate of fire and greater accuracy. This type of gun, however, took longer to move and emplace than the mobile model.

The difficulty was met by the REME detachment at Anti-Aircraft Command's HQ devising a steel mattress which did away with the necessity for an elaborate concrete emplacement, although it was not until June 27 that the first static guns had been relocated in the 'Diver' gun belt.

It was also at that date that two new items of equipment which permitted the accurate engagement of unseen targets started to come into service. These were the No. 10 Predictor and the American SCR 584 radar set. The latter was capable of a number of operational functions but for defence against flying bombs it was used entirely for controlling gun-fire against both visual and unseen targets. The No. 10 Predictor permitted more rapid and accurate tracking of targets than earlier models. The introduction of both sets of equipment at a time when operations were in progress involved a large and difficult retraining programme. No drill books, only a few instructors, and little training equipment were available.

Owing to the need to keep the guns in action, only a small number of personnel could be spared from a battery for instruction at any one time. These two pieces of equipment plus the VT proximity fuse, which was only used on an adequate scale after the middle of July, were the prime mechanical reasons for the success that eventually attended the work of the guns.

Balloons. No component of the defences was the subject of more experiments and suggestions for improvements than the balloon barrage. The arming of balloon cables commenced on June 19 and was completed for the first deployment of 480 balloons three days later. The next additions to the barrage — which more than doubled it — were also armed, as was the final strength of 1,750 balloons, though only after serious difficulties of supply had been overcome.

The arming device itself, the Double Parachute Length (DPL), was never entirely satisfactory. It had been designed to be actuated when piloted aircraft, travelling at speeds of 250 to 300 mph, hit the balloon cable, but in the case of the flying bomb, which was usually travelling at nearly 400 mph, by the time it reached the balloon barrage, the cable was not infrequently cut through before the DPL could operate. This had been appreciated before the attack, and it was for this reason that the first balloons to be deployed had been unarmed. However, when the DPL did function satisfactorily it was rare that the bomb escaped destruction, and it was by these means that the majority of the flying bombs were brought down.

There were often days of bad weather on which the barrage could only be raised for a few hours at a time. At one point the question of keeping the balloons in operation whatever the weather was discussed but, on examining the records of balloon destruction during the war through bad weather, it was agreed that unacceptably high wastage might result and the proposal was not adopted. There was also one good logistical reason: the shortage of hydrogen which would have been aggravated by heavy losses.

On the whole, the balloons did what was expected of them. They were responsible for a comparatively small proportion of the bombs that were destroyed but they were presented with fewer targets than the guns and fighters. That the Germans feared them is obvious enough from the steps that they took to fit at least some of the flying bombs with devices for warding off or cutting cables.

Just after midnight on June 21, a three-bomb salvo hit Bromley in Kent, one of the V1s exploding on Princes Plain School in Common Road. A US Signal Corps photographer was on the scene as soon as it was daylight.

Radar. The radar equipment that was located on the south and south-east coasts at the beginning of the attack was found not to be fully satisfactory. Sufficiently early warning of the approach of bombs was obtained for the purpose of giving the public warning; the tracking of bombs was fairly good and made possible the direct control from radar stations of interceptions by patrolling fighters, and an indication of the direction and height of attack could also be given to the gun operations rooms of Anti-Aircraft Command. However, none of these gave results as good as the situation required. In particular, the continuity of tracking was poor and during a heavy attack not all flying bombs were detected. The average range at which continuous tracking was possible was about 36-40 miles which was less than had been anticipated.

In one important respect results were definitely poor, namely the location of the sites from which bombs were being fired. This was especially poor for the area between the Seine and the Somme. Without accurate plotting of this kind, the bombing of the sites that were being used by the enemy was so much more difficult.

One of the main problems was to distinguish quickly between ordinary aircraft and flying bombs, a problem that was particularly difficult when aircraft were operating in strength over northern France. Thus one of the earliest modifications was to provide centimetre height-finding equipment at two of the best-placed CHL stations: at Beachy Head and Fairlight. This work was completed by July 14 and at two other stations, Swingate and Foreness, by August 9. The more accurate information that was obtained also facilitated the direction of defending fighters.

The design of a device for detecting propeller modulation was also hastened to be able to distinguish between air-

craft with a normal airscrew and jet or rocket-propelled aircraft. The first models were fitted at the Beachy Head and Hythe stations by August 8 but the trials were disappointing, and the effective contribution of the device to the efficiency of the warning system was very small. If it had worked well it would have been especially useful when flying bombs were being launched from piloted aircraft.

The earliest, and possibly the most important addition to existing radar facilities, was the re-siting of an American station — the Microwave Early Warning (MEW). This equipment, with its associated British Type 24 height-finding set, gave a longer range, better continuity of tracking, and also permitted the simultaneous plotting of more targets than any other radar set. It was useful, therefore, for all three of the

main functions of radar, viz: obtaining early warning of attack, controlling fighters, and analysing plots so as to locate the enemy's launching sites. It was for this last purpose that the equipment was initially used.

At the start of the attack the MEW equipment was located at Start Point to cover fighter operations over the invasion beaches in Normandy, and it was intended to move it to France as soon as possible. During the third week in June, however, arrangements were made through the commander of the American Ninth Air Force, Lieutenant General Lewis Brereton, for its use against flying bombs and it commenced operations at Fairlight on June 29. From August 4 it was used primarily as an interception station with analysis as a secondary function. However, It could not be withheld from France indefinitely and it was transferred there late in August.

Steps had been taken to produce an equivalent British set (the Type 26) late in June, constructed from a dismantled Type 20 station and certain American components which were obtained direct from the United States. It took the place of the MEW at Fairlight during the second week in August. A second Type 26 station was installed at St Margaret's Bay.

The only other important modification that came into operation during the main attack was intended — like the introduction of the MEW — to improve the location of the launching sites. This information was difficult to obtain by visual means under normal operating conditions owing to the weakness of the response from a flying bomb at long range, and also because so many tracks were frequently appearing at one and the same time. Special cameras were therefore installed at three stations, Beachy Head, Fairlight and Hythe, to take photographs every few seconds of the responses that were detected. The pictures from two or more stations could then be examined and collated yet this was not in use until July 25.

In September 2015, a huge row ensued when it was announced that the name was being changed to The Trinity Church of England Primary School.

IN LONDON BETWEEN 21.00 ON TUESDAY, JUNE 20, TO 20.59 ON WEDNESDAY, JUNE 21

21.00 Orpington	01.23 Poplar	05.05 Carshalton	09.02 Beckenham
22.45 Sutton & Cheam	01.43 Battersea	05.25 Erith	09.23 Chislehurst & Sidcup
00.20 Croydon	02.25 Wandsworth	05.45 Harrow	09.45 Woolwich
00.30 Bromley	02.35 Willesden	05.50 Lewisham	11.16 Banstead
00.55 Westminster	02.50 Wimbledon	05.55 Greenwich	12.35 Erith
00.55 Bromley	03.35 Greenwich	06.00 Greenwich	12.50 Esher
01.00 Bromley	04.15 Wimbledon	06.07 Stepney	13.19 Woolwich
01.01 Battersea	04.20 Croydon	06.30 Richmond	14.09 Esher
01.16 Chigwell	04.23 Woolwich	06.50 Lewisham	14.10 Beckenham
01.16 Surbiton	04.55 Poplar	08.00 Bexley	14.51 Croydon

IN LONDON BETWEEN 21.00 ON WEDNESDAY, JUNE 21, TO 20.59 ON THURSDAY, JUNE 22

00.10 City of London	05.35 Camberwell	06.52 Surbiton	08.47 Wandsworth
00.15 West Ham	05.50 Esher	07.00 Carshalton	08.55 Camberwell
01.33 Ilford	06.04 East Ham	07.07 Lewisham	09.10 Surbiton
01.36 New Malden	06.10 Banstead	07.08 Bromley	09.10 Mitcham
01.40 Wandsworth	06.20 Mitcham	07.10 Uxbridge	09.44 West Ham
04.43 Lewisham	06.20 Sutton	07.30 Surbiton	11.00 Beckenham
04.43 Surbiton	06.23 Beddington & Wallington	07.49 Acton	13.03 Carshalton
04.45 Camberwell	06.37 Wandsworth	07.55 Mitcham	18.45 Wandsworth
04.55 Lewisham	06.47 Lambeth	08.02 Hackney	18.50 Holborn
05.09 Lambeth	06.50 Wimbledon	08.25 Croydon	

The Beckton Road flying bomb that crashed just after midnight on June 22 was West Ham's worst with 17 killed and 31 seriously injured. *Top:* **This Signal Corps picture, taken by photographer Meyer, says that 'workmen begin to clear away debris after the explosion of a German robot plane'. Meyer took his photo from a first-floor window of a house bordering Beckton Road looking south-west towards St Luke's Church in Canning Town, the spire of which can be seen on the skyline. The whole block backing onto Watford Road has been taken out giving post-war planners free rein to add an additional carriageway to the A13 in 1959.** *Right:* **Today the Beckton Road of old has gone, including the name, as this is now Newham Way, the name adopted on the amalgamation of East and West Ham.**

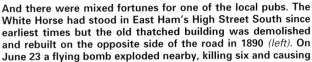

And there were mixed fortunes for one of the local pubs. The White Horse had stood in East Ham's High Street South since earliest times but the old thatched building was demolished and rebuilt on the opposite side of the road in 1890 *(left)*. On June 23 a flying bomb exploded nearby, killing six and causing widespread damage to over 2,000 properties. Three days later, workmen were still carrying out repairs when a second V1 fell at the rear of the pub; this time, six people were killed in the White Horse itself. A single storey replacement was put up on the site in 1965 but now even that has gone *(right)*.

IN LONDON BETWEEN 21.00 ON THURSDAY, JUNE 22, TO 20.59 ON FRIDAY, JUNE 23			
01.55 Lewisham	03.15 Beddington & Wallington	06.58 Wandsworth	09.37 Lambeth
02.03 Mitcham	03.18 Malden	06.59 Croydon	15.04 Dagenham
02.04 Wimbledon	03.30 Ealing	06.59 Croydon	15.05 Barking
02.05 Camberwell	03.42 Woolwich	07.10 Lewisham	15.05 Croydon
02.07 Croydon	03.58 West Ham	07.15 Lewisham	15.05 Woolwich
02.10 Camberwell	04.01 Ilford	07.56 Poplar	15.10 Greenwich
02.13 Merton & Morden	04.04 Lambeth	07.59 Wandsworth	15.31 Woolwich
02.16 Surbiton	04.10 Bermondsey	08.00 Beckenham	16.45 Lambeth
02.20 Leyton	04.20 Bermondsey	08.03 East Ham	16.56 Wandsworth
02.21 Paddington	04.43 Greenwich	08.05 Westminster	17.05 Mitcham
02.22 Croydon	05.05 Lewisham	08.05 Chislehurst	17.29 Dagenham
02.25 Greenwich	05.20 Greenwich	08.05 Greenwich	17.35 Camberwell
02.30 Holborn	05.25 Lewisham	08.05 Woolwich	17.57 Greenwich
02.35 Barking	05.35 Coulsdon & Purley	08.07 Mitcham	18.00 Wanstead & Woodford
02.47 Southwark	06.50 Deptford	08.15 Feltham	18.30 Croydon
03.00 Elstree	06.55 Woolwich	08.20 Lewisham	18.37 Bexley
03.05 East Ham	06.57 Barking	08.44 Orpington	18.52 Battersea

The first of two near misses on Buckingham Palace came just after midnight on June 20, when a doodlebug brought down this section of wall on Constitution Hill. A second flying bomb landed in the grounds five days later, yet the King and Queen continued to live in London to share in the ordeal alongside their long-suffering subjects.

The first flying bomb to strike Woodford on the north-east outskirts of London — the one I described visiting in my Introduction on page 7 — blasted the corner of Empress Avenue, killing five and injuring over 50, some seriously. At the end of the war,

the RAF's photo-reconnaissance squadrons were given the job of surveying the UK and large gridded photo-maps *(left)* were produced showing the wartime damage. *Right:* Looking across the road at the rebuilt corner of Empress Avenue today.

IN LONDON BETWEEN 21.00 ON FRIDAY, JUNE 23, TO 20.59 ON SATURDAY, JUNE 24

21.02	Stepney	23.22	Hammersmith	01.20	Lewisham	06.45	Lambeth
21.12	Surbiton	00.15	Sutton	02.30	Coulsdon & Purley	06.54	Southwark
22.00	Stepney	00.24	Banstead	03.07	Brentford	07.25	Deptford
22.27	Wimbledon	00.30	Hackney	06.29	Staines	07.50	Lewisham
22.30	Acton	00.30	Ilford	06.30	Finsbury	08.00	Croydon
22.35	Bromley	00.30	Wandsworth	06.30	St Marylebone	08.15	Lewisham
22.55	Lewisham	00.57	Lewisham	06.35	Epsom		

Progress of Counter-Measures, June 17 — July 15

It is against the background of these changes in tactics and equipment, few of which had yet made their contribution to a more effective defence, that the first month of flying bomb attack should be set. From the night of June 16/17, the attack continued on an average scale, in round figures, of 100 bombs every 24 hours although there were considerable daily and weekly variations. The worst day was the 24 hours following dusk on July 2 when 161 flying bombs came close to the coast or passed overland.

IN LONDON BETWEEN 21.00 ON SATURDAY, JUNE 24, TO 20.59 ON SUNDAY, JUNE 25

00,22	Enfield	01.55	Mitcham	03.11	Wanstead & Woodford	04,05	Lambeth
00,24	Lambeth	01.55	Westminster	03.21	Hammersmith	04.10	Southwark
00.43	Greenwich	02,03	West Ham	05.30	Walthamstow	05.50	Hornsey
01,10	Woolwich	02.15	Deptford	03.46	Lambeth	06.20	Friern Barnet

This London News Agency picture dated June 23 just states it was 'taken after the explosion of a flying bomb somewhere in Southern

England'. Watkins & Simpson were seed merchants trading in Drury Lane in central London . . . their building still survives.

On June 26, 1944, artist and photographer Reg Fowkes was on duty beside the Congregational Church at Woodford Green. (The Wanstead and Woodford Civil Defence control centre had been constructed nearby in 1938 in the rear garden of No. 13 Broomhill Road by the simple expedient of burying two Nissen huts beneath 18 inches of concrete, covered with three feet of earth.) Around 2 p.m., a flying bomb was heard approaching. Oddly enough in this case the motor continued running right up until it crashed, the church taking the main force of the blast. Reg had a lucky escape as it fell only about 70 feet away. This is his painting of the incident — a local coal merchant, Bill Day, was killed in his lorry, and his wife, Harriet, and six-year-old son, Victor, nearby.

IN LONDON BETWEEN 21.00 ON SUNDAY, JUNE 25, TO 20.59 ON MONDAY, JUNE 26

21.27 Chingford	01.15 Orpington	04.05 Fulham	14.42 Greenwich
21.36 Beckenham	02.00 Stoke Newington	04.15 Barking	14.59 Wanstead & Woodford
21.45 Coulsdon & Purley	02.06 Bethnal Green	04.40 Lewisham	15.05 Leyton
23.19 Greenwich	02.10 Croydon	05.34 Wandsworth	15.18 Deptford
23.30 Woolwich	02.10 Croydon	12.45 Bromley	15.26 Croydon
00.50 Lewisham	02.10 Ilford	12.50 Battersea	15.26 Wandsworth
00.54 Bromley	02.10 Lewisham	12.50 Croydon	15.30 Ilford
00.54 Deptford	02.24 Camberwell	13.01 Acton	15.47 Richmond
00.54 East Ham	02.43 Chislehurst & Sidcup	13.15 Islington	15.55 Wandsworth
01.00 Chigwell	02.56 West Ham	13.40 Southwark	15.55 Ilford
01.00 Beckenham	03.05 Croydon	13.40 Leyton	16.00 Camberwell
01.02 Camberwell	03.20 Croydon	13.45 Waltham Holy Cross	16.00 East Ham
01.15 Crayford	03.45 City of London	14.25 Harrow	

WOODFORD TIMES, FRIDAY AUGUST 9, 1946

Bombed Church to be demolished

WRECKED BY FLYING BOMBS in June, 1944, the Woodford Green Congregational Church has remained derelict ever since and is now likely to be demolished according to information obtained this week to the effect that the church is not to be rebuilt, the church membership being now merged in the Woodford Union Church. The church with its graceful 145 ft. spire has been a landmark on Woodford Green since the building was erected in 1873. The lecture hall and a parlour were added in 1905. (See story on Page One).

As we have just seen at the White Horse in East Ham, it was not unusual for a second bomb to land at almost the same place. This is what happened to the Woodford Congregational Church, which was struck on June 26 and June 29. The stonework was offered for sale and many local residents took the opportunity to beautify their gardens. The Sir James Hawkey Hall was erected on the site in 1955.

When Chesterfield Road School in Enfield was hit just after noon on June 27, a photographer from the *Daily Mail* was quickly on the scene. The school caretaker was slightly injured but the censor blocked publication until the damage was cropped out.

IN LONDON BETWEEN 21.00 ON MONDAY, JUNE 26, TO 20.59 ON TUESDAY, JUNE 27			
23.50 Orpington	01.11 Paddington	03.37 Bromley	12.07 Enfield
00.10 Chigwell	01.15 Hendon	04.15 Barking	12.46 Islington
00.10 Waltham Holy Cross	01.20 Chigwcll	04.18 Lambeth	14.00 Ilford
00.10 Westminster	01.20 Wood Green	04.30 Orpington	15.25 Hackney
00.10 Wandsworth	02.10 Carshalton	04.35 Orpington	18.32 Orpington
00.14 Battersea	02.10 Sutton	04.40 East Ham	18.33 West Ham
00.15 Chelsea	02.22 Chelsea	05.25 Orpington	18.36 Mitcham
00.16 Ilford	02.30 Poplar	05.26 Bromley	19.20 Richmond
00.18 Hornsey	02.32 Camberwell	06.47 Chislehurst & Sidcup	19.37 Acton
00.20 Greenwich	02.35 Merton	07.46 Coulsdon & Purley.	20.00 Greenwich
00.22 Wandsworth	02.37 Lewisham	08.35 Beckenham	20.16 West Ham
00.23 Wandsworth	02.45 Deptford	10.50 Epsom	20.20 Camberwell
00.25 Walthamstow	02.50 Battersea	10.55 Camberwell	20.34 Croydon
00.45 Cheshunt	03.06 Woolwich	12.04 St Marylebone	20.52 Carshalton
01.10 Richmond	03.07 Woolwich	12.05 Camberwell	

Having seen that the children were safe in the shelters, unfortunately the playground lady, Elsie Parnall, was caught in the blast.

With dozens of bombs blasting the South-East every day, in the first fortnight of the attack some 1,600 people had been killed, 4,500 seriously injured, and 5,000 slightly injured. However, the proportion of those killed was much lower, the reason for the high injury rate being that many people were caught out in the open during the day. By this stage of the war the authorities had realised the value of canine help for searching for buried victims and the unit which covered the 11 local authorities in Metropolitan Essex had its kennels in Loughton. Here the Light Rescue Team is pictured on the ruins of Seymour Court, Whitehall Road, Chingford, which was hit on June 28. At 7.59 a.m. on Wednesday, a flying bomb hit a large tree at the rear, causing serious damage to two blocks and demolishing 18 flats. A number of people were trapped including one resident taking his morning bath. Two deaths were reported: Mrs Ethel Smith of No. 32 and Mrs J. Morris of No. 33 who both died later in hospital from injuries received.

It appears that the weapon struck a large tree at the rear of the flats, causing serious damage to blocks 25-36 and 37-48.

Although not cleared for publication until August 3, these Associated Press photographs were the first to be released showing a flying bomb actually diving onto Central London.

The buildings in the foreground are the Royal Courts of Justice (Law Courts) on the north side of the Strand. The date is Friday, June 30 and the time just a few minutes after 2 p.m.

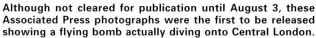

IN LONDON BETWEEN 21.00 ON WEDNESDAY, JUNE 28, TO 20.59 ON THURSDAY, JUNE 29			
21.30 Woolwich	02.00 Lewisham	05.55 Wanstead & Woodford	10.33 Wimbledon
22.25 Woolwich	02.24 Sutton	06.10 Malden & Coombe	10.46 Orpington
22.28 Croydon	02.44 Lewisham	06.20 Islington	10.47 Penge
22.35 Camberwell	02.58 Lambeth	06.26 Beckenham	10.52 Wandsworth
22.35 Heston	03.00 Carshalton	06.55 Croydon	12.00 Lambeth
23.00 Orpington	03.00 Wandsworth	07.16 Wandsworth	17.12 Esher
23.02 Croydon	03.15 Crayford	07.20 Beddington & Wallington	17.20 Croydon
00.01 Coulsdon & Purley	03.19 Bexley	08.00 Croydon	17.46 Twickenham
00.24 Penge	03.35 Beddington & Wallington	08.00 Wandsworth	18.25 Mitcham
00.33 Banstead	03.50 Esher	08.07 Hampstead	19.50 Kingston-on-Thames
00.55 Penge	04.00 Lewisham	08.15 Croydon	19.53 Wandsworth
01.40 Coulsdon & Purley	04.20 Elstree	08.33 Merton & Morden	20.56 Wimbledon
01.45 Croydon	04.29 Merton & Morden	08.40 Beddington & Wallington	
01.55 Twickenham	04.35 Lambeth	08.50 Croydon	

While the Associated Press photographer pictured the blast from the rooftops, a *Daily Mirror* cameraman, perhaps alerted by the sudden silence after the engine cut out, captured this incredible scene in Fleet Street of people carrying on regardless of the explosion in the background. The original caption as passed by the censor reads: 'Australia House in the Strand has been damaged in recent flying bomb attacks. Quite unconcernedly Londoners go about their business.'

22.40 Deptford	07,20 Greenwich	11,16 Penge	16.38 Hammersmith
00.15 Southwark	07.26 Heston	11.25 Wimbledon	16.40 Bermondsey
00.4-5 Esher	07.30 Greenwich	11.55 Esher	16.48 Wimbledon
00.50 Lewisham	07.45 Woolwich	12.15 St Pancras	17.10 Westminster
01,35 Beckenham	07.55 Bermondsey	12.40 Westminster	18.05 Crayford
01.25 Bromley	07.58 Poplar	13.28 Carshalton	18.06 Battersea
01.37 Beckenham	08.15 Harrow	13.35 Poplar	18.12 Leyton
02.10 Ruislip	08.50 West Ham	13.40 Beckenham	18.20 Enfield
03.00 Coulsdon & Purley	08.55 Lewisham	14.07 Westminster	18.29 Coulsdon & Purley
03.14 Orpington	09.05 Lambeth	14.56 Wandsworth	19.05 Ilford
03.37 Westerham	09.35 Camberwell	14.58 Wandsworth	19.55 Mitcham
03.55 Greenwich	09.55 Camberwell	15.03 Bromley	20,05 Beckenham
04.06 Finchley	10.25 Walthamstow	15.05 Wanstead & Woodford	20.06 Wandsworth
04.15 Mitcham	10,27 Wandsworth	15.12 Ilford	20.15 Heston
04.15 Croydon	10.35 East Ham	15.12 Ilford	20.34 Poplar
06.56 Mitcham	11.12 Camberwell	15.15 Esher	

On that Friday, Oberst Wachtel came within a few yards of scoring a direct hit on the Air Ministry at Aldwych (see page 18). Two flying bombs exploded within an hour of each other in the West End (Borough of Westminster), the first, shortly after midday, hitting the roof of the annexe to the Regent Palace Hotel in Brewer Street, killing a chambermaid. Yet it was the second bomb exploding in the street outside Adastral House just after two o'clock that resulted in the third-highest death toll of all the V1 incidents. The explosion had come at lunchtime on a fine sunny day when the street was crowded and most of the 200 casualties were passers-by. As Aldwych is only yards from Fleet Street it was inevitable that this incident would receive huge attention from the Press.

Photographers from the independent news agencies — Westminster Press, Planet News, the London News Agency, Sport & General, Keystone, Topical Press, Central Press — all descended on the scene as well as staff photographers from *The Times*, *News Chronicle*, *Daily Mirror*, *Daily Sketch* and the *Evening News*. All were immediately on the scene taking dozens of photographs, many duplicating each others' exposures like these two. This one, showing the search for survivors outside the blasted entrance to the Air Ministry, was taken by Sport & General. Their caption stated that 'the wall in the foreground claimed one victim'.

On the two lightest days, July 13 and 15, the comparable figure was 42 in each case. The week ending July 8, when 820 flying bombs were plotted, was the heaviest of the whole attack. The following week, however, the total fell by more than a third to 535.

Various factors account for these variations. That the Germans increased the weight of attack during cloudy weather, which hindered the defenders, is certain. We knew too that the supply of bombs to sites was hindered by inadequate transport, which was partly due to the attacks made specifically against 'Crossbow' targets.

The great majority of bombs were aimed at the London area yet many, owing to the inherent inaccuracy of the missile, fell at widely scattered points in the Home Counties and even beyond. The Solent area also received a small number of bombs. There was a definite attack on the night of June 25/26 when six bombs fell near Portsmouth, most of them to the west of the city within an hour. Other bombs may have been launched against the same area on June 19, and later, between July 10-22, some 60 bombs fell there at various times. They forced the withdrawal of two fighter squadrons from the main area of attack further east; otherwise their effect was negligible.

The attack on the Bristol area, which the orientation of certain sites in the Cherbourg peninsula had led us to expect, failed to materialise.

The attack, in short, was almost exclusively directed at London. The mean point of impact of the bombs was regularly calculated by the Operational Research Section at ADGB Headquarters and by the Deputy Directorate of Science at the Air Ministry. Excluding those bombs which were brought down by the defences, and all bombs aimed at the Solent area and those that fell more than 30 miles from the centre of London, on this reckoning the mean point of impact for the period up to the middle of July was at Alleyn's School in North Dulwich (see pages 108-109). In other words, the bombardment chiefly affected the boroughs south of the river in the area Wandsworth—Croydon—Woolwich, which received nearly 40 per cent of the bombs falling on Greater London.

Casualties and damage were by no means negligible. Up to July 15, approximately 3,000 people had been killed, 10,000 seriously injured and 12,000 slightly injured. Over 13,000 houses were irreparably damaged. Had the mean point of impact had been a few miles further north, where the density of population was greater, casualties would have been appreciably heavier. Moreover, the maintenance of a fairly constant mean point of impact meant that a number of bombs fell in places already devastated or partially evacuated. As the Germans were doubtless out to do as much damage as possible, it was assumed at the time that their aiming point was probably the centre of London, say Charing Cross.

To begin with, all bombs were launched from modified sites in northern France and came inland over the coasts of Sussex and Kent. Then on the night of July 9/10, bombs were plotted approaching London on a westerly course from the direction of the Thames Estuary. This suggested that sites had been constructed in the area round Dunkirk and Ostend where there had certainly been no sites prior to the middle of June. Photographic reconnaissance of the area could not be carried out owing to bad weather until July 28 but no new constructions could be seen. It was not until August 3 that it was firmly established that the bombs approaching London from the east were in fact being launched from piloted aircraft. However, the number fired by this method was small compared to those launched from sites on land, and it remains true to say that the attack of London at this period was almost entirely carried out from the sites in northern France.

Taking pictures alongside him was the man from the *Evening News* but, although he must have pressed his shutter within a second or so, for some reason his shot did not pass the censor. Alan Haylock was a 17-year-old working in the news-room of Reuters and was travelling on a bus up Fleet Street. 'The conductor called out: "Next stop the Law Courts", then the bus seemed to rear up like a frightened horse, settle for a moment, then veer over at an angle. Windows on both decks blew in and the roof of the bus in front peeled back as if by some giant tin-opener.'

'I walked slowly into the Strand and a scene of utter devastation', continued Alan. 'Bodies lay everywhere, some already dead, some dying, and some injured in varying degrees.' Three photographers were sent from Planet News but it was the chief photographer, Herbert 'Andy' Andrews, who took the most graphic pictures of the dead and dying, even though he must have known that they would never be passed for publication.

Alan: 'I looked down at a middle-aged woman seated on the pavement among the ankle-deep debris. She was propped up against a shop front and was deathly white. One shoe was missing and both her stockings were torn, she was terribly cut about the neck, face and head. She had auburn hair and was still clutching her handbag. I was about to bend down to see if there was anything I could do when I felt someone come up behind me. A voice said: "There's nothing you can do for her, chum. She's gone. Died about two or three minutes ago. We're just waiting for the ambulance." For a moment I stood and talked to the First Aid man, surveying the carnage around us. Then I turned round and took one last look at the lady. My eyes were moist, it was almost as if I knew her.'

On the opposite side of the road lay Australia House and Bush House which then housed the European section of the BBC. One of the post-boys there was Derrick Grady. 'Weather permitting, during our lunch hour, most of us younger boys used to go down to the Embankment. It was there that we heard the warning siren and as we entered the East Court of Bush House we could hear the alarm bells ringing inside the building that meant "Enemy action imminent". Just as we arrived at the side entrance we heard the V1 and its engine cut out.

One of my friends shouted: "There it is!" We saw it just above the north-east wing before it disappeared behind the buildings. We turned and flung ourselves to the ground. I was in the air when the blast hit me but I still have no idea why I wasn't hurt when there were injured people all around. I put my jacket under someone's head; when I found it later it was covered in blood.' Central Press took these photos of the activity outside Bush House as members of the public help soldiers and police to rescue victims. Forty-eight were killed that day.

The Bombing of Sites in northern France

This being the case, it followed that the bombardment of sites in that area remained a necessary counter-measure, despite the practical difficulties and the many other calls upon Allied bombing resources.

It will be recalled that up to June 23, bad weather had interfered with both the weight and accuracy of attacks upon 'Crossbow' targets, but there was every intention, at least on the part of Air Chief Marshal Tedder, of carrying out a heavy and sustained offensive. It will also be recalled that at that time the targets to be attacked were, in order of priority, the large sites, the supply sites and the 47 modified sites that had been identified in the area Somme—Pas-de-Calais.

On June 22, a beginning had been made in the attack on storage depots. General bombing policy from June 23 remained the same: that is to say that after the needs of the land battle had been met, the attack of 'Crossbow' targets had priority over all operations. No written directive embodying this policy appears to have been issued by the Deputy Supreme Commander; but on at least two occasions Tedder personally informed the commanders of the bomber forces of the relative priorities. Moreover, on June 29, AEAF Headquarters requested RAF Bomber Command and the US Strategic Air Forces to observe this programme: first 'Crossbow', second railways and bridges, and third fuel dumps. Air Chief Marshal Leigh-Mallory, who was still nominally responsible for 'Crossbow' operations, could properly issue such a request but there appears to have been nothing mandatory about it. Indeed, the organisation of the chain of command was such that the heavy bomber force commanders regarded themselves only under the direct command of the Supreme Commander or his Deputy.

A few days later, the London News Agency recorded the clear-up of the remains of the ten-foot-high blast wall which had protected the entrance to Adastral House. (See page 18 for the subsequent history of the building.) Note the pillbox situated on the corner of Kingsway.

Even so, although they knew what were the views of the Deputy Supreme Commander, Air Chief Marshal Harris and Lieutenant General Doolittle sent as many aircraft to attack strategic targets as 'Crossbow' targets. One half of the effort of the two forces was exerted against battlefield targets between the middle of June and the middle of July, one quarter against 'Crossbow', and one quarter against industrial towns in Germany, aircraft factories and oil targets. Moreover, the Chief of the Air Staff also considered that to prohibit them in order to bring to bear a heavier scale of attack on 'Crossbow' targets would be unwise. At a meeting of the War Cabinet 'Crossbow' Sub-Committee on July 11, Sir Charles Portal urged 'that nothing should be done to detract from what

Meanwhile the RAF was taking the battle to the enemy. On June 22, a combined force of 234 aircraft comprising 119 Lancasters, 102 Halifaxes and 13 Mosquitos bombed a number of V-weapon sites, like this one at Siracourt. Further attacks were made on the installation on June 25 and July 6 even though it was now realised that the flying bombs were being fired from the so-called 'modified' launch sites, not the bunker constructions which had by now been abandoned.

Left: **The tiny village of Flers, just south of Bapaume, was photographed on July 7 by Lieutenant Colonel John S. Blyth of the 14th Squadron of the US 7th Photo Reconnaissance Group based at Mount Farm in Oxfordshire. Although Flers lies over 70 miles inland, analysts at Medmenham identified it as a V1** ski site, the letter 'P' indicating the position of the ramp. Note also the Flak position — three light guns — top right. *Right:* **Lying right in the centre of the Somme battlefield, Flers is better known for the French battle in September 1914 and the tank battle by the 41st Division in September 1916.**

appeared to be the war-winning policy of air attack on the enemy's oil resources and essential support to the army'. He reminded the meeting that while the concentration on railways and communications prior to D-Day might have given the Germans time to complete their preparations for flying bomb attacks, it had also prepared the way for the consolidation of the Allied landings in France. In other words, he was implying that it was vital to keep a sense of proportion about 'Crossbow' and put it against the wider and far more important background of the land battle, but this does not alter the fact that between the formulation of general bombing policy during this period and its execution there was a gap which might have been filled.

The records of the campaign show that the bomber force commanders resented the effort that they had to make against 'Crossbow' targets but there is this to be said in their support. Throughout the first five weeks of the campaign, the policy governing the selection of 'Crossbow' targets, for which the Directorate of Operations at the Air Ministry was responsible, was unsatisfactory. In the first place, priorities for attack were frequently changed between June 15 and July 15. Large sites, supply sites, storage depots, and depots equally with certain production targets in Germany, were at different times first-call upon the bombers. This in itself reflected the imperfect current

intelligence of the place which each category of target occupied in the German organisation. Large sites were indeed thought not to be connected with flying bombs but with rockets, and their attack was an insurance against what as yet was only a threat. The bombing of supply sites gambled on their actually being in use of which there was no evidence. Nor did evidence to that effect become available during June and early July, yet attacks were made on them until July 10. Similarly, ski sites were still on the list of targets as late as June 27 although there was nothing to show that they were being used.

Where the position was most unsatisfactory from the point of view of Bomber Command and the Eighth Air Force was in the relative effort assigned to modified sites and storage depots. The fact was that the sites were an extremely unpopular target. They were small, hard to find and well defended, and there were a lot of them, 41 being identified between June 15 and July 15, making 88 in all. They were a difficult target for all types of bombers and a dangerous one for fighter-bombers. For heavy bombers they were an uneconomical target for a large weight of bombs had to be dropped to ensure the destruction of even a single site which, where there were so many, was no great loss to the enemy. In any case, sites could be repaired and new sites constructed very rapidly.

On the other hand, the storage depots, of which seven had been identified by the end of June, covering as they did a large area, could be very effectively attacked by the heavies, and the commanders of both forces were strongly in favour of concentrating against them and abandoning the attack of modified sites. These depots, and also supply sites and production targets in Germany, particularly those factories making gyro compasses, which were essential to flying bombs, were suggested as the best 'Crossbow' targets by the US Strategic Air Force Chief, Lieutenant General Spaatz, on June 30. On this occasion, Leigh-Mallory (who was still responsible for the execution of 'Crossbow' countermeasures) directed that, as an experiment, the modified sites should be left alone for a few days but both Portal and Tedder disagreed and on July 5 the attacks were recommenced.

Organisation. Such differences of opinion were, of course, partly a reflection of the inadequate intelligence of what the Germans were doing, which in turn led to a reluctance on the part of Air Intelligence to recommend a coherent target policy such as the operational commanders would have liked.

Intelligence and operational countermeasures were still nominally co-ordinated in the Directorate of Operations at the Air Ministry but this arrangement was not working well. That this was the case was common knowledge, and the matter came to a head on July 8 when

Major General Orvil Anderson of the US Strategic Air Forces formally recommended to Tedder that the organisation of 'Crossbow' intelligence should be overhauled, particularly in the sphere of target selection. Over the next few days, a scheme was agreed that meant that the routine work of intelligence was henceforth the entire responsibility of Air Intelligence at Air Ministry. From there it passed to an Anglo-American committee consisting of representatives of Air Intelligence and the operational staffs of Air Ministry and US Strategic Air Forces. The function of this body was to examine the collated intelligence daily and recommend what targets should be attacked and in what order. It was known as the Joint 'Crossbow' Target Priorities Committee and it held its first meeting on July 21.

At the same time a change was made in the structure of operational responsibility for 'Crossbow' bombing. So far Leigh-Mallory had been responsible for operational counter-measures against 'Crossbow' targets, but in both its defensive and offensive aspects it was little more than a nominal role. His prime task was the organisation of air support for the land battle and he had neither the inclination nor the time for any other matters. This was recognised as far as defence against flying bombs was concerned, and when the Chiefs of Staff later took exception to certain changes in defensive measures, it was Air Marshal Hill who suffered their dis-

pleasure, not Leigh-Mallory, although the former was nominally the latter's subordinate. As for the offensive, Leigh-Mallory had little control over the strategic bombers with the exception that he had 'general direction' of such as were allotted by the Supreme Commander to support the land battle. As these were the main arm of the offensive against 'Crossbow' (the components of AEAF being fully committed to the land battle) he asked Tedder on July 22 if he could be relieved of his 'Crossbow' responsibilities. The Deputy Supreme Commander agreed and decided that the planning of 'Crossbow' bombing should henceforth be done by the Combined Operational Planning Committee — a body on which all the bombing forces were represented — though the broad direction of operations would remain his own responsibility. The change merely clarified a situation that had existed since April when Tedder had taken up the position of Deputy Supreme Commander, giving him general responsibility to the Supreme Commander for air operations.

Operations. The Allied bombing during these weeks was by no means fruitless. Of the 88 modified sites that had been identified, 68 had been attacked by July 15. At least 24 of these had been made inoperative and eight others seriously damaged. By July 10 damage at the four most important large sites — Mimoyecques, Siracourt, Watten and Wizernes — was

such that they were thought unlikely to become operational before the middle of August. They were accordingly withdrawn from the schedule of targets. On the same date, three of the seven supply sites were also suspended from attack and no more attacks were made against this sort of target. A number of power stations and transformers in the Pas-de-Calais had been damaged and one château housing a headquarters unit was destroyed.

As for the storage depots, Nucourt and St Leu-d'Esserent were each attacked once in the last week in June by the Eighth Air Force but on July 3 it was decided that they should be left to RAF Bomber Command. Very heavy attacks were made on St Leu-d'Esserent on the nights of the 4th/5th and 7th/8th, when nearly 3,000 tons of bombs were dropped. At the time, Air Intelligence believed that up to 70 per cent of flying bomb supplies were being distributed through this depot. After the first attacks there were indications that supplies were being moved from there to Nucourt and it was reckoned that a notable blow had been struck. Nucourt then became more important than ever to the Germans and it was singled out for attack on the night of July 10/11. However, the target area was completely obscured by cloud, the pathfinder force failed to illuminate it, and the attack was a failure. A further attack by day on the 15th was also unsuccessful but Bomber Command persevered and hit the target hard that same night.

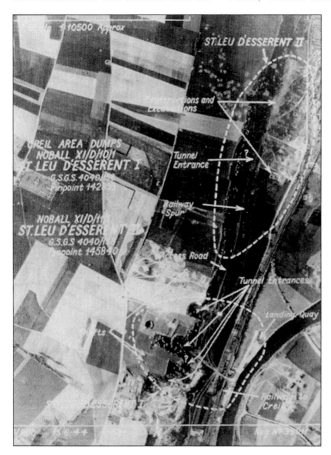

Late in June, Allied intelligence identified the caves at St Leu-d'Esserent, some 25 miles north of Paris, as one of the major underground V1 storage depots. It was initially bombed by the Americans and then on July 4/5 by the RAF in an attempt to collapse the tunnels. Finally, on July 7/8, a big raid by over 200 Lancasters successfully blocked the entrances using Tallboy bombs.

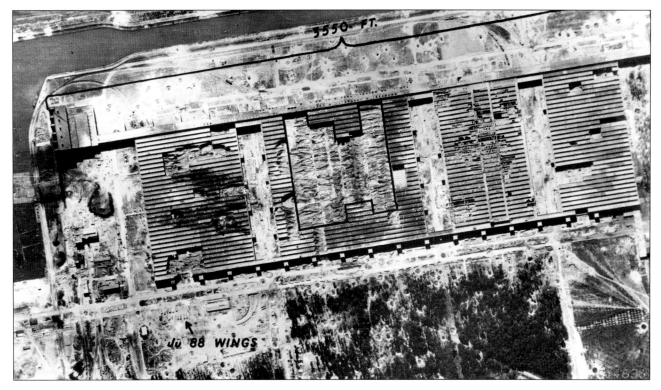

It was ironic that the major damage to the Volkswagen factory at Fallersleben, a main V-weapon production plant on the target list, was caused by an American pilotless aircraft! On April 29, the Eighth Air Force mounted a major raid on Berlin to be carried out by a mixed force of over 600 B-17s and B-24s.

When one aircraft was hit by anti-aircraft fire, the crew baled out leaving the bomber — believed to be a Fortress — to head south and eventually crash still with its bomb-load intact. Unfortunately, it has not been possible to identify the aircraft concerned from the 46 that failed to return from that raid.

Altogether, nearly 6,000 tons had been dropped on these two targets as they were suitable for attack by heavy bombers. It is significant, too, of the part that heavy bombers were playing in counter-measures that factories thought to be connected with rockets or flying bombs were once more being seriously considered as targets for the first time since February. The Volkswagenwerke at Fallersleben, near Brunswick, was one and it was attacked by the Eighth Air Force with excellent results as early as June 2 and again on June 29. Then three plants producing hydrogen peroxide (which was used in the launching of flying bombs) were listed for attack. They were at Peenemünde, Oberraderach, near Friedrichshafen, and Düsseldorf. A fourth site at Höllriegelskreuth, near Munich, was added on July 7 although none of these were attacked until after July 15.

Tell-tale signs of the repair to Hall 1 are indicated by the patchwork roof panels.

IN LONDON BETWEEN 21.00 ON FRIDAY, JUNE 30, TO 20.59 ON SATURDAY, JULY 1

21.45 Brentford	06.15 Wood Green	11.30 Woolwich	14.55 Esher
21.52 Lewisham	06.30 Battersea	12.00 Lewisham	15.25 Wandsworth
01.51 Ilford	06.47 Willesden	12.08 Greenwich	15.35 Fulham
02.05 Enfield	06.55 Poplar	12.10 Beddington & Wallington	16.22 Fulham
02.30 Banstead	06.56 Coulsdon & Purley	12.20 Greenwich	16.30 Southgate
02.50 Wimbledon	07.30 Croydon	12.25 West Ham	16.31 Beckenham
02.50 Croydon	08.29 West Ham	12.28 Greenwich	17.15 Chingford
03.00 Westminster	08.49 Carshalton	12.28 Croydon	17.45 Stepney
03.42 Lambeth	08.51 Chislehurst & Sidcup	12.35 Crayford	18.25 Camberwell
03.45 Greenwich	09.09 Croydon	12.38 Sutton	18.40 Westminster
04.01 Greenwich	09.20 Croydon	13.01 Bromley	18.50 Bermondsey
04.10 Greenwich	09.25 Mitcham	13.01 Wandsworth	18.50 Twickenham
04.14 Hendon	10.24 Croydon	13.12 Greenwich	19.58 Islington
04.27 West Ham	10.26 Bexley	13.35 Lambeth	20.01 Wandsworth
04.50 Lambeth	10.46 Coulsdon	13.35 Woolwich	20.30 Coulsdon
05.00 Deptford	10.50 Woolwich	14.24 Beddington & Wallington	20.50 Battersea
05.26 Orpington	10.57 City	14.30 Greenwich	
05.56 Beddington & Wallington	11.00 Chislehurst & Sidcup	14.30 Woolwich	
06.13 Lambeth	11.25 Beckenham	14.41 Wandsworth	

By the beginning of July, with no official pronouncement about the steps being taken to counter the increasing bombardment, Members of Parliament in the affected constituencies were agitating for action. As yet there had been no official word from the Ministry over evacuation plans; no announcement about any additional protection, including the opening of the deep shelters, and the warning system was losing its credibility, with either over-long alerts with no bombs heard, or no warning at all. Even worse was the overall veil of secrecy surrounding the whole matter with not even the admission by the Government that London was the main target. Although the combined defence of fighters, guns and balloons had achieved a kill rate of over 40 per cent of bombs launched, this was of no consequence to those Londoners trying to muster the courage to face the new Blitz — made worse by the psychological effect of the deadliness of the robot bombs which seemed to be unerringly guided like an arrow to pre-ordained targets.

The Attack on London; Work of the Defences

According to the most-reliable statistics, 2,930 flying bombs were reported by the defences between June 15 and July 15 of which all except about 30 were aimed at London. The number of bombs that came overland amounted to 2,579, of which 1,280 fell inside the London area. The defences destroyed 1,241 bombs, most of them falling in Kent and Sussex and the Channel, but 65 of them crashed on London. The rest of the bombs represented gross errors in accuracy.

Very few important industrial and commercial objectives, and no military ones, were directly affected by the attack, and there were less than a dozen major fires. This was only to be expected when the weapon was indiscriminate in its nature and relied on blast rather than incendiarism to cause damage. The long catalogue of incidents consisted almost entirely of damage to civilian property — houses, churches, hospitals, schools and the like. Similarly, the number of service casualties was barely five per cent of those

Almost spot on was the bomb which hit Nos. 79-81 Aldersgate Street at 10.57 a.m. on July 1, the picture (centre) being taken by the City of London Police. The Metropolitan Railway tunnel was breached and began flooding from a fractured water main, but the fact that it was a Saturday no doubt mitigated the casualties to five dead and 62 injured.

The heavy hand of censorship on this photo submitted for publication by the *Croydon Times*. On July 1-2, the borough suffered no fewer than 13 V1s within a 48-hour period yet all the photographs submitted by the paper were not approved for release until August and only then with the general description 'Southern England'.

IN LONDON BETWEEN 21.00 ON SATURDAY, JULY 1, TO 20.59 ON SUNDAY, JULY 2			
22.00 Hackney	01.30 Wandsworth	05.45 Croydon	11.06 Cheam & Sutton
22.03 Wandsworth	01.30 Croydon	07.18 Bromley	11.07 Camberwell
23.28 Wandsworth	02.10 Deptford	08.05 Bexley	11.15 Erith
23.30 Battersea	02.42 Croydon	08.08 Coulsdon	11.26 Camberwell
23.30 Surbiton	02.57 Hayes & Harlington	09.23 Lewisham	11.35 Greenwich
23.33 Lambeth	03.10 Beckenham	09.28 Penge	11.35 Wanstead & Woodford
23.33 Hendon	03.10 Esher	09.30 Orpington	11.36 Beddington & Wallington
23.34 Orpington	03.42 Beckenham	09.30 Croydon	11.50 Camberwell
23.35 Camberwell	04.20 Bromley	09.35 Lewisham	12.00 Hammersmith
23.37 Chigwell	04.30 Lambeth	09.35 Wandsworth	12.05 West Ham
23.38 Hayes & Harlington	04.30 Bexley	09.38 Coulsdon	12.08 Kensington
23.39 Fulham	05.10 Croydon	09.41 Barking	12.25 Croydon
00.01 Surbiton	05.17 Lewisham	10.40 Barnet	12.47 St Pancras
00.15 Merton & Morden	05.25 Chislehurst & Sidcup	10.49 Epsom	12.50 Croydon
00.50 West Ham	05.28 Bromley	10.57 Beckenham	13.15 Epsom
00.56 Islington	05.30 Deptford	11.00 Coulsdon	13.25 Enfield
01.23 Lambeth	05.30 Chislehurst & Sidcup	11.00 Beddington & Wallington	

suffered by the civil population, though the two most-serious incidents of the period — indeed of the whole attack — judged by loss of life, were ones in which service casualties predominated.

Throughout the period, the efficiency of the defences as a whole showed a tendency to improve. The percentage of bombs destroyed rose from 33 in the week June 15-21 to 50 in the week July 9-15. The improvement was almost entirely the result of the efforts of the fighters, whose percentage success doubled from approximately 20 to approximately 40. Guns and balloons destroyed only some 13 per cent and eight per cent respectively of their possible targets. Almost half the bombs that crossed the coast during the period succeeded in reaching the London area — a proportion that was considered far from satisfactory.

Now the location can be revealed: this is Whitehorse Road!

formations for reinforcements, for only the fastest fighters in service were able to register consistent success, and ADGB only possessed three squadrons of Tempest Vs and three of Spitfire XIVs. Therefore Air Marshal Hill's first move was to obtain, with the assent of Leigh-Mallory, one flight of Mustang IIIs from No. 316 Squadron of the Second Tactical Air Force. These aircraft began to operate on July 1 and straightway began to score successes. Consequently, a much larger reinforcement was negotiated whereby three squadrons — a complete wing — of Mustang IIIs were transferred to ADGB. They made their first flying bomb patrols on July 12. By that date, 13 single-engine fighter squadrons — three Tempest Vs, three Spitfire XIVs, one Spitfire XII, two Spitfire IXs and four Mustang IIIs — were being employed. Three Mosquito squadrons were also in use solely for flying bomb work, and six others were being used partly for flying bomb patrols and partly for work over the beaches. Two, Nos. 85

A notable incident on Sunday, July 2, occurred at West Ham when the Electricity Department of the Borough Council on the corner of Romford Road and Vicarage Lane received a direct hit. The Ministry logged it at 00.50 but the local report stated 00.58. Damage to over 1,100 properties was recorded.

Fighters. Most of the fighter squadrons that were employed were drawn entirely from the resources of ADGB and, in particular, of No. 11 Group, which, though it had extensive duties to perform over the Normandy beaches and the shipping lanes across the Channel, was also responsible for the defence of its own area which included the 'Diver' Defence Area. As a result it was necessary to call on other

Then two weeks later on July 19 a second bomb landed on the ruined southern end of the building at 04.42. Forest Gate photographer Mr W. Wedlake revisited Vicarage Lane to take this matching shot . . .

and 157, were with No. 100 Group under the control of Bomber Command when flying bomb attacks began. They were required to accompany the heavy bombers on attacks where night fighter opposition was anticipated, and for this they were equipped with one of the latest types of Mosquito — the Mark XII — and the most up-to-date model of AI radar, the Mark X. But despite the importance of their task, Air Marshal Hill felt justified in asking for their use against flying bombs and they commenced operations on June 27. However, Harris only agreed with reluctance, and eventually, under a ruling from Portal, the two squadrons divided their efforts about equally between bomber support and flying bomb patrols.

. . . and 70-odd years later we took this comparison, the building since having been converted into separate flats.

01.00 Dagenham	03.48 Coulsdon & Purley	08.09 Mitcham	16.12 Lewisham
01.00 Kensington	03.50 Deptford	08.20 Lewisham	16.25 West Ham
01.02 Lewisham	03.50 Camberwell	08.55 Camberwell	16.35 West Ham
01.05 Heston	03.50 Coulsdon & Purley	10.20 Beddington & Wallington	16.47 Lewisham
01.05 Lewisham	03.52 Lewisham	11.20 Coulsdon & Purley	17.32 Barking
01.05 Wembley	04.30 Croydon	12.20 Croydon	17.45 Coulsdon & Purley
01.08 West Ham	04.35 Epsom	12.25 Banstead	18.30 Wandsworth
01.08 Greenwich	04.45 Wandsworth	12.58 Bromley	18.40 Wandsworth
01.10 Epsom	04.56 Kensington	14.17 Esher	19.00 Wembley
01.10 Chislehurst & Sidcup	05.15 Merton & Morden	15.15 Kensington	19.05 Beckenham
01.10 Sutton & Cheam	05.35 Malden & Coombe	15.20 Wanstead & Woodford	19.20 Banstead
02.08 Merton & Morden	05.37 Stepney	15.25 Malden & Coombe	19.25 West Ham
02.11 Southall	06.34 Wandsworth	15.25 Greenwich	19.25 Carshalton
02.15 Epsom	06.37 Battersea	15.26 Hackney	19.40 Mitcham
02.25 Mitcham	06.40 Carshalton	15.32 City	19.50 Barking
02.28 Ealing	07.27 Sutton & Cheam	15.41 Wandsworth	20.05 Coulsdon & Purley
02.40 Beddington & Wallington	07.44 Chelsea	15.41 Wandsworth	20.10 Croydon
03.04 Camberwell	07.45 Greenwich	15.50 Mitcham	20.35 Croydon
03.45 Malden & Coombe	08.00 Merton & Morden	16.06 Croydon	20.50 Erith

Improvements in the equipment that was used consisted chiefly in concentrating the best and fastest fighters available in the south-east and increasing their speed to the utmost by various modifications. Fighters that were exclusively employed on flying bomb patrols were stripped of armour and all unnecessary external fittings. Camouflage paint was removed from the fuselage and wings and the surfaces polished; engines were modified to use 150-octane fuel and also accept higher boost pressure than normal. The three types of day fighters principally employed were made faster in this way by some 15-30 mph.

The alterations inevitably meant an extraordinary strain upon airframes and engines but this was accepted as speed was quite the most important factor in interception. For the same reason, increasing use was made of single-seater fighters at night, both by ordinary squadrons and by a flight of Tempests, manned by volunteers from Mosquito squadrons, which was placed under the Fighter Interception Unit. These

In the summer of 1942, Glenn Miller with his civilian band was at the pinnacle of his fame. In September he joined the United States Army and formed his orchestra in the spring of 1943. Then the following year he was sent to Britain to entertain the troops and on Thursday, June 29, the musicians of the Glenn Miller Army Air Force Band arrived at Euston Station after an overnight train journey from Gourock in Scotland. They arrived to be greeted by an air raid alert. Billets for the band had been arranged at No. 25 Sloane Court, Chelsea. However, surrounded by the frequent explosions of V1s, Captain Miller was far from happy with this situation and he drove out to Supreme Headquarters in Bushy Park, Teddington, to arrange for alternative accommodation to be made available outside London. The band members were only at Sloane Court for three nights, the transfer to Bedford being made on Sunday morning, July 2. It proved a narrow escape as the street was blasted by a flying bomb at 7.44 a.m. the following morning. The incident also proved to be the second-worst V1 incident and the one causing the most deaths to military personnel — in this case American.

IN MEMORY OF
THE 74 AMERICAN MILITARY PERSONNEL
OF THE UNITED STATES ARMY
AND THREE CIVILIANS
WHO WERE KILLED ON THE 3RD JULY 1944
BY A 'VI' FLYING BOMB
IN SLOANE COURT EAST / TURKS ROW

WE WILL REMEMBER THEM

The number of service victims was first given as 36 but was later revised upward to 64 with over 50 seriously injured. In 1998 a wall plaque unveiled at Turks Row opposite Sloane Court East now states that 74 Americans were killed and three civilians. There is also a Blue Plaque set in the pavement although this ignores the civilian dead.

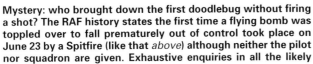

Mystery: who brought down the first doodlebug without firing a shot? The RAF history states the first time a flying bomb was toppled over to fall prematurely out of control took place on June 23 by a Spitfire (like that *above*) although neither the pilot nor squadron are given. Exhaustive enquiries in all the likely squadron records have drawn a blank, the earliest recorded reference appearing on July 4 when Flying Officer W. R. MacLaren of No. 56 Squadron tipped up a 'diver' after using up all his ammunition at 17.05 hours two miles south-east of Redhill — but that was in a Tempest.

aircraft began to operate regularly from Newchurch on the night of June 27/28 and scored many successes.

As the attack proceeded and our pilots gained in experience, so the comparatively standardised technique of interception and destruction that has already been outlined (see pages 77-78) was formulated. Then on June 23 a Spitfire pilot destroyed a flying bomb by tipping it over with his wing-tip and four days later a Tempest destroyed another by the pilot manoeuvring his aircraft so that its slipstream forced the bomb into a spin.

IN LONDON BETWEEN 21.00 ON MONDAY, JULY 3, TO 20.59 ON TUESDAY, JULY 4

21.36 Lambeth	09.10 Merton & Morden	12.46 Wanstead & Woodford	18.05 Bexley
21.45 Wandsworth	09.35 Stepney	13.10 Lambeth	18.33 Islington
22.25 Woolwich	10.00 Wimbledon	14.40 Yiewsley	18.40 Epsom
23.59 Lewisham	10.20 Orpington	15.25 Coulsdon & Purley	19.32 Hornsey
00.04 Deptford	10.40 Camberwell	15.32 Carshalton	20.20 Merton & Morden
01.12 Battersea	10.45 Surbiton	15.33 Mitcham	20.23 Sunbury
08.50 Lambeth	11.05 Croydon	15.41 Esher	20.29 Surbiton
08.50 Epsom	11.34 Wandsworth	17.19 Barking	20.50 Heston
09.04 Malden & Coombe	12.31 Epsom	17.55 Lambeth	

Tempests were armed with four Hispano 20mm cannon which delivered 40 shells per second. Wing Commander Roland Beamont, leading No. 150 Wing at Newchurch, had the guns on aircraft unofficially altered to converge at 300 yards (as opposed to the normal Fighter Command 'spread' pattern) to increase the firepower against the small, fast-moving target. The trick was so successful that he had all the Wing's Tempests re-adjusted, No. 3 becoming the top-scoring squadron with a bag of 258 V1s to their credit. 'It was certainly impressive to fly straight through the middle of a 2,000lb bomb explosion', wrote Beamont in his autobiography *Phoenix into Ashes*, 'but not many pilots were hurt doing it.' However, at least 70 pilots (and crewmen if the aircraft involved was a Mosquito) lost their lives in attempts to bring down flying bombs.

IN LONDON BETWEEN 21.00 ON TUESDAY, JULY 4, TO 20.59 ON WEDNESDAY, JULY 5

21.20 Croydon	02.00 Ilford	13.14 Willesden	18.08 Wandsworth
22.00 Croydon	03.10 Woolwich	13.15 East Barnet	18.20 Coulsdon & Purley
22.01 Greenwich	03.10 Wandsworth	13.47 Heston	18.23 Finsbury
22.31 Beckenham	03.40 Epsom	14.20 St Pancras	18.45 Barnes
23.10 Poplar	04.25 Camberwell	14.40 Ilford	19.10 Croydon
23.20 Lewisham	04.30 Lewisham	14.50 Wandsworth	19.29 Wanstead & Woodford
23.57 Epsom	05.00 Battersea	16.55 Coulsdon & Purley	19.35 Merton & Morden
00.23 Surbiton	05.15 Greenwich	17.00 East Ham	19.45 Kensington
00.25 Wanstead & Woodford	06.30 Leyton	17.00 Kensington	20.05 Bermondsey
00.25 Beckenham	08.10 Hampstead	17.18 Walthamstow	20.31 Twickenham
00.25 Wandsworth	12.29 Croydon	17.18 Kingston-on-Thames	20.35 Croydon
00.43 Lambeth	12.42 Wimbledon	17.28 Leyton	20.36 Finchley
00.58 Lewisham	12.50 Wandsworth	17.40 Wimbledon	20.42 Beckenham
01.10 Bermondsey	12.55 Wandsworth	18.04 Westminster	
01.10 Lambeth	13.02 Surbiton	18.05 Greenwich	

The V1s took a terrible toll on life and property across the south-east. Many were brought down by Britain's own defences and in a relatively small village such as Westfield in Sussex, it is quite astonishing that no less than 12 flying bombs fell in the parish. Lying just behind Hastings on the direct route of the V1s to London, several were exploded in mid-air by RAF fighters or anti-aircraft defences and, hard though it may seem, the difficult deci-sion had been made; they were less likely to cause devastation and death if downed over rural areas before they inevitably impacted on London. In total, the old Battle Rural District area had 374 of these bombs downed within its boundary. The next time you drive into the village, take the sharp left-hand bend into Church Lane and notice the bungalow directly ahead of you. It suffered damage from a falling V1.

> WESTFIELD (near HASTINGS). 1737. FLY destroyed. Slight damage to two houses. No casualties.
> 1740. FLY destroyed. 1 house seriously and 21 others slightly damaged. Farm buildings were also affected.

Spring Cottage lay further down the road and on July 3 it too suffered from a falling flying bomb. Ken Munday rushed to the scene only to hear Doris Linch, who was in an advanced state of pregnancy, screaming as she was pulled from the wreckage. As a teenager who had found the war exciting up to now, it had a profound effect on him and ever after Ken took it on himself to tend her grave in Westfield's churchyard. Although her name was inscribed on the village war memorial, the grave itself was unmarked so in February 2014 Ken rectified the situation by the addition of a steel cross of wartime pattern.

Guns. The fact that the performance of the guns was unsatisfactory up to the middle of July was freely acknowledged by Anti-Aircraft Command. During these first five weeks, those tactical difficulties of controlling fire against the bombs that have already been outlined (pages 78-79), were at their worst, and were likely to remain unsolved until the equipment that had been deployed originally was replaced, especially the heavy gun equipment. All turned, therefore, on the speedy emplacement of static, power-controlled guns, SCR 584 radar sets and No. 10 Predictors.

The necessary static guns, however, could only be found from the less-vulnerable gun-defended areas of the United Kingdom which meant a large movement of equipment that had not been designed for mobility. Thus it was not until July 8 that the first static, power-controlled guns were in position in the 'Diver' gun belt. By the same date, 60 SCR 584 sets and 48 No. 10 Predictors were available.

By the 15th the general position was as follows. There were 376 heavy and 594 light guns in action in the gun belt. On the coast there were a further 600 guns of 40mm and 20mm, most of them manned by units of the RAF Regiment, and also 3½ batteries of rocket guns. All heavy gun sites had been equipped with the SCR 584 and the No. 10 Predictor, but only 55 power-controlled guns had been placed in position, and only four of these were operational.

Home Security Intelligence Summary No. 3536 for 12 hours ending 06.00, Thursday 6th July, 1944: 'The enemy continued to send Flying Bombs against this country until 2208, when there was a lull which lasted until 02.10, after which time activity continued throughout the period. A total of 89 Flying Bombs were plotted, 52 of them over land. 25 were destroyed. 31 incidents have been reported from 24 boroughs in LONDON mostly in the central and eastern parts of the region. A serious fire in WANDSWORTH involved the Army Form Depot, OK Sauce Factory and the Metropolitan Dyers & Cleaners *(above)*. Warner Bros. Studio in TWICKENHAM was also damaged by fire and the borough electric sub-station in BERMONDSEY was seriously affected. Railway damage was reported from GREENWICH and SUTTON & CHEAM. All patients had to be evacuated from the Royal Free Hospital ST PANCRAS and serious damage was caused at Mile End Hospital, STEPNEY. Elsewhere 29 incidents have been reported, 17 of them in Sussex and 13 in Kent. None were serious except at CROWBOROUGH where a number of Service casualties were involved.' Later that day Churchill gave Parliament an eagerly-awaited statement on the V-weapon campaign.

Up to 6 a.m. today 2,752 people have been killed by flying bombs and about 8,000 have been injured and detained in hospital. The number of flying bombs launched up to 6 a.m. today was 2,754. The number of dead will be somewhat increased by people who die of their injuries in hospital. Many minor injuries have been caused by splinters of glass.

The firing points in France have been continually attacked for several months and the total weight of bombs so far dropped on these and rocket targets in France and Germany, including Peenemünde, have now reached about 50,000 tons.

The invisible battle has now crashed into the open. We shall now be able to watch its progress at fairly close quarters. Between 100 and 150 flying bombs, each weighing about one ton, are being discharged daily, and have been discharged for the last fortnight or so.

Considering the modest weight and small penetrative power, the damage done by blast effect has been extensive. It cannot be compared with the terrific destruction by fire and high explosive with which we have been assaulting Berlin, Hamburg, Cologne and scores of other German cities and war manufacturing points.

The House will be favourably surprised to learn that the total number of flying bombs launched have killed almost one person per bomb. It has kept pace week by week.

A very high proportion of the casualties have fallen upon London — now I have mentioned it the phrase 'Southern England' passes out of currency — which presents to the enemy a target 18 miles wide by 20 miles deep. It offers the unique target of the world for the use of a weapon of such inaccuracy. The flying bomb is a weapon literally and essentially indiscriminate in its nature, purpose and effect.

The House will ask: What of the future? Is this attack going to get worse? Will the rocket-bomb come? Will more destructive explosions come? Will there be greater ranges?

I can give no guarantee that any of these evils will be finally prevented before the time comes when the soil from which these attacks come has been finally liberated.

I must make it perfectly plain. I don't want any misunderstandings. We shall not allow the battle operations in Normandy, or the attacks we make against specific targets in Germany to suffer. They come first. We must fit in our own domestic arrangements in the general scheme. There is no question of the slightest weakening of the battle. It may be a comfort to some that they are sharing in no small way with the burdens of our soldiers overseas.

London will never be conquered and we will never fail.

WINSTON CHURCHILL, JULY 6, 1944

00.04 Hornsey	04.35 Chislehurst & Sidcup	13.35 Woolwich	18.23 Heston
00.09 Wandsworth	05.40 Orpington	13.37 Bromley	18.25 Orpington
00.50 Poplar	12.20 Orpington	14.35 Coulsdon & Purley	18.28 Hackney
01.02 Croydon	12.23 Dagenham	14.37 Deptford	20.00 Ilford
01.05 Southgate	12.25 Coulsdon & Purley	14.59 Hayes	20.32 Beddington & Wallington
01.40 Wimbledon	12.45 Lewisham	15.32 Mitcham	
01.45 Chingford	13.06 Mitcham	16.30 Malden	
03.45 Barking	13.14 Epsom	17.31 Mitcham	

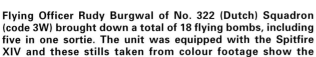

Flying Officer Rudy Burgwal of No. 322 (Dutch) Squadron (code 3W) brought down a total of 18 flying bombs, including five in one sortie. The unit was equipped with the Spitfire XIV and these stills taken from colour footage show the damage caused to one of the squadron's aircraft which has flown straight through the explosion of a V1 directly ahead. The unit claimed a total of 110 flying bombs shot down between June and October.

No. 12 Region (SOUTH EASTERN).

SUSSEX.

HAILSHAM. 1420. FLY. Shot down. Slight damage. No casualties.

CHIDDINGLY 1235. FLY. Shot down. Some damage. No casualties.
1240. FLY. Shot down. Slight damage. No casualties.

LAUGHTON. 1235. FLY. Shot down. Slight damage to 6 houses.
No casualties.

SALEHURST. 1450. FLY. Shot down. No damage. No casualties.

BROOMHILL. 1250. FLY. Shot down. No damage. No casualties.

HELLINGLY. 1710. FLY. Brought down.

KENT.

APPLEDORE. 1230. FLY. Shot down. Damage to livestock and
5 houses.slightly damaged.
1330. FLY. Shot down.

SHIPBOURNE. 0655. FLY. Shot down. Blast damage to houses.
No casualties.

BROOMFIELD. 1757. FLY. Shot down. Considerable damage.

BENENDEN. 1218. FLY. Shot down.

HAWKHURST. 1440. FLY. Shot down. Damage to houses. No casualties.

EASTWELL, near ASHFORD. 1645. FLY. Shot down.

GRAVESEND. 1740. FLY. Shot down. Slight damage.

The Ministry of Home Security produced detailed reports of incidents twice daily. Although this extract for July 6 is not specific as to whether the claims were due to fighters or AA guns, the score of the number of flying bombs brought down was still impressive.

Balloons. The original 500 balloons had hardly been deployed before Air Marshal Hill gave instructions for the barrage to be doubled, the intention being not to extend it geographically but to increase its density and thereby improve the chances of impact. The additions entailed eliminating every other barrage in the country except six. The move began on June 24 but owing to the short notice and the necessity of assembling crews from all parts of the country, it was completed less quickly than the initial 500. Even so, by July 1 a 1,000 balloons were in position.

Concurrently, Balloon Command Headquarters were working out the maximum number of balloons that could be flown, and on June 28 they reported that 1,750 could be provided by July 22. Five hundred of the additions were intended to increase still further the density of the barrage, the remaining 250 were to extend it further to the west. The order to move was given on July 8 and the deployment was completed a day earlier than scheduled.

While all these broad additions were being planned and executed, certain deficiencies in the original deployment were rectified. It was found that the northern edge of the barrage was so close to the built-up areas on the southern fringe of the London area that a number of flying bombs, after impact with balloon cables, were still doing damage to life and property. A number of key points in Kent and Surrey were also endangered by the barrage. Immediately after the second deployment had been completed, over 200 balloons were therefore moved from the north-western side of the barrage to the south. A further 50 balloons were withdrawn to allow a clearance of one mile in front of a number of key points.

During earlier operations for the air defence of the country, Fighter Command had normally exercised a close control over the flying of balloons so as not to endanger friendly aircraft, and barrages were frequently lowered or

grounded for this reason. But this was hardly practicable with a barrage as large as that now deployed. Moreover, the idea behind it was to present the flying bomb with a permanent and inescapable barrier. Consequently, on June 23, ADGB Headquarters issued a warning to pilots to keep well away from an almost certainly lethal obstacle that would be in the air continuously. To assist pilots, Royal Observer Corps posts near the barrage were issued with Schermuly ('Snowflake') rockets, which were fired when aircraft approached. Searchlights were also used for the same purpose.

The warning that the barrage would fly continuously was a deliberate exaggeration, made for the pilots' sakes.

This was certainly the theory but weather curtailed it being the practice. By the end of June the balloon and hydrogen resources of the country had been invested almost entirely in the 'Diver' barrage, and the heavy wastage that would have been incurred if the barrage had been flown during a gale or, even more dangerous, in an electric storm, could only have been replaced slowly. Thus, there were many periods when the barrage, wholly or in part, was grounded because of weather. The heavy responsibility of deciding whether to fly or not fell upon the Barrage Commander, who was located at the control centre of all the 'Diver' defences, the Biggin Hill Sector Operations Room.

Although it was not realised at the time, in the early hours of Saturday morning, July 8, III./KG3 launched its first V1 at London from a Heinkel flying over the North Sea in an effort to circumvent the Kent defences. The idea of firing the weapon from a moving platform was, in theory, a clever one. However, in practice accuracy suffered as both the course and distance had to be programmed in to the V1 before the mother aircraft took off. This gave no room for error and meant that the pilot had to position the aircraft precisely above the designated, yet unmarked, launch position to which he had to fly at low-level to avoid night fighters. He then had to pull up to around 500 metres and increase his speed to that of the bomb's launch speed of around 200 mph while the flight engineer started the motor of the V1. When the engine fired, the exhaust would light up the sky for miles around, attracting any fighters in the area like moths to a flame. Any discrepancy in navigation would correspondingly be transferred to the impact position.

IN LONDON BETWEEN 21.00 ON FRIDAY, JULY 7, TO 20.59 ON SATURDAY, JULY 8

21.10	Croydon	23.45	Wandsworth	00.28	Greenwich	01.16	Hackney
21.11	Finchley	23.57	Camberwell	00.34	Hammersmith	03.24	Greenwich
21.22	Camberwell	24.00	Hackney	00.36	Epsom	04.45	Greenwich
22.04	Twickenham	00.27	Leyton	00.40	Westminster	05.20	Mitcham

Difficulties of Co-ordinated Defence

The need for new equipment was not the only factor in the unsatisfactory results achieved by the guns. It was also the case that fighters and guns had not been working together with that smooth co-operation that was necessary if the best possible results were to be obtained. It proved in practice very difficult for pilots to recognise the boundaries of the gun belt and for gunners to cease fire in time to avoid endangering the fighters. Moreover, fighters were frequently fired on by anti-aircraft units outside the gun belt. The difficulties were most apparent when condition 'Pickle' applied, i.e. when the guns in the gun belt were allowed to fire up to 8,000 feet and fighters were prohibited from entering the gun belt except when in close pursuit of a flying bomb.

The first steps towards a solution were taken on July 10 at a conference called by Air Marshal Hill. It was agreed that when both fighters and guns were operating, the guns in the belt would have complete freedom of action and fighters would enter the belt at their own risk.

These projected arrangements contributed towards a more effective defence in that they established the principle of mutually exclusive spheres of action for fighters and guns, but within three days they were superseded as a result of a decision that maintained the new principle but radically altered the disposition of the whole of the gun defences.

BETWEEN 21.00 ON SATURDAY, JULY 8, TO 20.59 ON SUNDAY, JULY 9   (Airburst ✳)

21.27	Rye	22.36	Wandsworth	00.15	Biddenden	12.46	Duddingstone
21.29	Great Chart	22.37	Greenwich	00.31	Lambeth	12.47	Stoke Newington
21.34	Lewisham	23.10	Bothersden	00.32	Brasted	13.53	Jevington
21.34	Lewisham	23.10	Dover	00.50	Holmwood	13.54	Ilford
21.34	Orlestone	23.12	Aveley	00.52	Parham	14.03	Bermondsey
21.34	Stansted	23.13	Battle	00.53	Lewisham	14.15	Chevening
21.37	Wandsworth	23.15	St Marylebone	00.55	Carshalton	14.15	Aveley
21.37	Wandsworth	23.15	Langley	00.55	West Ham	14.28	East Ham
21.38	Lambeth	23.15	Hothfield ✳	00.55	Staplehurst	14.28	Hackney
21.40	Bilsington	23.16	Headcorn	01.09	Winchelsea	14.33	Woolwich
21.40	Mayfield	23.20	West Hamble	02.32	Lewisham	14.33	Cock Clarks
21.40	Oxted	23.20	Hadlow	04.10	Benenden	14.40	Bexley
21.43	Croydon	23.21	Camberwell	04.45	Iden	14.42	Horton Kirby
21.43	Beckenham	23.21	Camberwell	04.45	Stone	14.44	West Ham
21.47	Banstead	23.21	Watford	10.50	Willingdon	14.45	East Ham
21.48	Sedlescombe	23.22	Croydon	11.05	Sevenoaks	15.26	Barking
21.49	Framfield	23.23	Westerham	11.14	Willesden	15.55	Waltham Holy Cross
21.50	Eridge	23.25	Headley	11.30	Chelmsford	20.45	Linstead
21.57	Northiam ✳	23.26	Banstead	12.06	Hornsey	20.51	Coulsdon
21.58	Stepney	23.27	Hartfield	12.10	Dagenham	20.55	Chislehurst
22.01	Ewhurst ✳	23.30	Headcorn	12.20	Lamberhurst		
22.03	Rolvenden	23.38	Chislehurst	12.30	Leyton		
22.05	Ruckinge	23.40	Ticehurst	12.46	Twickenham		

Up to this date, the Home Office 'Pilotless Aircraft Reports' only covered V1 incidents in London. However, from here on, the listings were widened to include those occuring outside the capital, and also the ones that were classed as airbursts.

BETWEEN 21.00 ON SUNDAY, JULY 9, TO 20.59 ON MONDAY, JULY 10 (Airburst ✳)

21.00	Goudhurst	23.45	Croydon	09.19	Epsom	15.27	Effingham
21.00	Gosfield	23.50	Esher	10.36	Bletchingley	16.40	Beckley
21.18	Cranham	23.50	Ongar	10.40	Woolwich	17.00	Hailsham
21.23	Crayford	01.30	Southborough	10.41	Crayford	17.15	Heathfield
21.25	Wilmington	01.45	Orpington	10.44	Wandsworth	17.25	Barking
21.34	Radlett	02.17	Ovington	14.12	Benenden	17.39	Lewisham
21.40	Brookland	02.22	Rye ✳	14.23	Beckenham	17.57	Penge
21.46	Croydon	02.38	St Marylebone	14.23	Lewisham	19.15	Stone-cum-Ebony
21.50	Ulcombe	02.42	Battersea	14.23	Crawley	19.20	Burmarsh
21.57	Orpington	02.54	Wandsworth	14.43	Bethnal Green	19.20	Maidstone ✳
22.10	Lydd ✳	03.03	East Ham	14.45	Harrietsham	19.24	Bromley
22.16	Croydon	03.12	Broadstairs	14.45	Brenchley	19.35	Merton
22.16	Shorne	04.09	Enfield	14.46	Wandsworth	20.10	Hythe
22.25	Brookland	04.46	Barnet	14.55	Warbleton	20.15	Brightling
22.30	Goudhurst	09.08	Wimbledon	14.55	Seal ✳	20.50	Herstmonceux
22.53	Hellingly	09.11	Eynsford	15.03	Hornsey	20.53	Camberwell
23.15	Balcombe	09.14	West Ham	15.05	Charing		

The Operational Research Section of ADGB at the Air Ministry collated and analysed the Mean Point of Impact (MPI) for all 'untouched' V1s, i.e. excluding those brought down by guns and fighters, and those which fell more than 30 miles outside London. This established that the MPI for the period up to the middle of July was Alleyn's School at North Dulwich in the borough of Camberwell. The first flying bomb came on June 20 with follow-ups on the 22nd, two on the 23rd, one each on the 26th and 27th and two on the 30th. Nineteen bombs followed in July, the south wing of the school being hit at 22.37 on the 10th. Photographs of the boys assisting the clear-up were released after being censored with the name of the school deleted.

BETWEEN 21.00 ON MONDAY, JULY 10, TO 20.59 ON TUESDAY, JULY 11 (Airburst ✳)

21.00	Beddington	09.19	Headcorn	13.15	Bethersden	17.54	Camberwell
22.32	Ruckinge	09.23	Shoreham	13.20	Chigwell	17.55	Bermondsey
22.37	Camberwell	09.25	Banstead	14.25	Ashburnham	17.55	Leatherhead
22.42	Lower Beeding	09.25	Shoreham	14.34	Battle	17.56	Bromley
18.00	Banstead	09.30	Orpington	14.37	Sundridge	18.00	Banstead
00.30	New Forest	09.32	Sutton	14.41	Wandsworth	18.09	Penge
00.30	Denny Lodge	10.11	Mitcham	14.42	Paddington	19.20	Horsted Keynes ✳
00.32	New Forest	10.11	Bexhill	14.43	St Pancras	19.32	Smeeth ✳
00.35	Old Botley	10.12	Widdiham ✳	14.46	Mitcham	19.38	Battersea
00.40	Fur Copse	10.13	Watton	15.08	Shalford	19.40	Ninfield
00.45	Wood Copse	10.20	Pulborough	15.50	Burnham ✳	19.40	Lingfield
01.00	Itchen Stoke	10.41	Haywards Heath	15.54	Bansted	19.43	Charing
01.25	Bishops Waltham	11.24	Bermondsey	16.03	Sutton	19.45	Oxted ✳
01.35	Preshaw	11.25	Islington	17.40	Waddington	19.45	Rotherfield
01.55	Stoney Hurd	11.57	Kensington	17.45	Eastfield	19.45	Crowhurst
02.20	Springvale	12.15	Greenwich	17.47	Hildenborough	19.47	Stone
04.55	New Forest	12.27	Lambeth	17.48	Pembury	20.10	Flimwell ✳
05.00	Upham	12.50	Battle	17.48	Chelsham	20.14	Beddington
05.20	Curdridge	12.50	Hastings	17.49	Offham	20.50	Mountfield
05.25	Curdridge	12.57	City	17.50	Croydon	20.50	Biddenden ✳
05.32	Curdridge	12.59	Mitcham	17.50	Beckenham	20.51	Salehurst ✳
05.43	Fareham	13.00	Alderbury	17.50	Plaxtol	20.55	Widdersham ✳
05.45	Sarisbury	13.05	Lewisham	17.51	Malden	20.56	Biddenden
05.45	Basingstoke	13.05	Oxted	17.52	Lewisham	20.57	Chislehurst

BETWEEN 21.00 ON TUESDAY, JULY 11, TO 20.59 ON WEDNESDAY, JULY 12   (Airburst ✳)

21.00 Biddenden	08.40 Newchurch ✳	15.40 Orpington	17.50 Benenden
21.00 Iden	08.45 Brabourne	16.26 Mitcham	17.50 Burmarsh
01.20 Bitterne	08.48 Deptford	16.26 Pett	17.52 Beckley
01.25 Beaulieu	08.50 Poplar	16.28 Hoathfield	17.52 Boddington
02.40 Fairoak	08.54 Staplehurst	16.30 Sevenoaks	17.53 Cranbrook
02.50 Chandler's Ford	08.56 Charing	16.31 Dagenham	17.57 Penshurst
02.50 Coombe	08.57 Weald	16.32 Greenwich	18.01 Heston
02.50 Rustington	08.58 City	16.34 Fulham	18.12 Sandhurst
04.35 Longwood	09.00 Beckenham	16.35 Ticehurst	18.12 Stapleford Abbotts
04.50 Debden Bay	15.10 Capel le Ferne	16.36 Lyminge	18.13 Sutton
04.53 Southstoke	15.15 Charing	16.37 Old Romney	18.20 Burmarsh
04.56 Botley	15.15 Waltham	16.38 Waltham Holy Cross	18.20 Pembury
05.00 Bentworth	15.20 Orpington ✳	16.40 Ringmer	18.20 Ticehurst
05.10 Burseldon	15.20 Sutton	16.40 Wadhurst	18.20 Ticehurst
05.30 Brockenhurst	15.20 Wandsworth	16.40 Withyham	18.27 Hever
07.20 Laughton	15.21 Banstead ✳	16.43 Greenwich	18.28 Wandsworth
07.20 Snargate	15.22 Islington	16.44 Bexhill	18.43 Guestling
07.20 Stone-cum-Ebony	15.22 Lewisham	16.45 Oxted ✳	18.50 Broomhill
07.21 Kingsnorth	15.23 Brentford	16.47 Chigwell	19.10 Ewhurst
07.22 Dallington ✳	15.23 Carshalton	16.47 Twickenham	19.13 Greenwich
07.22 Sundridge	15.25 Bermondsey	16.48 Deptford	19.13 Tonbridge
07.23 Shenfield	15.25 Walton	16.50 Hambleton	19.14 Beckenham
07.25 Croydon	15.25 West Hoathley	16.50 West Ham	19.15 Camberwell
07.27 Esher	15.25 Willesden	17.00 Lewisham	19.15 Oxted
07.30 Betchworth	15.26 Merton	17.15 Rotherfield	19.16 Hackney
07.30 East Grinstead	15.30 Epsom	17.18 Southwark	19.16 Westfield
07.31 Bletchingley	15.32 Purfleet	17.24 Ashford	19.18 Benenden
07.35 Lympne ✳	15.33 Wembley	17.31 Kingsnorth	19.22 Nadehurst
07.55 Waldron	15.35 Carshalton	17.45 Boughton Malherbe	19.24 Shoreditch
08.40 Mayfield	15.38 Burmarsh	17.45 Crowhurst	

Fortunately, as the flying bomb struck at night there were only three injuries.

The original buildings, designed by Charles Barry, were completed in 1870, the replacement block in June 2016.

I had been involved in supplying misleading information to the Germans through the agents whom they supposed to be freely operating in Britain. The dilemma facing MI5 was that the Germans were now telling their supposed London agents to report the times and places of flying bomb incidents in London. If, to preserve the security of possible future deceptions, we were to supply truthful information to the Germans, this would be aiding the enemy. If, on the other hand, we supplied false information, then this could be checked by German photographic reconnaissance in which case the agents would be 'blown' and future deception plans ruined.

It immediately occurred to me that photographic reconnaissance could only reveal the points of impact, and not the times. Moreover, I knew from previous experience that while agents could usually define the place of an incident fairly well, they were likely to be wrong in other details, even the time.

I had noticed that in the Peenemünde trials the bombs tended to fall short of the target, and now knew from the plot of bombs for the first 24 hours that the operational bombs were also tending to fall short, the centre of gravity being in south-east London, near Dulwich. In a flash I saw that we might be able to keep the bombs falling short, which would mean fewer casualties in London as a whole, and at the same time avoid arousing any suspicions regarding the genuineness of the agents.

We could give correct points of impact for bombs that tended to have a longer range than usual, but couple these with times of bombs which in fact had fallen short. Thus, if the Germans attempted any correlation, they might be led to think that even the bombs which they had reason to believe might have fallen short, were instead tending to fall in north-west London. Therefore, if they made any correction at all, it would be to reduce the average range.

As I recommended this course of action, I realised well that what I was doing was trying to keep the mean point of impact in the Dulwich area.

Somehow the dilemma got out and it was discussed at the political level. I was not present at the meeting at which the deception policy was discussed when Herbert Morrison was in the chair in Churchill's absence. He finally ruled that it would be an interference with Providence if we were to supply the Germans with misleading information, because this might mean that some people would be killed through our action who might otherwise have survived.

Dr. R. V. JONES, 1978

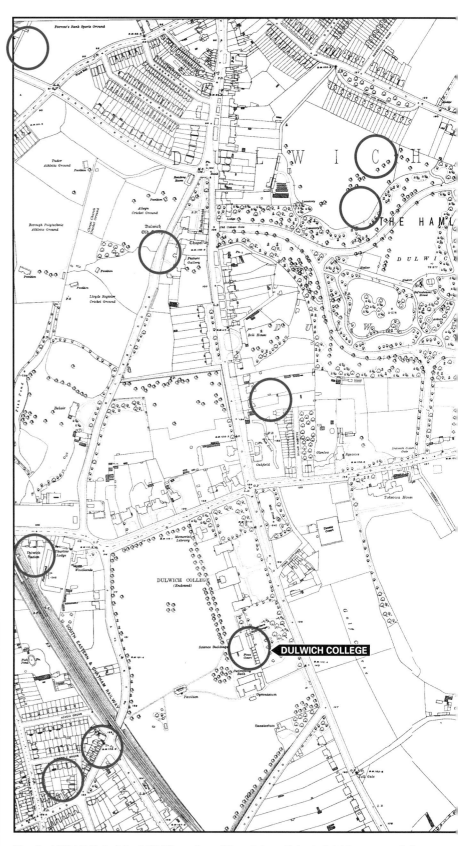

The first V1 hit Dulwich at 18.12 on June 20 and demolished eight houses and damaged another 100 centered on Friern Road and Etherow Street. A second flying bomb fell two days later at 05.26, followed on the 23rd by two more at 02.11 and 04.05. On the night of June 26, the clubhouse of the local golf club on Grange Lane was demolished; on the 27th another caused much damage on College Road, while the Old Allenians rugby ground suffered on the morning of June 30. Widespread damage was caused to Henslow and Underhill Roads in East Dulwich on the same day. July began with a prolonged bombardment by V1s for eight days in a row: Camberwell Old Cemetery on the 1st, Elmsworth Grove on the 2nd, Woodhall House in College Road on the 3rd, the Greenvale area on the 4th, Park Hall and Alleyn Roads on the 5th, Woodvale and Greendale by two V1s on the 6th, another on Park Hall Road on the 7th, and one

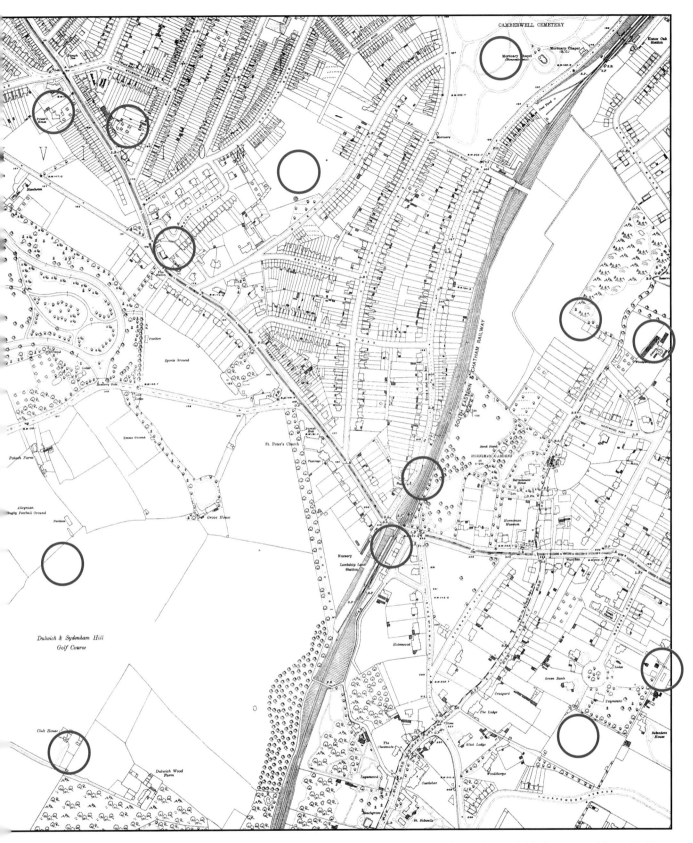

in Dulwich Park on the 8th. It was at 22.37 on June 10 that the South Wing, science block and rifle range of Dulwich College were severely damaged. The junction of Lordship Lane and Court Lane were hit on the 11th and Dulwich Hospital the following day. Lordship Lane suffered again on July 13, South Croxted Road on the 18th, and College Road again on the 19th. Three flying bombs landed on the 21st, one seriously damaging the Dulwich Picture Gallery. Three more V1s hit Dulwich on the 22nd followed by two in the Peckham Rye area on the 23rd and 27th. Lovelace Road was hit on August 1 and Crystal Palace Road two days later. One of South London's worst death tolls

came when the Co-op in Lordship Lane was hit at 16.45 on August 5, killing 23 persons. The next day damage was caused to two railway stations when bombs fell at Sydenham Hill and West Dulwich. Friern Road suffered more damage on the 7th, Rosendale Road, already struck twice, received another V1 on the 16th. The following day Therapia and Mundania Roads were badly damaged and Lordship Lane again on the 22nd. With the commencement of the V2 rocket attacks Dulwich had a brief respite but on November 1 a strike on Friern Road killed 24. The last recorded flying bomb incident at Dulwich, obviously air-launched, took place on March 4, 1945.

By now the problem of clashes between the guns and fighters had reached a stage where something had to be done — and fast. On Monday, July 10, a conference was called by Air Marshal Hill who, since June 20, had been flying V1 patrols himself to try to assess a solution. (He flew a total of 62 patrols in a sterling example of leadership from the top.) At that meeting it was agreed that when both guns and fighters were operating, the guns would be given complete freedom of action and any aircraft would enter the belt at their own risk.

'Southern England is still having fly bomb incidents. Here is one of them where rescue work is in progress while a fire is being fought by the NFS [National Fire Service]. You are fortunate not to be living in the south of England. If bombed people come amongst you, remember their experiences.' So wrote the Illustrations Bureau in Fetter Lane on their caption to this photo. The location was censored — it was in fact Montford Place, Kennington, where a V1 crashed on the night of July 8/9 — and release of the picture was banned until August 22.

The Redeployment of the Guns

In the original 'Diver' deployment, the area in which fighter interceptions had taken place had extended from offshore of Kent and Sussex to the southern edge of the gun belt. Usually fighters had been directed by the controlling radar stations on to flying bombs as they crossed the coast and interception and destruction had consequently taken place overland. So long as this was achieved before the built-up metropolitan area was reached, the fighter pilot had successfully defended the main target but it was obviously even more desirable to destroy bombs before they crossed the coast.

Up to the middle of July, by far the most successes had fallen to the fighters, but more than 50 per cent had crashed on land. Some improvement in successes over the sea could be expected when the radar stations obtained longer warning of the approach of bombs but not a great one owing to the small margin of speed that the fighter enjoyed over the flying bomb.

By July 10, as already noted, the answer was partly appreciated, i.e. to reduce the interference of guns and fighters by giving each complete freedom to operate within a defined sphere. The decision to do this was taken by Air Marshal Hill, as commander of the air defences as a whole, and his was the responsibility for its success or failure.

The revised solution was one that involved even more restrictions on the operations of the fighters and a correspondingly greater reliance on the performance of the guns for it involved

Following the new instruction, Air Marshal Hill asked the Deputy Senior Air Staff Officer at Air Defence of Great Britain, Air Vice-Marshal Geoffrey Ambler, to prepare a memo to explain the change to units of ADGB. In doing so, he came to the conclusion that it was wrong to maintain the guns inland, south of London, and instead they should be redeployed on the coast. Meanwhile Sir Robert Watson-Watt had been making an independent study of the fighters-versus-guns problem and devised a similar solution, and both men compared notes at ADGB Headquarters on July 13. The matter was put to Air Marshal Hill and the Senior Air Staff Officer, Air Vice-Marshal William Callaway. They were convinced of the sense of the idea and Sir Robert agreed to put the proposal immediately to General Pile. Within half an hour he had returned with the news that the chief of AA Command had enthusiastically endorsed the plan and it was formally approved at a conference at 5.30 p.m. that day. Thus, within a few hours, what was to prove to be the most-important decision in countering the flying bomb had been made, thereby saving hundreds of lives over the weeks that followed.

General Pile's speed in getting the new plan into operation was equally impressive. By dawn on the 17th — just three days later — all the heavy guns presently on the North Downs (over 400 pieces) had been moved and re-sited between St Margaret's Bay and Cuckmere Haven and by the 19th they had been joined by over 970 light guns. The new 'Diver' zone of action stretched 10,000 yards to seaward and 5,000 yards inland, with aircraft being allowed freedom of action forward of the 'Diver' gun belt, and between it and the static balloon barrage south-east of the Capital. A further 'Gun Box' had to be provided around the mouth of the Thames to cover against the new air-launches from the east and north-east at which time the forts in the Estuary really came into their own. [1] Nore (Army), [2] Red Sand (Army), [3] Shivering Sand (Army), [4] Tongue (Navy), [5] Knock John (Navy), [6] Sunk Head (Navy), [7] Roughs (Navy). In the 1960s, the forts unexpectedly had a new lease of life, even though it was short lived . . .

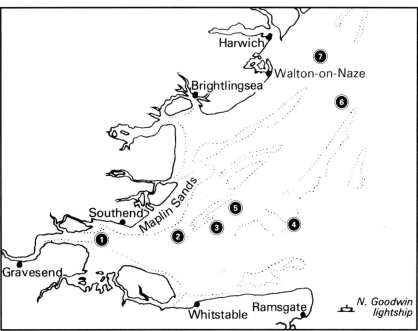

scrapping entirely the inland gun belt, moving it forward to the coast so giving the guns virtually complete freedom to engage at all times and in all conditions in their new positions. A decision to this effect was taken by Air Marshal Hill on July 13.

The new arrangements, which were to be put into effect by the morning of the 17th, involved moving the gun belt from its original position in front of the balloon barrage to a coastal strip between St Margaret's Bay and Cuckmere Haven, with a zone of 10,000 yards to seaward and 5,000 yards inland. Complete freedom of action against flying bombs was to be allowed to fighter

. . . when they were taken over by 'Pop Pirates' for radio stations. This is Red Sand fort.

aircraft forward of the balloon barrage and forward of the new gun belt, but not in the area covered by the latter.

Not all the old problems were solved by the new deployment: some indeed were aggravated. The security of coastal towns had to be considered so gaps were left in the siting of the guns near Eastbourne, Hastings, Bexhill, Scythe, Folkestone and Dover so that the risk of bombs being brought down on those places was lessened. Restrictions were also imposed on the guns near the radar stations at Beachy Head and Fairlight so as to lessen the chances of bombs falling on these important links in the chain of defence. These gaps had the secondary function of allowing fighters and aircraft in distress to cross overland without flying directly over the guns.

Such an immense deployment of guns, representing perhaps the densest concentration of anti-aircraft fire anywhere in the world, had to be so controlled that friendly aircraft were not imperilled. Careful arrangements were therefore made with the bomber force commanders in the United Kingdom to ensure the safe routing of aircraft and, in addition, non-operational flying in south-east England was prohibited. Instructions were also sent out to all forces to ensure that any friendly

After the initial redeployment of the guns to Kent, on June 30 General Pile took Churchill to visit 481 (H) AA Battery, at which the Prime Minister's daughter Mary was serving, in its new location on the North Downs. He saw the guns engage one bomb without bringing it down. It was followed by two more but this time the guns did not open fire because fighters chasing them were too close. Neither V1 was shot down.

BETWEEN 21.00 ON WEDNESDAY, JULY 12, TO 20.59 ON THURSDAY, JULY 13   (Airburst ✳)

21.10 Warehorne	10.08 Woodchurch	14.45 Plaxtol	17.46 Lambeth
21.15 Warbleton	10.08 Shipbourne	14.47 St Thomas Cambray	17.53 Lamberhurst
21.15 Benenden	10.09 Orpington ✳	14.55 Hartfield	18.03 Deptford
21.16 Ewhurst ✳	10.10 Battle ✳	14.56 Betchworth	18.06 Sidcup
21.17 Croydon	10.13 Wanstead	15.00 Coombe	18.54 Woolwich
21.25 Camberwell	10.14 Hastings	15.02 Crayford	18.54 Wandsworth
08.23 Heathfield ✳	10.15 Battersea	15.04 Sundridge	18.55 Woolwich
08.30 Falkington	10.15 Trimley St Martin	16.21 Ashford ✳	18.58 Hawkhurst
08.40 Brightling	10.17 Brede	16.25 Dagenham	19.53 Penge
09.43 Lewisham	10.18 Surbiton	17.19 Camberwell	
10.05 Herstmonceux	10.53 Wandsworth	17.22 Dagenham	
10.06 Goudhurst	14.11 Alfriston	17.26 Erith	

aircraft returning to England flew at a height of at least 10,000 feet, and in order not to confuse the radar stations, at no more than 200 mph, making at least one marked change of course and at no time flying in a direct line towards Greater London.

For the gunners it gave them a better sight of their targets; it improved the efficiency of their radar sets, which were not affected to the same extent as inland by ground echoes, and it enabled them to use VT-fuzed shells without restriction.

The task of the fighters, however, was made more difficult by the change. Whereas hitherto there had been an uninterrupted run for a patrolling fighter from the Channel to the southern edge of the gun belt, and even beyond if the fighter was in close pursuit, the new location of the gun belt meant that two separate fighter patrol areas had to be established, one forward of the guns, the other between the guns and the balloon barrage. And as each of these was restricted in space, the chances of successfully pressing home an interception were inevitably reduced.

Having been transferred to Kent from Hyde Park, the new location of the battery was in a large field at Four Elms which was only a few miles from Churchill's home at Chartwell. He had not set foot in the house at all that year so paid it a quick visit before returning to London.

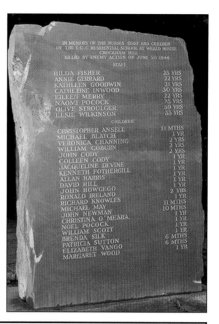

Earlier that morning, the worst single V1 incident involving children occurred at nearby Crockham Hill. Just after 3.30 a.m. on June 30 (see page 88), a flying bomb that had reportedly been damaged by the guns, instead of coming down in open countryside, struck a tree which deflected it into Weald House. This had been taken over by the London County Council as a home for evacuated children and 22 were killed along with eight female staff, there being only two survivors, of whom one was Peter Inwood whose mother was killed. *Below:* All the victims save for Alan Harris, who was taken back to London for burial, were laid to rest in a communal grave in St Peter and St Paul's Churchyard at Eden-bridge, near Sevenoaks, Kent. *Top right:* As there was no memorial in Crockham Hill itself, in 2018 the Downsview Monumental Company of Burgess Hill, West Sussex, spent three months producing a memorial, paid for by public subscription, for erection in the village. Weald House could not be repaired and has since been rebuilt and named Hoplands.

> Weald House was a very large house which enjoyed spectacular views over the Weald of Kent. From its lofty position it overlooked miles of open country-side. Because of this location the home was considered a place of relative safety for short-stay evacuated children from the London area. The children living there were all under three years of age and many were new arrivals. It was a warm summer evening and the children had been taken to bed for the night.
>
> Somewhere nearby a doodlebug on its way to London had been intercepted by anti-aircraft fire and had been badly damaged before it could reach its intended target. The doodlebug should have landed somewhere in the miles of open fields causing no loss of life, but it smashed directly into the children's home. Twenty-two infants and eight female staff were killed that night in one of Kent's worst tragedies of the Second World War.
>
> My Mother was a member of staff caring for the infants, and I understand she was killed instantly. I am told that I was one of only two or three infants to survive this terrible disaster, but I have no recollections or memories of what happened. Tragically not only did this devastating event deprive me of my Mother, but also of any roots or knowledge of my natural family.
>
> A year later I was adopted and taken to the north of England and it was not until 1989 that I discovered the truth of the terrible tragedy.
>
> I have since travelled to the site where the disaster took place, today it is a beautiful and peaceful place just as it had been before June 30, 1944. I can only reflect with great sadness on how my life would have been so very different but for the events of that fateful summer night in 1944.
>
> PETER INWOOD, 2004

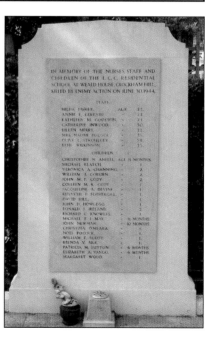

BETWEEN 21.00 ON THURSDAY, JULY 13, TO 20.59 ON FRIDAY, JULY 14			(Airburst *)				
01.10	Avington	09.05	Carshalton	09.57	Woolwich	18.05	Buxted
01.10	Worting	09.45	Forest Row	10.00	Hadlow Down	18.27	Pett *
01.23	Ditchling	09.45	Heathfield	15.15	Fluckley	18.30	Ewhurst *
01.35	Durley	09.49	Mitcham	15.15	Wye	18.30	Marden *
01.52	Sutton Sootney	09.49	Woolwich	15.25	Abbots Langley	18.33	Woodchurch *
08.09	Beckenham	09.50	Chiddingly	15.25	Tandridge	18.35	Woodchurch
08.12	Ticehurst	09.52	Brightling	15.43	Mitcham *	18.37	Battle
08.23	Sutton	09.52	St Marylebone	17.45	Bexhill	18.40	Greenwich
08.52	Croydon	09.52	Wimbledon	18.02	Capel le Ferne	20.58	Leyton

Reactions at the Air Ministry

It was partly on this account that the redeployment was unfavourably received at the Air Ministry. A minute to Portal on July 17 said: 'I am not in favour of the plan which must inevitably result in a reduction of the number of kills by fighters. It is doubtful whether this reduction will be made up for by an increased or even similar number of successes on the part of the AA gunners.'

But there were reasons of a constitutional as well as military character that account for the reception of the new scheme. Air Marshal Hill had taken the decision on July 13 and on the same day Anti-Aircraft Command had begun to plan the redeployment. By the 14th a massive movement of guns to the coast had already begun and on the following day Air Marshal Hill wrote to the Air Ministry to explain his action. He stated that the new plan was in effect only a tactical redeployment of the resources under his control, but as it involved a substantial change in the plan previously approved by the Air Ministry 'and

the other authorities concerned' he felt it his duty to report his action.

However, the Air Ministry held that it was not a matter that was within the competence of Hill to decide. Their point of view was that it had always been customary for any major alterations in air defence plans to be agreed upon in consultation with the Air Staff as the Air Ministry were constitutionally responsible for the air defence of Great Britain. The Chief of the Air Staff made this point at a meeting of the Chiefs of Staff on July 18, adding that the Chiefs of Staff had also been consulted when major changes were projected. He said that while he did not suggest that the deployment should be countermanded, he thought the responsibility for its success or failure should now rest with Air Marshal Hill.

It is clear that the Air Staff were not so much concerned that Air Marshal Hill had proceeded improperly on his own initiative, but that the decision had been taken as a result of pressure put upon him by Duncan Sandys' Sub-Com-

mittee, with the result that Anti-Aircraft Command had been given undue preference over ADGB. To put it brutally and colloquially, the fighters had been given a raw deal in favour of the guns because Sandys, as an ex-anti-aircraft officer, had wanted to give more chances to the guns. Also that he and General Pile had persuaded Air Marshal Hill (with the implication that it was against the latter's better judgement) to order a deployment that was originally their idea.

This, however, was not the case. The Sandys Sub-Committee had neither any formal executive authority, nor did it seek to exercise any on this particular matter. Although the result might well mean fewer successes for the fighters, Hill was anxious to obtain the best total results rather than to maintain the superiority of his own service which was, indeed, no more than his duty. Although he was an air officer, his task was to co-ordinate the operations of all the components of air defence in the most effective way.

On the night of July 11/12, a completely different target was attacked when III./KG3 loosed off bombs towards Southampton, with further attacks on July 14 and 15, giving London a few night's rest. However, of the 50-odd V1s launched, only two hit the city, the remainder being so widely scattered that Home Security thought that some may have been intended for Portsmouth. One of those that missed in the July 15 attack exploded here at 1.02 a.m. in the little village of Goodworth Clatford, 30 miles inland near Andover. The village school and Royal Oak public house were both destroyed along with 'The Thatch' (in the foreground), killing four: Mr and Mrs William Jones and their 17-month-old baby, who had only just arrived that weekend to get a break away from the bombing in Thornton Heath, and Mrs Sylvia Church. Miss Ellen Tatford and Mrs Florence Watton were also killed at nearby Manor Farm Cottages.

BETWEEN 21.00 ON FRIDAY, JULY 14, TO 20.59 ON SATURDAY, JULY 15			(Airburst *)				
00.15	Portsmouth	01.36	Fairoak	13.56	Bromley *	15.45	Croydon *
00.20	Froxfield	04.03	Bishops Waltham	14.25	Brenchley	15.47	Deptford
00.23	Isle of Wight	04.05	Catherington	15.15	Bethersden	17.26	Kingsdown
00.26	Beaulieu	04.06	Westend	15.19	Wanstead	17.30	Ashford *
00.39	Icklesham	04.40	Bitterne	15.20	Battersea	17.33	Poplar
00.43	Kilmeston	05.03	Chandler's Ford	15.20	Chigwell	17.34	Bredgar
00.57	Warmford	13.46	East Peckham	15.22	Lambeth	17.35	Kings Langley
01.02	Lower Clatford	13.50	Bermondsey	15.35	Eastling	17.45	Hadlow
01.18	Cheriton	13.54	Greenwich	15.43	City	17.50	Beckley *

Portsmouth had suffered grievously in the night Blitz of 1940-41 and endured the last two flying bombs that hit the city before the launch sites in France were overrun.

In 2015, Bob Hind of *The News* took this perfect comparison in Locksway Road, Milton. The pillar box stands on the corner of Meryl Road.

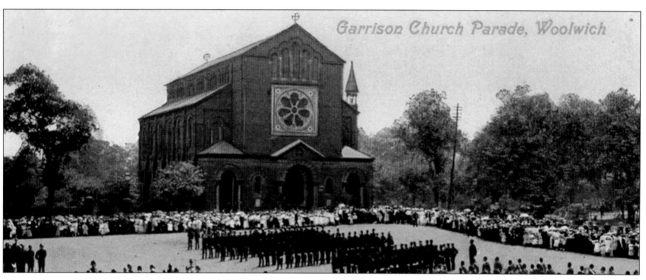

St George's Garrison Church was built on the orders of the then-Secretary of State for War, Lord Herbert. It was sited next door to the barracks in Woolwich to provide for the moral well-being of the soldiers of the Royal Artillery and, when completed in 1863, it was described as 'the first decent chapel provided for soldiers' use in the country'. While the patterned brickwork was typical of the Victorian period, the interior was richly decorated with mosaics illustrative of the Roman era. In 1915, a memorial was added with marble tablets inscribed with the names of those from the Royal Artillery awarded the Victoria Cross. The church had been damaged during the First World War when the rose window was blown out, but it was a flying bomb exploding at 18.55 on July 13 that resulted in a fire that gutted the interior. The upper parts of the walls were demolished in the 1970s while the surviving mosaics were protected by a temporary corrugated roof over the east end, replaced in 2011. A plaque now placed inside commemorates the church as a memorial garden. On the south and north aisle walls, copper plaques are attached with the names of Royal Artillery men killed in action or who died of natural causes after World War II. On November 11, 2015, a memorial was added by the Royal Borough of Greenwich marking Woolwich's history as a barracks town and commemorating the men and women who served or lived in Woolwich and gave their lives in the service of their country. Included are the names of the victims of the IRA bombing of the King's Arms in 1974, and Fusilier Lee Rigby who was murdered by Islamic terrorists in Woolwich in 2013.

On July 18, the Eighth Air Force mounted Mission 481 to attempt to destroy the hydrogen peroxide plant at Peenemünde used to produce fuel for the flying bombs. Mission 514 returned to the plant on August 4, the same day that the Americans launched the very first operation against 'Noball' sites in the Pas-de-Calais using radio-controlled 'Aphrodite' flying bombs. War-weary B-17s of the 562nd Bomb Squadron were packed with explosives and steered onto their target from a 'mother' aircraft after the pilot and co-pilot had parachuted out over England. In Mission 515, four of the B-17s were detailed to crash on Mimoyecques, Siracourt, Watten and Wizernes but one came down prematurely at Sudbourne and the others failed to hit their targets. This picture shows a B-17 of the 401st Bomb Group over Peenemünde on Mission 570 on August 25.

The Attack on London: July 16 to September 5

Attempts to divert bombs to different areas by misleading the Germans were echoed after a fashion by ordinary people in their secret prayers that the wretched motor would keep running to take the bomb elsewhere. 'Please pass over' or 'Keep going you bugger' were silent or vociferous pleas on many a lip. Already large numbers of people had left the capital under their own steam — upwards of half-a-million by mid-July — and on July 1 the London County Council, on behalf of the Government, was instructed to begin the official evacuation of two priority classes: mothers with children under five, and children of school age. The operation was limited by the amount of rolling stock committed to supplying the ports servicing the invasion beachhead, but the first parties left on July 3 and within two weeks it was estimated that 170,000 had left London. By September another 300,000 had gone under the official scheme with a further 500,000 being 'aided' by the provision of free rail tickets and billeting certificates. In the end it has been estimated that between 1.5 and 2 million people left London for safer areas of Britain during the flying bomb attacks.

Flying bombs had already been falling short like this one that crashed in East Grinstead, 25 miles from the aiming point, at 7.30 a.m. on July 12. Three people were killed in London Road. The church in the background is St Swithun's.

The Offensive against 'Crossbow' Targets, July 16 — August 15

The first weeks of the attack on London had seen the policy of counter-measures in the process of amendment in two important respects. First, the machinery for the selection of 'Crossbow' targets was being overhauled, and secondly the system of defence had been re-planned.

Attacks on storage depots at Nucourt and Rilly-la-Montagne were made on the 16th and 17th by RAF Bomber Command and the US Eighth Air Force respectively but neither attack achieved any significant damage. On the 18th, the Eighth sent 415 Fortresses to Peenemünde and dropped 953 tons of bombs on the hydrogen peroxide plant and the experimental station. Results were claimed as fairly good.

Attacks on launching sites in northern France continued to be made, chiefly by Bomber Command but Air Chief Marshal Tedder was still far from satisfied, and on the 18th he proposed a massive project for the attack of all types of 'Crossbow' targets on the same day and it was referred to the Combined Operational Planning Committee for examination. Such an attack would have the merit of damaging every part of the flying bomb organisation simultaneously.

Meanwhile, the scale of effort against 'Crossbow' remained low bearing in mind that it was still judged second in importance to the direct support of the land battle. Between July 19 and August 1, only 7,500 tons of bombs were dropped on 'Crossbow' targets out of some 50,000 tons delivered by the strategic bombers. Targets attacked in direct support of the armies themselves received a lesser weight of bombs (11,200) than oil and industrial targets. Moreover, the tonnage that was dropped on 'Crossbow' only partly reflected the order of importance that was given to the various types of target.

These had been very closely examined at the first meeting of the Joint 'Crossbow' Target Priorities Committee on July 21 as a result of which a short list of targets was agreed upon. This gave three storage depots and seven production targets in Germany as 'first priority' targets. Next came 57 modified sites, the proviso being that only harassing attacks should be made in which a high proportion of delayed-action bombs were to be used. Large sites were completely suspended from attack as well as those on power stations and headquarters. In short, the prime targets that were approved were those for which the heavy bomber force commanders had always expressed a preference.

Yet of the tonnage that was dropped during the rest of July, less than half was directed against storage depots and only one attack was made on a production target in Germany — the hydrogen peroxide plant at Höllriegelskreuth, south of Munich, which was bombed on July 19 by the Eighth Air Force. Otherwise, apart from the direct support of the land battle, the Eighth went for oil targets, aircraft and aero-engine factories, the German munitions industry and marshalling yards on the Franco-German frontier. Similarly, Bomber Command, in direct support of the armies, went for oil targets, railway centres and town centres. Its biggest effort against any one target was against Stuttgart on which nearly 5,000 tons were dropped on three nights during the last week in July.

However, on August 1 the Combined Operational Planning Committee presented its plan for a general offensive against 'Crossbow' targets. It was based on a plan for 1,500 sorties by the Eighth Air Force, 1,000 by Bomber Command, and 400 by the Tactical Air Forces. It envisaged three phases of attack: two by day and one by night, all being completed within 24 hours. In the first phase, the Eighth Air Force would go for Oberraderach, Düsseldorf, Fallersleben and Peenemünde, and the flying bomb storage depots at Méry-sur-Oise and Rilly-la-Montagne. Simultaneously, Bomber Command would attack the suspected 'Crossbow' storage depot in the Forêt de Nieppe and also six launching sites. In the second phase, which was planned to begin six hours later, the Eighth would attack 20 launching sites and Bomber Command 16. The Tactical Air Forces were to make their effort during these two phases against 40 modified sites. The third phase was to be a night operation by Bomber Command to attack the storage depots at Bois de Cassan and Trossy-St-Maximin. Basically, nearly every major 'Crossbow' target and all launching sites, known or suspected, were to be attacked.

The town had already suffered grievously a year earlier when 108 lost their lives when the Whitehall Palace Cinema was struck by conventional bombs. Another 235 persons were injured. Today, Timpson occupy the old foyer.

BETWEEN 21.00 ON SATURDAY, JULY 15, TO 20.59 ON SUNDAY, JULY 16   (Airburst ✳)

00.10	Chislehurst	00.59	Croydon	10.26	Lambeth	16.45	Icklesham
00.10	Cranbrook	04.24	Lympne ✳	10.28	Bermondsey	16.45	Stepney
00.10	Wrotham	04.28	Mill Down	10.37	Blue Bell Hill	16.55	Lydd ✳
00.12	Lambeth	04.31	Greenwich	10.38	Kingsnorth	17.10	Shipbourne
00.13	Wimbledon	04.32	Croydon	10.55	Yalding	17.20	Chingford
00.14	Beckenham	04.33	Hornsey	11.10	Camberwell	19.17	Crowhurst
00.19	Eastwell	04.35	St Pancras	11.10	Merton	19.18	Beckley
00.20	Chiddingstone	04.48	Mickleham	11.14	Westminster	19.18	East Farleigh
00.20	Margaretting	07.31	Hackney	11.26	Withyham	19.20	Shoreham
00.21	Orpington	07.45	Lambeth	12.12	Poplar	19.21	Penge
00.23	Bexley	10.20	Bredhurst ✳	12.38	Postling	19.24	Battersea
00.27	Beddington	10.20	Bredhurst ✳	12.53	Wimbledon	19.24	Carshalton
00.39	Kingsnorth	10.25	Battersea	16.42	Hastings		

However, the plan was not in fact carried out. Leigh-Mallory did not want the Tactical Air Forces to be taken away from their primary task as a moving battle was at last developing with an abundance of targets. The main practical difficulty was that for a powerful and successful blow to be struck by the heavy bombers against a series of widely dispersed targets, and targets which varied in type, good weather over practically the whole of northern France and northern and central Germany was required.

Early on August 1 there were slight prospects of this for some days to come so it was agreed that the plan should be attempted but the weather did, in fact, seriously interfere with operations. On the 1st, the Eighth Air Force could not go into Germany while of the 15 launch sites that they attempted to attack in France, only three were bombed, two with no success. Bomber Command sent 719 aircraft to bomb six modified sites and the suspected depot at Forêt de Nieppe, but only 74 aircraft were able

to attack. For the same reason, on the following day, the Eighth succeeded in attacking only five out of 15 sites that they set out to attack. Bomber Command were more successful. Over 300 tons were dropped on each of the storage depots at Trossy-St-Maximin and Bois de Cassan, and six modified sites and the Forêt de Nieppe were also attacked. The first two targets were accurately bombed but Harris considered that they would require a succession of attacks before they were completely neutralised.

July 17: Plashet Grove, Manor Park, in East Ham. Though the damage caused by the V1s was less than had been predicted, it **was still estimated that within two months London would suffer the same as during the whole nine months of the Blitz in 1940-41.**

BETWEEN 21.00 ON SUNDAY, JULY 16, TO 20.59 ON MONDAY, JULY 17

04.36	Tatsfield	05.00	Southwark	05.15	Battle	07.48	Coulsdon
04.37	Poplar	05.02	Epsom	05.27	Brentford	07.50	Bermondsey
04.38	Croydon	05.02	Islington	06.29	Battersea	07.55	Heston
04.41	Lewisham	05.04	Fulham	06.32	Crayford	08.06	Woolwich
04.55	Beddingham	05.10	Lambeth	07.44	Wandsworth	08.20	Darenth
04.55	Hildenborough	05.10	Leatherhead	07.45	Halstead	10.44	St Marylebone
04.58	East Ham	05.12	Ruckinge	07.45	North Chapel		

Over the next four days, Bomber Command made 12 attacks against these three targets, and one against the storage depot at St Leu-d'Esserent. During the same period, the Eighth attacked Peenemünde and Fallersleben, a storage depot at Méry-sur-Oise, two depots for flying bomb fuel, and over 20 launching sites. In short, while the original plan of attack was discarded as regards its time element, it was largely carried out within a week. However, the operation against the launching sites met with only moderate success: nine being were put out of action, making 41 that were reckoned Category A out of a total of 94 that had been identified up to date.

All told, nearly 15,000 tons of bombs were dropped on 'Crossbow' targets during the week August 2-9, three-quarters of this upon storage depots which were still believed to be the most profitable of the various sorts of targets. This represented quite the most determined effort that had so far been made within such a short space of time to vitally damage the flying bomb organisation. It had not, however, embraced the whole system which was what Tedder had in mind when he initiated the idea.

The week following the heavy 'Crossbow' attacks was one of increasingly rapid deterioration of the German position in Normandy, and the strategic bomber forces exerted most of their effort against targets connected with the battle on land. Strong attacks were made by Bomber Command and the Eighth Air Force on August 15 against seven airfields in Holland and Belgium from which those aircraft air-launching flying bombs were thought to be operating. It was significant for 'Crossbow' even though it was part of a wider onslaught that was carried out on that day against airfields in north-west Europe.

At the same time the Royal Air Force was also taking the battle to the enemy. This is the raid on Trossy-St-Maximin, a storage site near St Leu-d'Esserent north of Paris. It was bombed on August 4, a raid on which an Australian pilot, Squadron Leader Ian Bazalgette of No. 635 Squadron, was posthumously awarded the Victoria Cross. Hit by flak that knocked out both starboard engines, his Lancaster fell almost out of control but he managed to level out in time to let four members of the crew bale out. He even managed a crash-landing but he, the bomb-aimer and mid-upper gunner, all perished when the aircraft then exploded.

After their battering of the previous week, the storage depots were left alone, except for a further attack on Forêt de Nieppe by 126 aircraft of Bomber Command on the night of August 9. The two depots, Paris/Dugny and Pacy-sur-Armançon, that were thought to be handling flying bomb fuel were attacked again, the first by Bomber Command on August 10 when over 600 tons were dropped, the second by the Eighth Air Force on the 10th and again on the 11th, when 163 tons of bombs were dropped.

Altogether, some 31,000 tons of bombs were dropped on 'Crossbow' targets between July 15 and August 15, most in northern France.

When flying bombs began reaching London from an easterly direction, it became apparent that the Germans had perfected a method of air-launching V1s. After a survey of the likely airfields being used, these seven were targeted: [1] Venlo, [2] Eindhoven, [3] Gilze-Rijen, [4] Soesterberg and [5] Deelen in the Netherlands, and [6] Le Culot and [7] Brussels/Melsbroek in Belgium.

01.12 Bethersden	03.36 Poplar	06.20 Banstead	17.40 Tunbridge Wells
01.13 Wandsworth	03.37 Udimore	07.41 Croydon	18.15 Frittenden
01.14 Coulsdon	03.40 Yalding	07.50 Beckenham	18.19 Barking
01.14 Tonbridge *	03.56 Patrixbourne	07.52 Woodmancote	18.19 Stoke Newington
01.15 Fletching	04.45 Pett	08.03 Islington	18.30 Harrietsham
01.54 Walthamstow	04.52 Lewisham	15.17 Etchingham	19.39 West Ham
02.15 Bermondsey	06.11 Heaverham *	15.23 Brightling	19.39 Westwell
02.23 Minster in Sheppey	06.11 Lewisham	16.26 West Ham	19.40 Stansted
02.33 Staines	06.13 Bexley	16.29 Leybourne	20.25 Wadhurst
02.40 Cranbrook	06.14 Greenwich	16.32 Lambeth	20.31 Beckenham
02.44 Kensington	06.18 St Martha	17.37 Staplehurst *	

'Office staff clearing out wrecked offices in Southern England.' With no location or date, the late Roger Bell did well to trace the location in Essex Street, off the Strand, and he was delighted to find the building still standing.

22.08 Merton	03.40 Southall	09.58 Hadlow	12.43 Rolvenden
22.10 Biddenden	03.45 Enfield	10.05 Tenterden	12.45 New Romney
22.10 Brockham	03.48 Wonersh	10.07 Rolvenden	13.14 Bexhill
22.10 Lambeth	03.50 North Weald	10.09 Lewisham	13.20 Hastings
22.27 Gipping	03.52 Hackney	10.10 Seal	13.20 Hawkhurst
22.45 Ewhurst	03.53 Southgate	10.13 Sandon	13.20 Mayfield
22.45 Hawkhurst	03.53 Southgate	10.14 Wimbledon	13.28 Croydon
22.47 Flimwell	03.55 East Ham	10.30 Surbiton	13.30 Warbleton
22.50 Withyham	03.56 East Barnet	10.50 Staplehurst	13.36 Charing
23.26 Wrotham	04.00 Hythe End	10.53 Stepney	13.45 Northfleet
23.27 Rye	04.01 Lambeth	10.54 Brockham	14.00 Salehurst
00.15 Brenchley	04.42 West Ham	10.55 Stepney	14.33 Camberwell
00.26 Mitcham	04.43 Fulham	11.19 Banstead	14.42 Hackney
00.28 Southwark	04.47 West Ham	11.20 Beckley	14.50 Marden
00.29 Lambeth	06.11 Lewisham	11.25 Banstead	15.30 Biddenden
00.52 Banstead	06.40 Newington	11.32 East Farleigh	15.30 Harrietsham
01.26 Wandsworth	07.45 Stepney	11.35 Wittersham	15.35 Wanstead
01.28 St Marylebone	07.50 Yalding	11.45 Donington	15.37 Bexhill
01.28 Willesden	07.54 Camberwell	11.55 Lonham	16.50 Sissinghurst *
01.34 Yalding *	07.58 Battersea	11.56 Stone-cum-Ebony	17.26 Great Chart
02.12 Westminster	08.38 Addington	12.03 Camberwell	17.37 Battersea
02.53 Southfleet	08.38 City	12.10 High Halden	18.20 Frant
02.58 Kimblewich	08.38 East Ham	12.10 Stalisfield *	18.25 Forest Row
03.02 City	08.39 Lewisham	12.15 Ockley	18.30 Lamberhurst
03.32 Hackney	09.14 Marden *	12.15 Staplehurst	18.35 East Stratton
03.33 Cheshunt	09.20 City	12.18 Warnham	18.35 Sissinghurst
03.33 Darenth	09.27 Uxbridge	12.20 Ivychurch	19.30 Cobham

BETWEEN 21.00 ON WEDNESDAY, JULY 19, TO 20.59 ON THURSDAY, JULY 20 (Airburst ✳)

21.25	Ivychurch	01.06	Cranbrook	05.04	Poplar	08.25	Holmwood
22.32	Northiam	01.07	Goudhurst	05.45	Brede	08.30	Staplehurst
23.40	Sutton Valence	01.08	Hothfield	05.49	Nottlestead	08.32	Poplar
23.40	Hawkhurst	01.12	Ticehurst	06.16	Lamberhurst	09.27	Icklesham ✳
23.40	Konnardington	01.16	Wandsworth	06.33	Coppinghall	09.30	Trottiscliffe
23.45	Chigwell	01.26	Frant	06.38	Hunton	09.50	Forest Row
23.45	West Ham	02.34	Wandsworth	06.40	Deptford	09.55	Croydon
00.04	Epping Green	03.17	Smarden	06.42	Beckenham	10.00	Croydon
00.07	Ingatestone	03.20	Ryarsh	06.45	Hendon	10.03	Mitcham
00.11	Feltham	03.23	Orpington	06.45	Poling	10.20	Battle
00.12	Ealing	04.05	Broomhill	07.20	Ivychurch	10.20	Burmarsh
00.17	Hammersmith	04.05	Boughton Malherbe	07.25	Hastings	10.21	Acton
00.22	Enfield	04.26	Chingford	07.28	Hothfield	10.45	Woolwich
00.28	Poplar	04.40	Chigwell	07.29	Egerton	10.55	Rainham
00.28	Edmonton	04.46	West Ham	08.20	Boxley	11.09	Poplar
00.39	Stow Maries	04.52	Edmonton	08.23	Tonbridge	11.13	St Pancras
00.46	Enfield	05.01	Woolwich	08.25	Greenwich	11.18	Greenwich

The district of Penge suffered heavily from several flying bombs, particularly the High Street where the first exploded in the early hours of June 18 (see page 68) killing 11. Hit again three times on June 29 (see page 87), another bomb landed just before 7 a.m. on July 21 in Blenheim Road, just to the rear of the High Street, killing a family of three at No. 7.

BETWEEN 21.00 ON THURSDAY, JULY 20, TO 20.59 ON FRIDAY, JULY 21 (Airburst ✳)

23.18	Fairlight ✳	05.12	Merton	09.25	Gatton Park	12.51	Walthamstow
23.18	Blotchington	05.24	Kingston-on-Thames	09.27	Headley	12.52	Coulsdon
23.20	Hadlow	05.31	Horsham	09.30	Banstead	12.56	Banstead
23.20	Buxted	05.35	Orpington	09.30	Capel-le-Ferne	13.00	Bletchingley
23.22	Barking	05.35	Greenwich	09.40	Coulsdon	13.24	Wandsworth
23.23	Dunton Green	05.51	Chelsham	09.51	Kingston	13.30	Dorking
23.25	Herstmonceux	05.52	Lewisham	09.52	Banstead	13.31	Barking
23.26	Chislehurst	05.59	Chislehurst	10.15	Lambeth	13.35	Wembley
23.27	Banstead	06.26	Rainham	10.15	Reigate	13.36	Woolwich
23.30	Harrow	06.28	Oxted	10.16	Lullingstone	13.37	Titsey
23.31	Woolwich	06.30	Helllingley	10.22	Wandsworth	14.08	Brasted
00.01	Dymchurch	06.30	Rotherfield	10.25	Limpsfield	14.29	Charing
00.43	Burmarsh	06.51	Penge	10.27	Albury	14.32	Orpington
00.54	Reigate	06.56	Croydon	10.29	Linchmere	14.33	Leyton
01.01	Camberwell	06.58	Poplar	10.30	Newdigate	14.35	Nutfield
01.08	Hammersmith	06.58	Ascot	10.42	Orpington	15.28	Chelsham
01.30	Ashtead	07.43	Twickenham	11.08	Epsom	15.35	Buxted
01.34	Wembley	07.45	Mickleham	11.18	Shoreham	15.36	Beckenham
01.36	Battersea	07.47	Mitcham	11.21	Esher	15.56	Goudhurst
02.09	Croydon	07.57	Orpington	11.22	Banstead	16.46	Twickenham
02.09	Fairlight	08.09	Greenwich	11.25	Burstow	17.29	Carshalton
02.10	Lambeth	08.12	Lambeth	11.30	Wadhurst	18.11	Shipbourne
02.22	Camberwell	08.35	Redhill	11.35	Caterham	18.55	Fletching
02.39	Poplar	08.35	Kingston-on-Thames	11.48	Ealing	19.14	Chislehurst
02.45	Wotton	08.51	Brentford	12.05	The Warren	19.23	Goudhurst
03.06	Sutton	08.55	Chiddingly	12.10	Esher	19.52	Erith
03.08	Barking	09.03	Beddington	12.16	Lambeth	19.53	Godstone
03.20	Boxley	09.07	Sundridge	12.20	Croydon	20.02	Pembury
03.42	Greenwich	09.10	Banstead	12.25	Greenwich	20.20	Tenterden
04.02	Titsey	09.13	Newdigate	12.33	Camberwell	20.25	Wandsworth
04.13	Wandsworth	09.16	Windelsham	12.33	Merton	20.55	Monks Green
04.31	Croydon	09.23	Croydon	12.35	Dorking	20.58	Wrotham
04.49	Deptford	09.25	Waldron	12.43	Sutton		
04.58	Sutton	09.25	Brockham	12.50	Lingfield		

Scale of the German Attack, July 15 — August 15

The total number of flying bombs reported by the defences during this period was 2,667, compared with a total of 2,934 in the first five weeks of the attack. In other words, the Germans had succeeded in maintaining the original scale of attack but the number of bombs reported in the week following the very heavy attacks of August 2-9 fell by more than a half compared to that of the previous week. It was impossible to be certain that this decline was due to Allied bombing. The weather, which was good during this particular week, may have had some effect as the Germans tended to fire most heavily in dull and cloudy weather.

Insofar as the decline was down to bombing, it seemed to be due very largely to the attacks on storage depots rather than on launching sites. Some 41 of the latter had been destroyed by bombing up to the middle of August but that still left the Germans 53 sites, which was more than enough to maintain the average daily scale of attack.

It appeared to the Joint 'Crossbow' Target Priorities Committee that there was no proof that the 26,000 tons of bombs that had been dropped on launching sites between the middle of June and the middle of August had achieved anything worthwhile. On the other hand, they were equally convinced that storage depots, communications and production centres in Germany were valuable targets, and on August 15 Tedder was again asked to give a decision on the matter. However, he stood by his earlier ruling that attacks on launching sites must still be made though he agreed that they should only be carried out when bad weather prevented attacks on other types of 'Crossbow' target.

That the bombing had clearly failed to bring about any important reduction compared with the first five weeks, meant that the defences of London had still to deal with a dangerous weight of attack.

The V1 that struck Deepwater Road on Canvey Island bordering the Thames could well be one of the bombs launched from He 111s operating from the Low Countries. Eleven-year-old June Ward saw it come down on July 22: 'I was standing at the bus stop in the village with my sister when we saw the V1 being chased by one of our aeroplanes. He was firing at it to turn it towards the sea but it suddenly turned and landed on Lord Edward Scott's bungalow. He was killed as were Peter and Eric Howard, aged five and eight, next door.'

BETWEEN 21.00 ON FRIDAY, JULY 21, TO 20.59 ON SATURDAY, JULY 22   (Airburst ✳)

21.42 Rainham	03.04 Enfield	07.35 Lambeth	16.36 Ightham
22.37 Chislehurst	03.06 Steeple Creek	07.45 Woolwich	16.37 Hastings
00.54 Beckenham	03.07 Croydon	08.15 Chislehurst	16.38 Eynsford
00.56 Beckenham	03.14 Epping	08.37 Greenwich	16.56 Sittingbourne ✳
00.57 West Ham	03.15 Billericay	10.22 Camberwell	17.09 Wye
00.58 Camberwell	03.22 Wimbledon	10.23 Beckenham	17.09 Shadoxhurst
01.02 Wartling	03.27 Little Stambridge	11.14 Camberwell	17.26 Mersham
01.06 Beckenham	03.28 Hockley	11.33 Canvey Island	17.56 Ashburnham ✳
01.16 Crowborough	03.30 Cheshunt	12.12 Edenbridge	18.00 Pluckley
01.39 East Ham	03.36 Woolwich	13.19 Pluckley	18.00 Benenden
01.39 Esher	03.47 Dagenham	13.21 Chigwell	18.05 Rolvenden
01.40 Upminster	04.11 Tatsfield	13.24 Beckenham	18.05 Mayfield
02.06 Bromley	04.27 Shoreditch	14.05 Lydd	18.45 Marlow
02.06 East Ham	04.39 Portsmouth (in sea)	14.35 Orlestone	19.20 Etchingham
02.15 St Pancras	04.40 Aveley	15.02 Old Romney	19.25 Etchingham
02.15 Eynsford	04.45 Pevensey	15.17 Frant	19.25 Hawkhurst
02.31 Boughton Aluph	05.21 Poplar	15.18 Beckenham	19.26 Hadlow
02.34 Woolwich	05.32 Merton	15.20 Bexhill	19.28 Warbleton
02.47 Kelvedon	05.37 Bletchingley	15.27 Lewisham	19.32 Etchingham
02.53 Purfleet (in river)	06.14 Blindley	15.33 Sissingshurst	20.14 Chartham
02.54 Camberwell	06.25 Cooling	15.48 Lingfield	20.59 Wadhurst
02.54 East Ham	06.31 Wandsworth	16.32 Battle	
02.57 Galleywood	06.58 Lewisham	16.35 Bexhill	
03.00 Marden Park	07.33 Croydon	16.36 Goudhurst	

The Development of the Coastal Gun Belt

The working of the defence system was last considered at the stage where the decision to move the guns to the coast had been taken. The redeployment began on July 14 and by dawn on the 17th all heavy guns that had been deployed in the inland belt were now in action in their new positions on the coast. All the light guns were in action two days later having remained in their inland positions to cover the move. The speed of the redeployment was an achievement that was almost beyond praise, especially as the Command had little experience of large-scale movement.

The position on the morning of July 19 was that 412 heavy and 972 light guns were ready for action in the coastal belt; and there were also 168 Bofors and 416 20mm guns of the RAF Regiment, and 28 RAC light guns, and 2½ batteries of rocket guns in position. Amongst the heavy guns was one US Army battalion. From that point on, the numbers rose steadily until by August 15 there were 592 heavy guns, including five US Army battalions (80 guns) in the coastal belt and 701 light guns.

Comparable progress was also made in the programme of replacing mobile guns by static guns and bringing in SCR 584 sets and No. 10 Predictors. This unavoidably took longer to complete than the initial redeployment so it was not until July 22 that the first 30 static guns were in position. By the end of the month, 288 static guns were ready for action, the figure having risen to 379 by August 15. It was this gap between the completion of the first moves on July 17

When it was decided to move the gun belt forward to the coast, it involved the laying of 3,000 miles of cable for the inter-battery lines alone. Some 30,000 tons of stores and 30,000 tons of heavy gun ammunition were also moved into the coastal belt. In the first week of the move it was calculated that vehicles of Anti-Aircraft Command had covered 2¾ million miles. The redeployment began on July 14 and within three days all the 3.7-inch guns were in action. As there was no time to prepare concrete platforms, engineers improvised with ones like these on the sea front at St Leonards, Hastings. The light guns — the Bofors 40mm — followed two days later having been retained at their original locations to protect the move of the heavy guns.

and the bringing to bear in force of the most-efficient equipment, coupled also with the need to become familiar with the new positions, that accounts for the relatively poor results that were obtained in the week following the redeployment.

Andy Saunders pictured Hastings seafront for us in 2019 — little change since it was in the front line in 1944.

Great Eastern Street, EC2, on July 24, identified in the list of incidents on the opposite page as Shoreditch.

BETWEEN 21.00 ON SATURDAY, JULY 22, TO 20.59 ON SUNDAY, JULY 23			(Airburst ✳)
21.01 Frittenden	23.13 Hawkhurst	01.30 Camberwell	08.14 Mersham
21.03 Ticehurst	23.14 Orpington	01.30 Chelsham	08.25 Mersham
21.06 Charlwood	23.33 Orpington	01.44 Lewisham	08.26 Brasted
21.08 Lambeth	23.45 Icklesham	01.54 Rye ✳	08.29 Kingsnorth
21.11 Burmarsh	23.49 Chelsham	02.28 Off Littlestone ✳	08.56 Hackney
21.13 Cranbrook	23.53 Tangmere	02.49 Surbiton	09.00 Selling
21.17 Appledore	23.54 Birling	02.54 Southall	09.12 Burmarsh
21.17 Peasmarsh	23.55 Finsbury	03.10 Icklesham	09.13 Hackney
21.19 Snargate	23.58 Acrise	03.14 Sunbury	09.40 Elmstead
21.23 Smeeth	00.07 Beckenham	03.35 Fernhurst	14.17 Fairlight
21.40 Hornchurch	00.09 Richmond	03.53 Off Littlestone	14.24 Lympne
21.40 Appledore	00.14 Oxted	04.08 City	14.27 Off Fairlight ✳
21.45 Warbleton	00.17 Horne	04.29 Reigate	14.28 Wanstead
21.56 Woodchurch ✳	00.19 Littlestone ✳	04.36 Merton	14.35 Ewhurst
22.05 Off Hastings ✳	00.24 Mitcham	04.51 Hythe	14.37 St Pancras
22.07 Ewhurst	00.31 Off Littlestone	05.01 Hackney	15.18 Battersea
22.11 Hartfield	00.34 Romford	05.28 Off Dymchurch	15.19 Hornsey
22.45 Off Rye ✳	00.39 Off Bexhill	05.40 Chipperfield	15.20 Westerham
22.50 Walthamstow	00.43 Brill	05.47 Off Folkestone	15.20 Hever
22.50 Great Cheaton	00.44 Battle	06.00 Chiddingly	15.20 Warbleton
22.51 Chiddingstone	00.47 Barnes	06.10 Sandhurst	15.22 Charlwood
22.52 Deptford	01.14 Sutton	06.11 Wandsworth	15.38 Shipbourne
23.04 Chalfont St Giles	01.16 Fulham	06.33 Battle	15.42 Ticehurst
23.05 Abinger	01.17 Wandsworth	07.40 West Ham	16.23 Kensington
23.13 West Hoathley	01.18 Lambeth	07.42 Ripley	

From this date, the Air Ministry began including flying bombs shot down over the sea.

BETWEEN 21.00 ON SUNDAY, JULY 23, TO 20.59 ON MONDAY, JULY 24 (Airburst *)			
00.13 Appledore *	00.46 Off Goldhanger	04.43 Bodiam	16.33 Benenden
00.18 Deptford	01.52 Newington	04.45 Edmonton	16.34 Twickenham
00.19 Wandsworth	01.57 Broomfield	04.46 Enfield	16.38 Stepney
00.20 Tonbridge	02.00 Buxted *	04.47 Watton	16.38 Wilmington
00.22 Ilford	02.06 Ardingley	05.29 Brightling	18.24 Bromley
00.22 Waltham Holy Cross	02.14 Off Eastbourne *	05.29 Crundale	18.24 Shoreditch
00.22 Lambeth	03.34 Frant	15.04 Eastwell	18.29 East Ham
00.23 Cobham	03.39 Mayfield	15.05 Heathfield	19.55 Cranbrook
00.25 Canewdon	03.42 Westminster	15.06 Leyton	20.01 Purfleet
00.26 Chigwell	03.42 Merton	15.08 Bethnal Green	20.03 Newdigate
00.26 Nettleswell	04.10 Penshurst	15.09 Westminster	20.05 Leyton
00.36 High Wych	04.40 Willesden	15.13 Hooe	
00.38 Offham	04.40 Shenfield	16.23 Goudhurst	
00.38 Sacombe	04.42 Harold Park	16.32 Croydon	

The superior blasting power of the V1 caused much more damage to property than the same weight of conventional bombs. In the August 4 edition of the *Daily Mirror*, this photo was published under the headline 'Rooms still wanted'. The caption read as follows: 'Another buzz-bomb "incident" in Southern England. Firemen and Civil Defence rescuers catfoot over the debris of a vanished home, carrying stunned children to safety. The first care is always to get people out. And where do they go from here? Over 17,000 houses have been destroyed and 800,000 damaged, and still the bombs come. Rooms are still wanted, please.' The picture shows the aftermath of the flying bomb that had fallen on Arundel Road, Leyton, in the mid-afternoon of July 24. In 1972 the photo was published again in the IPC magazine *Headlines* at which point the little girl in the fireman's arms — then Mrs Eileen Alexander — wrote to identify herself. She could not recall the date the picture had been taken but we were able to advise her. She said that she had been playing ball in the street when the bomb came over with its frightening roar. When the engine stopped she made for the Anderson shelter in her back garden as fast as her legs would carry her, and as she dived through the door the explosion flung her to the far end.

Although the area where the bomb fell has been totally rebuilt, we plotted the exact spot where her house No.5 had stood and in 1990 took her back for our comparison photo. The second part of the conundrum was to try to identify her fireman but it was not until 1995, when the BBC broadcast an interview with Eileen on the 40th anniversary of VE-Day, that the mystery was solved. The programme resulted in a phone call from a Mrs Violet Sayers who revealed that the fireman was her husband Bill. Unfortunately, she said that he had died only two years before but that he was always wondering what had happened to that little girl. 'It's so nice to find out after all this time', said Violet. 'It was a hell of a night and not a stick was left standing where the doodlebug landed. A lot of people were killed and they were digging others out with their bare hands and it was next morning before Bill got home'. Eileen, also, had dearly wanted to meet her rescuer but the ironic thing was that he lived only a few miles from her home and she never knew. Eileen did meet his widow though, and said that it was a very moving experience.

BETWEEN 21.00 ON MONDAY, JULY 24, TO 20.59 ON TUESDAY, JULY 25   (Airburst ✳)

21.33 Wye	23.13 Penge	23.33 Off Eastbourne	00.30 Cheshunt
21.34 Bethersden	23.13 Harden	23.53 Broadstairs	02.52 Swanscombe
21.39 Woking	23.14 East Ham	23.58 Hendon	03.28 Meesdon
23.08 Off Hythe ✳	23.15 West Ham	23.58 Wood Green	03.56 Chingford
23.10 Off Icklesham	23.15 Oxted	24.00 Essendon	03.58 Edmonton
23.11 Barking	23.16 Greenwich	24.00 Hertford Heath	04.01 Edmonton
23.12 Off Eastbourne	23.18 Goudhurst	00.01 Standon	04.01 Nazeing
23.12 Off Romney	23.19 Hammersmith	00.11 Poplar	

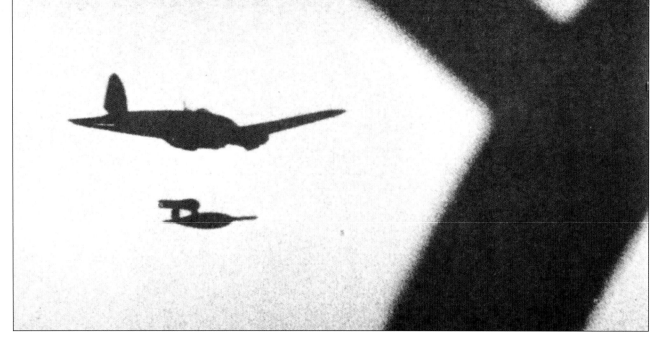

With the imminent break-out from Normandy and the consequent overrunning of the static sites, the Luftwaffe began air-launching V1s from over the North Sea using modified He 111s. Over 1,100 were sent on their way by this method but after the war the failure rate was estimated at 40 per cent. Sites for ground launches were also prepared in Holland.

Defence against Attack from the East

The immense task of redeployment was also complicated by the need for setting up a new defence system further north. It will be recalled that on the night of July 9/10, and subsequently, flying bombs had been plotted as they approached London from the direction of the Thames Estuary, but it was not until August 3 that it was confirmed that these bombs were being launched from German aircraft. As early as July 12, ADGB Headquarters had prepared a provisional plan for the defence of the capital against attacks from Belgium and Holland along the same lines as the original 'Diver' deployment. From July 9 to the middle of August, it is believed that 107 flying bombs were launched by air, all of them at night.

There was to be a belt of balloons west of a line from Rochester—Thames Haven, and a belt of anti-aircraft guns east of the balloons and west of a line from the north-east corner of the existing gun belt to Clacton. Forward of the guns there would be a patrol area for fighters which would be manned by squadrons operating from Manston under the control of the radar stations at Sandwich, Foreness and Foulness.

Further progress was held up for a week by the decision to redeploy the main gun belt but the matter was again examined at a meeting on July 18. By then an alternative plan had been produced. This, like the one to move the guns to the coast, emanated from ADGB Headquarters, and was based on a similar appreciation of what was required. It envisaged the extension of the new coastal gun belt from St Margaret's Bay — its present northerly limit — to the North Foreland, and from there further north across the Thames by mounting heavy anti-aircraft guns on a line of ships moored in the estuary. Anti-Aircraft Command preferred a more westerly deployment on the grounds that it would allow the continuous engagement of flying bombs by cross-fire as they passed up the river. In any case, as the alternative plan depended upon the provision of the necessary shipping, it was soon clear that vessels could not be provided in anything like the necessary quantity, so the original plan was adopted as far as it affected the guns.

At night, the launch aircraft were also vulnerable to attack when the pulse-jet engine was started, lighting up the sky.

126

Another difficulty arose over the disposition of the balloon defences that were required. The ADGB plan provided for two belts of balloons; one of 106 which would be an extension of the main barrage at its northern end, and another of 307 which was to be deployed to the north of the Thames between Tilbury and Brentwood. Anti-Aircraft Command held, however, that these would hinder the defence of the capital against the attack by ordinary aircraft as the balloon cables would interfere with the gun radar sets in and near London. The upshot was that while Balloon Command reconnoitred the sites that would be required north of the river, no balloons were flown from that area. The extension to the main barrage, bringing it up to the south bank of the estuary in the Gravesend area, was carried out and, by the beginning of August, 265 balloons had been added.

Also standing patrols of fighters in the Thames Estuary area was raised from two fighters to ten from July 30 while defence against attack from due east was largely left to Anti-Aircraft Command. General Pile was given discretion to redeploy the permanent defences east of London as he thought fit. These consisted chiefly of the guns in the Thames and Medway AA zones; and during the last week in July the movement of 64 of these was begun. The new positions that were taken up were in the quadrilateral Rochester—Whitstable—Clacton—Chelmsford, an area that was henceforth known as the 'Diver' Gun 'Box'. At the same time, four mobile HAA regiments of 21st Army Group, one Anti-Aircraft Command LAA regiment, and a number of RAF Regiment and naval units also began to move to positions in the box. By the end of July there were 136 heavy, 120 40mm and 324 20mm guns in action there.

As in the case of the coastal belt, to build up a high proportion of remotely-controlled static guns within the box took longer than to carry out the initial deployment, but by the middle of August 136 of the heavy guns in the box

To try to avoid being detected by radar while carrying the missile, the mother aircraft adopted a tactic called 'lo-hi-lo'. On leaving the coast, the Heinkel would fly at wave-top height until approaching the planned launch position. It would then rapidly climb, release the V1 before descending to a low altitude again for the flight back to base. The intended operational altitude for the flying bomb was originally set at 2,750 metres (9,000ft) but problems with the barometric fuel pressure regulator led to this being changed, halving the height and so bringing the V1 within the range of the Bofors.

(which by then contained 208 heavy guns all told) were of that type. The number of light guns had been increased by the same date to 174 40mm and 404 20mm. Gun-fire could also be brought to bear from a small number of guns on the Maunsell forts in the estuary, and from barges and converted pleasure steamers. The normal searchlight dispositions in Essex had also been thickened by the addition of two composite searchlights and LAA batteries.

BETWEEN 21.00 ON TUESDAY, JULY 25, TO 20.59 ON WEDNESDAY, JULY 26 (Airburst *)

23.30	Sudbourne	04.14	Barham	06.32	Chiddingstone	08.00	Aloiston
23.41	Cromer Hyde	04.14	Detling	06.32	East Peckham	08.00	Hollingbourne
23.43	Rettenden	04.14	St Thomas The Apostle	06.35	Warehorne	08.01	Oxhey
23.44	Cuffley	04.15	Aylesford	06.36	East Ham	08.10	Heathfield
23.45	Ayot St Lawrence	04.15	Eynsford	06.36	Great Chart	08.22	Battle
23.45	Novendon	04.16	Otterden	06.42	Carshalton	14.10	Folkestone
01.04	St Mary-in-the-Marsh	04.17	Leigh	07.10	Hampden	14.11	Tenterden
01.05	Charing	04.18	Wandsworth	07.26	Rotherfield	14.13	Stone-cum-Ebony
01.14	West Thurrock	04.19	Walthamstow	07.27	Beckenham	14.17	Doddington
01.17	Wanstead	04.20	Chigwell	07.31	Warbleton	14.19	Chelsham
01.20	Kingsdown	04.24	Barking	07.45	Ivychurch	14.20	Biddenden
01.24	Hornsey	04.35	Biddenden	07.50	Salehurst *	14.22	Uckfield *
01.49	Wanstead	04.35	Brenzett	07.50	Ticehurst	14.23	Croydon
01.50	Westminster	04.48	Lewisham	07.53	Rotherfield	14.23	West Wickham
01.57	Marden	04.50	Off Eastbourne	07.53	Sundridge	14.24	Selling
02.56	Wennington	04.56	Hildenborough	07.54	Orpington	14.25	Hinxhill
03.08	Mountfield	06.24	Burmarsh	07.55	Ditton	14.25	Wartling
03.23	Nazeing	06.24	Tenterden	07.55	Farningham	14.30	Crayford
03.25	Pilgrims Hatch	06.24	Wittersham *	07.55	Meopham	14.32	Guildford
03.27	Gilston	06.27	Saltwood	07.55	Wateringbury	14.39	Capel
03.27	Hastingwood	06.30	Hadlow	07.58	West Ham		

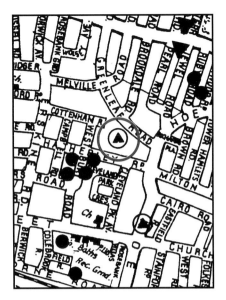

Many local councils maintained their own bomb plot maps, this one by the Borough of Walthamstow being published in 1945 with the enigmatic proviso that 'some flying bombs and rockets have had to be omitted owing to security regulations'.

The force of the explosion of a flying bomb, which was designed to detonate on the first surface it struck, was tremendous and old houses simply collapsed and even bricks were reduced to powder.

In Greenleaf Road at 04.19 on July 26, the bomb fell near a public surface shelter and demolished the parsonage from which the Vicar, his wife and child were safely extracted, having slept in their Morrison shelter. Unfortunately, a National Fire Service static water tank stood by the side of the public shelter, and this was lifted by the explosion and flung against the wall of the shelter. As the water weighed some 20 tons, it was reckoned by the experts that at the moment of hitting the shelter, the tank was exercising the force of a 60-ton battering ram! The shelter was soundly built and properly reinforced but something had to give way and Beatrice Green was killed inside by the collapse of part of the wall. The shock of the impact was also transmitted to the side walls and caused cracks near the roof. The blast area on this occasion affected Hoe Street almost from Forest Road to beyond the High Street.

TELEPHONE MESSAGE

Time Sent 19-00-19-30 Date 28-7-44 Sent by JS:5 a PBY

From Eastbourne Control To Chief Warden and Key Post.

S.T.P. Ltd. 5461

BOMB REPORT.

At 19.25 hours 27.7.44 an enemy "Flying Bomb" fell at Brassey Avenue, Hampden Park. Civilian Casualties. Injured and detained in hospital 10. Injured other cases. 23.

6. Houses demolished. Many others damaged. Widespread superficial damage.

RECEIVED
29 JUL 1944

On a day that saw one of the heaviest attacks on the United Kingdom, Eastbourne received its ninth flying bomb and fortunately the original message file has survived. The V1 hit the back garden of No. 68 Brassey Avenue in Hampden Park at 19.25, the first report being received three minutes later. The emergency services immediately swung into action. The rescue party arrived at 19.30 together with two ambulances, the Light Mobile Unit following nine minutes later with three more ambulances. Two more arrived at 19.46 and, because the mains had been ruptured, the Water Repair Party reached the scene at 20.20. The Presbyterian Hall at Elm Grove was opened for a rest centre at 19.38 and a canteen from the local authority was ordered out which arrived at the top end of the road. Twenty-four civilian casualties from Brassey Avenue, Nevill Avenue, Parkfield Avenue, Percival Road,

Freeman Avenue and Glynde Avenue were treated at the First Aid Point at Hampden Park, and nine casualties taken to St Mary's Hospital. Miss Mary DuPont in No. 64 Brassey Avenue was admitted to Princess Alice Hospital. There were 28 Service casualties, many from 126 Heavy Anti-Aircraft Battery suffering from severe deafness, and two Americans, Sergeant Henry Ondrej and Private Remingio Frenondel. Four servicemen, all with the Royal Artillery's 337th Searchlight Regiment of the Royal West Kents, lost their lives. Gunners George Kelly and Charles Hind were killed outright, Bombardier John Glasser dying on the 28th and Gunner Charles Dennison on July 29. By 20.21 all the casualties were reported as having been taken to hospital and stretcher-bearers were stood down. Six houses had been totally demolished with many seriously damaged.

BETWEEN 21.00 ON WEDNESDAY, JULY 26, TO 20.59 ON THURSDAY, JULY 27   (Airburst ✳)

22.00	Ewhurst	02.05	Lewisham	16.45	Headcorn	17.56	Woolwich
22.06	Salehurst	02.07	St Pancras	16.46	Croydon	17.58	Coulsdon
22.09	Off Rye	02.12	Aveley	16.46	Sundridge	17.58	Ilford
22.11	Dellington	02.23	Great Warley	16.47	Bromley	17.58	Merton
22.12	Heathfield	05.03	Buxted	16.48	Beckenham	18.01	Heston
22.12	Mountfield	05.05	Polegate	16.50	Capel	18.02	Sutton
22.17	Buxted	10.50	Lydd	16.50	Marden	18.02	Woolwich
22.43	Waldron	15.11	Hougham Without	16.50	Stondon Massey	18.04	Leyton
23.50	Off Hythe	15.21	Orpington	16.50	Wandsworth	18.23	Aveley
00.07	South Fambridge	15.22	Greenwich	16.54	Purfleet	19.13	South Ockenden
00.08	Ticehurst	15.22	Lewisham	16.55	Swanscombe	19.19	West Hythe
00.10	Hollingley	15.22	Maidstone	16.56	Twickenham	19.22	Warbleton
00.17	Lenham	15.23	Bexley	16.56	Woolwich	19.25	Eastbourne ✳
01.13	Off Hythe	15.24	Abridge	17.00	Sellindge	19.25	Frant
01.14	Kemsing	15.24	Heybridge Basin	17.44	Beckenham	19.29	Camberwell
01.17	Off Hythe	15.25	Bexley	17.45	Leyton	19.30	Greenwich
01.19	Crowhurst	15.25	Chislehurst	17.47	Lympne	19.30	Lingfield
01.20	Bromley	15.25	East Ham	17.50	Deptford	19.30	Mayfield
01.20	Lambeth	15.25	Horsmonden	17.51	Wanstead	19.30	Nutfield
01.23	Croydon	15.25	Lympne	17.52	Frimley	19.32	Barking
01.26	Ilford	15.26	Chislehurst	17.52	Lewisham	19.32	Lambeth
01.29	Barking	15.26	West Hoathley	17.53	Beddington	19.34	Woldingham
01.33	Haverhill	15.27	Beckenham	17.53	Croydon	19.35	Billericay
01.38	Lewisham	15.34	Beckenham	17.54	Broomhill	19.35	Camberwell
01.42	Wandsworth	15.37	Woolwich	17.54	Lewisham	19.39	Abberton
01.42	Wateringbury	15.40	Romford	17.54	Orpington	19.45	Rotherfield
01.44	Beckenham	16.10	Wandsworth	17.54	Wateringbury	20.03	Ticehurst
01.51	Wennington	16.30	Lyminge	17.55	Hackney		
01.53	West Ham	16.40	Battle	17.55	Hastingleigh		
01.55	Maresfield	16.42	Ticehurst	17.55	Sutton		

BETWEEN 21.00 ON THURSDAY, JULY 27, TO 20.59 ON FRIDAY, JULY 28			(Airburst *)
21.13 Ilford	22.45 Folkestone	23.59 Greenwich	13.25 Stanford-le-Hope
21.13 Herstmonceux	22.47 Wartling	23.59 East Peckham	13.25 Uckfield
21.15 Bilsington	22.50 Rotherfield	24.00 Lewisham	13.26 Leigh
21.15 Staplehurst	22.50 Woodchurch	00.01 Croydon	13.28 Malden
21.15 Kingsnorth *	22.52 Frant *	00.01 Hythe *	13.30 Bushey
21.17 Woodchurch	22.53 Chislehurst	00.03 Great Burstead	13.30 Croydon
21.18 Mayfield	22.53 Headcorn	00.06 Rye *	13.31 Kensington
21.20 Goudhurst	22.54 Wandsworth	00.07 Pett	13.32 Fulham
21.21 Beckenham	22.54 Croydon	09.44 Lewisham	13.32 Westminster
21.21 Goudhurst *	22.54 West Malling	09.44 Coulsdon	13.32 Ulcombe
21.26 Mitcham	22.58 Bletchingley	09.54 West Ham	13.32 Southborough
21.27 Capel	23.10 Coulsdon	09.55 Framfield	13.34 Lullingstone
21.32 Heathfield	23.30 Croydon	13.15 Broomhill	13.45 Surbiton
21.36 Deptford	23.39 Bromley	13.18 Brabourne	13.47 St Mary in the Marsh
21.37 Etchingham	23.56 Shadoxhurst	13.22 Smarden	13.51 Stepney
21.45 Orpington	23.58 Staplehurst	13.22 Saltwood	13.53 Waldron

The Protection of London

It has already been noted that during the four weeks succeeding the redeployment to the coast, the general scale of enemy attack was much the same as in previous weeks. In another respect, too, the position remained much the same: the mean point of impact of all the bombs falling in London was, as before, in the Dulwich district, approximately one mile east of Alleyn's School. The brunt of the attack therefore, continued to fall on the boroughs south of the Thames.

The toll of houses damaged and destroyed continued to rise, being near one million by the middle of August. Casualties, however, were lower by one half than in the first five weeks; which reflected the evacuation that had been going on, especially south of the river. Nor were there any single incidents so destructive of life like those that had occurred earlier in the attack. The three most serious were at Leyton, Kensington and Watford, where some 30 people were killed in each case.

One of the worst-hit areas was Croydon, the first flying bombs falling on the night of June 15/16. The Incident Officer recounted that 'the deep-throated roar was heard first. A blinding flash followed and an explosion rocked the Warden's Post. The projectile had fallen at the junction of Avenue and Warminster Roads. The race to the scene was through a nightmare fog of mortar and dust, the road being carpeted with leaves, glass and rubble. Injured and uninjured were rushing out, dazed and bewildered . . . the scene itself was desolation.' To date, over 100 V1s had fallen on the borough, the worst event in the central part of Croydon occurring one minute after midnight on July 27/28 when a low-flying bomb cut out over the Town Hall to come down in Cranmer Road. All the houses in the road were seriously damaged and a large number were destroyed, as was Cranmer Hall. Cranmer Road (this photograph shows the rear of the houses) is one of a series of parallel roads of small properties and the blast damage extended over a quarter of a mile radius. The casualty services worked all night and the next day as well. The dead on this night were 11 and the injuries 80, including 16 very serious. *Right:* Cranmer Road was never rebuilt, the opportunity being taken to lay out tennis courts.

When the attack was at its peak, Croydon's Town Clerk, Ernest Taberner, was invited to visit the guns on the coast near Rye in company with other Town Clerks from the London area. On that particular day, of the 107 bombs that came over, the guns brought down 91, some of them disintegrating in mid-air or, when hit, falling and exploding on touching the sea. The officials were also greatly impressed with the work of the ATS girls who were helping to man the guns.

On July 27 a very serious incident occurred in Forest Gate as West Ham fire chief Cyril Demarne explains. 'A particularly nasty, gory situation confronted us following a V1 explosion at the junction of Dames and Pevensey Roads. A trolleybus, crammed with home-going workers, had caught the full blast and the whole area was a sickening sight. Dismembered bodies littered the roadway; others were splattered over the brickwork of the houses across the way and the wreckage of the trolleybus was simply too ghastly to describe. I dictated my report to Firewoman Ball who raced away to telephone the message to Control.'

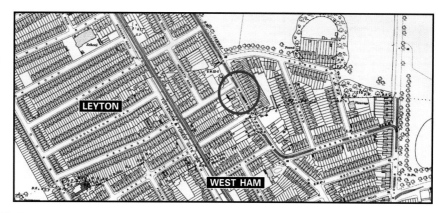

'Next morning there came a knock on my office door. Firewoman Ball entered, nervously fingering her cap. She had come to ask a favour; could she be excused from accompanying me as yesterday's experience had sickened her and she felt she could not repeat the operation without fainting. I understood her reaction so I arranged for a despatch rider to take over the duty.'

Cyril traced this photograph in 1991 for his book *A Fireman's Tale*: 'I cannot say with certainty that this is the trolleybus involved but it looks remarkably like it. The roof and upper deck, together with the passengers were blasted away. Standing passengers on the lower deck also were flung against the fronts of the houses on the other side of the road. The passengers seated on the lower deck were all dead.'

One problem with this incident is establishing the precise number of persons killed as the flying bomb came down on the boundary between West Ham and Leyton. At the time, an article in the *Stratford Express*, approved by the censor, only mentioned four fatalities. Then an odd report in the *Belfast Newsletter* stated that least eight had been killed and that Italian prisoners from the nearby POW camp on Wanstead Flats had helped in the rescue work. A report in the *Leytonstone Independent* in September then revealed that 'rescue workers recovered 34 bodies, among them the driver, and others died in hospital'. The *Walthamstow Guardian* increased the total to 41, some of whom were probably waiting at the bus stop.

Lewisham High Street was busy on Friday, July 28, when one eyewitness said: 'We were almost opposite Marks & Spencer when I suddenly heard a queer sound — a sort of crackling noise. I instinctively looked up at the very low clouds and there it was, right over the top of us like a huge black whale's head, coming through the white cloud almost at roof level. I saw it fall on Marks & Spencer and explode.' The Civil Defence recorded that 'the sirens had not been sounded. The flying bomb came over the borough at an unusually low altitude so it could not be seen. There was a complete lack of warning.' The market stalls *(right)* lined up in the street caught the full force of the blast, the Ministry of Home Security recording in that evening's report that 28 persons were killed and 83 seriously injured, but the final death toll is believed to be 52 with three unidentified.

Five M&S staff lost their lives including the manager, Sydney Spurling. A plaque dedicated to the 51 [*sic*] dead was set in the pavement outside the store but when this became worn, a new one was mounted on the façade and unveiled on the anniversary in 2011.

More than a dozen V1s came down in the Thames and on July 28 these police constables were pictured carrying a piece of wreckage that had been blown onto the Embankment. With Waterloo Bridge

in the background, this must have been the bomb that fell opposite Victoria Embankment Gardens. The bridge itself was then in the process of being rebuilt due to settlement of the foundations.

BETWEEN 21.00 ON FRIDAY, JULY 28, TO 20.59 ON SATURDAY, JULY 29 (Airburst *)							
21.32	Burmarsh	00.13	Lambeth	10.23	Rotherfield	18.27	Saltwood
21.33	Burmarsh	00.14	Camberwell	10.25	Frant	18.28	Luddenham
21.39	Hawkhurst	00.14	Wandsworth	10.29	Hackney	18.30	St Thomas the Apostle
21.40	Old Romney	00.14	Battersea	10.29	Hackney	18.31	Lower Beeding
21.40	Marden	00.15	Greenwich	14.13	Ninfield	18.31	Titsey
21.43	Herstmonceux	00.16	Northfleet	14.17	Staplehurst	18.33	Dagenham
21.44	Stepney	00.17	Harold Wood	14.18	Chislehurst	18.33	Lewisham
21.44	Westminster	00.21	Leyton	14.18	Hastingleigh	18.34	Chignall
21.45	Staplehurst	00.21	Ticehurst	14.19	Croydon	18.35	Folkestone
21.46	Stoke Newington	00.25	Chislehurst	14.20	Westminster	18.36	Lewisham
21.47	Stepney	00.31	Off Hythe	14.20	Ilford	18.36	Near Headcorn *
21.47	West Ham	00.33	Mitcham	14.20	Mitcham	18.39	Mountnessing
21.47	Merton	00.55	Hackney	14.20	Storrington	18.44	Wadhurst
21.51	St Marylebone	01.13	Bulphan	14.20	Billericay	18.53	Bexley
22.34	Hythe	01.15	Tenterden	14.20	Hastingwood	19.29	Hawkinge
22.35	Lympne	01.16	Laughton	14.23	Southwark	19.33	Headcorn
22.37	Tenterden	01.19	Beauchamp Roding	14.24	East Ham	19.38	Lewisham
22.38	East Farleigh	01.23	Kingston	14.25	Camberwell	19.38	Dagenham
22.40	Ticehurst	01.24	East Ham	14.25	Barking	19.39	Greenwich
22.42	Appledore	01.31	Finsbury	14.27	Wandsworth	19.39	Lewisham
22.45	Dallington	01.37	Long Melford	14.30	Coulsdon	19.40	Stepney
22.45	Bonhall	03.55	Wandsworth	14.31	Camberwell	19.40	East Guildford
22.46	Lamberhurst *	03.57	Chislehurst	14.35	North Mimms	19.42	Erith
22.46	Harrietsham	03.58	Bexley	14.39	Stepney	19.42	Sundridge
22.48	Westminster	03.59	Ingatestone	14.40	St Marylebone	19.43	Cranbrook
22.50	Hastingleigh	04.13	West Ham	14.40	Marden	19.45	Newchurch *
23.00	West Ham	05.06	Hurstpierpoint	18.23	Salehurst		
00.08	Ticehurst	05.14	Hornsey	18.26	Denton		

Left: A few days before, a V1 had hit Electra House, the head office of Cable & Wireless Ltd, in Temple Place at the northern end of the Embankment Gardens. Three members of staff were killed and 17 injured in the blast at 3.42 a.m. on July 24 (see page 125). The building next door was Accountants House

(Astor House) which had been built for the financier William Waldorf Astor in 1895. Its basement was flooded, destroying several priceless works of art. *Right:* Both were redeveloped after the war, Electra House becoming Globe House and Astor House Two Temple Place.

Moorfield's, the world-famous eye hospital on City Road, was struck by a V1 on the night of July 29. Seven patients were killed in the hospital itself and another 14 in a surface shelter alongside in Peerless Street. Police Sergeant Harley Wright's action in rescuing those trapped was borne out in statements from Sub-Divisional Inspector Stoneman and three civilians. The award of the George Medal was recommended by the Commissioner of the Metropolitan Police, and Sergeant Wright attended Buckingham Palace to be decorated in March 1945.

RECOMMENDATION FOR THE AWARD OF THE GEORGE MEDAL

At 1.30 a.m, on the 29th July, 1944, a Flying Bomb fell on the rear portion of Moorfield's Eye Hospital, City Road, E.C.1., destroying that part of the hospital, also part of a block of flats, and starting a large fire in the premises of the Anglo-American Fibre Company Ltd., Cayton Street, E.C.1., which adjoins the hospital.

Police Sergeant Wright and War Reserve Sexton, with others, immediately went to the scene of the incident. The Sergeant was aware of the fact that there was a public shelter in the basement of the burning premises and that a number of people were in the habit of using it at night. A search was made to find an entrance, but this was unsuccessful as the only known entrances had already been blocked by debris; further search by the Sergeant revealed a possible entrance in an area in Cayton Street, separated from the pavement by some railings. This area is some 8-10 feet below ground level. Debris blocked the area and had destroyed the steps down, but had not quite reached the doorway into the shelter itself.

In spite of the fact that the part of the building by this corner of the area was blazing and the walls and remaining floors were in imminent danger of collapse, the Sergeant without any hesitation, followed by the War Reserve, climbed the railings and dropped into the area itself. Additional danger arose from the fact that immediately over their point of entry there was a covered bridge joining the premises with a neighbouring building. This bridge was some 40 feet above the ground and at the time the officers went down into the area it was burning strongly and was obviously likely to collapse at any moment. It did in fact fall whilst the officers were in the shelter. So also did the first floor and side walls and the debris covered the remainder of the area.

After searching the shelter, the officers discovered two men and a woman, and they set about trying to find an exit, but in this they were badly hindered by the activities of one of the men who had lost control of himself. Their search was also made more difficult by the fact that the shelter was slowly flooding and was filled with smoke and debris, whilst electrical cables which had become detached from the walls were on fire.

During the course of their search for an exit an electric fuse-box exploded in the Sergeant's face causing temporary blindness and severe burns on his face and neck.

There was no chance of escape at the rear as another shelter had collapsed and blocked the exit and they realised that their only chance was by the way they had come in. So Sergeant Wright brought the people as near as possible to that point, making them lie down in the water in an endeavour to assist breathing, which was made difficult by the dense smoke and overpowering heat.

After some time, the officers discovered that the fire around the area had abated and it was decided to make an attempt to get out that way. With the assistance of Sergeant Wright, Sexton succeeded in climbing over the debris and railings and then ran to get assistance. Wright, who was by this time weak and badly burned, was unable to assist the others but he managed to get himself out and secured assistance for the remainder of the party, who were successfully extricated by means of ropes and a ladder.

After this had been carried out the officers allowed themselves to be taken to City Road Station and they were then removed to St Bartholomew's Hospital where it was found that Sergeant Wright had not sustained any apparent permanent injury to his eyesight as a result of the explosion mentioned above.

It has been impossible to obtain any accurate information as to the length of time the officers were in the shelter but it is estimated that they were there for well over an hour.

The fire went on burning strongly for nearly 24 hours and during the time the officers were in the shelter the heat was so intense that the firemen operating the hoses had to do so with their backs to the fire. The Fire Brigade were not finally withdrawn from the scene until six days after the incident.

It must have been plainly obvious to both officers before they started on this rescue that a complete collapse of the building was more or less inevitable owing to the fierceness of the fire, which at that time had not been attacked as the Fire Service had not arrived. It must also have been equally clear to them that their means of escape when once inside the shelter might be blocked and they knew there was no other way out as they had previously searched the building. There was also the danger that the ground floor, which formed the roof of the shelter, might collapse on them through the fire and the weight of the debris.

Inside the shelter and particularly when their escape was blocked there was no doubt that the behaviour of the two officers did much to help the morale of the persons trapped.

At Watford, early on July 30, Fred Coates was spotting from the top of the Catholic Church in Market Street when he saw the light of the flame from a missile as it approached from the direction of Harrow. 'It came towards me. It was so low I could have hit it with an air pistol.' He watched it disappear out of sight and it is believed that it came down at a shallow angle causing the blast to spread outwards. Ken Orvis was woken up at his home in Stanmore Road by 'the roaring sound above. That's what woke me. I thought it was the engine but then I realised they only fell when the engine stopped. Then came the explosion, the noise being audible for miles around.' Cyril Halsey was awakened by the blast. 'The windows came in and there was glass all over us but the only injury was to our dog. The back door blew in and hit him on the head. We rushed out and could see the flames. Our father, who was in the AFS, sent us back home as children were not allowed to stay around there.' *Right:* A mobile listening squad was called in to detect survivors buried under the rubble.

BETWEEN 21.00 ON SATURDAY, JULY 29, TO 20.59 ON SUNDAY, JULY 30			**(Airburst ✳)**
21.30 Kenardington ✳	23.09 Merton	00.57 Shipley	13.45 City
21.34 Hastingleigh	23.11 Merton	00.57 East Farleigh ✳	13.45 Ewhurst
21.35 Hadlow	23.11 Stone	01.26 Hollingbourne	13.45 Canvey Island
21.35 Beckley	23.12 Carshalton	02.32 Stapleford Abbotts	13.47 Buxted ✳
21.35 Boxley	23.14 Hawkinge	02.57 Leyton	13.50 Coulsdon
21.35 Off Dover ✳	23.29 Heston	03.04 Islington	13.50 Smarden
21.38 Chislehurst	23.36 St Leonards	03.04 Watford	13.51 Beckenham
21.39 Lambeth	23.54 Dagenham	03.10 Hampstead	14.07 Hackney
21.41 Leatherhead	23.54 Erith	03.21 Little Baddow	16.04 Bilsington
21.48 Brenchley	23.55 Purleigh	03.26 Forest Row	16.08 Sutton
21.53 Beckenham	23.56 Forest Row	03.34 Newhaven	17.28 Harrow
22.50 Aldington	23.58 South Weald	03.37 Ruislip	18.02 Chiddingly
22.57 St Mary-in-Marsh	00.02 Bethnal Green	13.35 Rochester	18.06 West Dean
22.58 Off Hythe ✳	00.03 West Ham	13.36 Croydon	18.06 Edenbridge
23.01 Lydd	00.36 Harrow	13.36 Leatherhead	18.07 Peasmarsh
23.01 Stanford	00.49 Wanstead	13.37 Kenardington	18.09 Croydon
23.04 Off Hythe ✳	00.49 Cranbrook	13.40 Bilsington	18.10 Hackney
23.07 Burwash	00.49 Off Hythe ✳	13.40 Fletching	18.10 Esher
23.08 Seabrook	00.52 Tandridge	13.40 Northiam	18.10 Wandsworth
23.08 Ewhurst ✳	00.54 Croydon	13.44 West Ham	18.14 Woolwich
23.08 Hutton	00.54 Tollesbury	13.45 Epsom	18.15 Hailsham
23.09 Fulham	00.57 West Ham	13.45 Beddington	18.16 City

At the time Dorrice Ephithite was visiting her daughter at No. 101 Sandringham Road. When the sirens sounded, she got up and dressed, lying down on the bed beside her husband in the back bedroom. 'At about three in the morning, a flying bomb struck the house. I was covered with debris. My husband was beside me. Men came in the dark to get me.' Two days later she identified the body of her husband and grand-daughter but it was not for a further eight months that her daughter, who had been misidentified in the confusion and mistakenly buried under another name, was officially declared dead and a death certificate issued. Twenty-one adult females, 13 males, two female children and one male child were taken from the debris: a total of 37 dead. Among the dead were understood to be American troops attending a party, and several of the fatalities were evacuees who had come from London to escape the bombing. Sixty-four were injured; 50 houses damaged beyond repair, 500 other houses damaged to a lesser degree and 100 shops in St Albans Road lost their windows.

The site today of what was Watford's worst tragedy. Alan Tomkins pictured the tell-tale break in Sandringham Road.

23.39 6 miles SSE of Dungeness	23.53 Twineham	03.44 Wembley	15.12 Croydon
23.42 Rolvenden	23.54 Ilford	03.54 Wembley	15.25 Westerham
23.43 Brede	23.55 Beddington	03.59 Harwell	18.08 Gooden (in sea)
23.44 Swanscombe	23.58 Harrow	14.54 Erith	18.10 Gooden (in sea) *
23.46 Challock	23.59 Stanford Rivers	14.55 Horne	18.12 Mayfield
23.47 Godstone	00.02 Wembley	14.55 Goudhurst	18.14 Woolwich
23.48 Hammersmith	00.10 Barnes	14.57 Sutton	18.15 Ticehurst
23.49 4 miles East of Fairlight	00.15 Framfield	15.01 Lewisham	18.15 South Ockenden
23.50 Battersea	00.21 Hackney	15.01 Chevening	18.16 Greenwich
23.50 Woolwich	03.34 Hornsey	15.02 Croydon	18.17 Epsom
23.50 Slaugham	03.38 East Barnet	15.03 Bermondsey	18.19 Heston
23.50 Kelvedon Hatch	03.38 Ealing	15.04 Hourdon	18.20 East Grinstead
23.52 Beddington	03.40 Fulham	15.10 Pembury	18.22 Lewisham
23.53 Croydon	03.40 Whinburgh	15.11 Wimbledon	

On the outbreak of war there were some 1,600 local fire brigades throughout the country, but there were no county, regional or national standards and no central supervision. Even the size of hose couplings varied. An Auxiliary Fire Service had been set up in 1938 with unpaid part-time volunteers to increase manpower but it was not until the aftermath of one of the heaviest raids on London in May 1941 that legislation was rushed through Parliament to bring a

National Fire Service into being. It became operational under Commander Aylmer Firebrace on August 18, 1941 and by the time that the flying bomb attacks began in 1944, the emergency services were well prepared. Although Planet News were unable to state the location in their captions for this sequence of photographs other than 'southern England', they were taken on June 23 so there are plenty of possibilities in London that day, (see page 82).

23.18 Monkton	07.01 Leatherhead	09.54 Dagenham	14.21 Wanstead
23.26 Canewdon	07.05 Bexley	09.54 Maresfield	15.20 Lydden
23.32 Foulness *	07.05 Sedlescombe	09.54 Rolvenden	15.25 Off Bexhill
23.33 City	07.16 Sutton	14.05 Northiam	15.25 Guestling
23.34 Barnet	09.45 Coulsdon	14.12 Dunton Green	15.27 Lower Beeding
23.35 Ramsden Bellhouse	09.48 Off Hastings	14.13 Seal	15.28 Chislehurst
06.49 Off Hythe *	09.48 Off Bexhill	14.14 Fulham	15.29 Camberwell
06.50 Off Hastings *	09.48 South Hornchurch	14.15 Lambeth	15.32 Stepney
06.57 Orpington	09.49 Beddington	14.15 Deptford	15.33 West Chiltington
06.58 Wandsworth	09.49 Greenwich	14.15 Bromley	15.36 Eastbourne
06.59 Beckenham	09.49 Penge	14.15 Westfield *	15.36 Eastbourne
07.00 Croydon	09.49 Stepney	14.17 Leyton	15.42 Croydon
07.00 St Nicholas at Wade	09.50 Camberwell	14.19 Reigate	15.57 Stepney

Their chief photographer 'Andy' Andrews (see page 90) was quickly on the scene and, as the Planet News office was in Johnson's Court, just off Fleet Street, he was most probably picturing the incident that day in the borough of Holborn.

One of the most iconic photographs taken that day featured the rescue of a screaming child. It has been published many times before as a classic illustration of the Blitz although, as seen here, it started out being very heavily censored. The Prime Minister said of the Blitz that it was 'a sad tale of human sorrow and suffering and wholesale destruction of homes'.

On August 2 Churchill had given a further report to Parliament at which he announced that the total number of flying bombs sent to Britain was then 5,375 which had killed 4,735. However, from the July high of 1,106 bombs falling in the London Civil Defence Region, the August total had dropped to 539 — less even than the June figure of 696. In the last week of the month only 37 V1s reached the Capital, the last major attack being on August 28 when, of the 94 flying bombs which approached the coast, all but four were destroyed — 65 by the guns, 23 by fighters and two by balloons. It was, said Churchill, 'a record bag', a day on which the V1 was truly mastered and, unaware of the new shell fuze, 'the Germans who keenly watched the performance of our guns from across the Channel were completely bewildered by the success of our artillery.' By now the Wachtel organisation was being forced to pull back into Holland to avoid the risk of capture by the British and Canadian troops rushing northwards following the defeat of the German armies in Normandy.

BETWEEN 21.00 ON TUESDAY, AUGUST 1, TO 20.59 ON WEDNESDAY, AUGUST 2 (Airburst *)

04.07	Barking	06.25	Beddington	08.34	Banstead	12.58	Tilford
04.07	Oxted	06.25	Croydon	08.34	Dagenham	12.59	Bromley
04.09	West Ham	06.25	Hooe	08.34	Newchurch	12.59	Chislehurst
04.11	Barking	06.26	Seal	08.40	Ightham	12.59	East Ham
04.11	Farningham	06.27	Swanscombe	12.45	Little Horsted	13.00	Beckenham
04.11	Feltham	06.28	Deptford	12.51	Hollington *	13.00	Beddington
04.11	Off Beachy Head	06.29	Kensington	12.52	Ewhurst	13.00	Dagenham
04.12	St Pancras	06.29	Lewisham	12.55	Lewisham	13.00	Framfield
04.14	Forest Row	06.30	Cranleigh	12.55	Sedlescombe	13.00	Woolwich
04.15	Leigh	06.34	Orpington	12.56	Beckenham	13.02	East Ham
04.24	Shoreditch	06.47	Leyton	12.57	Ightham	13.02	Woolwich
04.31	Chislehurst	08.19	Beckenham	12.57	Lewisham	13.03	Woolwich
06.15	Brightling	08.25	Linton	12.57	Off Dymchurch	13.05	Tring
06.21	Hooe	08.29	Lewisham	12.58	Frant	13.06	Hayes

West Ham United Football Stadium, the home of the 'Hammers' since 1904, was hit by a flying bomb shortly after 4 a.m. on August 2 (top). The Boleyn ground (also known as Upton Park) had to be vacated for 14 games, the team returning in December 1944 after having won nine away games on nine consecutive Saturdays.

Having been awarded a 99-year lease on the Olympic Stadium at Stratford, in May 2016, West Ham played its last game at Upton Park following the sale of the ground for £40 million for redevelopment. However, before demolition, it was featured in the finale of the film *Final Score*.

We have already explained that the only location permitted to be published was 'Southern England' which, without more clues, makes it difficult to trace where particular photographs were taken. *Right:* This *Daily Mail* photo from early August was simply captioned: 'A surface shelter in a working class district of Southern England received the full blast of a flying bomb. Some of those taking shelter came out uninjured, but none were killed.' Implying that there were also serious injuries, the print was stamped by the censor: 'Not to be published'. *Below left:* An interesting contrast is provided by this shelter in Central Road, Morden, which survived a near miss at 09.10 hours on July 4 (see page 100). The bomb landed 47 feet away and a detailed report, produced by the London Region about the damage, stated that the shelterers were unhurt. *Below right:* The cover to the GPO inspection chamber on the pavement remains to pinpoint the exact spot.

BETWEEN 21.00 ON WEDNESDAY, AUGUST 2, TO 20.59 ON THURSDAY, AUGUST 3 (Airburst ✳)							
00.38	Off Eastbourne	01.44	Brasted	03.51	Lewisham	07.37	Woolwich
00.40	Biddenden	01.45	Westminster	04.04	Orpington	08.14	Mitcham
00.43	Croydon	01.46	Hythe	04.16	Poplar	08.39	Ilford
00.44	Leyton	01.46	Off Burmarsh ✳	04.18	Wandsworth	08.56	East Ham
00.44	Wandsworth	01.47	Farningham	04.19	Croydon	09.10	Coulsdon
00.44	Enfield	01.49	Off Lydd	04.33	Banstead	09.17	Wandsworth
00.44	Old Romney	01.51	Croydon	04.40	Battersea	09.53	Greenwich
00.45	Greenwich	01.52	Leyton	04.48	Chislehurst	09.59	Wimbledon
00.45	Althorne	01.55	Northumberland	04.54	West Ham	10.20	Willesden
00.46	Barnes		Bolton	04.57	Orpington	10.23	Camberwell
00.47	Walthamstow	02.00	Orpington	04.58	Bexley	10.26	Epsom
00.50	Poplar	02.05	Igtham	05.00	Mitcham	10.35	Coulsdon
00.51	Bethnal Green	02.12	Off St Leonards	05.00	Lambeth	10.54	Beckenham
00.51	East Ham	02.14	Aldington	05.09	Beckenham	11.20	Penge
00.54	Merton	02.15	Tunbridge Wells	05.20	Coulsdon	11.32	Woolwich
00.55	Lewisham	02.19	Barking	05.20	Coulsdon	11.34	Woolwich
00.56	Camberwell	02.23	Wembley	05.21	Ilford	12.17	Beckenham
00.59	Mitcham	02.24	Stepney	05.23	Orpington	12.18	Beckenham
01.02	Carshalton	02.52	Poplar	05.40	Coulsdon	12.20	Beckenham
01.05	Barnes	02.56	Carshalton	05.44	Wandsworth	12.23	Bromley
01.14	Bethnal Green	02.56	St Pancras	05.54	Orpington	12.24	Esher
01.20	Dartford	02.57	Wandsworth	06.04	Croydon	12.31	Woolwich
01.21	Stepney	03.06	Battersea	06.21	Woolwich	23.32	Fulham
01.25	Dagenham	03.10	Croydon	06.22	Greenwich	23.36	Harrow
01.25	Southfleet	03.22	Poplar	06.50	Ilford	23.38	Edmonton
01.28	Wartling	03.22	City	06.50	Orpington	23.38	Hayes
01.30	Woolwich	03.22	Barking	06.50	Greenwich	23.40	Hackney
01.35	Hendon	03.23	Stepney	06.50	Greenwich	23.44	Aldershot
01.37	Walthamstow	03.28	Brentford	06.55	Coulsdon	23.53	Crawley
01.40	Ilford	03.38	Camberwell	07.03	Greenwich		
01.40	Old Romney	03.47	Islington	07.08	Uxbridge		
01.40	Biddenden	03.48	Wandsworth	07.20	Camberwell		

It was also notable that the heaviest attack so far occurred between dusk on August 2 to dusk on the following day. In dull, cloudy weather, 210 flying bombs crossed the coast and 103 fell in London; an exceptional day, not only in weight of attack, but in the proportion of bombs that penetrated to the capital.

For the period as a whole, only a little over 33 per cent of bombs reported by the defences succeeded in reaching their target compared to 44 per cent for the first five weeks of the attack. That this was so was largely due to the improved performance of the guns. Between July 17 and 24 — the first week in which the guns were operating in their new positions on the coast — the percentage of bombs destroyed by anti-aircraft fire was only slightly better than in the previous most-successful week. The next week, however, saw a notable improvement: out of nearly 600 possible targets, the guns destroyed 140, which represented a destruction rate of

Although Britain had lost the race with Germany to be the first in the field with a jet-powered aircraft, on July 27 the RAF's No. 616 Squadron at Manston received operational clearance to baptise the twin-engined Gloster Meteor. (The Luftwaffe had introduced their Messerschmitt Me 262 in April 1944 although the two aircraft never met each other in combat.)

24 per cent compared to 16 in the previous week. There was a further slight improvement in the period July 31 to August 7, a week of consistently bad weather, and one in which the Germans launched more bombs than in any previous week. Then, in the week August 7-14, the guns destroyed 120 of the 305 flying bombs that were presented to them as targets, and for the first time their percentage of successes exceeded that of the fighters.

The steady improvement reflected the introduction of the new equipment but it also signifies the success of the gun detachments in familiarising themselves with the new drills that were entailed. This was the case with the light guns as well as the heavy as in order that the Bofors could be fired at unseen

targets, the No. 3 Predictor — which hitherto had been used exclusively with heavy guns — was adapted and brought into use by LAA regiments.

Although the performance of the defences as a whole showed a notable improvement over the first weeks of the attack, the successes of the fighters had diminished. It was recognised that fighters patrolling over the sea would be compensated for the bisection of their patrol area by the gun belt only if an improved technique of control was achieved by the radar stations. For this, radar had to detect flying bombs at least 60 miles away, track them continuously and accurately, and provide the fighter pilot with precise information on the course of his target. All this had to be done sufficiently quickly to allow the pilot time to

BETWEEN 21.00 ON THURSDAY, AUGUST 3, TO 20.59 ON FRIDAY, AUGUST 4 (Airburst *)							
01.23	Lympne	15.44	Challock	16.35	Esher *	19.03	Ashford
01.25	Benenden	15.45	Off Pevensey *	16.37	Orpington	19.03	West Cock
01.27	Aylesford	15.46	Lewisham	16.40	Goudhurst	19.05	Barking
01.28	Off Littlestone *	15.47	Orpington	16.40	Biddenden	19.05	Coulsdon
01.30	Leyton	15.47	Off Hythe *	17.05	Lydd *	19.05	Merton
01.30	Staplehurst	15.48	Itchingfield	18.02	Off Folkestone *	19.05	Speldhurst
01.34	Stepney	15.48	Ashurst Wood	18.05	Tenterden	19.06	Tonbridge *
02.00	Charing	15.49	Woolwich	18.05	Little Horsted	19.19	Coulsdon
02.12	Benenden	15.49	Carshalton	18.07	Lewisham	19.23	Dallington *
02.13	Lydd	15.49	Laughton	18.08	Lewisham	19.35	East Peckham
02.20	Off Littlestone	15.50	Lewisham	18.09	Bermondsey	19.37	Lamberhurst
02.25	Hellingly	15.50	Woolwich	18.09	Langley	19.54	Carshalton
02.27	Leybourne	15.51	East Ham	18.09	Brightling	20.05	Udimore
02.28	Stanway	15.51	Goudhurst	18.09	Abinger	20.06	Lydd *
02.30	Hadlow	15.52	West Ham	18.10	Kenardington *	20.07	Goudhurst *
02.41	Ruckinge	15.53	Lewisham	18.10	Funtington	20.07	Woodchurch
02.44	Off Littlestone *	15.57	Battle	18.10	Ash	20.10	Off Broomhill *
02.53	Off Folkestone *	15.57	Battle	18.11	Betchworth	20.14	Linton
03.06	Off Littlestone *	16.20	Appledore	18.11	Off Beachy Head	20.14	Off Littlestone
03.10	Littlebourne	16.23	Marden *	18.12	Lewisham	20.15	Ash *
03.10	Maidstone	16.24	Off Lydd *	18.16	Hawridge	20.15	Framfield
03.13	Off Canvey Island	16.25	Coulsdon	18.19	Croydon	20.17	Beddington
03.14	Off Dymchurch	16.25	Ewhurst *	18.20	Aldington	20.17	Croydon
03.16	Great Parndon	16.25	Hadlow	18.20	Peasmarsh	20.20	Herstmonceux
03.21	Whitstable	16.27	Beckenham	18.26	Whatlington	20.20	All Hallows
03.22	Off Sheerness	16.27	Off Pevensey *	18.56	Off Eastbourne *	20.21	Seale
03.23	Hythe *	16.28	Chislehurst	18.56	Aldington *	20.23	Off Eastbourne *
03.23	Tenterden	16.29	Headcorn	18.56	Marden	20.24	Leigh
03.27	Barnet	16.30	Croydon	18.58	Off Littlestone	23.33	East Sutton
03.32	Gillingham	16.30	Chilham	18.58	Ashford *	23.46	Hendon
03.44	Off Hythe *	16.31	Camberwell	19.00	Orpington	23.46	Thornham
03.45	Benenden	16.31	Woolwich	19.00	Snargate	23.48	Much Hadham
03.48	Kemsing	16.31	Wadhurst	19.00	Chiddingly	23.49	Hendon
04.08	Broomhill *	16.32	Leyton	19.00	Speldhurst	23.49	Canterbury
04.26	Icklesham	16.32	Frant	19.03	Croydon		

The top speed of the Meteor at sea level — around 385 mph — was not really on a par with the Tempest's 408 mph, but No. 616 achieved its first success on August 4 when Flying Officer T. D. 'Dixie' Dean in EE216 tipped and destabilised a bomb with his wing after his gun jammed. *Left:* This is Frank Wootton's impression entitled: 'Meteor Strikes the First Blow'. *Right:* This tree at Headcorn, still very much alive and bearing its wartime scars, is reputedly the one hit by the V1 crashing at Headcorn at 16.29.

On August 4 the RAF were able to deploy six Meteors from their base at Manston. (The day before, Flight Lieutenant Graves had been denied a unique first when a Mustang flew between his aircraft and his target, thus preventing him from completing the first jet-interceptor destruction of a V1 flying bomb.) August 4 was a hazy morning with poor visibility that prevented any operational flying but by late afternoon the weather had cleared sufficiently to allow seven Meteors to scramble — the six operational machines and one of the two prototypes currently on the strength of the squadron. The Operations Record Book reports that 'today, 4th August, the first flying bomb was destroyed by a jet-propelled aircraft. This note in Squadron and, indeed, aviation history can be recorded to Flying Officer T. D. Dean. Flying Officer Dean took off from Manston at 15.45 to patrol an inland area under "Kingsley 11" [Biggin Hill] control. At 16.16 hours a Diver was sighted at 1,000 feet near Tonbridge [sic] on a course of 330 and at a speed of 365 I.A.S. Dean dived down from 4,500 feet at a speed of 450 mph and attacked from dead astern but his four 20mm cannons failed to fire owing to a technical fault which is now being investigated. Flying level alongside the bomb he manoeuvered his wing tip a few inches under the wing of the flying bomb and by pulling upwards sharply he sent the bomb diving to earth four miles south of Tonbridge [sic]. Flying Officer J. K. Rodger sighted a bomb at 16.40 hrs near Tenterden on a course of 318 degrees at 3,000 feet at a speed of 340 mph. Attacking from astern, Rodger fired two bursts each of two seconds and saw the Diver crash and explode five miles north-west of Tenterden. The Squadron, now thrilled at the first two kills, are ready for more!'

S E C R E T

CONSOLIDATED DIVER REPORT   62

NO. 616 SQDN.

R.A.F. STATION MANSTON.

F/O. T.D. DEAN

At 1545 hours I was "scrambled" (under Kinsley 11 Control) for Anti Diver Patrol between Ashford and Robertsbridge.

Flying at 4,500 feet 340 m.p.h. I.A.S. I saw one Diver 4 to 5 miles south east of Tenderton flying at 1000 feet on a course of 330° estimated speed of 365 m.p.h. (16.16 hours)

From 2½ miles behind the Diver I dived down from 4,500 feet at 470 m.p.h. Closing in to attack I found my 4 x 20 m.m. guns would not fire owing to a technical trouble now being investigated. I then flew my Meteor alongside the Diver for approx. 20 - 30 seconds. Gradually I manoeuvered my wing tip a few inches under the wing of the Diver, then pulling my aircraft upwards and sharply I turned the Diver over on its back and sent it diving to earth approx. 4 miles south of Tonbridge.

On return to Manston I was informed that R.O.C. had confirmed one Diver had crashed at position given by me.

This is the first Pilotless aircraft to be destroyed by a jet propelled aircraft.

Claim 1 "Diver" Destroyed

Date   4. 8. 44
Sqdn.   616
Aircraft   Meteor Mark 1
Pilot   F/O. DEAN
Call-
sign   HUGO 24.
Time up 1545 hrs. Time down 16.35 hrs.
Weather 3/10 cloud at 5,000 ft.
        visibility good.   Sgd. ....F/O

03.15 Hartfield	04.56 Off Dymchurch ✳	16.34 In Thames near Thurrock	18.53 Woodchurch ✳
04.32 Off Dymchurch	06.55 Hadlow	16.35 Pevensey	18.54 Framfield
04.34 Petham	07.00 Dymchurch ✳	16.35 Warbleton	18.54 Off Dymchurch ✳
04.34 Woodchurch	07.01 Off New Romney ✳	16.37 Epsom	18.55 Heathfield
04.36 Woolwich	07.03 Brede ✳	16.40 Beckley	18.57 Pevensey ✳
04.38 Lewisham	07.04 Cranbrook	16.40 Rotherfield	18.58 Snodland
04.39 Bromley	07.07 Brenchley	16.45 Camberwell	18.59 Slaugham
04.40 Wandsworth	07.09 Battersea	16.45 Greenhithe	19.03 Wartling
04.42 Oxted	07.09 Waldron	16.46 Chislehurst	19.04 Challock
04.43 Brenchley	07.12 Romford	16.46 Sutton	19.07 Off Rye
04.46 Off Burmarsh ✳	07.15 Weald	16.49 Croydon	19.31 Off Lydd ✳
04.46 Off Hastings	07.20 Burwash	18.15 Broomhill	
04.46 Stapleford Abbotts	16.26 Bodiam ✳	18.15 Wadhurst	
04.50 Mayfield	16.33 Mitcham	18.53 Tenterden ✳	

Before . . . then . . . and now. South London had no sooner picked itself up from the Lewisham bomb when it was smashed down again by another shopping incident, only this time it was at 4.45 p.m. on a Saturday afternoon, August 5. The Royal Arsenal Co-op on Lordship Lane, Camberwell, was crowded at the time with a queue of passengers waiting at the tram stop outside. The RAF history quotes 16 killed and 35 injured but other sources indicate 23 dead and 42 injured. Incidents in public places yielded the greatest problem with determining a precise head count as frequently the mortuary returns had to brutally state things like 'three baskets of remains', 'unidentified' or 'not fit to view'.

00.21 East Guildford	03.55 Marden	07.05 Lydd	17.04 Folkestone
00.27 Croydon	03.59 Chislehurst	07.08 Burwash	17.05 Tunbridge Wells
00.31 East Blatchington	04.40 Rye Harbour ✳	13.18 Pevensey ✳	17.05 East Peckham
00.33 Coulsdon	04.43 Framfield	13.21 Wadhurst	17.05 Burwash
00.36 Lewisham	04.43 Woodchurch	13.22 Off Burmarsh	17.05 Off Littlestone ✳
02.31 Off Littlestone	04.45 Four Elms ✳	13.23 Ashburnham	17.06 Bromley
02.37 Wadhurst	04.46 Westerham	13.25 Woodchurch	17.07 Tunbridge Wells
03.28 Woolwich	04.47 Falding	13.26 Brasted	17.08 Wandsworth
03.28 Wadhurst	04.48 Wandsworth	13.28 Orpington	17.08 Great Chart
03.29 Hornchurch	04.48 Off Broomhill	13.30 Ruckinge	17.09 Camberwell
03.30 Orpington	04.50 West Ham	13.30 Bidborough	17.09 Caterham
03.30 Off Beachy Head	04.52 Off Broomhill	13.32 Wandsworth	17.09 Brightling
03.36 Chevening	05.45 Goudhurst	13.33 Shoreditch	17.10 Orpington
03.37 Off Folkestone ✳	05.49 New Romney	13.33 Shoreham	17.10 Dartford
03.42 Broomhill ✳	05.52 Aldington	13.35 Wrotham	17.11 Camberwell
03.44 Off Littlestone ✳	05.55 Oxted	13.37 Singleton	17.11 Shoreditch
03.49 Tenterden	05.55 Brenchley	13.39 Croydon	17.13 Poplar
03.50 Broomhill	05.58 Lambeth	13.40 Gondhurst	17.13 Dagenham
03.51 Cranbrook	05.59 Croydon	13.40 Goldhanger	17.13 Woolwich
03.53 Wadhurst	06.00 West Ham	13.42 Stepney	17.17 Laughton
03.54 Deptford	06.05 Hatfield Park	13.43 Wandsworth	17.24 Ticehurst
03.55 Orpington	06.08 North Weald	13.45 Barcombe	17.29 Poplar
03.55 Bermondsey	06.13 Bexley	13.55 Iden	
03.55 East Ham	06.15 Brightling	16.59 Sellindge ✳	

It was a few minutes before 7 p.m on August 5 when a pilot in pursuit of a flying bomb that was approaching Maidstone shot it down only to have it crash in the built-up area of Snodland. Police Sergeant William Braddick and his wife Olive were killed in Elmfield Villas on Malling Road together with Anne Orpin, aged 14, Bernice Stokes and Horace Wells. The Brooker family were also killed in adjacent Maida Vale. Fred Collard was killed in the street and Narcissa Gladdish, who was injured, died later in hospital.

make interception and destroy the bomb before it reached the coastal gun belt. For once that happened, the bomb came within the exclusive sphere of the guns where all pilots were expressly forbidden to trespass. In the event, the problem was never satisfactorily solved.

Overland the difficulties of interception were not so great. Basically, the problem was the same as over the sea, i.e. to give the fighter the necessary informa-

tion, sufficiently early, for interception to be made and pressed home, but it was found in practice that the gun-fire from the guns on the coast gave the patrolling pilots an excellent indication of the course of a bomb. Very often pilots could wait behind the guns and fall on those that passed unscathed through the barrage. In addition, there were facilities for aiding interception over land that were absent at sea. The Royal Observer Corps centres at Maidstone and Horsham were used for the control of patrolling fighters, the advantage being that this cut out the transmission of information to the Group operations room. ROC posts and a number of searchlight units were also used to speed up the passing of information to the patrolling pilot. They were equipped with white Schermuly rockets that were fired to mark the course of a flying bomb. Red rockets were used to mark the southern boundary of the balloon barrage. Searchlight beams were also extensively used to mark patrol lines.

Yesterday a scene of high drama but today all has been restored.

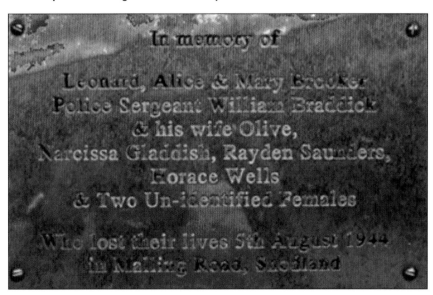

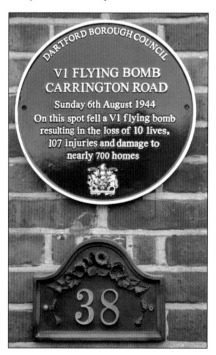

In recent years, many town councils have marked the sites of wartime tragedies, and at Snodland an 'In Memoriam' plaque *(left)* was unveiled at the Medical Centre in Catts Alley by Narcissa's brother John. *Right:* Further west, Dartford Borough Council have remembered the flying bomb that hit Carrington Road at 17.10 the following day.

143

On August 16 (page 153), a Canadian pilot, Flight Lieutenant John Malloy from No. 274 Squadron, was chasing a V1 as it crossed the coast at Dover. His attempts to shoot it down failed and an eyewitness at Newington (between Sittingbourne and Chatham) said that 'eventually the fighter drew level and with his wing-tip threw the weapon over. It then dived and exploded under the railway bridge in Oak Lane.' Just at that moment, the 3.35 p.m. train from Victoria to Ramsgate was approaching the bridge, about three-quarters of a mile from Rainham. To the driver's horror, at 16.47 the bridge suddenly exploded before his eyes. Although he instantly slammed on his emergency brakes, the engine crashed down into the gap and overturned, before rolling down the embankment. The second and third coaches ended up spanning the gap. In this incident eight people were killed and 16 seriously injured.

A temporary bridge was rapidly erected and trains were running over the line again within three days. This is the bridge today.

The result was that many more flying bombs were shot down overland than over the sea. In these four weeks the relative figures were 395 and 231 and there was no great decline from the rate of destruction that had been achieved by fighters in the first phase of the attack.

There was actually an increase in the number of V1s that were destroyed by fighters operating at night. This was partly explained by the move of the guns to the coast as it left the approaches to London free for the unimpeded operations of night fighters and searchlights.

It was due also to increased skill and efficiency on the part of night fighter crews and searchlight detachments, aided by the ground controls. It was significant that the most consistently successful night squadrons were those that

One other component of the defences improved on its performance prior to the middle of July; this was the balloon barrage. By the end of July, the planned total of 1,750 LZ balloons and 265 Mk VI balloons was deployed. Weather remained the chief factor affecting the flying of the barrage. In the last week of July, when the weather was very bad, the whole barrage was grounded for nearly one-fifth of the time. The following week, when the weather was better but still far from good, this figure fell to one-twentieth, while in the excellent weather of August 9-15 the barrage was fully operational for the whole week.

Destruction of bombs through impact with balloon cables reflected the expansion of the barrage. Expressed as a percentage of bombs destroyed to bombs passing into the barrage, it rose from eight during the second week in July to 15 in the next. It fell to 11 during the bad weather of the last week of the month and then rose again to 18 in the first week of August and 19 in the second. Altogether, 147 flying bombs were brought down by balloons during the period compared to 55 in the previous five weeks.

Later the same day, another V1 was brought down by a fighter at Little Chart, two miles south of Charing in Kent. Just after 8 p.m. that evening, the bomb blasted St Mary's Church in Pluckley Road.

specialised in the work: Nos. 96, 418 and 605 Squadrons, using Mosquitos and Tempests, and two Tempest squadrons — Nos. 3 and 486 — which flew chiefly by day, excelled in the number of bombs destroyed.

Although a replacement church was consecrated in 1958, the original, which had stood since 1500, was retained as a Scheduled Monument and granted Grade II listing. It now stands as memorial to all those who lost their lives from falling flying bombs.

CONFIDENTIAL	M. of H.S., & E. Dept. and AIR MISTRY		BOMB CENSUS	B.C.4.		Sheet No.
Region 12	County: Kent		Total Casualties:			Date: 16 8 44
Administrative Area	Swanscombe R D Balloon Barrage Belt		Killed M S/I M L/I M	F C F C F C		Warnings P and R 1642 Times N 1705
A	B	C	D	E		F
Bomb No & time of fall	Size & type of bomb & X or UX	Judged by F, C or D	Crater size and type of soil	Location and damage notes (Grid reference if no plot is made)		Additional notes by R. & E. Dept. Technical Officers
1 1648	FLY X	F	sand	G/R 115/033927 Sand pit, Western Cross Sand Pit, appr. 1 mile W. of Swanscombe. Sl. blast to 2 storey houses up to 300! Impact with cable Site 655 925 Sqdn G/R 115/065885		1812/4 Balloons

The balloon barrage also played its part: here is the report for the Swanscombe V1 brought down the same day.

The wartime captioning for this picture released on August 8 focusses on the fact that a Ford laundry van has been wrecked by a 'fly', but where and when? Beneath the censor's obliteration we can still just read 'Martins Bank' so a trawl through the 30 London branches revealed it to be at No. 208 Kensington High Street, opened in 1936. With the location found, this incident was one of the worst to strike the West End. The Home Security Report No. 3581 for July 28 simply states that 'a bomb fell in Kensington High Street near Earls Court causing damage to shops and to Troy Court block of flats. 22 persons were killed and 32 seriously injured.' The time was 13.31 (see page 130). Six weeks later the *Kensington News* were able to elaborate: 'Lyons, the Wooden Horse Restaurant, the Aerated Bread Company and another café were packed with diners and there were many shoppers in the streets outside'. However, the death toll by then had risen to 45 with 54 seriously injured and another 116 slightly injured. In fact, it was the worst of all

Kensington's 20 V1s and John Nicholls described how one schoolboy graphically remembered it. 'One day a Doodlebug fell at the top of Earls Court Road during the lunch hour. Over 2,000 people killed and I can remember the bodies being transported to the mortuary at the bottom of our mews using dustcarts. Feet were sticking out the back-end as the stacked bodies were shipped in. Us school kids used to climb up the mortuary windows to watch the bodies being dissected. Proper ghouls we were. Some of the older boys used to get inside the coffins in the playground store and others would then push the younger ones into the building. Huddling in the dark you can imagine the fear when all of a sudden a coffin lid started to open. But we were hardy then and had seen a lot so didn't need counselling like the kids would today. I remember the biggest boy was called Jackson. He smoked and was quite the hero to us small kids. Bit of a villain though and I think he ended up in gaol for burglary.'

Mosquito squadrons, which normally operated as 'Intruders', were first employed over the launch site area in northern France in order to try to spot the sites that were in action. They had little success, and from the middle of July usually patrolled to seaward of the gun belt. All told, 11 Mosquito squadrons and two USAAF P-61A night fighter squadrons, the 422nd and the 425th, as well as detachments from day fighter squadrons, were called upon for night patrols.

The general bombing policy during what was to prove the last fortnight of the main flying bomb attack, i.e. that launched from the belt of modified sites between the Seine and the Pas-de-Calais, showed little change. Compared to that of previous weeks, Air Chief Marshal Tedder still had difficulty in obtaining from the Eighth Air Force as big an effort against 'Crossbow' targets as he wished. Bomber Command's 'Crossbow' contribution was also small. During the week of August 16-22, only

In the mid-1960s Martins had over 750 branches in the UK but, reluctantly, in 1968 a decision had to be made to merge with Barclays. Now, with its façade changed, the old bank building has become a Post Office.

BETWEEN 21.00 ON SUNDAY, AUGUST 6, TO 20.59 ON MONDAY, AUGUST 7 (Airburst ✳)							
01.35	Off Rye ✳	06.06	Off Dover	07.30	Camberwell	10.56	Brenzett
01.35	Warbleton	06.08	Cranbrook	07.30	Darenth	10.57	Malden
01.40	Benenden ✳	06.10	Poplar	07.30	Havering	10.57	Swanscombe
01.44	Dagenham	06.15	Hawkhurst	07.35	Hughenden	10.59	Woolwich
01.44	West Ham	06.16	Poplar	07.38	Wanstead	11.00	Poplar
01.45	Laindon Hills	06.25	Withyham ✳	07.45	Elmstead	11.03	Bonnington
06.03	Boughton Monchelsea	06.28	Hornchurch	08.05	Off Burmarsh	11.05	Frant
06.04	Brenzett	06.30	Croydon	08.06	Hawkinge	23.09	Brasted
06.04	Off Dymchurch ✳	07.18	New Romney	08.07	Appledore	23.10	Frant
06.04	Smeeth	07.20	Dallington	08.16	Off Folkestone	23.14	Stepney
06.05	Cranbrook ✳	07.20	Orlestone	08.20	Cooling	23.16	Winkford
06.05	Goudhurst	07.24	Off Dymchurch ✳	10.50	Folkestone	23.17	Romford
06.05	Hooe	07.25	Ash	10.50	Off Littlestone		
06.06	Croydon	07.25	Monks Horton	10.52	Burmarsh		

1,100 tons out of a total of nearly 12,000 dropped by the two heavy bomber forces fell on 'Crossbow' targets.

During the next week, August 23-29, the proportion effort was higher: 4,528 tons were dropped on 'Crossbow' targets out of a total effort of more than 17,000 tons.

'Crossbow' bombing policy itself was complicated by the reappearance of targets connected with rocket as distinct from flying bomb-attack. This was as a result of the more-precise intelligence on rocket development and the imminence of rocket attack that had been received during the previous six weeks. Thus, the large sites at Watten and Mimoyecques were returned to the schedule of 'Crossbow' targets and were very heavily attacked by Bomber Command on August 25 and 27 respectively.

We have already seen how the 'Vergeltungswaffe Eins' disproved the old adage that lightning never strikes twice in the same place (see pages 84 and 98). A variation on that theme was when a building that had been badly damaged earlier in the war by conventional bombing, received a second dose . . . but this time from a flying bomb! Here is a very good example. Upton Lane School in West Ham was blitzed on the night of March 8/9, 1941. Then early on August 12, 1944 — fortunately a Saturday in the middle of the school holidays — the school took a direct hit from a V1. The building was too badly damaged to be repaired and the site was subsequently cleared to make way for the Stratford Grammar School which first opened its doors in 1959. Now, after a further change in 2015, it has rebuilt as the Stratford School Academy.

BETWEEN 21.00 ON MONDAY, AUGUST 7, TO 20.59 ON TUESDAY, AUGUST 8 (Airburst ✳)							
01.41	Off Bexhill ✳	05.13	Woolwich	06.01	Ticehurst	09.01	Amberley
01.48	Kemsing	05.16	Horsmonden ✳	06.03	Croydon	09.01	Chigwell
01.50	Buxted	05.16	Off Fairlight	06.05	Folkestone	09.01	Oxted
01.50	East Peckham	05.24	Islington	06.19	Esher	09.02	Bedmond
01.52	Boxley	05.50	Off Folkestone ✳	06.24	Camberwell	09.03	Banstead
01.52	East Peckham	05.54	Benenden	06.26	Esher	09.05	Crowhurst
01.54	Bexley	05.54	Mayfield	08.50	Cuxton	09.05	Ilford
01.55	Caterham	05.55	Lingfield	08.53	Off Winchelsea	09.06	Bidborough
05.03	Staplehurst	05.55	Lydd	08.55	Battle	09.06	Near West Thurrock
05.05	Hawkhurst	05.58	Cuckfield	08.57	Banstead	09.22	Poplar
05.08	Boughton Malherbe	05.58	Off Hythe	08.58	Banstead	23.08	Woodchurch
05.08	Lingfield	06.00	Hackney	09.00	Lewisham	23.11	Orpington
05.10	Off Folkestone ✳	06.01	Billingshurst	09.00	Leyton	23.17	West Hoathley
05.12	Esher	06.01	Rainham	09.00	West Ham	23.18	Eastbourne

BETWEEN 21.00 ON TUESDAY, AUGUST 8, TO 20.59 ON WEDNESDAY, AUGUST 9

06.24	East Ham	06.42	Staplehurst	23.04	Chislehurst
06.31	Lewisham	06.42	Lamberhurst	23.05	Hastings
06.33	Off Dover *	06.43	Ticehurst	23.07	Wennington
06.34	Off Folkestone *	06.45	Folkestone	23.07	Crowborough
06.35	Off Folkestone	06.46	Mitcham	23.12	Shipbourne
06.36	Off Hythe *	06.47	Wandsworth	23.13	Crayford
06.39	Off Hythe *	06.48	Shoreham	23.20	Darenth
06.41	Ightham	07.01	Off Bexhill *		
06.42	Croydon	07.15	Berwick		

BETWEEN 21.00 ON WEDNESDAY, AUGUST 9, TO 20.59 ON THURSDAY, AUGUST 10

03.58	Burwash	04.25	Cobham	17.42	Off Dymchurch
04.02	Rolvenden	04.25	Salehurst	17.43	Lympne
04.04	Off Fairlight *	04.25	Sutton-at-Hone	17.43	Off Hythe *
04.13	Chislehurst	04.26	Off Dymchurch	17.45	Rye *
04.14	Beckenham	04.31	Dorking	17.46	Merton
04.16	Laindon	04.35	Ilford	17.54	Capel-le-Ferne *
04.16	Northiam	04.38	Woodchurch	17.54	Stanford Rivers
04.22	Barking	04.44	South of Dover	17.57	Woking
04.22	Wrotham	17.38	Off Hythe	20.58	Off Dover
04.24	Barham	17.42	Hythe		

Meanwhile in Germany, the presses were beginning to roll on the latest issue of the Luftwaffe's house magazine featuring a double page spread on the V1. This is how the editor began the story: 'Even shortly before the start of the heavy barrage of revenge, the British themselves announced with great words that the whole of London and southern England represent one single offensive camp and weapon arsenal for the invasion. This space has for weeks now been the target of our V1, which is only the first link in a chain of new and strongest German weapons. The military significance of the deployment so far is beyond doubt. The V1, which is launched by a compressed-air installation, includes sufficient aiming apparatus that guarantee her accuracy of fire. She combines in her construction the most-modern ballistic novelties with the latest flight-technical experiences of the Luftwaffe. Churchill had to admit that the V1 threw up "the most serious problems for England"; yes, he even had to resign to admitting "that there were areas in which the damage wrought by the detonation is so large it cannot be repaired by the reserves in repair capabilities".'

At the same time, Churchill was speaking in the House of Commons: 'As long ago as February 22, I warned the House that Hitler was preparing to attack this country by new methods, and it is quite possible that attempts will be made with long-range rockets containing a heavier explosive charge than the flying bomb, and intended to produce a great deal more mischief. London, we may expect, will be the primary target on account of the probable inaccuracy of the rocket weapon. It is by no means certain that the enemy has solved the difficult technical problems connected with the aiming of the rockets, but none the less I do not wish to minimise the ordeal to which we may be subjected, except to say that I am sure it is not one we will not be able to bear. The weight of flying bombs launched against this country from the night of June 15 to the night of July 31 is estimated to be some 4,500 tons. During the same period the Allied Air Forces dropped approximately 48,000 tons of high-explosive bombs on Germany. Of course we try in the main to aim at important military objectives and consequently it may be that there is less loss of life in particular places than when a weapon is used which has no other object than the indiscriminate slaughter of the civilian population.'

The text and captioning is very bland and reveals nothing of substance, but nevertheless we thought it would be interesting to include it verbatim. 'First requirement for the successful deployment of the V1 was the secrecy, which was maintained right to the last. Even today, after the entire world speaks of the deeds of the men of the new weapon, they have not yet moved into the limelight of publicity. Secluded from the outside world, they enter the deep bunkers day after day, which since the deployment of the Vergeltungsfeuer [barrage of revenge], have become their second homes.'

'The men of the new weapon are excellent specialists. The target accuracy of the V1 also requires a precise knowledge of the present meteorological conditions. So that the V1 reaches its target without error the flight engineer here measures the wind speed.'

BETWEEN 21.00 ON THURSDAY, AUGUST 10, TO 20.59 ON FRIDAY, AUGUST 11

00.43 Ticehurst	07.30 Itchingfield	14.07 Kingsnorth	21.02 Great Chart
00.48 Etchingham	07.31 Elham	14.12 Horton Kirby	21.04 Bethersden
01.05 Waldron	07.33 Islington	14.15 Theydon Bois	21.05 Hawkinge
04.00 Frant	07.35 Bermondsey	14.16 Brabourne	21.05 Kenardington
07.22 Croydon	07.35 Barnes	14.17 St Marylebone	21.05 Ruckinge
07.25 Camberwell	14.05 Brabourne	14.20 Much Hadham	21.10 Lambeth
07.25 East Sutton	14.05 Folkestone	14.32 Aldington	21.20 Hinxhill
07.29 Boughton Malherbe	14.05 Stapleford Tawney	17.50 Capel-le-Ferne	21.23 East Ham

Left: 'A man of the new weapon. He was already there on the Eastern and Western Front, now he holds a responsible position with the V1. With visible joy he receives the order for action. In a few minutes a new missile will leave the launching site.' *Centre:* 'The tactical deployment of the V1 requires a well-functioning signal communications network. Through the hands of these men run the fire orders from the higher command.' *Right:* 'The Wachtmeister is in charge of the wireless. He too beams over his entire face as do all the men around the V1, because they know about the effect of the new weapon.'

'Another V1 is prepared for launching. The V1, an extraordinarily powerful creation of German aerial armament, is the first of the revolutionary weapons with which Germany strikes back hard and without pause at the enemy, who wanted to force it to its knees with its terror methods.'

We should remark on the technical excellence of the flying bomb as a weapon. Its simple construction made it cheap to produce, and it was designed to exploit the extraordinarily favourable situation in which the Germans found themselves, able to shoot at such a great target as London from an entire 90° arc running from east to south.

The bomb was hard to shoot down, and if we had not had so much prior warning our defences would have fared poorly. As it was, an analysis of the economics of the campaign showed a large balance in the German favour: the cost of our counter-measures, especially in bombing the sites, exceeded the estimated cost of the campaign to the Germans. But the fact was that we started from a potentially disastrous position geographically, with London a great 'hostage unto fortune' at the focus and mercy of the great French coastal arc; and the balance on which judgement must be passed is not between British and German expenditure but between our expenditure on counter-measures and the damage that would have ensued in lives, material and morale if those counter-measures had not been undertaken.

R. V. JONES, 1978

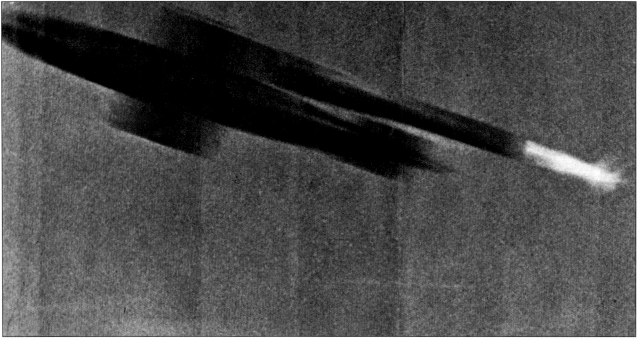

The final caption in the article translates: 'The V1 on its deathly course towards London. The air speed of this projectile is so high that the bomb can only be captured as a ghostly shade by the camera of the war reporter.'

BETWEEN 21.00 ON FRIDAY, AUGUST 11, TO 20.59 ON SATURDAY, AUGUST 12 (Airburst ✳)

01.15 Off Eastbourne	01.35 Boxford	03.09 Stepney	06.24 Wrotham ✳
01.18 Off Littlestone ✳	01.36 Orlestone	03.10 Burmarsh	06.25 West Ham
01.18 Withyham	01.43 South of Dover	03.10 South of Dungeness	06.46 Beddington
01.23 Hadlow	01.45 Gravesend	03.11 Lympne	22.58 Off Icklesham
01.24 Off Folkestone	01.50 Lewisham	03.12 Off Rye ✳	23.05 West Malling
01.26 Frant	01.53 Bexley	03.16 Greenwich	23.08 South of St. Leonards
01.26 Off Fairlight	02.37 Off Hythe	06.16 Off Dover	23.11 Ightham
01.28 Eythorne	03.00 Off Hythe ✳	06.17 Meopham	23.11 Kemsing
01.28 Off Littlestone ✳	03.02 South of Dungeness	06.19 Waltham Holy Cross	23.14 Caterham
01.32 Camberwell	03.03 Off Hythe	06.20 Marks Tey	23.16 Shoreham
01.33 Folkestone	03.06 Boughton Monchelsea	06.20 Penge	23.20 Croydon
01.33 Horton Kirby	03.09 Bermondsey	06.23 Romford	
01.33 Stapleford Abbotts	03.09 Croydon	06.24 Sunbury	

Back in September 1943, Oberst Wachtel had been told that mass production of the V1, mainly at the Volkswagen works at Fallersleben, would reach 5,000 per month by the end of the year, but by mid-November output was only 25 per month and the campaign was scheduled to open in February. However, problems with the compass and fuzing had still not been rectified yet only 38 bombs had been made available at Zempin for testing. Bearing in mind the vulnerability of the Volkswagen site, in March steps were taken to transfer production to the underground Mittelbau works at Nordhausen with a monthly target of 3,000 bombs. There were two other V1 factories, that of Fieseler in Kassel and a second Volkswagen plant at Magdeburg-Schönebeck, while the pulse-jet engine was supplied by Berlin-based Argus Motoren GmbH. By now though — mid-August 1944 — Wachtel was forced to begin to withdraw the left flank of his launching sites in France as the First Canadian Army threatened them.

BETWEEN 21.00 ON SATURDAY, AUGUST 12, TO 20.59 ON SUNDAY, AUGUST 13 (Airburst ✳)

00.10 Dover	04.22 Barking	06.18 Cockfield	08.00 Aldington
00.30 Hackney	06.08 Off Rye	06.18 Hythe	08.09 Off St Margaret's Bay ✳
01.20 Off Hastings	06.10 Goldhanger	06.23 South of Dover	08.10 Lambeth
01.25 Hawkhurst	06.10 Off Dover ✳	07.45 Off Hythe ✳	22.55 Whatlington
01.27 Lambeth	06.11 Off Hythe	07.45 Hythe	22.55 Off Winchelsea
01.46 South of Hastings	06.12 Ulcombe	07.47 Off Dover ✳	22.56 Cooden ✳
02.12 Camberwell	06.14 West Ham	07.52 Staplehurst	23.03 Brede
03.50 Off Eastbourne ✳	06.14 Mereworth	07.53 Wandsworth	23.04 Off Bexhill
03.55 Mayfield ✳	06.15 Throwley	07.54 Bermondsey	23.05 West Ham
03.55 Heathfield	06.15 Lydden	07.55 Westminster	23.05 Cooden
03.58 Lewisham	06.16 Hornsey	07.55 Wandsworth	23.05 Farningham
04.00 Seal	06.16 Orlestone	07.58 Chigwell	23.11 Send

BETWEEN 21.00 ON SUNDAY, AUGUST 13, TO 20.59 ON MONDAY, AUGUST 14 (Airburst ✳)

	04.24 Off Hythe	06.53 Off Hythe ✳	22.56 Off Bexhill
00.44 Off Hastings ✳	04.25 Dymchurch	06.54 Off Burmarsh	22.58 Off Seaford
00.45 Off Hastings	04.27 Rochester	06.57 Aylesford	22.58 Orpington
00.47 Leigh	04.29 Hammersmith	06.58 Bromley	23.05 Off Bexhill ✳
00.50 Eastbourne ✳	04.31 Off Dover ✳	07.00 Barnes	23.07 Yiewsley
04.18 Off Hythe ✳	04.31 Wandsworth	07.00 Leybourne	23.14 SE of Beachy Head
04.19 Off Hythe ✳	04.32 St Pancras	07.00 St Pancras	23.19 Twickenham
04.20 Off Hythe ✳	04.39 Croydon	07.01 Merton	
04.20 Off Icklesham	04.39 Off Dungeness	07.02 Fawkham	
04.23 Rye ✳	06.51 Off Burmarsh ✳	22.54 Off Bexhill	

Referring back to page 95, it was already known that the Volkswagen works was involved in V-Weapon production so on August 5 the plant was subjected to another 270 tons of bombs, delivered by the B-24s of the 93rd Bomb Group.

The attacks opened with one of the rare contributions of the US Fifteenth Air Force to 'Crossbow' counter-measures. On the 16th, 89 Liberators, operating from airfields in the Foggia district of Italy, attacked the hydrogen peroxide plant at Oberraderach, dropping 170 tons of bombs and achieving excellent results.

Apart from the light attacks by the Eighth Air Force against the fuel depot at Pacy-sur-Armançon and the airfields at Eindhoven and Roye/Amy, and light attacks by Bomber Command against modified sites, on which less than 200 tons of bombs were dropped, the only other 'Crossbow' attack during the week of August 16-22 was made by Bomber Command on the 18th against a storage depot at Forêt de l'Isle-Adam in the Oise valley north-west of Paris. Over 700 tons of bombs were dropped and the target area was well covered with craters but the density of trees in the area made any detailed assessment of damage difficult. This was the last attack that it was deemed necessary to make against the group of storage

BETWEEN 21.00 ON MONDAY, AUGUST 14, TO 20.59 ON TUESDAY, AUGUST 15 (Airburst ✱)							
02.02	Off Hythe ✱	04.25	St Mary in Marsh	14.08	Off Hythe	17.55	Snargate
02.03	Off Dover	04.27	Stanford	14.09	Off Hythe	17.56	Meopham
02.04	Lydd	04.28	Brede	14.10	Frant ✱	17.58	Cuxton
02.10	South of Rye	04.28	Hendon	14.10	Ruckinge	17.59	West Ham
02.11	Off Littlestone	04.29	Off Hythe ✱	14.14	Orpington	18.00	Croydon
02.12	Off Rye	04.40	Off Dungeness	14.14	Wanstead	18.03	Off Sandgate ✱
02.14	Ash	08.58	Dymchurch	14.15	Hougham	18.04	Hunsdon
02.14	Off Littlestone	09.00	Ulcombe	14.18	Hackney	18.05	Theydon Bois
02.14	Off Littlestone	09.01	Off Littlestone	14.22	Hythe	18.43	Dymchurch
02.16	Willesden	09.05	Brasted	14.25	Boughton Aluph	18.44	Off Dymchurch
02.17	Off Lydd	09.05	Kingsdown ✱	15.40	Dymchurch	18.44	Off Folkestone
02.18	Enfield	09.05	Mereworth	15.45	Boughton Monchelsea	18.45	Snargate
02.22	Ilford	09.08	Dymchurch	15.49	Camberwell	18.49	Beddington
02.23	Wandsworth	09.09	Wimbledon	15.49	Off Lydd	18.50	Sittingbourne
02.36	Off Dover	09.11	Enfield	15.50	Dartford	18.56	Southfleet
04.18	Off Dungeness	09.15	Off Folkestone	15.51	Off Dungeness	19.00	Rainham
04.19	Off Dymchurch ✱	09.20	Hougham ✱	15.59	Godmersham	19.00	South Stifford
04.22	Acrise	09.30	Hothfield	17.44	Lydd		
04.22	Hothfield ✱	09.38	Rainham	17.48	Off Littlestone ✱		
04.25	Off Hythe	14.07	Off Littlestone	17.55	Goudhurst		

The radio and armament factory at Weimar/Buchenwald, which was suspected of making rocket components, was also added to the list and was attacked by the Eighth Air Force on August 24. Five 'Benito' W/T stations in the Somme—Pas-de-Calais area, operating in a frequency band which it was expected would be used for tracking the rocket, were recommended for attack. Two of those stations were lightly attacked during the last week in August, as were five small liquid oxygen plants in northern France and Belgium. In addition, as the Allied armies advanced to the Seine, the storage depots in the Paris area were suspended from attack and the forward storage depots, rearward of the belt of modified sites, were substituted. These smaller depots were thought to be for rocket rather than flying bomb storage. In attacks of rocket targets between August 16-29, some 2,000 tons of bombs were dropped leaving only some 3,000 for targets connected with flying bombs, quite the smallest effort in any fortnight since flying bomb attacks had begun.

This is how the operation was described by the caption-writer in 1944: 'Nazi War Plant at Fallersleben, located about 20 miles north-east of Brunswick, formerly making motor transport and aircraft wings, shown under attack August 5 by US Eighth Air Force heavy bombers, is now believed to be manufacturing fuselages and other parts for robot bombs.'

It was at 09.53 on August 16 that Walthamstow in East London suffered one of its worst incidents. This is what Home Security first reported at 18.00: 'In Walthamstow there was considerable damage to property including some small factories and a cinema. 11 persons were killed and 78 others injured, 34 of them seriously.' *Left:* The bomb had landed on a busy Wednesday morning on the corner of Hoe Street and High Street where school outfitters Henry Taylor had their store. *Right:* Rescue workers battled throughout the day to recover the dead. Unfortunately, we have not been able to trace a photo of that actual clear-up but this still from a Pathe newsreel shows work underway on a similar incident in the borough.

BETWEEN 21.00 ON TUESDAY, AUGUST 15, TO 20.59 ON WEDNESDAY, AUGUST 16   (Airburst ✳)

05.21 Boughton Aluph	08.39 South-east of Hythe ✳	16.55 Headcorn	19.00 Peasmarsh ✳
05.25 Harrietsham	08.43 Off Dungeness ✳	17.20 Off Littlestone	19.02 Cranbrook
05.28 Off Hythe	08.44 Beddington	17.31 Ham Street	19.06 Teynham
05.29 Doddington	08.45 Fawkham	17.36 Hadlow	19.07 Speldhurst
05.30 Guston ✳	08.46 Barking	17.39 Guestling ✳	19.09 Croydon
05.31 Off Dover	08.46 Theydon Bois	17.39 Off Dymchurch ✳	19.09 Hothfield
05.31 Off Dover	08.47 Lewisham	17.40 Capel-le-Ferne	19.09 Wanstead
05.32 Birling	08.48 Great Sampford	17.40 Cranleigh	19.10 Brabourne
05.38 Off New Romney ✳	08.50 Chesham	17.40 Off Folkestone ✳	19.11 Ilford
05.39 Dover ✳	08.51 Croydon	17.41 Off Folkestone	19.18 Tring
05.39 Off Dover ✳	08.51 Off Dungeness	17.42 Ash	19.18 Wanstead
05.39 Off New Romney ✳	09.32 Off South Foreland ✳	17.43 Stone-cum-Ebony	19.20 Horsmonden
07.00 Brenzett	09.38 Newington	17.49 Lambeth	19.45 Aldington
07.05 Hawkinge	09.40 Folkestone	18.06 Folkestone	19.45 Tenterden
07.10 Off Hythe ✳	09.40 Harrietsham	18.10 Off Lydd	19.50 Appledore
07.10 Plaxtol	09.40 Off Dymchurch	18.12 New Romney	19.50 Orpington
07.10 Tuddenham	09.44 Off Dymchurch ✳	18.13 St Mary in the Marsh	19.50 Sutton Valence ✳
07.11 South-east of Dungeness	09.51 Waltham Holy Cross	18.16 Stone-cum-Ebony	19.57 Off Burmarsh ✳
07.13 Ash	09.53 Walthamstow	18.21 Hawkinge	19.58 Nonington
07.14 Barking	09.57 Off Burmarsh ✳	18.21 Lewisham	20.05 Little Chart
07.15 Barking	16.38 Off Dover ✳	18.22 Lewisham	20.07 East Tilbury
07.15 Thurnham	16.42 Hothfield	18.22 Lewisham	20.23 Throwley
07.16 Stapleford Tawney	16.42 Off South Foreland ✳	18.26 Off Lydd ✳	20.55 Dover ✳
07.17 Deptford	16.45 Snodland	18.27 Off Hythe ✳	20.58 Alkham
07.17 Off Littlestone	16.47 Newington	18.28 Off New Romney ✳	20.58 Newington
07.19 Aylesford	16.48 Frindsbury	18.30 Blean	21.00 Iwade
07.20 Headcorn	16.48 Swanscombe	18.30 Boxted	21.06 Barking
07.26 Off Littlestone ✳	16.50 Lambeth	18.31 Deptford	
08.34 Off New Romney ✳	16.51 Leyton	18.34 Ashford	
08.38 Lympne ✳	16.53 Chigwell	18.36 Off Lydd ✳	

Henry Taylor's was replaced by a rather nondescript arcade-like structure next to the Granada cinema that had been used at one time during the conventional bombings as a temporary mortuary. Local historian Brian Ward was seven at the time and, when he heard that the site was now due for redevelopment, he informed the council of its significance. 'I wanted a plaque to act as a memorial to the people who lost their lives but also to get people walking by today to look up what happened.' Finally in July 2015 a blue plaque was mounted on the new building listing the final death toll: 144 casualties including 22 dead.

Not much could be done about destroying the huge underground factory at Nordhausen, and when in 1945 the RAF did carry out raids on the town on the nights of April 3/4 and 4/5, over 1,450 slave labourers were killed when the Boelcke Barracks were hit. Six days later US ground forces reached the area and it was only then that the true extent of the Nordhausen factory was revealed.

plant. This was the fourth and last occasion on which Peenemünde was attacked. The same night, Bomber Command sent 412 aircraft to Rüsselsheim and 1,554 tons of bombs were dropped. Bombing was well concentrated on the Opel works, very little weight falling on the residential districts nearby. Severe damage was caused throughout the plant; almost all major units, including three assembly sheds, were hit. No further attacks needed to be made on this factory.

These attacks marked the end of the efforts of the heavy bomber forces to diminish the scale of flying bomb attack from northern France. They were not the only 'Crossbow' attacks that were made before the Germans were forced to abandon their launching sites as Bomber Command sent out very strong forces to attack nine forward storage depots in the Pas-de-Calais on the night of August 31/September 1, dropping nearly 3,000 tons of bombs. These targets were attacked more for the part they might be playing in the enemy's preparations for rocket attack.

depots in the area Paris—Beauvais—Compiègne—Rheims, which was in danger of being cut off from the modified sites by the Allied advance towards the Seine.

During the week August 23-29, a larger effort was made against modified sites, 1,100 tons of bombs being dropped on 20 sites with some success in five cases. All the sites were north of the Somme which reflected the change in the situation on land. Three airfields in Holland — Venlo, Eindhoven and Deelen — and Le Culot in Belgium, all of which were thought to be used by flying bomb launch aircraft, were attacked, chiefly by the Eighth Air Force.

The main attacks of the week were against Peenemünde and the Opel works at Rüsselsheim. The Eighth sent 180 aircraft to Peenemünde on August 25; 319 tons of bombs were dropped and further damage was caused to the hydrogen peroxide

Comprising a network of tunnels (see *After the Battle* No. 101), this was the scene outside Tunnel A, the exit for the V1 factory. Wire-wound compressed-air bottles are piled on the left with a V1 trolley in the foreground.

The complex had been dug under the Kohnstein mountain but this fell within the Soviet zone of Germany. After the Americans — and the British — had had their pick of the contents, which included enough parts to assemble 100 V2 rockets, the site was handed over to the Russians. They picked it clean before dynamiting the entrances in 1948.

06.10	Appledore	07.53	Hackney	13.21	Off Littlestone ✱	16.55	Off Hythe ✱
06.10	Kenardington	08.13	Off Dover ✱	13.29	Battersea	16.55	Off Hythe ✱
06.13	Icklesham	08.22	Enfield	13.31	Great Parndon	16.58	Warlingham
06.14	Off Folkestone ✱	08.23	Walthamstow	13.32	Epping Upland	17.00	Camberwell
06.15	Northiam	08.25	Off Dungeness	13.32	Hackney	17.01	Off Hythe ✱
06.22	Bermondsey	08.28	Lydd	13.48	Off Dymchurch	17.01	Off Hythe ✱
06.28	Denton ✱	08.40	Off Littlestone	13.51	Off Burmarsh ✱	20.32	Off Hythe ✱
06.30	Folkestone ✱	09.13	Hinxhill	13.51	Off Folkestone ✱	20.34	Lydd ✱
06.42	Camberwell	09.15	Alkham	13.53	Hollingbourne	20.35	Folkestone
06.55	Off Dungeness	09.16	Kingsnorth	13.54	Off Littlestone	20.35	Off Littlestone
06.55	Peasmarsh ✱	09.22	Bermondsey	14.46	Off Burmarsh ✱	20.37	Off Dover ✱
06.58	Linton	09.23	Esher	14.47	Off Dymchurch ✱	20.37	Off Dover ✱
07.08	Hythe	09.23	Off South Foreland	14.53	Stansted	20.37	Off Hythe ✱
07.09	Off Dymchurch	09.25	Southend	15.06	Alkham	20.37	Waltham
07.11	Off Folkestone ✱	09.37	Wrotham	15.06	Cheshunt	20.38	Ruckinge ✱
07.12	Throwley	09.41	Off Dymchurch ✱	15.54	Walthamstow	20.39	Off Littlestone ✱
07.14	Off Dymchurch ✱	09.42	Off Dungeness ✱	16.16	Off Dymchurch ✱	20.40	Broomhill ✱
07.19	Newington	09.42	Off Littlestone ✱	16.19	Hythe	20.47	Erith
07.40	Snargate	09.45	Off Littlestone ✱	16.19	Off Dover	20.53	Great Maplestead
07.40	Wye	13.19	Elham ✱	16.27	Aylesford	21.23	Off Littlestone
07.43	Frant	13.21	New Romney ✱	16.29	Dartford		

06.58	Off Hythe ✱	07.04	Ivychurch	07.05	Off Dungeness	07.15	Poplar
06.59	Off Dymchurch ✱	07.05	Cuckfield	07.06	Old Romney	07.23	Off Littlestone
07.00	Off Folkestone ✱	07.05	Hucking	07.09	Icklesham	07.39	Bealings

Scale of German Attack, August 16 — September 5

This last period showed a substantial reduction in the scale of attack on London, down to almost one-third compared to previous weeks. Between August 16 and September 1, 1,115 flying bombs were reported, representing an average daily rate of 74 bombs. There were, however, considerable variations from day to day. The two heaviest attacks were in the dusk-to-dusk periods of August 22-23 and 23-24 when 103 and 127 bombs respectively were reported. There were two unusually light periods, August 17-18 and 24-25, when 15 and 14 bombs only were plotted, and on the last day of the attack from modified sites, August 31-September 1, only eight bombs were reported. From then until the early hours of September 5 there was no activity at all but then, between 0500 and 0600 hours on the 1st, nine flying bombs, all of them launched from Heinkel He 111s, were

One point not generally known — even today — is that the flying bomb's greatest psychological aspect — the silent death dive — was completely unintentional. The weapon had been originally designed so that the propeller-driven distance log, which was pre-set before the launch, automatically deflected the elevators to dive the bomb when over the target. It was the sudden application of the negative G-force which caused fuel starvation resulting in the engine cutting out. When, late in the campaign, the German designers realised what was happening, they modified the system so that the elevators operated slowly, thus diving the bomb under power. Whether this was an advantage is debatable, as the glide descent with detonation on the surface undoubtedly led to greater blast effect. *Above: Widespread blast damage to the northwest part of Southend on the morning of the 17th — this is Shirley Road.*

155

On November 23, 1938, a question was asked in Parliament of the Secretary of State for Air whether, in view of air raid risks in central London, it was still considered advisable to locate the new Air Ministry offices in Berkeley Square, Westminster. Sir Kingsley Wood replied that additional accommodation was required immediately to relieve the congestion that now existed in Air Ministry buildings (see page 18), and to provide for further expansion. He said that 'it is also essential under present circumstances that the new premises shall be within reasonable distance of the headquarters of the Department, which must remain for the present in the Kingsway area. The decision to move part of the staff to Berkeley Square House was taken after full consideration of all relevant factors because it was the only large building which met our immediate requirements both as regards space and location'. One wonders if anyone on August 20, 1944 remembered this statement when at 11.51 a flying bomb came within an ace of hitting the building.

BETWEEN 21.00 ON FRIDAY, AUGUST 18, TO 20.59 ON SATURDAY, AUGUST 19 (Airburst *)			
03.08 Off Littlestone	06.40 Off Romney *	14.30 Off Dungeness *	21.02 Newchurch
03.09 Off Littlestone *	06.41 Stowting	14.34 High Halden	21.02 Off Hythe *
03.11 Off Rye	06.42 Rolvenden	14.35 Brookland	21.03 Off Hythe *
03.13 Lydd	06.42 Woodchurch *	14.37 Off Lydd	21.04 Off Littlestone *
03.14 Off Rye	06.43 Folkestone	14.38 Northfleet	21.05 Off Dover
03.16 Brasted	06.43 Off Dover *	14.38 Shoreham	21.05 Off Littlestone
03.18 Off Hythe	06.44 Lydd *	14.38 Slaugham	21.06 Off Hythe *
03.20 Bicknor	06.44 Sissinghurst	14.40 East Guildford	21.07 Teston
03.20 Hendon	06.47 Off Dungeness	14.40 Hoo	21.08 Kensington
03.20 Lydden	06.47 Wittersham	14.43 Off Rye	21.08 Off Rye
03.20 Udimore *	06.49 Woodchurch	14.45 Yalding	21.09 Beckley
03.21 Detling *	06.50 Woolwich	14.52 Polsingford	21.09 Stansted
03.25 Dartford	06.55 Ivychurch *	14.58 Faulkbourne	21.10 Horne
03.31 Malden	14.30 Bonnington	15.04 Off Dungeness	21.13 Waltham Holy Cross
06.36 Off Dungeness	14.30 Folkestone	15.06 Lydd	21.16 Off Dungeness
06.38 Off Dover	14.30 Off Dover *	20.57 Off Dungeness	

After the near miss on Adastral House (pages 88-92), it was a close call for another Air Ministry building as the main damage was to Stewart & Ardern's showroom in Landsdowne House on the south-east corner of the square.

BETWEEN 21.00 ON SATURDAY, AUGUST 19, TO 20.59 ON SUNDAY, AUGUST 20 (Airburst *)

06.07	Off Littlestone	09.03	Addington	12.00	Feltham	23.19	Off Dungeness
06.07	St Mary in the Marsh	09.04	Burnham Beeches	12.06	Richmond	23.20	Off Hythe
06.08	Off Littlestone *	09.07	Ealing	14.12	Merton	23.22	Off Hythe
06.15	Wimbledon	10.29	Off Hythe	14.13	Chislehurst	23.24	High Halden
06.17	Barking	10.30	Brentford	14.16	Lambeth	23.24	Off Hythe *
06.17	Esher	10.30	Off Sandgate	14.19	Off Littlestone *	23.25	Off Dymchurch *
06.18	Esher	10.40	Ealing	14.21	Stoner	23.25	Off Dymchurch *
06.20	Off Burmarsh *	10.40	Northaw	14.43	Folkestone	23.25	Off Littlestone
06.25	Beckenham	10.40	Wotton	14.55	Off Folkestone *	23.25	Off Littlestone *
06.30	Walton & Weybridge	10.42	Ealing	15.03	Capel-le-Ferne	23.26	Capel-le-Ferne
06.37	Speldhurst	10.54	Finchley	15.34	Southwark	23.26	Lydd
07.44	Lydd *	11.42	Burmarsh	15.44	Off Hythe *	23.26	Off Burmarsh *
07.45	Off Burmarsh *	11.44	Brenchley	15.47	Off Dymchurch *	23.34	Slough
07.50	Snargate	11.45	Pluckley	15.48	Off Burmarsh *	23.38	Off Burmarsh *
07.58	Kenardington	11.49	Paddington	15.51	New Romney *	23.42	Off Folkestone *
08.51	Off Folkestone *	11.51	Hendon	15.54	Cuckfield	23.43	Off Burmarsh *
08.51	Off Folkestone *	11.51	Wembley	16.08	Walthamstow	23.43	Off Sandgate *
08.55	Tonbridge	11.51	Westminster	16.23	Off Dungeness	23.44	Off Sandgate *
09.00	Wennington	11.58	Challock	16.41	Off Lydd		

reported in an attack that marked the end of the main offensive. With the exception of five bombs on the night of August 30/31, these were the only ones reported as being launched from aircraft during these final three weeks. This compares with about 120 during the previous month which may have been due to the concerted attack which Bomber Command and the Eighth Air Force made on August 15 against airfields in north-west Europe, including

Milton Avenue was a small cul-de-sac in West Croydon struck at 6 p.m. on August 15 (see page 152).

BETWEEN 21.00 ON SUNDAY, AUGUST 20, TO 20.59 ON MONDAY, AUGUST 21 (Airburst *)

02.15	Lydd	11.12	Off Folkestone *	12.38	Off Littlestone *	19.37	Off Burmarsh
02.19	Off Dungeness *	11.19	Off Burmarsh	12.40	Off Littlestone *	19.40	Old Romney
02.19	Off Littlestone *	11.20	Off Folkestone	12.45	Willesden	19.45	Ardingley
02.23	Brenchley	11.20	Sevenoaks	13.07	Send	19.45	Walton
02.23	Off Dungeness *	11.22	Ripley	13.12	Lydd	19.47	Sutton
02.25	Poplar	11.26	Shoreham	13.13	Twickenham	19.48	Off Dymchurch *
02.26	Epsom	11.31	Worplesdon	13.15	Acton	19.49	Willesden
02.27	Meopham	11.35	Harrow	13.15	Kenardington	19.51	Twickenham
02.30	Byfleet	12.19	East of Dungeness	13.19	Heston	19.51	Westcott
02.32	Dagenham	12.19	Off Burmarsh	14.30	Lydd	20.07	Off Burmarsh *
02.35	Dunmow	12.24	Leigh	14.38	South of Lydd	20.07	South of Sandgate *
02.36	Merton	12.25	Seal	14.45	Brentford	20.10	South of Littlestone
03.59	Lydd	12.25	Titsey	14.46	Kensington	20.15	Sevenoaks
04.05	Off Lydd *	12.27	Mereworth	14.49	Sundridge	20.18	Godstone
04.07	Westwell	12.30	Esher	14.49	Walton	20.18	St Marylebone
04.15	Woodchurch	12.31	Twickenham	14.49	Walton	20.20	Off Hythe *
04.24	South of Rye	12.33	Off Littlestone *	14.55	Shere	20.23	Off Hythe *
04.33	Surbiton	12.33	Woldingham	15.00	Walton		
11.11	Off Dymchurch *	12.36	Bonnington	19.36	Off Hythe *		

Wharncliffe Gardens had been built in the late 19th century to house workers whose homes had been demolished when the Great Central Railway arrived at Marylebone station. It was what was then called 'a model dwelling' but severe damage was caused on August 21 when a V1 hit the block just after 8 p.m.

After the war all six five-storey blocks were demolished and a new council estate was built on the site in the 1970s comprising 280 homes with 70 specially for elderly residents. And, as a reaction to the by-then unpopular tower blocks, all were of a maximum of four stories with some gardens and car parking.

My Mother, sister and myself had not long had our dinner. We were all sitting in the ground-floor flat of the five-storey building when we heard the terrible screech of the bomb. I ran to the side of the fireplace and my sister followed me but the next thing I knew I was pinned from my shoulders to my right arm across my chest. My left arm was free and I could just move that and was able to put it out at the side a little way.

It was difficult for me to make a sound, as my mouth seemed full of debris, but I tried to make as much noise as I could, and was greatly relieved when I felt somebody get hold of my hand. He said he would come back. It seemed a very long time but then I could feel that the wall at the back of me was being loosened and I was able to move the top part of my body. I was gradually dug out with the men taking turns to release me. There was a doctor giving me attention and I was given a drink through a tube and injections in my arm, but was conscious all the time. Finally, I was hauled up by ropes, put in an ambulance, and taken to Middlesex Hospital.

I arrived there about 4.20 a.m. I remember having my clothing cut off, and my ring being sawn off my finger, then I remember no more until I found myself in bed. I must have looked a terrible sight as I was black and blue, and I must have taken up all of the nurses' time with the attention I required. I had penicillin injections every four hours, my ears syringed twice a day. I was given oxygen twice a day and had my mouth washed out regularly on account of ulcers that had formed.

My right arm was badly crushed and I had a compound fracture and laceration to right leg; fracture to left leg and lacerations to left ankle. My left arm was also dressed and stitched.

On September 1 I was taken to Stoke Mandeville Hospital near Aylesbury in an American Red Cross ambulance. There I had penicillin injections for several weeks and also a blood transfusion of eight pints of blood. My left leg was put in a splint as my foot was giving me a lot of trouble where it was lacerated and was causing shooting pains up my leg. I also had pain in my chest and every time I breathed it hurt so for this I was poulticed and bound up. One morning I moved slightly and accidentally spilt boiling water over my crushed arm. Large blisters formed and I had to have a great deal of attention but it led to shock pneumonia.

Next I had an operation to have my right leg stitched. After having stitches out, I had to do exercises in bed. Then I had another operation to have my right knee moulded and another plaster put on. My left foot was still painful but my crushed arm and hand improved daily with exercises and finally I could use my hand. After a time, I had a walking plaster on my right leg and was taught to walk on crutches, and then using sticks.

I left hospital in December 1944, still with the plaster on and during the time in hospital I was paid an allowance of 24/6d per week.

MADGE HUNT

[Robert Hunt said that his aunt remained crippled for the rest of her life and could only walk with a stick. She never married and died aged 83 years of age in 1981.]

The emergency services reacted quickly and within 40 minutes six heavy rescue parties, three light rescue units and several ambulances were on the scene, followed at 9 p.m. by three

cranes and 17 tipper lorries. Thirty-three people had been killed and 38 persons seriously and 107 lightly injured. The last body was not recovered until 8 a.m. on the 23rd.

The caption that was authorised by the censor for this photograph, simply read: 'Flying bomb drops on Southern England, 22.8.44. Photo shows firemen fighting a fire which was caused when a flying bomb fell on a block of flats'.

BETWEEN 21.00 ON MONDAY, AUGUST 21, TO 20.59 ON TUESDAY, AUGUST 22 (Airburst *)			
00.55 Lewisham	03.53 Hammersmith	07.25 Off Burmarsh	12.29 Shoreditch
00.56 Shorcham	04.13 Off Hythe *	07.27 Lambeth	12.32 Kingston
00.57 Wimbledon	04.20 Off Dymchurch	07.33 Off Dymchurch *	23.12 Thames Estuary
00.58 Stapleford Abbotts	04.23 Westminster	07.39 Off Folkestone *	23.15 Brentford
00.59 Wandsworth	04.23 South of Hythe *	07.47 Seal	23.16 Wheathampstead
01.02 Malden	04.23 Seal	12.16 Off Folkestone	23.19 West Ham
03.27 Off Folkestone *	04.44 Westminster	12.21 South of Dover	23.19 Pirbright
03.30 Off Folkestone	07.17 Off Hythe *	12.24 Lenham	23.21 Colney Street
03.33 Off Littlestone *	07.18 Elham	12.27 Camberwell	23.23 Uxbridge
03.38 Thurnham	07.19 Off Burmarsh *	12.27 Bethnal Green	23.29 Hurstbourne Tarrant
03.46 Kensington	07.21 Off Folkestone *	12.28 Chigwell	

seven from which aircraft were operating against London. Otherwise, it is difficult to trace any relation between the scale of attack during this period and the 'Crossbow' counter-offensive.

The mean point of impact of flying bombs had not shown any significant variation during the first two months of the attack, but it changed considerably during the second half of August, In the week August 11-18, it moved appreciably to the north-east, falling just south of West Ham. The following week showed an even greater variation, the mean point of impact falling in Chiswick. For the last week of the main attack it was then plotted at a point in the Lambeth—Newington area, north of the Camberwell—Dulwich districts where it had fallen during every week but three. Whether the Germans deliberately changed their aiming points, or whether the evacuation of the sites south of the Somme and the approach of the Allied armies affected the accuracy of their shooting from new ramps, is not known.

One would have expected such damage to have resulted in complete demolition but Andrew Hyde, with his expert knowledge of the City, found the location for us on the corner of Boundary Street and Calvert Avenue, right in the shadow of St Leonard's Church, Shoreditch.

Fifty years later *Engineering News* looked back to 1944. 'The morning of Wednesday, 23rd August 1944, was grey and gloomy. By 7 a.m. there had already been two yellow warnings and at 7.50 a.m. came a red alert which meant the sirens were sounded. "Visibility", the official log recorded, "was now about 400 yards with very low cloud", and the look-out Reg Smith, peering south through the murk, was horrified to "see and hear the bomb just short of our main gate on the corner of Brunswick Park Road" about 300 yards away. I shouted over the factory speakers: "Lie down! For God's sake, lie down!" A few seconds later the bomb broke through the cloud and descended on Building 7 at 45 degrees, the engine cutting out half way. The time was 7.59 a.m. The bomb had landed at the very heart of the factory, between Building 8, a strong three-storey building of reinforced concrete, used for the assembly of airborne radio and radar equipment, and Building 6, a single-storey steel-framed and brick construction which contained the Woodwork Shop where Bailey bridge parts were being built. The explosion blew a crater four feet deep and 12 feet wide in the road, but the buildings on either side took the main force of the blast. The ominous silence that greeted the roll call confirmed more eloquently than words the scale of the disaster which had fallen upon the factory. As the bodies were removed from the wreckage they were laid out in rows in the entrance hall, close by the main surgery. A few, killed outright by blast, "looked", the sister in charge remembers, "as if they had just sat down" but some were unrecognisable or badly mutilated. The New Southgate flying bomb cost the lives of 33 people, 21 of whom died on the spot, and caused serious injury to about 200 others. Government figures and company records disagree slightly as to the casualties but the total of dead and seriously injured was 233, the highest of the whole campaign. The public knew little of what had happened, for the *Barnet Press* reported merely that some lives had been lost, when "a works had been hit and within two or three days, production had been re-started, even in the worst damaged buildings".'

Standard Telephones & Cables (STC) started life in London in 1883 as International Western Electric, becoming STC in 1925. The site alongside the Great Northern Railway in New Southgate (in the borough of East Barnet) had been acquired in 1922 and was developed into a manufacturing base for telecommunications equipment. The factory had effective black-out facilities which enabled 24-hour working, and it was successful in avoiding any stoppages until it was struck by a flying bomb.

Demolition under way for a second time when the site was being redeveloped into the North London Business Centre.

BETWEEN 21.00 ON TUESDAY, AUGUST 22, TO 20.59 ON WEDNESDAY, AUGUST 23 (Airburst ✳)

04.33	Off Dymchurch	05.22	Off Dymchurch ✳	08.22	Elham	20.45	Lydd
04.35	Off Dymchurch	05.23	Off Folkestone	08.32	Bulls Green	20.45	Off Winchelsea ✳
04.37	Off Burmarsh	05.24	Off Lydd	08.33	Brentford	20.47	Off Dymchurch
04.37	Off Sandgate ✳	05.25	Staplehurst	09.01	Off Folkestone	20.47	Off Dymchurch
04.42	Hammersmith	06.02	Lower Beeding	09.03	Womenswold	20.48	Bethersden
04.42	Kensington	07.49	Off Dymchurch	09.04	Lydd ✳	20.48	Thornham
04.43	Hendon	07.50	Broomhill	09.05	Off Folkestone ✳	20.49	Burmarsh
04.43	Orpington	07.54	Off Dungeness ✳	09.05	Pluckley	20.50	East Guildford ✳
04.43	Twickenham	07.56	Hendon	09.06	Elham	20.50	Off Burmarsh ✳
04.44	Waltham Holy Cross	07.56	Off Dover ✳	09.08	Godmersham	20.50	Otterden
04.45	Hampstead	07.58	Esher	09.09	Lydd ✳	20.53	Off Folkestone
04.46	Lydd	07.59	East Barnet	09.13	Chigwell	20.54	Esher
04.47	Hornsey	07.59	Slough	09.15	Navestock	20.54	Off Littlestone
04.50	Off Romney ✳	07.59	Wembley	09.17	Off Folkestone	20.55	Brenchley ✳
04.51	Off Burmarsh ✳	08.00	Godalming	09.17	Stoke Newington	20.55	Enfield
04.51	Off Romney ✳	08.00	Wembley	09.18	Potters Bar	20.55	Lambeth
04.53	Ringmer	08.02	Felsted	09.19	Stradishall	20.55	West Dean
05.02	Off Dungeness	08.03	Off Sandgate ✳	09.20	Great Chart ✳	20.57	Dungeness ✳
05.04	Off Bexhill ✳	08.08	Tunstall	09.20	Off Littlestone ✳	20.57	Esher
05.04	Off Littlestone ✳	08.17	Twickenham	09.21	Off Littlestone ✳	20.57	Richmond
05.09	Off Littlestone	08.18	Off Folkestone ✳	20.40	Ivychurch ✳	20.59	Esher
05.16	Cheshunt	08.19	Acrise	20.43	Lydd ✳	21.00	Thannington
05.20	Off Lydd	08.21	Off Littlestone ✳	20.44	Off Folkestone		

BETWEEN 21.00 ON WEDNESDAY, AUGUST 23, TO 20.59 ON WEDNESDAY, AUGUST 24 (Airburst *)

02.43 Off Dungeness	06.24 Off Dungeness	17.43 Aldington	19.13 Off Rye *
02.44 Off Dungeness	06.25 Off Folkestone *	17.43 Off Hythe	19.18 Plaxtol
02.45 Off Hythe	06.25 Off Lydd	17.44 Off New Romney *	19.20 Carshalton
02.47 Off Dungeness	06.25 Off Lydd *	17.51 Wandsworth	19.23 Great Canfield
02.48 Kingsnorth	06.25 Postling	17.52 Dorking	19.23 Stanford Rivers
02.48 Off New Romney	06.25 Pyrford	18.00 Coulsdon	19.24 Bermondsey
02.49 Off Dungeness	06.26 Off Rye	18.02 Sutton	19.24 Penge
02.52 Lydd *	07.27 Off Rye	18.09 Off Folkestone *	19.25 New Romney
02.52 Off Dungeness	07.28 Off Dymchurch *	18.10 New Romney *	19.25 Tottenham
02.53 Off Folkestone	07.29 Off Burmarsh	18.11 Off Folkestone *	19.25 Wateringbury
02.55 Icklesham	07.29 Off Folkestone	18.15 Elmstead	19.30 Holborn
02.55 Off Hastings	07.30 Off Fairlight	18.16 Off Folkestone *	19.36 Hackney
02.55 Southgate	07.30 Off Icklesham	18.17 Smarden	19.40 Off Eastchurch
02.58 Wembley	07.30 Stone-cum-Ebony	18.22 Barnes	19.48 Off Folkestone *
03.03 Wimbledon	07.31 Off Dymchurch *	18.22 Merton	19.48 Stelling Minnis
03.09 Brookland	07.33 St Mary in the Marsh *	18.25 Off Folkestone *	19.51 Dagenham
06.10 Off Greatstone	07.35 Newchurch	18.28 St Mary in the Marsh	20.07 Ockley
06.11 Off Lydd *	07.35 Off Littlestone *	18.36 Lambeth	20.12 Greenwich
06.12 Off Rye *	07.35 Stone-cum-Ebony	18.39 Malden	20.13 Off Folkestone
06.13 South of Lydd *	07.36 Off New Romney *	18.40 West Ham	20.16 Woolwich
06.15 Battle	07.37 Heathfield	18.41 Paddlesworth	20.17 Walthamstow
06.15 Burwash	07.39 Holborn	18.43 Off Burmarsh	20.19 Off Hythe
06.15 Ticehurst	07.42 Hampstead	18.43 Theydon Bois	20.24 Dagenham
06.16 Off Fairlight	07.43 Ealing	18.44 Off New Romney	20.24 Enfield
06.18 Off Dungeness	07.43 Molash *	18.45 Yalding	20.43 Off Hythe
06.21 St Mary in the Marsh	07.43 Off Dungeness	18.51 Wimbledon	20.44 Off Dymchurch *
06.22 Off New Romney *	07.44 Black Notley	18.52 East Barnet	20.45 Off Hythe
06.23 Twickenham	08.12 Woodchurch *	19.00 Hedsor	21.03 Rye
06.24 Dymchurch	17.42 Off Dymchurch	19.09 Higham	

The Defence of London, August 16 — September 5

The rate of improvement, which was noticed in the month following the redeployment of the guns to the coast, was well maintained. By the middle of August, the defences had reached their greatest strength. Fifteen day fighter squadrons and six night fighter squadrons of ADGB were engaged entirely on 'Diver' patrols, and two more night fighter squadrons were engaged on the work part-time. The balloon barrage consisted of 2,015 balloons of which over 1,600 were equipped with light wire armament. In the coastal gun belt there were 592 heavy and 922 light guns, and over 600 rocket barrels. In the gun 'box' there were 208 heavy and 178 light guns, 400 guns of 20mm and 108 rocket barrels.

Only 17 per cent of the 1,124 bombs that were reported between August 16 and September 5 fell in the target area, compared to 33 per cent during the previous month and 44 per cent during the first five weeks. During the last four days (i.e. excluding the small air-launched attack of September 5) when 192 bombs were reported, only 28 fell in London, The most-successful day for the defences was August 27-28 when, out of 97 bombs reported, no fewer than 87 were destroyed and only four fell in London. During these 24 hours, the anti-aircraft guns destroyed 82 bombs, fighters 19, balloons two, and guns and balloons shared the destruction of a further four.

The relative successes of the three sorts of defence on this day reflected the trend throughout these last three weeks. The percentage successes of the guns rose from 40 in the second week in August to 55 in the third, 57 in the fourth, and 63 in the final four days before the enemy abandoned their launching sites. Altogether, between August 16 and the end of the attack, the guns destroyed 791 flying bombs, compared to 669 during the whole of the previous nine weeks.

```
FLY Shot down in sea:

Off DOVER.  1 by Fighter.  0533/22.

Off FOLKESTONE.  4 by A.A., 1111 (2), 1120, 1216 on the 21st.
                 5 by A.A., 1936, 1946, 2005, 2020, 2054 and
                 2 cause unstated, 0325, 0420 on the 21st.

Off NEW ROMNEY.  3 by A.A., 0334, 0415, 0421, and 1 cause unstated,
                 0421 on the 21st.

Off HYTHE.  16 by A.A., 1129 (2), 1220 (2), 1904 (2), 1948,
            2008 (3), 2021, 2025, 0335 (2), 0430 (2) on the 21st.
```

August 24 marked the climax of the campaign . . . probably a last all-out effort by the Luftwaffe before the firing sites had to be abandoned. With British and Canadian forces poised to cross the River Seine into V1 country, the flying bomb weapon would soon be restricted to air-launches. Also, by now the defences had achieved the upper hand, for although V1s were still reaching London, those being brought down by the guns were now being listed in multiples in Home Security reports. Here is an extract for the 12 hours ending at 18.00 on August 22. The following day Hythe claimed 14 shot down and New Romney eight.

The V1 which crashed on the junction of Clerkenwell and Farringdon Roads at 07.39 hours on the morning of August 24 severely affected the commercial properties in the Hatton Garden area. Dozens of casualties were recorded in both Holborn and the adjoining borough of Finsbury. It was also somewhat of an own goal as it hit the lighting and heating specialists Falk, Stadelmann and Co in Farringdon Road. With its German origins, in the inter-war years it had become the largest oil lamp company in Britain using the German Veritas trademark. Planet News photographer 'Andy' Andrews was quickly on the scene picturing shattered buses but again his photographs were never released by the censor.

The spire of St James's on the right is the common reference point.

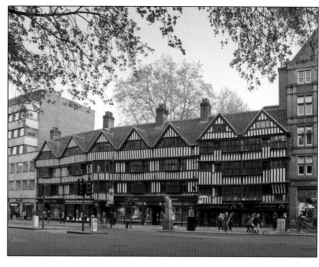

Staple Inn had stood in Holborn since the 16th century. On the night of September 2/3, 1666, John Evelyn led a gallant band of firefighters to prevent the Great Fire spreading to this part of the city, and it was undoubtedly due to his efforts that the building was saved. *Left:* However, another fire in 1756 led to the half-timbered façade being covered with 'fire-proof' plaster making it appear very different to how it looks today. *Right:* In 1884 the site was sold to a firm of builders, G. Trollope and Sons for £80,000. They sold Nos. 11 and 12 Staple Inn, which overlooked the garden from the south, to the Commissioners of Works and Public Buildings in June 1886, and later the same year a public auction was announced to sell the rest of the site, provoking impassioned public outcry against the loss of these historic buildings. The auction took place in November when the successful bid of £68,000 was that of the Prudential Assurance Company, who had occupied the distinctive offices on High Holborn since 1879. When the company restored Staple Inn, part of the work involved removing the covering to expose the timber.

It was then the most impressive surviving example of a timber building in London with a magnificent Elizabethan Hall at the rear. Occupied by the Institute and Faculty of Actuaries, on the evening of August 24 a flying bomb reduced the hall to matchwood although fortunately the side facing the street suffered only broken windows. The Ministry of Home Security report stated the area was under an air raid warning from 17.48 to 20.36 with the exact time of the impact being logged at 19.30. The bomb made a crater measuring 17 feet by two feet in the garden at the rear *(left)*. Two porters were rescued by some American servicemen but 70-year-old Jessie Hollingshead of Essex Road, Islington, who had worked at the Inn for 40 years, was not so lucky. *Below:* Using much of the material saved from the original building, the courtyard and hall were lovingly restored in 1955. The superior blasting power of the V1 caused much more damage to property than the same weight of conventional bombs.

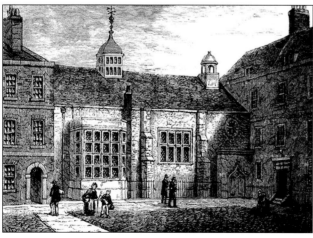

In the last days of August, the flying bomb attacks were dwindling as the launching sites in France were being evacuated. Yet before the month was over — almost as if it was a dying gesture — those V1s that reached Britain were sent over loaded with propaganda leaflets. Ron Gamage obtained this copy *(left and below)* from one of the first bombs that came down at 14.10 on August 28 at Madams Court Farm, Frinsted. Ron was told by the ARP Incident Officer for Hollingbourne Rural District Council who attended the incident that 'the leaflets came as a shock to the emergency services at the scene so it was immediately referred

to control'. A copy was sent to London and Churchill instructed that the Police and Military must make a thorough search to collect every last one. More were found in the V1s down at 14.15 at Stone, near Dartford, and 14.53 at St Mary's. The following day even more were sent over in two bombs which were brought down at Leigh and at Hougham Without at 14.00. Leaflets were also found in the Cheriton V1 shot down by a fighter at 17.30 and on August 31 more were sent over in the Aldington bomb (09.11) and Parkwood Hollingbourne at 10.15. Ron found these pieces of wreckage still scattered at the impact site *(right)*.

The victims: Women, children and old folks (Hamburg, July 27/28th, 1943)

"There are numbers of tenderhearted people who do not wish to see Berlin bombed, or common Germans experiencing any of the miseries that they have allowed their Government to inflict on other nations.
I am convinced that vigorous bombing, bombarding, town wrecking, and the like would be an entirely wholesome and chastening experience for them. ... let the Germans take their medicine now."
Don Iddon "Daily Mail", Jan. 26th, 1940
Citing H. G. Wells from the Am. Magazine "Liberty"

"Anyone who kills Germans is my best friend."
Captain H. H. Balfour, Under-Secretary for Air. "The Times", Dez. 1st, 1941

... that the Germans will scream for mercy."
Air Marshall A. T. Harris, in an interview with Mr. Trevor Smith, London editor of the Sydney Sun. "Daily Telegraph", Mai 6th, 1942

"What she has had in the past we can assure her will be chicken-feed compared with what she is going to get just as long as she persists in her aggression."
Air Chief Marshall Sir Arthur Harris. "The Times", Mai 31st, 1943

The victims of the terror-raid on Cologne, July 27/28th, 1943

"We are bombing Germany, city by city, and ever more terribly, in order to make it impossible for you to go on with the war. That is our object. We shall pursue it remorselessly. City by city: Lübeck, Rostock, Cologne, Emden, Bremen, Wilhelmshaven, Duisburg, Hamburg — and the list will grow longer and longer. Let the Nazis drag you down to disaster with them if you will. That is for you to decide."
Air Marshall Sir Arthur Harris, Commander-in-Chief. "The Times", July 29th, 1942

The victims: Women, children, old folks — terror-raid on Hamburg, July 27/28th, 1943

The demise of the flying bomb attacks led to a sudden increase in the shelling of Folkestone, Deal, Ramsgate and Margate by long-range guns sited in the Pas-de-Calais (see *After the Battle* No. 29). Dover received 28 shells on August 31/September 1,

Home Security recording that the most serious occurred when the entrance to a shelter was hit, killing five and injuring 15. The following night over 100 shells were reported falling in the Dover area and 43 at St Margaret-at-Cliffe on September 2.

......Hollingbourne........INCIDENTS.   WAR DIARY.   Date......28 – 8 – 44......

Time		Parish	Time of Incident	Type of Bomb	No.	Information	Casualties			Damage
Origin	Receipt						K.	S.I.	SL.I.	
14.50	14.57	Frinsted	14.10	C.C. Fly	I.	Fly grounded and exploded in field on Madamas Court Farm M.R. 332 745. Fly carrying leaflets		W 2 KC		Extensive to Lords Hill cottages.
15.50	15.53	"								
16.00	16.10	"								
16.35	16.37									

As the Canadians advanced up the coast, they came across the evidence of bombs that had failed like this one said to have only travelled a short distance after being launched and which came down without exploding.

Over the same period the successes of the fighters showed little variation. They destroyed 15 per cent of all possible targets until the last week, when their successes fell to 11 per cent probably because of the small number of bombs that were despatched. Fighters destroyed 263 flying bombs in those three weeks, bringing their successes since June 13 to 1,771.

The balloons maintained the improved rate of destruction that had followed the completion of the full barrage and the equipping of the majority of the balloons with additional wires. The barrage accounted for 45 flying bombs after August 15 making a total for the whole of the main attack of 232.

Certain changes in deployment and tactics were made during the period to meet the enemy's involuntary concentration on launching bombs from his more northerly sites. As early as August 14 the number of bombs fired from sites south of the Somme was very small. By the 21st it was appreciated that further launchings from this area were unlikely so the movement of a number of guns from the western end of the coastal belt began. By the 25th the full extent of these redispositions had been decided upon: 182 heavy and 48 light guns were to be moved from positions west of Covehurst Bay to thicken the eastern sections of the belt and slightly extend it, and were in fact moved by the end of the month. A similar change was made in the balloon barrage when 246 were withdrawn from its western end. Some were used in the area immediately south of the Thames which had until then been defended by Mk VI balloons while the remainder were redeployed within the barrage to increase its density. Instructions for the transfer were received by Balloon Command on August 22 and the move was completed by the 28th.

The new concentration of fire proved a disadvantage to the fighters. Although the area to be patrolled was no longer so extensive, the warning obtained, especially of bombs launched from sites near the Straits of Dover, was necessarily shorter than in the case of those fired from sites south of the Somme giving fighters even less time in which to intercept. Thus, while the fighters patrolling inland of the gun belt maintained their rate of destruction during these last three weeks, those operating out to sea were somewhat less successful. Their score fell from an average of over 10 per cent for the first two weeks of August to 6 per cent for the third week, and to 9 and 6 per cent respectively for the last two weeks of the attack.

Little could be done to remedy this. On August 23, ADGB Headquarters suggested to No. 11 Group that it might be possible to make interception east of Cap Gris Nez. No. 11 Group, however, held the idea impracticable because it would be impossible to keep the fighters out of the areas in the Pas-de-Calais that were strongly defended by heavy anti-aircraft guns and they ran the risk of sooner or later being shot down. If the patrolling fighters flew above the ceiling of the enemy's light flak, i.e. at about 6,000 feet, they would have little chance during daylight of seeing and catching a flying bomb. The proposal was therefore abandoned.

Also from August 26 the number of day fighter squadrons that were available for full-time employment on flying bomb patrols had been cut down from 15 to ten. On that day Leigh-Mallory had instructed Air Marshal Hill to release a number of Spitfires for fighter-bomber operations in the Lille—Arras—Douai area, which in turn would release the Ninth Air Force for the attack on railways further east and south-east. Five squadrons were accordingly withdrawn from 'Diver' work but were retained on their airfields in Kent on the understanding that they could be re-employed in their old role if the flying bomb situation warranted it.

The location was stated as Fourcarmont, between Dieppe and Amiens, although an alternative source says it was found near Rouen. An interesting film clip showing this V1 can be viewed on *https://www.youtube.com/watch?v=4hbev7_uPg0*.

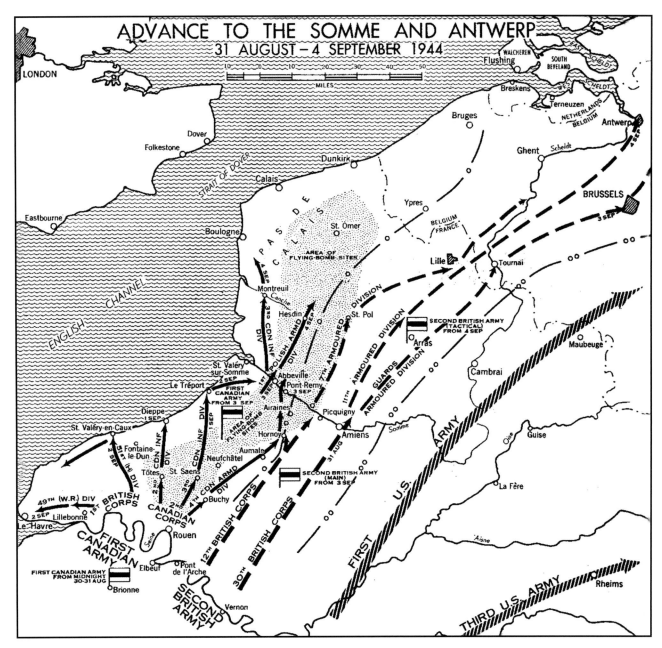

In clearing the Channel coast in September 1944, the Canadians eliminated the flying bomb sites from which the bombardment of London and south-eastern England had been maintained for three months.

Air Marshal Hill accepted this reduction of the forces employed against flying bombs for two reasons: first, the shrinkage of the German launching area meant a reduction in the patrol area which the fighters had to cover, and second because by this time the guns were achieving splendid results.

The conditions of the coastal gun belt were still further modified in favour of the guns during the last week in August. From the 26th all safety lanes that had been established for the passage of friendly fighters and distressed aircraft were abolished; the coastal gun belt and the gun 'box' were declared prohibited areas for flying below 7,000 feet so as to give the guns complete freedom of action at all times up to 6,000 feet. Fighter airfields within the gun areas continued to be used but to safeguard the aircraft, it was laid down that they should approach from landwards. Aircraft in distress were also provided for by passing warning of their approach to Biggin Hill or North Weald sector operations rooms from the fighter control

stations, and thence to the Anti-Aircraft Command gun operations rooms at Chatham or Southend as the aircraft was approaching the guns in the coastal belt or in the 'box'. These rules were in being when the main attack came to an end.

These measures signified that for defence against flying bombs, the anti-aircraft gun was the most effective weapon. It had taken over a month of heavy attack for this change to be appreciated but it was greatly to the credit of ADGB Headquarters that — without prompting from Anti-Aircraft Command — they had seen its necessity and revised the scheme of defence accordingly. The result was that London, the enemy's target, was much more effectively protected, to the extent that during the last three weeks of the attack only one out of every seven flying bombs that the enemy launched actually reached the capital.

The Contribution of Ground Forces

As early as the middle of August, the Germans had begun to withdraw from the launching sites south of the Somme, even though the Allied ground forces had not yet reached the Seine. These sites had probably been evacuated by August 20 as from dusk on that day only the sites north of the Somme remained operative.

The end came rapidly, so rapidly that an airborne expedition to land troops in the Pas-de-Calais on September 3 was cancelled. By August 30 the British 11th Armoured Division was in Amiens, and the US Third Army was well past Laon. The sites in the Pas-de-Calais were not captured by these moves but their communications with Germany were obviously about to be cut. Thus, on September 1, the sites ceased operating and personnel and equipment were moved east and north-east while there was yet time to escape.

167

BETWEEN 21.00 ON TUESDAY, AUGUST 29, TO 20.59 ON WEDNESDAY, AUGUST 30 (Airburst ✳)

00.09	Off Folkestone ✳	07.38	Off Dover ✳	12.04	Halling	22.51	Capel-le-Ferne ✳
00.09	Off Folkestone	07.42	Wye	13.10	Off Dover ✳	22.52	Off Dymchurch
00.21	Enfield	07.49	Woolwich	13.52	Freston	22.52	Off Littlestone ✳
00.25	Off Dymchurch ✳	07.49	Darenth	21.19	Merton	22.53	Off Hythe ✳
00.34	Stapleford Tawney	07.50	Hackney	22.21	Easton	22.58	Ruckinge
00.51	Off Folkestone	08.19	Off Hythe ✳	22.21	Brentford	23.02	Southgate
00.55	Of Folkestone ✳	08.19	Off South Foreland	22.23	Tottenham	23.10	Hammersmith
01.00	Stoke Newington	08.20	Elmsted	22.28	Chingford	23.30	Off Folkestone ✳
05.15	Newchurch	09.32	Off Hythe	22.28	Brill	23.32	Off Littlestone ✳
06.02	Off Hythe ✳	09.36	Boughton Aluph	22.50	Off Folkestone	23.42	Nazeing

Guided by a member of the French Resistance, a Canadian soldier inspects a wrecked launch site.

BETWEEN 21.00 ON WEDNESDAY, AUGUST 30, TO 20.59 ON THURSDAY, AUGUST 31 (Airburst ✳)

04.34	Capel St Mary	05.54	Off Lydd ✳	09.53	Off Dymchurch	11.56	Theydon Bois
04.35	Raydon	05.55	Bridge ✳	09.56	Folkestone	12.23	Off Dover
04.40	Great Wenham	05.59	Off Dymchurch	10.00	Woolwich	12.26	Off Dymchurch
04.42	Little Bromley	08.26	Chislehurst	10.01	Dagenham	12.28	Off Dungeness
04.48	Harleston	08.37	Chigwell	10.01	Dagenham	12.37	Hythe
04.58	Off Herne Bay	08.46	Monks Horton ✳	10.03	Greenwich	15.19	Off Dymchurch ✳
05.47	Off Dungeness	08.46	Off Dymchurch ✳	10.15	Hollingbourne	17.02	Off Folkestone ✳
05.47	Off Hythe	08.46	Off Folkestone ✳	10.30	Off Hythe	17.05	Beckenham
05.48	Off Hythe ✳	08.55	Isle of Grain	10.34	Off Folkestone	17.41	Hougham Without
05.50	Off Folkestone ✳	09.11	Aldington	10.34	Off Sandgate ✳	17.42	Off Folkestone
05.51	Lyminge	09.11	Off Folkestone ✳	10.53	East Ham		
05.53	Whitstable	09.24	Woolwich	11.55	Shorne		

BETWEEN 21.00 ON THURSDAY, AUGUST 31, TO 20.59 ON FRIDAY, SEPTEMBER 1

02.18	Ipswich	04.19	Off Littlestone	12.02	Chartham	12.55	Off Dover
02.22	Freston	11.34	Hawkinge	12.17	Folkestone	13.08	Clothall

BETWEEN 20.41 ON MONDAY, SEPTEMBER 4, TO 20.38 ON TUESDAY, SEPTEMBER 5

05.10	Felixstowe	05.36	Kings Waldon	05.42	Bardfield End Green
05.24	Eyworth	05.39	Dedham	05.43	Ware
05.24	Langham	05.42	Aldham	05.56	St Paul's Waldon

No V1s fell in Britain from September 2 to 4, no doubt due to the ongoing evacuation of V1 units from northern France and Belgium.

On August 26, General Bernard Montgomery, the Allied Land Forces commander, had issued a directive to the First Canadian Army to 'destroy all enemy forces in the Pas-de-Calais'. Having already overrun the southerly bomb-sites, early on the morning of September 1, General Harry Crerar's forces were approaching Abbeville when the Germans fired their last bomb from this area.

Although the German 15. Armee was retreating northwards, Oberst Wachtel's flying bomb regiment was meanwhile preparing to open an attack on Continental targets, and such equipment that he could save was now moved with his troops to depots in Holland and Germany. At the same time a new major offensive would soon be launched using super-sonic V2 rockets.

On September 6, the Vice-Chiefs of Staff reported that all areas from which flying bombs might be fired against London had been, or were about to be, occupied by Allied troops, going on to say that 'there should thus shortly be no further danger to this country from either of these causes, except for the possibility of the airborne launching of flying bombs'. Acting on this encouraging report, a press conference was arranged for September 7 to give the public at large the good news. Duncan Sandys, who was chairing the conference at Senate House, the Ministry of Information HQ in Bloomsbury, stood up to announce that 'except possibly for a few last shots, the Battle of London is over'. In this picture he is flanked by General Pile (left), commanding Anti-Aircraft Command, and Brendan Bracken, the Minister of Information. Mr Sandys' lengthy address was full, frank and details were given for the first time on the locations and casualties of the major incidents. He also revealed that '92 per cent of all the fatal casualties from the bombs occurred in the London Region', and said that during the 80 days, 2,300 V1s had got through to London.

It was in April 1943 that the Chiefs of Staff sent me four rather vague reports from secret agents which suggested that the Germans were developing a long-range bombardment weapon of some novel type. These four reports led us to suspect that the new weapon, if it existed at all, was being developed on the Baltic coast.

All doubts were removed when we discovered last November that the Germans were building all along the French coast from Calais to Cherbourg a whole series of concrete structures which had certain unmistakable features in common with those seen at the experimental station on the Baltic. Furthermore, we noticed that these sites in France were almost all of them oriented in the direction of London.

Heavy and persistent air attacks were kept up all through the winter. In the end, the Germans abandoned these launching sites altogether and started, round about last March, constructing an entirely new series of firing points.

During the period preceding the invasion a large proportion of our anti-aircraft guns were sited around the embarkation ports and assembly areas in the south and west. When the flying bomb attacks started these guns were immediately moved to prepared sites along the southern edge of the balloon barrage, stretching roughly from Maidstone to East Grinstead.

About the middle of July it was decided to take the bold step of moving the entire AA belt down to the coast, so that the guns should get an uninterrupted field of view.

From that time onwards the guns never looked back. In the first week after the redeployment the guns shot down 17 per cent of the bombs which entered the Gun Belt, and in the last week it was 74 per cent.

The AA defences have been in action day and night during the last two and a half months. The people of London owe much to the men and women of Anti-Aircraft Command and, in particular, to General Pile, to whose energy and personal leadership these achievements are in large measure due.

During the first few weeks of the flying bomb attacks the fighters shot down over 1,000 flying bombs. In the hours of darkness it was, of course, easy enough to spot the flaming tail of the flying bomb many miles away, but in order to bring down the bomb the pilot must fire his guns at a range of about 300 yards. If he fires when too far away he probably will not destroy the bomb. If he fires when he is too near the bomb may blow up and destroy him.

Our scientists gave much attention to this problem, which for a long time baffled us. Experiments were carried out with various elaborate radio equipments. Meanwhile, Professor Sir Thomas Merton produced a simple and ingenious range-finder which proved to be the complete answer. It was so simple that the whole device cost little more than one shilling.

As was noticed by many people, a small proportion of the bombs came in by night from a due easterly direction. We soon obtained information that these flying bombs were being launched from aircraft. This form of attack can, of course, be carried on from airfields in the heart of Germany. We cannot, therefore, as yet assure the public that flying bomb attacks will cease altogether.

During the 80 days of the bombardment, the enemy has launched over 8,000 bombs. Of these some 2,300 got through into the London region. Even of the bombs successfully launched, some 25 per cent were inaccurate or erratic. Many dived into the sea of their own accord. Others strayed as far as Norfolk and Northampton. The remainder were brought down by the combined efforts of guns, fighters and balloons.

In the first week about 33 per cent were brought down, while rather more than that reached London. By the end of the period there was a very different story to tell. Some 70 per cent of the bombs launched were being brought down by the defences and only nine per cent were reaching London. The record bag was obtained on August 28.

Although many hundreds of bombs were shot down by the guns along the south coast, only 11 of these fell in built-up areas. The understanding and restraint of the people living inside various defence zones in Kent, Sussex and Surrey are deserving of great praise. By their readiness to accept their share of London's dangers, the people of 'Bomb Alley' played a notable part in keeping down the overall casualties.

I am very glad to have the opportunity of expressing formally on behalf of His Majesty's Government our appreciation of the help which our American allies have given us in the battle against the flying bomb. They have thrown themselves into the job of beating the bomb with just as much determination and enthusiasm as if New York or Washington had been the victim of the attack.

DUNCAN SANDYS, SEPTEMBER 7, 1944

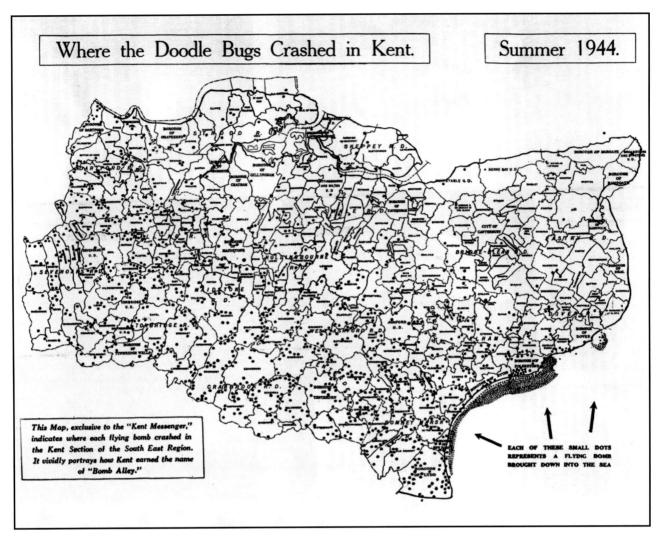

EACH OF THESE SMALL DOTS REPRESENTS A FLYING BOMB BROUGHT DOWN INTO THE SEA

This Map, exclusive to the "Kent Messenger," indicates where each flying bomb crashed in the Kent Section of the South East Region. It vividly portrays how Kent earned the name of "Bomb Alley."

There was also a relaxation concerning what could be revealed about the flying bomb in the Press, and many newspapers included maps like this one published in the September 15 edition of the *Kent Messenger.*

Rocket and Flying Bomb attacks: September 5 to November 25

The last flying bombs to be launched from the modified sites in the Pas-de-Calais fell in Kent in the early afternoon of September 1. By that date the position on land in northern France was such that within a day or two the whole of the Pas-de-Calais would have been overrun. Indeed, British forces were beginning their drive on Antwerp and there was little to stop them from reaching the Scheldt, Already the Germans had begun to evacuate the last of the sites and there was little likelihood of further bombs being launched against London from sites on land.

Left: The *Daily Mirror* caption to this picture reads as follows: 'Front-line fishermen at Folkestone repairing their nets of the damage caused by wreckage of Doodlebugs which did not reach London. These southcoastmen have carried on through shelling, machine-gunning, bombing and, until recently, Doodles were shot down into the sea all around them. Many have had their ships blown out of the water, riddled with shrapnel, and the timbers opened up. They get no compensation for damage to their gear, but their watchword is "Carry On".' *Right:* Comparison by the late Roger Bell.

Although the big bunker launch sites had now fallen into Allied hands, Generalmajor Walter Dornberger, in overall charge of the development of the A4 rocket programme, had an alternative up his sleeve, only this time the solution was even simpler than that adopted for the flying bomb. The rocket needed no ramp to take off as it rose vertically from the ground so the weapon could be fired from any small flat piece of concrete.

With unlimited freedom to move the launch pads around, a completely mobile organisation was set up under SS-Gruppenführer und Generalleutnant Dr Ing. Hans Kammler. The SS was now effectively in control as a result of the Reserve Army, commanded by Reichsführer-SS Heinrich Himmler who had taken over responsibility for the revenge weapons following the bomb plot against Hitler in July.

The possibility that air-launched attacks would continue could not, of course, be discounted but here also there were good grounds for optimism. Such was the Allied ascendancy over what remained of the German Air Force in the Low Countries, and so swiftly was the whole situation changing in the favour of the Allies, that few attacks were expected from this source unless the position on land stabilised before Belgium and Holland had been occupied.

As for attacks by rockets, it was known that the weapon had reached a stage of development and production where it could be used operationally but it was believed that the Allied ground forces would soon have occupied so much of Western Europe that no firing points for rockets could be established within range of London.

The first week of September was notable, therefore, for some of the most sanguine statements on what was to be expected from V-weapons. On September 6 the Vice-Chiefs of Staff reported that all areas from which flying bombs or rockets might be launched against London had been, or were about to be occupied by Allied troops and that 'there should thus shortly be no further danger to this country from either of these causes, except for the possibility

of the airborne launching of flying bombs'. On the following day, Duncan Sandys, in a lengthy review of the attacks that had taken place, spoke to the Press about the Battle of London being over 'except possibly for a few last shots'.

In fact, the battle was far from over for during the next six months over a 1,000 rockets and nearly 500 flying bombs fell in the United Kingdom. To understand how this came about, and how far the defences were caught unawares, it is necessary to trace the developments in our intelligence of the German preparations since the early months of 1944.

Intelligence on the Rocket, January — July 1944

In the sphere of Allied air operations, the eclipse of the rocket by the flying bomb was complete from December 1943 to June 1944, except for a small number of attacks on the large sites in the Cherbourg peninsula and the Pas-de-Calais. The intelligence investigation into the rocket, however, continued.

By December 1943, both weapons had been identified, but as the development work on each was concentrated at Peenemünde, and as the constructional works required for the operations of each were being carried out in the same

area of northern France, there was still some confusion between the two in the intelligence that was being received.

As far as was known at the time, Peenemünde remained the centre both of flying bomb and rocket development during the winter of 1943. To find out exactly what was happening there was even more difficult than it had been in the previous summer. German security noticeably improved after the raid in August and all foreign workers were transferred elsewhere, leaving as the sole intelligence agents in the district the sources that were investigating the activities of the Luft-Nachrichten-Versuchs-Regiment. As we have seen, their work on flying bombs was of great value but all that was learned from them about rockets was that firing trials were being carried out on a small scale. Photographic reconnaissances during the winter also added little to what was known, beyond establishing that Peenemünde was a production centre for hydrogen peroxide as well as an experimental establishment. And the most important questions: what was the weight of the rocket . . . how was it launched and controlled . . . what was its performance . . . what organisation would control its operations . . . all remained unanswered.

When Churchill spoke in the House of Commons early in August, although he could see a possible end to Germany's first weapon of revenge, the second threat was drawing nigh, yet up to June the precise size, weight, range and performance of the rocket were still in dispute amongst the British experts. Meanwhile, in Germany, despite the earlier bombing of the main research centre at Peenemünde and the necessity to relocate the test range to Blizna, plus building a whole new production line for the V2 at Nordhausen, everything was almost ready for lift-off. All that was needed was Hitler's order to open fire.

As long ago as February 22 I warned the House that Hitler was preparing to attack this country by new methods, and it is quite possible that attempts will be made with long-range rockets containing a heavier explosive charge than the flying bomb, and intended to produce a great deal more mischief. London, we may expect, will be the primary target on account of the probable inaccuracy of the new weapon. We therefore advise the classes for whom evacuation facilities have been provided by the Government, and others with no war duties here who can make their own arrangements, to take the opportunity of leaving the capital in a timely, orderly and gradual manner. It is by no means certain that the enemy has solved the difficult technical problems connected with the aiming of the rockets, but nonetheless I do not wish to minimise the ordeal to which we may be subjected, except to say that I am sure it is not one we will not be able to bear.

WINSTON CHURCHILL, AUGUST 2, 1944.

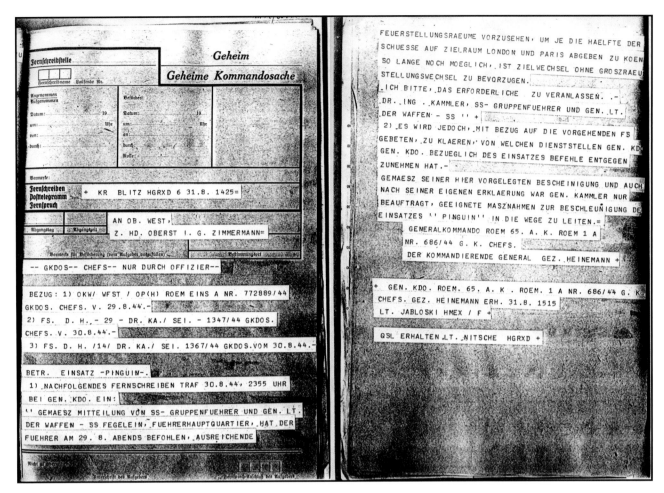

FEUERSTELLUNGSRAEUME VORZUSEHEN, UM JE DIE HAELFTE DER SCHUESSE AUF ZIELRAUM LONDON UND PARIS ABGEBEN ZU KOEN
SO LANGE NOCH MOEGLICH, IST ZIELWECHSEL OHNE GROSZRAEU
STELLUNGSWECHSEL ZU BEVORZUGEN.
ICH BITTE, DAS ERFORDERLICHE ZU VERANLASSEN. -
DR. ING. KAMMLER, SS- GRUPPENFUEHRER UND GEN. LT.
DER WAFFEN - SS '' +
2) ES WIRD JEDOCH, MIT BEZUG AUF DIE VORGEHENDEN FS
GEBETEN, ZU KLAEREN, VON WELCHEN DIENSTSTELLEN GEN. KD
GEN. KDO. BEZUEGLICH DES EINSATZES BEFEHLE ENTGEGEN
ZUNEHMEN HAT. -
GEMAESZ SEINER HIER VORGELEGTEN BESCHEINIGUNG UND AUCH
NACH SEINER EIGENEN ERKLAERUNG WAR GEN. KAMMLER NUR
BEAUFTRAGT, GEEIGNETE MASZNAHMEN ZUR BESCHLEUNIGUNG DE
EINSATZES '' PINGUIN'' IN DIE WEGE ZU LEITEN.=
GENERALKOMMANDO ROEM 65. A. K. ROEM 1 A
NR. 686/44 G. K. CHEFS.
DER KOMMANDIERENDE GENERAL GEZ. HEINEMANN +

+ GEN. KDO. ROEM. 65. A. K. ROEM. 1 A NR. 686/44 G. K
CHEFS. GEZ. HEINEMANN ERH. 31.8. 1515
LT. JABLOSKI HMEX / F +

QSL ERHALTEN LT. NITSCHE HGRXD +

Geheim

Geheime Kommandosache

+ KR BLITZ HGRXD 6 31.8. 1425=

AN OB. WEST,
Z. HD. OBERST I. G. ZIMMERMANN=

-- GKDOS-- CHEFS-- NUR DURCH OFFIZIER--

BEZUG: 1) OKW/ WFST / OP(H) ROEM EINS A NR. 772889/44
GKDOS. CHEFS. V. 29.8.44.-
2) FS. D. H., - 29 - DR. KA./ SEI. - 1347/44 GKDOS.
CHEFS. V. 30.8.44.-
3) FS. D. H. /14/ DR. KA./ SEI. 1367/44 GKDOS.VOM 30.8.44.-

BETR. EINSATZ -PINGUIN-.
1) NACHFOLGENDES FERNSCHREIBEN TRAF 30.8.44, 2355 UHR
BEI GEN. KDO. EIN:
'' GEMAESZ MITTEILUNG VON SS- GRUPPENFUEHRER UND GEN. LT.
DER WAFFEN - SS FEGELEIN, FUEHRERHAUPTQUARTIER, HAT DER
FUEHRER AM 29. 8. ABENDS BEFOHLEN, AUSREICHENDE

The order for 12,000 rockets was placed on October 19, 1943 of which some 3,000 are estimated to have been used on test flights. However, by the summer of 1944, only about 100 acceptable rockets were coming off the production line in the secret underground factory at Nordhausen each month against the planned total of 900. By September the figure was up to 600 but by then all the prepared launch sites north of the Somme had been lost to the advancing British and Canadians. *Above:* On August 31 Hitler's orders of the commencement of the offensive against London and Paris under the command of SS-Gruppenführer Kammler had given the green light to begin a new era in aerial warfare.

The Polish Trials

In March 1944, however, a fresh field for investigation came to light. When the operation on Peenemünde had been planned in the summer of 1943, it had been appreciated that it might prove almost too successful if it resulted in the evacuation of the station and the dispersal of the work that was going on there. As it was, development work continued there after the raid although a measure of dispersal was carried out. In November-December 1943, an organisation was set up at Blizna, near Debica, about 170 miles west of Warsaw (see map page 50), for testing and firing V-weapons, in which capacity it became as important as Peenemunde. It was controlled by the SS which reflected the growing importance of that organisation in the retaliation campaign.

The value of the move from the German point of view was not only that Blizna was unlikely to be attacked from the air but that it permitted firing overland and the recovery of the missiles for inspection. Intelligence in the United Kingdom was unaware of this new station until March 1944 when, thanks to the sources that had been covering the trials on the Baltic coast, it became clear that a flying bomb launching site had been built at Blizna from which bombs

were being fired. It then emerged that trials of a second long-range weapon were also being carried out at Blizna. To establish beyond doubt that this was in fact the A4 rocket took many weeks, and it was not until July that the matter was settled by the identification of a rocket at Blizna shown on a photograph taken on May 15. Concurrently with establishing this point, much valuable information, on the size, nature and effect of the rocket was transmitted by the Poles.

Evidence from Prisoners of War and the Swedish Rocket

In the meantime, fresh evidence had arrived from two directions, one of them entirely unexpected: from prisoners captured in Normandy and from the examination of a rocket fired from Peenemünde that accidentally fell near Malmö in Sweden on June 13. In other respects, too, the invasion of France marked the beginning of the solution of the problem for it released many of the officers of scientific Air Intelligence whose energies had been devoted to preparations for the invasion.

Evidence from prisoners who had been associated with V-weapon development was useful, chiefly in indicating that the rocket firing point was a *very*

simple affair and not the big and cumbersome mortar-like launcher that had been envisaged from the scientists' estimate of a rocket weighing 60 tons or more.

In addition, information was obtained that led to the discovery of three rocket storage depots, two of them underground in northern France. This, from the layout of their buildings and storage tunnels, provided valuable confirmatory evidence of the length and width of the rocket.

Something was also learned of the unit — the LXV. Armeekorps — which the Germans had formed specially for their retaliation campaign.

New information on the technical aspects of the rocket came from the one that had fallen in Sweden. Arrangements were made for two technical intelligence officers of A.I. 2(g) [Air Intelligence, Technical] to examine the remains and some useful information came from this inspection. In particular, the impression that had hitherto been held, that hydrogen peroxide was the main constituent of the fuel, was corrected as it appeared that liquid oxygen was used instead. However, it was decided that the most satisfactory way to exploit this fortunate occurrence was to arrange for the transport of the parts

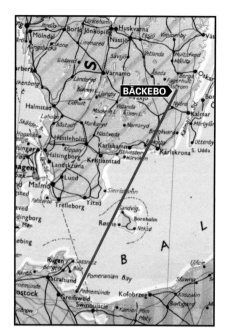

of the rocket to England for detailed examination and reconstruction. All this took time and was not in fact completed until the middle of August.

Until this examination was completed, the two main sources of intelligence were the Polish Secret Intelligence Service and German documents captured in France. The genius of the Poles for clandestine organisation proved invaluable. They set up an organisation to reach the sites of rocket incidents before the German search parties, and collect any small fragments of interest and photograph anything too large to be carried away.

They also planted agents in Blizna camp itself. By the end of June, they reported that the rockets were about 40 feet long and six feet in diameter and that radio control was employed. Their work was crowned by an exploit in which their leader was picked up in Poland and brought to the United Kingdom by way of Italy. He arrived on July 28 in a Dakota aircraft with all the documents and parts that he was able to carry, and

On June 13, the engineers at Peenemünde were testing a rocket under radio control when contact was lost. It continued out of sight flying north until it broke up over Sweden on re-entry, spreading itself over an area measuring four square kilometres at Bäckebo. Two tons of wreckage was recovered and taken to Stockholm for examination by the Military Aeronautical Research Institute under Colonel Henry Kjellson. Although Sweden was technically neutral, two officers from the RAF, Flight Lieutenants A. H. Burder and G. Wilkinson arrived late June to inspect the debris. They were permitted to take back some 112kg of components for examination at Farnborough while the heavier items, like the venturi, were flown to Britain at the end of July.

was able to clarify several points of detail in the reports that had previously been sent. In particular, he cleared up one point that had proved very puzzling: that many of the rockets fired from Blizna had burst high in the air. Previously, this had been thought to mean that a proximity fuse was fitted but from what the Polish leader said it was clear that the bursts were premature. In other words, although the A4 rocket had reached an advanced stage of development, it had not yet been perfected.

Before all the Polish evidence and that from Sweden had been absorbed, valuable information was revealed by a study of a series of captured documents

on the rocket sites in northern France. As a result, more firing sites and rocket storage depots were found together with an outline drawing of the rocket itself. Other documents showed what vehicles were required by a rocket-firing unit.

The most important feature of the rocket from the point of view of those who were likely to be its target was the weight of the warhead but it was not until August that this emerged, by which time the rocket had again become the major concern of the Government just like it had been in the summer and autumn of 1943. It is to what happened in this sphere from June to August that we must now turn.

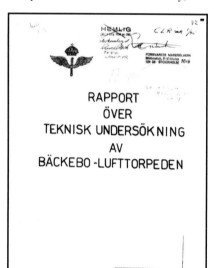

Left: The Swedish report, which included 45 photos, was available on July 21 which greatly helped Dr Jones in producing his analysis. *Right:* The impact crater left by the rocket engine has now been signposted some 200 metres past Gräsdals Glåd.

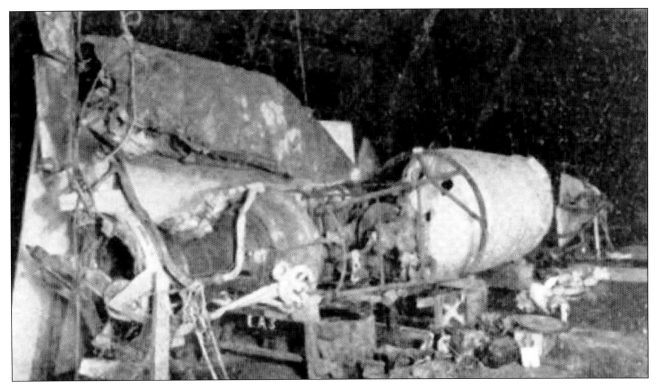

Renewed Interest of the War Cabinet

Although the first five months of 1944 had seen real progress in rocket intelligence, there was still so much that was incomplete and unsubstantiated. Up to the arrival of the flying bomb on June 13, little had been done to appraise the Chiefs of Staff that rocket development vigorously continued. The advent of one of the two V-weapons altered the position in that attacks upon the large sites recommenced, but these were attacks on suspicious constructions which it was well to destroy before they were virtually invulnerable more than upon targets known for certain to be connected with the rocket. And with their exception, active counter-measures against rocket attack necessarily waited for the crystallisation of the intelligence that was coming in from Peenemünde, Sweden and Poland.

Inevitably, however, the arrival of the flying bomb had led to a concern about the rocket and a demand from the departments concerned with the defence of the country for some statement, as authoritative and comprehensive as possible, on the possibilities of rocket attack.

Dr R. V. Jones was therefore required in the second week in July to prepare a report. He did so with some reluctance as all the results of the examination of the Swedish rocket were not yet to hand; photographic cover of Blizna was not complete; and the SOE operation to pick up the leader of the Poles investigating Blizna had still to be carried out. Consequently, his report, which was circulated to the Chiefs of Staff on July 16, emphasised the gaps in our knowledge, in particular on the launching points for the rocket, the radio control stations, the nature of the radio control, and also on the production and supply system and the field organisation.

Nevertheless, Jones made it clear that the rocket had reached the stage of series production, and that while it had not been perfected, it could probably be used operationally on a small scale. He went on to say that there were few indications of when bombardment might begin. On the weight of the rocket he said only that judging from craters seen at Peenemünde and Blizna, its warhead might weigh between three and seven tons. He repeated the opinion, shortly to be corrected, that hydrogen peroxide was the main constituent of the fuel, and also the mistaken view (which the Polish officer was to put right) that the rocket embodied a proximity fuse.

There was sufficient detail in the report, however, for the Prime Minister to come to the next meeting of the War Cabinet 'Crossbow' Sub-Committee on July 18 at which Churchill was critical of the Air Ministry's work on the rocket and their attitude to it, suggesting that they had been caught napping. He directed Dr Jones to keep his personal Scientific Advisor, Lord Cherwell, fully informed of all developments in intelligence.

He was no less critical at a further meeting of the Sub-Committee a week later. The previous day, a scientific subcommittee that Mr Sandys had set up under Professor Charles Ellis, Scientific Adviser to the Army Council, to study the rocket, had reported its opinions. Its report embodied intelligence that had recently arrived indicating that the firing point for the rocket was merely a slab of concrete and that its fuel was composed chiefly of liquid oxygen and, possibly, ethyl alcohol. It was more downright than Dr Jones had been concerning the weight of the rocket and advanced as approximations a total weight of 30 to 40 tons and a warhead of five to ten tons at a range of 150 miles. It concluded with the observation: 'Although we have as yet no reliable information about the movement of projectiles westwards from Germany, it would be unwise to assume from this negative evidence that a rocket attack is not imminent.'

At the meeting on the following day the Prime Minister, and also the Home Secretary, expressed surprise that so immediate a threat was not disclosed earlier. They were concerned lest Intelligence had failed in its duty, for the Government was now confronted with the information that the Germans had produced 1,000 rockets (this was the number indicated by the Swedish and Polish evidence) which could be fired from a simply constructed platform at ranges of 150 miles.

The suggestion that Intelligence had been weak was strongly resisted by Dr Jones who pointed out that the most-significant information had only come through in the past week (he had in mind the fuller report on the Swedish rocket and the arrival of the Polish officer). Nor would Jones accept that adequate warning of attack had not been given as attacks had not yet begun, nor was there any evidence of the movement of supplies towards northern France that would herald them.

In the light of the fuller report on the Swedish rocket, on August 2 Professor Ellis advanced a weight of no more than 24 tons with a warhead of at least four tons. A week later he reduced it still further in the light of the intelligence that was being received, and suggested that the rocket might have a range of 200 miles with a one-ton warhead and 140 miles with one of two tons.

As soon as the bulk of the wreckage arrived at the Royal Aircraft Establishment at Farnborough, work began to reconstruct the rocket. (After the war, all the wreckage was buried as infill for an extension of the runway.)

The Final Reconstruction of the Rocket

Nevertheless, it was a rocket with these approximate characteristics that the Germans had developed. The final links in the chain of intelligence were forged, as was typical, through the collation of several separate pieces of evidence. The general confirmation of the agents' reports of a comparatively low total weight came from the discovery from Swedish and Polish evidence that the fuselage of the rocket was simply a hollow metal shell which left as much space as possible for fuel, radio apparatus and explosive.

The next problem to be solved was the weight of the fuel. Peenemünde sources indicated that 4.3 tons of the main fuel was required for normal long-range shooting. The exact nature of the fuel was unspecified, but the most likely possibilities, after the hydrogen peroxide theory had been discounted, were thought to be liquid oxygen or alcohol. The examination of the Swedish rocket in July indicated the former, which fitted in with numerous agents' reports and information from prisoners, but it was not until documents captured in Normandy were examined during the second week in August that liquid oxygen could be regarded as almost certainly the main fuel. It was only then that Dr Jones would advance what he considered a reliable estimate of weight. He did this on August 10 at a meeting of the 'Crossbow' Sub-Committee, giving the total weight of the rocket as approximately 12 tons and that of the warhead as one ton.

This was so much lower than any previous authoritative estimate that the Sub-Committee demurred at accepting it. Within the next fortnight, however, confirmation came from a British source: the Royal Aircraft Establishment at Farnborough. There, since July 31, work had been proceeding on the reconstruction of the rocket that had fallen in Sweden. On the basis of the fragments of this missile, and a few dimensions from the documents captured in Normandy, the occupation of the volume of the rocket was accounted for. This gave a total weight of 13½ tons with a warhead of 1,900—2,000 lbs. What made this particularly important was that the Swedish rocket was known to be the result of series production; it was also fairly certain that it was rockets of this type that were to have been handled in the storage depots which had been captured in France.

Therefore, the position by August 24 was that the characteristics of the only rocket that the Germans were likely to fire against the United Kingdom in the near future were known with sufficient accuracy for the threat to be regarded with a good measure of objectivity. It was at least quite clear that unless Intelligence had failed completely, the rocket was not the devastating projectile that it had been made out to be when the threat was first apprehended.

Report by A.D.I. (Science) on August 27

The steps by which the problem had been solved, the state of our knowledge of the rocket, and an indication of when and on what scale attack might begin, were displayed in a 30,000-word report prepared by Dr Jones during the last week in August. This was the most-detailed statement on the rocket and the organisation that lay behind it that was prepared before attacks began. On August 27 it was circulated to every department and formation that had a direct interest in rocket attack thus ensuring that every authority concerned knew what to expect. However, Mr Sandys considered Jones's closing summation as unjustified and unfair to the many experts whom Sandys had called in, so the 40 copies of the report that had already been distributed were promptly withdrawn. Nevertheless, it was a valuable document, particularly insofar as it is evidence of the extent to which Air Intelligence had succeeded in discovering what the Germans were planning.

Dr Jones concluded: 'The Germans will launch the rocket against us as soon as they can amass sufficient effort. This may be soon, but the still-existing technical defects, the relatively small warhead, the increasing difficulties of supply, and our threat to the operational area, all lead us to believe that the magnitude of the menace is small.'

Counter-Measures, June — August

It will be recalled that from June to November 1943, Civil Defence preparations against rocket attack had been an important aspect of counter-measures. A warning system had been devised; reserves of Morrison shelters were concentrated near London and the Solent area, and plans covering evacuation of certain classes of the population from the threatened areas had been prepared.

The plans were made on the understanding that London was to remain the seat of Government and that essential war production in the London area was to be maintained. As investigations into the rocket continued during the summer and autumn of 1943, without confirming any of the earlier alarming reports about the danger and imminence of rocket attack, the War Cabinet decided in November that all plans for Civil Defence should simply be completed on paper. Then, with the emergence of the flying bomb as by far the more likely weapon for retaliation, all rocket plans were set aside early in 1944. It was only when it was reported at the meetings of the War Cabinet 'Crossbow' Sub-Committee in July that the rocket was in series production, that Civil Defence arrangements were again reviewed.

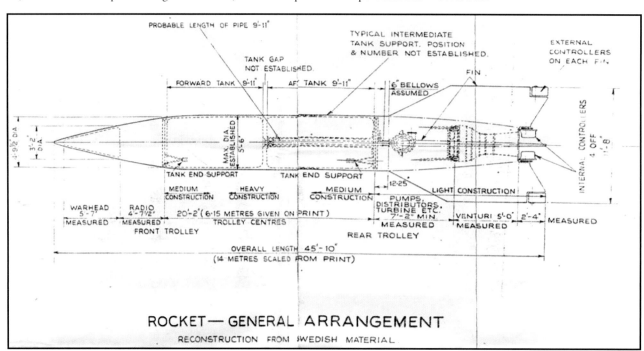

Although there was still over 800kg of the V2 missing, by August 18 the RAE were able to produce this detailed drawing.

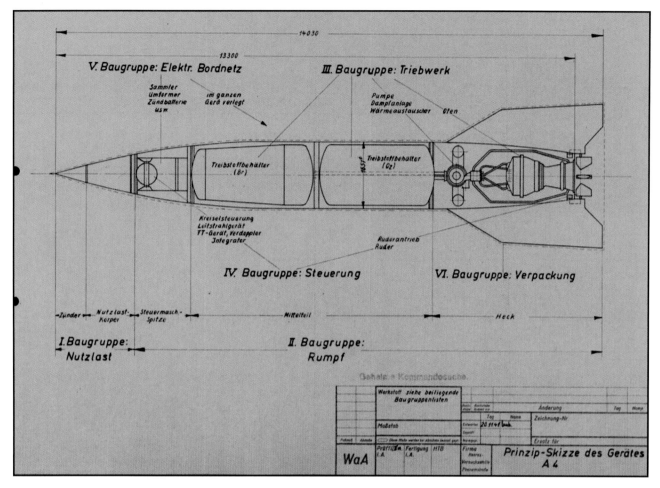

Diagram labels:
- V. Baugruppe: Elektr. Bordnetz
  - Sammler / Umformer / Zündbatterie usw
  - im ganzen Gerä verlegt
- III. Baugruppe: Triebwerk
  - Pumpe / Dampfanlage / Wärmeaustauscher / Ofen
- Treibstoffbehälter (Br)
- Treibstoffbehälter (Oz)
- Kreiselsteuerung / Leitstrahlgerät / TT-Gerät, Verdoppler / Integrator
- Ruderantrieb / Ruder
- IV. Baugruppe: Steuerung
- VI. Baugruppe: Verpackung
- Zünder / Nutzlast-Körper / Steuermasch.-Spitze / Mittelteil / Heck
- I. Baugruppe: Nutzlast
- II. Baugruppe: Rumpf
- Werkstoff siehe beiliegende Baugruppenlisten
- Maßstab / Änderung / Zeichnung-Nr
- Prüfstelle / Fertigung / HTB / Firma
- WaA
- Prinzip-Skizze des Gerätes A 4

It proved to be remarkably accurate when compared with a German drawing captured at the end of the war.

Herbert Morrison, as Home Secretary and Minister of Home Security, acted quickly. On July 26 he placed a memorandum before the War Cabinet in which he drew attention to the report that '1,000 rockets with a range of possibly 200 miles were believed to be in an advanced state of preparation and that the warhead weighs probably seven tons. The latest theory is that no elaborate launching sites are necessary and it is therefore reasonable to assume that the enemy will mount an attack on a fairly considerable scale, as he did in the case of flying bombs, even though the frequency and density may be less.'

So far the Civil Defence services were coping satisfactorily with flying bomb attacks although repairs to houses were hardly keeping abreast of the task. On the basis of the original plans for dealing with rocket attack it was quite clear that Civil Defence resources mobilised to their fullest extent would be exhausted after three or four days of attack at hourly intervals. Whether rocket attacks would be as frequent as this was uncertain but, on the basis of calculations made by the Research and Experiments Department of the Ministry of Home Security, it appeared that if the 1,000 rockets that the Germans were believed to have manufactured were fired against London, about 13,000 people would be killed, and at least as many, if not three times as many, seriously injured.

Material damage from a single rocket, assuming a seven-ton warhead, was expected to demolish or render uninhabitable all houses within a radius of 400 yards.

The implications were very serious. It seemed to the Home Secretary that the economy of London would be grievously strained if serious rocket attacks began, especially if flying bomb attacks continued. Hospital services might be swamped; the Civil Defence services would need considerable military assistance; a much bigger force than was already engaged on house repairs would be needed; and the police, railways and such emergency arrangements for accommodating and feeding evacuees as were in being might be overwhelmed by the exodus of people from the capital.

Nor were the effects likely to be confined to the civil population: they might well affect the conduct of Allied military operations. The Home Secretary argued that 'as the areas of sheer devastation grow under continued bombardment, I fear that the public will become angry, though whether the anger will be directed solely against the enemy may be doubted. We have boasted rightly of our air superiority and military strength. We shall be expected to use our resources to eliminate attacks on the metropolis by the new weapons as we have virtually eliminated raids by ordinary aircraft. It will be difficult to give convincing reasons why this cannot be done. In my view, the rocket attack

must from now onwards be regarded as a major effort by the Germans to avoid sheer defeat. It must be met by us by a corresponding effort both in active attack and passive defence, and not regarded as fatalistically inevitable or even as a by-product of enemy activity to be dealt with by the resources of the Fighting Forces which are not otherwise required to prosecute the war.'

Clearly, the Home Secretary was not disposed to minimise the gravity of the threat. Offensive counter-measures he did not attempt to deal with, but as for defensive preparations he concluded his paper by asking the War Cabinet to give a decision on the vital question of evacuation, the policy for which would largely dictate what was done in other spheres of civil defence. Also the Minister of Health felt that plans should be made to deal with an exodus considerably greater than that of the half million people for whom plans had been prepared in the summer and autumn of 1943 in which case some public announcement about the rocket would be desirable as a stimulant to voluntary evacuation before attacks actually began.

The Home Secretary's memorandum was considered by the War Cabinet on July 27. Its recommendations were accepted, it being agreed that 'plans should be made to meet the contingency of rocket attacks on the scale which now seemed possible, and certain action should be taken at once'.

The Government's plans for countering the rocket included the evacuation of children, just like the one that had taken place at the beginning of the war. Marchants Hill had been built at Hindhead, Surrey, in 1939 by the government-financed National Camps Corporation, and it was brought into use again in 1944.

Immediate action covered such matters as the evacuation of priority classes from London; shifting production, especially vital war production, from London to factories outside; evacuation of patients from London hospitals; and moving 10,000 Government employees from their present shelterless accommodation to safer premises either in London or elsewhere. The question of advising newspaper editors in confidence of what might happen was considered as was the advisability of extending Double Summer Time beyond the agreed date of August 13. Mr Churchill also did something to prepare the public in a speech in the House of Commons on August 2 (see page 172).

Throughout the whole of August, the work of planning and preparation went ahead vigorously. The position at the end of the month was as follows.

The areas earmarked for evacuation had been extended to include 27 boroughs and urban districts around the Metropolitan area, and facilities for evacuation had been made available to all mothers with children of school age or under, as well as to the usual priority classes. Organised and private evacuation had continued, and on August 31 it was estimated that nearly 1½ million people had left London, most of them doubtless because of flying bomb attacks. A voucher scheme designed to regulate the flow of refugees through the London stations was prepared, while to handle those who would move out of London by road in the event of heavy attack, temporary accommodation had been prepared in Rest and Reception Centres within 40 miles of the centre of London for a maximum of 700,000 people. It was a measure of the Government's appreciation of the problem that the possibility of providing accommodation for an even larger number of refugees was being examined.

Within the general plans for civilian evacuation, those for Government departments visualised the evacuation of about 85,000 of the 130,000 employed at headquarters in London of whom 13,000 were to stay in London in well-protected accommodation. The rest were to be dismissed or 'stood off'.

Also, by the end of August, good progress had been made in evacuating patients from London hospitals and thus leaving large numbers of beds vacant for receiving rocket casualties; 15,734 patients and staff had been evacuated and 23,249 beds in London hospitals were ready for casualties. A further 8,179 beds could have been made available at a few hours' notice by discharging patients to their homes.

In short, a good deal of time and energy had been expended on preparations of one sort or another. How far these would have helped London to withstand attack on the scale for which they were designed, it is impossible to say, for during the second half of August two new factors emerged which altered the whole situation. The first was the success of the Intelligence investigation into the rocket that pointed to a much less destructive weapon than had been appreciated in July. The second was the advance of the Allied armies in France, which increasingly threatened to drive the Germans from those areas of northern France from which it was presumed that rocket attacks would be launched.

As soon as Air Intelligence committed itself to a reliably low estimate of the weight of the rocket, Morrison asked the Chiefs of Staff what effect this might have on the possible scale of attack, taking into account also, so far as possible, the effect of the advance in France. He himself felt that some of the preparations that had been sanctioned were scarcely justified in view of the latest intelligence. In response to this request, an appreciation was obtained on August 28 from Mr Sandys who advanced as a basis for planning the possibility of up to 60 rockets falling daily on London during the first month of bombardment, reinforced by about 20 flying bombs. The reaction of the Civil Defence authorities was to amend their plans on the principle that the more-drastic measures that had been envisaged should be discontinued or remain plans on paper.

Then, as the first few days of September saw the situation further improve — the cessation of flying bomb attacks being only one of many good features — on September 7 Morrison recommended to the War Cabinet that such evacuation schemes as were actually being carried out should be halted and all preparations suspended. To this the War Cabinet agreed.

Today Marchants Hill lives on as a holiday camp and adventure school.

Radar and Radio

Amongst the first counter-measures against the rocket that were contemplated was the use of radar.

Five stations between the Isle of Wight and the North Foreland — Ventnor, Poling, Pevensey, Rye and Swingate — were specially fitted with Cathode Ray Direction Finding and photographic equipment to observe the flight of rockets, and a continuous watch had been maintained at them until March 1944. This watch was renewed on June 13 immediately after the first flying bomb attack.

Their equipment only permitted observation up to a height of about 50,000 feet, so during the early months of 1944 two other stations (Martin's Mill, near Dover, and Snap Hill, near Pevensey) were prepared to cover altitudes between 50,000 and 100,000 feet by the third week in August. By the same date, five more stations — at Ramsgate and Dymchurch on the south coast, and Bromley, Bawdsey and High Street on the east — had been equipped to the standard of the original stations. In addition, 11 Army radar sets (G.L. Mk II) were modified for the same purpose and deployed at intervals between Pevensey and Harwich. Special aerials, giving cover up to 400,000 feet, were also under construction at this time; four stations were to be fitted but were not expected to be ready for operations before October.

It was intended to use radar for two purposes: early warning and firing point location. As to the first, under the best conditions, i.e. if the attack was from northern France, if there was no jamming by the enemy and no interference through the presence of aircraft in the area under observation, a warning of about 3½ minutes was expected from the Cathode Ray Direction Finding stations, one of four minutes from the stations at Martin's Mill and Snap Hill, and one of 1½ minutes from the G.L. sets. But as to the second — firing point location — a mean radial error of two miles was the very best that could be expected. From the middle of June, units of the 11th Survey Regiment, Royal Artillery, were deployed near

As with the reporting of flying bomb attacks, No. 11 Group was once again set up as the central control for giving an early warning of approaching rockets. However, the supersonic speed of the V2 severely affected the ability to give a significant warning so it was decided that the new proposal of warning the public by the firing of maroons would be held in abeyance. Nick Catford of Subterranea Britannica visited the preserved HQ and took the photos.

No. 11 Group headquarters was based at Hillingdon House within the grounds of the RAF Depot at Uxbridge, but independent of it. The underground Operations Room was closed in 1958 and locked up but it has since been fully restored as a private museum although visits have to be arranged well in advance and there is a long waiting list.

Before entering the bunker, we were able to inspect the original 1930s standby generator building. Its control equipment is still in place and fully operational as was demonstrated when the generator was started for us. The building is typical of its type, a brick blockhouse with a brick blast wall around it, one of three on the base.

From the standby set building we walked the 50 yards to the bunker, an unobtrusive flight of steps down into the ground beside some bushes alongside the road. Apart from two small ventilator stacks, nothing else is visible as the whole area is grassed over. On the far side is a small wood where the emergency exit is located with a rectangular brick pillbox overlooking it. The emergency exit is slightly more substantial with its heavy blast door and two more ventilator stacks behind.

The two-level bunker, 60 feet below ground, is accessed by two flights of stairs. Between the two flights is one of two identical ventilation plant rooms (one used only as a back-up). These date back to the late 1930s when the bunker was built and are still fully operational. At the bottom of the

second flight of stairs we found ourselves in a rectangular ring corridor, with most of the rooms accessed from the inner part of the ring.

Half way along one of the long sides we entered the Operations Room at the lower floor. The room is really on two and a half levels. Above is the control room with curved glass panels to cut out reflection and noise, but at the back of the room steep wooden steps lead up to a low balcony overlooking the plotting table. The room has been restored to the state it was in during the Battle of Britain with the large irregularly shaped, angled plotting table taking up much of the floor.

We were able to enter most of the rooms around the corridor including areas not normally accessible to the public. These included the second plant room and emergency exit, ejector room for the sewage and GPO room complete with the original 1930s frame. All the original cables are still in place in cable runs along the wall and at the back there was a Lamson Tube message handling system.

Along the two long corridors are stairs to the upper level with three control rooms, one which would have been manned by members of the Royal Observer Corps. These look down into the Operations Room through curved and tinted glass windows, all original. These rooms now house the museum with a large number of exhibits in glass cases.

NICK CATFORD AND BOB JENNER, 2001

In preparation for firing, a launching site was cleared and roads made available to the area. The rocket was then transported to the site, followed by the launching platform on its trailer (Abschussplattform-Anhänger) which was placed in position directly behind the rocket trailer. The platform was then detached from its trailer, which was moved from the site. The platform was made level, and attached to the rocket trailer by holding brackets. While the rocket was in the horizontal position the nose fuze was attached to it. The cable trailers and power-supply trucks were now brought onto the site and the cables were placed in position. After the power cables had been laid, the elevating motor on the rocket trailer was started to drive the hydraulic pumps to move the elevating platform and rocket to the vertical position. This operation took approximately 12 minutes, until the rocket was hanging vertically above the launching platform. The legs of the platform were now wound up until it took the weight of the rocket. With the missile now placed upon the launching platform, the trailer was withdrawn approximately five feet from the rocket to allow the three platforms on the trailer to be lowered and the maintenance crews to commence checking the rocket. After the electrical and instrument tests had been carried out successfully, the rocket was reported ready. The fuel wagons were now brought onto the site and the rocket on the platform was rotated 90 degrees counter-clockwise for filling. After the rocket had been fuelled it was turned another 90 degrees in the same direction, so that fins I and III were pointing along the direction of fire. The erecting, servicing and testing of the rocket before launching required 32 vehicles and trailers. The time taken before actual launch in erecting and servicing was about four to six hours.

London and in the Margate—Hastings area to help in this work with their flash-spotting and sound-ranging equipment.

To make the best use of such warning as radar might give, the necessary telecommunications were installed to give direct speech between the radar stations and the Filter Room of No. 11 Group. From there, the warning system for the general public was to be put into effect.

However, much of the attention of the scientists and technicians was directed to the possibility of jamming the radio control of the rocket. Radio counter-measures of this sort were the responsibility of the Director General of Signals at the Air Ministry who worked in co-operation with Sir Robert Watson-Watt's Inter-Departmental Radiolocation Committee.

An essential preliminary step before any jamming measures could be carried out was to discover what signals were being transmitted by the Germans and for what purpose when rockets were being fired. As early as May 1944 a listening station had been set up to identify any signals that could be associated with the firing of rockets from Peenemünde. No information had been obtained from it up to the beginning of July by which time an extensive programme of investigations had been carried out. This entailed listening to and jamming enemy signals from ground stations, mostly in the United Kingdom, and from Allied aircraft. Listening from the air was naturally directed to the Blizna and Peenemünde. Suitable aircraft — Lightnings (P-38s) — for covering Blizna were earmarked by the Americans but owing to the Russian advance in Poland they were never used. During August the Baltic area was visited by Halifaxes of No. 192 Squadron, their operations being arranged to coincide with periods when Air Intelligence believed that rocket firing would be taking place at Peenemünde. However, no signals were intercepted.

Negotiations for the establishing of a listening station in southern Sweden were begun in late July but nothing was settled before rocket attacks began. It had also been appreciated at the beginning of the investigation into jamming that high-powered transmitters would be necessary if interference was to be effective. Accordingly, action was taken in July to provide 20 transmitters of 50 kilowatts. Two were already available and others could be obtained by modifying equipment in the hands of the BBC. At the same

There are virtually no photos of V2 launches in the field — this is an undated test at Peenemünde.

time three more were ordered from the United States. Eight such transmitters were in position by the end of August; a battery of six at Crowborough and two more at Brighton. All radio counter-measures were controlled by No. 80 (Signals) Wing of the Royal Air Force from a special control room,

established first at Beachy Head and later at Canterbury.

Thus a good deal of preparatory work had been carried out by the end of August for combating the anticipated attack by means of radio science but the location of much of the ground equipment had been dictated by the expecta-

tion of attack from northern France. With the increasing likelihood that the Germans would be unable to fire any rockets before the whole of northern France was occupied, it was possible to hope that the worst dangers had been avoided and extensive radio counter-measures would not be required.

All vehicles were then removed from the site with the exception of the radio test car, control car, power supply car and the trailer FR-Anhänger (S). The trailer was moved only 20 feet away from the rocket as it was still connected by cables to the platform, and steel protector plates were placed over the tyres. The rocket was then levelled and lined in azimuth. As soon as the orientation had been completed, a signal was given by the commanding officer or his deputy in the armoured control vehicle to denote that firing would take place in ten minutes. All personnel were then dispersed, with three engineers in the armoured control vehicle, one on each of the control panels (the radio panel, propulsion panel and power control panel) by which the rocket would be launched through ground cable connections. The control vehicle was parked 100 yards away from the rocket, the rest of the personnel taking up positions in slit trenches at about the same distance away. The rocket was then ready for firing. *Right:* At the end of the war, a Special Projectile Operations Group was set up in the British Zone of Occupation to test-fire a V2. Operation 'Backfire' was carried out on a firing range at Altenwalde near Cuxhaven in October 1945 using captured German rocket troops.

The region of The Hague in western Holland was the first and major area selected for the firing of V2s on Britain. Initially, in the summer of 1943, engineers arrived to carry out ground-pressure tests at the race course at Duindigt. Then, on September 7, 1944, a Sonderkommando of the SS descended on the Wassenaar district and the civilian population living on the streets Konijnenlaan, Koekoekslaan and Lijsterlaan were given two hours to vacate their properties. Electricity cables were then laid out via Rijksstraatweg and Rust en Vreugdlaan. The following morning a column of six trucks arrived to prepare for the firing of the first two V2s from street launch pads [1] and [2]. Other street launch sites are numbered in the believed order of their use.

Public Warning System

A scheme for giving warnings to the public had been one of the earliest counter-measures that had been pursued, and a system had been devised by the autumn of 1943. The problem was that only radio location could hope to detect a rocket sufficiently early in its time of flight of five to six minutes for a warning of sufficient length to be useful to be sounded. The need for speed also demanded that the number of channels through which radar information passed before reaching the public in the shape of an audible warning should be as few as possible. For the same reason, the warning itself had to be such that it could be operated centrally for the whole of a threatened area; it had also to be sharper and more arresting than the siren, to galvanise people into taking what shelter they could in the short time before the rocket arrived. The system that was established was as follows.

The specially-equipped radar stations that, from June 13, were keeping a watch for rocket firings were allotted land-lines for their exclusive use that linked them to the Filter Room of No. 11 Group. To the same room, 140 maroon-firing cannons in the London area and 21 in the Portsmouth/Southampton area were directly linked and could be fired by operating a single switch in the Filter Room. The procedure that was laid down was that on receipt of warning by the code-word 'Big Ben' from the radar stations, the Controller on duty in the Filter Room operated the switch and fired the maroons. Both areas would be put under warning as it was impossible for the radar stations to distinguish which was being attacked. If the system worked as it was intended to work, a warning of at least 1½ minutes — and at most 3½ minutes — would have been given to the public.

However, although the system could have been put into operation at any time during July and August, the preliminary announcement to inform the public about it was never made. There were a number of good reasons. In the first place, at best the warning was so short that there was some doubt whether it would be of any help except if attacks were heavy.

Then, the system itself could not be regarded as perfect. It depended entirely on the extent to which the radar stations detected rockets shortly after they had been fired, and what their proportionate success might be was doubtful. If there had been fair certainty of the scale of attack, these limitations might have been accepted, but in the circumstances nothing was done to warn the public and no decision was taken as to when the warning system might be brought into effect. It was, however, decided on September 5, by which time northern France had largely been cleared, that no warning need be given in the Portsmouth/Southampton area until there was evidence that the enemy intended to attack it.

Offensive Action and Plans

Up to the middle of July the bombing of targets connected with rocket attack was confined to four of the large sites — those at Mimoyecques, Watten, Siracourt and Wizernes — which were amongst the first targets associated with V-weapon attack in general to be bombed after the first flying bombs had landed in the United Kingdom. On July 10 bombing was suspended but when after six weeks, photographic reconnaissance revealed that construction was still going on at Watten and Mimoyecques, a further heavy attack was carried out (on August 25 and 27 respectively), by RAF Bomber Command. The results appeared inconclusive at the time but when the sites were later examined it

was evident that bombing over the whole period had very seriously retarded the progress of construction. Altogether, 7,469 tons of bombs were dropped on the large sites between the middle of June and their capture by Allied ground forces.

From early July other types of target were attacked. At that time, hydrogen peroxide was thought to be one of the main constituents of the fuel of the rocket as well as necessary for the launching of flying bombs so attacks took place on the hydrogen peroxide plants at Höllriegelskreuth and Oberraderach with this in mind. The three attacks on Peenemünde in July and August were also directed against the hydrogen peroxide plant there as well as the experimental station. An attack of the other main experimental station at Blizna would have been a very difficult operation and was hardly considered as during July the Russians were approaching the area. Instead, arrangements were made to send a mission to inspect it as soon as it was in Russian hands.

With one further exception, bombing operations during July and August were concentrated against targets within the areas from which it was expected that rocket attacks would be launched. The exception was an attack against a factory adjacent to the notorious Buchenwald concentration camp near Weimar. There was good evidence that it was making rockets, flying bombs and radio components so it was attacked on

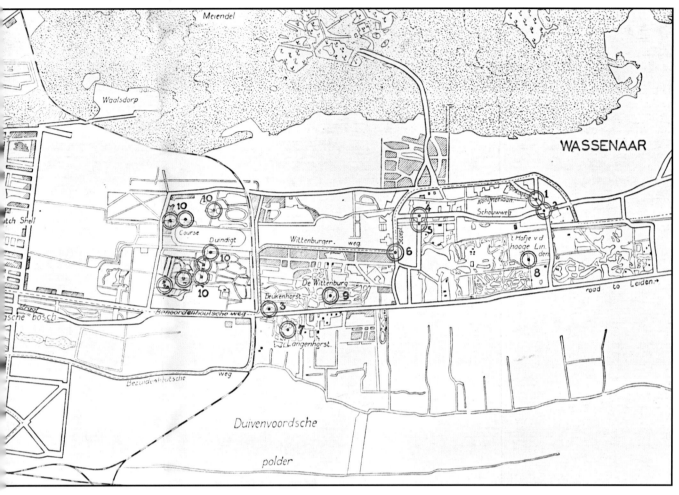

August 24 by 121 Fortresses of the Eighth Air Force which dropped 266 tons of bombs. Interpretation of photographs taken after the attack showed that a great part of both the armaments and the radio sections had been destroyed, and damage was caused to the SS camp and offices.

Otherwise, the main interest of the period lay in the planning of counter-measures that would be applied when rocket attacks were about to begin or had actually begun. The preparation of a plan was started by the Joint 'Crossbow' Target Priorities Committee early in August and completed by August 20.

The launching sites themselves were reckoned unprofitable targets, but the plan gave priority to armed reconnaissances in the area of the launching sites and near the rocket storage depots so that any fleeting chance might be taken of attacking any installations, vehicles or troops concerned with the transport, servicing, firing and control of the rocket.

Next, sustained attacks against nine forward storage depots and three rearward storage depots in the Rouen—Compiègne region were recommended, and also against a total of 18 liquid oxygen plants in France and Belgium.

The attack of the transport communications that the Germans would probably use for rockets was next in importance. Transport by rail was to be interfered with by attacks against what was known as the 'Third Ring of Rail Bridges'. This consisted of 30 bridges on or near the frontiers of Belgium, France and Germany. If these were cut, all railway traffic from Germany westward would be practically immobilised. The more northerly sections of it were brought under attack during the last week in August as part of the air support of the battle on land.

Interference with road and water transport was also advocated.

Events Immediately prior to the First Rocket Attack

As the first three days of September saw no check to the Allied advance in northern France, the future came to be regarded far more optimistically. The change was registered in a number of ways. On September 1, the Rocket Consequences Committee called a halt to the larger Civil Defence preparations. On September 4 the reconnaissances that ADGB had been carrying out were discontinued, and the Chief of the Air Staff recommended the cessation of the bombing of the German rocket organisation.

On the following day the future policy for counter-measures was outlined by the Vice-Chiefs of Staff. All bombing attacks against 'Crossbow' targets were to be discontinued, except for attacks against airfields from which aircraft launching flying bombs were known, or suspected, to be operating. With the rapid Allied advance, and so few signs of effective German resistance, the shelving of preparations against rocket attack is understandable, yet it was premature. Even if future operations such as the capture of the Rhine crossings at Arnhem, which had been decided upon by September 6, were successful, this still left the centre of London within the range of the whole of Holland west of a line from Amsterdam due south to the Belgian frontier.

This area, and part of Belgium also within 230 miles of London, was not in Allied hands on September 6, yet it seems to have been held by the Air Staff that the rocket had ceased to be a threat, a view that was not accepted by the Intelligence Staff at ADGB Headquarters. On September 6 they drew attention to the fact that as the range of the missile was known to be such that, so long as the Germans held western Holland, attacks on London were possible.

On September 4 the Chief of the Air Staff said that 'the Germans would have to make certain preparations of which we have no evidence and which in present circumstances are extremely unlikely'. This was a surprising statement for two reasons. First, it was well known that rocket-firing points discovered in northern France amounted to little more than half a dozen concrete slabs and two or three storage depots of which there was little or no information, and second, Holland had not been covered for signs of German preparations to anything like the same extent as northern France In short, the silence was a dangerous one . . . and events were soon to prove it so.

EINSATZ „A4"
bis 17.9.1944 ~ 2
M.: 1:1500000

zeichenerklärung:
Einsatzräume m. Angabe
der bekämpften Ziele
mot. Marsch - sond. Unt. Walcheren

'By order of the Reichsführer-SS, the date of the initial employment of the A4 was set for September 5, 1944. Two officers are provided with the necessary authority to bring the two groups North and South into action. Leader of Gruppe Nord is Major Mertin. Leader of Gruppe Süd is Major Schulz. Shortage of time and the problems of bringing a new weapon into action, as well as the uncertainty of activities at the front, will hinder these plans. The staff of the supply platoon has been divided. Oberst zum Eschenhoff remains in Gruppe Nord, Major Jester is transferred to Gruppe Süd for the supply task. Gruppe Süd is to receive a greater number of vehicles from Kraftfahrzeug-Abteilung 899. On Saturday, September 2, Batterie 444 travelled to Euskirchen with orders to proceed south to attack Paris. On Sunday, September 3, the 2. Batterie of 485 moves into Den Haag [The Hague] to set up operations against London. The influential suburb of Wassenaar has been chosen as the first launching location.' Gruppe Nord comprised the 1. and 2. Batterien of Artillerie-Abteilung 485 and 2. Batterie of Technische-Artillerie-Abteilung 91, while Gruppe Süd was made up of the 2. and 3. Batterien of Artillerie-Abteilung 836; Versuchs-Batterie 444, and the 3. Batterie of Technische-Artillerie-Abteilung 91.

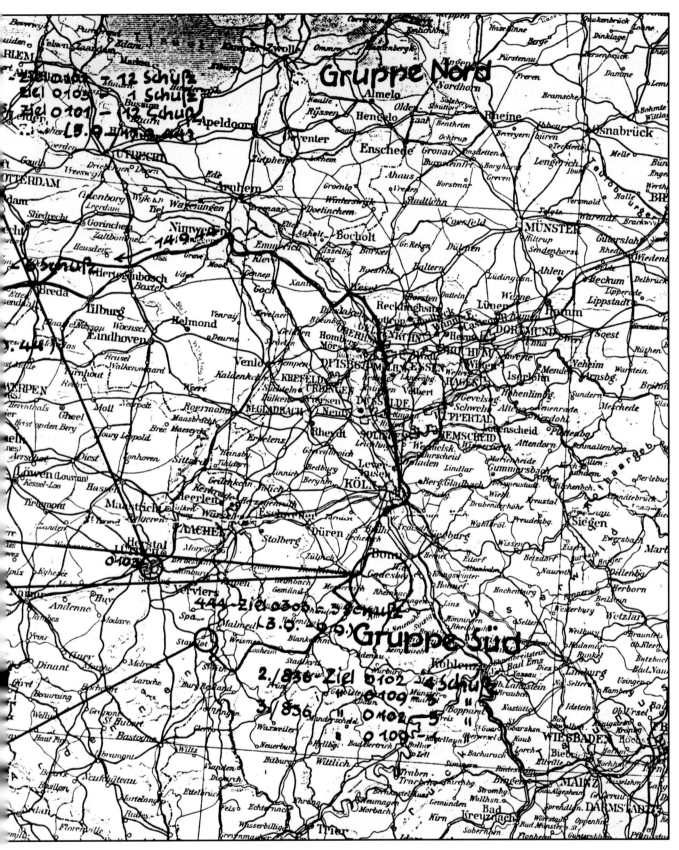

To launch the campaign, on September 6, Batterie 444 set up a pair of V2s at St Vith, 18 kilometres south-east of Malmedy in Belgium, with Paris as the intended target. The first V2 scheduled to be launched at 09.00 mis-fired, as did the second one at 09.40. Both rockets reached full power, lifted a few feet, but then set back on the launch pad, still vertical when engines were cut. The following day, Batterie 444 moved to a new location 17 miles south-east of former position near Houffalize and set up in a small village called Petites-Tailles. At 08.40 a V2 was fired from there at Paris but it was believed that it exploded at high altitude. A second rocket was made ready and launched at 11.00. This one was successfully impacted in Maisons-Alfort, in south-east Paris, killing six and injuring 36. (According to one captured prisoner, A4s had been fired earlier at Leningrad in 1943 although conclusive confirmation has never been forthcoming.) Meanwhile, the 2. Batterie of Artillerie-Abteilung 485 in Wassenaar was experiencing a heavy storm that even uprooted trees, one falling on the test tent. There were also problems with the new ground equipment which delayed the launches.

Reactions to the First Rockets

It was, therefore, without any prior warning from Air Intelligence such as had preceded the flying bomb offensive that the first rockets fell in the London area.

The first exploded at Chiswick at 18.40 on September 8, the second 16 seconds later at Parndon Wood near Epping. At Chiswick three people were killed and 20 injured, ten seriously, but there were no casualties at Epping.

From examination of the damage and fragments at Chiswick it appeared that the rocket used was essentially the same type as the Swedish rocket, and minor differences were thought to be due to the modifications necessary before a prototype could be produced in large numbers. The warhead was much the same as Air Intelligence had forecast, i.e. a total weight of just under 2,000 lbs of which 1,600 lbs was high explosive. The radar stations, although on watch, failed to give warning of the two rockets, but later examination of the photographic records of the Chain Home station at Bawdsey showed that plots had been obtained of one of them. Sound-ranging equipment in Kent gave good information of the Chiswick rocket but poorer information of the other. From both sets of data, it was thought that one launching had been from the Rotterdam area, and the other from somewhat further north.

Remarkable photo showing the firing of two V2s rockets from The Hague area. It must have looked very similar to those launched on the evening of September 8.

The first two from Wassenaar lifted off simultaniously at 18.35 from the crossroads of Lijsterlaan—Konijnenlaan—Koekoekslaan, and Lijsterlaan—Schouwweg. The first to impact came down in Staveley Road, Chiswick, demolishing seven houses and leaving the massive crater pictured here by the US Signal Corps. Three persons were killed and ten seriously injured.

Eileen Younghusband was on duty just ten miles away at the headquarters of No. 11 Group when she became the first WAAF to shout the words, 'Big Ben!' which signified the arrival of the very first V2. These American photos were taken by Signal Corps photographer McGaffin on September 9 although they were not released until March 26, 1946. The caption reads: 'An explosion of undetermined origin at Staveley Road, near the intersection of Burlington Lane, Chiswick, London, England, resulted in demolishing of several houses for several hundred yards.'

In September 1944 I was working as a Filterer Officer in the No. 11 Group Filter Room at Fighter Command HQ, Stanmore, where we handled and interpreted the radar information and early-warning systems for Britain. It was during one of my periods on duty that the first V2 landed on the London area. We had been warned of some new form of air attack and I happened to be the person who received the code-word 'Big Ben' from one of our radar stations. Immediately, I had to stand on a chair and shout out 'Big Ben' three times. The reaction was incredible, all hell was let loose but after several more of these attacks, we became used to them and things slipped back into the usual routine.

EILEEN YOUNGHUSBAND, 2005

On the morning of September 9 the Chiefs of Staff considered what counter-measures should be adopted. It is clear from the minutes of the meeting, though these only sketch the discussion, that they were not disposed to adopt any elaborate counter-measures while the situation on land was so promising. Moreover, only two rockets, little more destructive than flying bombs, had fallen in the country and a strong counter-attack was not yet called for. They advised the War Cabinet not to make any public announcement for the time being (none had been made by the Germans) and not to apply the drastic censorship measures which the original plan for security in the event of attack had envisaged.

It followed that the public warning system would not be put into operation as the radar stations specially equipped for observing rockets had been selected with an attack from northern France in mind, and were unsatisfactory for giving

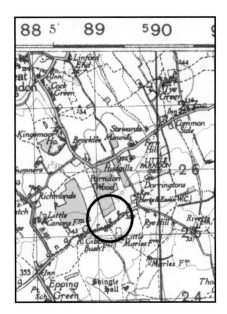

The second of the two rockets exploded on open farmland near Epping at grid reference 892254. These photos, taken by British photographers, were not released for publication by the censor until November 10.

warning of rockets fired from Holland. Sandys, who was present at the meeting, suggested that mobile radar or sound-ranging equipment should be sent immediately to Belgium to give better information on further firings than could be obtained from England. The Chiefs of Staff invited the Air Ministry to convene a meeting of the departments concerned to suggest measures for locating the firing points and providing an early-warning system.

First Counter-Measures

Although the Chiefs of Staff made no recommendations for counter-measures to be made by the air forces, nevertheless operations had begun soon after the first rockets had fallen. On the night of the 8th/9th, intruder aircraft, and on the following morning, day fighter squadrons of ADGB, were despatched on reconnaissance over south-west Holland, the beginning of an activity that was to continue until the last rocket had been fired against the United Kingdom. PRU aircraft began daily photographic reconnaissances over the suspected firing area, and aircraft of No. 100 Group were sent up to listen for and jam any radio signals that might have some connection with rocket firings. The listening and jamming stations of the radio counter-measures organisation that had been established in the United Kingdom carried out similar duties.

On the Continent, the Dutch resistance movement, through the Special Operations Executive, was briefed to provide intelligence of the location of firing points and the transport of rockets and fuel, and as early as September 11 a report was received in London that gave the location of three launching sites in the Wassenaar district northeast of The Hague.

Following the rockets which had fallen on the evening of the 8th, the next were reported from Fambridge, seven miles north of Southend, at 21.30 hours on the 10th, from Lullingstone, near Dartford, at 09.07 hours on the 11th,

Even so, this one, submitted by the *Romford Times*, still had the extent of the crater masked out!

How amazing would it be if the metalwork we found still rusting in the ditch bordering the Parndon Wood Nature Reserve on the outskirts of Harlow New Town in Essex came from the rocket!

In the early 1920s the American firm Chrysler Motors set up a factory just off Mortlake Road at Kew to enable them to beat UK import restrictions by assembling pre-made parts brought in from the USA, referred to as 'knock-down' kits. At 6.15 a.m. on September 12, blast from a V2 fired from Raaphorst near The Hague — the sixth to reach Britain — killed five employees. Three more persons were killed in West Park Avenue, seen lower left in the picture. Chrysler also owned Dodge and trucks known as Kew Dodge were the site's main product after the war. The factory closed in 1967, the Kew factory is now the location of the Kew Retail Park.

Aerial view of the Dodge manufacturing plant at Kew. Recent extensions and improvements have greatly increased production facilities. From these works, commercial vehicles are exported to over 50 countries throughout the world.

West Park Avenue backed onto the plant, Charles Lumley being killed in No. 40, Grace Hallet next door in No. 44, and John Cooper in No. 48. Note how the roof of the factory has been censored out.

and from Magdalen Laver, six miles north-east of Epping, at 09.30 hours, also on the 11th. Only one person was injured in the three incidents, in two of which the rocket was reported to have exploded in mid-air.

Between the 11th and midnight on the 16th, a further 15 rockets fell on land and three were reported to have fallen in the sea off the Essex coast. All told, therefore, 20 rockets fell in the United Kingdom between the 8th, when the attack began, and the 16th. Only ten of them fell within the London Civil Defence Region.

During these nine days the foundations of a policy of counter-measures were laid down. General responsibility lay, as for the flying bomb, with the Deputy Chief of the Air Staff. The channel between the Air Staff Directorate and the operational formations concerned was the Directorate of Operations (Air Defence). Although the Air C-in-C of the AEAF was ultimately responsible for the control of offensive air operations against the rocket organisation, due to the rapid advance on the

Continent — with its consequent strain on airfields and communications, and the continued importance of the land battle during September — the active participation of the tactical air forces was necessarily limited. The bulk of the

effort against rockets therefore fell upon the home-based air forces, and Air Marshal Hill at ADGB was responsible for directing and co-ordinating their activities as was the case with the flying bomb.

189

Another heavily censored photo as the Government did not officially admit the existence of the V2 until November 10. One of the typical explanations given out by the Ministry of Information was that a gas main had exploded but that excuse soon wore thin, people ridiculing the explosions as 'flying gas mains'! An eyewitness living in Ilford, one of the worst-hit boroughs, described the only sound similar to the ear-splitting crack of a V2 was a very close thunderclap. 'The initial explosion was accompanied by a blinding blue flash; then came a tremendous roaring as the sound of the rocket's descent caught up with it. Then came a secondary bang and a lesser roaring gradually fading to silence. We assumed that the second bang was a supersonic boom as the sound barrier was breached somewhere up in the stratosphere. At the top of the trajectory, the height was 60 miles, with a maximum speed on the flight of 3,466 mph. The velocity when the missile hit the ground was established as 2,200 mph. The only consolation for the unfortunate folk who were killed by these sinister monsters was the fact that they never knew what hit them — it was all over very quickly.'

Counter-Measures prior to Arnhem

The arrangements for the control of operations gave Air Marshal Hill the right to approach Bomber Command direct if he wanted a target attacked that was unsuitable for his own forces although there was nothing mandatory about such requests. On September 14 an attack by 37 aircraft of Bomber Command dropped 190 tons on a suspected rocket storage point near The Hague. Otherwise, armed offensive action was confined to patrols by day and night by ADGB aircraft over and near the launching area that by the 10th was known to be the stretch of wooded country between The Hague and Leiden. Between the 8th and 16th nearly 900 sorties were flown against a variety of targets.

Liquid oxygen plants, providing the main fuel of the rocket, were also considered as targets, but there was so little evidence about which of the many plants in north-west Europe were connected with the rocket organisation that a systematic offensive against them was held to be unwarranted so long as the

At Farnan Avenue, Walthamstow, struck at 04.53 on September 14, 24 houses on the western side were swept away with six fatalities and 74 injured, one of whom died later. This V2 was officially logged by the Air Ministry as Big Ben No. 10.

scale of rocket attack remained small. Intelligence reports during September had specified three small plants near Schiedam as producing liquid oxygen for rockets. Their bombing, however, raised a question that was to limit offensive action for the duration of the attack, namely, the safety of the Dutch people. The three plants were small and were in built-up areas and could not be attacked without inflicting casualties on civilians. Bombing was, therefore, ruled out. In its place, the Special Operations Executive was asked to arrange for their sabotage.

Up to the middle of September defensive counter-measures in the air were confined to a four-hour patrol every 12 hours by a Fortress of No. 100 Group from which all suspicious radio signals had been jammed. A continuous patrol for this task was organised during the third week in September, subject to the overriding claims of Bomber Command for the support of these aircraft and their specially-trained crews on bombing operations. In addition, Halifaxes of No. 100 Group maintained a listening watch over the North Sea but

Since the rocket offensive began there had been a hiatus in the arrival of flying bombs but that all changed on September 16 when a salvo of air-launched V1s began to make their landfall just before 6 a.m. (see comprehensive listing on page 195). The US Signal Corps sent two photographers to Barking on the eastern outskirts of London to picture the scene in St Awdry's Road.

Green Street's St Stephen's Church in East Ham was blasted by Big Ben No. 22 just after 6 a.m. on Sunday, September 17.

It had been fired by Batterie 444 from a new launch site on the Dutch island of Walcheren.

nothing significant was heard. From this, and from evidence from fragments of rockets examined in the United Kingdom, it was beginning to appear that radio control was not essential.

Most progress was made in the provision of equipment, both in England and on the Continent, for providing early warning of attack and for locating firing points. Certain measures had been put into operation by the middle of September; others were in process of being carried out.

In England, three radar stations had been added to those covering Holland making six between Dover and Lowestoft. One of them, Bawdsey, had been converted to a higher power, and two others were about to be converted. A number of the Army G.L. sets were also deployed in this area. The 11th Survey Regiment, RA, continued to employ its sound-ranging and flash-spotting equipment in Kent, and brought a small number of balloons into use to assist its observations.

The church had stood on the corner of St Stephen's Road since the 1880s but the damage was so great that a decision was taken in 1954 not to rebuild. Today this block of shops and flats seals off entry to the road from its western end . . . but beyond lies one of the East End's human tragedies.

Behind the church lay the home of the Burrell family at No. 3 that was totally demolished. Kevin Burrell explained that his father and grandfather were buried in the rubble but it was not

until another two days that his father's mother Elizabeth, grandmother Emma, two sisters Kathleen and Elizabeth, and his cousin Kathleen were found by an Alsatian dog — all dead.

This particular V2 was also unique as it provided the first photographs of major parts of the rocket — not that they were approved for release by the Press until November. Unfortunately, the relevant Home Office file on this particular incident has not survived as we were hoping that it would have given the location of this particular garden. Although the architecture of the houses seen in the background identifies it as St Stephen's Road, it would be pure guesswork to take a meaningful comparison. As well as the combustion chamber from the rocket motor *(above)*, this is the turbopump for the propellent *(right)*.

Thirty-nine low-power and four high-power ground transmitters for jamming were also in action by the middle of September. They were controlled from a centre set up under No. 80 (Signals) Wing at Eastbourne, which also controlled listening stations at Coulsdon and at Capel, near Tonbridge.

This considerable organisation had little to show for its activities. The radar stations and the survey unit had provided useful data for the location of firing points but, as these were thought to

All was collected together and taken to East Ham Police Station on High Street South. It closed in June 2014 and was sold for £3.4 million.

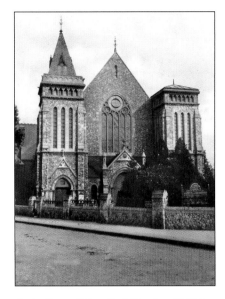

Just after midday that Sunday, British and American airborne troops began landing in Holland as the Allies launched Operation 'Market-Garden'. This had the object of capturing and holding bridges across the Rhine while XXX Corps began its drive north to the furthest bridge at Arnhem. It posed a serious threat to the rocket crews at their launch sites near the coast so, after one last shot on Monday evening, they pulled back to safer areas in eastern Holland to avoid being cut off. The V2 on September 18 was fired from Walcheren by Batterie 444 at 20.00 German time, crashing in Lambeth just after 7 p.m. The Baptist Chapel in Chatsworth Road had been built in 1877 by the London Baptist Association and the replacement *(below)* was constructed in 1959.

be changed frequently, the information was of little use for briefing purposes. Nor was the existing organisation reliable as a means of providing early warning of attack as in only six of the first 20 incidents could any warning have been given to the public.

The fact was that the original programme of radar and radio counter-measures had been based on the assumption that rocket attacks would be launched from northern France. Something was being done in this direction before the attack on Arnhem had been launched, even though success there might mean the end of the bombardment of London. On the 17th, the Deputy Chief of Air Staff reported to the Chiefs of Staff that 21st Army Group had provided a unit from the Royal Artillery (the 10th Survey Regiment) for employment in Belgium as an extension of the existing layout in the United Kingdom. It was intended to be in operation in the Antwerp area by September 23 though land-lines connecting it to the Canterbury headquarters of the system could not be provided until later. It was also agreed to set up an early-warning system on the Continent. Sites had been selected and the crews and necessary additional equipment were in transit by September 17.

So that the best use could be made of all these measures, it was essential that some form of control centre should also be set up in Belgium. For this purpose, a special unit, No. 105 Mobile Air Reporting Unit, was formed in ADGB during the second week in September. Its headquarters were to be at Malines and it was to be an advanced element responsible for the transmission of rocket warnings to No. 11 Group Filter Room at Stanmore, and for the correlation of all data received from the survey, radar and radio counter-measures units that would eventually come into operation on the Continent.

Effect of the Attack on Arnhem

On the morning of September 17, the airborne operations against the Lower Rhine were launched. Rockets continued to be fired from The Hague area throughout the day with five falling in England, all but one in the London region. This was the heaviest attack on one day since the bombardment had begun. Between the night of the 17th/18th and the morning of the 19th, when the Chiefs of Staff held their usual weekly meeting to consider 'Crossbow' policy, only one rocket fell — at Lambeth on the evening of the 18th. At that meeting a decision taken by the War Cabinet the previous evening was that no public announcement about rocket attacks should be made for a week during which time an appreciation should be made of the prospects of the continuance of the bombardment. Obviously, this entailed a forecast by the War Office of the situation on land by the 25th. The Chiefs of Staff, therefore, asked that this should be made and that the Deputy Chief of Air Staff, in consultation with Sandys, should prepare an appreciation of what threat would remain in the light of the War Office estimate.

In early September the German rocket force comprised over 6,300 men, a document dated on the 9th listing 173 officers, 69 officials and special commanders, 957 NCOs and 5,107 other ranks. All had to be relocated, Artillerie-Abteilung 485 actually withdrawing as far back as Münster in Germany. The experimental and testing unit, Lehr- und-Versuchs-Artillerie-Batterie 444, which by now had also been assigned to Gruppe Nord, pulled back to Zwolle to await the outcome of the 'Market-Garden' fighting. With the maximum range of the A4 being 200 miles, London was now too far away, but to keep up the offensive against Britain, SS-Gruppenführer Kammler now ordered Batterie 444 to open fire on two sizeable towns still within range: Ipswich and Norwich. Their new launch site was in Rijs Wood near Bakhuizen in Friesland on the north-eastern bank of the Zuider Zee. Meanwhile, Gruppe Süd began firing at targets in France and Belgium.

This appreciation, which also took account of flying bomb attacks, was circulated to the Chiefs of Staff on September 23 and was considered at their meeting on the 25th. By then two things had happened; first, the British forces had been checked at Arnhem and there was no immediate prospect of an advance across the Rhine; second, there had been no rocket incidents in the United Kingdom since the evening of the 18th. The two, as it were, balanced each other. From the first, it might follow that the attacks would continue as the launching area would remain in German hands. From the second, it appeared that the area had already been evacuated; there were, in fact, reliable intelligence reports that rocket supplies had been moving eastwards from The Hague and that the order to evacuate the area had been given on the 17th, the day the airborne attack was launched.

There was a further factor to be considered: even though the launching area remained in German hands, could they maintain a firing organisation there? The Deputy Chief of Air Staff and Mr Sandys thought it would be difficult and they reported that 'owing to the general state of disorganisation, especially as affecting communications in this area, it seems likely that few more rockets will be fired at London'.

The Chiefs of Staff agreed therefore that it would be best to wait a week before any public announcement about rocket attack was made. They also considered the question of giving a public warning of attack. Up to date, the performance of the radar and sound-ranging units had been such that it was decided that no warnings were to be given in the United Kingdom.

Similarly, nothing was done at this stage to increase the scale of Allied counter-measures. Armed reconnaissances continued to be made by ADGB though on a reduced scale owing to the contribution that was made in support of the airborne operations. Some 400 sorties were carried out in the week September 16-23, less than half that of the previous week.

V1 AND V2 INCIDENTS SEPTEMBER 1944

Flying bombs are indicated with a dagger †, rockets with their 'Big Ben' numbers. The times are those quoted in Air Ministry records. The fall-out from V2 airbursts (marked with an asterisk *) is often spread across a wide area, so locations in such cases are imprecise. See for example page 223.

September 8
18.43 Chiswick (1)
18.43 Parndon Wood, near Epping (2)

September 10
21.30 Fambridge, near Southend (3)

September 11
09.07 Lullingstone, near Dartford (4)
09.30 Magdalen Laver (5)

September 12
06.15 Kew Gardens (6)
08.19 Dagenham (7)
08.52 Biggin Hill (8)
17.55 Paglesham, near Rochford (9)

September 14
04.53 Walthamstow (11)
11.05 Sea off Colne Point (10)
07.25 Woolwich (12)
13.16 Rotherfield (13)

September 15
04.09 Sunbury (14)
14.20 River North of All Hallows (15)

September 16
05.49 Bradwell-on-Sea †
05.52 Barking †
05.58 Felsted †
05.59 Woolwich †
05.59 Off Clacton †
06.10 Saffron Walden †
06.15 Latchingdon †
07.33 Southgate (16)
08.28 Wembley (17)
10.28 Yiewsley (18)
15.20 Willingdon, near Eastbourne (19)
22.38 Noak Hill, near Romford * (20)

September 17
05.11 Knockholt, near Westerham * (21)
06.04 East Ham (22)
12.05 Hockley, near Southend (23)
13.11 Coulsdon (24)
18.56 Brockley, Lewisham (25)
20.42 Canewdon †
20.45 Easthorpe †
20.49 St Marylebone †

September 18
19.02 Lambeth (26)

September 19
04.16 Hornchurch †
04.20 Metheringham †
04.20 Rettenden †
04.24 Wetherfield †
04.27 Mitcham †
04.29 Hornchurch †
04.33 Tollesbury †

September 20
01.40 Cockfield †
01.42 Rushden †
01.43 Little Baddow †
01.48 Maldon †
01.48 Lawford Manningtree †
01.53 Dunmow †
01.55 Bethnal Green †
02.12 Essendon †
20.41 Chediston †
20.54 Richmond †
21.00 Poplar †
21.04 Codicote †
21.25 Wandsworth †
21.33 Waltham Holy Cross †
21.34 Wix †

September 21
04.20 Great Totham †
04.27 Bawdsey †
04.35 Hatfield Park †
04.44 Hatcheston †

September 22
20.35 Bradwell-on-Sea †
20.37 Enfield †
20.43 Little Heath †
20.48 Hatfield †

September 23
21.40 Thaxted †
21.43 Wormingford †
21.47 Braughing †
21.59 Codicote †

September 24
04.41 Swainsthorpe †
04.45 Framsden †
04.50 Pirton †
05.00 Burwell †
21.52 Chertsey †
22.04 Hessett †
22.08 Tilbury Juxta Clare †

September 25
05.15 Enfield †
05.29 Chigwell †
19.10 Hoxne (27)
22.55 Henham †
23.01 Gt Bromley †

September 26
16.30 Ranworth (28)

September 27
03.45 Sible Hedingham †
03.51 Ardleigh †
03.51 St Lawrence †
03.53 Edmonton †
10.47 Horsford, north of Norwich (29)
16.25 Kirby Bedon, SE of Norwich (30)
17.50 Beighton, ESE of Norwich (31)

September 28
14.20 8 miles NE of Happisburgh (32)

September 29
05.15 Chelmondiston †
05.19 Audley End †
05.27 Sutton Gault †
05.32 Edwardstone †
05.46 Bernstone †
05.55 Bygrave †
05.59 Barrow †
13.12 Hemsby, near Yarmouth (33)
19.45 Horstead/Coltishall (34)
20.42 Thorpe, near Norwich (35)
20.44 Rockleys †
20.45 Baythorn End †
20.50 Shudy Camps †
21.24 Off Felixstowe †
21.37 Walthamstow †

September 30
04.23 Off Felixstowe †
04.25 Imworth †
04.36 Off Southend †
04.40 Meopham †
04.40 Rudgwick †
04.42 Nazeing †
12.14 Tunstall, east of Norwich (36)

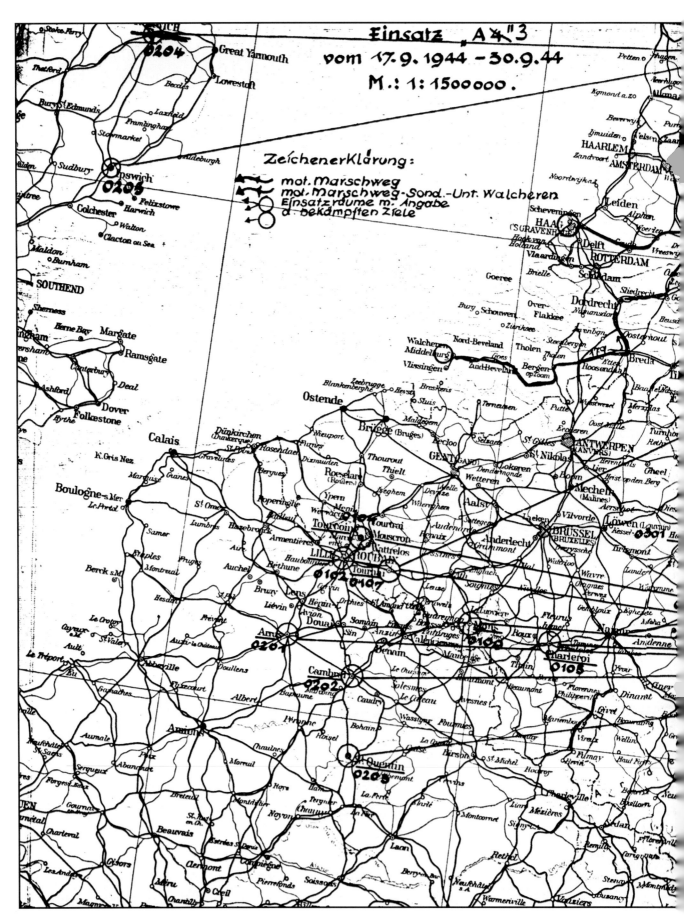

Einsatz „A𝕏"3
vom 17.9.1944 – 30.9.44
M.: 1:1500000.

Zeichenerklärung:
mot. Marschweg
mot. Marschweg-Sond.-Unt. Walcheren
Einsatzräume m. Angabe
d. bekämpften Ziele

However, by the 25th, with 'Market-Garden' not having achieved its aim, it was difficult to predict if, and when, the Germans would begin launches again. The Chiefs of Staff accepted that 'it was a sound policy to keep the public informed'; nevertheless they still decided to hold off for another week. That same day the attack recommenced, aimed now at East Anglia where Norwich appeared to be the main target. The new direction of attack was from south-west Friesland. Meantime, Gruppen Nord and Süd were back in business directing their fire at towns in Belgium and Northern France.

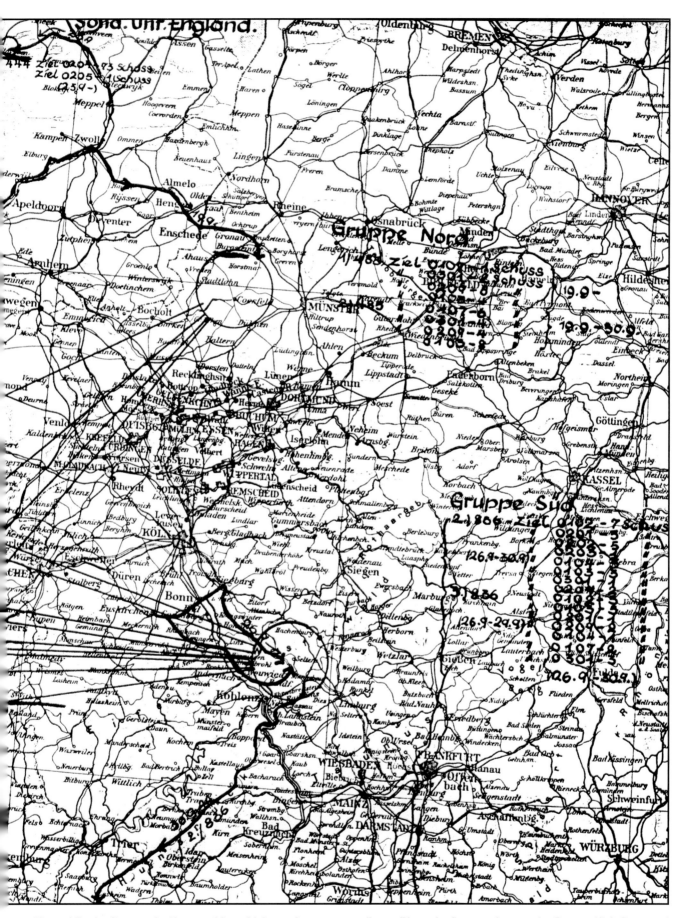

Meanwhile, the Germans had been waiting with increasing annoyance for a response in the British Press but none was forthcoming due to the restriction placed on mentioning the rocket by the Chiefs of Staff. As we shall see, it was not until Wednesday, November 8 that the German News Agency finally broke the silence: 'Not quite five months ago, the German High Command startled the world on the employment of a novel explosive missile; this is the case again today. Once again everyone is burning to hear details. The thanks of the Fatherland today go out to the innumerable hands which have worked on the V2 to put it into use.'

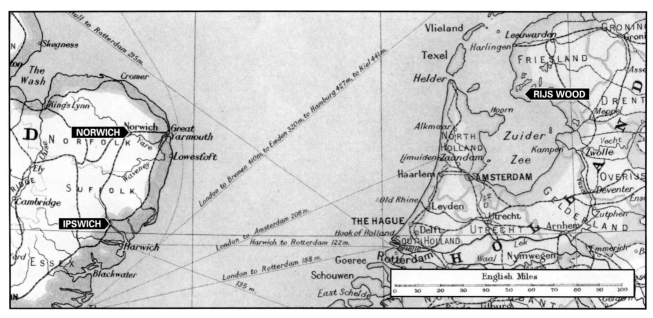

Switch to the Attack on Norwich; Rocket Attacks on the Continent

The lull in attacks on the United Kingdom continued throughout most of September 25. Then, at 19.10 hours, a rocket fell at Hoxne in Suffolk. The next came down nearly 24 hours later at Ranworth, eight miles north-east of Norwich. The following day, three more fell within nine miles of Norwich. This city now appeared to be the target, and from September 25 to the night of October 3/4, 16 rockets were reported from this district. No rockets were reported during the period from the London area.

Radar information and intelligence reports first established that the new direction of attack was from an area some ten miles west of Apeldoorn. Later, it appeared that an area in the south-west corner of Friesland was in use and possibly Vlieland and Terschelling in the Frisian Islands. As the most southerly of these areas was just over 250 miles from London, the main target, the bombardment of Norwich signified that the maximum operational range of the rocket was certainly under 250 miles. If London was again to be attacked, the Germans would therefore have to return to south-west Holland. However, there was no indication of such a move for over a week after the attacks on Norwich had begun and counter-measures continued after the pattern of the previous fortnight. ADGB flew 667 sorties over the suspected launching areas between September 23-30 and photographic reconnaissances over western Holland continued.

During the week, No. 105 Mobile Air Reporting Unit was established at Malines. Two of the G.L. sets that 21st Army Group had provided were set up in the Ostend area, and the 10th Survey Regiment, RA, was deployed around Antwerp. Radio counter-measures were maintained from ground stations in England and in Belgium, and aircraft of No. 100 Group continued to listen to jam suspicious signals even though there was still no evidence that the Germans were using radio control.

The scale of attack against the United Kingdom was such that counter-measures involving any diversion of force from the offensive against Germany were considered unwarranted but on September 14 a number of French and Belgian towns began to suffer rocket attacks. More than 20 incidents were reported between the 14th and the 25th, the majority in or near Lille and Liège. Up to the end of the month, no reliable reports of the areas from which the attacks were being made had been received in London. A week later, however, by which time there had been more than 80 Continental incidents, an area near Enschede on the Dutch-German frontier was indicated. This was only 120 miles from Liège and less than 200 miles from Lille, and the accuracy of attack against both places was better than in the attacks that had so far been made against London and Norwich.

Not surprisingly, therefore, the view was expressed by the Chief of the Imperial General Staff at a meeting of the Chiefs of Staff on October 2 that henceforth the main targets for rocket attack might well be areas important for 21st Army Group, such as Brussels and Antwerp. The observation was made when a request from 21st Army Group for the return of the 10th Survey Regiment from its rocket duties was being discussed.

The first arrival on October 3 exploded in a field at Beeston St Lawrence Park at 09.32 (Big Ben 38) causing little damage save for this centuries-old oak which still bore its wartime scars when Bob Collis photographed it in 1989.

About this time, however, the Supreme Commander was also becoming concerned at the potential threat to his forces not only from rockets but also flying bombs, for intelligence was received late in September indicating that the Germans were preparing flying bomb launching sites south-west and east of Cologne and Bonn. During October, therefore, a special section was set up in SHAEF for the control of a Continental 'Crossbow' organisation. All the radar and signals units that had been sent to Belgium to improve the defence of the United Kingdom were transferred to General Eisenhower's control, although the signals link with No. 11 Group Filter Room was maintained. A number of Fighter Command officers experienced in defence against V-weapons were transferred to the new section of Supreme Headquarters. As part of the general arrangement, the 10th Survey Regiment returned to its normal duties with 21st Army Group, its place being taken by the 11th Survey Regiment from England. This unit could be spared as the performance of the British radar stations had noticeably improved since the end of September. Very few rockets were not being observed and in nearly all cases the area from which firing had taken place was being indicated.

Although some 30 V2s were fired at East Anglia, it is surprising that there are virtually no contemporary photographs of identified impact sites. At 09.25 on October 6, Big Ben 56 came down on the outskirts of the village of Shotesham All Saints, the explosion blasting the windows of the village school 100 yards away. Joy Leighton recalled that 'it was a Friday morning and our teacher was reading us *Wind in the Willows*. All of a sudden there was an almighty crash and we all dived under our desks.' David Jackson remembered that 'there were pieces of the V2 laying all over the village several fields away from where it landed'. Now, the crater that lies off the footpath behind the church has been marked by a small interpretation board as a unique 'heritage' monument to the Second World War.

Some photographs are frustratingly difficult to identify. As this original print dated October 4 has the stamp of the SHAEF Field Press Censor on the reverse, we can assume that it was not taken in Britain. On that day, the 2. Batterie of Artillerie-Abteilung 836 was based at Merzig on the Franco-German border, 35 kilometres south of Trier, firing at Paris. These are the possible locations where hits were scored: Lizy-sur-Ourcq, Deuille-la-Barre, Dammartin, Noisy-le-Sec and Pantin. The caption explains that the 'hulk of the V2 has been gathered for inspection by experts'.

Renewed Attacks on London

The decision to release the survey unit was taken on October 7 by which time the direction of attacks against the United Kingdom had once more been changed. The lull in the bombardment of London that had set in on September 19 had coincided with intelligence reports that the German firing batteries had moved from The Hague north-east towards Utrecht, and, as we have seen, it had been from the northern half of Holland that rockets had been fired

On the evening of October 6 a flying bomb crashed in the business district of the City of London. A fire broke out in Gresham Street and Old Jewry and several policemen were injured in the nearby police headquarters. The V1 had scored a direct hit on one of the oldest firms in the City, the lawyers Freshfields Bruckhaus Deringer, at No. 32 Old Jewry. Before he died, Roger Bell visited the site for us and *(below)* **was thrilled to find the same post box still standing on the corner of Frederick's Place.**

against Norwich. On October 3, however, a report was received from an agent that certain launching crews had returned with equipment and rockets to south-west Holland and that rockets might be expected soon from an area

south of The Hague. The intelligence was promptly confirmed that same night when a rocket, which was subsequently plotted as coming from near The Hague, fell in Wanstead at 23.05 hours.

Between then and October 14, both Norwich and London were under fire, with more attention being paid to London as the period advanced, 39 incidents being reported, 21 the result of rockets aimed from The Hague area at London. However, the accuracy of the German fire was poor and more than half the rockets fell nearer to Southend than to London. Nevertheless the attack had recommenced and there was no prospect of it ceasing until such time as south-west Holland was liberated or some counter-measures, more effective than any that had been employed so far, were brought to bear.

The government was still imposing a total news black-out on anything to do with the V2, partly for morale at home but also to keep the Germans guessing. The official view was that to disclose details might help the enemy technically and would provide succour to her civilians now suffering increasing air attacks from the RAF that had once again turned its attention to Germany. However, on October 6 the *New York Times*, not under the thumb of the British censor, let the cat out of the bag when they published a revealing article on the rocket attacks by their Military Editor Hanson Baldwin. An Air Ministry representative in Washington cabled the news to London but the War Cabinet still decided to retain the ban, and it would appear that the Germans did not read the *New York Times*! The secrecy was maintained, even when the subject was raised again at a meeting on October 16. Then, on November 8, the German News Agency released the following statement: 'The German High Command announces that the V1 bombardment of the Greater London area, which has been carried out with varying intensity and only brief interruption since June 15, has been supplemented for the last few weeks by another far more effective explosive missile, the V2.' It was now obvious that the ban could no longer be sustained so on November 10 the Prime Minister at last spoke in the House of Commons. After the weeks of silence Churchill's statement made front-page news.

After the pocket occupied by the airborne troops at Arnhem was eliminated
in the last week of September, and the
Allied advance from the south had been
checked, the Germans were confident
enough to move back to recommence
V2 operations against London. The first
shot in the renewed attack was fired on
the evening of Wednesday, October 3.
Fighter Command listed it as Big Ben
43, giving the location as Leytonstone
although it actually fell in the adjacent
borough of Wanstead in Blake Hall Crescent on the edge of Wanstead Flats.
Eight people were killed and 12 injured.
Cyril Demarne, the West Ham fire chief,
attended the incident and, as he
observes on the opposite page, attack
by flying bombs was still relentless.

Then, on October 9, a V2 exploded on the anti-aircraft gun site on the nearby Wanstead Flats (Big Ben 59).

I returned to my office after an incident near the Wanstead Golf Course and settled into a chair for a snooze. I was awakened by the roar of an approaching V1 and moved to a corner of the room away from the window. The bomb passed over and, almost immediately, the engine cut out and I had the feeling of being suspended in space as I waited for the explosion. It came, a resounding boom, after the usual ten-second pause and not very far off. 'V1 explosion in Blake Hall Crescent, Wanstead, Sir. Your car has been ordered.'

Oh God; here we go again. What frightful scenes should we encounter this time? We had become accustomed to rows of shattered houses and shops and the back street factory with a dozen girls entombed; to the heart-rending cries of the bereaved and to children screaming for their parents; to the torn and hideously mangled bodies to be recovered from debris; and to the little corner shop, a heap of ruins, with customers slashed by flying glass, lying amid bundles of firewood and tins of corned beef.

As we toiled, several V1s roared across the sky and there came a chorus of 'Sieg Heil! Sieg Heil!' from hundreds of German throats in the POW camp, a few hundred yards along the road. How I prayed for one of them to come down smack in the centre of that compound but my prayer went unanswered.

The POW camp came near to disaster about a week later, when a flying bomb crashed on the anti-aircraft rocket installation on the opposite side of Woodford Road, killing a number of gunners and ATS girls. The blast set fire to dry grass on the site and it was by a narrow margin only that the NFS stopped the fire before it reached the magazines — crude corrugated-iron sheds with openings screened with hessian curtains protecting the rockets laid out in racks. It was a close shave.

CYRIL DEMARNE, 1980

V1 AND V2 INCIDENTS OCTOBER 1944
Flying bombs are indicated with a dagger, rockets with their 'Big Ben' numbers.   (Airburst ✳)

October 1
17.55   Bedingham, NW of Bungay (37)

October 3
09.32   Beeston St Lawrence (38)
14.41   Hopton, NW Lowestoft (39)
16.55   Mill Farm, Gt Witchingham (40)
19.45   Hellesdon (41)
20.10   Darrow Farm, Denton (42)
23.05   Wanstead (43)

October 4
08.15   Eastchurch, Isle of Sheppey ✳ (44)
12.22   Sea 8 miles off Yarmouth (45)
13.40   Rockland St Mary, Norwich (46)
16.47   Crostwick, near Norwich (47)
17.36   Spixworth ✳ (48)

October 5
04.22   Goose Green, Hoddesdon (49)
07.36   Sea off Great Yarmouth (50)
09.04   Taverham Hall Farm, Norwich (51)
11.38   Peasenhall (52)
13.28   Surlingham ✳ (53)
16.09   Tunstall (54)
17.44   Little Plumstead (55)
19.50   Off Orfordness †
19.54   Orford †
19.54   Stutton †
19.54   Colchester †
19.56   Noak Hill †
19.57   Great Coggeshall †
20.03   Bookham †
20.03   Surbiton †
20.06   Harrow †
20.07   Heston †
20.09   Addlestone †

October 6
09.25   Shotesham All Saints (56)
19.54   Bicknacre †
19.58   Off Southwold †
19.59   Off Foulness †
20.06   Orpington †
20.07   City †
20.24   Latchington †
20.32   Weybridge †
20.36   Mayland †

October 7
08.53   Pitsea, near Southend (57)
19.58   Off Orfordness †
19.59   Off Orfordness †
20.02   Off Orfordness †
20.09   Cheshunt †
20.17   Little Yeldham †
20.28   Greenstead †
20.44   Sutton-at-Hone †
20.45   Purfleet †

October 8
08.03   Linford (58)
20.00   Assington †
20.01   Marks Tey †

October 9
00.30   Off Southwold †
00.30   Wangford †
00.35   Assington †
00.47   Kelsale †
00.52   Hornsey †
05.07   Thwaite St Mary †
05.52   Wanstead Flats (59)
09.50   Havengore Island (60)
10.45   Cantley, SE of Norwich (61)
10.50   Brooke, SE of Norwich (62)
13.50   Hyde Marsh, near Fambridge (63)
18.30   Sea off Orfordness (64)

October 10
00.01   Off Lowestoft †
00.17   Thurleigh †
00.19   Billericay †
00.36   Hampstead †
04.39   Off Lowestoft †
04.43   Potters Bar †
04.58   Hatfield †
07.19   Sea off Clacton (65)
10.25   Navestock, NW of Brentwood (66)
16.00   Harwich Harbour ✳ (67)
17.35   Bramerton, SE of Norwich (68)

October 11
00.45   Rawreth, NW of Southend (69)
05.20   North of Ockendon (70)
06.50   Southend (71)
08.10   Haddiscoe, near Beccles (72)
10.51   Rockland St Mary, Norwich (73)
14.21   Playford, NE of Ipswich (74)
20.13   Felsted †
20.14   Off Orford †
21.22   Off Leiston †
21.23   Off Southwold †
21.34   Off Tillingham †

October 12
00.12   Walthamstow (75)
02.53   Sea off Clacton (76)
07.40   Ingworth, north of Aylsham (77)
10.58   Rawreth, NW of Southend (78)
23.44   Off Aldeburgh †
23.46   Capel St Andrews †
23.45   Salcott †
23.47   Framlingham †
23.50   Navestock †
23.51   Maldon †
23.56   Harlington †

Further Attacks by Flying Bombs

Any increase in counter-measures had to be considered in relation to the air offensive against Germany and to the weight and effectiveness of attack on England. So much depended on the first, that to reduce it in order to strike at the German V-weapon organisation would be justified only if the second was such as to impair seriously the Allied offensive effort. About the middle of October, when it was clear that the Germans would be holding most of Holland until the early spring, a reliable statement was needed as to the scale of future attacks. This question, however, could not be answered in terms of rocket attacks alone, for flying bombs were still reaching England. It is these attacks that must now be considered.

V1 AND V2 INCIDENTS OCTOBER 1944
Flying bombs are indicated with a dagger, rockets with their 'Big Ben' numbers.   (Airburst ∗)

October 13
05.04	Coggeshall †
05.08	Wanstead †
05.36	Friern Barnet †
06.48	Great Burstead, Brentwood (79)
07.24	Little Wakering, Southend (80)
21.32	Great Fransham †
21.44	Cressingham †
21.45	Westley †
21.51	Stretton †
21.55	Haynes †
21.58	Ranson Moor †

October 14
02.22	Potters Bar (81)
03.27	Dagenham †
03.28	Worlington †
03.31	Beazley †
03.44	South Green †
20.05	Southwold †
20.08	Off Corton †
20.10	Lowestoft †
20.12	Off Aldeburgh †
20.13	Off Kessingland †
20.16	Off Dunwich †
20.28	Hopton †
23.50	Barking Marshes (82)

October 15
01.47	13 miles east of Foulness Point †
01.49	18 miles east of Harwich †
01.51	Steeple †
01.52	Camberwell †
01.55	Tillingham †
01.59	Dovercourt †
02.00	Cheshunt †
02.03	Northaw †
02.08	Nayland †
02.09	Great Totham †
02.09	Off Covehithe †
05.05	Rettendon, SE of Chelmsford (83)
22.40	Luddesdown †
22.42	Rochford †
22.45	Off Seaford †
22.48	Mepal †

October 16
04.55	West Benacre †
04.55	Off Clacton †
04.58	Off Southwold †
04.58	NNW of Felixstowe †
04.59	Near Kessingland †
04.59	Off Leiston †
05.00	Off Leiston †
05.06	Sidcup †
05.08	Near Southend †
05.12	Near Benacre †
20.05	Off Sales Point †
20.07	Kirby-le-Soken †
20.07	10 miles SE of Clacton †
20.09	Off Tillingham †
20.19	Kirby-le-Soken †
20.26	Ongar †
20.32	Dartford †

October 17
15.50	Little Baddow, Chelmsford (84)
21.48	Off Orfordness †
21.54	Off Aldeburgh †
21.55	Kirby-le-Soken †
21.57	Off Leiston †
21.58	Off Southwold †
21.58	Off Covehithe †
21.58	Off Dunwich †
22.05	Dengie (Maldon RD) †
22.12	West Thurrock †

October 18
06.32	Chislet, NE of Canterbury (85)
23.27	Ipswich †
23.28	Edmonton †
23.29	Weeley †
23.30	Off Orfordness †
23.35	Frinton & Walton †
23.38	Thorrington †

October 19
04.59	Off Holliwell Point †
05.11	Thurlton †
05.12	Oulton Broad †
05.15	Off Leiston †
05.17	Off Alderton †
05.23	Alpheton †
07.17	Borough Green, Sevenoaks (86)
20.16	Capel St. Andrews †
20.22	Off Dunwich †
20.24	Off Aldeburgh †
20.26	Off Tillingham †
20.27	Off Canvey Island †
20.30	Off Orfordness †
20.32	10 miles east of Felixstowe †
20.32	Off Aldeburgh †

October 20
04.58	Off Felixstowe †
04.59	Off Felixstowe †
04.59	Off Clacton †
05.00	Off Aldeburgh †
05.03	Ramsey †
05.10	Fyfield †
05.15	Great Bentley †
05.17	Potters Bar †
05.18	Brookman's Park (Hatfield RD) †
20.15	South Norwood (87)

October 21
01.15	Hayes (88)
04.49	Barking †
04.49	Great Wakering †
04.53	Off Felixstowe †
06.25	Skippers Island †
23.13	Rivenhall †
23.18	Cheshunt †
23.20	Navestock †
23.20	Rayleigh †
23.23	Chingford †
23.24	Hackney †

October 23
03.44	Sea 1 mile SW of Clacton (89)
14.10	Felmore Farm, Billericay (90)
16.53	St Mary's at Hoo, Chatham (91)
19.18	Navestock Heath (92)
19.34	Off Sales Point †
19.37	Lamarsh †
19.44	Grays, Thurrock †
19.45	Ashtead †
19.47	Pound Hill †
19.51	Woolwich †

October 24
00.28	Langdon Hills, Tilbury (93)
00.49	Off Foulness †
00.50	Off Tillingham †
00.55	Snape †
01.00	Hartlip †
01.01	Fittleworth †
01.02	Off Bridgewick †
01.04	Dunton †
01.07	Hoddesdon †
02.07	Sear near Queenborough (94)
05.02	Rushmere St Andrew (95)
19.41	16 miles east of Felixstowe †
19.43	Off Shoeburyness †
19.47	Off Havengore †

October 24 (continued)
19.49	Off Tillingham †
19.49	Off Shoeburyness †
19.49	Hartfield †
19.55	Detling †
19.55	Latchingdon (Maldon RD) †
20.44	Bulphan, Essex (96)
20.47	Orsett, Essex (97)
22.27	Canvey Island (98)
23.58	Off Hollesley †

October 25
00.10	Laindon (Billericay UDC) †
12.40	Rawreth, Essex (99)
19.25	20 miles east of Dunwich †
19.26	Off Southwold †
19.27	Brightwell †
19.32	Boughton-under-Blean †
19.35	Margaretting †
19.37	Off Dunwich †
19.39	Orpington †
19.49	Off Leiston †
19.54	Richmond †

October 26
08.10	Walthamstow (100)
08.40	Bermondsey (101)
09.00	Barley, 3m SE of Royston (102)
10.14	Welborne, 10m W of Norwich (103)
11.35	Sheering (104)
13.41	Sea off Clacton (105)
18.45	Palmers Green (106)
22.50	Ilford (107)

October 27
06.55	Windsor Great Park (108)
10.15	In field near Swanley (109)
11.21	Wanstead (110)
12.05	Chingford, forest land (111)
18.54	Buckhurst Hill (112)
23.25	West Ham (113)
23.47	Lewisham (114)

October 28
04.59	Ashford, near Staines (115)
11.07	Deptford ∗ (116)
18.15	Shalford, near Braintree (117)
18.20	Camberwell ∗ (118)

October 29
05.10	Hollesley †
05.22	Danbury †
05.33	Off Leiston †
05.43	Banstead †
23.57	Shenfield, Essex (119)

October 30
05.15	Beckton, near Barking (120)
12.30	West Ham, Victoria Dock (121)
12.31	West Ham, Forest Lane (122)
16.23	Plumstead (123)
18.47	Wapping, Hermitage Wharf (124)
20.38	Elstree, Ridge Hill (125)

October 31
02.56	Hanwell Golf Course ∗ (126)
06.34	Off Walton-on-the-Naze †
06.36	Off Walton-on-the-Naze †
06.41	Off Bridgewick †
06.49	Coulsdon †
07.40	Surrey Commercial Docks (127)
07.52	Sudbourne †
08.03	West Ham †
08.17	Wigborough †
08.59	Wandsworth †
18.11	Bexleyheath (128)
18.36	Victoria Dock (129)
21.03	Hendon, Kingsbury ∗ (130)
23.40	Orpington (131)

From documents captured after the war, between the night of July 7/8 and November 10/11, Kampfgeschwader 3 (and its replacement from early October, KG53) air-launched 1,176 V1s against London. We are told that the failure rate was 40 per cent!

Flying Bombs, September 15 — October 14

It will be recalled that the main phase of the flying bomb attack on London came to an end in the early morning of September 5 when eight V1s fell at scattered points north and east of London. They were the last of a considerable number of bombs that had been launched since July 8, concurrently with launchings by He 111s of I./KG53 operating concurrently from airfields in Holland.

The optimism in the United Kingdom on the first week in September was tempered by the realisation that similar attacks might continue though it was thought that their scale would be so small that no modifications need yet be made to the existing scheme of defence. During the next ten days, Air Intelligence regularly reported the intensification of trial launchings in the Baltic area

so it was no surprise when air-launched flying bombs again came over England. This was in the early morning of September 16, the ten-day lull since the last attacks being accounted for by the move of I./KG53 from its Dutch bases to airfields in north-western Germany, of which Varrelbusch, Aalhorn and Rheine were thought to have been taken over. About 15 He 111s participated in the attack that took place between 05.30 and 06.30 hours, seven flying bombs being reported by the defences. Two came down in London, the rest fell at various widely separated points in Essex.

Attacks continued to be made on most nights during the rest of September, and by the end of the month 80 bombs had been plotted by the defences on 12 nights. Of these, 72 came overland but only 14 reached the London area. Twenty-three bombs

were destroyed: ten by fighters (two over the sea); ten by guns of Anti-Aircraft Command (three over the sea); two by naval gun-fire from Royal Navy ships at sea, with one shared by Anti-Aircraft Command and the Navy.

The attack continued on a similar scale during the next fortnight. Sixty-nine flying bombs were plotted of which 53 came overland and 12 fell in the London area, a slightly higher proportion of those that were plotted than in the previous fortnight. However, against this, the defences had been almost exactly twice as successful. From September 15-30, 29 per cent of the flying bombs plotted had been destroyed, whereas in the period October 1-14 this figure had risen to 55 per cent. Thirteen bombs were shot down by fighters, three over the sea; 23 by Anti-Aircraft Command, 11 over the sea; and two by naval gunners.

Anti-Aircraft Command claimed that 50 per cent of the bombs crossing the coast were destroyed by its guns. In this dramatic shot, a V1 approaching from the left is hit, the resulting explosion momentarily projecting a circle of light on the clouds above.

A good idea of the size of the crater caused by a V1 is shown here in Cambridge Heath Road, Bethnal Green, not that far from where the bomb in the very first salvo had landed. This particular V1 crashed at 01.55 on September 20. Home Security reported the crater as 20 feet diameter and four feet deep.

Counter-Measures, September 15 — October 14

These figures reflect a departure from the 'stand fast' defensive policy that, in default of anything better, had followed the end of the main attack from northern France. When air-launched attacks recommenced, the great majority of the guns that had been in action against flying bombs were still deployed in the Gun Belt on the south-east coast and the Gun Box in Essex, The latter, it will be remembered, had been established expressly to deal with air-launched attacks against London from the outer Thames estuary. Some of the renewed attacks were also launched from this direction but others were made from further north, the bombs crossing the coast between Clacton and Harwich.

The first defensive measures to be taken — apart from interception sorties by ADGB night fighters — therefore involved the reinforcement of the Gun Box and the deployment of additional batteries along the coast between Clacton and Harwich. Between September 16 and 19, 16 heavy and nine light anti-aircraft batteries were ordered to move. This was a considerable force although it was not the intention at this stage to establish a coastal gun-belt in East Anglia similar to that which had been so effective in the south-east. The scale of attack was not sufficient to warrant the great concentrations of fire-power that had been employed in the south-east. Moreover, to permit unrestricted fire during darkness — and it was expected that the German attacks would continue to be made exclusively at night — would endanger the aircraft of Bomber Command which normally flew out and home over the East Anglian coast.

Accordingly, the rules for engagement for guns in the Clacton—Harwich strip permitted 'seen' fire at flying bombs below 6,000 feet but 'unseen' fire only when the No. 11 Group Controller was certain that there were no friendly aircraft in the area. Night fighters, however, were instructed to regard the new deployment as they did the Gun Box and Gun Belt: that is to say they were not to pursue flying bombs closer than six miles to the coast from seaward and five miles from landward. Additional searchlights were set up near the coast to mark the boundaries of the area.

A conference was held at ADGB Headquarters on September 21 to consolidate these first measures and work out a comprehensive plan for defence

against the new attacks. By that time, it was clear that the use of what can well be described as a highly mobile launching site — the bomber aircraft — conferred a great advantage on the enemy. He could launch flying bombs from any point over the North Sea so long as it was within 130 miles (the range of the flying bomb) from London. Indeed, by the 21st there was good evidence that flying bombs aimed at London had crossed the coast even further north than Harwich but to protect the whole coast of East Anglia round to the Wash was reckoned to be unjustifiable. Instead, it was decided to establish a coastal gun zone, 5,000 yards deep, from Clacton, where the existing Gun Box had its northerly limit, to Great Yarmouth. It was to embrace the permanent anti-aircraft defences of places like Harwich, Lowestoft and Great Yarmouth. The total number of guns to be deployed, including those already in the Gun Box and in permanent defences, was 516 heavy guns and 611 light weapons. Forward of the gun zone, patrol areas for Mosquito night fighters were established. Inland of the zone, Tempests of No. 501 Squadron were to operate in co-operation with searchlights.

The order to redeploy to the north of Harwich was issued to all batteries concerned in the early morning of September 22. Some preliminary work in selecting sites and in preparing stocks of steel mattresses for static guns had already been carried out and it was intended to complete the move by September 26. On the 23rd, General Pile, allowing himself a little more grace, informed the War Cabinet 'Crossbow' Sub-Committee that the deployment should be complete by the 30th, with the majority of guns statically emplaced. However, the deployment was unsatisfactorily handled. The needs of the forces in Europe limited the amount of railway and road transport available, and the staff work of Anti-Aircraft

The new railings and repairs to the stonework mark the spot.

Command and Nos. 1 and 2 Anti-Air-craft Groups was not accomplished as well as was carried out in the great deployment to the south-east coast in the middle of July. It was not until October 13 that the deployment was substantially complete when 498 heavy guns and 609 light guns were finally ready for action in the Gun Box and the new Gun Strip.

There were important differences between the new situation to the one that had applied when flying bombs had been coming from sites in northern France. First, in the earlier attack, all bombs aimed at London had to fly over a comparatively restricted stretch of coastline whereas in an air-launched attack a much wider area had to be covered. Second, in the earlier case, a permanent 'attack in progress' had been assumed but in the new one there were restrictions on fire. Third, in the new form of attack, flying bombs were crossing the coast often as low at 1,000 feet, compared to 2,000-3,000 feet in the attacks of the summer, and this created a difficult problem of low-angle engagement for the 3.7-inch guns and for searchlights. Fourth, the enemy aircraft were approaching the points at which they launched their bombs at very low altitudes, usually below 300 feet, which meant that there was frequently little warning of attack. Moreover, the radar equipment of the night fighters operating out to sea was not at its best when searching for aircraft at very low altitudes. Frequently, contact was first obtained only when the launching aircraft climbed to 2,000 feet or so prior to releasing its bomb. After release the aircraft usually dived to sea level and flew hard for home which again made its interception difficult.

Various measures were adopted during October to meet some of these difficulties. Radar and R/T facilities were improved at the stations at Trimley, Hopton and Greyfriars, other stations in East Anglia being modified later. The possibility of using naval fighter-direction ships was examined but nothing came of it until the following month. Also to improve fighter interception, the development of a Wellington fitted

On the other hand, a V2 crater was larger and deeper although it was said that this reduced the blast area compared with the V1 which exploded at surface level.

with an ASV Mk VI set to act as an airborne fighter control station was put in hand but it was not until January 1945 that it was ready for operations.

To assist guns in engaging at very low altitudes, a new piece of control equipment (R.0.3) was brought into service. Its supply, however, was slow and by the middle of October only some 40 guns could be controlled by it. The normal fire-control instruments with which the rest of Anti-Aircraft Command was equipped were specially sited for controlling low-angle fire though to do this meant some sacrifice of early warning. The problem as it affected searchlights was met by substituting a spacing of 3,000 yards for the normal one of 6,000 yards within a belt 16 miles wide from Saffron Walden and Sudbury in the north to Southend and Brightlingsea in the south. Over and near this swathe of country, patrol lines were established for Tempest night fighters.

Rules for the engagement of flying bombs by the guns in the Gun Box and Gun Strip were agreed upon by the third week in October. They marked a compromise between the views of Bomber Command on the one side and Fighter and Anti-Aircraft Commands on the other. Flying below 6,000 feet over the box and strip areas was normally prohibited during the hours of darkness, and the guns were free to engage flying bombs up to a height of 4,000 feet. Provided Bomber Command gave prior warning to Fighter Command, aircraft could fly at any height over the Gun Strip, though not the Gun Box. At such times the guns were permitted to engage only those bombs below 4,000 feet that could be visually recognised. Finally, the Fighter Command Controller had the right to restrict or withhold fire to safeguard any friendly aircraft that were forced to fly over the Gun Strip.

This is Big Ben 75 which decimated Evesham Avenue, Walthamstow, on October 12. Comparison looking from Chingford Road.

Yet, despite the difficulties that hampered the defence, a high proportion of the flying bombs which came overland or approached the coast during the first month of the attack were destroyed. Between September 15 and October 14, 149 flying bombs were plotted by the radar stations and Royal Observer Corps. Of these, 125 came overland but only 26 fell in the London area. Sixty-one bombs were destroyed and the rest fell short, chiefly in Essex. Casualties were small: 91 people being killed with 217 seriously injured.

Moreover, there was evidence from Air Intelligence that I./KG53 was finding the operations a strain on the crews. Up to October 14, No. 25 Squadron — the Mosquito night fighter unit that was employed up to this date to intercept launching aircraft — claimed four He 111s destroyed, two probably destroyed and two damaged. Although these were not heavy casualties to have been suffered in the course of a month for a unit 30 aircraft strong, it was believed that they were also incurring a high accident rate as the pilots were required to operate at very low altitudes with overloaded aircraft.

However, no immediate diminution in the scale of German attack was expected. Throughout late September and the first half of October, Air Intelligence was regularly reporting intensive training in the Baltic area in the launching of flying bombs, and there was reason to believe that one or possibly two Gruppen were being prepared to supplement the operations of I./KG53.

The heavy hand of the censor had all but eliminated the background on this print when returned to the *Daily Express* on November 27 — well after the embargo on the V2 was lifted. This rocket (Big Ben 71) had exploded in the mud about 70 yards west of Southend Pier on October 11. Parts crashed through the Pier Pavilion, and windows and roofs were blasted on The Royal Terrace, Marine Parade and the High Street.

Mr Spence, the photographer, wrote that 'it weighed nearly three tons and was shot up into the air. It went through the roof, a stack of folded deck chairs, the floor and girders and landed in the mud 30 feet beneath the pier'.

The airfields from which the latter was operating were an obvious target for counter-measures, in fact they were the only possible targets without striking deep into Germany at factories concerned in flying bomb production. Varrelbusch, Zwischenahn, Aalhorn and Münster/Handorf were the airfields principally in use.

Regular photographic reconnaissances were flown over them from the middle of September, and Bomber Command and the Eighth Air Force were asked to collaborate in their attack although few were made during this first month. Münster/Handorf was attacked by 23 aircraft of Bomber Command on the night of September 23/24 but results were poor. Five light attacks, in which 217 tons of bombs were dropped, were made by Bomber Command and the Eighth Air Force during the first week of October against the same airfield with better results and photographs showed many craters on the runways and two He 111s severely damaged,

On October 12 a big strike by Liberators against airfields in north-west Germany, including Varrelbusch and Zwischenahn, was planned but bad weather prevented the operation from taking place.

When Batterie 444 relocated to south-west Friesland, the circuitous route to reach the Rijs Wood launch site (see map page 198) was not without its problems. After arriving by train at Heerenveen, each 46-foot rocket had to be offloaded by crane onto a light-weight trailer which had to be towed for six miles around the narrow Dutch roads.

Rocket and Flying Bomb Attacks, October 15 — November 25

By the middle of October, a defensive system had been brought into operation that was succeeding in restricting to insignificance the number of flying bombs that were reaching London. In those circumstances, more powerful counter-measures by bombing were not called for and on October 10, in reply to a suggestion by Duncan Sandys that there might have been 'an imperceptible slackening-off' in counter-measures, the Chiefs of Staff made it clear that they had no intention of interfering with what was being done unless the attack increased in strength. This was the point of view of the Chiefs of Staff and Air Ministry at this time. They preferred to wait for developments in the German attacks rather than approve further counter-measures of a precautionary nature that might prove unnecessary for there was no certainty that the scale of bombardment of the United Kingdom would notably increase.

There was evidence that more German units might soon be employed in launching flying bombs from the air but their likely dispositions were such that they could be used against Continental towns as much as London. Moreover, the building of launching sites for flying bombs in western Germany, and the already heavier scale of rocket attack against French and Belgian towns than against England, indicated that any increase in the total V-weapon effort of the enemy might affect the Continent rather than Great Britain. It was, of course, appreciated that for political and psychological reasons, the Germans would continue to attack London for as long as they could although they could do themselves more good, militarily, by concentrating upon towns along the lines of communication of the Allied armies, especially Antwerp whose proper functioning as a base port was essential to future Allied operations.

Relative Effort against England and the Continent

During the third week of October there was little to show how the Germans would allot their effort as the scale of rocket attack against British and Continental targets was small. Only eight rockets fell in Great Britain: all were launched from The Hague area and they were widely scattered between London and Southend. Rather more were launched against Continental towns and for the first time Antwerp was a target, the first rocket being reported from there on October 13.

Up to October 21, flying bomb attacks continued to be made exclusively against London. The week of October 14-21 was, in fact, the heaviest since the attacks had recommenced, 84 flying bombs being reported of which only five got through to London.

Then, on the 21st, flying bomb attacks began against Continental targets from the sites that the Germans were known to have been preparing in western Germany. For the first three days Brussels was the target where some 20 incidents were reported. On the night of the 23rd, the attack switched to Antwerp that was to be the sole target for the next fortnight and over 100 incidents were reported from that district before the end of October. About the same time, the enemy's rocket attacks against Continental targets were concentrated on Antwerp, nearly 100 being reported between October 21 and the end of the month. In short, Antwerp had become the main target for attack by V-weapons.

The next few weeks confirmed this. By November 25, 250 rockets had been recorded as falling in the United Kingdom, or sufficiently near its shores to

To reach and cross the bridge across the Lutz Canal, German engineers adopted the simple policy of felling the trees lining the very narrow Houtdijk approach road. The rockets fired from Rijs Wood were destined for East Anglia, the parting shot for this short-lived offensive arriving at 07.40 on October 12 in a field on Manor Farm, Ingworth (Big Ben 77).

The major Belgian port of Antwerp was entered by the British 11th Armoured Division on September 4, these German POWs were pictured the following day being marched across Koningin Astridplein into captivity. The Allies, desperate for a port to bring in supplies, were amazed to find most of the harbour facilities in working order, and Eisenhower wrote later that 'we were electrified to learn that the Germans had been so rapidly hustled out of the place that they had not time to execute extensive demolitions'.

However, the German High Command was very much alive to the situation, and the necessity of stemming the Allied advance by targetting transportation targets, and on October 7 the first flying bomb fell on Antwerp. Launched from the Cologne-Trier-Koblenz area of Germany, 131 V1 and 160 V2s landed in the city in October alone, and over 850 in November. One of the worst incidents occurred on November 27 when a military convoy was hit in Teniers Square killing 157.

be reported. Of these, about 200 had been aimed at London, the rest at Norwich. Rocket incidents reported on the Continent up to the same date (attacks having started in strength a week later than against London), amounted to 559, of which 430 fell in or near Antwerp. In short, the Germans were making twice the effort against Antwerp that they were against London. The scale of attack against the latter remained fairly constant. Between September 16 and October 21, when London was the sole target, 253 flying bombs were reported by the defences. Between October 21 and November 25, when London and also Continental targets were being attacked, 237 flying bombs were reported in the United Kingdom, but no less than 698 on the Continent, about 80 per cent being aimed at Antwerp. That is to say that nearly three times as many flying bombs were being launched against Antwerp as against London.

Today the Teniersplaats junction is the busiest in Antwerp; we are looking towards the Keyserlei.

Counter-Measures against Flying Bombs

German activity over the whole period was to some extent conditioned by the state of the moon, the heaviest attacks being launched on clear nights of little or no moon. The fluctuations over the six weeks, in terms of those bombs that were plotted weekly by the defences, were as follows: 84, 40, 12, 108, 42, 35. According to Air Intelligence, the long-expected second Luftwaffe unit commenced operations during this period (October 31 was thought to have been the date of its first attack) and during the following week more bombs were reported than in any other week since September 16. However, the increased effort was not maintained. An attack on the night of November 5/6,

The carnage was horrendous, 29 of the victims being servicemen.

when a number of bombs crossed the Kent coast, was thought to have been the work of the new unit. The novel direction of attack was put down to the unit's inexperience rather to any intention of outflanking the gun defences.

Such alterations as were made to the defences were matters of detail. From November 5 a regulation came into force, by agreement between Bomber and Fighter Commands, by which all friendly aircraft, other than night fighters, were prohibited from flying during darkness below 500 feet over an area bounded by Southend and Cromer and extending some 70 miles out to sea. Within the area night fighters were permitted to engage any aircraft flying below 300 feet without first establishing

The rocket had been fired by the 1. Batterie of Artillerie-Abteilung 836 and it impacted in the street just after midday.

I was at the HQ in Antwerp when another platoon, in which a friend of mine was serving, reported in. After a meal we decided to go to an ENSA show but it was a full house so we crossed the road to the Rex cinema. A cowboy film was showing so we decided to go in.

We all settled in our seats when just after three o'clock, there was a spear-shaped flash with many colours in it and a roaring explosion with the spearhead flash becoming longer and longer. Everything around us was breaking away into thousands of pieces, crashing down, and the noise was tremendous. It was so great that words cannot fully explain the situation but after a few minutes came the opposite: deadly silence. No shouts for help or cries of agony. It was as if everyone were dead.

A telegram to my parents stated that I was buried under ten tons of rubble. There was death everywhere. Somehow a soldier had been forced across my head but was still alive. My friend's left leg was less damaged compared with his right and I had suffered most damage to my left leg and my foot was hanging on by a quarter-inch of flesh. This meant

at the end of the day my friend lost his left leg below the knee, and his right leg above the knee whereas I lost my right leg below the knee and my left leg above. One young lad buried near me had his left leg almost torn off and a doctor amputated the boy's leg as he lay there.

There was no lifting gear but they managed to get hold of a coal-miner who knew how to shore up the wreckage to prevent a collapse. The night progressed until it was possible to release us. Along came the REs with a monster drill. I had no idea of the time, but I was in that situation until 6.30 a.m. the next morning. Finally, it was my turn to be freed. The drilling commenced just by my head right down to my feet. I had to shout a warning when the bit came to within a couple of inches of my face. At last I was free — good old REs. Even now I often wonder if the sapper chappie is still alive who said: 'Your shoe is nearly off mate. I'll take it off. My reply must have knocked him for six: 'That's my foot!'

JIM MILLS, 1992

Left: Three weeks later a rocket fired by the SS-Werfer-Batterie 500 from Hellendoorn, 60 kilometres north-east of Arnhem, exploded on the roof of the Rex cinema in Antwerp. This was located at No. 15 Keyserlei, just yards from Teniers Square. On that Saturday afternoon, December 16, an audience of some 1,200 civilians and servicemen were watching *The Plainsman*. At 15.20, just at the point in the film when Gary Cooper is told by a captured Indian that General Custer and his troops have been wiped out, there was a blinding flash followed by the sudden collapse of the ceiling and balcony. There were some miracle escapes but it took nearly a week to recover all the dead, some victims being found still sitting in their seats. A total of 569 people had been killed, including 296 Allied servicemen, of whom another 194 were injured. It was the highest-ever death toll from one V2 during the war. *Right:* The Rex was rebuilt in 1947 but closed in 1993 and was demolished two years later. The site in now occupied by one of the UGC chain.

At the beginning of October, the 2. Batterie of Artillerie-Abteilung 485 moved from its firing site at Burgsteinfurt, 40 kilometres north-west of Münster, back to The Hague, and on the night of the 20th/21st opened a double attack on London during a long period which had been dominated by flying bombs. The first rocket — Big Ben 87 — crashed at just after 8 p.m. at South Norwood, killing six including Charles and Florence Jupp and their six-year-old son Geoffrey at No. 7 Sunny Bank.

its identity. The purpose of the regulation was to help night fighter pilots and observers, and operators at coastal radar stations, to take action against launching aircraft without delay.

For the same purpose, various modifications were made during November to seven radar stations (Bawdsey, Hopton, Happisburgh, Trimley, Neatishead, Patrington and Greyfriars) on the East Anglian coast, the object being to improve the range of the stations at the low heights at which the He 111s were operating. A very flexible system of fighter control was introduced by which any radar station detecting a suspicious 'echo' could immediately take over the direction of the nearest Mosquito.

Trials were also carried out during November in controlling fighters from a frigate, HMS *Caicos*, but early results were disappointing as the effective range of the ship's radar was only some 20 to 30 miles.

There was one important alteration to the system of fighter interception inland where Tempests were operating in conjunction with searchlights. It was found in practice that it was more of a hindrance than a help to have a thick carpet of searchlights as the danger of a pilot, flying a single-engined fighter at high speeds and low altitudes, being dazzled by the beams, was considerable. Moreover, the altimeter of the Tempest was not as accurate as it ought to have been. So, by the end of November, all searchlights that had been moved into Essex to improve the spacing between lights were kept doused. It was found that searchlights operating at the normal interval of 6,000 yards gave a sufficiently good indication of the course of flying bombs for a high proportion of interceptions to be made.

It had recently been announced by the government that so far 130,000 properties in London had been destroyed and 720,000 needed repair. One lady bombed out of Sunny Bank said that 'the only clothes we had were those that me and my son stood in but we were finally fixed up handsomely by the American Red Cross'. The widespread destruction wrought by the V2s resulted in whole swathes being redeveloped after the war. This is Sunny Bank today.

Then in the early hours of the following morning, the second V2 (Big Ben 88) struck Gledwood Drive, off Uxbridge Road, Hayes. Six individuals received serious injuries but there were no fatalities. The Signal Corps captions to these photos stated that the crater in soft earth was about 35 feet deep and 40 to 50 feet in diameter, and that this house had its roof caved in although it was standing 'a block away'. The photograph was not officially released until June 14, 1945.

Defence Region, though some of those which fell short, and some which were shot down over land, caused damage and casualties in East Anglia. Most of the claims went to the credit of Anti-Aircraft Command and, as the majority of fighter interceptions fell to the aircraft patrolling inland of the guns, but the greater the successes of the guns, the fewer bombs were available for the fighters. Altogether, 203½ were destroyed by Anti-Aircraft Command, 40½ by Fighter Command, and four by naval gunners. In addition, 127½ of the successes by the guns and 15 of those of the fighters were obtained over the sea. In addition to these 15 flying bombs, Mosquitos of Nos. 25, 68, 96 and 488 Squadrons claimed nine He 111s destroyed, two probably destroyed and one damaged.

In the Gun Box and Gun Strip only minor alterations were made. There was a reduction in the number of light guns deployed, which were comparatively ineffective, and an increase in that of heavy guns, which by the middle of November totalled 540 but it was with some difficulty that these were kept in action. Manpower cuts, replacement of all men under 35 who were medically able by older or less fit men, and the need for building winter quarters for the great majority of sites, created grave administrative problems.

The results achieved by the defences were very good. Out of the 321 flying bombs that were reported between October 14 and November 25, 248, or 77 per cent were destroyed. Of the rest, only 25 reached the London Civil

Some of what were referred to at the time as 'sun houses' still have their flat roofs.

This end of Southwark Park Street in Bermondsey was hammered twice by V2s, Big Ben 101 coming at 08.40 on the morning of October 26, a second rocket on November 5 almost striking the same spot beside the railway line into London Bridge station.

Nevertheless, the flying bomb was still the primary weapon, exceeding the rocket by two to one during October. On the last day of the month, St Maries Hotel at Coulsdon was destroyed by a V1 at 6.49 a.m. Some 400 houses were damaged or destroyed and initial reports stated 15 deaths, ten seriously wounded, with some still missing.

two factors that would have reduced their 'Crossbow' effort to very small proportions. First, there was the paucity of targets connected with the production of rockets, and second, the difficulty of finding suitable targets in the launching areas.

Something was learned during October about rocket production from a factory in Luxembourg that had been making one of the components. It was now apparent that the Germans had planned to produce over 12,000 rockets by October 1944 with an eventual rate of production of 1,000 a month. Production had certainly fallen short of this; nevertheless, it was likely that at least 2,000 rockets had been produced by the end of September and that something approaching the planned output each month was being achieved. Therefore, allowing for an expenditure of some 700 rockets on trials and operations up to the end of October, a substantial reserve existed for the scale of effort at that time.

Counter-Measures to Rockets

Just as counter-measures against flying bombs fell largely upon the air defences of Great Britain, so those against rockets were principally carried out by Fighter Command. The Second Tactical Air Force assisted in the work of armed reconnaissance by attacking transport targets over much of Holland leaving the rocket launching areas used for the attack of London to Fighter Command. However, these activities were all part of the constant offensive against communications between the battle area and western Germany. While they were useful in straining communications and supply between the rocket launching areas and Germany, a detailed consideration of them is more appropriate to the subject of the air support of the Allied armies.

The heavy bomber forces were not used in this period directly against rocket targets. Even if it had not been the case that there were many better targets — notably oil plants, railway centres and the enemy aircraft industry — claiming their attention, there were

The entrance to the hotel was in Olden Lane with the property extending eastwards along Dale Road (above). A block of flats now stands on the site and all that now remains are stretches of the original flint garden wall.

When Luton received its first V2 — another one fired by Batterie 444 — on the morning of November 6, the rocket landed between the dispatch department of the Commer Car Works and the houses in Biscot Road. If key industrial targets were ever hit, the censor was careful not to let through any clues as to the location and, apart from deleting the damage to the factory, even the word 'LUTON' has been obliterated from the side of the council lorry.

Left: The area of damage, still unrepaired, shows up clearly in this 1945 aerial photograph. Commer had been owned by the Rootes Motor Group since 1934.

Right: Commer Dodge (UK) and Karrier were brought together in the 1960s and moved to Dunstable, the name subsequently being acquired by Peugeot-Citroën in 1979.

The mystery of the V1 that got away! This series of *Daily Mirror* photographs are dated November 8 (released by the censor on the 10th) illustrating the impact of a 'mystery explosion' in Epping Forest.

In the sequence above, the individual with his back to the camera on the left suddenly turns around to warn the photographer from taking photos. We checked the Air Ministry list of incidents for November 8 but nothing matches, whether it be a flying bomb or rocket, and there are no clues in the Ministry of Home Security report. The only way to resolve the issue was to consult local ARP records and fortunately they survive in our files for the Waltham Holy Cross district but there was still nothing that matched on November 8. However, Incident 592, listed on *August* 8, records that a flying bomb crashed at 09.52 at map reference 870183 and damaged the Keeper's Cottage on Woodredon Hill. Yet the V1 list on page 147 still does not include this particular bomb so it appears to have escaped the attention of both the Air Ministry and Home Security. However, it is still a mystery as to why the photos were embargoed for three months.

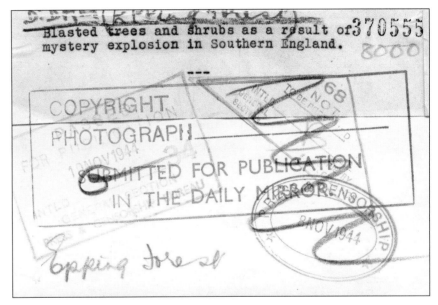

We found that even after 70 years the impact site was still clearly identifiable in the forest opposite the Keeper's Cottage.

Kammler's rocket troops fired 21 V2s on November 10 of which three by Batterie 444 reached mainland Britain. The first exploded at 8.15 a.m. destroying over a dozen properties in Tottenham Lane in Hornsey.

Documents discovered at the factory, supported by evidence from prisoners, suggested that a very important, if not the only component assembly plant, was located at Niedersachswerfen, near Nordhausen in the Harz Mountains. It was at any rate the only assembly factory of which there was positive and irrefutable evidence, so inevitably the question of its attack arose.

It had been under consideration for some time as a producer of Jumo jet engines but the difficulties of attacking it were known to be very great. To reach the plant was not the main problem so much as to damage it effectively. It consisted of two parallel tunnels about one-mile-long which had been constructed in former gypsum quarries and lay for the most part under some 200 to 300 feet of this mineral. The only bombs available to the Allied air forces which might penetrate to the tunnels were the 12,000lb, 'Tallboy' bombs used by Bomber Command. Production of the bombs during the autumn of 1944 was small and they were needed for the attack of the battleship *Tirpitz* whenever the opportunity arose, and for certain vital communication targets in Germany. The attack of Niedersachswerfen was therefore shelved.

The great majority of targets in the areas from which rockets were being fired at the United Kingdom were no less difficult for heavy bombers, but for different reasons. The areas themselves were known, lying between The Hague and Leiden, and The Hague and Hook of Holland. Much of this country was heavily wooded and the precise location of firing points and storage depots was not always known. Also, where the hand of nature was not an obstacle, that of man was, for targets that lay in or near built-up areas could only have been attacked by heavy bombers at the cost of civilian life. The less devastating attacks of fighter-bombers against targets of this type were also prohibited out of concern for the Dutch population for most of this period.

In these circumstances, the offensive took the form of sweeps and reconnaissances in which fighters and fighter-bombers attacked targets of opportunity rather than specific, pre-selected objectives. This was work better suited to the Second Tactical Air Force as they were based within easy reach of the areas to be attacked, whereas Fighter Command squadrons had to fly over 100 miles across the sea before they reached western Holland.

The sorties flown over Holland and north-west Germany by the two forces reflect the differences: for the period October 15 to November 25 they were only 600 by Fighter Command but nearly 10,000 by the Second Tactical Air Force. Much German transport was destroyed in this offensive: 40 barges, 40 locomotives, over 200 railway vehicles and nearly 200 motor vehicles were claimed as destroyed by the two forces.

The German strength in and near The Hague was not directly attacked which was far from being a satisfactory situation to Fighter Command. It was appreciated that the scale of rocket attack was low and did not warrant any important diversion of bomber forces. It was also appreciated that the heavy bombers and tactical air forces had more-important tasks than the bombing of 'Crossbow' targets, yet intelligence during October indicated that the Germans were accumulating supplies of rockets near The Hague which might be the prelude to a heavier attack. In a letter to the Deputy Chief of Air Staff on October 24, Air Marshal Hill argued, therefore, that a small offensive effort immediately might avoid a heavier effort later at a time when it might be embarrassing to the conduct of the offensive against Germany.

Then at 2.51 p.m. a V2 fired from Wassenaar scored a direct hit on a tenement block in Middlesex Street, more popularly known as Petticoat Lane after its famous marketplace. Here over 20 persons lost their lives.

There were, in particular, two areas near The Hague that were believed to be actively employed both for firing and storing rockets. They were at Bloemendaal and Ockenburg Kliniek that adjoined and together covered an area of about 600 by 500 yards, well away from any important built-up area, and on October 17 it was recommended as a target to Bomber Command, but by November 10 their importance was judged to have diminished and they were not attacked.

Fighter Command had no better response from Second Tactical Air Force to requests made on October 16 and 18 for the attack on two stations at Leiden, through which rocket supplies were thought to be passing, and on the Hotel Promenade at The Hague which was used as a vehicle park.

In the 12 days from October 15-26, only 19 rocket incidents had been reported in the United Kingdom. All were from missiles aimed at London but only two fell in the London Civil Defence Region, but on the 26th alone, eight incidents were reported and seven on the following day. By November 4 a further 27 incidents had occurred. The attack was not only heavier than any hitherto made in a similar period, it was also more accurate. Thirty-three of the incidents occurred in the London Civil Defence Region and a further seven within 25 miles of Charing Cross. The mean point of impact of these 40 rockets was in Poplar.

A small section of the building on the left can still be seen.

219

The first serious incident for Romford occurred on November 15 when Ainsley Avenue was blasted.

The following day it was the fate of Collier Row Lane — both locations victims of Batterie 444. Of the 83 casualties at the latter incident 13 were fatal — one of the most serious in Essex. Over 30 houses were demolished and another 800 damaged.

By that time the existence of the rocket had been publicly recognised by the Government. On November 8 the German Home Service for the first time announced that 'V2' attacks were being made on London. Two days later, the Prime Minister made the long-delayed announcement (see page 201) but without specifying that London was the German target. No decision had yet been taken whether to give warning of attack to the general public. For one thing, nine of the G.L. sets that formed part of the system were transferred to SHAEF in the middle of November to complete the radar cover of Brussels and Antwerp. Even if they had remained in England, the prospects of establishing an efficient early-warning system were not good as a large number of unnecessary warnings would have been sounded in London.

By the middle of November, the general position was such that when the AOC-in-C Fighter Command again raised the question of direct attacks on the launching areas near The Hague, the response was more favourable than before. Air Marshal Hill wrote to the Air Ministry on November 17, making his letter the occasion for a thorough

The attack did not slacken. In the fortnight following November 4 it increased a little, 62 incidents being reported in the United Kingdom. Accuracy, however, fell away as only 26 of the incidents occurred in the London Civil Defence Region. During the week ending November 25 the accuracy of fire again improved as did its weight: 45 incidents were reported in the United Kingdom, 33 of them in the London area.

Casualties in the weeks following October 25 rose sharply. In the seven weeks up to that date rockets had killed only 82 people and injured 164 in the United Kingdom whereas in the following month 406 people were killed and 1,002 injured. The first single incidents causing heavy loss of life were recorded during these weeks. Seven incidents each caused the deaths of more than 20 people while on November 25 a rocket hit a crowded Woolworths in New Cross Road, Deptford, store killing 160 and injuring 108.

Despite having one rocket explode on the launch pad, November 19 saw Batterie 444 successfully fire eight V2s at the London area. Illustrated here is Big Ben 215 that came down in Hazelhurst Road, Tooting. Thirty-five fatal casualties were reported, the worst of the destruction being at No. 30 where Mr and Mrs Benjamin Farmer and their three sons perished, and next door at No. 32 where five members died from the family of Private John Gardner, then serving with the Corps of Military Police.

review of the difficulties under which Fighter Command had been operating. He pointed out that armed reconnaissance had to be carried out by Spitfires in daylight whenever weather permitted, and as winter approached their scale of effort was being seriously affected. Moreover, the majority of sorties had to be flown at low altitudes if the pilots were to identify suitable targets and attack them with cannon and machine-gun fire, and this in an area where the Germans had deployed a large number of light anti-aircraft guns was a dangerous proceeding. Altogether, armed reconnaissance seemed to him to be ineffective unless combined with other forms of offensive action.

Here, Bomber Command and the Second Tactical Air Force could help though so far they had done very little. A number of sorties were also being flown by bomb-carrying Spitfires of Fighter Command whose pilots were, however, under strict instructions not to bomb if there was any risk of causing civilian casualties.

It was particularly in this last connection that Air Marshal Hill wanted a revision of policy. He maintained that the positions of certain targets were known accurately and that the civilian population had been moved away from rocket launching points. In his view, therefore, it was 'a question of balancing the certain injury to British civilian life and property against the possible injury to Dutch civilian life and property' and he asked that bombing attacks should be permitted in spite of the risk.

He also asked for suitable rocket targets and the airfields used by aircraft launching flying bombs against England to be placed on a higher priority for attacks by Bomber Command.

The whole question was considered at a conference on November 21 under the chairmanship of the Deputy Supreme Commander. Air Marshal Hill and members of the Dutch Government were present. The latter agreed that if bombing attacks on launching points and storage sites were indeed considered necessary and likely to prove effective, they would raise no objection at this stage. Air Marshal Hill was therefore given authority to undertake such attacks even against targets near built-up areas, provided he considered them 'reasonably discriminating'.

This applied only to Fighter Command and its fighter and fighter-bomber aircraft. No alteration was made in 'Crossbow' policy as it affected Second Tactical Air Force and Bomber Command. Air Chief Marshal Tedder put

All has now been swept away as the whole area has been transformed into the Hazelhurst Estate, Tooting being part of the Borough of Wandsworth.

V1 AND V2 INCIDENTS NOVEMBER 1944
Flying bombs are indicated with a dagger, rockets with their 'Big Ben' numbers.   (Airburst ✳)

November 1
02.15   Woolwich (132)
03.13   Dulwich (133)
18.32   Wanstead Flats (134)
18.32   Brockley (135)
22.45   Dartford (136)

November 2
03.30   Ditton (137)
10.05   Lewisham ✳ (138)
17.00   Banstead (139)
20.58   Long Reach, Thurrock (140)

November 3
00.58   Hornchurch (141)
04.38   Lewisham (142)
10.45   Barking, Creekmouth (143)

November 4
10.56   Ilford (144)
17.25   Sutton-at-Hone (145)
18.05   Great Wakering (146)
19.14   Stratton Hall †
19.19   Off Dunwich †
19.19   Off Aldeburgh †
19.20   Off Orfordness †
19.23   Breckles †
19.27   Off Southwold †
19.27   Hutton †
19.33   Berners Roding †
19.42   Radwinter †
19.43   Off Orfordness †
19.47   Off Leiston †
19.51   Southminster †
21.47   North of Romford (147)

November 5
00.36   Romford (148)
01.30   Penshurst (149)
07.45   Wandsworth (150)
10.55   Bermondsey (151)
12.45   Rainham, near Barking (152)
16.41   Dagenham ✳ (153)
17.12   Islington (154)
19.35   Winchelsea †
19.37   Shoreham †
19.41   Greatham †
19.45   Frant †
19.51   Detling †
20.02   Off Southwold †
20.02   Worth †
20.04   Henfield †
20.14   Telscombe †
20.16   Off Worthing †
20.21   Off Thorpeness †
20.21   Aldeburgh †
20.44   Kennington †

November 6
09.45   Luton (155)
10.51   Yalding, SW of Maidstone (156)
14.58   Bexleyheath (157)
17.50   Little Warley, nr Brentwood (158)
20.18   Westleton †
20.20   Off Felixstowe †
20.20   Off Hollesley †
20.28   Tendring †
20.28   Bapchild †
20.28   SE of Dunwich †
20.30   Off Aldeburgh †
20.32   Foulness Island †
20.32   Kelsale †
20.32   Off Leiston †
20.42   Great Oakley †

November 7
01.08   Weeley, near Clacton (159)
09.04   Canvey Island area (160)

November 8
20.25   Hucking †
20.25   Northbourne †
20.28   East of Bradwell †
20.35   East of Bradwell †
20.39   NE of Sheerness †
20.43   East of Southend †
20.44   NE of Sheerness †
20.45   Rochester †
20.48   Lenington †
20.49   Roding †
20.49   Swanscombe †

21.02   Chiddingstone †
21.02   10 miles NE of North Foreland †
21.03   Luddesdown †
21.04   Ightham †
21.07   Stifford †
21.08   50 miles east of Naze †
21.14   Frant †
21.21   Stockbury †

November 9
18.56   Off Bradwell †
18.59   Off Bradwell †
19.01   Off Orford †
19.05   Off the Naze †
19.08   Walthamstow †
19.08   Off Southend †
19.09   South of Clacton †
19.10   Lullingstone †
19.12   Throwley †
19.20   East Grinstead †
19.28   Dengie †
21.45   Off Orford †
22.03   Ramsey †
22.05   Brentwood †
22.06   South Orford †
22.26   Minster †
22.27   South Orford †

November 10
06.45   Sea off Shoeburyness (161)
08.15   Hornsey (162)
11.50   Belvedere (163)
14.51   Middlesex Street, Stepney (164)
15.10   Fulbourn, near Cambridge (165)
19.32   Off Orfordness †
19.32   Off Orfordness †
19.36   Off the Naze †
19.39   Off Leiston †
19.39   Off Hollesley †
19.40   Off Bradwell †
19.41   Off Hollesley †
19.41   In River Crouch Estuary †
19.41   Off Aldeburgh †
19.43   Wymondham †
19.47   Writtle †
19.47   Off Leiston †
19.48   Ufford †
19.53   Harwich Borough †
19.54   Off Harwich †
19.55   Off Aldeburgh †
19.55   Off Orfordness †
19.58   Shotley †
19.59   Off Hollesley †
20.00   Off Felixstowe †
20.01   Ash †

November 11
01.30   Off Aldeburgh †
01.33   Sudbourne †
01.34   Off the Naze †
01.38   Off Aldeburgh †
01.39   Off Hollesley †
01.39   Off Felixstowe †
01.42   St Lawrence †
01.45   Off Clacton †
01.46   Eynsford †
01.47   Hunsdon †
01.52   Great Warley †
01.53   Beckenham †
01.57   Dagenham †
15.40   Cliffe-at-Hooe (in woods) (166)
18.37   Brook Hotel, Greenwich (167)
19.09   Monkton, Kent (168)
23.44   Sundridge (169)

November 12
00.08   Rochester Gardens, Ilford (170)
02.29   Noak Hill, NE of Romford (171)
11.35   Nazeing, Essex (172)
17.30   Stone, near Dartford ✳ (173)
20.53   Westminster ✳ (174)
21.56   West Ham (175)
23.43   Swanscombe (176)

November 13
04.32   Ockenden (177)
05.08   West Ham (178)
08.12   Sea NE of Clacton (179)
12.49   Erith (180)

16.38   Gravesend (181)
18.05   Off Orford †
18.10   Off Orford †
18.13   Off Orford †
18.18   Off Orford †
18.18   Off The Naze †
18.22   Hockley †
18.24   Eastchurch †
18.25   Off Thames Haven †
18.26   Sible Hedingham †
18.26   Cooling †
22.17   Langdon Hills, Brentwood (182)
22.47   Southborough (183)

November 14
06.21   Orpington (184)
09.38   Eltham (185)
09.40   Greenwich (186)
18.53   Off Leiston †
18.55   Off Aldeburgh †
18.55   Middleton †
18.55   Little Glemham †
18.56   Off Hollesley †
19.00   Falkenham †
19.07   Off Aldeburgh †
19.08   Cuxton †
19.09   Friern Barnet †
19.14   Martlesham †
19.17   Berkhamsted †
21.37   Dartford ✳ (187)
22.16   Rayleigh (188)
22.25   Bermondsey (189)

November 15
00.08   Stratford, Leytonstone Road (190)
00.13   Croydon †
00.14   Rayleigh †
00.15   Felsted †
00.15   Off Bradwell-on-Sea †
00.20   Pembury †
00.23   St Pancras †
00.31   Little Bentley †
00.40   Off Clacton †
00.51   Fyfield †
00.57   Sutton & Cheam †
02.06   Southgate (191)
05.12   Romford (192)
05.44   Bethnal Green †
05.50   Surbiton †
05.50   Great Parndon (193)
09.19   Sea off Southend (194)
12.50   Lewisham (195)
16.43   High Ongar (196)
17.18   Finchley (197)

November 16
02.45   Islington (198)
07.40   Collier Row (199)

November 17
02.40   Barking (200)
03.27   Erith (201)
04.50   West Ham (202)
06.15   Wanstead ✳ (203)
10.56   Sea off Clacton (204)
19.02   Off Southend †
19.03   Thames Estuary †
19.15   Off Foulness Point †
19.20   Orsett †
19.24   Hadleigh †
19.26   Rayleigh †
19.28   Margaretting †
19.30   Buntingford †
21.45   Rainham (205)

November 18
11.13   Stanford Rivers (206)
11.16   Chadwell Heath (207)
11.28   Woolwich (208)
16.07   Theydon Mount, SE Epping (209)
16.08   Erith (210)
19.48   East Ham (211)
22.32   Dagenham (212)

November 19
02.10   Walthamstow (213)
07.05   Peckham (214)
08.31   Wandsworth (215)
10.58   Hackney (216)
16.25   Warren Hill, Chigwell (217)

V1 AND V2 INCIDENTS NOVEMBER 1944
Flying bombs are indicated with a dagger, rockets with their 'Big Ben' numbers. (Airburst ✻)

19.22	Bexley (218)	00.54	Off Felixstowe †	11.30	Great Warley (254)
19.57	Carlton Colville †	00.58	Great Burstead †	12.26	Deptford (255)
20.07	Off Orfordness †	00.59	Off Bradwell-Juxta-Mare †	**November 26**	
20.16	Off the Naze †	00.59	Off Felixstowe †	02.25	9 miles SE of Clacton (256)
20.17	Copford †	01.01	Wherstead †	05.40	Ilford (257)
20.22	Off Felixstowe †	01.11	Sudbourne †	08.10	In sea off Orfordness (258)
20.24	Off the Naze †	01.18	Harlow †	11.01	Rainham (259)
20.26	Off Felixstowe †	01.55	Silvertown (240)	11.34	Chigwell (260)
20.30	Off Felixstowe †	19.32	Westwick (241)	12.51	Walthamstow (261)
20.30	Off Felixstowe †	20.13	Finsbury (242)	13.45	Poplar (262)
20.31	Off Walton †	20.15	Bowers Gifford (243)	13.55	Billericay (263)
20.41	Hertford Heath †	**November 24**		17.43	Cranham, 4m SE of Romford (264)
21.18	Bromley (219)	03.37	West Ham (244)	20.06	Horndon, 5m NE of Tilbury (265)
November 20		05.44	Kirby Cross †	21.07	Hertingfordbury (266)
01.02	Harrow (220)	05.44	Off Hollesley †	23.25	Canvey Island (267)
10.00	East Ham (221)	05.45	Harwich †	**November 27**	
13.15	Stapleford Airfield (222)	05.47	Colchester †	16.16	Sidcup (268)
18.52	Plumstead Marshes (223)	05.47	Off Felixstowe †	22.05	Woolwich (269)
20.54	Waltham Holy Cross ✻ (224)	05.52	Off Little Oakley †	23.13	Chingford (270)
November 21		05.54	Off Foulness Point †	**November 28**	
02.52	Shorne (225)	06.00	Off the Naze †	16/20	Sea 8m S of Foulness Point (271)
05.37	Purfleet Marshes (226)	06.07	Springfield †	20.15	Stepney ✻ (272)
12.00	Walthamstow (227)	06.10	Polstead †	22.03	East Newlands (273)
12.03	Little Waltham (228)	08.00	Waltham Cross (245)	23.35	Burwash (274)
13.20	Erith (229)	10.45	Braughing, Herts (246)	**November 29**	
15.17	Laindon (230)	10.52	Ilford (247)	03.13	Barling (275)
18.02	Orpington (231)	12.02	West Ham (248)	10.55	Sandon (276)
23.14	Battersea (232)	13.59	Childerditch (249)	15.14	Bradwell (277)
November 22		20.32	Poplar (250)	19.50	Poslingford (278)
13.27	Bradwell Marshes (233)	**November 25**		20.20	Woolwich (279)
15.04	All Hallows (234)	04.55	Great Bentley †	21.11	Bexley (280)
16.02	Great Wakering (235)	04.56	Off Hollesley †	23.38	Gravesend (281)
19.40	Bethnal Green (236)	04.57	Broadstairs †	23.55	Edmonton (282)
20.34	Chislehurst (237)	05.00	Off Bridgewick †	**November 30**	
21.07	Ilford (238)	05.04	Hampstead †	00.09	Leyton (283)
23.15	Dagenham Marshes (239)	09.25	Woodford (251)	01.10	Greenwich (284)
November 23		10.35	Chislehurst ✻ (252)		
00.52	Off Orfordness †	11.16	High Holborn (253)		

the claims of the battle on land on Second Tactical Air Force higher than the needs of rocket counter-measures. However, the current operations of this force included attacks on the railway bridges at Deventer, Zwolle and Zutphen, which carried communications to The Hague.

As for Bomber Command, their operations were to continue to be governed by the instruction from the Combined Chiefs of Staff whereby the greatest possible effort, particularly by visual bombing — and it was this sort of attack which was needed for 'Crossbow' targets — was to be made against oil targets and communications, especially those affecting the Ruhr.

Although the medium and heavy bombers thus remained inoperative against both rocket and flying bomb targets, the decisions of November 21 mark the beginning of more-active counter-measures. They mark also a new interest on the part of Fighter Command in the rocket attacks. Hitherto, apart from its comparatively small effort in armed reconnaissance, its task had been largely passive: i.e. to utilise its system of intelligence and communications for the warning system that, in one important respect, the warning of the general public, had not been put into operation. Henceforth, it was to attempt a specific task, one which was unique in the history of the Command and one more-usually undertaken by a bomber force, namely the attack at its source of an organisation, itself attacking the United Kingdom.

The air-burst on November 20 was recorded by the Air Ministry as having occurred at 20.54 over Woodford Bridge but Chief Warden Ted Carter at Waltham Cross found the combustion chamber about four miles away at Fairmead Bottom. He wrote that High Beech Post B.1 had reported an unexploded missile on their patch and 'would I go and have a look at it. We drove down Fairmead Road and a short walk brought us to the "object". It was absolutely as if H. G. Wells' story of *The War of the Worlds* had come true, and here was a missile from Mars! In the dim light of our torches we could make out that its apparent length was about six feet, with more out of sight where it was buried. Although it was over an hour since the missile had fallen, the metal was still too hot to touch with the bare hand, and the heat inside it almost overpowering.'

It had now been determined that V2s were being fired from areas in Holland still in German hands, yet the ability to use any flat piece of tarmac made it virtually impossible to destroy the actual sites. Instead, Fighter Command had to rely on attacking fixed targets like possible storage areas. One important location was the Promenade Hotel on Oude Scheveningse-weg as it was believed that it had been taken over for the quartering of the rocket troops stationed in The Hague. Consequently, it was subjected to several attacks over the following months. In actual fact, the hotel was used for storage, but rocket personnel was indeed billeted in the same street and in nearby Parkweg and Van Stolkweg.

November 25, 1944 to March 29, 1945

Fighter-Bomber Attacks against The Hague, November 25 — December 16

During the first fortnight after Fighter Command had been allowed greater liberty of action, the weather was poor and only spasmodic attacks could be made. Conditions improved during the first week in December when a more sustained offensive was undertaken.

No. 12 Group of Fighter Command, being more suitably located than No. 11, had by now been made responsible for operations against The Hague area and a list of targets suitable for attack by fighter-bombers was issued to it on November 29. It included a suspected storage area and a depot for motor vehicles in the Haagsche Bosch; suspected storage areas near Wassenaar, at Voorde and Huis te Werve. Also listed was a vehicle park and storage area and billets believed to be occupied by rocket-firing troops in the Hotel Promenade at The Hague. Light attacks had been made on some of these targets on November 21, and between then and December 4 some 13½ tons were dropped by Spitfires armed with 250lb bombs. The accuracy of the bombing was considered very high but many of the targets were well concealed, particularly in the Haagsche Bosch, and observation of results was often difficult or impossible. Nevertheless, the enemy was at least being harassed, and many targets that had hitherto enjoyed complete immunity were now being attacked for the first time.

The building was so badly damaged that it was pulled down in 1945-46. A new hotel was built on the same plot of land in 1970 although the Promenade of old has now become the Crown Plaza Hotel of today.

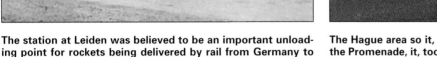

The station at Leiden was believed to be an important unloading point for rockets being delivered by rail from Germany to

The Hague area so it, too, was singled out for attack. And, like the Promenade, it, too, has been transformed since the war.

Operations against these targets continued during the next fortnight. An attack was also made on December 10 on the main railway station at Leiden through which rocket supplies were known to pass. Four Spitfires dropped eight 250lb bombs of which at least four hit the target. Altogether, between November 25 and December 16, nearly 300 sorties were flown by Fighter Command over Holland on which 25 tons of bombs were dropped.

The Second Tactical Air Force was also indirectly assisting in the offensive against The Hague area by mounting attacks against German communications south of the Zuider Zee. Railway lines were cut south-west of Zwolle by fighter-bombers, a bridge north-east of Rotterdam was destroyed, and Leiden station was bombed by Typhoons. The important communication points at Deventer, Zwolle and Zutphen were attacked by medium bombers.

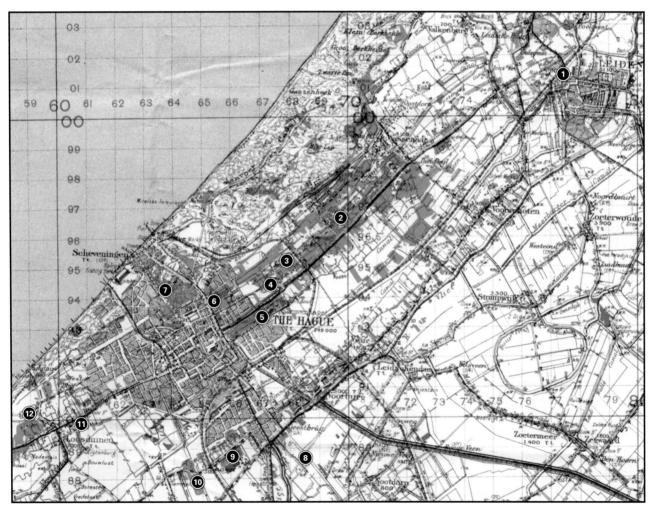

The locations in and around The Hague connected with the V2 are superimposed on the War Office map of 1944 (GSGS No. 2541) Amsterdam. [1] Leiden Railway Station. [2] Rust en Vreugd Estate. [3] Duindigt Racecourse. [4] Filmstad (film studios). [5] Haagsche Bosch. [6] Headquarters building of the Bataafsche Import Company. [7] Promenade Hotel. [8] Ypenburg Airfield. [9] Huis te Werve Estate. [10] Voorde. [11] Loosduinen Tramway Depot. [12] Ockenburgh Airfield.

In July, a V1 had hit Lewisham High Street killing 60 people and destroying Marks & Spencer (see page 132). Woolworth's staff in the nearby store on the High Street at New Cross in Deptford were shocked as there had been a friendly rivalry between the staff of the two store chains for years, with regular football matches and competitive events for charity. The staff immediately went to the aid of their M&S comrades, providing first aid and refreshments. A few days later, after discussion with his District Office, the Store Manager offered to lend them half of his own floor space. His offer was accepted and the two firms traded side-by-side until the Marks & Spencer store was rebuilt. Then, on Saturday, November 25, Britain suffered its worst single V2 incident. It was 12.26 when a rocket struck the rear of the flat roof of the New Cross Woolworths. After a moment's silence the walls bowed, and the building collapsed. The Royal Arsenal Co-operative Society store next door and the queue of people waiting for a tram in the street outside were caught in the blast. As the dust settled, shards of glass and debris stretched ankle-deep all the way to New Cross Station, half a mile away. In the hours that followed, local people helped the emergency services to search the rubble by hand. As it was cleared the full horror was evident: 168 people had died — both customers and staff — and 122 passers-by suffered injuries.

Rocket Attacks, November 25 — December 16

Offensive action by Fighter Command during these three weeks was small when measured by the weight of bombs dropped and, by that token alone, not much could be expected from it in reducing the scale of German attack. However, it was in this way that the new policy of counter-measures could be most strikingly justified.

In the first week of the period (November 25 — December 1) there were 45 rocket incidents reported in the United Kingdom; in the next week 29, and in the following one 25. Activity, therefore, decreased as Fighter Command's efforts increased but whether the two were directly connected was not demonstrable. It was perhaps evidence against it that the scale of rocket attack against Antwerp increased as the Ardennes offensive gathered strength. In other words, it was possible that in order to increase the rate of fire against the main Allied base in Belgium while the German offensive was in progress, the scale of attack on other targets had to be reduced.

The community was devastated and it was to be 15 years before the store reopened. Woolworths had lost 26 British stores during the war but the casualties in the one incident had exceeded the losses of all other Woolworth stores worldwide, including all the staff who had fallen in battle across the globe.

In memory of the 168 people who died and those injured in the V2 rocket attack that landed here 25th November 1944

Big Ben 255 had been fired by Batterie 444 from Loosduinen, a former village in the Netherlands that was a municipality until 1923 when it was annexed by The Hague (see map page 225). The tramway depot there belonged to the Westlandsche Stoomtramweg-Maatschappij and the RAF bombed it on February 9 after it was suspected of being associated with the V-weapons. However, the bombing of targets in built-up areas in Holland was only carried out if civilian casualties could be avoided. On November 25, Batterie 444 had already fired four rockets from the Loosduinen yard, before it sent the Woolworth's missile on its way. The first V2, which they fired at 08.14 disappeared without trace, the second at 09.20 landed at Woodford at 09.25, the one at Chislehurst fired at 10.29 hit at 10.35 and Great Warley in Essex at 11.30, having been fired at 11.24.

Earlier, at 11.16, a direct hit was scored on Warwick Court, a small alleyway off Holborn. Being close to Fleet Street, several photographers reached the scene just as people trapped on the top floor were being rescued from the roof of the White Hart.

It was cameramen from the US Signal Corps who covered the rocket that struck the West End of London on December 6. That evening Batterie 444 carried out two night launches, the first missile going astray at 21.13 and the second, fired from Scheveningen, landing on the Red Lion pub on the corner of Duke Street and Picton Place.

However, it was also noticeable that the accuracy of attack against London fell away after Fighter Command began regular bombing. In the first week of the period, over half the incidents occurred in the London Civil Defence Region but in the next two, only a third. Perhaps most significant was the fact that whereas up to the beginning of December the enemy effort was fairly equally divided between day and night, in the following fortnight only about one-fifth of the incidents were by day. It seemed fair to assume, therefore, that the more-determined efforts of Fighter Command in daylight had forced the Germans to fire mostly at night.

All rockets launched against the United Kingdom continued to come from the general area of The Hague but a wider dispersal of launching points was discerned at this time. Three districts were in use: one south of Leiden, one in The Hague—Wassenaar district, and one three or four miles east of the Hook of Holland. It was thought that supplies of rockets were brought to Leiden by rail, and were then taken by road to field storage depots near the launching areas for final assembly. Liquid oxygen was believed to be conveyed by rail as far as The Hague. Intelligence on the German field organisation made it fairly clear that operational control was being exercised by the SS which was known to provide at least one of the eight firing troops in action. Certainly two, and possibly three of these were thought to be firing against England, the others at Antwerp.

Continued Offensive against The Hague; Request by Home Secretary for Stronger Counter-Measures

Fog affected operations in the week December 17-24 and only 83 sorties were flown over The Hague by Fighter Command. They included, however, the heaviest single attack that had yet

been mounted. This was the work of 33 Spitfire XIV aircraft of Nos. 229, 453 and 602 Squadrons against Marlot, a block of flats near the Haagsche Bosch which was believed to be the headquarters of the rocket-firing troops in that district. The Spitfires each carried one 500lb bomb in addition to two of 250lbs. Photographs were taken during the attack, which was made on Christmas Eve, from an accompanying Mustang but they showed only one direct hit. Later photographs, however, showed that considerable damage had been done and shortly after the attack the building was evacuated. One Spitfire was destroyed by anti-aircraft fire.

The German effort against London during this week was also low as there were only 28 incidents of which seven were in the London area. As in the previous fortnight, most of the firing was at night. There were no incidents where there were heavy casualties.

However, on December 22, the Home Secretary suggested to the Chiefs of Staff that more powerful counter-measures should be applied against The Hague area. His was the main responsibility for the security of the civilian population, and certain developments in that sphere threatened an effect out of all proportion to the moderate scale of rocket bombardment. These originated from doubts that had been expressed about the safety of the London underground railways under rocket attack. It was feared that rockets might penetrate the tunnels running under the Thames and cause flooding with heavy loss of life, especially at night when thousands of people were sheltering in 'tube' stations. Accordingly, during December, the transmission of special warnings to the London Passenger Transport Board was considered so that the under-river floodgates of the 'tubes' could be closed during attacks.

Known as 'the Duke Street bomb', it was the first and only V-weapon to land in Mayfair. The rebuilt pub is now called The Henry Holland.

Directly opposite was the Selfridges department store, the rear annexe of which was occupied by the US Base Transportation Office. Although the blast walls protecting the ground floor held, extensive damage was still caused to the building and eight Americans were killed plus ten British civilians.

recommended that heavy bombers should not be employed against targets near The Hague. Their reasons were twofold. First, they were sure that the attacks would mean heavy loss of life amongst Dutch civilians and the destruction of much Dutch property without achieving anything more than a temporary interruption of rocket firings; second, for the eight to ten known or suspected targets to be attacked effectively, some 1,200 to 1,500 sorties by Lancasters would be needed, and this effort, it was felt, could not be justified.

Consideration of Stronger Counter-Measures

Nevertheless, the possibility of widening the scope of counter-measures by bombing was much to the fore at this period. During December, the Deputy Chief of Air Staff asked the Economic Advisory Branch of the Foreign Office and the Ministry of Economic Warfare to review again the liquid oxygen factories that might be providing fuel for rockets and a detailed paper was prepared and circulated on December 18. It emphasised that Germany required liquid oxygen for industrial purposes and for high-altitude flying as well as for rockets and that it was impossible to say

Mr Morrison was anxious, therefore, that rocket attacks should be reduced below even the present low level. He recognised that the scale of attack had fallen during the first three weeks in December, and this he credited to the attacks of Fighter Command and the Second Tactical Air Force, but he suggested that heavy bomber attacks upon The Hague launching areas would reduce it still further. He also argued that according to the Air Ministry the morale of all the German firing troops, not only those attacking England, was being affected by the present attacks, so heavy bomber operations against rocket targets would contribute to the security of the lines of communication of the Allied forces in Belgium as well as to the defence of the United Kingdom.

The Home Secretary's views were considered at a meeting of the Chiefs of Staff on December 23, which strongly

The bridge which connected the main store with the annexe is no longer there.

Above left: **In December, Wim Berssenbrugge took this picture of an A-Stoff Kesselwagen (V2 fuel tanker) parked opposite his parent's home at No. 27 Laan van Meerdervoort in The Hague.**

Below left: **Then, from the rear window, he captured the actual missile in flight as it rose above the Vredespaleis (League of Nations Peace Palace). Karel Margry took both of the comparisons.**

what were the requirements for each or what factories provided them. There were indications that the Germans would probably rely for liquid oxygen for rockets on plants producing at least 15 to 20 tons per day, supplemented by deliveries from such of the smaller plants as lay within 50 miles of rocket launching points. There were in Holland eight plants that the Germans might be using, five in western Germany and five elsewhere in Germany. None of the German plants, however, could be positively identified as producing fuel for rockets and, consequently, none were attacked. Those in Holland continued to be studied, and the one at Loosduinen was eventually bombed by Fighter Command, although the evidence was never conclusive that the Germans used these plants for rocket fuel.

Another type of target which if successfully attacked might affect the scale of attack from The Hague was studied in January 1945: this was the road and rail communications system between Germany and western Holland. A report on the subject by the Deputy Chief of Air Staff was presented to the Chiefs of Staff on January 13. Leading from northern Germany to enemy-occupied Holland, there were four main railway and four main road bridges, all of which crossed the River IJssel between Doesburg near Arnhem and Kampen near Zwolle. All were strongly constructed, some 400 yards in length, and heavily defended by anti-aircraft guns. For their destruction, the employment of the tactical air forces appeared most suitable, and it was estimated that about 600 sorties by fighter-bombers or 400 by medium bombers would be needed to destroy the railway bridges and a similar effort for the road bridges. Even then, the interdiction would not be complete as it would be necessary to prevent attempts to repair the bridges or to convey supplies across the IJssel by pontoon bridges or barges. The possible diversion of road traffic to the northern route across the Zuider Zee causeway would also have to be reckoned with. For such extensive operations the approval of the Supreme Commander was necessary but neither the Air Staff at the Air Ministry nor SHAEF headquarters considered that they were justified. Consequently, plans for the full interdiction of supplies to The Hague were left at the paper stage against the possibility that their execution would be necessary if rocket attacks substantially increased.

Thus, no radical change was made in the policy of counter-measures which relied on the attacks carried out by Fighter Command, supplemented by the Second Tactical Air Force. This applied until all attacks upon the United Kingdom, both by rockets and flying bombs, had ceased.

Back in September, as soon as the V2s began to fall, Air Marshal Hill immediately considered how Fighter Command in the UK could best help mitigate the launches which were obviously being made from Holland. Operation 'Big Ben' was the code-name given to his plan to allocate four squadrons to try to knock out the mobile rocket launch sites by dive-bombing. The best positioned aerodromes to carry out the task were in north Norfolk, some 200 miles (or 30 minutes flying time) from The Hague, and instructions (see extract below) were issued by No. 12 Group on September 18. Initially, some Tempest squadrons were earmarked but these were soon switched for those equipped with clipped-wing Spitfires. The Mark XVIs could carry a 250lb bomb under each wing and, if the target demanded it, a 500lb under the fuselage. The main base was Matlask, a relief aerodrome for the pre-war RAF station at Coltishall, but when this all-grass airfield became unusable due to it becoming waterlogged, aircraft switched to Coltishall and its satellite Swannington that had become operational in April 1944.

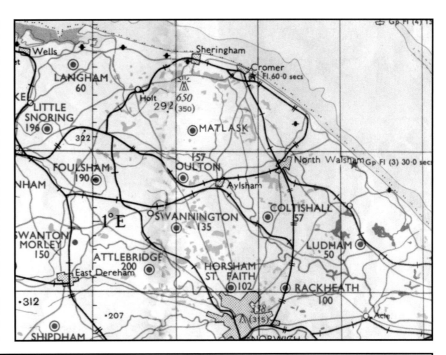

INFORMATION
1. The enemy is launching long-range radio-controlled rockets against this country from sites in Holland, this operation being known as 'Big Ben'. The sites from which the rockets are fired are not large permanent structures as was originally thought, but consist simply of numerous well-concealed concrete platforms. The firing equipment, radio control apparatus and operating personnel are transportable and may therefore afford, if spotted, only a fleeting target.

2. In addition, No. 12 Group is being reinforced and has been made responsible for:
(i) The provision of fighter aircraft to special aircraft of No. 100 Group employed for observing 'Big Ben' activity and taking radio-counter measures.
(ii) Armed anti-rocket reconnaissance patrols.
(iii) The immediate despatch of fighters to attack 'Big Ben' sites and radio installations when located.

4. No.100 Group aircraft employed on 'Big Ben' counter-measures will be operating as follows:
(i) Pairs of Halifax or Wellington aircraft operating together will patrol continuously throughout the 24 hours.
(ii) A patrol of one Fortress aircraft will be operating throughout the 24 hours.

5. The rocket launching area, known as the 'Big Ben' area, consists of that part of Holland bounded on the South by Latitude 51.20'N; on the East by Longitude 05.10'E on the West by the coast and on the North by Latitude 53.00'N.

INTENTION
In conjunction with No. 100 Group to locate and destroy:
(i) Erections, personnel, vehicles either road or rail, and waterborne traffic, which appear to be connected with the rocket firing.
(ii) The Radio Control stations connected therewith either static or mobile.

EXECUTION
Forces Available
7. The following fighter forces will be available in the Coltishall Sector to meet the commitment:
(i) COLTISHALL. Nos. 80 and 274 Tempest V Squadrons, No. 229 Spitfire IX Squadron.
(ii) MATLASK. Nos. 3, 56 and 486 Tempest V Squadrons.

Armed Reconnaisance
9. Should the No. 100 Group aircraft be unable to operate for any reason, a continuous patrol consisting of one Section in the Northern part of the 'Big Ben' area and one Section in the Southern part of the 'Big Ben' area, will be maintained in an endeavour to locate the launching points of any rockets. If seen, they are to be reported immediately, after which the section concerned is to take immediate offensive action against any enemy activity on the site.

10. In addition to the escort to the No. 100 Group force, or to the armed reconnaissance patrol in their absence referred to above, squadrons will be employed on armed reconnaissance over the 'Big Ben' area, operating either as a Squadron, Sections of eight, or Sections of four. It is most likely, however, that standing patrols of four aircraft will be required throughout the hours of daylight.

Strike Force
11. One squadron will be held at readiness to attack sites reported to be operating.

Tactics
14. Sites will not be attacked by the Section Leader until his R/T report has been acknowledged.

15. Fighters attacking vehicles which appear to be connected with the firing, should not go below 1,000 feet in view of the possibility of very large explosions.

16. Since the sites will be extremely well camouflaged, armed reconnaissance patrols are to be carried out above light flak height.

19. It is considered that flak may be considerable, but is unlikely to open fire until aircraft commence to attack.

20. All pilots are to be instructed to be particularly observant when passing over or operating in the 'Big Ben' area and are to make note of any installations or activities that might connect with the long-range rockets, especially if there is any indication of rocket firing.

Reports on Rocket Firing
21. All reports on rocket firing received by R/T or from pilots on landing will be passed immediately to No.12 Group Controller, in order that the Readiness Squadron may be despatched.

ADMINISTRATION
24. Nos. 80 and 274 Tempest V Squadrons will move to Coltishall on 19th September, 1944.

25. Nos. 3, 56 and 486 Tempest V Squadrons (150 Wing) will move to Matlask on 20th September, 1944 and will be administered by RAF Coltishall.

The Haagsche Bosch (Forest of The Hague) is the oldest forest in the Netherlands and it once stretched from the Hook of Holland right past Amsterdam but by the 20th century all that remained was a rectangular wooded park in the Haagse Hout district of The Hague, reaching from the old city centre in the south-west to the border of Wassenaar in the north-east. At the northern end of the park the Germans had taken over the former film studios as a base for launching V-2 rockets. It also housed the Technische Batterie, the unit supporting the Schiessende Batterie (Firing Battery).

Fighter-Bomber Attacks against The Hague, December 17 — February 1

Up to the middle of January the striking force that Fighter Command maintained for attacks against The Hague amounted to four squadrons of Spitfires: Nos. 229, 303, 453 and 602. All operated under No. 12 Group, chiefly from the Coltishall sector. No operations were flown against the area at night. The intruder resources of the Command were at this time fully committed to the support of Bomber Command, and although the question of using intruder pilots under training was considered nothing came of it.

During the first month of this period operations were affected by the weather and only some 300 sorties were flown, of which nearly one-third had to be abandoned. As this was also the period in which there was heavy fighting in the Ardennes, the effort by the Second Tactical Air Force was largely confined to the support of the Allied ground forces, and few operations were carried out which might have affected The Hague area.

As weather permitted, attacks were carried out in accordance with a list of targets agreed upon between Air Intelligence and the Director of Operations (Air Defence) at the Air Ministry and Fighter Command. The list initially comprised 11 targets: seven wooded areas near The Hague, Wassenaar and Hook of Holland which were in use for storing rockets preparatory to firing; one headquarters building at The Hague; one supply depot (the Leiden goods station); one liquid oxygen depot (the Staatsspoor station at The Hague), and the billets and vehicle park at the Hotel Promenade. The list was supplemented during the next two months as intelligence indicated fresh targets, and

by the middle of February there were 17 targets listed between the Hook of Holland, The Hague and Leiden which were judged to be connected with rockets and where attack had been approved. The main consideration in clearing a target for attack, when its connection with the German organisation had been established, was the danger to Dutch civilians. Very great care had to be taken in briefing pilots, selecting aiming points and planning the method and direction of attacks in order to minimise possible civilian casualties.

During November 1944, there had seemed to be a possibility of carrying out attacks on particular launching sites at times when rockets were about to be fired. It was hoped to make use of the wireless traffic between the headquarters and sub-formations of the German rocket batteries, which was being intercepted by units in Belgium, to obtain warning of attacks by individual launching sites.

A study of the intercepts up to the end of November indicated that a warning of about an hour would usually be obtained, which was sufficient for aircraft either of Fighter Command or the tactical air force to be over the site at the time of firing. Further study showed, however, that there would be little or no indication of which of the sites within a battery would be firing; and while the wireless traffic proved a valuable source of information on changes in the dispositions of the German firing troops, it was never used as a basis for operations against particular sites.

During the weeks December 17 — January 16, Fighter Command only operated on 15 days and a high proportion of the sorties that were flown had to be abandoned in which case bombs were either jettisoned in the sea or brought back to England. Altogether, 258 fighter-bombers were despatched of which 92 were unable to find their targets. In addition, 68 armed reconnaissances were flown in which machine-gun and cannon attacks were made on rocket storage areas and rail and road transport near The Hague. A small number of bombing attacks, four in all, were made at squadron strength (12 aircraft), although the normal strength, both for bombing attacks and armed reconnaissances, was four aircraft. There was also the attack by the three squadrons on the Marlot flats that were in use as headquarters.

Several attempts were made to destroy both the storage facilities in the wooded park and the technical facilities in the film studios, and this unfortunately would lead to serious collateral damage to the adjacent Bezuidenhout district.

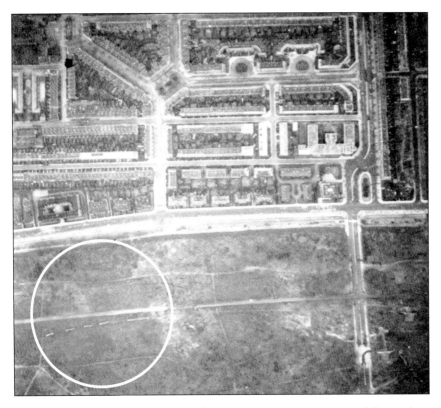

A photo-reconnaissance aircraft was fortunate to capture a convoy of five rockets lined up in the park on February 6. It has been estimated that over 100 rockets were fired from the park and launch sites in the city area. In late January/early February 1945, the V-weapon units were re-organised into the Armeekorps zur besonderen Verwendung (Armeekorps z.b.V.), comprising the 5. Flak-Division for the V1 units, and the Division zur Vergeltung for the V2 units. As part of the reorganisation Artillerie-Abteilung 485 became Artillerie-Regiment (motorised) z.V. 902.

With the exception of the latter attack and four attacks upon the Hotel Promenade at The Hague, all bombing was against storage areas. The Haagsche Bosch, where enemy activity was believed to be heaviest and where rockets were actually photographed from the air during December as they lay in side roads cut through the trees, was attacked on five occasions. Four attacks were made on two more storage areas at The Hague, Voorde and Huis te Werve; and three areas at Wassenaar, north-east of The Hague, received nine attacks. Altogether, just under 50 tons of bombs were dropped during the period.

It was very difficult for the fighter-bomber pilots to assess results at the time of attack. The Hague area was heavily defended, and while losses due to enemy fire during the month amounted to just one Spitfire, it was highly dangerous for pilots to descend below 3,000 feet, either to bomb or to observe results. Nor, since most of the bombs were dropped in wooded country, was photographic reconnaissance after an attack really fruitful. What appeared undeniable, however, was that the effort against launching areas ought to be as sustained at least throughout the hours of daylight, and, if possible, by night also. Night sorties, as we have seen, were not possible at this time owing to the commitments of Fighter Command in support of Bomber Command's attacks against Germany. Moreover, a sustained effort by day during the winter months meant that a large number of sorties against specific objectives would be failures owing to bad weather.

The scale of attack during the second half of January remained low. Only nine bombing attacks were carried out, all of them against rocket storage areas. A tenth attack was attempted but had to be abandoned owing to cloud. Armed reconnaissances fared no better; seven were attempted but only two were carried out. The weather was particularly bad towards the end of the month and no operations were carried out during the last week. The most notable attack on a suspected rocket target during this period was in fact not the work of Fighter Command but of the Second Tactical Air Force. On January 22 four squadrons of Spitfire fighter-bombers were sent to attack a liquid oxygen factory at Alblasserdam in western Holland. The tactical air force was more active at this time against communications east of The Hague than it had been at any time since the middle of December.

However, the first half of February saw these attacks, and those of Fighter Command, increase in response to a decision of the War Cabinet on January 27 that Fighter Command should intensify its attacks on The Hague area and that Second Tactical Air Force should supplement the attacks on communications which Fighter Command was already planning.

Two more Fighter Command squadrons — Nos. 124 and 603 — began to participate in the offensive and a list of secondary targets, more suitable for attack in bad weather than the targets near The Hague, was prepared. These were stretches of railroad and railway junctions in the rear of The Hague, in the area Gouda—Utrecht—Amersfoort as the junction at the latter place was particularly important.

The results were apparent from February 3 which was the first clear day for nearly two weeks. In the succeeding fortnight, February 3-16, a total of 38 attacks, involving 286 sorties, were attempted against targets near The Hague compared to 16 attacks and 74 sorties in the previous fortnight. With the exception of three armed reconnaissances, all were bombing sorties although 40 of them could not be carried out, some through mechanical troubles, but most because of bad weather.

Today, the Haagsche Bosch (better known these days as Haagse Bos) is the 'Central Park' of The Hague.

Altogether, 31 bombing attacks were undertaken, mostly against rocket storage areas. The Haagsche Bosch was attacked on seven occasions, the Staalduinsche Bosch, near the Hook of Holland, on five, and Rust en Vreugd at Wassenaar on three. Four more attacks were carried out on storage areas at The Hague and Wassenaar and the Hotel Promenade was attacked three times. In accordance with the new policy four attacks were made on secondary railway targets but the one against which the greatest effort was made was of a type which had not previously been carried out by Fighter Command.

As a result of the close study of the possible sources of liquid oxygen supply that had been made back in 1944, it had appeared that no major offensive against likely plants was possible, but in December Fighter Command had been asked to consider the attack on three factories in Holland which held promise as targets. One of these at Alblasserdam was attacked by the Second Tactical Air Force on January 22 with great success. Another, at IJmuiden, consisted of two buildings in the middle of a large factory area and precision attacks upon it would have been exceptionally difficult. The third possibility was a suspected liquid oxygen plant in a former tramway depot at Loosduinen, south-west of The Hague, but it was a difficult target as there was civilian property on three sides of the factory. It was, therefore, with some reluctance that Fighter Command undertook its attack, especially as there was no reliable evidence that even complete success would affect rocket supplies. The Intelligence officers at Fighter Command believed that all the oxygen that was required for the existing scale of rocket attack could be transported from Germany.

Two attacks were carried out upon Loosduinen on February 3 followed by one on the 8th and two on the 9th. In all but one attack, the bomb runs were made over the side of the factory that was free of housing, and the technique adopted by the pilots has been well described as 'trickling their bombs towards the target'. For this reason, five attacks had to be made. Altogether, 78 fighter-bombers, carrying nearly 30 tons of bombs, attempted to attack the factory but only about one-third of their bombs fell in the target area. However, with the last attack, the factory was sufficiently badly damaged to be ignored in the future.

V1 AND V2 INCIDENTS DECEMBER 1944
Flying bombs are indicated with a dagger, rockets with their 'Big Ben' numbers.   (Airburst *)

December 1
08.03	Enfield * (285)
08.03	Woolwich (286)
09.00	Barking Marshes (287)
09.31	Lapwater Hall, nr Brentwood (288)
10.24	Barking (289)
10.24	Leyton (290)
13.01	Hornchurch (291)
13.08	Great Burstead (292)
18.25	Hornsey (293)
21.12	Paglesham, Southend (294)
21.47	Walthamstow (295)

December 2
07.35	Ramsholt (296)
08.20	Sea off Clacton (297)
08.31	Benfleet (298)
11.08	Dagenham (299)
20.29	Lambeth (300)
21.34	North Stifford (301)

December 3
06.13	Rainham (302)
07.41	Wennington, SE of Rainham (303)
09.29	Burnham-on-Crouch (304)
09.46	Greenwich * (305)
10.30	Herongate, SE of Brentwood (306)
12.31	Downham (307)
14.51	In River Thames, Erith (308)
17.08	Grays, Thurrock (309)
21.00	Bexley (310)

December 4
02.31	Tilbury (311)
09.36	Canewdon, E of Rochford (312)
19.11	Off Dovercourt Bay †
19.12	Off the Naze †
19.24	Off Shoeburyness †
19.25	Off Leiston †
19.26	Off Sheerness †
19.51	Off Tillingham †
20.01	East Malling †

December 5
20.23	Swale †
20.23	Off Orfordness †
20.25	Manuden †
20.27	Takeley †
20.27	Off Hollesley †
20.28	Off Hollesley †
20.30	Chignall St James †
20.35	Walthamstow †
21.38	Dagenham (313)
22.30	Rettendon (314)

December 6
02.31	Great Burstead (315)
02.33	Camberwell (316)
04.46	Woodham Ferrers (317)
05.47	25m E of Foulness (318)
07.15	Crayford (319)
10.04	15m E of Naze (320)
23.07	Marylebone, Duke Street (321)

December 7
01.23	Hackney (322)
02.03	Great Saling (323)
18.36	Off Orfordness †
18.37	Off Orfordness †
18.38	Thames Estuary †
18.40	Off Tillingham †
18.41	Off Tillingham †
18.43	Off Tillingham †
18.45	Off the Naze †
18.47	Dunton †
18.48	Foulness Island †
18.49	Off Bridgewick †
18.50	Foulness Island †
18.54	Chelmsford †
18.56	West Mersea †
18.56	Off Bridgewick †
19.07	Off Foulness Point †
20.08	Hayes (324)

December 8
03.24	Woodford (325)
12.45	Canewdon (326)
22.11	½m S of Brentwood (327)
23.51	East of Tiptree (328)

December 9
04.49	Hornchurch (329)
05.24	Canvey Island (330)
07.45	Enfield (331)
22.36	Bowers Gifford (332)

December 10
00.38	Erith * (333)
04.50	Lewisham (334)
18.49	Off Felixstowe †
18.50	Frinton & Walton †
18.51	Levington †
18.54	Chelmondiston †
18.57	Off Harwich †
18.57	Tottenham †
18.58	Off Felixstowe †
18.58	Great Barford †
19.00	Off Felixstowe †
19.01	Henlow †
19.01	Kirby-le-Soken †
20.50	20m N of North Foreland (335)

December 11
22.43	Hopton †
23.06	Foulness Island †
23.08	West Hanningfield †
23.11	Beddington †
23.17	Rainham †
23.33	Shipbourne †
23.39	Longfield †

December 12
01.21	10m SW of Clacton (336)
04.24	Southwark * (337)
05.15	Greenwich (338)
06.23	Burnham-on-Crouch (339)
17.58	Chislehurst (340)

19.17	Off Aldeburgh †
19.22	Stansted Abbot †
19.24	Off Orford †
19.27	Off Aldeburgh †
19.28	Off Lowestoft †
19.30	Fingringhoe †
19.31	Off Aldeburgh †
19.40	Northaw †
19.44	Off Shoeburyness †
19.50	Fressingfield †
20.34	Creeksea (341)
22.42	Notting Hill (342)

December 13
00.18	Sea SW of Clacton (343)
03.23	Little Warley (344)
07.21	Woolwich (345)
22.05	2m N of Foulness Point (346)
22.33	Canvey Island (347)

December 14
01.09	Mouth of River Crouch (348)
02.16	Bowes Park (349)
05.01	Nuthampstead, Herts (350)
17.17	Southwark (351)
20.42	4m E of Foulness Point (352)
21.06	Great Stanbridge (353)
23.39	Writtle, near Chelmsford (354)

December 15
00.14	Latchingdon (355)
02.03	High Ongar (356)
02.50	9m E of Shoeburyness (357)
04.05	Mottingham, Sidcup (358)
21.48	3m east of Clacton (359)

December 16
10.43	Sea 9m SW of Clacton (360)
20.13	7m SE of Foulness Point (361)

December 17
16.02	Leyton (362)
18.54	Camberwell (363)

December 18
00.57	Tillingham Marshes (364)
03.48	Off Felixstowe †
03.51	Off Alderton †
03.51	Off Lowestoft †
03.52	Off Felixstowe †
03.52	Trimley St Martin †
03.52	Off Orford †
03.58	Off Alderton †
03.59	Cedgrave Marshes †
04.03	Off Alderton †
04.08	Stanmore †
04.09	Off Felixstowe †
04.10	Radlett †
04.12	Off Alderton †
04.12	Clophill †
04.21	Off Orford †
04.25	Newport †
04.30	Shottisham †
04.35	Tilton on the Hill †

In attacks on other targets, 50 tons were dropped, chiefly on the two storage areas most used by the Germans — the Haagsche Bosch and the Staalduinsche Bosch at which over 30 tons were aimed. The accuracy of bombing was high and only seven tons of bombs were estimated to have fallen outside the two areas. Moreover, 500lb bombs were frequently used whereas previously loads had consisted almost exclusively of 250 pounders. The change had been made possible by an arrangement with Second Tactical Air Force that Fighter Command aircraft could land to refuel and re-arm at an airfield at Ursel, near Ghent.

Even so it was hard to estimate what damage had been done. Occasionally, heavy explosions in the woods indicated that rockets had been detonated and it was known that even slightly damaged rockets had to be returned to Germany for repair before they could be fired. Yet it was more from the indirect evidence of changes in the scale and character of attacks on London than from direct evidence of damage in and near The Hague that the effect of the offensive could best be assessed.

With the exception of the fighter-bomber attack on Alblasserdam, and two unsuccessful attempts by medium bombers to deny communications across the IJssel at Zwolle and Deventer, the efforts of the Second Tactical Air Force over the period January 17 to February 16 took their usual form of attacks on communications south of the Zuider Zee. Over 3,000 sorties were flown and impressive numbers of barges, railway locomotives, rolling

You will realise from the following how important it is to bring this thing off: the enemy now knows all about the flying bombs. He has of course completely rebuilt some of them. We know that. He is already producing them. There is no doubt that, just as we are harassing England's industrial areas all the time with these flying bombs, they will be able practically to demolish the Ruhr area by massive use of them. There is no protection against them. We should not even be able to use fighters against them. I would rather not talk about the heavy rockets. There's absolutely no defence against them. Everything therefore indicates that we must clear up this situation before the enemy gets super-weapons of this sort into service.

The German people have breathed more freely in the last few days. We must make sure that this relief is not followed by lethargy — lethargy is the wrong word, I mean gloom. They have breathed again. The mere idea that we were on the offensive again has had a cheering effect on the German people. And if this offensive can continue, as soon as we get our first really great victories — and we shall have them for our situation is no different from that of the Russians in 1941 and 1942 when everything was against him, when he had an enormous front but when we went over to the defensive and he was able to push us slowly back by limited offensives. If the German people see this happening, you may be sure they will make every sacrifice which is humanly possible. They will answer every call. They will be afraid of nothing — whether I order a new levy on clothing or a new levy on something else, or whether I call for men — the young men will come forward with enthusiasm. The German people will react. I must say that the nation acts as well as anybody could expect. There are no better people than our Germans. Individual bad examples are merely the exceptions which prove the rule.

ADOLF HITLER, DECEMBER 28, 1944.

'I have asked you to come here before an operation on the successful conclusion of which further blows in the West will depend.' So began Adolf Hitler in his 6,500-word address to officers assembled at his at Ziegenberg headquarters on December 28 — a critical stage in his 'Wacht am Rhein' operation, more commonly described as the Battle of the Bulge.

stock and motor vehicles were destroyed, and railway lines were cut at no less than 139 points. But, as in the case of the operations by Fighter Command, the precise effects of this upon the enemy's position in Holland could not be estimated, nor upon his rocket organisation in particular. Again, it was in the attacks upon England that any evidences of success would be apparent.

04.35	Great Braxted †	18.49	Bexley (383)	**December 26**	
04.48	Chelmondiston †	19.40	Hackney ✳ (384)	21.05	Nazeing (390)
05.00	Cretingham †	20.28	20m E of Shoeburyness (385)	21.26	Islington (391)
05.45	Stebbing †	23.46	West Row, Suffolk ✳ (386)	21.45	Corringham (392)
05.46	Orford †			21.56	Dartford Marshes (393)
05.50	Titsey †	**December 24**			
05.53	Orford †	05.21	Rossington †	**December 27**	
06.03	Langford †	05.30	Buxton †	01.19	Navestock (394)
06.45	Boreham †	05.32	Worsley †	02.48	Downham area (395)
16.29	Clacton Foreshore (365)	05.34	Grange Moor †	04.56	Waltham Holy Cross (396)
		05.38	Woodford, Northants †		
December 19		05.39	Near Newport †	**December 29**	
00.47	Hazeleigh Lodge, Maldon (366)	05.40	Stockport †	06.14	Southminster (397)
01.25	1m N of Chelmsford (367)	05.41	Redbourne †	09.06	1m NE of Mundon (398)
06.05	Ilford (368)	05.44	Beighton †	09.16	1m NE Burnham-on-Crouch (399)
11.31	Bradwell Marshes (369)	05.44	Turton †	19.31	Tillingham (400)
23.25	Lewisham (370)	05.45	Chapel-en-le-Frith †	19.54	3m E of Brentwood (401)
		05.45	Willerby †	20.06	Barking (402)
December 20		05.46	Epworth †	22.38	Croydon (403)
02.59	Crayford (371)	05.46	Oldham †	23.20	Shotgate, 2m E of Wickford (404)
12.08	Brentwood (372)	05.46	Oswaldtwistle †		
14.15	Little Berkhamstead Hill (373)	05.46	Midhope Moor †	**December 30**	
17.00	Cuffley (374)	05.47	South Cliffe †	08.59	West Ham (405)
19.20	Sea, Foulness Point (375)	05.49	Radcliffe †	20.58	Ilford (406)
20.01	Nevendon (376)	05.50	Tottington †	21.34	Northfleet (407)
		05.50	Henbury †	22.34	Sutton-at-Hone (408)
December 21		05.54	Didsbury †	22.47	Stansgate Abbey, nr Maldon (409)
01.44	Noak Hill (377)	05.54	Sowerby Bridge †	22.49	Orsett, Essex (410)
04.34	Rayleigh (378)	05.55	Sturton-le-Steeple †		
04.40	Rawreth (379)	06.02	Ollerton †	**December 31**	
09.42	Bradwell-on-Sea (380)	06.08	Tudhoe †	00.35	Ramsden Heath (411)
10.43	Fairstead (381)	06.08	Brindle †	02.09	Enfield (412)
16.17	Barking (382)	06.08	Barmby Moor †	02.55	Rush Green, Romford (413)
		06.14	Macclesfield Forest †	03.40	Noak Hill, near Brentwood (414)
December 23		06.18	Hyde †	19.12	Stow Maries, near Maldon (415)
07.06	Off Orfordness †	06.24	Kelsall †	19.46	In Sea E of Shoeburyness (416)
07.08	Ightham †	06.25	Burbage †	20.41	Canvey Island (417)
07.12	Off Orfordness †	07.37	Wanstead (387)	23.40	Islington (418)
07.42	Off Felixstowe †	09.37	Eastwood (388)		
07.53	Grazeley †	23.23	Lambourne End (389)		

Rocket Attacks, December 17 — February 1

During the last fortnight of December, the scale of rocket attack on London remained low. Only 57 rockets were reported compared to 80 during the first half of the month and 86 in the second half of November. The majority of rockets continued to be fired at night, only 14 incidents occurring during daylight. This alone meant some relief for London as the number of casualties from rockets falling at night tended to be less

Ball-bearings were a vital wartime commodity and, just like the US Eighth Air Force targeted similar plants in Germany, in turn the Luftwaffe had made several attempts to hit Britain's leading company: Hoffmann's at Chelmsford. Now the rocketeers at the Duindigt racecourse at The Hague came close to achieving a direct hit on December 19. The death toll was 39 with another 138 suffering injuries.

than in daytime. The accuracy of the German fire also remained poor as only 15 rockets fell within the London Civil Defence Region. Casualties were, in fact, slightly higher than during the first half of the month (176 killed and 352 seriously injured compared to 128 and

310) chiefly because of two serious incidents in Islington and one in Chelmsford in which 124 people were killed and 168 injured. They were, however, less than half of those of the last fortnight in November when the firing troops at The Hague had been operating undisturbed.

Three days before, German ground forces had launched the offensive in the Ardennes with the intention of splitting British and American forces in a spearhead advance to Antwerp. In the early stages it was touch and go as fog denied the Allies the advantage of their superiority in the air. Rockets, on the other hand, were not so restricted and on December 26, when a real pea-souper blanketed London, a V2 hit the junction of Mackenzie Road (formerly St James's Road) and Chalfont Road in

Islington. Boxing Day festivities were in full swing in the Prince of Wales when the rocket exploded at 09.26 p.m. in the road outside, blasting a crater 40 feet across. First reports on the following morning indicated eight dead and 81 injured but that total eventually increased to 68 dead and over 250 injured, of whom nearly 100 were very serious. Post-war research indicates that this was another rocket launched at 21.21 by Batterie 444 from the Duindigt area.

While the London County Council were maintaining their colourful map record of damage to the capital (V2 hits are circled), in April 1945 Flight Lieutenant S. D. Devon was flying low over London making his own record for the RAF. Clearance work was still in progress on the Mackenzie Road site where more than 20 buildings were totally destroyed as well as the Prince of Wales. In December 2016, Bill Patey, writing in the *Islington Gazette*, argued the case for a permanent memorial to be erected to the memory of those that died. The response to this appeal was the addition of an information board on the railings of Paradise Park.

The LCC graded the severity of the damage using different colours (see page 74).

Lambeth was struck a fatal blow in the evening of January 4, when a V2 fired by Batterie 444 at the Duindigt launch site exploded on the junction of Lambeth and Kennington Roads.

This photo was taken from the north-western corner with the Surrey Lodge flats in the foreground. Beyond are the ruined public baths that stood near the south-western corner.

V1 AND V2 INCIDENTS JANUARY 1945
Flying bombs are indicated with a dagger, rockets with their 'Big Ben' numbers.   (Airburst ✳)

January 1
01.55	Laindon (419)
04.58	Leyton (420)
05.25	Halstead (421)
06.22	Sandon (422)
08.52	Off Foulness Point (423)
20.40	30m E of Bradwell (424)

January 2
03.35	Barnes (425)
09.20	Waltham Cross (426)
12.15	Beckenham (427)
15.35	Greenwich (428)
15.46	Doddinghurst (429)
18.19	Stapleford (430)
18.51	Ramsden Heath (431)
21.42	Greenwich (432)

January 3
03.32	Billericay (433)
08.39	Edmonton (434)
08.50	Chelsea (435)
13.05	Southminster (436)
18.36	Aldeburgh †
18.40	Off Kessingland †
18.45	Wainford †
18.50	Off Covehithe †
18.50	Off Felixstowe †
18.51	Harlow/Sheering (437)
18.53	Off the Naze †
18.55	Off Bawdsey †
18.55	Off Hollesley †
18.57	Deopham †
18.59	Tendring †
19.00	Castor †
19.01	Bredfield †
19.01	Ellough †
19.04	Off Aldeburgh †
19.05	Godmanchester †

19.12	Shelley †
19.40	Heydon †
19.43	Sutton †
19.47	Off Orfordness †
19.50	Lothingland †
19.50	Lound †
19.51	Sutton †

19.55	Off Leiston †
20.00	Topcroft †
20.03	Tonbridge (438)
20.05	Langham †
20.06	Off Covehithe †
20.09	Hempnall †
20.14	Lewisham †

This was Lambeth's worst wartime incident, 43 people losing their lives — ironically just a stone's throw from the premises of the Imperial War Museum. The following night a flying bomb smashed houses a mile away in Fentiman Road.

20.17	Moulsoe †	**January 11**		11.21	Barking ✳ (567)
20.17	Off Felixstowe †	10.25	Battlesbridge (504)	13.15	East Barnet (568)
20.20	Langham †	**January 12**		16.09	East Horndon (569)
20.25	North Weald †	11.04	South Green (505)	16.10	Navestock (570)
20.25	Langham †	17.38	Marden Ash (506)	16.37	Riverhead (571)
20.28	Lowestoft †	17.39	Trimley (507)	18.08	Broxbourne ✳ (572)
20.33	Off Bawdsey †	17.55	Writtle (508)	19.23	Greenwich (573)
20.34	North Weald †	19.35	Boreham (509)	19.52	Tottenham (574)
23.50	Hornsey (439)	19.46	Sea off Clacton (510)	22.49	Woodford (575)
January 4		20.45	Ilford (511)	**January 21**	
04.19	Hoddesdon (440)	22.16	Orpington (512)	02.05	Plaxtol (576)
12.30	West Ham (441)	**January 13**		12.11	Hendon (577)
12.36	Titsey Hill (442)	00.59	Toot Hill (513)	14.43	Laindon ✳ (578)
12.56	Rayleigh (443)	02.31	Wood Green (514)	15.46	Noak Hill (579)
15.43	Runwell (444)	06.00	Islington (515)	16.50	Greenwich (580)
16.13	Hackney (445)	06.05	Capel St Andrew †	18.52	Rainham (581)
16.13	Little Thurrock ✳ (446)	06.09	Great Holland †	18.57	Woolwich (582)
18.35	Clothall (447)	06.31	Gravesend †	19.12	South Ockenden (583)
19.32	Ilford (448)	06.35	Irthlingborough †	**January 22**	
20.29	Lambeth (449)	06.52	North Cray †	10.12	West Thurrock (584)
21.06	Stepney (450)	07.08	Poplar (516)	12.15	Friern Barnet (585)
21.21	Sea off Southwold (451)	07.49	Watton at Stone (517)	14.37	Kingston-on-Thames (586)
22.54	Dulwich ✳ (452)	08.57	Broadoak End (518)	17.14	Southwark (587)
January 5		11.30	Chigwell (519)	**January 23**	
00.12	Bromley (453)	11.53	Enfield ✳ (520)	08.37	Hither Green (588)
00.43	Navestock (454)	12.58	West Ham (521)	09.26	Waltham Holy Cross ✳ (589)
03.36	Wanstead (455)	14.11	South Hornchurch (522)	10.50	Mayland (590)
09.27	Layham (456)	16.35	West Tilbury (523)	11.45	Edmonton (591)
14.12	E of Billericay (457)	16.43	Off Foulness (524)	15.51	Stapleford Tawney airfield (592)
15.25	Tolleshunt D'Arcy (458)	17.58	Hockley (525)	19.14	Dagenham (593)
22.15	Off Orfordness †	**January 14**		21.52	Horton Kirby ✳ (594)
22.19	Orford †	01.50	West Wickham †	**January 24**	
22.25	Hatfield Peverel †	01.50	Orpington †	09.07	Waltham Holy Cross (595)
22.25	Langford †	01.55	Southwark †	10.50	Enfield (596)
22.26	Beckenham †	01.55	Stoke Newington †	11.43	Enfield (597)
22.29	Woodford †	01.56	Mitcham †	16.19	Greenwich (598)
22.45	Lambeth †	02.00	Epping † ✳	20.05	Navestock (599)
22.45	Addington (459)	02.01	Orpington †	**January 25**	
January 6		02.07	Southminster † ✳	07.12	Enfield (600)
02.15	Darenth (460)	02.10	Enfield †	08.19	Willesden ✳ (601)
07.49	Hatfield (461)	02.12	Hornsey †	08.33	Langdon Hills (602)
08.32	Toot Hill (462)	10.56	Foulness Island (526)	12.01	Hatfield Heath (603)
13.43	Deptford (463)	11.35	Abbess Roding (527)	19.18	Dengie Marshes (604)
16.28	Northaw (464)	12.12	Barking (528)	21.45	Greenwich (605)
16.46	West Ham (465)	13.47	Brickenden (529)	**January 26**	
17.06	Dulwich (466)	15.29	Cheshunt (530)	06.11	Shenley (606)
19.46	Erith ✳ (467)	15.50	Ilford (531)	06.24	Wanstead (607)
22.01	Beazley End (468)	16.13	Lewisham (532)	06.32	Woolwich ✳ (608)
22.46	Camberwell (469)	17.38	Shoreditch (533)	09.05	Leyton (609)
January 7		20.59	Barking (534)	09.40	Ardleigh Green, Hornchurch (610)
01.45	Dagenham (470)	**January 15**		09.54	Aveley ✳ (611)
02.16	Twickenham (471)	05.18	Off Shoeburyness (535)	10.40	Clapham (612)
04.56	Edmonton (472)	09.07	Chingford (536)	12.10	Dagenham ✳ (613)
05.25	Greyshott, Hampshire ✳ (473)	11.13	Near Whitstable (537)	14.43	Ilford (614)
06.12	Great Baddow (474)	17.17	Off Palling (538)	18.17	Croydon (615)
12.14	Leytonstone (475)	18.54	Hackney (539)	23.01	Woolwich (616)
15.40	Cheshunt (476)	23.12	Rainham (540)	**January 27**	
16.48	Ilford (477)	**January 16**		00.04	East Ham (617)
17.15	Islington (478)	03.00	Havering-atte-Bower (541)	02.14	Wickford (618)
17.36	Hutton (479)	09.09	Near Herne Bay (542)	03.40	Latchingdon area (619)
18.13	Brightlingsea (480)	10.59	Chigwell ✳ (543)	03.45	East Ham (620)
January 8		15.00	Goldhanger (544)	03.55	Stanmore (621)
10.43	High Beech (481)	19.10	Sidcup ✳ (545)	03.56	Walthamstow (622)
11.23	Islington (482)	20.32	Cock Clarks (546)	09.45	Mountnessing (623)
12.13	Lewisham (483)	21.01	Harlow (547)	12.26	Tillingham (624)
12.37	Hornsey (484)	21.54	Banstead (548)	16.01	Battersea (625)
13.14	Wilmington (485)	**January 17**		16.25	Datchworth Green (626)
14.13	Barking Marshes (486)	08.18	Mayland (549)	**January 28**	
15.18	Barking ✳ (487)	11.42	Bengeo (550)	00.19	Forest Row (627)
16.02	Datchworth (488)	12.17	Essendon (551)	00.43	West Ham (628)
16.33	West Hampstead (489)	14.17	Corringham Marshes (552)	02.29	Willesden (629)
18.22	Clapham Common (490)	16.42	Childerditch (553)	03.30	Benenden (630)
19.44	Sidcup (491)	16.59	Hatfield Broad Oak (554)	05.07	Bromley (631)
22.29	Stoke Newington (492)	18.34	Much Hadham (555)	06.51	Chislehurst (632)
January 9		19.37	Chingford (556)	07.30	Kirby-le-Soken (633)
10.50	Beckenham (493)	**January 19**		10.30	East Ham (634)
14.05	South Ockenden (494)	23.09	Barking (557)	**January 29**	
17.16	Little Hallingbury (495)	23.10	Woodford (558)	05.55	Bradwell (635)
18.02	Basildon (496)	23.41	Great Parndon (559)	06.33	Waltham Holy Cross (636)
19.28	Deptford (497)	**January 20**		07.36	Great Amwell (637)
22.15	Great Warley, Essex (498)	01.16	Upminster (560)	08.52	Darenth (638)
January 10		02.57	Canewdon (561)	09.22	Shotgate (639)
00.27	Edmonton (499)	05.00	Walthamstow ✳ (562)	09.53	Bridgemarsh Island (640)
11.00	Great Totham (500)	06.39	East Ham ✳ (563)	10.02	Stoke Newington ✳ (641)
11.14	Stoke Newington (501)	08.55	Takeley (564)	15.35	Bradwell Bay airfield (642)
14.20	Henlow/Arisley (502)	10.06	Bishop's Stortford (565)		
14.31	Broomfield (503)	10.52	Potters Bar (566)		

Ted Carter, Chief Warden for the Urban District of Waltham Holy Cross, January 2, 1945: 'At 09.20 this morning a shattering explosion heralded the arrival of a rocket, followed quickly by the usual second explosion and the long reverberation. Phoned Control and was told "Swanfield Road, Waltham Cross". Took Francis and Windle up, visualising streets of collapsed houses. Swanfield Road was alright but not the brush factory of Chadwick & Shapcott. The V2 had fallen right on the boiler house and coal dump of this factory, and the majority of the buildings, being only timber structures, complete wreckage had resulted. Fire was raging round the remains of the boiler house where firemen, rescue workers and soldiers tugged and heaved at the wreckage. Casualties everywhere and we loaded a stretcher on an ambulance, some poor fellow with a face a mass of blood and black dirt.'

The comparative lull in the attack of London was soon broken. Beginning with the first week in January, the number of rockets reported weekly in the United Kingdom jumped from an average of 34 for December to 59. There was no decline during the rest of the month when 167 incidents were reported, making a total for the month of 226, compared to 137 for December. On January 26 there were 17 incidents, 13 of them in the London area, the highest so far recorded in one day. The first half of February saw still heavier attacks. Up to and including the 16th, 142 rockets were reported, and again on one day, the 13th, there were 14 incidents, 11 in the London area. With this increase there was for most of the period an improvement in accuracy. During December, only one-third of reported incidents were in the London area but in January the proportion rose to exactly a half, and this was maintained during the first few days of February. Then, however, during the week of February 10-16 which saw the heaviest activity since the rocket attacks had begun, only a little over one-third of the incidents were in the London area.

Where the total number of incidents was comparatively small, no great significance was attached to these variations in accuracy. What was undoubtedly significant, however, was the change in the distribution of the German fire between day and night. Whereas in December only one-third of the incidents in the United Kingdom had occurred during daytime, in January nearly 60 per cent were in daytime, and a similar percentage in the first half of February. It appeared, therefore, that despite the greater activity of Fighter Command over The Hague area, the Germans were not restricted to the hours of darkness for firing as much as they had been when the fighter-bomber offensive opened.

With the improvement in accuracy, the higher rate of fire and the increase in daylight attacks, casualties during this period sharply increased compared to December. Between January 1 and February 16, 755 people were killed and 2,264 seriously injured by rockets,

Carter wrote in his diary that 'this was the biggest, dirtiest incident I've been on so far with seven killed and 108 injured. Standing upon a box a woman clerk, herself cut and bleeding and dirty, called the roll and ticked off the names as the folk answered.'

This is where the factory of Chadwick & Shapcott once lay. During the last week of December, when the Ardennes battle was at its height, 217 rockets had been fired at Antwerp. On January 2, when the brush factory was one of the eight UK locations hit by V2s, Continental targets suffered 18 rockets.

Big Ben 435 demolished part of the Royal Hospital (the retirement home for ex-soldiers of the British Army) at Chelsea. The Germans had bombed the building on the night of February 16/17, 1918, killing five, and again in April 1941. Now, at 08.50 on January 3, 1945, Batterie 444 scored a direct hit with the loss of four lives.

a weekly casualty rate twice as high as that of December. There were 13 incidents, mostly in east and north-east districts of London, in each of which more than 20 people were killed.

The greater weight and effect of the attack during these first weeks of 1945 must be placed against the background of the counter-offensive. During January, the Operational Research Section at Fighter Command Headquarters carefully collated the scale of rocket attack and of the fighter-bomber offensive against The Hague. A simple balancing of the two sets of data was hardly sufficient evidence to support any positive conclusions about the effect of the offensive. It did appear, however, that it was only in the period December 4-15, when Fighter Command had been able to make sustained attacks on The Hague, that the weight of German fire had been affected. Moreover, during that period, the accuracy of fire by day had been considerably, and by night slightly, affected. On the whole, it seemed that neither sporadic nor sustained attacks by day had much effect on the enemy's scale of effort or accuracy by night. What was needed was a sustained effort by both day and night, and a recommendation to this effect was made by the Chief Intelligence Officer of Fighter Command on January 22.

The shortage of suitable night fighters made it impossible to conduct a continuous counter-offensive, but, as we have seen, from the beginning of February the weight of attack by day against The Hague area was notably increased. Even so, the scale of rocket attack remained higher than at any time previously. This was not to say that the counter-offensive was failing; at least it might be saving London from still heavier bombardment. For even though assessment of the results achieved was not easy, it was beyond doubt that damage was being

caused to targets in The Hague area that were known for certain to be connected with rocket attacks.

However, it was still not certain which targets or what type of targets were most precious to the enemy so on February 15 the Chief Intelligence Officer at Fighter Command recommended a new target policy. This proposal entailed concentrating for a week on one of the three main targets (Haagsche Bosch, the woods near Ockenburg, and Staalduinsche Bosch) rather than spreading the effort of the Command over a dozen targets. The recommendation was accepted and the new policy was applied from February 20. Its results will be considered at a later stage.

Defensive Reactions

Between the middle of December and the middle of February there were some notable developments in defensive aspects of our counter-measures. By this time the radar stations in the United Kingdom, through No. 105 Mobile Air Reporting Unit at Malines, were detecting a large number of rockets sufficiently early for warnings to have been sounded in the London region. If a warning of 50 to 60 seconds had been acceptable to the Civil Defence authorities, the existing system would have sufficed, but something better would be required if ever the scale of attack became such that public warnings were essential. At a meeting on January 15, Sir Robert Watson-Watt's Inter-Departmental Radio Committee was asked to investigate what would be required to permit warnings of up to four minutes. In the meantime, no public warnings were sounded in London.

However, on January 2, the War Cabinet decided to put into operation the scheme for issuing special warnings to the London Passenger Transport Board so that the floodgates of the 'tube' railways under the Thames could be closed. Warnings began to be given on the afternoon of January 8 and during the ensuing months 201 warnings were passed, of which only nine were false and only four rockets fell in the London region without warning.

The reliability of the warning system also came under review in connection with a proposal by Anti-Aircraft Command to attempt the destruction of rockets by gun-fire. The question was first raised outside Anti-Aircraft Command at a meeting at Fighter Command Headquarters on December 19. General Pile indicated the possibilities of predicting the passage of rockets through a pre-defined area that would be covered by anti-aircraft fire and the rockets thus exploded in mid-air. Its success depended on the accuracy of the prediction of the trajectory of the

The damaged wing was rebuilt in 1965, following the original design by Sir Christopher Wren. It was opened in January the following year by the then Prime Minister Harold Wilson.

The Hippodrome Theatre in Ilford opened in November 1909 with 2,500 seats and 500 standing places. It survived as a top variety theatre, even through the advent of the 'Talkies', and only very occasionally was it forced to show films for the odd week or two. In between the wars all the top entertainers played there and Max Miller, Richard Tauber, Gracie Fields, George Formby, and Flanagan and Allen were all special favourites. The very young singer Vera Lynn was proudly acknowledged as a 'local' girl. The 1944/45 pantomime was Lew Grade's *Robinson Crusoe* with Renée Houston and Donald Stewart and it was during the second performance on the January 12, when Renée was on stage singing her opening number *The Fleet's In*, that a V2 rocket struck some cottages behind the building. The blast destroyed the theatre's rear wall and dressing rooms, sent Renée flying into the orchestra pit, and showered dust and debris into the auditorium.

Within seconds the stage manager grabbed a microphone and appealed for calm. As soon as he finished, the orchestra struck up in spite of injuries and the fact that they were being sprayed by water from broken pipes. This prompt reaction immediately evoked cheers and applause from the audience which then began an orderly evacuation from the building.

Rescue workers and some of the audience spent the night digging out performers and stagehands from the rubble. Over 100 people had been injured. Although there had been fatalities in the cottages behind the theatre, miraculously no one in the Hippodrome had been killed. Two days later the roof collapsed, bringing the gallery down into the stalls. Like so many of the nation's bombed buildings, the derelict shell remained for many years until finance was available and it was finally pulled down in 1957.

rocket and on the efficiency of the G.L. radar sets which would be employed for the purpose. The sets had improved in performance during the latter half of 1944, but for the purpose in mind it was essential that they should receive a pre-liminary warning from the Chain Home stations of the RAF. Close co-ordina-tion of the two types of radar was there-fore necessary to give this longer warn-ing and also ensure that virtually all rockets were observed.

A report on the subject was given to the War Cabinet 'Crossbow' Sub-Com-mittee on January 15 by Sir Robert Watson-Watt. He held that the require-ment of comprehensive warning — this being taken as 80 per cent of all rockets — could be met but that at present warnings of only 60 to 75 seconds could be given on those rockets that would fall in London, which left only 15 sec-onds for computing where the rocket would fall. Resiting certain stations might lengthen the time for computa-tion, but this would give rise to certain practical difficulties and increase the danger of jamming by the enemy.

On the chances of a successful engage-ment there were varied opinions, from one in 100 to one in 1,000. Consequently, until more-effective results could reason-ably be claimed, the Sub-Committee agreed that it would be premature to ask the permission of the War Cabinet for the necessary firing trials. Anti-Aircraft Command were asked to continue their investigation of the scheme and Sir Robert Watson-Watt's committee were invited to examine means for improving existing methods of predicting the course of rockets. The proposition was to be examined again in March.

The following month it was the turn of Ilford's Super Cinema. On Thursday, February 8, a queue had formed outside the cinema which had just opened its doors for the afternoon's performance of *The Impatient Years* starring Jean Arthur, Lee Bowman and Charles Coburn. It was early closing in Ilford and the street was busy with last-minute shoppers before the stores shut for the day. It was amazing therefore that not one person in the street was killed, although over 140, many of them pedestrians, were treated for injuries from flying glass from shop windows or falling debris. Of the 14 people that died in the blast, seven worked in the clothing factory opposite the cinema; two were usherettes, one was a NFS fireman and four were occupants of nearby houses.

Radio warfare was the sphere of another important development in defensive measures. It will be recalled that a good deal of care had been taken to build up an organisation for interfer-ing with the radio control which it was expected would be applied to the rocket, and listening for radio signals and jamming them both from ground and air had been amongst the first counter-measures to be applied. By the middle of December, however, there had been no evidence that any rockets fired against either the United Kingdom or the Continent contained radio-control equipment. In consequence, existing and proposed radio counter-measures were largely abolished.

The Super stood on the corner of Ley Street and Balfour Road opposite the station, the whole area now having been redeveloped into The Exchange. Although Bodgers store was closed when we took our photograph the rear section still shows the repaired end of the building.

During the last big assault by Kampfgeschwader 53, a salvo of flying bombs was released on the night of December 17/18. One particular V1 travelled over 100 miles inland to crash in a field at Glebe Farm, near Tilton on the Hill in Leicestershire. The farmer and his family were awoken by the explosion at 04.35, fortunately all were unharmed.

The Last Air-Launched Flying Bomb Attacks, November 25 — January 14

Air-launched flying bomb attacks on London were last considered at a stage when a second German unit had begun to take part in the offensive. The week following its appearance the scale of attack was heavier than in any previous week, but then, in the last two weeks of the period, November 11-25, there had been a sharp decline in the German effort. After the last attack of this period, activity ceased for more than a week, probably because of the full moon, and it was not until the night of December 4/5 that launchings again took place. These were the work of a third Luftwaffe unit that Air Intelligence had previously identified as being under training. The strength of these three Gruppen, which together formed KG53, was about 100 aircraft.

This meant that there should be a maximum strength for sustained operations of between 60 and 70 aircraft, each of which could launch one flying bomb. In fact, nothing like that number of bombs was regularly launched. In the week December 4-11, attacks were made on four nights and only 37 flying bombs were reported. The following week saw one night of heavier activity than usual: this was December 17/18 when 29 bombs were reported. Otherwise there was activity on only two nights and the total number of bombs reported during the week was 45. Thereafter, with one exception, the Germans operated on only four nights January 3/4, 5/6, 12/13 and 13/14. On the night of the 12th/13th, 28 bombs were reported and on the remainder only 23 all told. And with the attack of January 13/14, the last air-launched flying bomb landed in the United Kingdom.

That this form of attack had come to an end was not, of course, appreciated at the time. A close watch was kept on Schleswig and north-west Germany, from which the German units had been operating but, after a month had elapsed without further attacks being made, Air Intelligence reported that bad weather, unserviceable airfields and a full moon could account for the inactivity. Nevertheless, it seemed hardly likely that a shortage of flying bombs had brought air-launchings to an end, for firings against Continental targets continued on a large scale. (During the period November 25 to January 15, 1,654 flying bombs were reported.) Moreover, there was good intelligence evidence that the enemy held large stocks of bombs and there was no evidence that the aircraft and aircrew losses of KG53 had not been replaced.

January 14 saw the end of the air-launch stage of Wachtel's eight-month V1 campaign. *Left:* One of the last fell at 01.55 on houses on the east side of Horseman Road, Southwark, the explosion blasting the railway arches but leaving the track undamaged. *Right:* Much of the road was lost in post-war rebuilding and this end of Horseman Road has now disappeared.

	M. of H.S., R. & E. Dept. and AIR MINISTRY		BOMB CENSUS	FORM B.C.4.	Serial No............ Sheet No. *P.B.F.Y.*......

Region 5		County: 6A		Total Casualties: ?				Date: 13/14.1.45
Adminis-trative Area		*Enfield*		Killed S/I L/I	M M M	F / F / F	C / C / C /	Warnings 'P............. and R..0150...... Times W..0216......

A	B	C	D	E	F
Bomb No & time of fall	Size & type of bomb & X or UX	Judged by F, C or D	Crater size and type of soil	Location and damage notes ——— (Grid reference if no plot is made)	Additional notes by R. & E. Dept. Technical Officers
1 / 0210	Flying Bomb X	F	No Crater	*Whitewebbs Rd. Enfield. Map Reference 775 187. Bomb hit trees on edge of Whitewebbs Park + 105 yds S.S.W. of King James + Tinker Inn, Whitewebbs road. Damage :– 0 to adjoining property*	

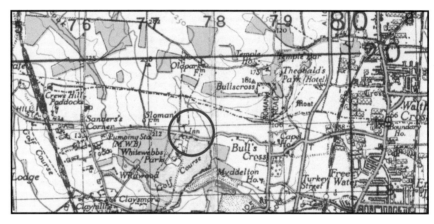

The penultimate bomb landed in Enfield. The Technical Intelligence Officer was Mr C. B. Fellows and this is his report and sketch map which were produced for every incident. According to the Enfield Historical Society, the King and Tinker pub in Whitewebbs Lane was seriously damaged but the only casualty was an elderly lady who had to be treated for shock. A nearby chapel was also damaged as was the roof of Whitewebbs old people's home. To date, over 1,500 flying bombs had been released from aircraft at the UK and 8,900 from ramps in France. Some 3,500 had eluded the defences and the number of incidents reported in the London Civil Defence Region was 2,419.

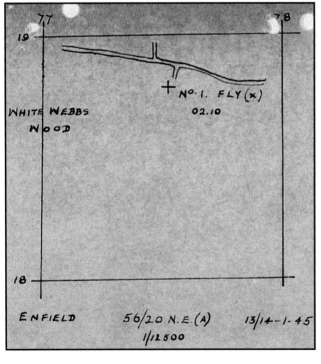

WHITE WEBBS WOOD

+ No. 1. FLY (X)
02.10

ENFIELD   56/20 N.E. (A)   13/14–1–45
1/12500

Almost as a last throw of the dice, on Christmas Eve Oberst Wachtel mounted a surprise attack on the Midlands, striking at targets across ten counties. One of the first V1s hit Garners Lane in Davenport, near Stockport.

The Attack on Manchester

Before KG53 ceased operations, it mounted an attack which, while it caused little material damage, sharply displayed the potential threat from air-launched bombs if the Germans had possessed all the resources for a sustained offensive. The attack took place in the early morning of December 24 and was directed at Manchester. Thirty bombs were reported by the defences and from this, and from intercepted wireless traffic, it appeared that probably about 50 Heinkel 111s — nearly the maximum operational strength of KG53 — took part. All the bombs reported came overland, and while a number came down over 30 miles from Manchester, and only one fell within the city boundary, the attack was as accurate as any that had been launched against London. Six bombs came down within ten miles of the centre of Manchester and 11 within 15 miles. The casualties were 37 killed and 67 seriously injured.

The attack was launched from off the Yorkshire and Lincolnshire coasts between Skegness and Bridlington, the first bomb falling at 05.21 hours, the last at 06.25 hours. The position of launching and the direction of attack outflanked the guns deployed on the East Anglian coast, and although seven bombs passed over the Humber Gun-Defended Area and were engaged, none were shot down. No launching aircraft or bombs were intercepted by fighters.

Defensive Reactions

The Germans had undoubtedly sprung a surprise. There had been no prior intelligence that the attack would be launched against the Midlands and there were no defences in the north of England suitably placed to intercept it. Nevertheless, the attack was not unexpected; as early as the previous October Air Intelligence had reported that additional units of the Luftwaffe were training to launch flying bombs. Anti-Aircraft Command had therefore begun to prepare detailed plans for a rapid deployment along the coast north of the Wash, and No. 5 Group of Anti-Aircraft Command had carried out preliminary reconnaissances for the selection of suitable gun-sites.

Ann Chanley was just six years old living at No. 173 when the bomb struck, the brunt of the explosion demolishing No. 89 where William Etchells, aged 69, was killed. She said that 'I was in bed when my Mum came rushing up and dragged me under the table. You could hear the "put-put" as it went over sounding like a motorbike. My Mum would say you don't have to worry when you can hear it, only when the noise stops. For a long time afterwards I had recurring nightmares about the noise — I was on the pavement outside and a motorbike was driving straight at me. It was a more sombre Christmas as we all knew we'd had a lucky escape and I still remember it every Christmas Eve.' On the anniversary in December 2014, the *Manchester Evening News* pictured Ann when she returned to the spot to lay flowers in William's memory.

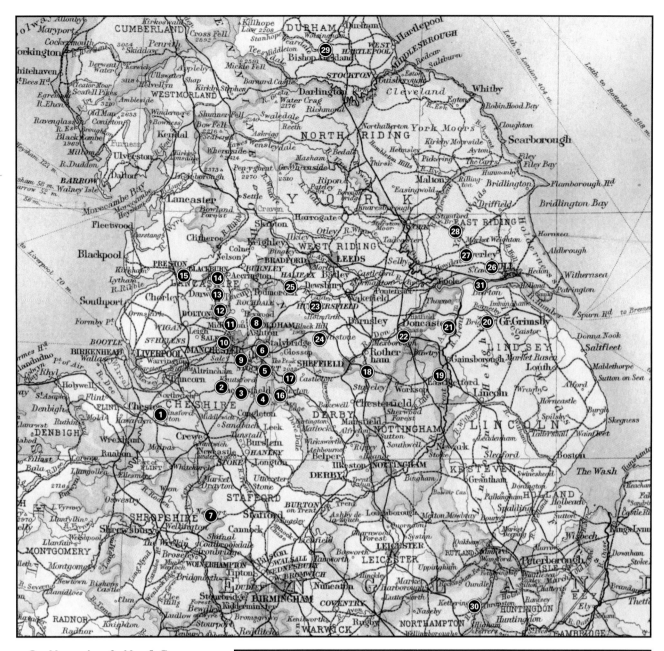

On November 2, No. 5 Group was ordered to reconnoitre the coast between Skegness and Whitby, and by the 19th a plan of deployment had been completed. It provided for what was termed a Gun Fringe between Skegness and Whitby that would be manned by 59½ batteries of guns but no moves had been ordered before the attack on Christmas Eve.

However, all this preliminary work proved useful when on the same day as the Manchester attack, and following it, Air Marshal Hill ordered the immediate deployment of 60 heavy anti-aircraft guns between Skegness and Filey. Two days later four troops of light guns were ordered to move to sites in the Gun Fringe and four troops of searchlights were deployed to provide navigational aids to night fighters and bombers flying over the Fringe. Similar rules for the engagement of targets as applied in the Gun Strip and Gun Box further south, were introduced. On January 11 a full scheme for the Fringe involving 212 heavy guns was approved by the Chiefs

CHRISTMAS EVE V1 ATTACK ON THE MIDLANDS

CHESHIRE (6 bombs)
6.22 Kelsall [1]
6.05 Ollerton [2]
5.45 Henbury [3]
6.10 Macclesfield Forest [4]
5.30 Stockport [5]
6.25 Hyde [6]

SHROPSHIRE (1 bomb)
5.40 Newport [7]

LANCASHIRE (8 bombs)
5.50 Oldham [8]
5.30 Didsbury, Manchester [9]
5.30 Worsley [10]
5.56 Radcliffe [11]
5.50 Tottington [12]
5.44 Turton [13]
6.00 Oswaldtwistle [14]
5.28 Brindle [15]

DERBYSHIRE (3 bombs)
5.50 Buxton [16]
5.45 Chapel-en-le-Frith [17]
5.40 Beighton [18]

NOTTINGHAMSHIRE (1 bomb)
5.45 Sturton le Steeple [19]

LINCOLNSHIRE (2 bombs)
5.40 Redbourne [20]
5.48 Epworth [21]

YORKSHIRE (7 bombs)
6.00 Rossington [22]
5.35 Grange Moor [23]
5.45 Midhope Moor [24]
6.00 Sowerby Bridge [25]
5.45 Willerby [26]
5.45 South Cliffe [27]
5.50 Barmby Moor, Pocklington [28]

COUNTY DURHAM (1 bomb)
6.05 Tudhoe, Spennymoor [29]

NORTHAMPTONSHIRE (1 bomb)
5.30 Woodford [30]

IN HUMBER ESTUARY (1 bomb)
— Reads Island [31]

It is believed that 45 to 50 Heinkels were used by KG53 to loose the 31 flying bombs that crossed the East Coast between Skegness and Bridlington so presumably a dozen or so never made landfall. Two V1s went widely astray but half came within 20 miles of the target: Manchester. The most serious loss of life occurred at Oldham where the bomb struck Abbey Hills Road, blasting the terrace houses that lined the road on both sides.

of Staff. Schemes were also prepared, but never carried out, for coastal gun zones for the defence of the areas Tyne—Tees and Forth—Clyde. By the end of January, there were 88 heavy and 16 light guns deployed in the Fringe which extended from Skegness as far north as Flamborough Head. Heavy guns were steadily added until the Fringe reached its greatest strength during the first week in March when 152 heavy and 16 light guns were ready for action.

The majority of these guns were found by redeploying guns available in No. 5 Group and few calls were made upon the batteries on the East Anglian coast. There, throughout the attacks on London of December and January, the strength of the defences remained much the same. At the beginning of the period beginning on November 25, there were 346 heavy guns and eight light guns in the Gun Strip and 138 heavy and 36 light in the Gun Box. By January 14 the position was unaltered except that the Gun Strip was stronger by 20 heavy guns.

It was these guns that were the principal defence against the German attacks on London. Of the 138 flying bombs that were reported as being launched against London during this period, 83 were shot down by anti-aircraft fire. Naval gunners shot down three and fighters eight.

Over 500 sorties were flown on patrols inland, over the sea and on intruder work by Fighter Command. Three He 111s were claimed as destroyed and one damaged by Mosquitos over the North Sea, and one Heinkel was believed to have been destroyed and one unidentified aircraft damaged on the night of January 5/6 by intruding Mosquitos over airfields in north-west Germany used by KG53.

Altogether, 79 flying bombs, excluding the Manchester attack, came overland during this period, but only 15 of them managed to reach London and explode there. Outside London only one person was killed and six seriously injured. In London the casualties were 61 killed and 151 injured; four incidents accounted for 48 killed and 105 injured between them. Thus, approximately three bombs were being launched against London for the death of one Londoner.

The task of searching for, and recovering the dead, ended with 31 bodies being accounted for. However, of 62-year-old Miss Hannah Holmes, who lived at No. 145 on the left-hand side of the road, no trace was ever found.

At Tottington, 12 miles to the north-west, in the second-worst incident, the bomb fell on a terrace in Chapel Street, directly opposite St Anne's Chapel. A total frontage of over 50 feet was wiped out and the street blocked with debris that also littered the churchyard opposite. The chapel itself was also badly damaged. In all, some 27 houses were seriously damaged, eight being rendered inhabitable, with another 350 suffering from the effects of the blast.

Today the Whitehead Memorial Garden lies where seven people lost their lives. A plaque explains what happened.

Bombs were scattered in all parts of the forest, which was nearly two miles long and half a mile wide at its widest point, but particular attention was paid to the north-west corner where a group of movie studio buildings known as the Filmstad was in use as a storage depot. It was first attacked on the morning of the 22nd by 12 Spitfires of No. 453 Squadron. Most of the bombs hit the target causing very heavy explosions and, when No. 602 Squadron attacked shortly afterwards, the pilots were assisted by a column of smoke rising from the buildings. Their bombing was also accurate. The buildings continued to burn throughout the day and photographs taken later from a Mustang of No. 26 Squadron showed that about 80 per cent of them had been destroyed. The following day, the 23rd, the weather was bad and only one sortie, on which no bombing was possible owing to cloud, was flown.

After the effort that the Command had made on the previous two days, it resulted in a marked decline in the scale of German attack. From February 17-23, the attack on London had continued on a scale as heavy as in the first two weeks of the month: 79 rockets were reported in the United Kingdom of which 31 fell in the London region. Then, between dusk on the 23rd and the morning of the 26th, only one rocket fell in the United Kingdom — on the morning of the 24th. Photographic reconnaissance on that day showed that, for the first time since December when photographs first revealed rockets in the Haagsche Bosch, there were no rockets to be seen.

The Duindigt racecourse lies just off the north-eastern corner of Haagsche Wood.

Heavier Attacks against The Hague, February 17 — March 16

Bad weather during the third week in February coincided with the change in the target policy of Fighter Command whereby bombing was to be concentrated on a small number of targets, and it was not until February 21 that the Haagsche Bosch came under heavy attack. Ten attacks had been attempted on the previous two days, nine against the Haagsche Bosch and one against the Hotel Promenade, but only two were carried out. In one case the primary target could not be bombed and instead attacks were made on road and rail transport in northern Holland along the line of communication between the causeway over the Zuider Zee and The Hague area. In the other operation, six Spitfires of No. 124 Squadron successfully dropped their bombs in the Haagsche Bosch in a typical attack in which the pilots dived down from 11,000 to 5,000 feet before bombing,

Late on the 20th the weather began to clear and the next two days were fine. Fighter Command made the most of them. Twenty-two bombing attacks were carried out on the 21st, and 17 on the 22nd, only five of them being mounted against areas other than the Haagsche Bosch. The total number of sorties flown on the two days was 214 and 40 tons of bombs were dropped. Only one aircraft was lost.

It became one of the main launch sites in The Hague and several craters caused by the explosion of misfires can be seen.

and that while new arrangements were being made, launchings had had to cease.

It was some days before this evidence had been sufficiently studied for a new target policy to be formulated. Meanwhile, the main target remained the Haagsche Bosch, particularly the northern part near the racecourse. From February 24-28, 88 attacks were attempted involving 400 sorties, all with the Haagsche Bosch as the primary target. The weather was cloudy and 12 operations had to be abandoned. Twenty-eight others were made against secondary railway targets, widely-dispersed over the communications system between Gouda, east of The Hague, and Alkmaar in northern Holland. Three attacks were made on the Ockenburg storage area at The Hague and one on Rust en Vreugd at Wassenaar, northeast of The Hague. Four attacks on the Haagsche Bosch and Ockenburg were made with cannon and machine-gun fire. The rest, 40 in all, were against the Haagsche Bosch.

In this enlargement, Medmenham identified a V2 and its support vehicles being prepared for firing.

The same photographs showed four rockets in the Duindigt area contingent to the Haagsche Bosch to the north where there was a racecourse from which rockets were known to have been launched. When firing was resumed on February 26 after a lull of over 60 hours, radar evidence indicated that the rockets had come from this area, while on the same day a photograph taken from a Mustang of No. 26 Squadron showed a rocket in position for launching in the woods east of the racecourse. It seemed a fair enough inference, therefore, that storage facilities in the Haagsche Bosch had been so badly damaged that they had been vacated at least temporarily,

The same area photographed after being attacked by the Spitfires as part of Operation 'Big Ben'.

In many of these attacks, after bombing the primary target, squadrons carried out low-level reconnaissances over western Holland, attacking road and rail transport. The most successful was by No. 602 Squadron which destroyed a large number of vehicles in an MT park north-west of Rotterdam on the 25th. The total weight of bombs dropped in all these operations was 70 tons, of which 40 were dropped on the Haagsche Bosch and 25 on railways. Bombs of 250lbs were exclusively employed in these attacks.

On February 28, the Chief Intelligence Officer at Fighter Command recommended certain alterations to targets. He did not suggest that the Haagsche Bosch should be removed from the list of targets even though there was still no sign that rockets were being stored there. The aiming points for attack, however, were so selected that the northern portion of the area, including part of Duindigt, would be covered. There was photographic evidence available by this time

The Filmstad movie studio complex (see page 232) was also wiped out.

The Spitfire pilots of No. 12 Group were very mindful of the necessity to avoid casualties to the Dutch living around the target area. On March 3, No. 603 Squadron dispatched six machines to The Hague but while they were en route a message was received to instruct them instead to abort and attack their secondary target as the Second Tactical Air Force was about to bomb the Haagsche Wood lying adjacent to the Bezuidenhout residential area using a combined force of 56 Bostons and Mitchells.

that a limited number of rockets — up to six, compared with 20 to 30 that had sometimes been seen in the forest — were being stored under camouflage netting in Duindigt. This area was to be one target. A second was to be the rest of Duindigt and a third was to be the storage and maintenance area of Rust en Vreugd. Fifty per cent of the effort of Fighter Command was to be devoted to the first location, 30 per cent to the second, and 20 to the third. In the event of bad weather railway targets were to be attacked rather than other storage areas. This policy was approved and all concerned were informed on March 1.

It was recognised by the Intelligence section at Fighter Command that there was an element of doubt about the Haagsche Bosch target and strenuous efforts were made to identify another storage depot that might have taken over the very important place which the Haagsche Bosch had hitherto occupied

The Spitfire pilots watched in horror as the medium bombers plastered the area resulting in the deaths of 535 Dutch civilians with over 3,300 homes and buildings totally destroyed. A protest was made by the Netherlands Embassy in London and Churchill fired off a stinging rebuke to the Chiefs of Staff. 'The matter requires a thorough explanation. We have had numerous accounts of the pin-point bombing of suspected Gestapo houses in Holland and of other specialised points. But good indications are given in this account of the wood where the rockets are stored and of the railway lines which, if interrupted, would hamper the supply of rockets. All this ought to have been available from Air Intelligence. Instead of attacking these points with precision, all that has been done is to scatter bombs about this unfortunate city without the slightest effect on their rocket sites but much on the innocent human lives and the sentiments of a friendly people.'

The reason that the bombing missed the target by over 500 yards was due to a combined error in map reading, the overcast conditions on the day, and an incorrect allowance given for the prevailing wind. This is Louise de Colignyplein.

in the German V2 organisation. For even if the Germans had completely evacuated the Haagsche Bosch, which was not absolutely certain, they had found other means for maintaining the scale of attack on London.

In the week following the resumption of firing — February 26 to March 5 — 66 rockets were reported in the United Kingdom, 33 of them in London, compared to 71 and 32 in the week before the lull. Yet until new storage areas were found, it was considered prudent to maintain the attack on the Haagsche Bosch. The northern portion, where there was a network of roads and also a bridge across a wide and deep anti-tank bridge between the forest and Duindigt, in particular offered good opportunities for denying it to the Germans.

Consequently, on the first two days of March, attacks continued almost exclusively against the Haagsche Bosch, Thirty-four attacks were attempted, of which eight could not be made because of the weather. Twenty-three were carried out against the Haagsche Bosch and three on other storage areas including Rust en Vreugd. On the 3rd, half the 28 attacks were aimed at the Haagsche Bosch, the rest at Rust en Vreugd and

Staalduinsche Bosch, the latter being the storage area for rockets fired from the neighbourhood of the Hook of Holland.

The attack on the 3rd was notable as it was one of the rare interventions by the Second Tactical Air Force directly against a rocket target. Arrangements had been made during February that this force should attack the Haagsche Bosch with medium bombers when it had the aircraft to spare, and between 09.00 and 09.20 hours, two wings (Nos. 137 and 139) of Mitchells and Bostons bombed the area.

There was much to be said for such an attack. A much heavier weight of bombs could be dropped simultaneously than by fighter-bombers; heavier bombs could be used, and the area could be deeply and extensively cratered. All told, 56 aircraft were employed and 69 tons were dropped but the bombing was very inaccurate. As far as could be judged, the nearest bombs to either of the two aiming points were some 500 yards away, and the largest concentration of bombs was over a mile away in a densely populated area. Severe damage to Dutch property and heavy civilian casualties were reported

and a strong protest was lodged by the Netherlands Embassy in London. The cause of the accident appeared to be the application of an incorrect allowance for wind that resulted in abnormal bombing errors. As a result, instructions were given by the AOC-in-C of the Second Tactical Air Force that no further attacks by medium bombers were to be made against The Hague.

Nor was the Haagsche Bosch attacked again by Fighter Command. All the intelligence at this stage pointed to Duindigt as the only profitable target though it was also clear that extensive storage facilities did not exist there. There was some evidence that Staalduinsche Bosch, Rust en Vreugd and Ockenburg were being used but not extensively. A target of a different character that was also selected early in March was the headquarters of the Bataafsche Import Company that was believed to be in use as billets and offices by the firing troops in The Hague area. One attack was made upon it on March 4 by four Spitfires of No. 602 Squadron. It was a difficult target as there was much property on two sides and no bombs hit the building. Moresuccessful attacks were to be made later.

The sculpture of Juliana van Stolberg (1506-1580), the mother of William of Orange, the founding father of the Dutch Republic, that dominated the square was unveiled by her namesake Princess Juliana of the Netherlands in 1927. When the Bezuidenhout was rebuilt after the war, the square disappeared and the sculpture was moved to a spot nearby at the corner of Koningin Marialaan and Juliana van Stolberglaan. Today it also serves to remember those who died in March 1945.

On January 28, the 3. Batterie of Artillerie-Abteilung 485 fired four rockets from one of the launch pads in the Scheveningse Bosch. The first from The Hague at 00.38 landed virtually on the boundary of East and West Ham at 00.43, just to the east of the football stadium, seen here in the lower right-hand corner of this photo, another one in the series taken by Flight Lieutenant S. D. Devon in April 1945. When the second V2 exploded on the launch pad at 01.30, the 3. Batterie had to relocate to the Duindigt site. The third rocket was successfully sent on its way from there at 03.23 but it disintegrated over Benenden in Kent. The fourth rocket fired at 06.50 impacted at Chislehurst.

The white rectangle shows the same area but the image has deliberately been enlarged to show the demise of West Ham United's football stadium in the foreground in 2018-19. The ground had already received a direct hit from a flying bomb in August (see page 138), and now there was further blast damage from Big Ben 628.

On February 9, a V2 exploded just after 4 p.m. in front of the Presbyterian Hall in Regent Square, London, although the censor described it on these photos as Judd Street which runs close by. A conference was being held in the hall and several dozen people were killed there along with others walking in the street and in adjacent houses. Reported casualties were 34 dead and 121 injured. The rocket had been fired from The Hague area by the 3. Batterie of Artillerie-Abteilung 485.

From the 4th to the 8th of the month, the effort of the Command was devoted to the three storage and firing areas mentioned above, with secondary railway targets being attacked when the weather was poor. Altogether, 47 operations were flown, 20 against Rust en Vreugd, 12 against Duindigt, and the rest against Ockenburg and the Staalduinsche Bosch. Weather, as had been only too often the case during the last four months, seriously interfered and none of the operations on the 6th, 7th and 8th could be pressed home, and 16 of those attempted on the 4th and 5th had to be abandoned. On eight occasions the primary target was obscured by cloud and the railway system in the triangle The Hague—Rotterdam—Utrecht was attacked instead.

In the light of the latest intelligence, on March 8 a new list of priorities was issued by Fighter Command. The first target was to be Duindigt which remained the only area on which satisfactory information was available. The second was a wood at Ravelijn, a mile to the north of the racecourse, where recent photographic reconnaissances had revealed a small number of rockets, and the third was the Bataafsche Import Company's building in The Hague. The railway system east of The Hague was to provide secondary targets. Seventy per cent of the effort of Fighter Command was to be devoted to Duindigt and the rest to Ravelijn. The third target, the Bataafsche Import Company, was to be the object of a single attack — if possible by a full squadron — to achieve its destruction. In fact, it was not attacked until the latter half of March by which time the target policy of Fighter Command had again been altered. From March 9-16 inclusive, with the exception of three attacks on Rust en Vreugd on the first day of the period, all attacks were against Duindigt, Ravelijn and railway communications.

A considerable effort was brought to bear during that week, many aircraft landing at Ursel, near Ghent, after a first attack, re-arming and refuelling there, and carrying out a second attack before returning to England. Altogether, 108 bombing attacks and 26 armed reconnaissances were attempted, involving 586 sorties of which 110 were carried out though not always against the primary target. Secondary railway targets, particularly between Gouda and Utrecht, were attacked as much as the storage area at Ravelijn, nearly 20 tons of bombs being dropped on each. Some 70 tons were dropped on the Duindigt area as it was there that there was the most obvious return for the efforts of the Command. Much of the target area was heavily pitted with craters (it was remarked at the time that it looked as if Bomber Command and not Fighter Command had been attacking it) and on several occasions heavy explosions followed bombing. To crown it all, from March 13 there was evidence, which was confirmed by photographs on March 18, that the enemy had abandoned the area.

Under the re-organisation of V-weapon units effected in late January, this unit was now being referred to as the 7. Batterie of

Artillerie-Regiment (motorised) zur Vergeltung (for revenge) 902. The Air Ministry labelled the incident Big Ben 709.

On February 2, East Ham was hit by two V2s within two hours, the first at 10.41 and the second at 12.43, both having been fired by the 3. Batterie of Artillerie-Abteilung 485 (now Artillerie-Regiment 902). This is Navarre Road where 12 people were killed and 119 injured, but one wonders what they would have thought if they had known that, behind the scenes, MI5 was trying to shorten the range of the rockets, thus reducing a greater loss of life further west.

Scale of Rocket Attacks, February 17 — March 16

During these four weeks in which so much thought and effort had been devoted to the counter-offensive against The Hague, a dividend seemed to be discernible not only in the photographic evidence of the evacuation of the Haagsche Bosch and Duindigt areas but also in a reduction in the scale of attack on London. This was not apparent in the first week, February 17-23, when the comparatively heavy attacks of the first half of the month were maintained, and 79 rockets fell in the United Kingdom that week, 31 of them in the London Civil Defence Region.

During the following week, during which a lull was forced on the Germans by the bombing of the Haagsche Bosch, the number of rockets reported reaching the United Kingdom fell to 57. There was something of a recovery in the week March 3-9, when 66 rockets were reported, but only 50 in the week March 10-16 during which Duindigt was abandoned, the lowest weekly total of incidents for over a month. For the whole period, just under half of the rockets reported fell in London. In the

John Masterman, the Chairman of the 'Double-Cross' Committee, explained how MI5 developed a similar method to the one used the previous year (see page 108) to shorten the range of flying bombs fired from France: 'Early in September the rocket attacks (V2) started, and presented us with similar problems and similar opportunities to those connected with V1. Consequently, our deception was also on similar lines. There was, however, a technical difference. In the flying bomb attacks location had been the important factor, because it was doubtful whether the enemy could tie the times we gave them to particular shots; in the rocket attacks timings were vital because the enemy could calculate accurately the time of arrival of any shot, and link this up with any information which we gave him. It was therefore decided to give real incidents which would show a Mean Point of Impact (MPI) in Central London, but to give as the times for these incidents the times of shots falling some five to eight miles short. In this way over a period of some months we contrived to encourage the enemy steadily to diminish his range; thus in the four weeks from 20 January to 17 February 1945 the real MPI moved eastward about two miles a week and ended well outside the boundary of London region. It would be only fair to claim that the deception was a very real triumph for HDE [Home Defence Executive]. In spite of a good deal of opposition, they succeeded in pushing through their policy, and succeeded also, if we may judge by results, in causing the Germans to shorten their range considerably. When a report was made to the W. Board on the year's work of double-cross agents after the conclusion of hostilities, DMI [Director of Military Intelligence] gave a brief summary of a document which he had recently received. This was an appreciation by a scientific expert who had calculated the approximate extra number of lives which would have been lost had the Germans' MPI been five miles further west each week than it was. The expert had no knowledge of our work and supposed that the location of the MPI was simply due to German miscalculation. We, however, were surely entitled to feel that the double-cross system had done its full share in the saving of those many thousands of lives'. This is Big Ben 645 which struck Barnby Road, West Ham, on February 1, killing 30.

week of March 3-9, the number rose as high as 60, only to be followed in the next with a fall, coincident with the fall in the scale of attack, to one of 40.

It was perhaps not insignificant that whereas in the first week of the period two-thirds of rocket incidents occurred during daylight, the proportion fell as the counter-offensive against The Hague continued. In the second week only 40 per cent of rockets were launched in daylight, dropping to 37 in the third week and 26 in the fourth. Moreover, the hours of heaviest activity were in the early morning before dawn, and the lightest during the last hours of daylight and the earliest of the night. The implication was not that the presence of Fighter Command aircraft over The Hague almost throughout the day was forcing the Germans to fire at night, but that the enemy's storage facilities had been so affected by the counter-offensive that rockets were having to be brought up to launching points during the night and fired as quickly as possible. In other words, no reserves of rockets were being held in the field.

The perceptible slackening in the German offensive was not accompanied by a relief in the number of casualties. The fall of rockets in London was, as before, chiefly in eastern and north-eastern districts. The point of greatest concentration during the period was in East Ham, and a number of serious incidents swelled casualty lists to figures comparable with those of previous weeks. In the four weeks preceding February 14, 473 people had been killed and 1,415 seriously injured by rockets in the United Kingdom, of whom only 17 were killed and 107 injured outside London. In the four weeks following

Inevitably, Ilford, the adjoining borough to the east, suffered equally and the impacts of over 30 V2s were recorded in the area. On February 20 it was the turn of the photographic manufacturing plant of Ilford Ltd when their factory in Roden Street and Audrey Road was struck by Big Ben 830. Now the site is occupied by a Sainsbury store.

that date, 580 were killed and 1,220 seriously injured, of whom 50 were killed and 121 injured outside London. The death toll depended very much on the absence of really serious incidents, underlined by the fact that whereas 114 rockets fell in London during those four weeks, six rockets alone killed 308 people and seriously injured 318. The heaviest casualties were caused by one that fell on Smithfield Market in Farringdon Road at 11.02 a.m. on the morning of

March 8; 110 people were killed and 123 seriously injured.

No alterations were made to the warning system during the period beyond the deployment near Lowestoft of one additional G.L. radar set. Sir Robert Watson-Watt's committee continued its examination of what an effective public warning would entail but the only warnings that were given were to the London Passenger Transport Board.

Walthamstow, five miles to the west, suffered its worst rocket on February 19 when one fell opposite W. B. Bawn's factory in Blackhorse Lane. The whole of the office block was destroyed and all except one of the office staff lost their lives including two directors. In total, 18 people were killed outright while another three died later as a result of their injuries. A further 35 people were listed as seriously wounded while an additional 120 suffered minor injuries.

V1 AND V2 INCIDENTS FEBRUARY 1945
Flying bombs are indicated with a dagger, rockets with their 'Big Ben' numbers.   (Airburst *)

February 1
01.33	North Weald (643)
02.08	Althorne (644)
03.03	West Ham (645)
04.03	Harrow * (646)
05.19	Chiddingstone (647)
06.11	Walthamstow (648)
07.31	Walkern (649)
07.46	Chingford (650)
10.10	Chingford (651)
14.00	Hackney * (652)
14.06	Chingford (653)

February 2
06.13	Woodham Mortimer (654)
08.08	Southminster (655)
08.22	Deptford (656)
10.13	Dagenham in River Thames (657)
10.41	East Ham (658)
12.43	East Ham (659)
12.55	Walthamstow (660)

February 3
11.25	Epping Forest (661)
13.16	Barking (662)
15.15	Ilford (663)

February 4
14.48	Near Danbury * (664)
15.05	Ilford (665)
15.06	Dagenham * (666)
17.26	West Ham * (667)
17.31	Ilford (668)
17.37	Theydon Garnon (669)
18.13	Doddinghurst (670)
18.15	Hackney (671)
22.21	Woodford (672)
23.51	Hornchurch (673)
23.57	Rettendon (674)

February 5
01.59	Chingford (675)
02.39	Hackney (676)
05.35	Epping Upland (677)
08.14	Willingale (678)
09.41	Watton at Stone (679)
21.09	Waltham Holy Cross (680)

February 6
04.58	Paglesham * (681)
06.38	Essendon (682)
07.34	Tottenham * (683)
09.48	St Mary Cray (684)
09.51	Ramsden Heath (685)
12.56	Bradwell Bay (686)
18.05	Crockenhill (687)
19.16	Wanstead Flats (688)
21.46	Woolwich (689)

February 7
11.52	Ilford (690)
12.10	Barking (691)
15.59	Waltham Holy Cross (692)

February 8
00.32	Bacton * (693)
01.08	Walthamstow (694)
02.18	In sea off Sheringham (695)
03.03	Chislehurst (696)
09.18	Fobbing (697)
10.57	Bethnal Green (698)
12.06	Erith (699)
12.35	Ilford (700)
15.43	Rettendon (701)
17.43	Sidcup (702)
17.50	Charlton (703)
20.12	Cock Clarks (704)
22.38	Dagenham (705)

February 9
05.42	Navestock (706)
07.26	Stow Maries (707)
14.08	Poplar (708)
16.08	St Pancras (709)
17.25	Bromley (710)
19.03	In sea south of Clacton (711)
21.34	Chislehurst (712)

February 10
00.33	Basildon (713)
04.59	Bexley (714) *
06.34	Radley Green (715)
08.28	Leyton (716)
09.24	In sea at Bradwell (717)
10.58	Woolwich (718)

11.27	Rawreth (719)
12.47	Purleigh (720)
15.03	In sea at Clacton (721)
15.29	Margaretting (722)
16.01	Purfleet (723)
19.14	Oxted * (724)
20.01	Writtle (725)

February 11
01.03	Collier Row (726)
01.50	Chertsey Mead (727)
04.40	Stoke Common (728)
12.31	Stratford * (729)
13.31	Bromley (730)
14.51	Walthamstow (731)
16.07	Collier Row (732)
18.16	East Ham (733)
22.00	Lewisham (734)

February 12
05.15	Leatherhead (735)
07.16	Sea off Clacton (736)
07.22	Beauchamp Roding * (737)
10.30	Bayfordbury (738)
13.46	Mountnessing (739)
16.04	Great Warley (740)
18.45	Great Totham (741)
18.46	Dengie (742)
20.28	Walthamstow (743)
23.05	Hackney (744)

February 13
02.24	Sea off Orfordness (745)
03.42	West Halstead (746)
06.17	Cheshunt (747)
15.49	High Laver (748)
15.53	Thames Haven (749)
16.15	Braxted Park (750)
16.33	Erith (751)
16.39	Depden (752)
16.44	Wood Green (753)
18.45	Harold Wood (754)
18.52	West Ham (755)
19.15	Bexley (756)
22.58	Ilford * (757)
23.47	Horndon on the Hill (758)

That afternoon, London Civil Defence Group 7 telephoned Chief Warden Ted Carter at Waltham Abbey to attend and photograph the operation. His log records that he found 'a very nasty incident involving a factory and a number of small houses. Gas main broken and alight with scores of rescue men man-han-dling the debris in their search for casualties. A mobile crane was already at work, field telephone installed, and a searcher dog standing by — in fact all the hundred and one things that go to make up a big incident. Said to be about 17 dead and up to 20 still missing. One located still alive, while I was there.'

February 14					
00.32	Platt (759)	08.10	Wickford ✻ (802)	17.53	Heston (846)
02.21	Farningham (760)	08.17	Canvey Island (803)	20.11	Sea off Clacton (847)
03.02	Cranham (761)	09.40	Aveley (804)	21.02	West Romford (848)
05.03	Rawreth (762)	10.15	Dartford Heath ✻ (805)	21.48	Althorne (849)
05.36	Canvey Island (763)	12.01	Rochester (806)	22.48	Warley (850)
09.55	Camberwell (764)	12.18	Bexley (807)	22.51	Greenwich (851)
14.41	Chislehurst (765)	14.41	Poplar ✻ (808)	**February 23**	
14.55	Havering-atte-Bower (766)	15.21	Canewdon (809)	00.04	East Ham (852)
17.00	Havering-atte-Bower (767)	18.06	Sea off Clacton (810)	01.03	Waltham Holy Cross (853)
17.11	Finsbury ✻ (768)	19.44	Bexleyheath (811)	04.37	Chigwell ✻ (854)
17.12	Mountnessing (769)	19.52	Eltham (812)	07.46	Dagenham ✻ (855)
20.23	South Green (770)	**February 19**		09.08	Chigwell ✻ (856)
21.58	Hammersmith (771)	00.44	Ilford l(813)	09.45	Sevenoaks (857)
22.31	Hackney (772)	04.46	Off East Anglian coast (814)	11.24	Cheshunt (858)
23.57	Mundon (773)	04.56	Berners Roding (815)	12.42	Sea off Folkestone (859)
February 15		07.19	Epping Forest (816)	13.39	1m NW of Epping (860)
00.55	Erith (774)	07.27	Wanstead (817)	14.25	Blackmore (861)
07.04	Crayford (775)	07.42	Crayford ✻ (818)	16.43	Purleigh (862)
09.30	Iver Heath (776)	11.06	Woolwich ✻ (819)	16.59	Chelmsford (863)
11.22	Shoreham (777)	11.44	Blackheath (820)	**February 24**	
11.36	Corringham Marshes (778)	13.57	Off Clacton (821)	07.40	Dagenham (864)
14.47	In sea off Foulness (779)	14.19	Walthamstow (822)	**February 26**	
February 16		22.21	Stoke (823)	09.10	Plumsted (865)
16.10	Shenfield (780)	22.55	Laindon (824)	09.11	Bobbingworth (866)
21.24	South Hanningfield (781)	**February 20**		09.22	In sea off Clacton (867)
21.35	West Hanningfield ✻ (782)	01.16	Greenwich (825)	09.35	Ilford (868)
21.54	Woolwich (783)	04.32	Poplar ✻ (826)	11.27	Belvedere (869)
23.44	Leyton (784)	08.44	Mundon (827)	16.11	Sea off Clacton (870)
February 17		09.57	Earl Stonham ✻ (828)	18.26	Leyton (871)
00.41	Steeple (785)	11.21	Upminster (829)	20.25	West Ham (872)
00.49	Thorpe-le-Soken (786)	11.37	Ilford (830)	23.05	Pitsea Marshes (873)
00.54	Dunton (787)	13.23	Rainham ✻ (831)	**February 27**	
03.32	Aylesford (788)	13.37	Waltham Holy Cross (832)	01.23	West Thurrock Marshes (874)
03.41	Althorne (789)	15.38	Blackmore (833)	01.25	Dagenham (875)
04.28	Garston Park (790)	17.56	Woolwich (834)	02.24	Kelvedon Hatch (876)
05.42	Ilford (791)	20.35	Romford (835)	02.29	Ilford (877)
05.33	Poplar (792)	20.47	Chingford (836)	04.43	Chevening (878)
06.22	Rawreth (793)	22.55	Foulness Island (837)	05.33	Theydon Garnon (879)
08.10	Lynsted (794)	23.29	Barking (838)	07.45	North Stifford (880)
08.49	Shenfield (795)	**February 21**		09.21	Swanscombe (881)
11.32	Willingale (796)	09.17	Sidcup (839)	10.51	Ingatestone (882)
14.22	High Halstow (797)	11.21	Beckenham (840)	**February 28**	
February 18		12.58	Ilford (841)	00.22	Newhall Green (883)
00.55	Chingford (798)	16.17	South Ockendon (842)	01.21	Chingford (884)
01.16	Conningham (799)	22.18	Ilford (843)	03.14	East Ham (885)
04.25	Ilford (800)	**February 22**		05.07	Erith (886)
07.32	Woodham Ferrers (801)	09.21	Epping (844)		
		14.46	Eynsford (845)		

As we have seen, the launching of flying bombs from fixed ramps in France ceased back in September with the capture of firing sites. Air-launches were dependent on available aircrews and aircraft, the weather, and the accuracy of the release, so there was no substitute to railed launch ramps accurately aligned on London. The Dutch coast was still in German hands but the only drawback was that the range of the bomb needed to be increased from 130-140 miles to at least 230 miles. This was achieved through modifications enabling extra fuel to be carried.

March 3-29: The Last Flying Bomb Attacks from Sites in German-occupied Territory

The lot of Londoners during March was made no easier by a resumption of flying bomb attacks after an interval since January 14. Attacks against Antwerp had continued throughout the period, all from sites on land in western Germany, and late in January from the Rotterdam—Dordrecht area, but there had been no sign of a resumption of air-launched attacks against the United Kingdom. This was the only means of attacking Britain unless the Germans were able to increase the range of the flying bomb beyond the 130 miles that had so far been the limit of its operations. However, evidence began to accumulate in February 1945 that it was precisely this that the Germans were attempting to do. It appeared that by reducing the weight of the wing of the bomb by using a large proportion of wood instead of steel in its construction, and perhaps also the weight of the warhead by replacing the usual steel casing with wood, the amount of fuel that could be carried — and therefore the endurance and range of the bomb — had been increased. Wreckage that was recovered in February from flying bombs that had crashed in Belgium indicated that both sorts of alteration had been embodied in production.

Operation 'Pappdeckel' started at 02.30 on March 3 when the 12. Batterie of the II. Abteilung of Flak-Regiment 155 (W) began launches from three sites in Holland: at Vlaardingen (Launch Site 536), Delft (Launch Site 537) and Ypenburg (Launch Site 538). A total of 17 V1s were sent on their way that day of which the British defences brought down seven. Only two reached the London Civil Defence Region, one landing at Bermondsey at 03.01 and Wood Green at 16.09. Once the launch sites had been identified by photo-reconnaissance, they were subjected to a sustained attack by the Royal Air Force. Ypenburg was destroyed and Vlaardingen heavily damaged, causing the Germans to abandon these two sites and prepare new ones further north at Lisse and Vogelenzang. In all, between March 3 and March 29, a total of 276 V1s were fired against London from south-western Holland. Of these, four were brought down by fighters, 87 by the guns, leaving 32 to cross the English coast of which 13 reached Greater London.

OPERATION 'PAPPDECKEL' [PASTEBOARD]

I have today entrusted Oberst Wolf with the task of seeking out and beginning the construction of sites for Target Area 0101 [London], at a distance of 350 to 370 km, for the Holland V1 operation.

Careful choice of V1 sites for firing bring Greater London within easy reach (over 370 km). Operation on London begins around 20.3.45. For this operation, sites which are low-lying as far as possible should be selected. It must be noted that these missiles should not be fired when the wind is coming from the rear.

SS-GRUPPENFÜHRER HANS KAMMLER,
TELEPRINTER ORDER, FEBRUARY 5, 1945

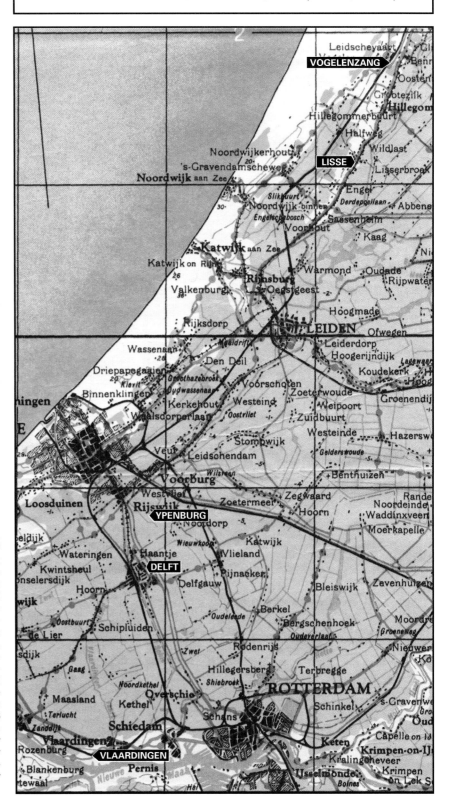

The launch site at Ypenburg airfield was subjected to heavy attacks by Typhoons of the Second Tactical Air Force and Spitfires from Fighter Command.

On February 25 the Chiefs of Staff were informed by Air Intelligence that in view of these changes, attacks on the United Kingdom might resume, and that if London was to be the target the Germans would have to construct launching sites in south-west Holland. There was so far no evidence that they had done so but comprehensive photographic reconnaissance of the area was being flown. The Chiefs of Staff were told that assuming the trials of the modified weapon were successful, operations could be expected to start about one month later. What the scale of attack might be was doubtful. As far as was known, only one regiment had been trained to fire flying bombs and at least half of it was committed to the attacks on Antwerp. However, Air Intelligence estimated that sufficient crews might be deployed to launch attacks on London on a scale of around 30 flying bombs every 24 hours.

On the day following this meeting, photographs taken over south-west Holland showed that two launching sites, oriented on London, were being constructed, one near The Hague at Ypenburg airfield, which was no longer in use, the other in a factory district at Vlaardingen, six miles west of Rotterdam. In each case the Germans had taken great care to conceal the components of the site among adjacent buildings. Both sites, therefore, were difficult targets and no attacks were made on them for some time to come.

Defensive Preparations

On February 26 a conference was held at Fighter Command Headquarters to consider what could be done about the new threat. Since the question of defence against flying bombs had arisen over a year before, now without question the guns would be allotted the

main role. Flying bombs aimed at London from sites on land in south-west Holland could be expected to converge on the capital over the coast between the Isle of Sheppey and Orfordness. Accordingly, the basis of the plan that was made was the reinforcement of the gun defences of this area, which was already covered by the Gun Box and the southern sectors of the Gun Strip, by the addition of 96 heavy guns, i.e. 12 batteries. These were to be found by redeploying 12 batteries from the northerly sectors of the Gun Strip, half of which would be replaced by mixed Royal Artillery and Auxiliary Territorial Service batteries then under training. Instructions for the move were given on February 27 and on the following day four of the batteries were ready for action in the Gun Box. By March 4 a further two batteries had been added to the Gun Box and three to the southern Gun Strip. On that date there were now 196 heavy guns and 16 light in the Gun Box and 304 heavy and eight light in the Gun Strip.

The rules governing the fire of the guns were designed to give them almost as much freedom as they had enjoyed in the later stages of the deployment on the south-east coast the previous August. A permanent 'attack in progress' was declared by day and arrangements were made with Bomber Command whereby the Controller at No. 11 Group Filter Room could remove all height restrictions on gun-fire if flying bombs were reported and if there was no large-scale friendly activity near the gun zones. The procedure came into effect on the night of February 28/29. To reduce the chances of friendly aircraft being fired on, flying was restricted over the quadrilateral North Foreland—Gravesend—Orfordness—Ostend.

Considerable fighter defences were planned for the expectation of 30 flying bombs every 24 hours. This implied a scale of attack approaching half that which had caused so much destruction in the summer of 1944. Six squadrons of Mustangs, their engines boosted to give

It is pictured here after it had been abandoned by the 12. Batterie.

After Ypenburg and Vlaardingen had been put out of action, the Germans switched to three new sites some 20 miles further up the coast. Manned by the 11. Batterie, they opened fire at 19.30 on March 22 although by then it was really far too late and they were only in action for eight days until March 29 when Lisse was demolished.

extra speed, were selected to operate by day, three between the guns and London and three to seaward of the guns. No. 616 Squadron, which was equipped with Meteors, was also transferred from the Second Tactical Air Force to Fighter Command for patrol duties overland. By night, two Mosquito squadrons were to patrol to seaward and the Tempests of No. 501 Squadron overland. To improve radar reporting, the Admiralty was asked to return the fighter-direction ship, HMS *Caicos*, but this proved impossible as there were few ships of this kind to meet extensive naval requirements. For the same purpose, a direct link was laid between the radar stations of Second Tactical Air Force in Belgium that covered the Dutch coast and No. 11 Group.

The Attacks; Success of the Defences

The new German attack began in the early morning of March 3. The first flying bomb to be reported penetrated the defences and fell in Bermondsey at 03.01. Six more were reported in the next three hours, followed by a lull until the middle of the afternoon. Then, from 14.30 until 22.30, seven bombs were plotted. Another lull ensued until shortly before 11 o'clock the following morning when three bombs were plotted during the next hour. There was an even longer pause before the next bombs came over, which was not until 11.00 on March 5. So far, therefore, the weight of attack had been nothing like that anticipated.

Of these first 21 flying bombs, seven penetrated to London and exploded there, and ten were shot down by anti-aircraft fire which was not as high a proportion of destruction as the gunners had achieved, either during the later stages of the attack from sites in France or against air-launched flying bombs, but thereafter the performance of the guns exceeded even their previous best.

From the evening of March 5 until the early afternoon of the 29th when the attacks ceased, 104 flying bombs were plotted. Activity did not continue daily — there were five days (March 9-13) when it ceased altogether — and on other days the average number of bombs was less than ten. No less than 81 bombs were shot down, 76 by Anti-Aircraft Command, four by fighters of Fighter Command, and one shared by gunners of the Royal Navy and Anti-Aircraft Command. For the whole of the attack, therefore, out of the 125 flying bombs that came close enough to the coast to be reported, 91 were shot down, 86 by Anti-Aircraft Command. Only 13 bombs came down within the London Civil Defence Region. Twenty others escaped destruction but fell outside London. The total number of bombs the Germans launched is unlikely to have been less than 150, therefore, only some nine per cent of their effort reached the target area.

The scale of attack proved to be so much less than had been expected that with the exception of one Mustang squadron and the Tempests of No. 501 Squadron, defence against it was left entirely to Anti-Aircraft Command and the reporting system of radar stations and the Royal Observer Corps. The other Mustang squadrons, which had been originally allocated to flying bomb defence, reverted to escort duties with Bomber Command early in March and No. 616 (Meteor) Squadron returned to Second Tactical Air Force. Radio counter-measures against signals from the transmitters, with which a proportion of flying bombs were fitted, were applied throughout the attack.

Few bombing counter-measures were initiated directly against the German flying bomb organisation in south-west Holland as the success of the close defences of London was such that they were not urgently required. Little was known about the means of supply to the launching sites; there were certainly no storage depots comparable to those that had been established in 1944 in northern France. Vlaardingen and Ypenburg appeared to be the only launching sites that were being employed against London, though shortly after activity had ceased, there was evidence that a third site near the Delftsche Canal had also been used. Both Vlaardingen and Ypenburg were attacked, the first by Typhoons of Second Tactical Air Force, the second by Spitfires of Fighter Command. Vlaardingen was attacked on March 23 when one of the essential buildings was destroyed, and shortly afterwards the Germans dismantled the launching ramp. Ypenburg was first attacked on March 20 by four Spitfires of No. 124 Squadron, and, later on the same day, in separate attacks, by Nos. 451, 453, 603 Squadrons and again by No. 124, 24 Spitfires taking part in all. In this case also, an essential component of the site was destroyed. On the 23rd, two attacks were carried out by 12 Spitfires of No. 451 Squadron. The bombing was accurate and photographs taken after the attack showed that the launching ramp had been dismantled.

It appears that the RAF was also unaware of the existence of the two ramps at Vogelenzang before they, too, were destroyed and abandoned by the launch crews.

The firing point at Delft (Launching Site 537) had been built on the property of the Lijm en Gelatinefabriek Delft (Glue and Gelatine Factory Delft) on Oude Rotterdamse Straatweg, which lay alongside the Oude Schie Canal. It was an ideal location as the ramp was built parallel to an existing track, four metres high, used for moving wagons dumping coal from barges on the canal. This track was not only precisely aligned towards London but it also served as perfect camouflage. However, the Dutch resistance soon got wind of it and sent in numerous reports, and an RAF photo-reconnaissance aircraft took very good photos of the installation, even before it was brought into use. Nevertheless, unlike Vlaardingen and Ypenburg, for some reason it was never attacked. It was destroyed by the Germans after the final launch had taken place. (The mean point of impact of the 32 V1s in March not destroyed by the defences was now at Hackney.)

Casualties in the United Kingdom were very small: 26 killed and 106 seriously injured, of whom 22 were killed and 83 injured in London. The last flying bombs to fall in London exploded at 07.54 and 07.55 hours on March 28 at Chislehurst and Waltham Holy Cross respectively. The last to fall anywhere in the United Kingdom was shot down by anti-aircraft fire and fell at Iwade, near Sittingbourne, Kent, at 09.59 on March 29. The last to approach the coast was also shot down by anti-aircraft fire off Orfordness at 12.43 on the 29th.

This last flurry of flying bomb activity against London during March was clearly a failure. It is hard to see in it any serious military purpose other than the testing of a modified type of flying bomb. It did not divert any Allied forces, other than a single Mustang squadron, from the offensive against Germany, and such forces as were used against it were part of the air defences of Great Britain and would have continued in that role whether or not flying bomb attacks had been launched.

The London Civil Defence Region received its last flying bomb on the morning of March 28 — Chief Warden Ted Carter at Waltham Cross went to investigate. 'The siren at about 07.45 hours was followed shortly after by the sound of a doodle. By the noise of the engine it was not far away, but before we could get outside to see him, there was a bump but not nearly so loud as expected. Almost immediately Control phoned that it was at Claverhambury, just inside the London Region. Took Smith and Francis and found it in one of the paddocks attached to Claverhambury Kennels. Very slight damage round about but quite small crater. Apparently it had hit a tree and exploded almost before it reached the ground. The usual smell of burnt earth and hot metal. It was a Type "C.C" with the new plywood wings.' All told, Flak-Regiment 155 (W) claimed to have ground-launched a total of 12,263 flying bombs of which 9,251 appear to have been fired at Britain. Of these, 5,672 crossed the coast, 4,261 were destroyed and 2,419 reached the London area.

Oude Rotterdamse Straatweg is today the Rotterdamse Weg and the factory is now the Lijm en Cultuur BV (Glue and Culture Ltd). There are still a few original buildings and a car park now occupies the area where the railway track and V1 ramp were sited.

In 1990 Denis Huxter (left) took local historian Bryn Elliott to show him the exact spot at Claverhambury where the last V1 to fall in the London region crashed.

The first major incident on Warden Carter's own patch had taken place on March 7 when a rocket launched by the 3. Batterie of Artillerie-Regiment 902 from the Duindigt racecourse (Big Ben 953) hit the centre of the main road in Waltham Abbey. The huge crater measured more than 75 feet across and it rapidly filled with water from the shattered mains necessitating Incident Control Points being set up on both sides. The Abbey, burial place of King Harold, stands unscathed in the background.

The Last Rocket Attacks on London, March 17-27

The month of March 1945 also saw the end of the rocket bombardment of London. The situation was last considered at the stage which had been reached by the middle of the month when Fighter Command had for some time been attacking the storage areas at Duindigt and Ravelijn which were the only ones for which there was any reliable evidence of employment. However, photographs taken during the second week in March strongly indicated that the Germans had been driven out of both areas. Consequently, in default of any other targets in The Hague area which could be attacked without probable hurt to civilians, an entirely new policy was decided upon, one which was to be applied until the enemy's attacks had ceased.

It took the form of concentrating upon attacking the railways leading to The Hague, particularly upon the stretches of track between Haarlem and Leiden, Utrecht and Leiden, and The Hague—Gouda—Alphen, along which rocket supplies were known to pass. The policy was not rigidly applied as the large building of the Bataafsche Import Company at The Hague remained on the list of targets as well as a Ford garage, near the Kurhaus Grand Hotel at Scheveningen, where the Meilerwagen transporters were believed to be housed. Duindigt and Ravelijn also received a small number of attacks between March 17 and 19 as insurance against resumption of activity there. From the 24th, by which time there was evidence that firing, though not storage, had been resumed in the Duindigt district, armed reconnaissances were flown daily over the area. However, during the rest of March, no other targets associated with either the storage or the firing of rockets were bombed. There was a report late in the month that

The blasted area when cleared provided space for the introduction of a roundabout in later years.

Smithfield — in the Victorian era reputed to be the greatest wholesale meat market in the world — occupied a huge covered building erected in 1865 on the corner of Farringdon Road and Charterhouse Street. On the morning of March 8, the 3. Batterie, Artillerie-Regiment 902, were making ready to fire their sixth rocket of the day, and at 10.58 it was sent streaking on its way from the launch site at Wassenaar. Being a Thursday the market was crowded when at ten minutes past eleven one eyewitness, George Campbell, who just happened to be looking skywards at the time, recounted seeing a whole punched in the clouds as the V2 descended at over 3,000 mph. *Right:* This photographer was standing in the middle of Farringdon Road looking across to the building on the northern corner of Charterhouse Street, struck by Big Ben 964.

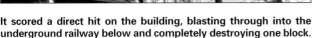

It scored a direct hit on the building, blasting through into the underground railway below and completely destroying one block.

The dead numbered 110 with another 123 suffering serious injuries . . . it was the third-highest death toll from a V2.

a large hall at Rijnsburg, near The Hague — in happier times a flower market — was being used for storage but the evidence was not held to be sufficient to justify its attack.

The Bataafsche Import Company's building was attacked on March 18 by six Spitfires of No. 602 Squadron. The attack appeared to the pilots to be very accurate and six 500lb and 12 250lb bombs were released with only one cluster missing the target. Later, photographs indicated that the damage was not as great as had been thought; though an intelligence report of March 25 stated that the German organisation occupying the building had been evacuated. A heavier attack was made on March 30 by No. 603 Squadron, when 12 Spitfires took part, each refuelling and re-arming at Ursel after the first attack and bombing again on the homeward journey. Over ten tons of bombs were dropped and at least six direct hits were scored on the building and eight near misses.

The Kurhaus garage at Scheveningen was also accurately bombed in the heaviest single attack made by Fighter Command during the whole of its offensive against The Hague. This took place on March 22 when 24 Spitfires of Nos. 453 and 603 Squadrons, each carrying a 500lb bomb and two of 250lb attacked the

garage section by section. The squadrons refuelled and re-armed at Ursel and attacked again just over three hours later. In all, over 20 tons of bombs were dropped. The full extent of the damage was not apparent, but a ramp leading from the roadway to the first floor of the garage collapsed under the bombing and the approaches were heavily cratered. A nearby transformer station was also hit. Intelligence officers at Fighter Command were doubtful whether the Germans had been driven out of the garage, but no more attacks were made upon it.

With these exceptions, the efforts of the Command were entirely directed against railways. Between March 17 and April 3, which was the last day on which any bombing attacks were made, a total of 1,572 sorties were flown by Fighter Command against western Holland. Nearly 1,400 were against railway targets,

An amazing comparison in 2019 with a section of the old building still standing.

It was on March 18 that a final operation was carried out on a target suspected as being involved in the launching of rockets from The Hague. The office block of the Bataafsche Import Company (BIM) was situated within the built-up area north of the Haagsche Bosch (see map page 225), so there was a risk of civilian casualties. Earlier in the war, the RAF had carried out very successful pin-point attacks on various Gestapo headquarters using Mosquitos from Nos. 21, 464 and 487 Squadrons. However, in the case of the BIM building, six Spitfires from No. 602 Squadron, instead of their usual dive-bombing attacks, would now attack at zero feet using delayed-action bombs. The intention was to try to 'skip' their bombs into the building like a pebble skimmed on a pond, but it appears that only superficial damage was caused and there was no let-up in V2 launches.

the rest, including the attacks on Ypenburg, were against specific objectives directly connected with the German rocket troops. Against the latter targets, some 70 tons were dropped compared to over 400 tons on railways. The weight of bombs dropped in this period of less than three weeks was in fact higher than at any other stage of the offensive, partly because the weather was better and partly because more use was made of Ursel airfield for refuelling and re-arming, which allowed double attacks to be made and 500lb bombs to be carried.

According to the interpretation of photographs, no less than 220 cuts were made in the line; three railway bridges and two road bridges were destroyed with 14 more damaged, but little movement was taking place on Dutch railways at this time. Certain stretches of railway remained unrepaired after being broken, but others were repaired shortly after bombing.

V1 AND V2 INCIDENTS MARCH 1945
Flying bombs are indicated with a dagger, rockets with their 'Big Ben' numbers. (Airburst ✱)

March 1
01.08	Erith (887)
02.34	Little Leighs (888)
05.07	Barnet (889)
05.09	Stapleford Tawney (890)
05.46	Woolwich (891)
07.32	Eltham (892)
08.06	Shoreditch (893)
08.23	Orpington (894)
15.27	Walthamstow (895)
16.10	Wickford (896)
17.28	Horndon on the Hill (897)
23.13	West Ham (898)

March 2
01.02	Ashington (899)
02.19	Havering-atte-Bower (900)
04.49	Greenwich (901)
04.52	Orpington (902)
05.41	Epping Forest (903)
05.48	Chigwell ✱ (904)
05.51	N of Fambridge (905)
07.39	Thorndon Park (906)
07.50	High Halstow (907)
08.18	Sea off Southend (908)
09.22	Brentwood (909)
11.06	Greenwich (910)
12.21	Orpington (911)
23.03	Chigwell (912)
23.11	Bermondsey (913)
23.15	Woking ✱ (914)

March 3
01.14	Foulness Island (915)
02.32	Edmonton (916)
03.01	Bermondsey †
03.05	Off Southend † ✱
03.35	Theydon Bois (917)
03.47	Woolwich ✱ (918)
04.39	Woowich ✱ (919)
04.49	Sevenoaks (920)
03.55	Off Foulness † ✱

04.05	Off Southend †
04.55	Frinton & Walton † ✱
04.56	Off Walton † ✱
05.49	Off Clacton † ✱
06.01	Ilford (921)
06.14	Sea off Clacton (922)
12.17	Deptford (923)
14.39	Stapleford †
14.43	Cuffley †
16.09	Wood Green †
16.56	Off Foulness † ✱
21.03	Off Clacton † ✱
21.58	Off Foulness † ✱
22.32	Off Foulness †

March 4
01.35	Havering-atte-Bower (924)
04.52	Penshurst (925)
05.38	Bermondsey ✱ (926)
08.20	Chingford (927)
09.08	Mouth of the Thames (928)
10.44	Camberwell †
10.47	Chertsey †
12.02	Redbourne †

March 5
11.06	Barking †
11.06	Deptford †
12.32	Enfield †
12.32	East Barnet †
20.07	Woolwich (929)
22.08	Foulness Island †
22.32	Rainham (930)
22.59	Off Orfordness † ✱

March 6
00.57	Bexley (931)
03.07	Rainham (932)
03.09	West Ham (933)
04.35	St Mary Cray (934)
06.18	Barking (935)
08.35	Woolwich (936)
12.33	Bowers Marshes (937)

12.57	Wandsworth (938)
14.24	Sandon †
16.58	Walthamstow (939)
17.46	Fambridge †
17.48	Off Clacton † ✱
19.38	Wandsworth (940)
19.38	West Ham (941)
21.44	Woolwich (942)
21.50	St Nicholas at Wade †
23.02	Shelley †
23.24	Ilford (943)
23.26	Chigwell (944)

March 7
01.59	Near Navestock (945)
03.13	Stanford Rivers (946)
03.20	Deptford (947)
06.03	Edmonton (948)
08.37	Greenwich (949)
10.33	Sidcup area ✱ (950)
12.57	Poplar (951)
14.55	Raveningham (952)
17.00	Waltham Holy Cross (953)
21.59	Ilford (954)
23.32	Dagenham (955)

March 8
00.49	Chigwell (956)
01.37	Eltham (957)
01.52	Woolwich (958)
03.24	Writtle (959)
04.21	12 ESE of Clacton (960)
04.36	St Mary Cray (961)
05.04	Ilford (962)
09.12	West Ham (963)
11.02	Finsbury (964)
12.06	Blackheath (965)
14.55	Sidcup (966)
19.27	Off Shoeburyness † ✱
19.30	Bradwell †
19.53	Horton Kirby (967)
20.17	Dunton (968)

21.46 Berden (969)
21.51 Harold Wood (970)
23.03 Sea off Canvey Island (971)

March 9
00.40 Kenton (972)
02.18 Marden (973)
04.06 Pitsea (974)
04.27 Greenwich ✳ (975)
08.29 Greenwich (976)
08.38 Sea 3m SSW of Southend (977)
11.06 In Thames at Woolwich (978)
13.51 Waltham Holy Cross (979)
22.59 South Ockenden (980)

March 10
00.01 Beckenham (981)
00.16 Biggin Hill (982)
01.26 Pilgrims Hatch (983)
01.50 Enfield ✳ (984)
04.22 1m SSW of Rawreth (985)
09.57 Westmill ✳ (986)
10.01 Welling (987)

March 11
07.09 Near mouth of River Crouch (988)
07.40 West Ham (989)
10.02 Westerham (990)
20.04 Brockley (991)
20.40 Canvey Island (992)
21.51 Bulphan (993)

March 12
00.11 Ilford (994)
00.26 Upminster (995)
01.29 Greenstead (996)
02.05 Sea 6-7m SE of Clacton (997)
02.33 Chislehurst (998)
02.40 Sidcup (999)
04.45 Little Warley (1000)
04.47 Hainault Forest (1001)
05.05 NW of Hornchurch (1002)
07.01 Eltham (1003)
07.18 Althorne (1004)
09.03 Stanford-le-Hope ✳ (1005)
11.17 Lower Kirby (1006)
21.19 Epping (1007)
23.46 Nazeing (1008)

March 13
03.27 Tillingham Marshes (1009)
06.29 Shenfield (1010)
08.30 Erith (1011)

March 14
00.39 Havering-atte-Bower (1012)
07.20 Off Foulness Point † ✳
09.23 Ealing †
21.22 Rainham (1013)
23.27 Sutton at Hone (1014)

March 15
00.16 In Thames near Erith (1015)
01.01 Beckenham (1016)
02.42 In Thames at Dagenham (1017)
03.33 In Thames at Woolwich (1018)
03.34 Off Walton † ✳
03.35 Off Walton † ✳
03.35 Off Clacton † ✳
05.21 Off Foulness Point † ✳
06.24 Rayleigh (1019)
09.11 Richmond Park (1020)
13.27 Tottenham (1021)
22.26 Hornchurch (1022)
22.57 Neasden (1023)
23.45 Near Maldon (1024)

March 16
02.34 Willesden (1025)
02.54 Sea off North Foreland (1026)
03.58 Off Clacton † ✳
04.03 Off Foulness Point † ✳
05.23 Off Foulness Point † ✳
05.31 Dartford †
06.34 Leyton (1027)
06.51 Stock (1028)
08.53 East Ham (1029)
09.37 Dengie (1030)
23.06 Basildon (1031)

March 17
00.09 3m S of Upminster (1032)
00.55 Near Hornchurch (1033)
03.34 Wennington Marshes (1034)
05.16 Hampstead (1035)
07.36 Dartford ✳ (1036)

08.11 Woolwich (1037)
12.45 Greenwich (1038)
13.20 Stepney (1039)
22.26 Barking (1040)

March 18
00.38 West Ham (1041)
01.33 Cranham (1042)
01.41 Battlesbridge (1043)
02.03 Epping (1044)
02.48 Off Felixstowe † ✳
02.50 Off Bridgewick † ✳
02.59 Somersham †
03.40 Ightham (1045)
06.07 Off Hollesley † ✳
06.09 Off Bradwell † ✳
06.30 Aylesford (1046)
06.40 Hutton (1047)
06.46 Barking (1048)
09.34 Marble Arch (1049)

March 19
00.05 Theydon Garnon (1050)
00.06 Netteswell (1051) ✳
01.33 South Hornchurch (1052)
01.37 Nutfield (1053)
05.45 Off the Naze † ✳
08.19 Great Parndon †
08.40 Off Foulness Point † ✳
09.16 Thorndon Parva †
09.17 Shipbourne †
10.08 Cockpole Green (1054)
10.31 Erith (1055)
15.55 Woolwich (1056)
22.20 Theydon Bois (1057)
22.45 Hatfield Broad Oak (1058)

March 20
01.27 Sutton Valence †
01.28 Little Warley (1059)
04.10 West Hanningfield (1060)
05.37 Hornchurch (1061)
07.03 Parslow Common (1062)
08.20 Sidcup (1063)
09.53 Mayland (1064)

March 21
00.40 Wanstead (1065)
03.06 Off Bridgewick † ✳
03.07 Off Shoeburyness † ✳
09.36 Heston (1066)
11.39 Hampstead (1067)
13.43 Ruislip ✳ (1068)
18.44 NE of Romford ✳ (1069)
21.33 Little Saling (1070)
22.40 Woodham Ferrers (1071)
23.54 Frinton & Walton †
23.55 Stansted (1072)

March 22
02.06 Off Blackwater River (1073)
02.36 Near Canewdon (1074)
02.43 Epping (1075)
03.35 Harrow (1076)
03.40 Off Clacton † ✳
03.42 Off Foulness † ✳
03.57 St Mary's Hoo (1077)
05.22 Stock (1078)
05.47 Boreham, NNE Chelmsford (1079)
06.02 Leyton ✳ (1080)
06.25 Off Bawdsey †
06.28 Great Holland † ✳
07.02 Brightlingsea (1081)
07.44 Sea 5m off Bradwell (1082)
08.13 Dagenham (1083)
09.52 Woodham Ferrers (1084)
10.30 Dagenham ✳ (1085)
19.45 Off Bawdsey †
19.45 Off Foulness Point † ✳
19.47 Off the Naze † ✳
21.45 20m SE of Yarmouth (1086)
22.48 Off Clacton † ✳
23.00 Off Foulness Point † ✳
23.21 Dartford (1087)
23.42 Southminster (1088)

March 23
01.40 Brockley ✳ (1089)
03.15 Sea off Clacton (1090)
03.19 Off Clacton † ✳
04.30 Stepney ✳ (1091)
05.03 Off Foulness Point † ✳
06.26 Theydon Garnon (1092)

06.49 Studham (1093)
06.58 Elham †
07.14 Thorpe-le-Soken †
09.41 Latchingdon (1094)
12.32 Stapleford, Herts (1095)
23.16 Waltham Holy Cross (1096)

March 24
01.31 Poplar (1097)
03.17 Chicksands †
07.07 Stondon Massey †
07.21 Braughing †
07.57 Paddington †

March 25
07.50 Buttsbury †
07.55 Stanford Rivers †
07.57 East Grinstead †
22.33 St Pancras (1098)
23.00 Enfield (1099)
23.44 Stepney (1100)

March 26
00.05 Lambourne (1101)
00.41 Leysdown †
00.54 Tillingham Marshes † ✳
01.19 Off Clacton † ✳
01.25 Off Clacton † ✳
01.28 Great Bromley †
02.22 Off Clacton † ✳
02.32 Dagenham †
03.44 Off the Naze † ✳
04.04 Cheshunt (1102)
04.20 Bermondsey (1103)
04.42 Hornchurch (1104)
09.03 Navestock (1105)
14.43 Ilford ✳ (1106)
15.22 Bromley (1107)
19.08 Romford (1108)
22.30 Noak Hill (1109)

March 27
00.22 Edmonton (1110)
02.44 Berners Roding †
03.02 Cheshunt (1111)
03.20 Off Foulness Point † ✳
03.30 Ilford (1112)
03.30 Off Clacton † ✳
03.44 Bradwell † ✳
04.04 Hutton Park (1113)
04.07 Off Foulness Point † ✳
05.21 Chelsham †
05.25 Orpington †
06.28 Off Whitstable †
07.21 Stepney (1114)
07.36 Off Foulness Point † ✳
09.25 Off Foulness Island †
16.54 Orpington (1115)

March 28
01.35 Off Bridgewick †
01.44 Off the Naze † ✳
02.37 Off Hollesley † ✳
02.39 Off Orfordness † ✳
02.43 Off Felixstowe † ✳
03.42 Off Felixstowe † ✳
03.57 South of Orfordness † ✳
06.05 Off Frinton-on-Sea † ✳
07.54 Chislehurst & Sidcup †
07.55 Waltham Holy Cross †
21.35 Off Sheerness † ✳

March 29
00.04 Great Holland †
00.41 Off the Naze †
00.44 Hanford Rivers †
02.17 Off Foulness †
02.30 Off Sheerness † ✳
03.00 Off Brightlingsea †
03.22 Off Bradwell †
03.28 Off Orfordness † ✳
03.37 Burnham-on-Crouch †
04.29 Off Bradwell †
05.51 Off Brightlingsea † ✳
07.32 Great Wakering †
08.58 Datchworth †
09.37 Little Oakley †
09.52 Great Wigborough †
09.59 Iwade †
10.07 Off Foulness †
10.25 Off Walton † ✳
12.43 Off Orfordness † ✳

That same day in London, one of the capital's iconic edifices was nearly struck by a V2 launched at 09.25 from the Haagsche Bosch by the 1. Batterie of Artillerie-Regiment 902. It exploded at 09.34, killing three people close by Marble Arch, the triumphal gateway designed by John Nash in 1827 to be the state entrance to Buckingham Palace. However, 24 years later it was dismantled and moved to form an impressive northern entrance to Park Lane which was in the process of being widened. Yet, isolated on a traffic island, it was rarely used as only members of the Royal Family and the King's Troop of the Royal Horse Artillery were permitted to pass through its arch.

There was, however, some evidence that the Germans were at least inconvenienced by the attacks. Since the autumn of 1944, the Intelligence officers concerned had accepted that Leiden was the only railhead for rocket supplies and the stations there had not been attacked only because of the

The crater lay on the other side of the carriageway at 'Speaker's Corner', which has been the traditional site for public speeches and debate since 1872. In former times this was Tyburn, the dreaded site of public executions.

congestion of civilian property in the neighbourhood. On March 18 photographs taken by No. 26 Squadron of Fighter Command revealed — both at Leiden and The Hague — the easily-recognisable long railway wagons on which rockets were transported. Five days later a similar train was photographed in Rotterdam station, and others were seen at Amsterdam in the latter part of March. The evidence was slight enough but it bore the interpretation that the direct lines from western Germany through Amersfoort and Utrecht to Leiden were being interrupted and that other routes, and possibly railheads additional to Leiden, were being improvised.

The Odeon Marble Arch, on the corner of Oxford Street and Edgware Road, boasted the largest screen in London but it closed in 2016 and was demolished the same year. The Cumberland Hotel, built by J. Lyons in 1933, stands on the right.

On the basis of this intelligence, the effort of Fighter Command during the last few days of March and the first three days of April was concentrated on the railways Leiden—Woerden, The Hague—Gouda, Amsterdam—Hilversum and Amsterdam—Utrecht. Special attention was paid to a bridge at Elinkwijk which carried the Utrecht—Woerden railway over the Merwede Canal and to a junction of tracks on the line Woerden—Breudijk. Repair work was vigorous at both places and, although many hits were scored, photographs taken on April 2 when the offensive was almost over indicated that the lines were still serviceable.

Throughout the period, the Second Tactical Air Force was operating further to the east in support of the advance across the Rhine and also scored many hits on railway communications. The damage caused would not make the Germans' task in bringing up rockets for firing any easier, but to what extent the rate of fire was affected by these attacks could not be determined.

Enemy Activity; Reactions of the Defences

After the abnormally low scale of attack during the week March 10-16, when only 50 rockets had fallen in the United Kingdom, there was a slight recovery, and between the 17th and 23rd some 65 rockets were reported. One rocket impacted on March 24, with three on the 25th, nine on the 26th, and six on the 27th. The last V2 crashed at 16.54 hours on the 27th in Kynaston Road, Orpington, making it the 1,115th rocket to be reported in the United Kingdom. There was one casualty, the very last of the V-weapon campaign against Britain.

Of the final 80 rockets, 34 fell in London representing an accuracy similar to that of earlier weeks and making a total of 518 rockets in the London Civil Defence Region since September 8.

On the night of March 25/26, all three batteries of Artillerie-Regiment 902 fired off seven rockets, three at targets on the Continent and four at Britain. Twenty-eight people lost their lives, nine of which occurred at the Whitfield Tabernacle in Tottenham Court Road. It was just after 10.30 p.m. that the Central Mission of the Congregational Church was hit and totally destroyed, the search for victims continuing during the night under floodlights.

The tendency to fire principally at night, which had been noticed towards the end of February and was an index of the effectiveness of the counter-offensive, remained very marked as only 36 per cent arrived in daylight.

Casualties would have been light during the period compared to earlier weeks but for the ill-fortune which saw the last rocket but one fall on a block of flats, Hughes Mansions, in Stepney. The building was hit at 07.21 on the 27th, killing 134 people seriously injuring 49. Casualties for the last fortnight totalled 308 killed and 604 seriously injured compared to 394 killed and 763 seriously injured in the previous fortnight. This brought the total casualties from rockets for the whole period of attack to 2,511 killed and 5,869 seriously injured in London and 213 killed and 598 seriously injured elsewhere.

A new chapel was built in 1957 which today houses the American International Church and the London Chinese Lutheran Church.

Most V2s were now being despatched at night and on March 27 the 3. Batterie of Artillerie-Regiment 902 fired its first of the day at 00.14. A second followed at 03.24 and the next at 03.59 but then there was a lull until 07.12. That rocket was the last to reach London and the penultimate of Kammler's campaign. It struck at Stepney in East London at 07.21 on Tuesday morning, just as the residents of Hughes Mansions in Vallance Road were getting ready for work. With 134 dead, it was the second-highest number of casualties since the Woolworths store was hit the previous November (see page 226).

The system for warning the London Passenger Transport Board remained in operation to the end. Only five rockets escaped detection during these last days and warnings were transmitted in all other cases. If these had been given to the general public in London it would have meant 75 warnings for a total of 34 rockets falling in London. In other words, approximately twice as many warnings than were strictly necessary would have been sounded. This was one of the factors affecting the findings of the

In May, the King and Queen made a special journey to the East End to view the site.

Inter-Departmental Radio Committee on the feasibility of an effective public warning system. A warning time of some four minutes could have been obtained by reliance on existing Chain Home stations but the number of warnings given to the London area for rockets that fell outside would have been over 60 per cent of all warnings sounded.

A similar decision was passed on the proposal by Anti-Aircraft Command for shooting at rockets which was again considered during the last week in March. On March 21, General Pile wrote to Duncan Sandys and asked for permission to carry out experimental firing as the time available was clearly becoming very short. He did not advance any scientific estimate of the chances of detonating rockets as there were so many imponderables but an improved G.L. radar set had recently

been developed and he considered that the chances of predicting where rockets would fall were sufficiently high to justify opening fire. A meeting of the 'Crossbow' Sub-Committee was held on March 26 and a panel of scientists reported the same day that on the assumption by Anti-Aircraft Command that 400 rounds were to be fired against one rocket, the chances of securing a hit were at best one in 30. Immediately General Pile again asked for permission to fire, pointing out the possible value in the future of the experiment and stating that he would attempt to treble the number of rounds fired and thus treble the chances of a hit. The proposal came before the Chiefs of Staff on March 30 when it was decided that the chances of success were too small to justify the possible adverse effect on public morale, and permission was therefore refused.

By then, the site had been cleared of the ruins of the middle block, the local paper reporting that a large number of people were waiting, lining the large open square. 'As soon as their Majesties made their appearance, the crowd began spontaneously to sing the National Anthem. Waving flags, the people surrounded their Majesties singing *There'll Always Be An England.'*

At six o'clock on the evening of April 27, Churchill gave a statement to the effect that the rocket attacks had now finished, praising the RAF, Navy and the British Army for the part they had played in bringing them to an end. He quoted some of the worst cases and ended by saying that the last one fell at Orpington. It was there that came the final tragedy.

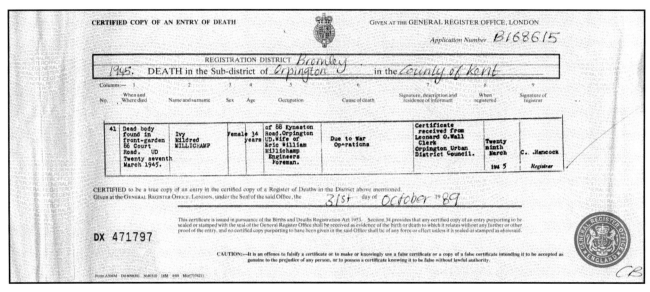

REGISTRATION DISTRICT Bromley

1945. DEATH in the Sub-district of Orpington in the County of Kent

No.	When and Where died	Name and surname	Sex	Age	Occupation	Cause of death	Signature, description and residence of informant	When registered	Signature of registrar
41	Dead body found in front-garden 86 Court Road. UD Twenty seventh March 1945.	Ivy Mildred MILLICHAMP	Female	34 years	of 88 Kynaston Road, Orpington UD. Wife of Eric William Millichamp Engineers Foreman.	Due to War Operations	Certificate received from Leonard O. Wall Clerk Orpington Urban District Council.	Twenty ninth March 1945	C. Hancock Registrar

CERTIFIED to be a true copy of an entry in the certified copy of a Register of Deaths in the District above mentioned.
Given at the GENERAL REGISTER OFFICE, LONDON, under the Seal of the said Office, the 31st day of October 1989

Withdrawal of the German Batteries; Cessation of Counter-Measures.

By April 3 it was obvious that further rocket attacks on the United Kingdom from Holland were unlikely (though it was to be late in April before there was positive evidence that the launching troops had been withdrawn). On that day, Air Marshal Hill stopped all fighter-bomber attacks against western Holland and substitued armed reconnaissances. These were maintained by sections or pairs of fighters until April 25. Flying bomb attacks were considered even less likely in view of the photographic evidence that the sites at Vlaardingen and Ypenburg had been dismantled and that no new sites were being constructed.

Both flying bomb and rocket attacks against Antwerp had also come to an end at much the same time as those against London: in each case the last were fired on March 28. The flying bomb sites in the Deventer—Hengelo area of Holland, which were the last in action against Antwerp, were destroyed in the last days of March. To complete the picture of retreat and abandonment, there was good evidence that KG53, which had last launched flying bombs in the middle of January, had been disbanded.

As for rocket-firing troops, as early as March 21 units previously attacking Antwerp had begun to withdraw to avoid being trapped by the Allied advance across the Rhine. It was believed at the time that they had instructions to retire to Nordhausen in

the Harz mountains where the higher headquarters of the rocket organisation had been concentrated.

In consequence, April was a month of reduction and the standing down of all formations engaged in rocket countermeasures. On the 13th the watch for rockets was discontinued at all Chain Home radar stations and on the 20th the Chiefs of Staff agreed that all flying restrictions over the flying bomb defence zones could be cancelled. They also instructed the Joint Intelligence Sub-Committee to report the possibilities of further attacks on England. On receipt of the report, which stated that there was no risk of flying bomb attack and only a very slight chance of rocket attack, they approved the discontinuance of all counter-measures.

At 16.48, the 1. Batterie of Artillerie-Regiment 902 fired their very last rocket towards London from the Statenkwartier launch site in The Hague. It came to earth at Orpington, killing Ivy Millichamp — the last civilian casualty.

Then . . . and now in Deptford. After the 3. Batterie of Artillerie-Regiment 902 wrecked this corner of south London in the early morning of March 7, in later years the Borough of Lewisham decided to completely raze the area centered on Folkestone Gardens and Oareboro Road to create a quiet refuge of reflection. The area was cleared in the late 1960s to establish a six-acre park, appropriately named Folkestone Gardens after the street of railwaymen's houses. Here 52 persons lost their lives.

In 1957, the number of civilian casualties caused by all forms of enemy attack were declared as 146,777. Of these, flying bombs had accounted for 6,184 deaths and rockets 2,754. In addition, nearly 25,000 people had been seriously injured by both forms of attack. Nine-tenths of the casualties had occurred in the London Civil Defence Region. (Service casualties were not included.)

Photo released in June 1945 showing the damage caused by the V2 which impacted in West Ham at 19.38 on March 6.

Index

COMPILED BY PETER B. GUNN

Note: Page numbers in *italics* refer to illustrations. There may also be textual references on these pages.

A4 rocket (later V2) 8, *9*, 19, *20*, 30, *50*, 56, *172*, 173, 174
  see also V2 rocket
Abberton, V1 strikes 129
Abbess Roding, V2 strikes 239
Abbeville 20, *24*, 36, 48, *169*
Abbots Langley, V1 strikes 114
Abinger, V1 strikes 124, 140
Abridge, Epping
  V1 strikes 129
Acrise, V1 strikes 124, 152, 160
Acton, V1 strikes 63, 81, 83, 84, 85, 121, 157
Adastral House, Kingsway (Air Ministry) *18*, *88–92*, 156
Addington
  V1 strike 157
  V2 strike 239
Addlestone, V1 strike 203
Der Adler 148–150
Air Ministry 217
  AA defence 114
  Adastral House *18*, *88–92*, 156
  Berkeley Square *156*
  Directorate of Operations 28, 68, 93, 189, 232
  and German weapons development 10, 21, 28, 37
  Operational Research Centre 48, 89, *106*
  Radio counter-measures 180
Aircraft
  B-17 'Aphrodite' flying bombs *30*, *116*
  B-17 Flying Fortress *116*, 191
  Boston 49
  FZG 76 *see* V1 flying bomb
  Halifax 180, 191
  Heinkel He 111 *22*, *24*, *122*, *126–127*, 155, *205*, 208, 213, 214, 246, *248*
  Heinkel He 177 *35*

Aircraft — continued
  Henschel Hs 293 glider bomb 9
  Liberator 208
  Messerschmitt Me 262 *140*
  Messerschmitt Me 410 60, *62*
  Meteor *140–141*, 262
    EE216 *141*
  Mosquito 48, 77, 98, 99, 145–146, 206, 208, 213, 214, 248, 262, *266*
  Mustang *48*, 77, 98, *141*, 228, 250–251, 261–262
  P-38 Lightning 180
  P-61A night fighter 146
  PH17 *19*, 20
  Queen Bee 18
  Spitfire 77, 98, *100*, 221, 224–225, 228, *231*, 233, 250, *251–252*, 253, *261*, 262, 265, *266*
  Tempest 77, 98, 99, *100*, *141*, 145, 206, 207, 213, *231*, 262
  Typhoon *47*, *48*, 77, *261*, 262
  Wellington 207
  see also V1 flying bomb; V2 rocket
Aircraft Production, Ministry of 18, 21
Airfields
  Aalhorn 205, 208
  Biggin Hill *76*, 104, *141*, 167
  Bradwell Bay V2 strike 239
  Brussels/Melsbroek *119*
  Coltishall *231*, 232
  Deelen *119*, 154
  Eindhoven *119*, 152, 154
  Fairlop, V2 strike 204
  Gilze-Rijen *119*
  Le Culot *119*, 154
  Longues, Normandy (B11) *66*
  Manston 126, *140–141*
  Matlask *231*
  Mount Farm *93*
  Münster/Handorf 208
  Newchurch *100*
  North Weald 167
  Ockenburgh *225*
  Peenemünde-West *22*, *27*
  Rheine 205
  Roye/Amy 152
  Soesterberg *119*
  Swannington *231*
  Ursel, Ghent 235, 255, 265, 266

Airfields — continued
  Varrelbusch 205, 208
  Venlo *119*, 154
  Westhampnett (later Goodwood) *47*
  Ypenburg *225*, *260*, *261*
  Zwischenahn 208
  see also Farnborough RAE
Alblasserdam, Netherlands 233, 234, 235
Albury, V1 strikes 121
Aldeburgh, V1 strikes 203, 204, 222, 234, 238
Alderbury, V1 strikes 106
Aldershot, V1 strikes 139
Alderton, V1 strikes 204, 234
Aldham, V1 strikes 168
Aldington
  V1 propaganda leaflets *164*
  V1 strikes 120, 135, 139, 140, 142, 149, 151, 153, 161, 168
Aldwych, *see* Adastral House
Alexander, Mrs Eileen *125*
Alfriston, V1 strikes 112
Alkham, V1 strikes 153, 155
Alkmaar, Holland 251
All Hallows
  V1 strikes 140
  V2 strikes 195, 223
Aloiston, V1 strikes 127
Alphen 264
Alpheton, V1 strike 204
Altenwalde, Cuxhaven *181*
Althorne
  V1 strike 139
  V2 strikes 258, 259
Amberley, V1 strikes 147
Ambler, AVM Geoffrey *110*
American Red Cross *43*, 158, *213*
Amersfoort 233, 268
Amiens 20, 167
Amsterdam 183, 268
Anderson, Maj.-Gen. Orvil 94
Anderson air-raid shelters *125*
Andrews, Herbert 'Andy' *90*, *137*, *162*
Antwerp 171, 194
  Allied objective *236*
  Rex cinema, Keyserlei *212*
  targeted by V2s 198, 209, *210–212*, 220, 226, 228, *240*, 272
  V1 strikes 260, 261

Apeldoorn, Netherlands 198
'Aphrodite' flying bombs *30, 116*
Appledore, Kent, V1 strikes 103, 124, 125, 133, 140, 147, 153, 155
Ardennes offensive 226, 232, *236, 240*
Ardingley, V1 strikes 125, 157
Ardleigh, V1 strike 195
Ardleigh Green, Hornchurch, V2 strike 239
Arisley, V2 strike 239
Arnhem *212*, 230
   and Operation 'Market-Garden' *194*, 195, *202*
Arras 166
Arthur, Jean (actor) *243*
Ascot, V1 strikes 121
Ash, V1 strikes 140, 147, 152, 153, 222
Ashburnham, V1 strikes 106, 122, 142
Ashford, Kent, V1 strikes 107, 112, 114, 140, 153
Ashford, Staines, V2 strikes 204
Ashington, V2 strike 266
Ashtead, V1 strikes 121, 204
Ashurst Wood, V1 strikes 140
Assington, V1 strikes 203
Associated Press *87*
Astor, William Waldorf *133*
Atlantic Wall *24*
Audinghem 29
Audley End, V1 strikes 195
Auxiliary Fire Service (AFS) *135, 136*
Auxiliary Territorial Service (ATS) *130*, 261
Aveley
   V1 strikes 105, 122, 129
   V2 strikes 239, 259
Avington, V1 strikes 114
Axthelm, Genlt Walter von *24*
Aylesford, Stoke Mandeville Hospital 158
Aylesford
   V1 strikes 127, 140, 151, 153, 155
   V2 strikes 259, 267
Ayot St Lawrence, V1 strikes 127

Babington-Smith, Flt Off. Constance *27*
Bäckebo, Sweden *174*
Bacton, V2 strike 258
Balcombe, V1 strikes 106
Baldwin, Hanson *201*
Ball, Firewoman *131*
Balloon defences 38, *41, 43, 79*, 126–127, 145, 161, 166, 170
Banstead
   V1 strikes 67, 68, 73, 81, 83, 87, 96, 99, 105, 106, 107, 120, 121, 138, 139, 147, 204
   V2 strikes 222, 239
Bapaume *93*
Bapchild, V1 strike 222
Barcombe, V1 strikes 142
Bardfield End Green, V1 strikes 168
Barham, V1 strikes 127, 148
Barking
   Creekmouth V2 strike 222
   St Awdry's Road V1 strike *191*, 195
   V1 strikes 60, 63, 67, 82, 84, 85, 86, 97, 99, 100, 102, 103, 105, 106, 120, 121, 126, 127, 129, 133, 138, 139, 140, 148, 151, 153, 157, 204, 266
   V2 strikes 222, 234, 235, 239, 258, 259, 266, 267
Barking Marshes, V2 strikes 204, 234, 239
Barley, Royston, V2 strike 204
Barling, V2 strikes 223
Barmby Moor, Pocklington, V1 strike 235, 247
Barnes
   V1 strikes 86, 100, 124, 136, 139, 149, 151, 161
   V2 strikes 238
Barnet
   V1 strikes 97, 106, 136, 140
   V2 strikes 266
Barnet Press 160
Barrow, V1 strikes 195
Barry, Charles (architect) *107*
Basildon, V2 strikes 239, 258, 267
Basingstoke, V1 strikes 106
Bataafsche Import Company (BIM), The Hague 253, 255, 264, 265, *266*
Battersea
   St John's Hill *67*
   V1 strikes 67, 68, 81, 82, 84, 85, 88, 96, 97, 99, 100, 106, 112, 114, 118, 120, 121, 124, 133, 136, 139, 142, 155
   V2 strikes 223, 239

Battle, V1 strikes *101*, 105, 106, 112, 114, 118, 121, 122, 124, 127, 129, 140, 147, 161
Battle of Britain 179
Battle of the Bulge 235
   see also Ardennes offensive
Battlesbridge, V2 strikes 239, 267
Bawdsey, Suffolk
   radar station 179, 186, 192, 213
   V1 strikes 195, 238, 239, 267
Bayfordbury, V2 strikes 258
Baythorn End, V1 strikes 195
Bazalgette, S/Ldr Ian, VC *119*
BBC *73, 91, 125*, 180
Beachy Head
   CHL radar station 78, 80, 112
   radio counter-measures 181
   V1 strikes 138, 140, 142, 151
   V1 tracking 72
Bealings, V1 strikes 155
Beamont, W/Cdr Roland *100*
Beauchamp Roding
   V1 strikes 133
   V2 strikes 258
Beaulieu, V1 strikes 107, 114
Beauvais 154
Beauvoir 55, 60, 62
Beazley, V1 strike 204
Beazley End, V2 strike 239
Beckenham
   V1 strikes 63, 67, 81–88, 96, 97, 99, 100, 105, 106, 107, 114, 118, 120, 121, 122, 124, 127, 129, 130, 135, 136, 138, 139, 140, 148, 157, 168, 222, 239
   V2 strikes 238, 239, 259, 267
Beckley, V1 strikes 106, 107, 114, 118, 120, 135, 142, 156
Beckton, Barking, V2 strike 204
Beddingham, V1 strikes 118
Beddington, V1 strikes 63, 67, 68, 81, 82, 87, 96, 97, 99, 103, 106, 118, 121, 129, 135, 136, 138, 140, 151, 152, 153, 165, 234
Bedford *99*
Bedingham, V2 strike 203
Bedmond, V1 strikes 147
Beeston St Lawrence, V2 strike *198*, 203
Beighton, Derbys, V1 strikes 235, 247
Beighton, Norwich, V2 strikes 195
Belfast Newsletter 131
Belhamelin, Cherbourg 54, *56, 58*
Belvedere, V2 strike 222, 259
Benacre, V1 strike 204
Benenden, Kent
   V1 strikes 103, 105, 106, 107, 112, 122, 125, 140, 147, 165
   V2 strikes 239, *254*
Benfleet, V2 strikes 234
Bengeo, V2 strike 239
Bentworth, V1 strikes 107
Berden, V2 strike 267
Berkhamstead, V1 strikes 222
Berlin *27, 35, 69, 95*
   Argus Motoren GmbH *151*
   Askania electrical plant 16
Bermondsey
   Southwark Park Street V2 strikes 204, *215*
   V1 strikes 63, 68, 82, 86, 88, 96, 100, *102*, 105, 106, 107, 114, 118, 120, 136, 140, 142, 149, 151, 155, 161, *260*, 262, 266
   V2 strikes 222, 266, 267
Berners Roding
   V1 strikes 222, 267
   V2 strikes 259
Bernstone, V1 strikes 195
Berssenbrugge, Wim *230*
Berwick, V1 strikes 148
Betchworth, V1 strikes 107, 112, 140
Bethersden, V1 strikes 106, 114, 120, 126, 149, 160
Bethnal Green
   Cambridge Heath Road V1 strike *206*
   Grove Road V1 strike 60, *61–62*
   V1 strikes 7, *72*, 84, 86, 106, 125, 135, 139, 159, 195, 222
   V2 strikes 223, 258
Bexhill
   AA defences 112
   V1 strikes 106, 107, 114, 120, 122, 124, 136, 147, 148, 151, 160

Bexley
   V1 strikes 61, 63, 68, 81, 82, 86, 87, 96, 97, 100, 102, 105, 118, 120, 129, 133, 136, 139, 142, 147, 151
   V2 strikes 223, 234, 235, 258, 259, 266, 267
Bexleyheath, V2 strikes 204, 222, 259
Bicknacre, V1 strike 203
Bicknor, V1 strikes 156
Bidborough, V1 strikes 142, 147
Biddenden, V1 strikes 105, 106, 107, 120, 127, 139, 140
Biggin Hill, V2 strikes 195, 267
Billericay
   Felmore Farm V2 strike 204
   V1 strikes 122, 129, 133, 203
   V2 strikes 223, 238, 239
Billingshurst, V1 strikes 147
Bilsington, V1 strikes 105, 130, 135
Birling, V1 strikes 124, 153
Bishop's Stortford, V2 strikes 239
Bishops Waltham, V1 strikes 106, 114
Bitterne, V1 strikes 107, 114
Black Notley, V1 strikes 161
Blackheath, V2 strikes 259, 266
Blackheath Park, London 61
Blackmore, V2 strikes 259
Blackwater, River, V2 strike 267
Blean, V1 strikes 153
Bletchingley, V1 strikes 106, 107, 121, 122, 130, 165
Blindley, V1 strikes 122
Blizna, Poland *17, 172*, 173, 174, 175, 180, 182
   see also Heidelager (Heath Camp)
Bloemendaal, Netherlands 219
Blotchington, V1 strikes 121
Blue Bell Hill, V1 strikes 118
Blyth, Lt Col John S. *93*
Bobbingworth, V2 strikes 259
Boddington, V1 strikes 107
Bodiam, V1 strikes 125, 142
Bognor Regis, V1 strikes 165
Bois Carré, Abbeville *24–26, 58*
Bois de Cassan 117–118
Bonhall, V1 strikes 133
Bonn, possible flying bomb launch sites 199
Bonnington, V1 strikes 147, 156, 157
Bookham, V1 strike 203
Books
   A Fireman's Tale (Demarne) *131*
   Phoenix into Ashes (Beamont) *100*
   The War of the Worlds (Wells) *223*
Boreham, Chelmsford
   V1 strike 235
   V2 strikes 239, 267
Bornholm island *19*, 24
Borough Green, Sevenoaks, V2 strike 204
Bothersden 105
Botley, V1 strikes 107
Bottomley, AM Sir Norman 21, *38*, 50, 56
Boughton Aluph, V1 strikes 122, 152, 153, 168
Boughton Malherbe, V1 strikes 107, 121, 147, 149
Boughton Monchelsea, V1 strikes 147, 151, 152
Boughton-under-Blean, V1 strike 204
Boulogne, weapon sites *28, 30*, 36
Bowers Gifford, V2 strikes 223, 234
Bowers Marshes, V2 strikes 266
Bowes Park, V2 strike 234
Bowman, Lee (actor) *243*
Boxford, V1 strikes 151
Boxley, V1 strikes 121, 135, 147
Boxted, V1 strikes 153
Brabourne, V1 strikes 107, 130, 149, 153
Bracken, Bernard (Minister of Information) *170*
Braddick, Olive *143*
Braddick, Police Sgt William *143*
Bradwell-on-Sea
   V1 strikes 195, 222, 223, 266, 267
   V2 strikes 222, 235, 238, 239, 258, 267
Bradwell Bay, V2 strikes 258
Bradwell Marshes, V2 strikes 223, 235
Bramerton, Norwich, V2 strike 203
Brasted, V1 strikes 105, 121, 124, 139, 142, 147, 152, 156
Brauchitsch, FM Walter von *11*
Braughing, Herts
   V1 strikes 195, 267
   V2 strikes 223

Braun, Dr Wernher von, and rocket development 9
Braxted Park, V2 strikes 258
Breckles, V1 strikes 222
Brede, V1 strikes 112, 121, 136, 142, 151, 152
Bredfield, V1 strikes 238
Bredgar, V1 strikes 114
Bredhurst, V1 strikes 118
Brenchley, V1 strikes 106, 114, 120, 135, 142, 157, 160, 165
Brentford, V1 strikes 83, 96, 102, 107, 118, 121, 139, 157, 159, 160, 168
Brentwood
　balloon defences 127
　V1 strikes 222
　V2 strikes 234, 235, 266
Brenzett, V1 strikes 127, 147, 153, 165
Brereton, Lt Gen. Lewis H. 39, 66, 80
Breudijk 268
Brickenden V2 strikes 239
Bricquebec, Cherbourg peninsula 72
Bridge, V1 strikes 168
Bridgemarsh Island, V2 strike 239
Bridgewick, V1 strikes 204, 223, 234, 267
Bridlington 246, 248
Brightling, V1 strikes 106, 112, 114, 120, 125, 138, 140, 142
Brightlingsea
　AA screen 207
　V1 strikes 267
　V2 strikes 239, 267
Brighton, radio counter-measures 181
Brightwell, V1 strike 204
Brill, V1 strikes 124, 168
Brindle, Lancs, V1 strike 235, 247
Bristol
　air defences 38, 41
　V-weapons threat to 39, 44, 54, 56, 89
Broadoak End, V2 strikes 239
Broadstairs, V1 strikes 106, 126, 223
Brockenhurst, V1 strikes 107
Brockham, V1 strikes 120, 121
Brockley, V2 strikes 195, 222, 267
Bromley, Kent
　Princes Plain School, Common Road (later Trinity C of E Primary) 80
　radar station 179
　V1 strikes 63, 68, 81, 83, 84, 85, 88, 96, 97, 99, 103, 106, 114, 122, 125, 129, 130, 136, 138, 139, 142, 151
　V2 strikes 223, 239, 258, 267
Brooke, Gen. (later FM) Sir Alan (CIGS) 40
Brooke, Norwich, V2 strike 203
Brooker family 143
Brookland, V1 strikes 106, 156, 161, 165
Brookman's Park, Hatfield, V1 strike 204
Broomfield, Kent
　V1 strikes 103, 125
　V2 strike 239
Broomhill, Sussex, V1 strikes 103, 107, 121, 129, 130, 140, 142, 155, 160, 165
Brown, Arthur, fitter at A.C.E. Machinery Company 7
Broxbourne, V2 strike 239
Bruneval 12
Brunswick 95
Brussels, as V2 target 198, 209, 220
Buchenwald concentration camp 152, 182–183
Buckhurst Hill V2 strikes 204
Bug, River 51
Bulls Green, V1 strikes 160
Bulphan
　V1 strikes 133
　V2 strikes 204, 267
Buntingford, V1 strikes 222
Burbage, V1 strike 235
Burder, F/Lt A. H. 174
Burgrove, Harry 7
Burgsteinfurt, Münster 213
Burmarsh, V1 strikes 106, 107, 121, 124, 127, 133, 139, 142, 147, 151, 153, 155, 157, 159, 160, 165
Burnham Beeches, V1 strikes 157
Burnham-on-Crouch
　V1 strikes 106, 267
　V2 strikes 234, 235
Burrell family (East Ham) 192
Burseldon, V1 strikes 107

Burstow, V1 strikes 121
Burwash
　V1 strikes 135, 142, 148, 161
　V2 strikes 223
Burwell, V1 strikes 195
Bushey, V1 strikes 130
Buttsbury, V1 strike 267
Buxted, V1 strikes 114, 121, 125, 129, 135, 147
Buxton, Derbys, V1 strike 235, 247
Byfleet, V1 strikes 157
Bygrave, V1 strikes 195

Calais, weapon sites 12, 15, 24, 28, 30, 36
Callaway, AVM William 110
Calvados department 54
Camberwell
　Royal Arsenal Co-op, Lordship Lane, V1 hit 142
　V1 strikes 63, 67, 68, 77, 81–88, 96, 97, 99, 100, 102, 105, 106, 107, 112, 118, 120, 121, 122, 124, 129, 133, 136, 139, 140, 147, 149, 151, 152, 155, 204, 266
　V2 strikes 204, 234, 239, 259
　see also Dulwich
Campbell, George 265
Canewdon, Rochford
　V1 strikes 125, 136, 195
　V2 strikes 234, 239, 259, 267
Canning Town, St Luke's Church 81
Canterbury
　radio counter-measures 181, 194
　V1 strikes 140
Cantley, Norwich, V2 strike 203
Canvey Island
　Deepwater Road 122
　V1 strikes 122, 135, 140, 204
　V2 strikes 204, 222, 223, 234, 235, 259, 267
Cap Gris Nez 166
Capel, radio counter-measures 193
Capel St Andrew, V1 strikes 203, 204, 239
Capel St Mary, V1 strikes 168
Capel-le-Ferne, V1 strikes 107, 114, 121, 127, 129, 130, 148, 149, 153, 157, 168
Cardiff 41
Carlton Colville, V1 strikes 223
Carshalton, V1 strikes 73, 81, 85, 87, 88, 96, 99, 100, 102, 105, 107, 114, 118, 121, 127, 135, 139, 140, 161
Carter, Chief Warden Ted 223, 240, 259, 263, 264
Castor, V1 strikes 238
Caterham
　AA defence 41
　V1 strikes 121, 142, 147, 151
Catford, Nick 179
Catherington, V1 strikes 114
Causley-Windram, Maj. James 71
Cedgrave Marshes, V1 strikes 234
Cemeteries
　Camberwell Old Cemetery 108
　Edenbridge, Sevenoaks, St Paul's Churchyard 113
　Westfield 101
Central Press 89, 91
Chadwell Heath, V2 strikes 222
Chain Home radar stations see Radar
Chalfont St Giles, V1 strikes 124
Challock, V1 strikes 136, 140, 142, 157
Chandler's Ford, V1 strikes 107, 114
Chanley, Ann 246
Chapel-en-le-Frith, Derbys V1 strike 235, 247
Charing, Kent, V1 strikes 106, 107, 120, 121, 127, 140, 145
Charlton V2 strikes 258
Charlton, Westmoor Street, A.C.E. Machinery Company 6–7
Charlwood, V1 strikes 124
Chart Sutton, V1 strikes 165
Chartham, V1 strikes 122, 168
Chartwell 112
Château du Pannelier 55
Chatham 144
　AA ops room 167
　see also St Mary's at Hoo
Cheam
　V1 damage 102
　V1 strikes 67, 81, 97, 99, 222
Chediston, V1 strikes 195
Chelmondiston, V1 strikes 195, 234, 235

Chelmsford
　AA defences 127
　Hoffmann's company bombed 236
　V1 strikes 105, 234
　V2 strikes 235, 259
Chelsea
　Royal Hospital V2 strike 238, 241
　Sloane Court V1 strike 99
　V1 strikes 85, 99
Chelsham, V1 strikes 106, 121, 124, 127, 267
Cherbourg peninsula, weapon sites 22, 24, 29, 44, 46, 54, 55, 58, 72, 89, 172
Cheriton
　V1 propaganda leaflets 164
　V1 strikes 114
Chertsey, V1 strikes 195, 266
Chertsey Mead, V2 strikes 258
Cherwell, Lord (Prof. Frederick Lindemann) 13, 21, 62, 175
Chesham, V1 strikes 153
Cheshunt
　V1 strikes 85, 120, 122, 126, 155, 160, 203, 204
　V2 strikes 239, 258, 259, 267
Chevening
　V1 strikes 105, 136, 142
　V2 strikes 259
Chichester 63
Chicksands, V1 strike 267
Chiddingly, Sussex, V1 strikes 103, 114, 121, 124, 135, 140
Chiddingstone
　V1 strikes 118, 124, 127, 222
　V2 strikes 258
Chiefs of Staff
　bombing of V-weapon sites 43, 50–51, 55, 56, 60, 66, 67, 94, 261
　end of V-weapon campaign 272
　and home defence 39, 41, 42, 65, 114, 178, 247–248
　V2 campaign and public information 196
　V2 counter-measures 187, 188, 194, 195, 198, 209, 223, 228, 230, 270
　and weapon development 10, 21, 28, 32, 40, 44, 170, 175
　see also Joint Intelligence Sub-Committee
Chignall, V1 strikes 133
Chignall St James, V1 strikes 234
Chigwell
　V1 strikes 81, 84, 85, 86, 97, 106, 107, 114, 121, 122, 125, 127, 147, 151, 153, 159, 160, 168, 195
　V2 strikes 223, 239, 259, 266
　Warren Hill V2 strike 222
Childerditch, V2 strikes 223, 239
Chilham, V1 strikes 140, 165
Chingford
　Seymour Court, Whitehall Road 86
　V1 strikes 84, 86, 96, 103, 118, 121, 126, 168, 204
　V2 strikes 204, 223, 239, 258, 259, 266
Chipperfield, V1 strikes 124
Chipperfield Common, Herts 73
Chislehurst
　V1 strikes 63, 68, 81, 82, 84, 85, 96, 97, 99, 103, 105, 106, 118, 121, 122, 129, 130, 133, 135, 136, 138, 139, 140, 142, 148, 157, 168, 254, 263, 267
　V2 strikes 223, 227, 234, 239, 254, 258, 259
Chislet, Canterbury, V2 strike 204
Chiswick
　Burlington Lane 187
　Grove Park 69
　Staveley Road, first V2 strike 186, 187, 195
　V1 strikes 68, 159
Choats Manor Way, East London 62
Christiansen, Lt Cdr Hasager 19
Church, Mrs Sylvia 114
Churchill, Mary 112
Churchill, Mrs Clementine 37
Churchill, Winston 40, 137, 220, 271
　approves RAF bombing of German cities 8
　bombing of weapon sites 30, 31, 39, 66
　first V-weapon targets 62
　and flying bomb propaganda leaflets 164
　and German weapon development 10, 12, 13, 21, 148, 175
　home defence 65, 112
　Netherlands bombing casualties 252
　speeches in Parliament 102, 138, 148, 172, 178, 201

Civil Defence *138*, 176–178, 183, 241
Clacton
  AA defences 126, 127, 206
  V1 strikes 195, 204, 222, 266, 267
  V2 strikes 203, 204, 222, 223, 234, 235, 258, 259, 266, 267
Clapham, V2 strikes 239
Clapham Common, V2 strikes 239
Claverhambury, last V1 strike *263*
Cliffe-at-Hooe, V2 strike 222
Clophill, V1 strikes 234
Clothall
  V1 strike 168
  V2 strike 239
Coates, Fred *135*
Cobbold, Lt-Col John *71*
Cobham
  AA defence 41
  V1 strikes 120, 125, 148
Coburn, Charles (actor) *243*
Cock Clarks
  V1 strike 105
  V2 strikes 239, 258
Cockfield, V1 strikes 151, 195
Cockpole Green, V2 strike 267
Codicote, V1 strikes 195
Coggeshall, V1 strikes 204
Cohen, Dora *61*
Colchester, V1 strikes 203, 223
Collard, Fred *143*
Collier Row, V2 strikes 258
Colne Point, V2 strikes 195
Colney Street, V1 strikes 159
Cologne
  1000 bomber raid *8*
  possible flying bomb launch sites 199, *210*
Colt, Mrs Margaret Sloan *43*
Coltishall/Horstead, V2 strike 195
Compiègne 154, 183
Comps, André *24–25*
Coningham, AM Sir Arthur *39*, *66*, 69
Cooden, V1 strikes 151
Cooling, V1 strikes 122, 147, 222
Coombe, V1 strikes 68, 86, 87, 99, 100, 107, 112
Cooper, Gary (actor) *212*
Cooper, John *189*
Copford, V1 strikes 223
Coppinghall, V1 strikes 121
Corringham Marshes, V2 strikes 235, 239, 259
Corton, V1 strike 204
Coulsdon
  radio counter-measures 193
  St Maries Hotel, Olden Lane/Dale Road
    V1 strike 204, *215*
  V1 strikes 63, 67, 68, 77, 82, 83, 84, 85, 87, 88, 96, 97, 99, 100, 103, 105, 118, 120, 121, 129, 130, 133, 135, 136, 139, 140, 142, 161, 165
  V2 strikes 195
Covehithe, V1 strikes 204, 238
Covehurst Bay 166
Cranbrook, V1 strikes 107, 118, 120, 121, 124, 125, 133, 135, 142, 147, 153, 165
Cranham, Romford
  V1 strikes 106
  V2 strikes 223, 259, 267
Cranleigh, V1 strikes 138, 153, 165
Crawley, V1 strikes 106, 139
Crayford
  V1 strikes 63, 84, 87, 88, 96, 106, 112, 118, 127, 148
  V2 strikes 234, 235, 259
Creeksea, V2 strike 234
Crerar, Gen. Harry *169*
Cressingham, V1 strike 204
Cretingham, V1 strikes 235
Cripps, Sir Stafford 21
Crockenhill, V2 strikes 258
Crockham Hill, Weald House, V1 strike *113*
Croisette *33*
Cromer, night fighter defence screen 211
Cromer Hyde, V1 strikes 127
'Crossbow', Operation
  'Crossbow' code-name *39*
  'Crossbow' Sub-Committee established 28, *57*, 65–69
  flying bomb counter-offensive 28, 30, 31, 33, 40, 42, 43, *45*, 51, 52, 89, 92–94, 117–119, 122, 146–147, 152, 154, 159, 206

'Crossbow', Operation — continued
  V2 counter-measures 183, 194, 199, 215, 219, 221, 223, 243, 270
  V2 intelligence-gathering 175–176
Crostwick, Norwich, V2 strike 203
Crouch, River, V2 strike 267
Crouch river estuary V1 strike 222, 234
Crow, Dr Alwyn (Min. of Supply) 10, 20
Crowborough
  radio counter-measures 181
  V1 strikes *102*, 122, 148
Crowhurst, V1 strikes 106, 107, 118, 129, 147
Croydon
  Avenue Road *130*
  Cranmer Road *130*
  Milton Avenue flying bomb strike 152, *157*
  V1 strikes 63, 67, 68, 73, 77, 81–89, 96, 99, 100, 102, 103, 105, 106, 107, 112, 114, 118, 120, 121, 122, 125, 127, 129, *130*, 133, 135, 136, 138, 139, 140, 142, 147, 148, 149, 151, 153, 222
  V2 strikes 235, 239
  Warminster Road V1 strike *130*
  Whitehorse Road V1 strike *97*
Croydon Times 97
Crundale, V1 strikes 125
Crüwell, Gen. Ludwig *11*
Cuckfield 60
  Sparks Farm (now Mizbrooks Farm) *62*
  V1 strikes 147, 155, 157
Cuckmere Haven *111*
Cuffley
  V1 strikes 127, 266
  V2 strike 235
Cunningham Adm. of the Fleet Sir Andrew 40
Curdridge, V1 strikes 106
Cuxton, V1 strikes 147, 152, 222

Dagenham, Essex
  V1 strikes 63, 68, *69*, 82, 99, 103, 105, 107, 112, 122, 133, 135, 136, 138, 139, 142, 147, 157, 161, 168, 204, 222, 267
  V2 strikes 195, 222, 234, 239, 258, 259, 266, 267
Dagenham Marshes, V2 strikes 223
Daily Express 208
Daily Herald 201
Daily Mail 85, *139*
Daily Mirror 87, *89*, *125*, *171*, *217*
Daily Sketch 89
Dallington, V1 strikes 107, 133, 140, 147
Dammartin *199*
Danbury
  V1 strike 204
  V2 strike 258
Darenth
  V1 strikes 118, 120, 147, 148, 168
  V2 strikes 239
Dartford
  Carrington Road V1 hit *143*
  V1 strikes 139, 142, 152, 155, 156, 204, 267
  V2 strikes 267
Dartford Heath, V2 strikes 259
Dartford Marshes, V2 strike 235
Datchworth
  V1 strike 267
  V2 strike 239
Datchworth Green, V2 strike 239
Day, Bill *84*
Day, Connie *61*
Day, Harriet *84*
Day, Victor *84*
De Gaulle, Gén. Charles *31*
Deal, shelled by long-range guns *164*
Dean, F/O T. D. 'Dixie' *141*
Debden Bay, V1 strikes 107
Dedham, V1 strikes 168
Delft
  Glue and Gelatine Factory *263*
  V1 launch site *260*, *263*
Delftsche Canal 262
Dellington, V1 strikes 129
Demarne, Cyril *131*, *202*, 203
Dengie, Maldon
  V1 strikes 204, 222
  V2 strikes 239, 258, 267
Dennison, Gunner Charles *129*
Denny Lodge, V1 strikes 106

Denton
  Darrow Farm V2 strike 203
  V1 strikes 133, 155
Deopham, V1 strike 238
Depden, V2 strikes 258
Deptford
  Folkestone Gardens/Oareboro Road V2 strike 266, *273*
  New Cross Road Woolworths V2 strike 220, 223, *226*
  Royal Arsenal Co-operative Society *226*
  V1 strikes 63, 82–85, 88, 96, 97, 99, 100, 102, 103, 107, 112, 114, 121, 124, 125, 129, 130, 136, 138, 142, 153, 266
  V2 strikes 204, 223, 239, 258, 266
  see also Lewisham
Der Adler 148-150
Desvres *28*
Detling, V1 strikes 127, 156, 204, 222
Deuille-la-Barre *199*
Deventer 223, 225, 235, 272
Devon, F/Lt S. D. *237*, *254*
Didsbury, Manchester, V1 strike 235, 247
Dieppe 24, 46
Dimbleby, Richard 76
Ditchling, V1 strikes 114
Ditton
  V1 strikes 127
  V2 strikes 222
Doddinghurst, V2 strikes 238, 258
Doddington, V1 strikes 127, 153
Doesburg 230
Domléger 60, 62, 69
Donington, V1 strikes 120
Doolittle, Lt Gen. James 42, *43*, 69, 92
Dordrecht 260
Dorking, V1 strikes 72, 121, 148, 161
Dornberger, Oberst (later Genmaj) Walter, and rocket development *9*, *172*
Douai 166
Dover
  AA defences 36, 112
  radar coverage 36, 179, 192
  shelled by long-range guns *164*
  Straits of 78
  V1 shot down 161
  V1 strikes 105, 135, 147, 148, 151, 152, 153, 155, 156, 159, 160, 165, 168
  V1 tracking *144*
Dovercourt, V1 strike 204
Dovercourt Bay, V1 strike 234
Downham, V2 strikes 234, 235
Downsview Monumental Company, Burgess Hill *113*
Duddingstone 105
Duindigt racecourse, The Hague *182*, *236*, *238*, *250–251*, 252–253, *254*, 255, 256, *264*
Dulwich
  Alleyn's School, North Dulwich 89, *106–107*, 130
  College Road *108*
  Etherow Street *108*
  Friern Road *108*, *109*
  Grange Lane *108*
  Henslow Road, East Dulwich *108*
  Lordship Lane *109*
  Park Hall Road *108*
  Peckham Rye *109*
  Sydenham Hill *109*
  Underhill Road, East Dulwich *108*
  V1 strikes 89, *106–109*, 159
  V2 strikes *109*, 222, 239
  Woodvale and Greendale *108*
Dungeness, V1 strikes 136, 151, 152, 153, 155, 156, 157, 160, 161, 165, 168
Dunkirk 20, 89
Dunmow, V1 strikes 157, 195
Dunstable, Peugeot-Citroen *216*
Dunton
  V1 strikes 204, 234
  V2 strikes 259, 266
Dunton Green, V1 strikes 121, 136
Dunwich, V1 strikes 204, 222
DuPont, Miss Mary *129*
Durley, V1 strikes 114
Düsseldorf 95, 117
Dymchurch
  radar station 179
  V1 strikes 121, 124, 138, 140, 142, 147, 148, 151, 152, 155, 157, 159, 160, 161, 165, 168

Eaker, Gen. Ira C. 14, 33, 42
Ealing, V1 strikes 68, 82, 99, 121, 136, 157,
 161, 165, 267
Earl Stonham, V2 strikes 259
East Barnet
 V1 strikes 73, 100, 120, 136, 160, 161, 266
 V2 strikes 239
East Blatchington, V1 strikes 142
East Fairlight, V1 strikes 136
East Farleigh, V1 strikes 118, 120, 133, 135
East Grinstead
 London Road 117
 St Swithun's Church 117
 V1 strikes 107, 117, 136, 222, 267
 Whitehall Palace Cinema 117
East Guildford, V1 strikes 133, 142, 156,
 160
East Ham
 Navarre Road V2 strike 256
 Plashet Grove, Manor Park, V1 strike
  118
 Police Station, High Street South 193
 St Stephen's Church, Green Street V2
  strike 192, 195
 St Stephen's Road 192–193
 V1 strikes 63, 68, 81, 84, 85, 88, 100, 102,
  105, 106, 120, 122, 125, 126, 127, 129,
  133, 138, 139, 140, 142, 148, 149, 168
 V2 strikes 222, 223, 239, 254, 256, 257,
  258,259, 267
 White Horse pub, High Street South,
  V1 strike 82, 84
East Horndon, V2 strikes 239
East Malling, V1 strikes 234
East Newlands, V2 strikes 223
East Peckham, V1 strikes 114, 127, 130, 140,
 142, 147, 165
East Stratton, V1 strikes 120
East Sutton, V1 strikes 140, 149, 165
East Tilbury, V1 strikes 153
Eastbourne
 AA defences 112
 Brassey Avenue, Hampden Park 129
 Freeman Avenue 129
 Glynde Avenue 129
 Nevill Avenue 129
 No. 80 (Signals) Wing 193
 Parkfield Avenue 129
 Percival Road 129
 Presbyterian Hall, Elm Grove 129
 St Mary's Hospital 129
 V1 strikes 125, 126, 127, 129, 136, 139, 140,
  147, 151
Eastchurch, Isle of Sheppey
 V1 strikes 161, 222
 V2 strike 203
Eastfield, V1 strikes 106
Easthorpe, V1 strikes 195
Eastling, V1 strikes 114
Easton, V1 strikes 168
Eastwell, Kent, V1 strikes 103, 118, 125
Eastwood, V2 strike 235
Economic Warfare, Ministry of 14, 29, 30,
 229
Edenbridge, V1 strikes 122, 135
Edmonton
 V1 strikes 86, 121, 125, 126, 139, 195, 204
 V2 strikes 223, 238, 239, 266, 267
Edwardstone, V1 strikes 195
Effingham, V1 strikes 106
Egerton, V1 strikes 121
Eisenhower, Gen. Dwight D.
 and Antwerp port 210
 and the V-weapon threat 39, 50, 51, 67,
  199, 230
Elham, V1 strikes 149, 155, 159, 160, 165,
 267
Elinkwijk bridge 268
Elizabeth, Queen 43, 82, 270–271
Elliott, Bryn 263
Ellis, Prof. Charles 10, 175
Ellough, V1 strikes 238
Elmstead, V1 strikes 124, 147, 161
Elmsted, V1 strikes 168
Elser, Georg 34
Elstree
 Ridge Hill V2 strike 204
 V1 strikes 82, 87
Eltham, V2 strikes 222, 266, 267
Emergency Services, Directorate of 74

Enfield
 Chesterfield Road School V1 strike 85
 V1 strikes 63, 73, 83, 88, 96, 97, 106, 120,
  121, 122, 125, 139, 152, 155, 160, 161,
  168, 195, 266
 V2 strikes 234, 235, 239, 267
 Whitewebbs Lane (King and Tinker pub)
  V1 strike 239, 245
Engineering News 160
Enigma code 19
ENSA (Entertainments National Service
 Association) 212
Enschede 198
Ephithite, Dorrice 135
Epping
 V1 strikes 122, 239
 V2 strike, Parndon Wood 186, 188, 195
 V2 strikes 259, 267
Epping Forest
 Keeper's Cottage, Woodredon Hill, V1
  strike 217
 V2 strikes 259, 266
Epping Green, V1 strikes 121
Epping Upland
 V1 strike 155
 V2 strike 258
Epsom, V1 strikes 63, 67, 68, 83, 85, 97, 99,
 100, 103, 105, 106, 107, 118, 121, 135, 136,
 139, 142, 157, 165
Epworth, Lincs, V1 strike 235, 247
Eridge 105
Erith, Kent
 V1 strikes 69, 73, 81, 97, 99, 112, 121, 133,
  135, 136, 155
 V2 strikes 222, 234, 239, 258, 259, 266, 267
Erith Marshes, V2 strikes 223
Eschenhoff, Oberst zum 184
Esher, V1 strikes 68, 73, 81, 87, 88, 96, 97,
 99, 100, 102, 106, 107, 121, 122, 135, 139,
 140, 147, 155, 157, 160
Essendon
 V1 strikes 126, 195
 V2 strikes 239, 258
Etchells, William 246
Etchingham, V1 strikes 120, 122, 130, 149
Euskirchen 184
Evening News 89
Evening Standard 64
Eversley, V1 strikes 165
Ewell 67
Ewhurst, V1 strikes 105, 107, 112, 114, 120,
 124, 129, 135, 138, 140
ExxonMobil HQ (ex-Adastral House) 18
Eynsford
 V1 strikes 106, 122, 127, 222
 V2 strikes 259
Eythorne, V1 strikes 151
Eyworth, V1 strikes 168

Fairlight
 MEW and CHL radar stations 77–78, 80,
  112
 V1 strikes 121, 124, 147, 148, 151, 161, 165
Fairmile Bottom, V2 strike 223
Fairoak, V1 strikes 107, 114
Fairstead, V2 strikes 235
Falding, V1 strikes 142
Falkenham, V1 strikes 222
Falkington, V1 strikes 112
Fallersleben 117, 119
 Volkswagen works 31, 95, 151–152
Fambridge
 Hyde Marsh V2 strike 203
 V1 strikes 266
 V2 strikes 188, 195, 266
Fareham, V1 strikes 106
Farmer family, Tooting 221
Farnborough, Royal Aircraft Establishment
 10, 174, 175, 176
Farningham
 V1 strikes 127, 138, 139, 151
 V2 strike 259
Faulkbourne, V1 strikes 156
Fawkham, V1 strikes 151, 153
Fécamp 36
Felixstowe, V1 strikes 168, 195, 204, 222,
 223, 234, 235, 238, 239, 267
Fellows, C. B. (Tech. Intell. Officer) 245
Felmore Farm, Billericay, V2 strike 204
Felsted, V1 strikes 160, 195, 203, 222

Feltham, V1 strikes 73, 82, 121, 138, 157
Fernhurst, V1 strikes 124
Fields, Gracie (singer) 242
Fieseler, and V1 development 52
Filey, AA screen deployed 247
Finchley
 V1 strikes 63, 73, 88, 100, 105, 157
 V2 strikes 222
Fingringhoe, V1 strikes 234
Finsbury
 Smithfield Market, Farringdon Road V2
  strike 257, 265, 266
 V1 strikes 68, 83, 100, 124, 133, 162
 V2 strikes 223, 259
Firebrace, Cdr Aylmer 136
Fittleworth, V1 strike 204
Flamborough Head AA zone 248
Flanagan and Allen (entertainers) 242
Flers 93
Fletching, V1 strikes 120, 121, 135
Flimwell, V1 strikes 106, 120
Flos, Ingenieur Werner 15, 22, 23, 28, 29, 49
Fluckley, V1 strikes 114
Fobbing, Essex, V2 strikes 258
Foggia, Italy 152
Folkestone
 AA defences 36, 112
 shelled by long-range guns 164
 V1 strikes 124, 127, 130, 133, 140, 142, 147,
  148, 149, 151, 152, 153, 155, 156, 157,
  159, 160, 161, 165, 168
 V1s shot down 161, 171
 V2 strikes 259
Foot, Dorothea 7
Foot, Violet 7
Foreign Office 229
Foreness radar station 80, 126
Forest Gate
 Dames Road 131
 Pevensey Road 131
 V1 strikes 131
Forest Row
 V1 strikes 114, 120, 121, 135, 138
 V2 strikes 239
Forêt d'Éperlecques 15
Forêt de l'Isle-Adam 152
Forêt de Nieppe 117–119
Formby, George (entertainer) 242
Forth-Clyde AA zone 248
Foulness Island
 radar station 126
 V1 strikes 136, 203, 204, 222, 234, 266, 267
 V2 strikes 239, 259, 266
Foulness Point
 V1 strikes 204, 222, 223, 234, 267
 V2 strikes 223, 234, 235, 238
Four Elms, Kent
 AA battery 112
 V1 strikes 142
Fourcarmont 166
Fowkes, Reg 84
Framfield, V1 strikes 105, 130, 136, 138, 140,
 142
Framlingham, Suffolk, V1 strikes 63, 203
Framsden, V1 strikes 195
Frankenthal, Klein Schanzlin Becker 31
Frant, V1 strikes 120, 121, 122, 125, 129, 130,
 133, 138, 140, 147, 149, 151, 152, 155, 222
Frenondel, Pte Remingio 129
Fressingfield, V1 strikes 234
Freston, V1 strikes 168
Friedrichshafen 43, 95
 I.G. Farben 14, 16
 Maybach and Zeppelin works 30, 31
Friern Barnet
 V1 strikes 83, 204, 222
 V2 strikes 239
Friesland, V2 rocket launches 195, 196, 198, 209
Frimley, V1 strikes 129
Frindsbury, V1 strikes 153
Frinsted, Madams Court Farm 164, 165
Frinton-on-Sea, V1 strikes 204, 234, 266, 267
Frisian Islands 198
Frittenden, V1 strikes 120, 124, 165
Froxfield, V1 strikes 114
Fulbourn, Cambridge, V2 strike 222
Fulham, V1 strikes 68, 73, 84, 96, 97, 107,
 118, 120, 124, 130, 135, 136, 139
Funtington, V1 strikes 140
Fur Copse, V1 strikes 106

Fürstenwalde, Julius Pintsch 30–31
Fyfield, V1 strikes 204, 222

Galleywood, V1 strikes 122
Gamage, Ron 164
Gardner, Pte John (CMP) 221
Gardner family, Tooting 221
Garston Park, V2 strikes 259
Gatton Park, V1 strikes 121
Gell, AVM William 67
George Medal, Wright, Sgt Harley 134
George, Mr Bruce 71
George VI, King 43, 82, 270–271
German Democratic Republic (East
  Germany) 14
German News Agency 201
Germany
  post-war British Zone of Occupation 181
  post-war Soviet Zone of Occupation 154
Gestapo 252, 266
Ghent 56, 235, 255
Gillingham, V1 strikes 140
Gilston, V1 strikes 127
Gipping, V1 strikes 120
Gladdish, Narcissa 143
Glasser, Bombardier John 129
Godalming, V1 strikes 160
Godmanchester, V1 strikes 238
Godmersham, V1 strikes 152, 160
Godstone, V1 strikes 121, 136, 157
Goebbels, Dr Joseph 34
Goldhanger
  V1 strikes 125, 142, 151
  V2 strikes 239
Gooden, V1 strikes 136
Goodhart-Rendel, Harry 71
Goodnestone, V1 strikes 165
Goodwood racetrack 47
Goodworth Clatford
  Manor Farm Cottages 114
  Royal Oak pub 114
Göring, Reichsmarschall Hermann 35
Gosfield, V1 strikes 106
Gossage, AM Sir Leslie 43
Gouda, Netherlands 233, 251, 255, 264, 268
Goudhurst, V1 strikes 106, 112, 121, 122,
  125, 126, 130, 136, 140, 142, 147, 152
Grade, Lew, Robinson Crusoe 242
Grady, Derrick 91
Grange Moor, Yorks, V1 strike 235, 247
Gräsdals Glåd, Sweden 174
Graves, F/Lt 141
Gravesend, Kent
  AA defences 261
  balloon defences 127
  V1 strikes 72, 103, 151, 239
  V2 strikes 222, 223
Grays, Thurrock
  V1 strike 204
Grazeley, V1 strike 235
Great Amwell, V2 strikes 239
Great Baddow, V2 strikes 239
Great Barford, V1 strike 234
Great Bentley, V1 strikes 204, 223
Great Braxted, V1 strikes 235
Great Bromley, V1 strikes 195, 267
Great Burstead, Brentwood
  V1 strikes 130, 223
  V2 strikes 204, 234
Great Canfield, V1 strikes 161
Great Chart, V1 strikes 105, 120, 127, 142,
  149, 160
Great Cheaton, V1 strikes 124
Great Coggeshall, V1 strike 203
Great Fransham, V1 strike 204
Great Holland, V1 strikes 239, 267
Great Maplestead, V1 strikes 155
Great Oakley, V1 strikes 222
Great Parndon
  V1 strikes 140, 155, 267
  V2 strike 222, 239
Great Saling, V2 strikes 234
Great Sampford, V1 strikes 153
Great Stanbridge, V2 strikes 234
Great Totham
  V1 strikes 195, 204
  V2 strikes 239, 258
Great Wakering
  V1 strikes 204, 267
  V2 strikes 222, 223

Great Warley
  V1 strikes 129, 222
  V2 strikes 222, 223, 227, 239, 258
Great Wenham, V1 strikes 168
Great Wigborough, V1 strike 267
Great Witchingham, Mill Farm, V2 strike
  203
Great Yarmouth
  AA zone defences 206
  V2 strikes 203, 267
Greatham, V1 strikes 165, 222
Greatstone, V1 strikes 161, 165
Green, Beatrice 128
Greenhithe, V1 strikes 142
Greenstead
  V1 strike 203
  V2 strikes 267
Greenwich
  Brook Hotel V2 strike 222
  V1 strikes 63, 68, 81, 82, 83, 84, 85, 88, 96,
    97, 99, 100, 102, 105, 106, 107, 114, 118,
    120, 121, 122, 126, 129, 130, 133, 136,
    139, 151, 161, 168
  V2 strikes 222, 223, 234, 238, 239, 259, 266,
    267
Greyfriars radar station 207, 213
Greyshott, Hampshire, V2 strike 239
Griffiths, Cdr Leslie 7
Griffiths, Mabel 7
Guestling, V1 strikes 107, 136, 153
Guildford
  V1 strikes 127, 165
Gurney, David 71
Guston, V1 strikes 153

Haagsche Bosch (Haagse Bos - Forest of
  The Hague) 224, 225, 228, 232–233, 234,
  235, 241, 250–253, 256, 266, 268
Haarlem 264
Hackney 263
  V1 strikes 67, 68, 81, 83, 85, 86, 97, 99, 102,
    103, 105, 107, 118, 120, 124, 129, 133,
    135, 136, 139, 147, 151, 152, 155, 161,
    168, 204
  V2 strikes 222, 234, 235, 239, 258, 259
Haddiscoe, Beccles, V2 strike 203
Hadleigh, V1 strikes 222
Hadlow, V1 strikes 105, 114, 120, 121, 122,
  127, 135, 140, 142, 151, 153
Hadlow Down, V1 strikes 114
Hailsham, Sussex, V1 strikes 103, 106, 135
Hainault Forest, V2 strike 267
Hallet, Grace 189
Halling, V1 strikes 168
Halsey, Cyril 135
Halstead
  V1 strikes 118
  V2 strikes 238, 258
Ham Street, V1 strikes 153
Hambleton, V1 strikes 107
Hamburg, RAF raids 20
Hammersmith
  V1 strikes 83, 86, 88, 97, 105, 121, 126, 136,
    151, 159, 160, 168
  V2 strikes 259
Hampden, V1 strikes 127
Hampstead
  V1 strikes 77, 86, 87, 100, 135, 160, 161,
    203, 223
  V2 strikes 267
Hanford Rivers, V1 strike 267
Hannover, Hanomag works 31
Hanwell Golf Course, V2 strike 204
Happisburgh
  radar station 213
  V2 strikes 195
Harden, V1 strikes 126
Harleston, V1 strikes 168
Harlington, V1 strikes 73, 97, 203
Harlow
  V1 strikes 223
  V2 strikes 238, 239
Harold Park
  V1 strikes 125
  V2 strikes 267
Harold Wood
  V1 strikes 133
  V2 strikes 258
Harrietsham, V1 strikes 106, 120, 133,
  153

Harris, ACM Sir Arthur (AOC-in-C
  Bomber Command)
  bombing campaign 8, 42
  V-weapon targeting 43, 66, 69, 92, 98, 118
Harris, Alan 113
Harrow
  V1 strikes 73, 81, 84, 86, 88, 121, 135, 136,
    139, 157, 203
  V1 track 135
  V2 strikes 258, 267
Hartfield, V1 strikes 105, 112, 124, 142, 165,
  204
Hartlip, V1 strike 204
Harwell, V1 strikes 136
Harwich
  AA zone defences 206
  radar station 179
  V1 strikes 204, 222, 223, 234
  V2 strike 203
Harz mountains 17, 272
Hastingleigh, V1 strikes 129, 133, 135
Hastings
  AA defences 112, 123
  radio counter-measures 180
  St Leonards sea front 123
  V1 strikes 106, 112, 118, 120, 121, 122, 124,
    136, 142, 148, 151, 161
Hastingwood, V1 strikes 127, 133
Hatcheston, V1 strikes 195
Hatfield
  V1 strikes 195, 203
  V2 strike 239
Hatfield Broad Oak, V2 strikes 239, 267
Hatfield Heath, V2 strike 239
Hatfield Park, V1 strikes 142, 195
Hatfield Peverel, V1 strike 239
Hatton Garden
  Clerkenwell Road 162
  Farringdon Road, Falk, Stadelmann & Co.
    162
Havengore Island
  V1 strike 204
  V2 strike 203
Haverhill, V1 strikes 129
Havering-atte-Bower
  V1 strikes 147
  V2 strikes 239, 259, 266, 267
Hawkhurst, Kent, V1 strikes 103, 112, 120,
  121, 122, 124, 133, 147, 151
Hawkinge, V1 strikes 133, 135, 147, 149,
  153, 168
Hawridge, V1 strikes 140
Hay, Lt-Col The Lord Edward (Grenadier
  Guards) 71
Hayes
  Gledwood Drive, Uxbridge Road V2
    strike 204, 214
  V1 strikes 73, 97, 103, 138, 139
  V2 strikes 234
Haylock, Alan 89–90
Haynes, V1 strike 204
Haywards Heath, V1 strikes 106
Headcorn, V1 strikes 105, 106, 129, 130, 133,
  140, 141, 153, 165
Headley, V1 strikes 105, 121
Headlines (IPC magazine) 125
Health, Ministry of, Special Repair Service
  (SRS) 74–75
Heathfield, V1 strikes 106, 112, 114, 125,
  127, 129, 130, 142, 151, 161
Heaverham, V1 strikes 120
Hedsor, V1 strikes 161
Heerenveen, Netherlands 209
Heidelager (Heath Camp), Blizna, Poland
  50
Hellendoorn, Netherlands 212
Hellesdon, V2 strike 203
Hellingly, Sussex, V1 strikes 103, 106, 121,
  140
Hempnall, V1 strikes 238
Hemsby, Great Yarmouth, V2 strikes 195
Henbury, Cheshire, V1 strike 235, 247
Hendon
  Kingsbury, V2 strike 204
  V1 strikes 85, 96, 97, 121, 126, 139, 140, 152,
    156, 157, 160
  V2 strikes 239
Henfield, V1 strikes 222
Hengelo, Netherlands 272
Henham, V1 strike 195

Henlow
  V1 strike 234
  V2 strike 239
Herbert, Lord Sydney, 115
Herne Bay
  V1 strike 168
  V2 strike 239
Herongate, Brentwood, V2 strike 234
Herstmonceux, V1 strikes 106, 112, 121, 130, 133, 140
Hertford Heath, V1 strikes 126, 223
Hertingfordbury, V2 strikes 223
Hessett, V1 strikes 195
Heston
  V1 strikes 73, 87, 88, 99, 100, 103, 107, 118, 129, 135, 136, 157, 203
  V2 strikes 259, 267
Hever, V1 strikes 107, 124
Heybridge Basin, V1 strikes 129
Heydon, V1 strikes 238
Hidrequent, Calais 44, 45
High Beech, V2 strikes 239
High Halden, V1 strikes 120, 156, 157, 165
High Halstow, V2 strikes 259, 266
High Laver, V2 strikes 258
High Ongar, V2 strikes 222, 234
High Street, radar station 179
High Wych, V1 strikes 125
Higham, V1 strikes 161
Hildenborough, V1 strikes 106, 118, 127, 165
Hill, AM Roderic
  anti-'Diver' defence 41, 98, 104, 105, 110, 111, 114, 166–167
  appointed to command ADGB 38, 39
  ends offensive operations 272
  intruders against V1 launch sites 62, 67, 77, 94
  V1 assault on the Midlands 247
  V2 counter-measures 189–190, 219, 220–221, 231
Hilversum, Netherlands 268
Himmler, Reichsführer-SS Heinrich
  and revenge weapons 50, 172
  V2 deployments 184
Hind, Bob (The News) 115
Hind, Gunner Charles 129
Hindhead, Surrey, Marchants Hill 178
Hinxhill, V1 strikes 127, 149, 155
Hither Green, V2 strikes 239
Hitler, Adolf
  address to officers 235
  July 1944 bomb plot 172
  Munich Löwenbräu address 34
  orders abandonment of Wizernes site 29
  orders retaliation for RAF bombing 8
  orders V2 offensive 173
  'putsch' of 1923 34
  and 'revenge' weapons 7, 31, 35
  and rocket development 9
  timing of 'V' campaign 66
  visits Peenemünde 20
Hoathfield, V1 strikes 107
Hobbs Offen & Co Ltd 6
Hockley, Southend
  V1 strikes 122, 222
  V2 strikes 195, 239
Hoddesdon
  Goose Green, V2 strikes 203, 239
  V1 strike 204
Hollard, Michael (Picardy Resistance) 24
Hollesley, V1 strikes 204, 222, 223, 234, 238, 267
Hollingbourne, V1 strikes 127, 135, 155, 165, 168
Hollingbourne Rural District Council 164
Hollingley, V1 strikes 129
Hollingshead, Jessie 163
Hollington, V1 strikes 138
Holliwell Point, V1 strike 204
Höllriegelskreuth, Munich 95, 117, 182
Holmes, Miss Hannah 248
Holmwood, V1 strikes 105, 121
Home Defence Committee/Executive, and civil defence 14, 28, 34, 256
Home Office 'Pilotless Aircraft Reports' 105
Home Security, Ministry of 70, 102, 103, 132, 163, 206, 217
  Research and Experiments Dept. 177
  threat from enemy weapons 13, 28, 52, 66, 114, 161

Hoo, V1 strikes 156
Hooe, V1 strikes 125, 138, 147
Hook of Holland 218, 228, 232, 234, 235, 241, 253
Hopkins, Albert 7
Hopton, Lowestoft
  radar station 207, 213
  V1 strikes 204, 234
  V2 strike 203
Hornchurch
  V1 strikes 124, 142, 147, 195
  V2 strikes 222, 234, 258, 267
Horndon on the Hill, V2 strikes 223, 258, 266
Horne, V1 strikes 124, 136, 156
Hornsey
  Tottenham Lane V2 strike 218
  V1 strikes 63, 83, 85, 86, 100, 103, 105, 106, 118, 124, 127, 133, 136, 151, 160, 203, 239
  V2 strikes 222, 234, 239
Horsford, Norwich, V2 strikes 195
Horsham
  ROC centre 76, 78, 143
  V1 strikes 121
Horsmonden, V1 strikes 129, 147, 153
Horstead/Coltishall, V2 strike 195
Horsted Keynes, V1 strikes 106
Horton Kirby
  V1 strikes 105, 149, 151
  V2 strikes 239, 266
Hothfield, V1 strikes 105, 121, 152, 153
Houffalize, V2 deployment 185
Hougham, V1 strikes 152
Hougham Without
  V1 leaflets dropped 164
  V1 strikes 129, 165, 168
Hourdon, V1 strikes 136
Houston, Renée 242
Houtdijk, Netherlands 209
Howard, Eric 122
Howard, Peter 122
Hoxne, V2 strike 195, 198
Hucking, V1 strikes 155, 165, 222
Hughenden, V1 strikes 147
Humber area AA screen 246
Hunsdon, V1 strikes 152, 222
Hunt, Madge 158
Hunt, Robert 158
Hunton, V1 strikes 121
Hurstbourne Tarrant, V1 strikes 159
Hurstpierpoint, V1 strikes 133
Hutton
  V1 strikes 135, 222
  V2 strikes 239, 267
Hutton Park, V2 strike 267
Huxter, Denis 263
Hyde, Cheshire, V1 strike 235, 247
Hyde Marsh, Fambridge, V2 strike 203
Hythe
  radar station 78, 80
  V1 strikes 106, 124, 126, 129, 130, 133, 135, 136, 139, 140, 147, 148, 151, 152, 153, 155, 157, 159, 161, 165, 168
  V1s shot down 161
Hythe End, V1 strikes 120

Icklesham, V1 strikes 114, 118, 121, 124, 126, 140, 151, 155, 161, 165
Iden, V1 strikes 105, 107, 142, 165
I.G. Farben factories 14, 16
Ightham
  V1 strikes 122, 138, 139, 148, 151, 222, 235
  V2 strikes 267
IJmuiden, Netherlands 234
IJssel, River, bridges over 230, 235
Ilford
  Hippodrome Theatre V2 strike 239, 242
  Ilford Ltd, Uphill Road, V2 strike 257, 259
  Rochester Gardens V2 strike 222
  Super Cinema, Ley Street/Balfour Road, V2 strike 243, 258
  V1 strikes 63, 68, 81, 82, 83, 84, 85, 88, 96, 100, 102, 103, 105, 125, 129, 130, 133, 136, 139, 147, 148, 152, 153
  V2 strikes 190, 204, 222, 223, 235, 257, 258, 259, 266, 267
Imworth, V1 strikes 195
Information, Ministry of
  Senate House HQ 170
  and V2 campaign 190

Ingatestone
  V1 strikes 121, 133
  V2 strikes 259
Ingworth, Aylsham, Manor Farm V2 strike 203, 209
Intelligence see Joint Intelligence Sub-Committee
Inwood, Peter 113
Ipswich
  V1 strikes 168, 204
  V2 threat to 195
Irish Republican Army (IRA) 40
Irthlingborough, V1 strike 239
Isle of Grain, V1 strikes 168
Isle of Sheppey 261
  see also Eastchurch
Isle of Wight
  Lake 73
  radar 36, 179
  V1 strikes 73, 114
Isleworth
  V1 strike 73
Islington
  Essex Road 163
  Mackenzie Road (formerly St James's Road)/Chalfont Road V2 strike 235, 236–237
  V1 strikes 63, 68, 82–88, 96, 97, 100, 102, 105, 106, 107, 118, 120, 135, 139, 147, 149
  V2 strikes 222, 239
Islington Gazette 237
Ismay, Gen. Sir Hastings, and German weapon development 10
Itchen Stoke, V1 strikes 106
Itchingfield, V1 strikes 140, 149
Iver Heath, V2 strikes 259
Ivychurch, V1 strikes 120, 121, 127, 155, 156, 160
Iwade, V1 strikes 153, 263, 267

Jackson, David 199
Jester, Maj. (Gp Süd V2) 184
Jevington 105
Joint Intelligence Sub-Committee (of Chiefs of Staff) 21, 28, 30, 53, 272
Jones, Dr (later Prof.) Reginald
  and German weapon research 10–12, 21, 27, 29, 31, 53, 174, 175–176
  V-weapon campaign 62, 108, 150
Jones family, Goodworth Clatford 114
Juliana, Princess 253
Jupp family, South Norwood 213

Kammler, SS-Gruppenf. und Genlt Dr Ing. Hans 172, 173, 195, 218, 260, 270
Kampen, Netherlands 230
Karlshagen, Luftwaffe test centre 20
Kassel, Fieseler 151
Kelly, Gunner George 129
Kelsale, V1 strikes 203, 222
Kelsall, Cheshire, V1 strike 235, 247
Kelvedon, V1 strikes 122
Kelvedon Hatch
  V1 strikes 136
  V2 strikes 259
Kemsing, V1 strikes 129, 140, 147, 151
Kenardington, V1 strikes 135, 140, 149, 155, 157
Kendall, W/Cdr Douglas 27, 58
Kennington
  Montford Place, V1 strike 110
  V1 strikes 222
Kensington
  Earls Court, V1 strike 146
  V1 strikes 67, 68, 73, 97, 99, 100, 106, 120, 124, 130, 138, 156, 157, 159, 160, 165
Kensington News 146
Kent Messenger 171
Kenton, V2 strikes 267
Kessingland, V1 strikes 204, 238
Keston Mark, Towerfields 76
Kew
  Chrysler Motors, Mortlake Road, V2 strike 189
  West Park Avenue 189
Kew Gardens, V2 strikes 151
Keystone 89
Kilburn Grammar School 73
Kilmeston, V1 strikes 114
Kimblewich, V1 strikes 120

Kings Langley, V1 strikes 114
Kings Waldon, V1 strikes 168
Kingsdown, V1 strikes 114, 127, 152
Kingsnorth, V1 strikes 107, 118, 124, 130, 149, 155, 161
Kingston-on-Thames
  V1 strikes 77, 87, 100, 102, 121, 133, 159
  V2 strikes 239
Kirby Bedon, Norwich, V2 strikes 195
Kirby Cross, V1 strikes 223
Kirby-le-Soken
  V1 strikes 204, 234
  V2 strike 239
Kirdford, V1 strikes 165
Kjellson, Col Henry 174
Knockholt, Westerham, V2 strikes 195
Koblenz 210
Kohnstein mountain, Nordhausen 154
Konnardington, V1 strikes 121
Krakow, Poland 50

La Sorellerie 55
Laindon, Billericay
  V1 strikes 148, 204
  V2 strikes 223, 238, 239, 259
Laindon Hills, V1 strikes 147
Lamarsh, V1 strike 204
Lamberhurst, V1 strikes 105, 112, 120, 121, 133, 140, 148
Lambeth
  Chatsworth Road Baptist Chapel, V2 strike 194, 195
  Fentiman Road V1 strike 238, 239
  Lambeth/Kennington Roads V2 strike 238, 239
  V1 strikes 68, 73, 81–88, 96, 97, 100, 102, 105, 106, 112, 114, 118, 120, 121, 122, 124, 125, 129, 133, 135, 136, 139, 142, 149, 151, 153, 157, 159, 160, 161, 165
  V2 strikes 234
Lambourne, V2 strike 235, 267
Langdon Hills, Tilbury/Brentwood, V2 strikes 204, 222, 239
Langford, V1 strikes 235, 239
Langham, V1 strikes 168, 238, 239
Langley, V1 strikes 105, 140
Laon 167
Lapwater Hall, Brentwood, V2 strike 234
Latchingdon, Maldon
  V1 strikes 195, 203, 204
  V2 strikes 234, 239, 267
Latimer House, Bucks 11
Laughton, Sussex, V1 strikes 103, 107, 133, 140, 142
Lawford Manningtree, V1 strikes 195
Laycock, Maj.-Gen. Robert 37
Layham V2 strike 239
Leatherhead
  V1 strikes 106, 118, 135, 136
  V2 strikes 258
Leiden, Netherlands, targeted by RAF 190, 218, 219, 225, 228, 232, 264, 268
Leigh
  V1 leaflets dropped 164
  V1 strikes 127, 130, 138, 140, 151, 157, 165
Leigh-Mallory, ACM Sir Trafford 38, 39, 48, 50, 51, 66, 67, 92–94, 98, 118, 166
Leighton, Joy 199
Leiston, V1 strikes 203, 204, 222, 234, 238
Lenham, V1 strikes 129, 159
Leningrad, as V2 target 185
Lenington, V1 strikes 222
Leuna, I.G. Farben 14
Levington, V1 strike 234
Lewisham
  Cressingham Road 72
  Granville Park 72
  Lewisham Hill 72
  Marks & Spencer, High Street, V1 strike 132, 226
  V1 strikes 63, 67, 68, 77, 81–88, 96, 97, 99, 100, 102, 103, 105, 106, 107, 112, 118, 120, 121, 122, 124, 127, 129, 130, 132, 133, 136, 138, 139, 140, 142, 147, 148, 151, 153, 159, 238
  V2 strikes 204, 222, 234, 235, 239, 258, 273
  see also Deptford
Ley Green, V1 strikes 165
Leybourne, V1 strikes 120, 140, 151
Leysdown, V1 strike 267

Leyton
  Arundel Road, V1 strikes 125
  V1 strikes 82, 84, 88, 100, 105, 114, 121, 129, 130, 131, 133, 135, 136, 138, 139, 140, 147, 153
  V2 strikes 223, 234, 238, 239, 258, 259, 267
Leytonstone, V2 strikes 202, 239
Leytonstone Independent 131
Liège 198
Lille 166, 198
Limpsfield, V1 strikes 121, 165
Linch, Doris 101
Linchmere, V1 strikes 121
Lindemann, Prof. Frederick see Cherwell, Lord
Linford, V2 strike 203
Lingfield, V1 strikes 106, 121, 122, 129, 147, 165
Linstead 105
Linton, V1 strikes 138, 140, 155
Lisse, V1 launch site 260, 262
Little Baddow, Chelmsford
  V1 strikes 135, 195
  V2 strikes 204
Little Bentley, V1 strikes 222
Little Berkhamsted Hill, V2 strike 235
Little Bromley, V1 strikes 168
Little Chart
  St Mary's Church, Pluckley Road, V1 strike 145
  V1 strikes 153
Little Glemham, V1 strikes 222
Little Hallingbury, V2 strike 239
Little Heath, V1 strikes 195
Little Horsted, V1 strikes 138, 140
Little Leighs, V2 strike 266
Little Oakley, V1 strikes 223, 267
Little Plumstead, V2 strike 203
Little Saling, V2 strike 267
Little Stambridge, V1 strikes 122
Little Thurrock, V2 strike 239
Little Wakering, Southend, V2 strike 204
Little Waltham, V2 strikes 223
Little Warley, Brentwood, V2 strikes 222, 234, 267
Little Yeldham, V1 strike 203
Littlebourne, V1 strikes 140
Littlestone, V1 strikes 124, 140, 142, 147, 151, 152, 153, 155, 156, 157, 159, 160, 161, 165, 168
Lizy-sur-Ourcq 199
London
  air defences 38, 41, 61
  Aldersgate Street 96
  Australia House, Strand 87, 91
  BBC Broadcasting House 73
  Berkeley Square
    Air Ministry 156
    Stewart & Ardern's, Landsdowne House 156
  Buckingham Palace 71, 82, 134, 268
  Bush House 91
  Cayton Street 134
  Charing Cross 89, 219
  City
    V1 strikes 68, 81, 84, 96, 99, 106, 107, 114, 120, 124, 135, 136, 139
    Gresham Street/Old Jewry V1 strike 200, 203
  Civil Defence 138, 176–178, 214, 219, 220, 228, 236, 245, 256, 260, 262, 263, 269
  Constitution Hill 82
  Downing Street 40
  Drury Lane, Watkins & Simpson 83
  Electra House (Cable & Wireless Ltd), Temple Place 133
  Embankment 133
  Essex Street, Strand 120
  Euston Station 99
  evacuation policy 34, 96, 113, 116, 178
  Fleet Street 87–89
    Johnson's Court 137
  Greater London Council (1985) 75
  High Holborn, Warwick Court V2 strike 223, 227
  Holborn
    Hatton Garden 162
    Staple Inn 163
    V1 strikes 81, 82, 137, 161, 162–163
  Hyde Park 112

London — continued
  Judd Street 255
  'Little' ('Baby') Blitz 35
  Marble Arch
    The Odeon Cinema 268
    V2 strike 267, 268
  Marylebone (St Marylebone)
    'Duke Street bomb' (V2 strike) 228–229, 234
    Marylebone Railway Station 158
    V1 strikes 83, 85, 86, 105, 106, 114, 118, 120, 133, 149, 157, 195
    Wharncliffe Gardens 158
  Metropolitan Railway 96
  Middlesex Street (later Petticoat Lane)
    V2 strike 219, 222
  Moorfields eye hospital, City Road, V1 strike 134
  Netherlands Embassy 252, 253
  Paddington, V1 strikes 68, 82, 85, 106, 157, 267
  Peerless Street 134
  Piccadilly 73
  Regent Palace Hotel, Brewer Street 88
  Regent Square Presbyterian Hall V2 strike 255
  Royal Courts of Justice 87
  St James's Park 65
  St Pancras
    ARP Committee 74
    Goodge Street 74
    Royal Free Hospital 102
    V1 strikes 63, 68, 73, 88, 97, 100, 106, 118, 121, 122, 124, 129, 138, 139, 151, 222
    V2 strikes 258, 267
    Whitfield Street 74–75
    Windmill Street 74
  St Paul's Cathedral 61
  Senate House (Min. of Information) 170
  Smithfield Market V2 strike see Finsbury
  Strand 87–92, 120
  threat from V-weapons 7, 13, 18, 21, 23, 24, 25, 31, 39, 44, 52–54, 56, 59, 150, 172
  Tottenham Court Road
    Central Mission Hall 269
    Police Station 74
    Whitfield Tabernacle V2 strike 269
  Tower of, WW1 100th anniversary 43
  Trafalgar Square 73
  V1 strikes (general) 136, 138, 140, 155, 161, 170, 205, 214, 248, 256, 260, 262
  V2 offensive ordered by Hitler 173, 184
  V2 strikes (general) 189, 209, 210, 240–241, 253, 256, 264
  Wellington Barracks, Birdcage Walk 71
  Westminster
    Central Hall 73
    Hungerford Bridge 70
    Rutherford Street 70
    V1 strikes 61, 68, 73, 81, 82, 83, 85, 88, 96, 100, 105, 118, 120, 125, 127, 130, 133, 139, 151, 157, 159, 165
    V2 strikes 222
  Whitehall 40
    New Public Offices 65
  see also Adastral House (Air Ministry) and other individual boroughs
London County Council 74, 113, 116, 237
London News Agency 89, 92
London Passenger Transport Board 228, 241, 257, 270
Long Melford, V1 strikes 133
Long Reach, Thurrock, V2 strike 222
Longfield, V1 strike 234
Longwood, V1 strikes 107
Lonham, V1 strikes 120
Loosduinen see The Hague
Lothingland, V1 strikes 238
Lottinghem 28, 29, 44, 47, 49
Loughton, Essex 86
Lound, V1 strikes 238
Löwental, Dornier assembly works 43
Lower Beeding, V1 strikes 106, 133, 136, 160
Lower Clatford, V1 strikes 114
Lower Kirby, V2 strike 267
Lowestoft
  AA defences 206
  radar coverage 192, 257
  V1 strikes 203, 204, 234, 239

Lubbock, Isaac (Asiatic Petroleum Co.) 20
Lübeck, RAF bombing 8
Lublin 50
Luddenham, V1 strikes 133
Luddesdown, V1 strikes 204, 222
Ludwigshafen, I.G. Farben 14, 16
Lullingstone
    V1 strikes 121, 130, 222
    V2 strikes 188, 195
Lumley, Charles 189
Luton, Commer Car Works (later Rootes
    Motor Group), Biscot Road, V2 strike
    216, 222
Lutz Canal 209
Luxembourg, V2 production 215
Lydd, V1 strikes 106, 118, 122, 129, 135, 139,
    140, 142, 147, 152, 153, 155, 156, 157, 160,
    161, 165, 168
Lydden, V1 strikes 136, 151, 156
Lyme Bay 60
Lyminge, V1 strikes 107, 129, 168
Lympne, V1 strikes 107, 118, 124, 129, 133,
    140, 148, 151, 153
Lynn, Vera 242
Lynsted, V2 strikes 259
Lyons, Sylvia (and son Paul) 73

Macclesfield Forest, Cheshire, V1 strike
    235, 247
MacDonald, Malcolm (Minister of Health) 75
McGaffin (US Signal Corps) 187
MacLaren, F/O W. R. 100
Magdalen Laver, V2 strikes 189, 195
Magdeburg-Schönebeck, Volkswagen plant 151
Maida Vale, V1 strikes 143
Maidstone
    ROC centre 76, 78, 143
    V1 strikes 106, 129, 140
Mainz 31
Maisoncelle V1 launch site 57
Maisons-Alfort, Paris 185
Major, Prime Minister John 40
Malden, V1 strikes 67, 68, 73, 82, 87, 99, 100,
    103, 106, 130, 147, 156, 159, 161
    see also New Malden
Maldon
    Hazeleigh Lodge V2 strike 235
    V1 strikes 195, 203
    V2 strike 267
Malines (Mechelen) 194, 198, 241
Malloy, F/Lt John 144
Malmedy, Belgium 185
Malmö, Sweden 173
Manchester, V1 assault on 246, 247, 248
Manchester Evening News 246
Mannheim 31
Manuden, V1 strike 234
Marden
    V1 strikes 114, 120, 127, 129, 133, 140, 142
    V2 strikes 267
Marden Ash, V2 strikes 239
Marden Park, V1 strikes 122
Maresfield, V1 strikes 129, 136
Margaretting
    V1 strikes 118, 204, 222
    V2 strikes 258
Margate
    radio counter-measures 180
    shelled by long-range guns 164
Marks Tey, V1 strikes 151, 203
Marlow, V1 strikes 122
Marquise-Mimoyecques 22, 29, 30, 31, 44,
    45, 69, 94, 116, 147, 182
Martin's Mill, Dover, radar station 179
Martinvast, Cherbourg peninsula 22, 29, 44,
    46, 49
Martlesham, V1 strikes 222
Marylebone see London
Masterman, John (MI5) 256
Maunsell forts, Thames Estuary 127
    see also Thames Estuary
Mayer, Hans Ferdinand (physicist) 10
Mayfield, V1 strikes 105, 107, 120, 122, 125,
    129, 130, 136, 142, 147, 151
Mayland
    V1 strike 203
    V2 strikes 239, 267
Medmenham, RAF Central Interpretation
    Unit (CIU) 12, 26, 27, 28, 56–57, 93, 251
Medway, River, AA zone 127

Meesdon, V1 strikes 126
Memorials
    Crockham Hill 113
    Dartford, Carrington Road 143
    Deptford, Lewisham, New Cross Wool-
        worths V2 strike 226
    Islington, Paradise Park, Mackenzie Road
        V2 strike 237
    Lewisham, Marks & Spencer store 132
    New Southgate, Standard Telephones &
        Cables (STC) 160
    Shotesham All Saints V2 strike 199
    Snodland, Malling Road 143
    The Hague, Bezuidenhout 253
    Tottington, Whitehead Memorial Garden
        (V1 strike) 249
    Turks Row, Sloane Court East, London 99
    Walthamstow
        Blackhorse Lane, W. B. Bawn's factory
            V2 strike 259
        Hoe Street/High Street flying bomb 153
Meopham, V1 strikes 127, 151, 152, 157, 195
Mepal, V1 strike 204
Mereworth, V1 strikes 151, 152, 157
Merifield, S/Ldr John 27
Mersham, V1 strikes 122, 124
Mertin, Maj. (Gp Nord V2 deployment) 184
Merton, V1 strikes 68, 73, 82, 85, 87, 97, 99,
    100, 106, 107, 118, 120, 121, 122, 124, 125,
    161, 168
Merton, Prof. Sir Thomas 170
Merwede Canal 268
Méry-sur-Oise 117, 119
Merzig 199
Metheringham, V1 strikes 195
MI5 108
    'Double Cross' Committee 256
    shortening range of V-weapons 256
MI6, and German weapon development 10
Mickleham, V1 strikes 118, 121
Middlesex Hospital 158
Middleton, V1 strikes 222
Midhope Moor, Yorks, V1 strike 235, 247
Milch, Feldmarschall Erhard 20, 24
Mill Down, V1 strikes 118
Miller, Glenn 99
Miller, Max (entertainer) 242
Millichamp, Ivy, last rocket victim 7, 272
Mills, Jim 212
Milton, Portsmouth, Locksway Road 115
Mimoyecques see Marquise-Mimoyecques
Minster in Sheppey, V1 strikes 120, 222
Mitcham, V1 strikes 68, 73, 81, 82, 83, 85, 87,
    88, 96, 99, 100, 103, 105, 106, 107, 114, 120,
    121, 124, 130, 133, 139, 142, 148, 195, 239
Mittelbau, see Nordhausen
Molash, V1 strikes 161
Monks Green, V1 strikes 121
Monks Horton, V1 strikes 147, 168
Monkton,
    V1 strikes 136
    V2 strikes 222
Montgomery, Gen. Bernard 169
Moorfields eye hospital, City Road see under
    London
Morden 82, 86, 87, 97, 99, 100
    Central Road, V1 near miss 139
Morgan, Lt-Gen. Frederick 39
Morris, Mrs J. 86
Morrison, Herbert (Home Secretary and
    Min. of Home Security) 13, 37, 64, 72,
    108, 177, 178, 229
Morrison air-raid shelters 34, 37, 128, 176
Mottingham, Sidcup, V2 strikes 234
Moulsoe, V1 strikes 238
Mountfield, V1 strikes 106, 127, 129
Mountnessing
    V1 strikes 133
    V2 strikes 239, 258, 259
Much Hadham
    V1 strikes 140, 149
    V2 strike 239
Munday, Ken 101
Mundon, V2 strikes 235, 259
Munich, Löwenbräukeller 34
Münster 195, 213
Museums
    Blizna 51
    Imperial War Museum 238
        Cabinet War Rooms 65

Museums — continued
    Peenemünde Historical Museum 17
    Uxbridge, Hillingdon House (ex-RAF 11
        Gp) 179
    Wizernes, La Coupole Museum 29, 49

Nadehurst, V1 strikes 107
Nash, John 268
National Camps Corporation 178
National Fire Service (NFS) 110, 128, 136, 243
Navestock, Brentwood
    V1 strikes 160, 203, 204
    V2 strikes 203, 235, 239, 258, 266, 267
Navestock Heath, V2 strike 204
Nayland, V1 strike 204
Naze, The
    V1 strikes 222, 223, 234, 238, 267
    V2 strikes 234
Nazeing, Essex
    V1 strikes 126, 127, 168, 195
    V2 strikes 222, 235, 267
Neasden, V2 strike 267
Neatishead radar station 213
Netherlands see individual locations
Nettleswell,
    V1 strikes 125
    V2 strike 267
Nevendon, Essex, V2 strikes 235
New Forest, V1 strikes 106
New Hall Green, V2 strikes 259
New Malden 68, 73, 81, 102
    see also Malden
New Romney
    V1 strikes 120, 142, 147, 153, 155, 157, 161
    V1s shot down 161
New Southgate
    Brunswick Park Road 160
    Standard Telephones & Cables (STC)
        (later North London Business Centre)
        160
New York Times 201
Newchurch, V1 strikes 107, 133, 138, 156,
    161, 165, 168
Newdigate, V1 strikes 121, 125
Newenden, Kent, V1 strikes 165
Newhaven, V1 strikes 135
Newington, V1 strikes 120, 125, 144, 153,
    155, 159
Newport, Essex, V1 strike 234
Newport, Shropshire, V1 strike 235, 247
Newport, Wales, balloon barrage 41
News Chronicle 89
Nicholls, John 146
Niedersachswerfen, Nordhausen: rocket
    assembly 218
Ninfield, V1 strikes 106, 133
Noak Hill, Romford
    V1 strike 203
    V2 strikes 195, 222, 235, 239, 267
Noisy-le-Sec 199
Nonington, V1 strikes 153
Nord-Pas-de-Calais region 29
Nordhausen 218, 272
    Boelcke Barracks 154
    Mittelbau works complex 151, 154, 172–173
Normandy invasion beaches 80, 116, 126,
    138
North Chapel, V1 strike 118
North Cray, V1 strike 239
North Downs, anti-aircraft defences 38, 41,
    111, 112
North Dulwich see Dulwich
North Foreland
    AA defences 126, 261
    radar screen 179
    V1 strike 222
    V2 strikes 234, 267
North Mimms, V1 strikes 133
North Stifford, V2 strikes 234, 259
North Weald
    V1 strikes 120, 142, 239
    V2 strikes 258
Northampton 170
Northaw
    V1 strikes 157, 204, 234
    V2 strike 239
Northbourne, V1 strikes 222
Northfleet
    V1 strikes 120, 133, 156
    V2 strike 235

Northiam, V1 strikes 105, 121, 135, 136, 148, 155, 165
Northumberland Bolton, V1 strikes 139
Northwood 67
Norwich
  V2 strikes 203
  V2 threat to 195, 198, 200, 201, 210
Notting Hill, V2 strikes 234
Nottlestead, V1 strikes 121
Novendon, V1 strikes 127
Nucourt 69, 72, 94, 117
Nutfield
  V1 strikes 121, 129
  V2 strike 267
Nuthampstead, Herts, V2 strikes 234
Nye, Lt-Gen. Sir Archibald 10

Oberraderach 95, 117, 152, 182
'Oboe' target marking 14–15, 46, 48
Ockenburg, Netherlands 219, 241, 251, 253, 255
Ockendon, V2 strikes 203
Ockley, V1 strikes 120, 161
Offham, V1 strikes 106, 125, 165
Old Botley, V1 strikes 106
Old Romney, V1 strikes 107, 122, 126, 133, 139, 155, 157, 165
Oldham, Lancs, Abbey Hills Road V1 strike 235, 247, 248
Ollerton, Cheshire, V1 strike 235, 247
Ondrej, Sgt Henry 129
Ongar, V1 strikes 106, 204
Operation
  'Backfire' 181
  'Big Ben' 39, 182, 187, 190, 231, 251
  'Diver' 39, 41, 65, 67, 76, 77–79, 98, 102, 104, 110, 111, 126–127, 161, 166
  'Hydra' 15, 17
  'Market-Garden' 194, 195, 196, 202
  'Millennium' 8
  'Noball' 39, 47, 66, 116
  'Pappdeckel' 260
  'Pointblank' 14, 43, 51
  'Steinbock' ('Little' ('Baby') Blitz) 35
  'Wacht am Rhein' 235
  see also 'Crossbow'; 'Overlord'
Oppau, I.G. Farben 14, 16
Orford, V1 strikes 203, 222, 234, 235, 239
Orfordness
  defensive screen 261
  V1 strikes 203, 204, 222, 223, 234, 235, 238, 239, 263, 266, 267
  V2 strikes 203, 223, 258
Organisation Todt 22, 29
Orlestone, V1 strikes 105, 122, 147, 151
Orpin, Anne 143
Orpington, Kent
  Kynaston Road V2 strike (last) 7, 267, 269, 271, 272
  V1 strikes 63, 67, 68, 81, 82, 84, 85, 87, 88, 96, 97, 100, 103, 106, 107, 112, 118, 121, 124, 127, 129, 130, 136, 138, 139, 140, 142, 147, 151, 152, 153, 160, 165, 203, 204, 239, 267
  V2 strikes 204, 222, 223, 239, 266, 267
Orsett, Essex
  V1 strike 222
  V2 strike 204, 235
Orvis, Ken 135
'Oslo Report' 9, 10
Ostend 89, 198, 261
Oswaldtwistle, Lancs, V1 strike 235, 247
Otford, V1 strikes 165
Otham, V1 strikes 165
Otterden, V1 strikes 127, 160
Oude Schie Canal 263
Oulton Broad, V1 strike 204
'Overlord', Operation 33, 38, 39, 40, 41–43, 51, 58, 59, 65, 67
  air forces created for 66
Ovington, V1 strikes 106
Oxhey, V1 strikes 127
Oxted
  V1 strikes 105, 106, 107, 121, 124, 126, 138, 142, 147
  V2 strikes 258

Pacy-sur-Armançon 119, 152
Paddington see London
Paddlesworth, V1 strikes 161

Paglesham, Rochford/Southend, V2 strikes 195, 234, 258
Palling, V2 strike 239
Palmers Green, V2 strike 204
Pantin 199
Parham 105
Paris 154
  as V2 target 173, 184, 185, 199
Paris/Dugny 119
Parkwood Hollingbourne, V1 propaganda leaflets 164
Parnall, Elsie 85
Parndon Wood, Epping, V2 strike 186, 195
Parslow Common, V2 strike 267
Pas-de-Calais 152, 166, 169, 171, 172
  long-range artillery 164
  weapon sites 15, 22, 29, 36, 44–45, 54, 56, 66, 69, 72, 92, 94, 116, 146, 154, 167
Patey, Bill 237
Pathe News 74, 153
Patrington radar station 213
Patrixbourne, V1 strikes 120
Peasenhall, V2 strikes 203
Peasmarsh, V1 strikes 124, 135, 140, 153, 155
Peckham, V2 strikes 222
Peek, F/Sgt Ernest 12
Peenemünde 20, 21, 24, 25, 50, 95, 108, 116, 117, 119, 154, 175, 180, 182
  Historical Museum 17
  V2 launches 14, 180–181
  V2 rocket development 8–9, 11–17, 172, 173, 174, 176
Peltz, Genmaj. Dietrich 35
Pembury, V1 strikes 106, 107, 121, 136, 222
Penge
  Blenheim Road 121
  High Street 121
  V1 strikes 68, 87, 88, 97, 106, 112, 118, 121, 126, 136, 139, 151, 161
Penshurst
  V1 strikes 107, 125
  V2 strikes 222, 266
Petham, V1 strikes 142
Petites-Tailles, V2 deployment 185
Pett, V1 strikes 107, 114, 120, 130
Pevensey
  radar station 179
  V1 strikes 122, 140, 142
Pile, Gen. Frederick 38, 39, 41–42, 67, 110–112, 127, 170, 206, 241, 270
Pilgrims Hatch
  V1 strikes 127
  V2 strikes 267
Pinner, V2 strikes 223
Pirbright, V1 strikes 159
Pirton, V1 strikes 195
Pitsea, Southend, V2 strikes 203, 235, 259, 267
Pitsea Marshes, V2 strikes 259
Planet News 89, 90, 136, 137, 162
Platt, Sevenoaks
  V2 strike 259
  Winfield Farm V1 strike 60, 62
Plaxtol
  V1 strikes 106, 112, 153, 161
  V2 strikes 239
Playford, Ipswich, V2 strike 203
Pluckley, V1 strikes 122, 157, 160
Plumstead Marshes, V2 strikes 204, 223, 259
Plymouth 56
Poland
  Secret Intelligence Service 174
  underground agents 51, 174
  see also Blizna
Polegate, V1 strikes 129
Poling, nr Arundel
  radar station 36, 179
  V1 strikes 121
Polstead, V1 strikes 223
Poplar
  V1 strikes 63, 81, 82, 85, 86, 88, 96, 100, 102, 103, 107, 114, 118, 120, 121, 122, 126, 139, 142, 147, 155, 157, 195
  V2 strikes 219, 223, 239, 258, 259, 266, 267
Portal, MRAF Sir Charles (Chief of Air Staff) 8, 18, 30, 38, 40, 47, 49, 92–93, 98
Portsmouth
  early warning systems 182
  evacuation from 34

Portsmouth — continued
  threat to 25
  V1 strikes 89, 114, 115, 122
Poslingford
  V1 strikes 156
  V2 strikes 223
Postling, V1 strikes 118, 161
Potters Bar
  V1 strikes 160, 203, 204
  V2 strikes 204, 239
Pound, Adm. Sir Dudley 40
Pound Hill, V1 strike 204
Preshaw, V1 strikes 106
Press and Censorship Bureau 6
Pulborough, V1 strikes 106
Purfleet
  V1 strikes 107, 122, 125, 129, 203
  V2 strikes 223, 258
Purleigh
  V1 strikes 135
  V2 strikes 258, 259
Purley, V2 strikes 63, 67, 68, 77, 82, 83, 84, 85, 87, 88, 96, 99, 100, 103
Pyrford, V1 strikes 161

Queenborough, Sear V2 strike 204

Raaphorst, The Hague 189
Radar
  American SCR 584 radar 79, 102, 123
  ASV radar 207
  Cathode Ray Direction Finding (CRDF) 36, 179
  H2S navigational equipment 31
  and HMS Caicos 213, 262
  MEW equipment 80
  No. 3 Predictor 140
  No. 10 Predictor 79, 102, 123
  'Oboe' target marking 14–15, 46, 48
  and radio counter-measures 35–36, 36, 180–181, 188–189, 191–194, 207, 243, 262
  stations 36, 77–78, 80, 179–181, 182, 186, 262, 272
  and V2 rocket campaign 198, 199, 220, 241, 243, 257, 270
  see also individual stations
Radcliffe, Lancs, V1 strike 235, 247
Radlett, V1 strikes 106, 234
Radley Green, V2 strike 258
Radwinter, V1 strikes 222
Rainham, Barking
  Oak Lane railway bridge V1 strike 144
  V1 strikes 121, 122, 147, 152, 234
  V2 strikes 222, 223, 234, 239, 259, 266, 267
Ramsden Bellhouse, V1 strikes 136
Ramsden Heath, V2 strikes 235, 238, 258
Ramsey, V1 strikes 204, 222
Ramsgate
  radar station 179
  shelled by long-range guns 164
Ramsholt, V2 strikes 234
Ranson Moor, V1 strike 204
Ranworth, V2 strike 195, 198
Ravelijn, The Hague 255, 264
Raveningham, V2 strike 266
Rawreth, Essex, V2 strikes 203, 204, 258, 259, 267
Raydon
  V1 strike 168
Rayleigh
  V1 strikes 204, 222
  V2 strikes 222, 234, 235, 239, 267
Reads Island, Humber Estuary V1 strike 247
Red Cross, American 43, 158, 213
Redbourne, Lincs, V1 strikes 235, 247, 266
Redhill
  V1 strikes 121
  V1 track 100
Reigate, V1 strikes 121, 124, 136
Renescure 60
Resistance
  Dutch 188, 263
  French 168
  in Haute-Savoie 47
  in Poland 51, 174
  and the V-weapon sites 24, 47
Rettendon, Chelmsford
  V1 strikes 127, 195
  V2 strikes 204, 234, 258
Reuters 89
Rheims 154

Rhine, River
  Allied crossing of 183, 268, 272
  bridges and Operation 'Market-Garden' *194*
Richmond
  V1 strikes 73, 81, 84, 85, 124, 157, 160, 165, 195, 204
  V2 strikes 267
Ridgewell, Mary 7
Rigby, Fusilier Lee 115
Rijnsburg, The Hague 265
Rijs Wood, Bakhuizen, Friesland *195, 209*
Rilly-la-Montagne 117
Ringmer, V1 strikes 107, 160
Ripley, V1 strikes 124, 157
Rivenhall, V1 strike 204
Riverhead, V2 strike 239
Rochester
  AA defences 126, 127
  V1 strikes 135, 151, 222
  V2 strikes 259
Rochford, V1 strike 204
Rockland St Mary, Norwich, V2 strikes 203
Rockleys, V1 strikes 195
Rodger, F/O J. K. *141*
Roding, V1 strikes 222
Rogers, Willie *61*
Rolvenden, V1 strikes 105, 120, 122, 136, 148, 156, 165
Romford
  Ainsley Avenue V2 strike *220*, 222
  Collier Row Lane V2 strike *220*, 222
  V1 strikes 124, 129, 142, 147, 151
  V2 strikes 222, 259, 267
  see also Noak Hill
Romford Times 188
Romney, V1 strikes 156, 160
Romney Marsh, V1 strikes 165
Rossington, Yorks, V1 strike 235, 247
Rotherfield
  V1 strikes 106, 107, 121, 127, 129, 130, 133, 142, 165
  V2 strikes 195
Rotherhithe 61
Rotterdam 186, 225, 251, 255, 260, 261, 268
Rouen *166*, 183
Royal Observer Corps
  centres 76, 78, 143
  detecting enemy aircraft 76
  fighter operations 67, 262
  Schermuly ('Snowflake') rockets 104
  tracking flying bombs 60, 208
  Uxbridge, No. 11 Gp HQ 179
Ruckinge, V1 strikes 105, 106, 118, 140, 142, 149, 152, 155, 165, 168
Rudgwick, V1 strikes 195
Rügen island 24
Ruhr dams *29*
Ruislip
  V1 strikes 67, 86, 88, 135
  V2 strike 267
Rust en Vreugd, Wassenaar 234, 251, 252, 253, 255
Runwell, V2 strike 239
Rush Green, Romford, V2 strike 235
Rushden, V1 strikes 195
Rushmere St Andrew, V2 strike 204
Rüsselsheim, Opel works 31, 154
Rustington, V1 strikes 107
Ryarsh, V1 strikes 121
Rye
  AA defences *130*
  Chain Home radar 36, 179
  V1 strikes 105, 106, 120, 124, 129, 130, 142, 147, 148, 151, 152, 156, 157, 161, 165

Sacombe, V1 strikes 125
Saffron Walden
  AA screen 207
  V1 strikes 195
St Catherine's House *see* Adastral House
St George's Garrison Church 115
St Lawrence, V1 strikes 195, 222
St Leonards, V1 strikes 135, 139, 151
St Leu-d'Esserent 72, *94, 119*
St Margaret-at-Cliffe, shelled by long-range guns *164*
St Margaret's Bay
  AA defences *111*, 126
  radar station 80
  V1 strikes 151

St Martha, V1 strikes 120
St Martin-l'Hortier 69
St Mary Cray, V2 strikes 258, 266
St Mary in the Marsh, V1 strikes 127, 130, 135, 152, 153, 157, 161, *164*, 165
St Marylebone *see* London
St Mary's Hoo, V2 strikes 204, 267
St Nicholas at Wade, V1 strikes 136, 266
St Omer, weapon sites *15, 28*, 46
St Pancras *see under London*
St Paul's Waldon 168
St Pol *22, 23*, 48
St Thomas Cambray, V1 strikes 112
St Thomas The Apostle, V1 strikes 127, 133, 165
St Vith, Belgium, V2 deployment *185*
Salcott, V1 strike 203
Salehurst, Sussex, V1 strikes 103, 106, 120, 127, 129, 133, 148
Sales Point, V1 strikes 204
Saltwood, V1 strikes 127, 130, 133
Sanders, Col Terence 23, *28, 31*
Sandgate, V1 strikes 152, 157, 160, 165, 168
Sandhurst, V1 strikes 107, 124
Sandon
  V1 strikes 120, 266
  V2 strikes 223, 238
Sandwich radar station 78, 126
Sandys, Duncan
  counter-measures 35, 114, 178, 188, 209
  'Crossbow' Sub-Committee 66, 175
  and German weapon research *10*, 11, *12–13*, 18, 20–21, *31*, 176
  reviews V1 campaign *170*, 172
  V2 rocket threat 194, 195, 270
Sarisbury, V1 strikes 106
Sarnaki, Poland 50, *51*
Saunders, Rayden *143*
Sautrecourt 60, 69
Savidge, Alec 61
Sayers, Bill (fireman) *125*
Sayers, Mrs Violet *125*
Scheldt, River 171
Scheveningen, Netherlands *228*
  Kurhaus Grand Hotel 264, 265
Scheveningse Bosch, The Hague *254*
Schiedam, Netherlands 191
Schleswig 244
'Schotterwerk Nordwest' *see* Wizernes
Schulz, Maj. (Gp Süd V2 deployment) *184*
Schweinfurt 30
Scott, Lord Edward *122*
Scythe, AA defences 112
Seabrook, V1 strikes 135
Seaford, V1 strikes 151, 204
Seal, V1 strikes 106, 120, 136, 138, 151, 157, 159, 165
Seale, V1 strikes 140
Sear, Queenborough, V2 strike 204
Searby, G/Capt. John *15*
Sedlescombe, V1 strikes 105, 136, 138, 165
Seine, River 146, 152, 154, *161*, 167
Sellindge, V1 strikes 124, 127, 129, 142
Send, V1 strikes 151, 157
Sevenoaks
  V1 strikes 105, 107, 157, 165
  V2 strikes 222, 259, 266
Shadoxhurst, V1 strikes 122, 130
Shaftesbury 41
Shalford, Braintree, V2 strike 204
Shalford, Surrey, V1 strike 106
Sheering, V2 strikes 204, 238
Sheerness, V1 strikes 140, 222, 234, 267
Shelley, V1 strikes 238, 266
Shenfield, Essex
  V1 strikes 107, 125
  V2 strikes 204, 259, 267
Shenley, V2 strikes 239
Sheppard-Jones, ATS Subaltern Elizabeth *71*
Shere, V1 strikes 157
Sheringham, V2 strike 258
Sherman, Lennie *61*
Shipbourne, Kent, V1 strikes 103, 112, 118, 121, 124, 148, 234, 267
Shipley, V1 strikes 135
Ships
  Caicos (frigate) 213, 262
  Tirpitz (battleship) 218
Shoeburyness
  V1 strikes 204, 234, 266, 267
  V2 strikes 222, 234, 235, 239

Shoreditch
  Boundary Street/Calvert Avenue *159*
  Great Eastern Street *124*
  St Leonard's Church *159*
  V1 strikes 107, 122, *124*, 125, 138, 142
  V2 strikes 239, 266
Shoreham
  V1 strikes 106, 118, 121, 142, 148, 151, 156, 157, 159, 222
  V2 strikes 259
Shorne,
  V1 strikes 106, 168
  V2 strike 223
Shotesham All Saints, V2 strike *199*, 203
Shotgate, Wickford, V2 strikes 235, 239
Shotley, V1 strikes 222
Shottisham, V1 strikes 234
Shudy Camps, V1 strikes 195
Sible Hedingham, V1 strikes 195, 222
Sidcup
  V1 strikes 68, *73*, 81, 84, 85, 96, 97, 99, 103, 112, 204, 267
  V2 strikes 223, 239, 258, 259, 266, 267
Silvertown, V2 strikes 223
Singleton, V1 strikes 142
Siracourt *22–23, 28*, 29, *33*, 44, 47, 69, *92*, 94, *116*, 182
Sissinghurst, V1 strikes 120, 122, 156
Sittingbourne *144*
  V1 strikes 122, 152
Skegness 246–247, *248*
Skippers Island, V1 strike 204
Slaugham, V1 strikes 136, 142, 156
Slough, V1 strikes 157, 160
Smarden, V1 strikes 121, 130, 135, 161, 165
Smeeth, V1 strikes 106, 124, 147
Smith, Mrs Ethel (Chingford) *86*
Smith, Reg (New Southgate) *160*
Smith, Sir Frank, investigates enemy weapons 13
Smuts, FM Jan 21, 66
Snap Hill, Pevensey, radar station 179
Snape, V1 strike 204
Snaresbrook
  Eagle Lane 7
  Woodford Road 7
Snargate, V1 strikes 107, 124, 140, 152, 155, 157
Snodland
  Elmfield Villas, Malling Road *143*
  V1 strikes 142, *143*, 153
Solent 34, 41, 89, 176
Somersham, V1 strike 267
Somme area 54, 56, 69, 92, *93*, 152, 154, 166, 167, *173*
Sottevast, Cherbourg peninsula 29, *44*, 47
South Cliffe, Yorks, V1 strikes 235, 247
South Fambridge, V1 strikes 129
South Foreland
  V1 strikes 153, 155, 168
  V1 track 72
South Green
  V1 strike 204
  V2 strikes 239, 259
South Hanningfield, V2 strike 259
South Hornchurch
  V1 strikes 136, 165
  V2 strikes 239, 267
South Norwood, Sunny Bank V2 strike 204, *213*
South Ockenden
  V1 strikes 129, 136
  V2 strikes 239, 259, 267
South Orford, V1 strikes 222
South Stifford, V1 strikes 152
South Weald, V1 strikes 135
South Woodford
  Cowslip Road 7
  Empress Avenue 7, *83*
  Onslow Gardens 7
  St Alban's Crescent 7
Southall, V1 strikes 73, 99, 120, 124, 165
Southampton
  air defences 38
  bombed *114*
  early-warning systems 182
  evacuation from 34
  V-weapons threat to 39

Southborough
  V1 strikes 106, 130
  V2 strikes 222
Southend
  AA screen 167, 207
  night fighter defence screen 211
  Royal Terrace/Marine Parade/High Street *208*
  Shirley Road V1 strike *155*
  V1 strikes 195, 204, 222, 266
  V2 hit on Pier 203, *208*
  V2 strikes 201, 209, 222, 266, 267
Southfleet, V1 strikes 120, 139, 152
Southgate
  V1 strikes 96, 103, 120, 161, 168
  V2 strikes 195, 222
Southminster
  V1 strikes 222, 239
  V2 strikes 235, 238, 258, 267
Southstoke, V1 strikes 107
Southwark
  Horseman Road V1 strike 239, *244*
  V1 strikes 63, 68, 77, 82, 83, 84, 86, 88, 107, 118, 120, 133, 157
  V2 strikes 234, 239
Southwold
  V1 strikes 203, 204, 222
  V2 strike 239
Soviet zone of Germany (post-war) 154
Sowerby Bridge, Yorks, V1 strike 235, 247
Spaatz, Lt Gen. Carl 43, 50, 93
Special Operations Executive (SOE) 37, 175, 188, 191
Speer, Albert, as Minister of Munitions *8*
Speldhurst, V1 strikes 140, 153, 157
Spixworth, V2 strike 203
Sport & General (news agency) *89*
Springfield, V1 strikes 223
Springvale, V1 strikes 106
SS (Schutzstaffel)
  controls V2 operations 228
  and revenge weapons *172*, 173
  Sonderkommando *182*
Staalduinsche Bosch, Hook of Holland 234, 235, 241, 253, 255
Staines, V1 strikes 63, 73, 83, 120
Stalisfield, V1 strikes 120
Standon, V1 strikes 126
Stanford, V1 strikes 135, 152
Stanford Rivers
  V1 strikes 136, 148, 161, 267
  V2 strikes 222, 266
Stanford-le-Hope,
  V1 strikes 130
  V2 strike 267
Stanmore
  RAF No. 11 Gp Filter Room 182, *187*, 194
  V1 strike 234
  V2 strike 239
Stansgate Abbey, Maldon, V2 strike 235
Stansted,
  V1 strikes 105, 120, 155, 156
  V2 strike 267
Stansted Abbot, V1 strikes 234
Stanway, V1 strikes 140
Stapleford
  V1 strikes 266
  V2 strikes 238
Stapleford, Herts, V2 strike 267
Stapleford Abbotts
  V1 strikes 107, 135, 142, 151, 159
  V2 strikes 239
Stapleford Tawney
  V1 strikes 149, 153, 168
  V2 strikes 223, 239, 266
Staplehurst, V1 strikes 105, 107, 120, 121, 130, 133, 140, 147, 148, 151, 160
Stebbing, V1 strikes 235
Steeple
  V1 strike 204
  V2 strike 259
Steeple Creek, V1 strikes 122
Stelling Minnis, V1 strikes 161
Stepney
  Hughes Mansions, Vallance Road, V2 strike 267, 269, *270–271*
  Mile End Hospital *102*
  V1 strikes 68, 73, 81, 83, 96, 99, 100, 105, 118, 120, 125, 130, 133, 136, 139, 140, 142, 147, 151
  V2 strikes 223, 239, 267

Stewart, Donald (entertainer) *242*
Stewart, Peter (photo interpretation) *12*
Stewart, Sir Findlater (Home Defence Executive) 14, 34
Stifford, V1 strikes 222
Stock, V2 strikes 267
Stockbury, V1 strikes 165, 222
Stockholm, Military Aeronautical Research Institute *174*
Stockport, Garners Lane, Davenport, V1 strike 235, *246*, 247
Stoke, V2 strikes 259
Stoke Common, V2 strikes 258
Stoke Mandeville Hospital 158
Stoke Newington
  V1 strikes 68, 84, 105, 120, 133, 160, 168, 239
  V2 strikes 239
Stokes, Bernice *143*
Stolberg, Juliana van *253*
Stondon Massey, V1 strikes 129, 267
Stone-cum-Ebony
  V1 leaflets dropped *164*
  V1 strikes 105, 106, 107, 120, 127, 135, 153, 161, 165
  V2 strikes 222
Stoneman, Police Ins. *134*
Stoner, V1 strikes 157
Stoney Hurd, V1 strikes 106
Storrington, V1 strikes 133
Stow Maries, Maldon
  V1 strike 121
  V2 strikes 235, 258
Stowting, V1 strikes 156
Stradishall, V1 strikes 160
Stratford
  Leytonstone Road V2 strikes 222
  Olympic Stadium *138*
  V2 strikes 258
  see also West Ham
Stratford Express 131
Stratton Hall, V1 strike 222
Stretton, V1 strike 204
Studham, V2 strike 267
Sturton-le-Steeple, Notts, V1 strike 235, 247
Stuttgart 117
Stutton, V1 strike 203
Subterranea Britannica *179*
Sudbourne, V1 strikes 127, 204, 222, 223
Sudbury, AA screen 207
Sunbury
  V1 strikes 100, 124, 151, 165
  V2 strikes 195
Sundridge,
  V1 strikes 106, 107, 112, 121, 127, 129, 133, 157
  V2 strike 222
Supply, Ministry of, and weapon development 10, 20, *23*
Surbiton, V1 strikes 67, 81, 82, 83, 97, 100, 112, 120, 124, 130, 157, 203, 222
Surlingham, V2 strike 203
Surrey Commercial Docks V2 strike 204
Sutton, V1 strikes 67, 68, 81, 83, 85, 87, 96, 97, 99, *102*, 106, 107, 114, 121, 124, 129, 135, 136, 142, 157, 161, 222, 238
Sutton Gault, V1 strikes 195
Sutton Sootney, V1 strikes 114
Sutton Valence, V1 strikes 121, 153, 267
Sutton-at-Hone
  V1 strikes 148, 203
  V2 strikes 222, 235, 267
Swainsthorpe, V1 strikes 195
Swale, V1 strike 234
Swanley, V2 strikes 204
Swanscombe
  V1 strikes 126, 129, 136, 138, *145*, 147, 153, 222
  V2 strikes 222, 259
  Watling Street V1 strike *60*
Swansea 41
Sweden *19*, 53
Swinemünde 9
Swingate CHL radar station 78, 80, 179

Taberner, Ernest *130*
Takeley
  V1 strike 234
  V2 strike 239
'Tallboy' earthquake bombs *23, 29, 30, 94*, 218

Tandridge, V1 strikes 114, 135
Tangmere, V1 strikes 124
Tatford, Miss Ellen *114*
Tatsfield
  Clarks Lane Farm *79*
  V1 strikes 118, 122
Tauber, Richard (entertainer) *242*
Taverham Hall Farm, Norwich, V2 strike 203
Tedder, ACM Sir Arthur 51, 66, *67*, 68, 69, 92–94, 117, 119, 122, 146, 221
Teddington
  Bushy Park Supreme HQ *99*
Tees, River 248
Television House *see* Adastral House
Telscombe, V1 strikes 222
Tendring, V1 strikes 222, 238
Tenterden, V1 strikes 120, 121, 127, 133, 140, *141*, 142, 153, 165
Terschelling, Netherlands 198
Teston, V1 strikes 156
Teynham, V1 strikes 153
Thames, River
  AA zone 127
  tunnels under 228
  V1 air launches 206
  V1 strikes *69, 133*, 142
  V2 strikes 266, 267
  V2 strikes nr Erith 234, 267
Thames Estuary 89, 126, 127
  Knock John fort *111*
  Nore fort *111*
  Red Sand fort *111*
  Roughs fort *111*
  Shivering Sand fort *111*
  Sunk Head fort *111*
  Tongue fort *111*
  V1 strikes 159, 222, 234
  V2 strikes 267
Thames Haven
  balloon defence 126
  V1 strikes 222
  V2 strikes 258
Thannington, V1 strikes 160
Thaxted, V1 strikes 195
The Hague (Den Haag), Netherlands
  Bezuidenhout district *232, 252–253*
  Hotel Promenade (later Crown Plaza) 219, *224–225*, 232, 233, 234, 250
  Huis te Werve 224, *225*, 233
  Laan van Meerdervoort *230*
  Loosduinen *225, 227*, 230, 234
  Staatsspoor station 232
  Statenkwartier V2 launch site *272*
  targeted by RAF 190, 218, 223, 224–235, *224–225, 227, 231*, 240–241, 257, 264, 268
  V2 launches from 7, *182–184, 186, 189*, 194, 195, 200, 201, 209, *213*, 224–235, *230*, 250–253, *254–255*
  Voorde 224, 233
  Vredespaleis (League of Nations Peace Palace) *230*
  Wassenaar *182–184, 186*, 188, *219*, 224, 228, *232*, 233, 234, 251, 252, 253, 255, *265*
  see also Duindigt racecourse; Haagsche Bosch, Ravelijn
Theydon Bois
  V1 strikes 149, 152, 153, 161, 168
  V2 strikes 266, 267
Theydon Garnon, V2 strikes 258, 259, 267
Theydon Mount, Epping, V2 strikes 222
Thoma, Gen. Wilhelm von *11*
Thorndon Park, V2 strikes 266
Thorndon Parva, V1 strike 267
Thornham, V1 strikes 140, 160
Thornton Heath *114*
Thorpe, Norwich, V2 strike 195
Thorpe-le-Soken,
  V1 strike 267
  V2 strike 259
Thorpeness, V1 strikes 222
Thorrington, V1 strike 204
Throwley, V1 strikes 151, 153, 155, 222
Thurleigh, V1 strike 203
Thurlton, V1 strike 204
Thurnham, V1 strikes 153, 159
Thurrock, in R. Thames, V1 strikes 142
Thwaite St Mary, V1 strike 203
Ticehurst, V1 strikes 105, 107, 114, 121, 124, 127, 129, 133, 136, 142, 147, 148, 149, 161

Tilbury
  balloon defences 127
  V2 strikes 234
  see also Langdon Hills
Tilbury Juxta Clare, V1 strikes 195
Tilford, V1 strikes 138
Tillingham
  V1 strikes 203, 204, 234
  V2 strikes 235, 239
Tillingham Marshes
  V1 strikes 267
  V2 strikes 234, 267
Tilton on the Hill, Leics, Glebe Farm V1
  strike 234, *244*
The Times 89
Tiptree, V2 strikes 234
Titsey, V1 strikes 121, 133, 157, 165, 235
Titsey Hill, V2 strike 239
Todt organisation *see* Organisation Todt
Tokyo, bombing of *43*
Tollesbury, V1 strikes 135, 195
Tolleshunt D'Arcy, V2 strike 239
Tonbridge 193
  V1 strikes 107, 120, 121, 125, 140, *141*, 157
  V2 strikes 238
Toot Hill, V2 strike 239
Tooting *see* Wandsworth
Topcroft, V1 strikes 238
Topical Press *89*
Tottenham
  V1 strikes 63, 86, 161, 168, 234
  V2 strikes 258, 267
  see also Tottenham Court Road *under* London
Tottington, Lancs, Chapel Street V1 strike
  235, *247*, *249*
Tourcoing 56
Trier *199*, *210*
Trimley
  radar station 207, 213
  V2 strike 239
Trimley St Martin, V1 strikes 112, 234
Tring, V1 strikes 138, 153
Trossy-St-Maximin 117–118, *119*
Trottiscliffe, V1 strikes 121
Tuddenham, V1 strikes 153
Tudhoe, Spennymoor, V1 strike 235, 247
Tunbridge Wells, V1 strikes 120, 139, 142
Tunstall, Norwich
  V1 strikes 160
  V2 strikes 195, 203
Turton, Lancs, V1 strike 235, 247
Twickenham,
  V1 strikes 68, 73, 87, 96, 100, *102*, 105, 107,
    121, 125, 129, 151, 157, 160, 161, 165
  V2 strike 239
Twineham, V1 strikes 136
Tyne, River 248

Uckfield, V1 strikes 127, 130
Udimore, V1 strikes 120, 140, 156
Ufford, V1 strikes 222
Ulcombe, V1 strikes 106, 130, 151, 152
Units, Allied
  Allied Expeditionary Air Force (AEAF)
    42, 47–48, 51, *67*, 68, 92, 94, 189
  SHAEF (Supreme Allied HQ), V2 rocket
    campaign *199*, 220, 230
Units, British
  21st Army Group 38, 40, 41, 127, 194, 198, 199
  Corps, XXX Corps *194*
  Divisions
    11th Armoured Div. 167, *210*
    41st Infantry Div. (WW1) *93*
  Brigade of Guards, King's Guard *71*
  Anti-Aircraft Command *38*, *39*, 41, 65–67, 76,
    78–80, *102*, *110*, 114, *123*, 126–127, 167, *170*,
    205, 206–207, 214, 241, 243, 262, 270
    No. 1 AA Group 207
    No. 2 AA Group 207
    No. 5 AA Group 246–247, 248
    126 (H) AA Battery 129
    481 (H) AA Battery *112*
  Balloon Command *43*, 66, 67, 104, 127, 166
  Combined Operations 37, 94, 117
  Combined Services Interrogation Centre *11*
  Regiments, Royal West Kent *129*
  Royal Artillery (RA)
    10th Survey Regt 194, 198, 199
    11th Survey Regt 36, *179*, 192, 199
    337 Searchlight Regt *129*

Units, British — continued
  Royal Engineers (RE) *31*
  Royal Horse Artillery, King's Troop *268*
  Royal Electrical and Mechanical
    Engineers (REME) 79
  Second Tactical Air Force 32–33, *38*, *39*,
    42, 54, *66*, 69, 98, 215, 219, 221, 223, 225,
    229–230, 232–235, *252*, 253, *261*, *262*, 268
  RAF Commands
    Air Defence of Great Britain (ADGB)
      89, 98, 104, *110*, 126–127, 161, 166–167
      countering flying bombs 41, 65–66, 206
      intruders over weapon sites 62, 198
      Re-formed *38*, *39*
      V2 threat 183, 188, 189, 190, 195
    Bomber 29–30, *30*, 31, 42, 47, 66, 68, 69,
      92–94, 117–119, 146–147, 154, 157, 182,
      208, 261, 262
      Berlin bombed *35*
      and home fighter threat 206, 207, 211
      Peenemünde hit 14, *15*
      radio counter-measures 191
      V2 sites 190, 218, 219, 221, 223
    Fighter
      attacking V-weapon sites 29, 215, 219,
        221, 223–235, *224*, *231*, 240–241, 248,
        250–253, 255, 257, *261*, 264–265, 268
      balloon control 104
      defence against flying bombs 207, 211,
        214, 262
      monitoring V2 operations *202*
      redesignated ADGB *38*
      Stanmore HQ 187
  RAF Groups
    No. 2 Group 42, 49
    No. 10 Group 41
    No. 11 Group 41, 67, *76*, 98, 166, *179*,
      180, 182, *187*, 194, 199, 206, 224, 261, 262
    No. 12 Group 224, *231*, 232, *252*
    No. 100 Group 98, 188, 191, 198, 231
  RAF Wings
    No. 80 (Signals) Wing 193
    No. 137 Wing 253
    No. 139 Wing 253
    No. 150 Wing *100*
    No. 180 (Signals) Wing 181
  RAF Squadrons
    No. 3 (RAF) 145
    No. 19 (RAF) *48*
    No. 21 (RAF) *266*
    No. 25 (RAF) 208, 214
    No. 26 (RAF) 250, 251, 268
    No. 56 (RAF) *100*
    No. 68 (RAF) 214
    No. 83 (RAF) *15*
    No. 85 (RAF) 98
    No. 96 (RAF) 145, 214
    No. 124 (RAF) 233, 250, 262
    No. 132 (RAF) *66*
    No. 157 (RAF) 98
    No. 192 (RAF) 180
    No. 229 (RAF) 228, 232
    No. 245 (RAF) *47*
    No. 274 (RAF) *144*
    No. 303 (RAF) 232
    No. 316 (RAF) 98
    No. 418 (RAF) 145
    No. 451 (RAF) 262
    No. 453 (RAF) 228, 232, 250, 262, 265
    No. 464 (RAF) *266*
    No. 486 (RAF) 145
    No. 487 (RAF) *266*
    No. 488 (RAF) 214
    No. 501 (RAF) 206, 262
    No. 540 (RAF) *12*, *23*, *27*
    No. 541 (RAF) *26*, *30*, 44, *46*
    No. 602 (RAF) 228, 232, 250, 251, 253, 265, *266*
    No. 603 (RAF) 233, *252*, 262, 265
    No. 605 (RAF) 145
    No. 616 (RAF) *140–141*, 262
    No. 617 (RAF) *23*, 29, *30*, 69
    No. 635 (RAF) *119*
  RAF Units
    Fighter Interception Unit 99
    Medmenham, RAF Central
      Interpretation Unit (CIU) *12*, 26, 27, 28,
      56–57, *93*, *251*
    No. 105 Mobile Air Reporting Unit 194,
      198, 241
  RAF Regiment 102, 123, 127

Units, Canadian, First Army *151*, *169*
Units, German
  Armies
    15. Armee *169*
    Reserve Army *172*
  Corps
    Armeekorps z.b.V. *233*
    LXV. Armeekorps 173
  Divisions
    5. Flak-Div. *233*
    Div. z.V. *233*
  Gruppe Nord (V2 deployment) *184*, *195*, *196*
  Gruppe Süd (V2 deployment) *184*, *195*, *196*
  Artillerie-Abt. 485 *184*, *185*, *195*, 213, *254*
    later Artillerie-Regt (mot.) z.V. 902 *233*,
      255, *256*, *264*, *265*, *268*, *269*, *270*, *272*, *273*
  Artillerie-Abt. 836 *184*, *199*, *212*
  Kraftfahrzeug-Atb. 899 *184*
  Technische Artillerie-Abt. 91 *184*
  Lehr- und-Versuchs-Artillerie-Batterie 444
    50, *184–185*, *192*, *194*, *195*, *209*, *216*, *218*,
    220, *221*, 227–228, *236*, *238*, *241*
  Luftwaffe
    Luftflotte 3 *19*
    Flak-Regt 155 (W) *20*, *22*, *24*, *27*, *60*, *71*,
      260, *261*, *262*, *263*
    Luft-Nachrichten-Versuchs-Regt 24, 26,
      172
    KG3 *205*
    III./KG3 *105*, *114*
    KG53 *244*, *246*, *248*, 272
    I./KG53 *205*, 208
  SS (Schutzstaffel)
    Werfer-Batterie 500 *212*
    Sonderkommando *182*
Units, Soviet, 2nd Belorussian Front *14*
Units, United States
  1st US Army Group 41
  Armies, Third 167
  US Signal Corps *67*, *70*, *73*, *80*, *186*, *187*,
    191, *228*
  USAAF
    Eighth Air Force
      airfields bombed 157, 208
      Berlin targeted 69, *95*
      industrial plants targeted *236*
      Operation 'Pointblank' *43*
      V-installations targeted 14, *15*, *17*, *23*,
        29–30, 33, 42, 47–51, 55, 60, 68,
        93–94, *116*, 117–119, *152*, 154, 183
    Ninth Air Force 29, *30*, *39*, 42, 48, 49, *66*,
      80
    Fifteenth Air Force 152
  USAAF Commands, IX Bomber 32–33
  USAAF Groups
    7th Photo Reconnaissance *93*
    93rd BG *152*
    401st BG *116*
  USAAF Squadrons
    14th Photo Reconnaisance *93*
    422nd FS 146
    425th FS 146
    562nd BS *116*
Upham, V1 strikes 106
Upminster
  V1 strikes 122
  V2 strikes 239, 259, 267
Usedom island 27
Utrecht 200, 233, 255, 264, 268
Uxbridge
  RAF No. 11 Group *76*
  HQ Hillingdon House *179*
  V1 strikes 67, 81, 120, 139, 159

V1 flying bomb
  air-launched *105*, 122, 126–127, 155, *191*,
    205, *244*, *248*, *260*
  British tally *138*, 140, 144–145, *161*, *164*,
    166, 214
  design *52–53*
  first launches *20–22*, 27
  FZG 76 *19*, *22*, *24*, *25*, *52*
  London targeted *6–7*, *148*
  modified launch sites *54–58*, 59, 60, 66, 69,
    72, *92*, 94, 171
  shortening range *256*
  sites overrun by Canadians 167, *169*
  'ski' launch sites *25*, *32–33*, 46, 48, 50, 51,
    53, *54*, *56*, *57*, 58–60, 66
  targets and strikes *see individual locations*

V2 rocket
  capture by resistance *51*
  development *see* Peenemünde
  first launches *182–197 passim*
  last strike on Britain *see* Orpington
  London as target *7, 172*
  Nordhausen production *154, 172–173*
  shortening range *256*
  targets and strikes *see individual locations*
V3 'revenge' weapon *31*
V4 'revenge' weapon *31*
Valognes *72*
Vavilov, Maj. Anatole *14*
Ventnor, Chain Home radar *36, 179*
Victoria Cross, Bazalgette, S/Ldr Ian *119*
Vlaardingen (V1 launch site) *260, 261, 262, 263, 272*
Vlieland *198*
Vogelenzang, V1 launch site *260, 262*

Wachtel, Oberst Max *20, 22, 24, 27, 60, 62, 66, 71, 88, 138, 151, 169, 244, 246*
Waddington, V1 strikes *106*
Wadhurst, V1 strikes *107, 120, 121, 122, 133, 140, 142, 165*
Wainford, V1 strikes *238*
Walcheren Island, V2s fired from *192, 194, 201*
Waldron, V1 strikes *107, 121, 129, 130, 142, 149*
Walkern, V2 strikes *258*
Wallington, V1 strikes *63, 67, 68, 81, 82, 87, 96, 97, 99, 103*
Wallis, Barnes *29*
Waltham, V1 strikes *107, 155*
Waltham Abbey, V2 strikes *264*
Waltham Holy Cross *217, 223, 263*
  Chadwick & Shapcott factory V2 strike *238, 240*
  V1 strikes *84, 85, 86, 105, 107, 125, 151, 153, 156, 160, 195, 263, 267*
  V2 strikes *223, 235, 239, 258, 259, 266, 267*
Walthamstow
  Blackhorse Lane, W. B. Bawn's factory V2 strike *258–259*
  Chingford Road *207*
  Evesham Avenue V2 strike *207*
  Farnan Avenue V2 strike *190*
  Forest Road *128*
  Greenleaf Road V1 strike *128*
  Hoe Street/High Street V1 strikes *128, 153*
  V1 strikes *63, 68, 83, 85, 88, 100, 120, 121, 124, 127, 139, 155, 157, 161, 195, 222, 234*
  V2 strikes *195, 203, 204, 222, 223, 234, 239, 258, 266*
Walthamstow Guardian 131
Walton, V1 strikes *107, 157, 165, 204, 223, 234, 266, 267*
Walton-on-the-Naze, V1 strikes *204*
Wandsworth
  Hazelhurst Road Tooting V2 strike *221, 222*
  V1 strikes *63, 67, 68, 73, 77, 81–89, 96, 97, 99, 100, 102, 103, 105–107, 112, 118, 120–122, 124, 125, 127, 129, 130, 133, 135, 136, 139, 142, 148, 151, 152, 159, 161, 195, 204*
  V2 strikes *222, 266*
Wangford, V1 strike *203*
Wanstead
  Blake Hall Crescent V2 strike *200, 202, 203*
  Hermon Hill *7*
  V1 strikes *82, 83, 84, 87, 88, 97, 99, 100, 112, 114, 120, 124, 127, 129, 135, 136, 147, 152, 153, 204*
  V2 strikes *222, 227, 235, 239, 259, 267*
Wanstead Flats
  POW camp *131, 203*
  V2 strikes *203, 222, 258*
  Woodford Road V1 strike *203*
Wanstead and Woodford Civil Defence *84*
Wapping, Hermitage Wharf V2 strike *204*
War Cabinet
  and German weapon development *12, 21, 28, 30, 34*
  home defence preparations *35, 177, 206, 241, 243*
  and V2 news blackout *196, 201, 208*
War Office
  and enemy weapon development *10, 18*
  V2 rocket threat *194*
Warbleton, V1 strikes *106, 112, 120, 122, 124, 127, 129, 142, 147*

Ward, Brian (Walthamstow local historian) *153*
Ward, June, Canvey Island flying bomb *122*
Ware, V1 strikes *168*
Warehorne, V1 strikes *112, 127, 165*
Warley, V2 strikes *259*
Warlingham, V1 strikes *155*
Warmford, V1 strikes *114*
Warnham, V1 strikes *120*
The Warren, V1 strikes *121*
Wartling, V1 strikes *122, 127, 130, 139, 142*
Wassenaar district *see* The Hague
Wateringbury, V1 strikes *127, 129, 161*
Watford
  St Albans Road *135*
  Sandringham Road *135*
  Stanmore Road *135*
  V1 strikes *81, 105, 130, 135*
Watson-Watt, Sir Robert
  radiolocation and radar *14, 35, 110, 180, 241, 243, 257*
Watten *12, 44*
  Forêt d'Éperlecques *15*
  targeted by Allied bombers *14, 16, 22, 29, 47, 69, 94, 116, 147, 182*
Watton, V1 strikes *106, 125*
Watton, Mrs Florence *114*
Watton at Stone, V2 strikes *239, 258*
Weald, V1 strikes *107, 142*
Weber, Maj. Wolfgang *50*
Wedlake, Mr W. *98*
Weeley, Clacton
  V1 strike *204*
  V2 strikes *222*
Weimar, Buchenwald armaments factory *152, 182-183*
Welborne, Norwich, V2 strike *204*
Welling, V2 strikes *267*
Wells, Horace *143*
Wembley
  V1 strikes *77, 99, 107, 121, 136, 139, 157, 160, 161*
  V2 strikes *195*
Wennington, Rainham
  V1 strikes *127, 129, 148, 157*
  V2 strikes *234*
Wennington Marshes, V2 strike *267*
West Benacre, V1 strike *204*
West Chiltington, V1 strikes *136, 165*
West Cock, V1 strikes *140*
West Dean, V1 strikes *135, 160*
West Ham
  Barnby Road V2 strike *256, 258*
  Beckton Road (now Newham Way) *81*
  Boleyn ground (Upton Park Football Stadium) *138, 254*
  Electricity Dept *98*
  Forest Lane V2 strike *204*
  Romford Road *98*
  Upton Lane School (later Stratford Comprehensive School), double bombing *147*
  V1 strikes *63, 68, 77, 82–85, 88, 96, 97, 99, 102, 105, 106, 107, 120, 121, 122, 124, 126, 127, 129, 130, 131, 133, 135, 139, 140, 142, 151, 152, 159, 161, 165, 204*
  V2 strikes *138, 204, 222, 223, 235, 239, 254, 258, 259, 266, 267*
  Vicarage Lane V1 strike *98*
  Victoria Dock V2 strikes *204*
  see also Stratford
West Hamble *105*
West Hampstead, V2 strikes *239*
West Hanningfield
  V1 strike *234*
  V2 strikes *267*
West Hoathley, V1 strikes *107, 124, 129, 147*
West Hythe, V1 strikes *129*
West Malling, V1 strikes *130, 151*
West Mersea, V1 strike *234*
Westmill, V2 strikes *267*
West Romford, V2 strikes *259*
West Row, Suffolk, V2 strike *235*
West Thurrock
  V1 strikes *127, 147, 204*
  V2 strikes *239*
West Thurrock Marshes, V2 strikes *259*
West Tilbury, V2 strikes *239*
West Wickham, V1 strikes *127, 239*

Westcott, V1 strikes *157*
Westend, V1 strikes *114*
Westerham
  V1 strikes *88, 105, 124, 136, 142*
  V2 strikes *267*
Westfield
  Church Lane *101*
  V1 strikes *107, 136*
Westleton, V1 strike *222*
Westley, V1 strike *204*
Westminster *see under* London
Westminster Press *89*
Westwell, V1 strikes *120, 157*
Westwick, V2 strikes *223*
Wetherfield, V1 strikes *195*
Weybridge, V1 strikes *157, 203*
Whatlington, V1 strikes *140, 151*
Wheathampstead, V1 strikes *159*
Wherstead, V1 strikes *223*
Whinburgh, V1 strikes *136*
Whitby *247*
Whitehall *see under* London
Whitstable
  AA defences *127*
  V1 strikes *140, 168, 267*
  V2 strikes *239*
Whittaker, Ken 'Curly' *7*
Wickford, Essex, V2 strikes *239, 266*
Wickford Ramsden, V2 strikes *259*
Widdersham, V1 strikes *106*
Widdiham, V1 strikes *106*
Wiener Neustadt, Henschel works *31*
Wigborough, V1 strike *204*
Wilkinson, F/Lt G. *174*
Willerby, Yorks, V1 strike *235, 247*
Willesden
  All Souls Avenue *37*
  V1 strikes *73, 81, 86, 96, 100, 105, 107, 120, 125, 139, 152, 157, 165*
  V2 strikes *239, 267*
Willingale, V2 strikes *258, 259*
Willingdon
  V1 strikes *105*
  V2 strikes *195*
Wilmington
  V1 strikes *106, 125*
  V2 strikes *239*
Wilson, Harold (Prime Minister) *241*
Wilton Park, Bucks *11*
Wimbledon, V1 strikes *67, 68, 73, 77, 81, 82, 83, 87, 88, 96, 100, 103, 106, 114, 118, 120, 122, 136, 139, 152, 157, 159, 161, 165*
Winchelsea, V1 strikes *105, 147, 151, 160, 222*
Windlesham, V1 strikes *121, 165*
Windsor Great Park, V2 strike *204*
Winkford, V1 strikes *147*
Withyham, V1 strikes *107, 118, 120, 147, 151*
Wittersham, V1 strikes *120, 127, 156, 165*
Wix, V1 strikes *195*
Wizernes *12, 22, 29, 44, 49, 94, 116, 182*
Woerden, Netherlands *268*
Woking
  V1 strikes *126, 148*
  V2 strikes *266*
Woldingham, V1 strikes *129, 157*
Womanswold, V1 strikes *160*
Wonersh, V1 strikes *120*
Wood, Sir Kingsley *156*
Wood Copse, V1 strikes *106*
Wood Green
  V1 strikes *67, 85, 86, 96, 126, 260, 266*
  V2 strikes *239, 258*
Woodchurch, V1 strikes *112, 114, 124, 130, 140, 142, 147, 148, 156, 157, 161, 165*
Woodcraft, Mrs Ellen *61*
Woodcraft, Tom *61*
Woodford, London
  V1 strikes *82, 83, 84, 87, 88, 97, 99, 100, 239*
  V2 strikes *223, 234, 239, 258*
Woodford, Northants, V1 strikes *235, 247*
Woodford Green
  Broomhill Road *84*
  Congregational Church *84*
  Sir James Hawkey Hall *84*
Woodham Ferrers, V2 strikes *259, 267*
Woodham Mortimer, V2 strikes *258*
Woodmancote, V1 strikes *120*

Woolwich
  Royal Military Repository 61
  V1 strikes 63, 67, 68, 81–89, 96, 100, 103,
    105, 106, 112, 114, *115* 118, 121, 122, 129,
    135, 136, 138, 139, 140, 142, 147, 156,
    161, 165, 168, 195, 204
  V2 strikes 195, 222, 223, 234, 239, 258, 259,
    266, 267
Wootton, Frank (artist) *141*
Works, Ministry of, Flying Squad 75
Worlington, V1 strike 204
Wormingford, V1 strikes 195
Worplesdon, V1 strikes 157
Worsley, Lancs, V1 strike 235, 247
Worth, V1 strikes 222
Worthing, V1 strikes 222

Worting, V1 strikes 114
Wotton, V1 strikes 121, 157
Wren, Sir Christopher, and the Royal
  Hospital Chelsea *241*
Wright, Sgt Harley, GM *134*
Writtle
  V1 strike 222
  V2 strikes 234, 239, 258, 266
Wrotham, V1 strikes 118, 120, 121, 142, 148,
    151, 155
Wye, V1 strikes 114, 122, 126, 155, 168
Wymondham, V1 strike 222

Yalding, Maidstone
  V1 strikes 118, 120, 156, 161
  V2 strikes 222

Yeovil, AA defence 41
Yiewsley
  V1 strikes 63, 100, 151
  V2 strikes 195
Younghusband, Eileen (WAAF) *187*
Ypenburg, V1 launch site *260, 261, 262, 263,*
    266, 272
Yvrench *24, 26*

Zempin, Germany 20, 24, 25, 27, *151*
Ziegenberg *235*
Zuider Zee *195*, 225, 230, 235, 250
Zutphen, Netherlands 223, 225
Zwolle, Netherlands *195*, 223, 225, 230, 235

This is the damage resulting from one of the last V2s to hit Britain (Big Ben 962) which exploded at the junction of Wanstead Park Road and Endsleigh Gardens in Ilford, on March 8. Nine people were killed, 15 seriously injured and 19 slightly injured. **Eight houses were totally destroyed and a further 16 had to be demolished, with over 100 others being very badly damaged. In this picture clearance work is still in progress on the site between Endsleigh Gardens and De Vere Road (bottom).**